www.wadsworth.com

www.wadsworth.com is the World Wide Web site for Thomson Wadsworth and is your direct source to dozens of online resources.

At *www.wadsworth.com* you can find out about supplements, demonstration software, and student resources. You can also send email to many of our authors and preview new publications and exciting new technologies.

www.wadsworth.com
Changing the way the world learns®

COLLEGE READING AND STUDY STRATEGIES

Dianna L. Van Blerkom
University of Pittsburgh at Johnstown

Patricia I. Mulcahy-Ernt
University of Bridgeport

THOMSON

WADSWORTH

Australia • Canada • Mexico • Singapore • Spain • United Kingdom • United States

Executive Manager: Carolyn Merrill
Technology Project Manager: Joe Gallagher
Advertising Project Manager: Linda Yip
Project Manager, Editorial Production: Catherine Morris
Creative Director: Rob Hugel
Print/Media Buyer: Doreen Suruki
Permissions Editor: Sarah Harkrader
Production Service: Carol O'Connell, Graphic World
            Publishing Services

Text Designer: Andrew Ogus
Illustrator: Graphic World Illustration Studio
Cover Designer: Lisa Delgado
Cover Image: © Jose Luis Pelaez/CORBIS
Compositor: Graphic World, Inc.
Text and Cover Printer: Edwards Brothers, Incorporated

For more information about our products, contact us at:
Thomson Learning Academic Resource Center
1-800-423-0563
For permission to use material from this text or product, submit a request online at http://www.thomsonrights.com.
Any additional questions about permissions can be submitted by email to thomsonrights@thomson.com.

Library of Congress Control Number: 2003114337

ISBN 0-534-58420-9

Thomson Wadsworth
10 Davis Drive
Belmont, CA 94002-3098
USA

Asia
Thomson Learning
5 Shenton Way #01-01
UIC Building
Singapore 068808

Australia/New Zealand
Thomson Learning
102 Dodds Street
Southbank, Victoria 3006
Australia

Canada
Nelson
1120 Birchmount Road
Toronto, Ontario M1K 5G4
Canada

Europe/Middle East/Africa
Thomson Learning
High Holborn House
50/51 Bedford Row
London WC1R 4LR
United Kingdom

Latin America
Thomson Learning
Seneca, 53
Colonia Polanco
11560 Mexico D.F.
Mexico

Spain/Portugal
Paraninfo
Calle Magallanes, 25
28015 Madrid, Spain

To my husband Steven and son Jonathan,
With love,
Patricia

To my husband Mal,
With love,
DVB

Brief Contents

PART III   COLLEGE READING STRATEGIES

Detailed Contents

II COLLEGE STUDY STRATEGIES

6 IMPROVING CONCENTRATION   142

III COLLEGE READING STRATEGIES

Activities Contents

1 INTRODUCTION TO COLLEGE LEARNING STRATEGIES

3 INTRODUCTION TO COLLEGE READING STRATEGIES 44

4 GENERAL READING STRATEGIES FOR COLLEGE TEXTBOOKS 71

5 USING VOCABULARY STRATEGIES   103

II COLLEGE STUDY STRATEGIES

6 IMPROVING CONCENTRATION   142

7   IMPROVING MEMORY   161

8   TAKING LECTURE NOTES   184

9 TAKING TEXT NOTES   207

10 PREPARING FOR EXAMS   232

13 LOCATING SPECIFIC DETAILS   316

14 ANALYZING KEY POINTS   342

15 SUMMARIZING AND SYNTHESIZING TEXTS   380

16 EVALUATING INFORMATION   414

To the Instructor

In order to be successful in college, many students need to improve their reading and study strategies. What are the most critical reading and study strategies that students need for college success? *College Reading and Study Strategies* provides a new answer to that question. This text features the most essential reading and study strategies for college students. We designed a text that provides foundational reading and study strategies in Part I and then presents more in-depth study and reading strategies in Parts II and III. Although the study strategies are presented first, you can present the reading strategies first or mix and match the chapters to best meet the needs of your students.

Many new college students experience anxiety and frustration because they have had little or no instruction in reading or study strategies. For many of these students, learning how to read college texts, how to take notes, and how to prepare for and take tests can make the difference between success and failure. Practicing these strategies on authentic text material in psychology, history, biology, mathematics, literature, and sociology, for example, will help students learn to modify and adapt the strategies to the lectures, texts, exams, and assignments for their other courses. This is one of the goals of every reading and learning strategy course.

Our goal in this text is to present a model of reading that integrates study strategies and shows literal, inferential, and critical comprehension skills. In this textbook, students learn to locate important details in both academic and nonacademic material. They learn to find and infer main ideas. They learn critical comprehension strategies of analysis, synthesis, and evaluation. The importance of these comprehension strategies has been well documented in literacy research.

It is our belief that learning to read should always be tied to reading to learn, so students practice their skills on interesting magazine articles, newspaper articles, and authentic text materials from a wide variety of subject areas. In many instances, they are, at the same time, learning to learn as they learn to read their college textbooks. As students improve their ability to read their college texts, they are also learning new strategies for mastering the content of those texts. Learning these reading and study strategies provides students with feelings of confidence and increases their ability to be successful in their coursework.

UNIQUE FEATURES OF THIS TEXT

You might expect to find many of the important aspects of this book in any comprehensive reading and study strategies text. However, we believe there are many features unique to this text:

➤ Emphasis on active learning throughout.

➤ Integration of reading and writing tasks throughout the text.

➤ A wide array of wonderful examples showing students how to use a range of study techniques and reading strategies.

➤ Dedicated chapters for specific comprehension strategies at the literal, inferential, and critical comprehension levels.

➤ Excerpts from newspapers and magazines so that students can practice the strategies with real-life, authentic text material.

➤ Longer excerpts from college textbooks in many disciplines to help students practice strategies immediately.

➤ Exercises and applications for immediate practice and to enhance transfer to the students' own course materials.

➤ Longer text selections for practice, which simulates the real college experience better than short excerpts found in competing texts.

➤ Four entire text chapters from college texts (available on the *College Reading and Study Strategies* Web site) for additional practice.

➤ Hands-on experiential approach, which supports the best theories about how students really learn.

➤ Critical comprehension strategies reinforced through multiple types of texts.

➤ Well-written and engaging text with a modern and student-friendly design.

➤ Flexible, straightforward format and organization that appeals to a variety of instructors.

➤ Boxed feature, "Tip Blocks" to summarize important strategies.

➤ InfoTrac College Edition® packaged with this text.

➤ Internet and InfoTrac College Edition activities in each chapter.

IMPORTANT ASPECTS OF THIS BOOK
INSTRUCTION

This text provides clear, easy-to-read explanations of reading and study strategies. Each chapter contains strategy, instruction, exercises for practice, and activities for self-evaluation.

The study strategies chapters include strategies for improving motivation, managing time, taking lecture and text notes, improving concentration, and preparing for and taking exams. Because every student learns differently, a number of different strategies are presented in the text. Students are encouraged to try all of the strategies and then permitted to select the ones that work best for them. But learning to read and study effectively and efficiently requires more than just *knowing* a new strategy. It also requires *using* that strategy. In many cases, understanding why particular strategies work helps motivate students to use them in their other courses. We present explanations and rationales for using these strategies so that students understand why one strategy may work in one particular situation while others may not.

In the reading strategies chapters, students learn essential strategies for literal, inferential, and critical comprehension. They learn how to locate important details in text passages and find the main ideas. They also learn how to analyze text passages and write summaries of them. Students also learn how to work with single and multiple texts and how to synthesize key ideas. In addition, the students learn how to evaluate text material. These critical reading strategies enable students to better understand their reading assignments, participate in class discussions, complete written assignments, and study for exams. By integrating both reading and study strategy instruction, you will be able to help your students develop the essential strategies that they need to succeed in college.

PRACTICE

One of the most important goals of any successful reading and learning strategies course is getting students to transfer what they learn to their other course work. In order to help students achieve this goal, well over 200 activities have been designed to get students to practice the strategies they have learned. Each of the activities has been strategically placed within the chapter so that students can practice the new strategy immediately after it has been introduced. In addition, a number of the activities encourage students to practice older strategies as they are learning new ones. Many of these activities are based on excerpts from other college textbooks. In this way, students are afforded practice with material that is similar to the course material they are currently using. Finally, many of the activities require students to practice the strategies using their own course materials and text reading outside of college. In this way, students transfer the strategies they have learned to their other courses while at the same time increasing their understanding of the material for their other courses. In many cases, this leads to overall higher success, something that helps students see the real value of reading and study strategy instruction.

JOURNAL ACTIVITIES

To foster written fluency, a key goal for college performance, we have included Journal Activities in this text. As students learn essential reading comprehension and study strategies, this textbook features multiple opportunities for students to reflect and respond to text. These practice exercises give students time to think about what they have read and/or allow them to reflect upon topics that are critical to their college success. The journal activities also help students become more fluent in their academic writing, a critical skill for college success.

SELF-EVALUATION

Many of the activities in the text are designed to help students monitor their own learning. The "Where Are You Now?" activities provide a quick check of the number of effective strategies students have before beginning each unit and the number they have made a part of their repertoire at the end of the unit. Some instructors choose to have students complete the end-of-chapter survey activity at a later date to allow more time for the students to incorporate the strategies. In addition, activities throughout the text ask students to evaluate many of the strategies that are presented in the text. Finally, the review questions at the end of each chapter allow students to evaluate whether or not they have mastered some of the key points covered in the text. They are not meant to be all-inclusive, but rather to give students some feedback on their reading and learning.

SUPPLEMENTARY MATERIALS
Instructor's Manual and Test Bank

The Instructor's Manual and Test Bank includes an overview of each chapter, teaching suggestions, course materials and handouts, and multiple-choice, completion, short-answer, and essay/discussion questions. Also included is a list of key concepts with definitions from each chapter and transparency masters.

Although we have presented a sequence of reading and study strategies that build on each other, the Instructor's Manual features different variations of introducing the strategies and chapters. These different variations provide flexible options to instructors who teach reading and study strategies courses that emphasize one area over the other. Therefore, although we offer one option for presenting the strategies, you are encouraged to select the chapter sequence that best meets the needs of your program and students.

InfoTrac College Edition

InfoTrac College Edition, an online database with current full-text articles from hundreds of scholarly and popular publications, is available bundled with this text. Both you and your students can receive unlimited online use for one academic term. Activities that help students use InfoTrac College Edition are included in each chapter of the text.

College Reading and Study Strategies Web Site

Students using this text will have access to the *College Reading and Study Strategies* book-specific Web site. In addition to the answers to the end-of-chapter review questions, students will have access to text excerpts and full chapters from a variety of college textbooks for transfer practice activities, handouts on topics related to college success, planning calendars and forms, a self-scoring version of the learning style inventory, college success links, and many other special features.

The Wadsworth College Success Resource Center

The College Success Web site at http://www.success.wadsworth.com offers a variety of downloads and links designed to enhance the freshman seminar for students.

ACKNOWLEDGMENTS

Creating a new textbook is an intriguing and challenging task. However, we have been fortunate to have had a wonderful team who helped guide us through the development of *College Reading and Study Strategies*. Special thanks to Elana Dolberg for helping us develop the original proposal, to Annie Mitchell for guiding us through the development of the manuscript, and to Carolyn Merrill for taking the text to the production process. Thank you for all of your time, effort, and wonderful ideas.

We also appreciate the support of Amanda Santana, Catherine Morris, and the Wadsworth team responsible for all the work behind the scenes preparing this book for production. A special acknowledgment is extended to Carol O'Connell and the entire production team of Graphic World Publishing Services for their invaluable expertise in bringing this book to print.

This book was a team effort of Diane's expertise for the study strategies sections of the text and Patricia's expertise for the reading sections of the text. However, we would like to extend a special thanks to Mal Van Blerkom for writing the section about the Information Processing Model in Chapter 7.

We are especially grateful to our families for their patience and encouragement during the many months while this work was in progress. We are also grateful to all of our students who constantly inspire us and challenge us with their insights and questions.

We have been very fortunate to have a group of reviewers who shared their time and expertise with us. Thank you for sharing your suggestions on how you teach your classes and how this text can best meet the needs of your program and your students. Your insight and experience in teaching college students have been invaluable in the development of this text:

Rebecca S. Casey, Kennesaw State University

Kara L. Craig, University of Southern Mississippi

Ava Drutman, SUNY/Westchester Community College

Susan L. Farley, Murray State University

Arden Hamer, Indiana University of Pennsylvania

Carlotta W. Hill, Oklahoma City Community College

Maxine Keats, Framingham State College

Patricia A. Malinowski, Finger Lakes Community College

Maritza Martinez, University at Albany, SUNY

Martha Olsen, Oklahoma State University

Darlene Pabis, Westmoreland County Community College

Carolyn A. Plaa, McLennan Community College

Jori B. Psencik, University of Texas at Dallas

Victoria M. Rey, Kean University

Kathleen Riepe, University of Wisconsin-Parkside

Kathryn M. Ryder, Broome Community College

Annette Ragland Sanchez, Nashville State Tech

Catherine A. Seyler, Palm Beach Community College

Terry Sheban, Youngstown State University

Sarah Spreda, University of Texas at Dallas

To the Student

This text introduces and explains many useful reading and study strategies that will help you achieve your academic goals. If you are using this text before or during your first semester in college, you should be well prepared for the challenges ahead of you. If you have already attended one or more semesters in college, you may be enrolled in a reading and study strategies course because you were not satisfied with your previous academic performance. By learning and applying new reading and study strategies, you can improve your academic performance.

To become a successful student, you need to learn new strategies and apply them to your own college assignments. If you use the new strategies in this textbook to complete your reading assignments, take your lecture notes, and prepare for and take exams, you'll be successful in college. By trying out each of the new strategies for managing your time, reading your texts, taking text notes, and preparing essay answers, you can evaluate the effectiveness of each strategy and choose the one that works best for you—you can become an active, strategic learner.

Once you put your newly learned strategies into practice, you should begin to see your grades improve in each of your courses. This kind of improvement doesn't result from just being told what to do differently but rather from hard work and persistence in applying effective reading and learning strategies to your own course material. Becoming a successful student takes time and effort—there are no miracles involved. If you're willing to learn new strategies and are also motivated to use them when doing your own course assignments, you, too, can achieve your goals.

Speaking of goals, we have four goals for you in your use of this text. First, we want you to learn new strategies that will make learning, reading, and studying much more effective. Second, we want you to use those strategies in your own course work, so that you can achieve your academic goals. Third, we want you to feel better about yourself both as a student and as a person—we want you to have self-confidence. Fourth, we want you to actually learn to enjoy school. Instead of dreading a class, an assignment, or even an exam, we'd like you to look forward to them because you will know how to be successful in understanding your text assignments, taking notes, writing that report, and preparing for and taking that exam. If you apply what you're learning, you should see an improvement in your grades, have more time for leisure activities, feel less stressed about your academic work, feel better about yourself, and even begin to enjoy learning.

HOW TO USE THIS BOOK

There are many resources available in this text to help you make a successful transition to college learning. Each of the following text resources will provide you with additional information to help you achieve your goals.

CONCEPT MAPS

The concept maps on the first page of the chapter are designed to give you a brief introduction to the main topics in the chapter. Think about what you already know about each of the topics before you begin reading the text. You may also find that they can serve as a template for your own map of the chapter. See Chapter 9 for more information on how to map the information in your textbook.

WHERE ARE YOU NOW? ACTIVITIES

By completing the "Where Are You Now?" activities before reading the chapter, you can evaluate your current strategy use related to the topics in each chapter. Once you identify your strengths and weaknesses, you can focus on those areas where you need the most assistance. You may notice after completing one of these activities that they provide you with an overview of some of the strategies that will be discussed in the chapter. After you complete the chapter, or even two or three weeks later, complete the activity again in the text (using a different color pen) or do it online at the *College Reading and Study Strategies* Web site (http://success.wadsworth.com/vanblerkom-mulcahy)

TIP BLOCKS

The Tip Blocks found in each chapter include additional strategies for both traditional and nontraditional students. You'll find practical suggestions in each chapter that will save you time, help you apply your strategies to your other course work, or give you tips for making reading and studying more interesting and challenging.

STUDENT EXAMPLES

The student examples shown in the text serve as models for many of the strategies that are described in each chapter. Although it has become almost a cliché, a picture is worth a thousand words to students who aren't sure how to take lecture notes, create recall questions, and set up study sheets, just to name a few of the applications you may find useful in this text. Occasionally, poor examples are included that contain common errors students make. These examples are designed to keep you from making those same mistakes.

SELF-MONITORING ACTIVITIES

Each chapter contains self-monitoring activities. By completing these activities you can learn how to monitor your learning. These activities help you monitor your performance in your other course work and the strategies that you are using. Knowing whether or not you are using effective strategies can help you make changes, if they are necessary, in order to be more successful in college.

GROUP ACTIVITIES

The group activities in each chapter are designed to encourage collaborative work. Many students enjoy working with others and find that they learn much more when working in a group. Sharing ideas, resources, and strategies all help you succeed in college. If you haven't already discovered the advantages of collaborative work, you may find that these activities will demonstrate how effective it can be.

JOURNAL ACTIVITIES

The journal activities in each chapter are designed to help you reflect on your reading and learning experiences as you move through the text and your course work. By writing about how you applied each of the strategies to your reading or coursework, you can evaluate how effective they were in helping you achieve your goals. Many students find that writing about their progress is very motivating and provides them with feelings of accomplishment as well. The journal activities also provide you with an opportunity to create well-developed, coherent responses to text material—a skill that is important for success on essay exams, term papers, and written reports.

INQUIRY ACTIVITIES

The Inquiry Activities provide a variety of exercises for you to apply the strategies presented in each chapter. Some of the activities ask you to think about what you've just read and jot down a quick response. Other activities ask you to read excerpts from college-level textbooks; some ask you to read magazine articles. As you complete these activities, you will gain the practice needed to transfer the strategies to your own courses.

INFOTRAC COLLEGE EDITION ACTIVITIES

The InfoTrac College Edition activities are designed to help you develop research skills so that you can make use of this powerful full-text database. Beginning with the activity in Chapter 1, each activity is designed to help you search the database in progressively more sophisticated ways. You will learn how to search using both keywords and the subject index. This will help you locate articles on any topic related to your own course work for papers, projects, and presentations.

COLLEGE READING AND STUDY STRATEGIES BOOK-SPECIFIC WEB SITE

The *College Reading and Study Strategies* book-specific Web site contains a wealth of information to help you succeed in college. You'll find answers to the multiple-choice and completion items from the end-of-chapter reviews. There are handouts on topics such as calculating your GPA, additional examples, and calendars for time-management activities. You'll also find a self-scoring form of the Learning Style Inventory described in Chapter 1. There are additional text excerpts for note-taking practice and practice tests for objective and essay exams. You'll also have access to four entire text chapters from a variety of academic disciplines. College success links and many other features can be found on this new Web site. Check it out at http://success.wadsworth.com/vanblerkom-mulcahy.

REVIEW QUESTIONS

The review questions at the end of each chapter are designed to help you monitor your learning. You'll find a list of key terms you should know, followed by completion, multiple-choice, and essay questions. You'll be able to check your answers on the Web site listed above.

A FINAL NOTE

If the strategies in this book helped you, we would be delighted to hear about your success. If you were successful during your first semester, first year, or even during your college career because of the use of this text, we'd love to hear from you; drop us a note and let us know how *College Reading and Study Strategies* helped you. Also, if you have any suggestions for how this book can be improved in order to help other students succeed in college, please let us know. You can contact us by writing to:

Editor, College Success
Wadsworth/Heinle
25 Thomson Place
Boston, MA 02110
USA

Introduction to College Learning Strategies

1 Getting Ready to Learn

In this chapter you will learn more about:

- ➤ Characteristics of successful students

- ➤ Getting motivated to learn

- ➤ Using learning styles to enhance performance

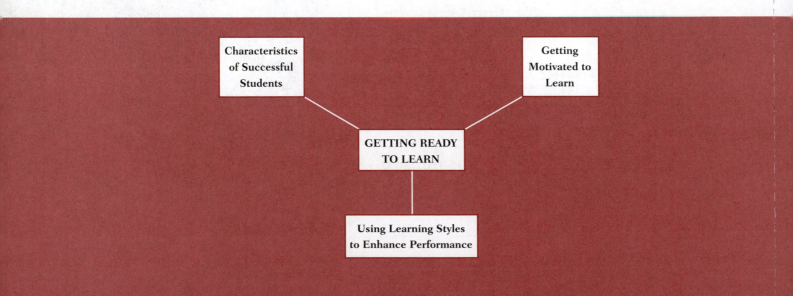

ACTIVITY 1.1 ▶ *Where Are You Now?*

Take a few minutes to answer *yes* or *no* to the following questions.

	YES	NO
1. Do you just skim through your reading?	_____	_____
2. Do you predict quiz and test questions when you do your reading assignments?	_____	_____
3. If you miss class, do you expect your professor to go over the material with you at a later date?	_____	_____
4. Do you know your preferred learning style?	_____	_____
5. Do you plan to take a lighter course load during your first semester in college?	_____	_____
6. Do you attend class regularly and stay up-to-date with your assignments?	_____	_____
7. Do you know how to increase your motivation?	_____	_____
8. Do you monitor your learning after you complete your work?	_____	_____
9. Have you really thought about why you are in college?	_____	_____
10. Do you expect college to be the same as high school?	_____	_____
Total Points	_____	

Give yourself 1 point for each *yes* answer to all questions except 1, 3, and 10 and 1 point for each *no* answer to questions 1, 3, and 10. Now total up your points. A low score indicates that you need some help adjusting to college. A high score indicates that you already have realistic expectations.

CHARACTERISTICS OF SUCCESSFUL STUDENTS

What makes some students succeed in college and others fail? Faculty, administrators, and students have discussed that question for years. Although there is no exact formula for success, research indicates that there are some factors that do lead to success. Successful students are actively involved in their learning. In addition, successful students are more likely to plan, monitor, and evaluate their learning—they are strategic learners. Finally, successful students take responsibility for their own learning—they are independent learners.

BECOMING AN ACTIVE LEARNER

How do you typically prepare for a quiz or an exam? When I ask my students that question at the beginning of the semester, most say they read over the material. Is that what you said? You may be thinking that reading over the material worked well for your high-school exams. Unfortunately, you'll have to use more active study strategies for college exams, because they contain much more information and occur much less frequently. Many college exams cover two to three hundred pages of text and four weeks of lecture material. You can't learn all of that information just by reading over it a few times. Instead, you need to identify, organize, and condense the information. Next, you need to use active study strategies such as taking notes, predicting questions, making word and question cards, developing study sheets, participating in study groups, and self-testing to learn the material.

Active learners talk and listen, write, read, and reflect on (think about) what they are learning.[1] Talking about the information and listening to others discuss the information in a study group, for example, gets you actively involved in the learning process. In addition to reviewing the information, you are elaborating on it by putting it in your own words. You can also learn by reading actively. Active reading involves previewing, highlighting, predicting questions, and thinking critically about the material, all of which force you to interact with the printed word. These strategies help you activate your prior knowledge (what you already know about the topic), identify the key information, check your understanding of it, and form connections within the material. Writing summaries, taking notes, developing concept maps and study sheets, and writing out answers to predicted essay questions help you organize and synthesize (combine the parts into a whole) the information as you learn it. Reflecting on the information helps you gain a deeper understanding of the material and form connections between the new information and your prior knowledge. Getting actively involved in your learning is the first step toward succeeding in college.

ACTIVITY ▶ **1.2** *How Do You Compare to Successful Students? (Optional)*

If your instructor has ordered the College Success Factors Index with your textbook, you can go to www.success.wadsworth.com and see how you compare with other students in areas proven to be determinants of college success by completing the 80 self-scoring statements. Then read about each of the factors to see how you can be even more successful in college.

BECOMING A STRATEGIC LEARNER

Another way to be more successful in college is to become a strategic learner. According to Weinstein and Hume, "Strategic learners are students who view studying and learning as a systematic process that is, to a good degree, under their control."[2] Weinstein's model of strategic learning involves three main components: skill, will, and self-regulation.

Skill

Strategic learners possess a wide variety of skills to aid their learning. These skills include knowledge about yourself as a learner, knowledge about different types of academic tasks, knowledge about strategies for learning, prior content knowledge, and knowledge about the contexts in which that knowledge could be useful.[3] Let's look at the first three of these components briefly.

---

[1]Chet Meyers and Thomas B. Jones, *Promoting Active Learning: Strategies for the College Classroom* (San Francisco: Jossey-Bass, 1993).
[2]Claire E. Weinstein and Laura M. Hume, *Study Strategies for Lifelong Learning* (Washington, DC: American Psychological Association, 1998).
[3]Claire E. Weinstein, "Strategic Learning/Strategic Teaching: Flip Sides of a Coin," in Pintrich, Brown, and Weinstein, Eds., *Student Motivation, Cognition, and Learning: Essays in Honor of Wilbert J. McKeachie* (Hillsdale, NJ: Lawrence Erlbaum, 1994).

You already know many things about yourself as a learner. You know which subjects you excel in, which types of classes you like, and which types of assignments you do best. You know something about your ability as a student from your grades in high school or scores on standardized tests. However, you may not know much about your learning style—about how you learn best—and you probably aren't aware of many of the study and learning strategies that you'll need to use to be successful in college. In this text, you'll learn more about yourself as a learner and about many of the learning strategies; you'll learn how to use them, why they work, and how to adapt or change them when they don't work.

After completing twelve years of formal schooling, you have a great deal of knowledge about completing academic tasks. You know how to do math problems, write a paper, and read a chapter in a textbook, just to name a few. However, some of the tasks that you will be asked to complete in college are different from anything you've done before; they will require you to complete new tasks and, possibly, to apply new strategies for learning.

Although you've learned some study strategies in the past, you will need to develop many new ones to succeed in college. Many of the tasks you will be asked to complete will be new to you. In addition to the increased amount of information you will have to learn, you also will be expected to understand the material rather than just memorize it. To achieve these goals, you must learn new strategies and learn how to match them appropriately to the task.

Will

Just knowing how to prepare for an exam or take lecture notes, though, is not enough. A strategic learner must have the will to put that knowledge into practice. Will involves setting goals, selecting appropriate study strategies, and believing in your own ability and in the study strategies that you have chosen. In addition, strategic learners are motivated—they are willing to work hard to achieve their goals.

Have you ever met a student who didn't do well in college? Most people assume that the students who fail or quit are those who can't do the work or don't have enough ability to succeed. However, most studies indicate that it is just as often the brightest students (as defined by test scores or academic histories) who do not succeed. Why does this happen? Look around your own classroom. You probably will notice that some students are absent. Not attending class, not doing reading assignments, not preparing for exams and many other similar factors contribute to college failure. These activities depend on a student's willingness to do what is necessary to be successful in college. Will is an equally important factor in college success.

Self-Regulation

Finally, strategic learners are self-regulated learners. They manage their time well, monitor their learning, evaluate the results of their effort, and approach learning in a systematic way.[4] Self-regulated learners are self-directed, not other-directed. They are what we often call independent learners—they take the initiative for their own learning. In high school, your parents and teachers often took the responsibility for your learning; they made sure that you completed your assignments, remembered to study for exams, and

---

[4]Claire E. Weinstein and Laura M. Hume, *Study Strategies for Lifelong Learning* (Washington, DC: American Psychological Association, 1998).

often felt responsible if you were not successful. In college, you have to take that responsibility—you have to become an independent learner.

If you miss class, *you* are responsible for the material and the assignment. Don't expect your TA (teaching assistant) or professor to repeat the lecture for you privately at your convenience. Instead, you should ask another student for the notes. If you fail a quiz or exam, you need to see your professor to talk about your performance. Don't expect your professor to call you in for a conference. Instead, you need to take the initiative and schedule the appointment. Your professors expect you to take the responsibility for your education.

Self-regulated learners plan before starting a task, select strategies that they know are appropriate for the task, and monitor their own learning as they are completing the task and after the task is completed. Self-regulated learners know what they have to do to be successful. They set goals and design plans that help them complete their work on time. They also know a wide variety of study skills and strategies and choose the appropriate strategies for each task and testing situation. For example, self-regulated learners prepare differently for multiple-choice and essay exams. They use different strategies for completing a reading assignment that will be followed by a quiz and one for which they must only attend class and take notes.

Finally, self-regulated learners monitor their learning. They pause to check their understanding when reading, ask questions in class when they don't understand something, compare lecture notes with friends, and self-test before exams. Self-regulated learners also make adjustments when they find their strategies are not working.

You'll have the opportunity to use new learning strategies in many of the text activities, and, I hope, you will use them in your other course work. By using the strategies in your own work, monitoring their effectiveness, and making changes when necessary, you can become a strategic learner.

ACTIVITY 1.3 *Discuss Strategies for Success*

Make a list of at least ten strategies that college students need to use to be successful. Then share your ideas with a group of your classmates. As a group, select the ten strategies or activities that are most representative of successful students. Think about how many of the strategies you currently use and select three that you plan to use this semester to increase your success.

GETTING MOTIVATED TO LEARN

Psychologists have been trying to explain why some people work hard at a task while others choose not to do so. Think of a task that you recently completed. Did you put all your energy into completing it? Did you understand what you were trying to accomplish? Did you continue working on the task even though it was difficult? How you answered each of these questions may give you a better understanding of how motivation affects college success. Motivation affects whether or not you do your work, which study strategies you decide to use, when you do your work, how long you work on a task, how well you concentrate on it, how much effort you expend doing it, and what you learn from completing the task. Motivation can be described as something that energizes, directs, and sustains behavior toward a particular goal. Understanding more about the factors that influence motivation and the strategies that can be used to increase it can help you be more successful in college.

FACTORS THAT INFLUENCE MOTIVATION

Although many factors influence motivation, your goals, your self-efficacy, and your level of effort are perhaps the most important ones for college success.

Goals

Your goals influence your motivation to complete a task. Without challenging, realistic goals, you may not know where to direct your efforts. You may have noticed that your motivation (or lack of motivation) varies depending on the tasks that you need to complete. Many students find that they are more motivated to work on a task when they have a personal interest in completing it or find it challenging to do so. If you are personally interested in learning how to use a computer program, for example, you may be highly motivated to achieve your goal. Working on a task because you want to learn or do something (even when you don't have to) can be described as intrinsic motivation.

On the other hand, you may also be motivated by the promise or expectation of earning rewards, grades, or other types of external gain. Being motivated by external factors can be described as extrinsic motivation. If you were told to learn to use a computer program as part of a course assignment but have little personal interest in using it, you may find that you are less motivated. Many times, our efforts are motivated by a combination of intrinsic and extrinsic motivation. You may begin to read a textbook chapter, for example, because you are concerned about your grade in the course (extrinsic motivation). However, as you are reading, you may find that you become interested in the material itself and want to learn more about the topic (intrinsic motivation). Your increased interest in the material may actually increase your motivation to complete the task, perhaps with even more effort.

Self-Efficacy

Your belief in your own ability to successfully complete a task can also affect your level of motivation. If you believe that you can successfully complete a task, you are more likely to be motivated to work on it. This belief in your ability to successfully complete a task is often described as self-efficacy. Each time that you are successful in accomplishing one of your goals (completing a task), it increases your self-efficacy (self-confidence) so that you can complete a similar or even more difficult task in the future. Students who have high self-efficacy are also more likely to persist on a task when it is difficult. For these reasons, many psychologists believe that past successes lead to future successes.

Effort

Your motivation is also affected by the strength of your belief that the amount of effort you put forth on a task can affect your performance. If you attribute your successes and your failures to your level of effort, you are more likely to be motivated to work on and complete a task. The amount of effort that you exert when working on a task is something that you can control. Unlike luck, which is out of our control, we can exert a lot of effort, very little effort, or no effort in completing a task. Many study skills experts believe that students need to work hard at the beginning of the semester so that they can see that the amount of effort they put toward their academic tasks does have a positive effect on their performance. Early success (knowing you can learn the material and achieve your grade goals) is very motivating for new college students. This early success can therefore lead to even more success. You may find the following formula will help you put all of this together: M↑→ E→S (Motivation leads to increased effort, which leads to success).

STRATEGIES TO INCREASE MOTIVATION

There are hundreds of strategies that students can use to increase motivation. Just go to a bookstore and check out the reference or self-help shelf. Books on how to get motivated or increase your motivation at home, at school, and at work are plentiful. Many of the chapters in this text in fact contain strategies that will help you increase your motivation. The Tip Block contains a number of basic strategies that can help you get more motivated now.

ACTIVITY 1.4 ▶ *Describe Your Motivational Problems*

List three academic tasks that you worked on recently. On a scale of 1 to 10 (with 1 being the least effort you ever put into a task and 10 being the most effort you ever put into a task) how would you rate the amount of effort you put into each task? Did you continue to work on the task when it became difficult? When it became boring?

Write a paragraph or two describing each of the tasks you rated and why you had trouble getting motivated or staying motivated when completing one or two of your academic tasks earlier this week. What strategies did you use to try to complete your work? Which strategies presented in this chapter may have been even more effective? Why?

GETTING YOUR MONEY'S WORTH

A college education is your key to the future, but it is also one of the most expensive investments you or your parents will ever make. A college education can cost anywhere from $20,000 to $100,000. If you break down your tuition costs, you may find that you are paying several hundred to several thousand dollars for each course you take. Divide that number by the number of class sessions that you have in each course. You may be astounded by the actual cost of each of your classes. What's the point of all of this math? Well, it's to help you realize that every time you miss a class, you're wasting money. Some students are excited when a professor cancels a class or doesn't show up. But students who are paying the bill or attending college on loans—which they'll have to repay—often feel angry because they believe that they are not getting their money's worth. In the same way, each time you cut a class, sleep through one, or show up unprepared, you aren't get-

TIP

STRATEGIES TO INCREASE MOTIVATION

SET CHALLENGING BUT REALISTIC GOALS. We are more motivated to complete tasks when we feel that they are challenging and yet attainable, within our reach. You may also find that thinking of each task as a step toward achieving your long-term personal or career goals can also help keep you motivated.

SET LEARNING GOALS. Decide what facts, concepts, or ideas you want to learn before you begin working on a task.

SEE THE VALUE IN THE TASK. Understanding why you are doing the task—seeing the importance of the task—can help motivate you to complete it.

HAVE A POSITIVE ATTITUDE. As you begin a task, think about similar tasks that you completed in the past. Knowing that you've done it before can increase your motivation. Reminding yourself that you are good at math can help motivate you to study for your upcoming math exam.

USE POSITIVE SELF-TALK. When working on a long or difficult task, you may find that telling yourself that you can do it, why it's important, or that you are almost done with the task can keep you going.

WORK HARD. Not working on a task or exerting very little effort often results in reduced motivation the next time you need to complete a similar task.

USE ACTIVE STUDY STRATEGIES. Knowing which strategy to use for a specific task and that it will work can help you be more motivated to work hard as you complete your academic tasks.

BREAK DOWN TASKS. By breaking down the task into parts (and working on them one at a time), you can increase your motivation. Checking off or crossing off each part of the task as it is completed can give you a sense of accomplishment, which motivates you even more.

MONITOR YOUR LEARNING. Answering your own self-test questions, taking end-of-chapter or online tests, or reciting from memory are just a few ways of monitoring your learning. When you know your time, effort, and study strategies are working to help you learn, you'll be more motivated to continue working. On the other hand, you may find that you get motivated when you find out that you don't know the information for a test.

LEARN FROM YOUR MISTAKES. Learning why you were unable to successfully complete a task can also help increase your motivation. Knowing what you need to do differently can help you be more motivated the next time you need to complete a similar task.

ting your money's worth, either. To get your money's worth and maximize your success, go to class and stay up-to-date with your assignments.

Working hard will also help you get your money's worth. In high school, many students did just enough to get by. Did you "cruise" through high school? Did you spend only one hour a day doing homework assignments or studying for tests? If you answered yes to either of these questions, you'll have to change your study patterns in college. To get your money's worth, you need to put school first; you need to spend twenty to thirty-five hours or more each week reading, doing assignments, and preparing for exams.

ACTIVITY 1.5 *Are You Getting Your Money's Worth?*

Are you getting your money's worth out of every class? Do you ever cut a class to sleep in? Do you ever sleep in class or do other assignments? Do you daydream or look out the window? How much are *you* paying for each of your classes?

INCREASE YOUR LEVEL OF INTERACTION

You're probably wondering how you could possibly spend that much time studying. Think about how you completed your last reading assignment. Did you just skim it? If so, you probably exerted very little effort and put very little time into the task. Unfortunately, you probably didn't get much out of the chapter, either. During the first week of the semester, I try to get my students to increase their level of interaction with their reading assignments. I developed a hierarchy of tasks that shows increasing levels of involvement with the material. Take a look at my list (see Figure 1.1) and put a check mark at your level of involvement.

Some of you may find that your check mark is near the top of the list, and I'm sure that some of you are working somewhere in the middle. I hope one or two of you are working very hard and your checkmark is near the bottom of the list. I don't expect you to jump from the top of the list to the bottom overnight—you may not have a good knowledge of all the skills involved. However, as you move through the text and acquire many of the skills that were listed, I hope you will increase your level of interaction as you complete your assignments. You'll also learn how to get more actively involved in taking lecture notes, doing math assignments, writing papers, and preparing for exams in later chapters. You may find that you are willing to work harder in some classes and put less effort into others. Ideally, you should make the greatest effort in all of your classes, but your prior knowledge, your time constraints, and your goals all are factors that will determine your effort. Remember, the more actively involved you are with the task, the more you will learn. If you work hard, you'll get your money's worth and a good education, too.

MAKE THE TRANSITION TO LEARN

Attending college requires a certain amount of adjustment for most students. If you started college immediately after high school graduation, you will experience many changes in your life. You may be on your own for the first time—you may have to take on many of the responsibilities that your parents or teachers previously handled. If you are a commuter or a returning adult learner, you will have to make adjustments, too. Although juggling work, school, and home responsibilities is a challenging task, many students do it every day. College life offers many exciting new experiences, and many new freshmen want to join in on the activities.

Attending college can be very stressful, however. Learning to manage stress and to use good decision-making strategies can help make the transition to college an easy one. New students have to make academic transitions, too. College courses are much more difficult than high school classes. Many resources are available on your college campus

FIGURE 1.1
Levels of Interaction

When you read this chapter or another assignment did you:

- Just skim it?

- Just read it?

- Read it and highlight the important information?

- Read it, highlight, and take notes?

- Read it, highlight, take notes and predict questions in the margin?

- Read it, highlight, take notes, predict questions, and do some of the activities?

- Read it, highlight, take notes, predict questions, do some of the activities, and think about how you would use some of the strategies?

- Read it, highlight, take notes, predict questions, do some of the activities, think about how you would use some of the strategies and apply one or two of them to your own work?

- Read it, highlight, take notes, predict questions, do some of the activities, think about how you would use some of the strategies, apply one or two of them to your own work, and quiz yourself on the material to test your understanding?

to help you deal with both your social and your academic problems. The suggestions in the Tip Block should help you make a successful transition.

WHY ARE YOU IN COLLEGE?

As you are getting ready to learn, maintain a positive attitude toward your progress. Think about why you're in college and what you plan to accomplish during your college career. Take some time to visit the career services office on your campus and explore the job opportunities available in your major field of study. Talk to other students and to your professors about the options available to you. Having a clear set of goals can be very motivating and can help you over some of the hurdles that you will have to face. If you haven't chosen a major yet, that's okay, too. Use your first year or two of college to explore various courses and majors. Make an appointment to discuss your interests with your advisor, the department chairperson, or with someone in the counseling or career services office. Colleges offer courses of study that you never even heard of in high school—one of them may be the right one for you. You may even think about changing your major. Most college students do change their major at least once; many change their major several times. The important thing to remember is that career goals help motivate you to set and achieve your academic goals, which help motivate you to set and achieve your study goals. Why are you in college? Think about it.

TEN TIPS FOR MAKING THE TRANSITION TO COLLEGE

BELIEVE THAT COLLEGE IS THE RIGHT DECISION FOR YOU. Many students come to college feeling uncertain of their ability to succeed. Give yourself at least one or two semesters to make the transition; don't give up too soon.

MAKE ACADEMICS YOUR TOP PRIORITY. Some college students get so caught up in social activities that their grades suffer. If you aren't working full time, you should have enough time to get your course work done and still have time for leisure activities. Set a goal to get your course work done before you participate in social activities.

TAKE A LIGHT COURSE LOAD YOUR FIRST SEMESTER. Many college freshmen think that taking five or six classes will be as easy as it was in high school. However, they don't realize how much time they will be expected to spend on each course outside of class. Taking the lightest full-time course load available will help you do well during this transitional semester.

MAKE USE OF THE RESOURCES AT YOUR COLLEGE LEARNING CENTER. If you find that you aren't getting the grades that you expected on papers, quizzes, or exams, go to your college tutoring or learning center immediately. If you wait until after you've gotten two or three low test grades, it may be too late to change your course grade.

TAKE A REFRESHER COURSE TO BUILD YOUR SKILLS. If you haven't used your math, writing, or study skills for ten years or more, you probably have become a bit rusty. Taking a refresher course or two will help you upgrade your skills.

GET TO KNOW YOUR COURSE INSTRUCTORS. Stop by your TA's or professor's office to introduce yourself or chat about the course. Making this initial contact will help you feel more comfortable about asking for help when you have a question or problem.

DEVELOP A SUPPORT NET AT HOME. Talk to your family and friends about why you are in school. By sharing what you're doing, what you're learning, and how you're feeling, you can get their support, too. Plan activities with your family and friends at least one or two hours each week and during semester breaks.

GET INVOLVED IN CAMPUS ACTIVITIES. Early in the semester, you'll have an opportunity to join clubs and organizations on campus. Pick one or two that interest you, but don't join everything. Clubs provide you with opportunities to enjoy extracurricular activities and make new friends.

REDUCE STRESS. College can be stressful for many students. You can reduce or cope with feelings of stress by taking action—by doing something about it. Talking with friends, family, and campus counselors is also helpful. Giving yourself some time for relaxation is also important in restoring your inner strength.

TAKE CARE OF YOURSELF. It's important to eat well-balanced meals, get enough sleep, and get some exercise. If you don't take care of yourself physically, you may find that you aren't able to concentrate on your work or even stay awake during class. If you don't take care of yourself, you may also lower your resistance to infection and miss class.

ACTIVITY 1.6 *Describe Why You Are in College*

Use the Journal Entry Form on the *College Reading and Study Strategies* Web site or your own paper to write an essay describing the reasons you chose to attend college. Did anyone or anything influence your decision?

USING LEARNING STYLES TO ENHANCE PERFORMANCE

Your learning style also affects your ability to succeed in college. Researchers in education and psychology have been investigating the issue of learning styles since the 1950s. In this section, you'll discover more about how you learn best, how to match learning strategies to specific tasks and subject areas, and how using your preferred and non-preferred learning style will affect your performance in college.

WHAT ARE LEARNING STYLES?

The term *learning style* refers to the preferred way that you acquire, process, and retain information—the way you learn best. We learn new tasks in different ways; we each have our own style or preference for learning. The time of day you study, the kinds of strategies you use, whether you work alone or with a group, and even the place you study are all aspects of your learning style.

However, your learning style involves more than these factors. Researchers have explored the nature of learning styles in many different ways. Some relate learning style to cultural factors that affect the expectations that teachers, parents, and students have about learning in the classroom and at home. Others have investigated the relationship of learning styles to whether we are left-brained or right-brained learners (whether we tend to process information in a linear, analytical manner like a computer or in a more holistic, visual manner like a kaleidoscope).[5] Many learning styles are based on Kolb's theory that some people approach new situations through "feeling" and others through "thinking."

ACTIVITY 1.7 *What's Your Learning Style?*

Complete the Learning Style Inventory in Figure 1.2A or use the self-scoring inventory on the *College Reading and Study Strategies* Web site. As you read each of the statements, check *yes* or *no* to indicate the response that describes you best. Then use the information in Figure 1.2B to determine your preferred learning style.

CHARACTERISTICS OF LEARNING MODALITIES

The Learning Style Inventory in Figure 1.2 is an informal inventory that can provide you with information about your preferred learning modality (learning through the senses). Are you a visual learner, an auditory learner, a kinesthetic learner, or do you have preferences in two areas? As you read through the following descriptions, you may find that you have some of the characteristics of each style. You probably do. We all have some strengths in each of the three learning modes. As you discovered by completing the inventory on page 14, however, one of the styles is your preferred style for learning new information.

Visual Learners

If you found that you're a visual learner, you learn best by seeing things. Reading; looking at pictures, diagrams, and charts; and watching films, videos, and demonstrations are all ways that you can learn new information. You probably have found that you understand your pro-

---

[5]Sharon L. Silverman and Martha E. Casazza, *Learning & Development: Making Connections to Enhance Teaching* (San Francisco: Jossey-Bass, 2000).

FIGURE 1.2A
Learning Style Inventory

As you read each of the following statements, put a check mark for *yes* or *no* to indicate the response that describes you best.

	YES	NO
1. I remember things better if someone tells me about them than if I read about them.	_____	_____
2. I'd rather read about "tapping" (extracting the sap from) trees than take a field trip and actually tap a tree.	_____	_____
3. I enjoy watching the news on television more than reading the newspaper.	_____	_____
4. I'd rather build a model of a volcano than read an article about famous volcanoes.	_____	_____
5. When I'm having trouble understanding my text chapter, I find that reading it out loud helps improve my comprehension.	_____	_____
6. If I had to identify specific locations on a map for an exam, I would rather practice by drawing and labeling a map than reciting the locations out loud.	_____	_____
7. I tend to better understand my professor's lecture when I read the text material ahead of time.	_____	_____
8. I would rather take part in a demonstration of how to use a new computer program than read a set of directions on its use.	_____	_____
9. If someone asked me to make a model for a class project, I would rather have someone explain how to make it than rely on written directions.	_____	_____
10. If I were preparing for an exam, I'd rather listen to a summary of the chapter than write my own summary.	_____	_____
11. I would prefer my professor to give me written directions rather than oral directions when I have to do a writing assignment.	_____	_____
12. I'd rather listen to the professor's lecture before I read the chapter.	_____	_____
13. If I had to learn to use a new software program, I'd prefer to read the written directions rather than have a friend describe how to use it.	_____	_____
14. If I have trouble understanding how to complete a writing assignment, I prefer to have written directions than have someone explain how to do it.	_____	_____
15. I like to listen to books on tape more than I like to read books.	_____	_____
16. When I have to learn spelling or vocabulary lists, I prefer to practice by reciting out loud rather than writing the words over and over again.	_____	_____
17. If I had a choice, I would prefer to watch a video of someone else doing chemistry experiments than actually perform them myself.	_____	_____
18. When I have trouble with a math problem, I prefer to work through the sample problems rather than have someone tell me how to do them.	_____	_____

fessor's lecture better if you read the text chapter ahead of time. Note-taking strategies such as outlining and mapping, which will be discussed in Chapter 9, work well for visual learners. Think about how you study for exams. You probably reread your text and lecture notes, rewrite your notes, and fill in study guides or make study sheets. During an exam, you may be able to "see" the correct answer in your mind's eye. Have you ever closed your eyes and

FIGURE 1.2B

Scoring Instructions

Your responses in both the *yes* and *no* columns are important in determining your preferred learning style. Tally your responses using the following scoring key and then use the chart to total your responses.

1. **A (Auditory) style.** Look back at your responses and circle the numbers of the *yes* responses for items 1, 3, 5, 9, 10, 12, 15, 16 and the *no* responses for items 6, 7, 11, 13, 14, 18. Write the totals in the appropriate blocks in the A column on the chart.

2. **V (Visual) style.** Look back at your responses and circle the numbers of the *yes* responses for items 2, 7, 11, 13, 14, 17 and the *no* responses for items 1, 3, 4, 5, 8, 9, 12, 15. Write the totals in the appropriate blocks in the V column on the chart.

3. **K (Kinesthetic) style.** Look back at your responses and circle the numbers of the *yes* responses for items 4, 6, 8, 18 and the *no* responses for items 2, 10, 16, 17. Write the totals in the appropriate blocks in the K column on the chart.

	A (Auditory)	V (Visual)	K (Kinesthetic)
Number of *yes* responses			
Number of *no* responses			
Total points			
Cutoff score	8	8	5

Add up your score for each column. To determine your preferred learning style, compare your total score for each column to the *cutoff score* for that column. If your score is equal to or higher than the cutoff score, then you tend to show a preference for that learning style. The higher your score is, the stronger your preference for that style of learning. You may find that you have high scores in two areas; that's okay. You may learn well using more than one learning style. Note: Your total points for the A, V, and K columns should add up to 18.

---

pictured the information on the textbook page, the chalkboard, or your study sheets? In Chapters 7 and 10, you'll learn many new test-preparation strategies that are designed for visual learners. Check them out now if your current study methods aren't paying off.

Auditory Learners

If you're an auditory learner, you learn best by hearing information. Unlike the visual learner, you probably prefer to go to your class and listen to the lecture before you read the text chapter. Have you found that you can understand the text much more easily after you hear the professor's lecture? Reading difficult text passages out loud is also a good idea for the auditory learner. Discussing the course material, mumbling information as you read and study, asking and answering questions out loud, and listening to study notes on tape are some strategies that you may already use if your preferred learning style is auditory. You may find that you can actually "hear" the professor's lecture when you try to recall the specific point you need to answer a particular test question. Many new test-preparation and memory strategies that are designed for auditory learners are included in Chapters 7 and 10.

Kinesthetic Learners

If you're a kinesthetic learner, you learn best by doing things. You prefer hands-on tasks that allow you to touch and feel. Many of the strategies used by visual and auditory learners also appeal to kinesthetic learners. For example, in Chapter 9 you'll learn a strategy called mapping—creating visual diagrams or representations of written and oral information. Whereas the visual learner can recall the information from a concept map by seeing it, the kinesthetic learner will be able to remember it by the feel of how he or she created it. Kinesthetic learners also learn well from doing experiments or replicating the tasks they will later have to perform in the testing situation. Many auditory learners use flash cards to recite definitions or information about a topic. The kinesthetic learner also learns well from making up the flash cards as well as from the action of self-testing. Kinesthetic learners like to get actively involved in what they are learning. In Chapters 7 and 10, you'll learn how to create study sheets, make up self-tests, construct models, and work problems in order to prepare for upcoming exams.

Integrated Learning Styles

Although each of us has a preferred learning style, most of us learn information by using our less preferred learning styles, too. In fact, some courses, assignments, or exams may require you to use one or more of your less preferred learning styles in order to complete the task. When you are forced to complete a hands-on activity, for example, you may find that using a kinesthetic approach is more successful. Even though it's not your best way to learn *most* material, it may be the best way to learn *that* material. Although my preferred learning style is visual, I always call the software hotline when I run into a problem with a computer program. The advantage for me is that the technical support personnel tell me how to fix my problem, and they stay on the line and assist me as I complete each of the steps on the computer. By using my two less preferred learning styles together, I learn better than by using my preferred style.

Using a combination of auditory, visual, and kinesthetic strategies will help you benefit from all the ways that you can learn information. As you learn about note-taking, text-reading, and test-preparation strategies in later chapters, keep your preferred learning style in mind. However, the most successful students are often the ones who can use strategies that take advantage of all of the ways they learn or those who can switch styles depending on the demands of the course or the assignment.

When tasks are familiar—similar to ones we've done in the past—like preparing for a history exam or writing a narrative composition, students generally use their preferred learning style to complete the tasks. However, when tasks are unfamiliar, some students may find that their preferred style doesn't work, which leads to feelings of frustration or self-doubt. The reason for their difficulty may be that the new task involves more characteristics of their less preferred learning styles—they have difficulty because they're using the wrong style, not because they're less capable students.

Other Characteristics of Learning Styles

The inventory in Activity 1.8 should help you find out more about how you learn best. Take a few minutes to complete it now, before you continue reading. One of the interesting outcomes of completing this activity is that many students find that they aren't always aware of some of the characteristics of their own learning style. In fact, you may want to experiment with some of these issues in order to test your responses further. For example, you may have indicated that you learn best when you study in the morning, but in fact you

ACTIVITY 1.8 *Find Out More About How You Learn Best*

Rank the four responses to each item according to the following scale in order to determine more about how you learn best: 4—best, 3—good, 2—fair, 1—poor.

1. I learn best when I study
   _____ in the morning.
   _____ in the afternoon.
   _____ in the evening.
   _____ late at night.

2. I learn best when I study
   _____ in complete quiet.
   _____ with soft background noise.
   _____ with moderate levels of noise.
   _____ in a noisy environment.

3. I learn best when I study
   _____ by myself.
   _____ with my regular study partner.
   _____ with a small group.
   _____ in a large-group review session or recitation class.

4. When I take exams, I generally
   _____ just guess to get done.
   _____ pick the first answer that looks right.
   _____ read all the possible answers before I choose one.
   _____ eliminate incorrect responses before I select the correct answer.

actually do most of your work in the late evening. This may be a habit you established in high school or for some other reason. However, now that you know that you learn best in the morning, you should change your time schedule to work in your preferred learning style. When and where you work are often dependent on each other, so look at your rankings to items 1 and 2. If you find that you often do your assignments late at night, it may be because that's the only time you can find a quiet place to study.

Your response to question 3 may explain why you work best when you're asked to do group projects, or why, for you, they're often something you dread. Many students study best when they work by themselves, whereas others find that everything falls into place when they work in groups. Although question 4 appears to focus on how you should take a test, it really assesses how impulsive (acting without thinking) or reflective (thinking before acting) you are in learning situations. If you tend to be impulsive, you may have more difficulty completing certain types of academic tasks—especially problem-solving tasks. Students who are more reflective tend to think through things more slowly and carefully. Reflective learning styles are generally more suited to academic learning and success. If you tend to be an impulsive learner, you can learn to be more reflective by using many of the learning strategies that will be presented in the remainder of the text.

A Word of Caution

The results of the learning style inventories that you completed in Activities 1.7 and 1.8 may not be accurate. These informal surveys have not been scientifically tested. In addition, these (and all) learning-style inventories are self-report questionnaires. That means that you determine your own score. Your mood, the way you interpret the statements, and how you feel at the time you do the activity all affect your score. You may want to do the inventories again, perhaps later in the semester or even next semester, to verify your results. You could also complete another learning style inventory in your college testing or learning center.

When faced with a new learning task, try working within your preferred learning style first, but if that doesn't work, don't give up. Instead, try using one of your less preferred learning styles. Through experimentation you'll find the right learning style and the most effective learning strategies for each of your courses and academic tasks.

If you are intrigued by some of the ways of looking at learning styles that were discussed earlier, go to your college learning center, counseling center, or testing center and ask to take a formal learning style inventory. Some of the more common ones (which are much too long and complex to include here) are the LSI (Kolb's Learning Style Inventory); the 4MAT System developed by Bernice McCarthy; the Learning Style Inventory by Dunn, Dunn, and Price; and the MBTI (the Myers-Briggs Type Indicator).

ACTIVITY 1.9   *What Type of Learner Are You?*

Find out more about what kind of learner you are by taking the quiz at the Personality Type Web site (www.personalitytype.com). This interactive quiz, based on the MBTI, is short, easy, and self-scoring. After identifying your type, be sure to take some time to explore the information available on the Web site.

WHY YOUR LEARNING STYLE IS IMPORTANT

One of my students, Staci, shared her frustrations about one of her courses. She said, "No matter what I do, it just doesn't work." What she meant was that no matter how much she studied, she continued to fail her exams. Have you ever felt that way? After some discussion, we decided that Staci may not be approaching the course material correctly. Soon after she began working with a tutor, her grades improved. Two things occurred that made a difference for her. First, her tutor was able to explain the material in a manner that better matched her learning style; the tutor modified his style of instruction to match her style of learning. Second, Staci changed her study strategies to better match the instructor's teaching and testing style.

Knowing more about how you learn best will help you improve your chances of succeeding in college. Do you tend to do well in some classes but have difficulty in others? For instance, let's say you are taking History and Biology this semester. Given the same level of effort and time spent in preparation, you may think that you should do equally well in both courses. However, if you earned an A in History but got only a C in Biology, you probably would feel frustrated and confused. In fact, you might start to question your ability to succeed in college if you always got As in high school biology but could pull only Cs in college biology. Even though college biology probably is harder than high school biology, that may not be the reason for your poor performance. You may have more difficulty in college biology because the instructor's teaching style did not match your learning style or because you didn't use the appropriate learning style when preparing the biology assignments.

Many professors teach the way that they learn best; they use their preferred learning style. Professors who are auditory learners typically lecture and involve students in class discussions. Visual learners present material primarily through handouts, videos, and transparencies and by writing key information on the chalkboard. Kinesthetic learners often teach through demonstrations, class activities, experiments, and other hands-on methods. If you learn best through the method that your professor uses, you probably feel very comfortable, in control, or "in your element" in that particular course. If, on the other hand, your learning style doesn't match your professor's teaching style, you may feel uncomfortable in class, have difficulty completing assignments, and perform poorly on exams. This mismatch can lead to frustration and even failure.

Understanding how you learn best can also improve your concentration. When you are working in your preferred learning mode, you probably find that you are better able to concentrate on your study tasks. Approaching a task from your preferred style results in a better fit or match—studying feels right. When things are "going well" during a study session, you'll probably complete your work efficiently and effectively. Working outside of their preferred style or using a learning style that does not fit the task may be the reason some students put in a lot of time on their studies but don't get the results they expect.

ACTIVITY 1.10   *Evaluate Your Instructors' Teaching Styles*

Use the chart to evaluate three of your instructors' teaching styles. Check the appropriate space if your instructor uses any of these activities. Then count the check marks for visual, auditory, and kinesthetic activities to determine your professors' preferred teaching styles. Do your professors' teaching styles match your learning style?

Instructional Mode	Instructor's Name:	Instructor's Name:	Instructor's Name:
1. Lectures			
2. Writes on board			
3. Uses transparencies			
4. Shows videos			
5. Uses handouts			
6. Includes discussions			
7. Does experiments			
8. Does demonstrations			
9. Gives directions orally			
10. Gives directions in writing			
11. Uses group activities			
Instructor's preferred teaching style			
Your preferred learning style			

ACTIVITY 1.11 *Use InfoTrac College Edition to Locate College Survival Tips*

If you are using the InfoTrac College Edition, access it using the Internet address: www.infotrac-college.com/wadsworth and type in your password (located on your access card available with this text). Click on the EasySearch Help button and click on the *link* (the underlined phrase) Introduction. Use the BACK button on the top left-hand corner of the tool bar to return to the EasyTrac main screen to learn how to use it to do simple searches. Use the *subject* guide to locate information on the topic: college. Type the word *college* into the search entry box and click the SEARCH button. You'll find a long list of related topics. Scan the subject headings for one related to freshmen or college survival. View the list of articles and then click on the *link* to read one or two that look interesting. List three topics that most closely match the information you want to find. After reading several articles, list three practical strategies that you plan to incorporate in your survival plan this semester.

ACTIVITY 1.12 *Where Are You Now?*

Now that you have completed Chapter 1, take a few minutes to repeat the "Where Are You Now?" activity, located on the *College Reading and Study Strategies* Web site. What changes did you make as a result of reading this chapter? How are you planning to apply what you've learned in this chapter?

Summary

Many factors contribute to your college success. One of the most important, though, is your commitment to the academic demands of your course work. Becoming an active, strategic, and independent learner will help you achieve that success. You also have to become a self-regulated learner—you need to manage your time, monitor your learning, and evaluate the results. Getting motivated to work hard and learn is critical to your college success. Your goals, your self-efficacy, and your level of effort all influence your level of motivation. Choosing to use some of the strategies to increase your motivation can make a difference. Attending college involves making transitions and taking on new responsibilities. Balancing your commitments at work, home, and school may be your most challenging task during your first year in college. Determining your learning style, how you learn best, will help you learn to select the appropriate study strategies to use for each of the study tasks you will need to complete. Becoming aware of how you learn best can help you better understand why you're more successful in some classes than in others. Using your preferred learning style or the most suitable learning style for the task can help you become more successful in all of your classes.

Review Questions

Terms You Should Know: Make a flashcard for each term.

Active learners	Kinesthetic learners	Self-regulated learners
Auditory learners	Learning style	Skill
Extrinsic motivation	Mapping	Strategic learners
Independent learners	Motivation	Visual learners
Intrinsic motivation	Self-efficacy	Will

Completion: Fill in the blank to complete each of the following statements.

1. Reading over your notes is an example of _____ learning.

2. The most common learning style for college professors is _____.

3. Strategic learners are students who view studying and learning as a _____ process that is, to a good degree, under their control.

4. You can get your money's worth in college by _____ all classes.

5. Taking a _____ course load during your first semester or first year can help make the transition to college easier.

Multiple Choice: Circle the letter of the best answer for each of the following questions. Be sure to underline key words and eliminate wrong answers.

6. When you do assignments, you need to increase your level of _____ with the material.
    A. motivation
    B. efficiency
    C. interaction
    D. time

7. A kinesthetic learner learns best by:
    A. reading.
    B. listening.
    C. doing.
    D. integrating all three learning modalities.

Short Answer–Essay: On a separate sheet, answer each of the following questions.

8. What are the three factors that influence motivation? Describe each briefly.

9. What is a self-regulated learner?

10. Describe the characteristics of successful students.

2 Managing Your Time

In this chapter you will learn more about:

➤ How to analyze your use of time

➤ How to organize your study time

➤ How to use time-management strategies to stay motivated

➤ How to reduce procrastination

➤ How to reevaluate your time plan

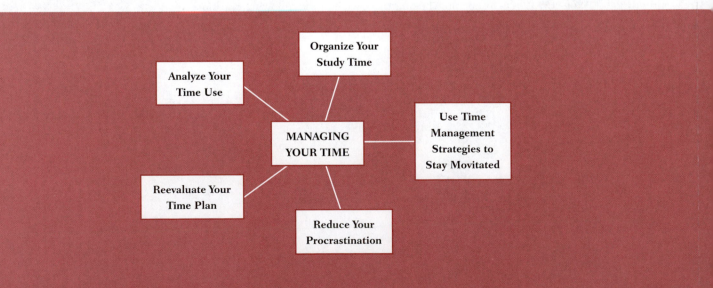

ACTIVITY 2.1 ▶ *Where Are You Now?*

Take a few minutes to answer *yes* or *no* to the following questions.

	YES	NO
1. Have you estimated how many hours you need to study this semester?	_____	_____
2. Do you tend to complete your assignments on time?	_____	_____
3. Have you estimated how long it takes you to read ten pages in each of your textbooks?	_____	_____
4. Do you begin working on long-term assignments early in the semester?	_____	_____
5. Do you make lists of things to do in your head rather than on paper?	_____	_____
6. Do you find that you go out even when you know you should be studying?	_____	_____
7. Do you schedule time to study for exams?	_____	_____
8. Are you working at a job more than twenty hours a week?	_____	_____
9. Do you know exactly what you are going to work on when you sit down to study?	_____	_____
10. Do you do the assignments from your favorite class first?	_____	_____
Total Points	_____	

Give yourself 1 point for each *yes* answer to all questions except 5, 6, 8 and 10, and 1 point for each *no* answer to questions 5, 6, 8, and 10. Now total up your points. A low score indicates that you need some help in managing your time now. A high score indicates that you are already using many good time-management techniques.

ANALYZE YOUR USE OF TIME

You can establish a good time plan once you know how you actually spend your time. Identifying how much time you have available for study and how much time you need for study can help you decide whether or not you should make any changes in your current time plan.

WHY IS TIME MANAGEMENT IMPORTANT?

Time management is the way you regulate or schedule your time. You can make more efficient use of your study time and complete your work in less time by using good time-management skills. The key to successful time management is allowing enough time to complete your work while still finding time to complete all of your other responsibilities.

Unlike high school students who are in class for almost thirty-five hours a week, most college students are in class for only twelve to fifteen hours a week. To a college freshman, this seems like a breeze. However, in college, most of your work must be completed outside of class. And, even though you may not want to admit it, you can't get all that work done in just a few hours every evening. To achieve your goals, you also need to make use of your available daytime hours for study.

Good time-management skills can actually save you time. A few minutes each week spent on planning can make a real difference in how your study time is organized and spent. Once you learn good time-management skills, you may be surprised to find that you can do all the things you want to do. You may find that for the first time, you are in control of your life. The first rule of good time management is: *Don't let time manage you; you must learn, instead, to manage your time.*

HOW DO YOU MANAGE YOUR TIME NOW?

The first step in learning better time management is to evaluate how you actually use your time now. The score you received in Activity 2.1 gave you an indication of your ability to manage your time. However, you also can find out a lot about your own time use by writing down how you actually spend your time.

Keep a Time Diary

Although most students think that they spend enough time on academic tasks, many of them don't. By keeping a time diary, you will be able to see how much or how little time you are actually spending. A time diary is a record of what you do each hour of the day for one week. To create your own time diary, just write down what you did in the morning at lunchtime, what you did in the afternoon at dinnertime, and what you did in the evening at bedtime. Some students prefer to carry an index card to record their activities and then copy them on to the time diary (available on the *College Reading and Study Strategies* Web site) at a later time. If you wait until the end of the day, you may have trouble remembering what you did. Split hours by drawing a diagonal line, but don't worry about five- or ten-minute activities.

You may find it helpful to color code your time diary. Highlight all of your academic tasks (classes, meetings with professors or tutors, and study time) in one color, your sleep hours in another, and the rest of your life (work, social time, meals, and so on) in a third. If you're working full-time, you may want to use a separate color for those hours, too. A quick glance can tell you a lot about how effectively you're using your time now. To get a more accurate picture, create a time-use chart (Figure 2.1) to count the number of hours you used for each of the various activities. You'll need to modify the categories depending on your own activities.

If you're a full-time student, you should divide your total hours into three overall categories. You should spend about 56 hours a week sleeping (one-third of your time), about 56 hours for academics (classes, study time, tutoring, review sessions, and meetings with your professors or advisor), and 56 hours for the rest of your life. If you are working full-time and attending college on a full-time basis, you won't have time left over for many social activities or home responsibilities. Looking realistically at how you're using your time *now* can help you make some necessary changes to be more successful in college.

FIGURE 2.1
Time-Use Chart

	Sleep	Meals	Class	Study	TV	Work	Internet	Social time	Commute	Get ready	Total hours
Monday											
Tuesday											
Wednesday											
Thursday											
Friday											
Saturday											
Sunday											
Total Hours											(Should total 168 hours)

	Sleep	Academics	The rest of my life

Note: A full-size version of this chart is available on the *College Reading and Study Strategies* book-specific Web site.

ACTIVITY 2.2   *Keep a Time Diary*

Keep a time diary for one week using the calendar available on the *College Reading and Study Strategies* Web site. Write down how you spent each hour of the day, being as specific as possible. Create a chart or use the time-use chart available on the Web site, indicating how many hours you spent in various activities (attending class, working, sleeping, eating, studying, commuting, completing personal tasks, watching television, playing video games, socializing, exercising, and so on) each day and then for the entire week. Then write several paragraphs describing any patterns that you noted in your use of time. Consider the amount of time that you spent on various activities as well as whether you did the things that you planned (or needed) to do. Discuss the changes that you plan to make in your time plan as a result of monitoring your use of time.

Complete a Prospective-Retrospective Calendar

Learning to manage your time effectively also depends on how well you can stick to a schedule. A Prospective-Retrospective Calendar allows you to compare what you *plan* to do on a given day (prospective) with what you *actually* do (retrospective). Fold a piece of notebook paper in half and write *Prospective* at the top of one column and *Retrospective* at the top of the other. Then give yourself a checkmark each time you do what you planned to do. What you do during each hour of the day is not important here. Instead, the key is how well you stick to your plan.

Just setting up a plan for each hour of the day often provides sufficient motivation for completing it. Some students who try this activity are surprised to find that they faithfully follow their time plans. Other students find that they have a great deal of difficulty staying on a schedule. Their most common problem involves getting study assignments done as planned. Do you?

IDENTIFY TIME AVAILABLE FOR STUDY

Identifying how much time you have available for study is the next step in setting up a good time plan. This involves looking at how much of your time is committed to other activities and also how much time you, as an individual, need to complete your work.

To establish how much of your time is committed to other activities, you should complete a Fixed Commitment Calendar.[1] What are fixed commitments? If you said classes, work hours, or even mealtimes, you were right. Fixed commitments are things you do the same time every day or every week. When completing your calendar, you should first write in your classes. You also should write in hours when you are asleep (normal sleep hours, not naps), mealtimes (setting regular times for meals helps you stay on a schedule), and work hours. If your work hours vary, don't write them in yet; we'll talk more about study and work later in this section. If you're involved in clubs, organizations, or sports, you may need to include additional hours for regularly scheduled meetings (same time each week) or practices and games. If you have family responsibilities such as dropping off or picking up your children at school or day care (or other regularly scheduled tasks), write them in, too. If you know that you will be socializing on most Friday and Saturday evenings, you should write in those times even though your plans are not definite. If you plan to sleep in Saturday or Sunday morning or attend religious services, include those hours as well.

After you have written in all the regularly committed hours, you should begin to see some patterns in your uncommitted time. You may have some very short blocks of time between classes, some two- or three-hour blocks in the morning or afternoon, and some longer blocks in the evenings and on weekends. Think of these time blocks as time available for study rather than free time. You also may notice that you have a lot of time to study on certain days but very little on others. All this information will be useful as you begin to schedule your study time.

After determining your available study time, trace around the perimeter of each time block (see the sample in Figure 2.2). Use a brightly colored marker to outline each block. Being able to see at a glance the hours when you have time to study can be very helpful when scheduling study time.

Some students, unfortunately, have work schedules that change each week. If your work schedule varies, this calendar is even more important for you. Before you put your work hours on the schedule, make a photocopy of the calendar for each week of the semester. As you get your work schedule each week, go through and write in your hours. This will save you a lot of time because you won't have to start from scratch each week.

---

[1]Adapted from Time Analysis Worksheet in Nancy V. Wood, *Reading and Study Skills,* 3d ed. (New York: Holt, Rinehart & Winston, 1986), pp. 18–20.

FIGURE 2.2
Greg's Fixed Commitment Calendar

	Monday	Tuesday	Wednesday	Thursday	Friday	Saturday	Sunday
7:00 A.M.	sleep	sleep	sleep	sleep	sleep	sleep	sleep
8:00 A.M.	shower/dress/eat	shower/dress/eat	shower/dress/eat	shower/dress/eat	shower/dress/eat	sleep	sleep
9:00 A.M.	Algebra class	lift weights	Algebra class	lift weights	Algebra class	sleep	sleep
10:00 A.M.	lift weights	lift weights		lift weights	lift weights	shower/dress	shower/dress
11:00 A.M.	English class	History class	English class	History class	English class	eat	eat
12:00 P.M.		eat		eat		work	watch football
1:00 P.M.	eat		eat		eat	work	watch football
2:00 P.M.	Sociology class		Sociology class		Sociology class	work	watch football
3:00 P.M.						work	watch football
4:00 P.M.	practice	practice	practice	practice	practice	work	watch football
5:00 P.M.	practice	practice	practice	practice	practice		work
6:00 P.M.	eat	eat	eat	eat	eat	eat	work
7:00 P.M.							work
8:00 P.M.					out	out	work
9:00 P.M.					out	out	work
10:00 P.M.					out	out	
11:00 P.M.	TV	TV	TV	TV	out	out	
12:00 A.M.	sleep	sleep	sleep	sleep	out	out	sleep
1:00 A.M.	sleep	sleep	sleep	sleep	out	out	sleep
2:00 A.M.	sleep	sleep	sleep	sleep	sleep	sleep	sleep
Hours Available for Study __34__				Hours Needed for Study __32__			

As a final step in preparing your Fixed Commitment Calendar, count the number of hours you have available for study. If you are not working, you may find that you have fifty to seventy hours available for study. If you are working, however, this number may be substantially smaller, depending on the number of hours that you work each week.

Greg (see Figure 2.2) has only thirty-four hours available for study. He is working ten hours a week and is participating in sports. He spends one or two hours a day lifting weights and another two hours a day practicing. To complete his assignments, Greg will have to make efficient use of his time.

Rayna's schedule (see Figure 2.3) is even tighter because she works full time and attends college three evenings a week. She has very little study time available during the week and spends most of the weekend completing her study tasks. Do you think that Rayna could handle a full-credit load this semester?

ACTIVITY 2.3   *Complete a Fixed Commitment Calendar*

Now fill out the Fixed Commitment Calendar available on the Web site. Write in your activities that are regularly scheduled for class, work, meals, and other obligations. Then box in the times that are available for study. Indicate the total number of available study hours at the bottom of the page. You will be able to determine the hours that you need for study soon. Leave that space blank for now.

IDENTIFY TIME NEEDED FOR STUDY

Knowing how much time you have available for study is useless until you identify how much time you need for study. Formulas, such as those that allot one hour of outside study time for every hour in class or two hours of outside work for every hour in class, are designed to simplify the task of determining how much time you need for study. Some educators believe students need two hours of study time for each hour that they are in class. So, a student who is taking fifteen credits would need thirty hours of study time per week. However, this figure is based on the average number of hours students study. Remember, too, that the average grade earned by students is a C. To get a more accurate figure, you need to consider a number of other factors.

Consider Your Credit Load

The first indicator of how much time you really need for study is your credit load. If you are taking fifteen credits, you should figure a *minimum* of two hours of study time for every hour in class. Remember that this is a minimum and probably will change when you consider the other factors—the goals you have set, how quickly or slowly you work, and the difficulty of your courses.

Consider the Difficulty Level of Your Classes

You may need to increase your study hours if you're taking very difficult classes. Certain classes at every school seem to have a reputation for being "killer" classes. If you're enrolled in a "killer" class, you may have to increase your study ratio to 3 to 1 (three hours of outside work for every hour in class) or even 4 to 1. Even if you're not taking a "killer" course this semester, you may find that one particular class is especially difficult for you. Calculus can be a tough course if you haven't used your math skills for a few years. A history class can be difficult for a student who is a slow reader. If you're taking a course that is especially demanding, you should allow three or four hours of outside work for every hour that you are in class.

FIGURE 2.3
Rayna's Fixed Commitment Calendar

	Monday	Tuesday	Wednesday	Thursday	Friday	Saturday	Sunday
5:00 A.M.	shower/ dress	shower/ dress	shower/ dress	shower/ dress	shower/ dress	sleep	sleep
6:00 A.M.	breakfast/ drive	breakfast/ drive	breakfast/ drive	breakfast/ drive	breakfast/ drive	sleep	sleep
7:00 A.M.	work	work	work	work	work	sleep	sleep
8:00 A.M.	work	work	work	work	work	sleep	sleep
9:00 A.M.	work	work break	work break	work break	work break	shower/ dress	sleep
10:00 A.M.	break work	work	work	work	work	breakfast	shower/ dress
11:00 A.M.	work	work	work	work	work	clean apartment	breakfast
12:00 P.M.	work lunch	work lunch	work lunch	work lunch	work lunch		
1:00 P.M.	work	work	work	work	work		
2:00 P.M.	work	work	work	work	work		buy groceries
3:00 P.M.	work	work	work	work	work	lunch	lunch
4:00 P.M.	drive home	drive home	drive home	drive home	drive home		
5:00 P.M.	drive	drive	drive				
6:00 P.M.	Biology	Anthropology	Study Skills				
7:00 P.M.	Biology	Anthropology	Study Skills	go to laundromat			
8:00 P.M.	Biology	Anthropology	Study Skills	go to laundromat	out to dinner		dinner
9:00 P.M.	drive home/ dinner	drive home/ dinner	drive home/ dinner	dinner	out to dinner	dinner	
10:00 P.M.					out to dinner	dancing	sleep
11:00 P.M.	sleep	sleep	sleep	sleep	sleep	dancing	sleep
12:00 A.M.	sleep	sleep	sleep	sleep	sleep	dancing	sleep
1:00 A.M.	sleep	sleep	sleep	sleep	sleep	dancing	sleep
2:00 A.M.	sleep	sleep	sleep	sleep	sleep	sleep	sleep

Hours Available for Study __28½__   Hours Needed for Study __21__

Consider Your Grade Goals

You may also need to increase your study time if you want to get As or Bs in one or more of your courses. You'll have to spend more time on your course work to earn high grades. This may involve editing your notes (see Chapter 8), annotating your text as you do your reading assignments as a weekly review (see Chapter 9), and studying more actively for quizzes and exams (see Chapter 10). You may need to spend more time on doing your assignments to ensure that they reflect your best effort. Some students also work with tutors or form a study group to maximize their grades. All these activities take additional time.

Learn How Long It Takes to Do Your Assignments

You also can learn to judge your time needed for study by estimating how long it takes you to do individual assignments. You should have a pretty good idea now about how much time you need to complete your overall study goals; learning to estimate the time needed for smaller, individual assignments can be extremely helpful as well. Time yourself the next time you read one of your textbooks. Finding out how long it takes to read ten pages in each of your texts will help you plan more accurately. You can also time yourself as you complete math assignments and writing assignments or as you review your notes. Knowing approximately how long it takes to do the routine work will allow you to plan more effectively.

Consider Long-Term Assignments

Many students forget to build in weekly study time for long-term assignments. You need to allow time to study for exams, prepare term papers, and complete semester projects. Some students expect the regular assignment load to disappear when test or paper deadlines roll around. Unfortunately, this doesn't happen. If you don't adjust your study schedule for these long-range assignments, you may find that you have to "steal" time from your regular work in order to prepare for them. As a result, you may fall behind in everything else.

Monitor Your Current Study Time

One way to get a better estimate of how much time you actually need for study is by monitoring your current study time. By keeping track of how many hours you actually study (read, take notes, edit lecture notes, do math or writing assignments, and so on) during a typical week, you can evaluate the accuracy of your estimate of study time needed. You can also repeat the experiment during a week that is not so typical. Choose a week in which you have one or more exams and a paper or project due.

You may also find it helpful to keep a study log. A study log is a calendar where you write in the number of hours you spend doing assignments and studying for each of your courses. Use the chart available on the Web site. By keeping track of exactly how many hours you spend each day (and each week) on each of your courses, you can monitor your time use. You may find that you don't spend enough time studying during the week or that you don't spend enough time on one class. You may also notice that on some days you spend a lot of time on academic tasks and very little time on other days. Look for patterns that will help you correct any problems early in the semester. Compare the total hours for each of your classes to the time goals that you set when you completed the study ratio chart. Like many of my students, you may find that keeping a study log will help motivate you to put more time into your work.

ACTIVITY 2.4   *Keep a Study Log*

Use the study log on the Web site to keep track of how much time you spend studying every day for the next week. (Be sure to include weekends.) List each of your classes. How closely does this total match your estimated time needed for study? What patterns did you notice? Did you complete all of your work?

ACTIVITY 2.5 *Evaluate Time Needed for Study*

Go back to your Fixed Commitment Calendar in Activity 2.3 and write in the number of hours that you need this semester for study. Remember that this number will change each semester, depending on your schedule of classes and your goals. Now compare the time available for study to the time that you need. Do you have enough time to complete all your work? Do you have any additional time left for relaxation and personal goals?

ORGANIZE YOUR STUDY TIME

Once you've set up a time plan that allows you enough time to complete all your work, you need to learn how to organize your time so that it can be used efficiently. By learning to plan and schedule your study time, you can begin to take control of your time.

CREATE A SEMESTER CALENDAR

One of the best ways to organize your study time is to make a semester calendar. A semester calendar includes all of your assignments, quizzes, and exams. Seeing what you have to do for each day of the semester is the first step in planning your study time.

The easiest way to prepare a semester calendar is to use a blank block calendar similar to the one in Figure 2.4. Write in the name of the month, and number the days of the month. Next, pull out your course syllabi. Write all your assignments on your calendar. (You may have reading assignments, math exercises, and an English paper all due on the same day.) If some of your professors don't give you a day-to-day syllabus, you will need to add assignments to your calendar as you learn of them. You may find it helpful to put the assignments for each separate course in a different color or list them all in black ink and then use colored markers to differentiate each subject. By color coding your assignments, you can quickly identify the work that you have to do each day. Make exams stand out on your calendar by writing them in large capital letters and putting a box around them.

After you've completed your calendars for each month of the semester, post them where you can see them easily—for example, on your refrigerator or bulletin board—and make sure that you're able to see two months at any one time. There is nothing more frustrating than turning the page on your calendar too late and realizing that you missed an important event. This is true for assignments and exams, too. Look at the sample calendars in Figures 2.4 and 2.5. The last week of September looks like a pretty easy week—after the Sociology exam on Monday. There is a little reading to do, but the workload definitely seems to be on the light side. If this were your calendar, you might think that you could take it easy for a week. Now look at the first week of October. You have exams in History, Algebra, and Study Skills, three papers due for English, and two chapters of reading. If you had waited until the beginning of October to turn the page of your calendar, it would have been too late to prepare for your exams and complete your papers.

FIGURE 2.4
Sample Semester Calendar for September

Month _____September_____

Sunday	Monday	Tuesday	Wednesday	Thursday	Friday	Saturday
2	**3**	**4** H - Ch 1 SS - Ch 1	**5** A - 1.1 & 1.2 E - 1-35 Journal	**6** H - Ch 2 SS - Ch 2	**7** A - 1.3 & 1.4 E - 38-52 Journal Soc - Ch 1 (2-24)	**8**
9	**10** A - 1.5 & 1.6 E - Experience essay-draft	**11** H - Ch 3	**12** A - 2.1 & 2.2 Soc - Ch 2 (26-48)	**13** SS - Goal statements	**14** A - 2.3 & 2.4 E - Experience essay	**15**
16	**17** A - 2.5 & 2.6 E - 53-56 Soc - Ch 3 (52-74)	**18** H - Ch 4 SS - Ch 3 To Do lists	**19** A - 3.1 & 3.2 E - Observation essay-draft	**20** SS - Ch 4 & H.O. Calendars due	**21** A - 3.3 & 3.4 E - Observation essay due	**22**
23	**24** A - 3.5 & 3.6 SOC-EXAM 1	**25** H - Ch 5 SS - Ch 5 notes due	**26** A - 4.1 & 4.2 Soc - Ch 4 (75-103)	**27**	**28** A - 4.3 & 4.4 E - 65-81	**29**
30						

A = College Algebra   H = Western Civilization   SS = Study Skills
E = English Composition   Soc = Sociology

FIGURE 2.5
Sample Semester Calendar for October

Month _____October_____

Sunday	Monday	Tuesday	Wednesday	Thursday	Friday	Saturday
	1 A - 4.5 & 4.6 E - Exposition essay-draft	**2** H - EXAM 1 SS - Text marking due	**3** A - EXAM 1 E - Revision Soc - Ch 5 (105-130)	**4** H - Ch 6 SS - EXAM 1	**5** A - 5.1 & 5.2 E - Exposition essay due	**6**
7	**8** A - 5.3 & 5.4 E - 82-111 Soc - Ch 7 (162-189)	**9** H - Ch 7 SS - Ch 9 text notes	**10** A - 5.5 & 5.6 E - Revision due	**11** SS - Predicted questions	**12** A - 6.1 & 6.2	**13**
14	**15** A - 6.3 & 6.4 E - Portfolio due	**16** H - Ch 8 SS - Ch 6 & H.O.	**17** A - 6.5 & 6.6 Soc - Ch 8 (191-240)	**18** SS - Ch 7	**19** A - 7.1 & 7.2 E - 112-125	**20**
21	**22** A - 7.3 & 7.4 E - Definition essay-draft SOC - EXAM II	**23** H - Ch 9 SS - Ch 10	**24** A -7.5 & 7.6 E - 127-140	**25** H - Ch 10 SS - Study plan due	**26** A - EXAM II E - Definition essay due Soc - Ch 11 (278-310)	**27**
28	**29** A - 8.1 & 8.2 E - Argument essay due	**30** H - EXAM II SS - EXAM II	**31** A -8.3 & 8.4 E - 141-162			

A = College Algebra   H = Western Civilization   SS = Study Skills
E = English Composition   Soc = Sociology

ACTIVITY 2.6   *Fill In Your Semester Calendar*

Print the blank calendars available on the Web site, purchase blank calendars in your college bookstore or a local office supply store, or use a computerized calendar program. Begin filling in your calendar by writing in the months and the dates for the entire semester. Then use your syllabi to list all your assignments on the calendar. Remember to color code your assignments. Don't forget to write exams in capital letters and to box them in so that they really stand out. Do you see any patterns in when your work is due?

USE DAILY "TO DO" LISTS

After you create a semester calendar you need to begin to plan when you're going to do your work. A "To Do" list is a list of the tasks that you want to complete each day. Look at your semester calendar and write down what you need to do for the next week. Break down some of the tasks from that list. You might decide to read your History assignment over the next two days or work on writing your English essay for one hour every day during the week.

Putting your personal goals on the list is important, too. This further reinforces your commitment to put all your plans in writing. In addition, writing your personal goals on your "To Do" list will help you stay more organized. The more organized you are in completing your personal goals, the more time you will have to complete your academic goals.

Making "To Do" lists can become habit forming, so by all means get started immediately. Don't worry if you don't accomplish everything on your list; few people do everything they set out to do every day. Just move the one or two tasks that were left uncompleted to the top of the list for the next day. Remember, though: It is important that you plan realistically. A pattern of planning too much to do and then moving half of your tasks to the next day can lead to procrastination.

Consider prioritizing some of your tasks. Use numbers, a star, or another symbol to indicate that certain tasks need to be done first. Look at the "To Do" lists in Figure 2.6. In the first example, Jean mixed study goals and personal goals together. As you might expect, the personal goals were completed, and the study goals were left undone. Put your academic goals at the top of the page and your personal goals at the bottom. By putting your study goals first, you are reinforcing your commitment to academics. By setting priorities, Robin was able to complete all of her study tasks before beginning her personal goals (Figure 2.6).

Many students use professional planners (available in college bookstores or office supply stores) to keep track of assignments and personal goals. Many planners are designed with space for hour-by-hour planning, blocks for listing tasks due each week, and monthly calendars. Using a professional planner can help you organize all your study, work, and personal goals in one place. Remember: It doesn't matter what kind of planner you use; the important thing is to plan ahead and write down what you plan to accomplish each day.

ACTIVITY 2.7   *Complete Your "To Do" Lists*

Write "To Do" lists every day for the next week. Be sure that you break tasks down, number them to show their priority, and check off completed tasks. Were you able to complete all your assignments? Did using the "To Do" lists help?

FIGURE 2.6
Sample "To-Do" Lists

JEAN'S "TO DO" LIST	ROBIN'S "TO DO" LIST
DAY ___Wednesday___	DAY ___THURSDAY___
Study Goals:	**Study Goals:**
✓1 Go to student aid office	✓2 MAKE COPY OF SPEECH OUTLINE
✓2 Do laundry	✓3 PRACTICE SPEECH
7 Final draft Engl paper	✓4 READ PP. 135-145 IN BLACK LIT
✓6 Go copy Fr tape Ch 3	✓1 READ ESSAY 2 IN POL SCI
✓3 Get card for Grandma B-day	✓8 DO FEB. CALENDAR
11 Make to do list for tomorrow	✓6 READ PP. 146-156 IN BLACK LIT
5 Study Ch 2 Fr	✓5 READ 10 PPS. OF CH. 1 POL SCI
✓8 Read Art pp 53-63	✓7 READ PP. 163-173 IN SS
9 Do Alg Ch 2-5	✓9 DO "THINGS TO DO" FOR TOMORROW
✓4 Dentist Appt. 2:30	
✓10 Meet Tom 5:30	
Personal Goals:	**Personal Goals:**
	✓10 WRITE LETTER HOME
	✓11 CHECK MAIL
	✓12 GO TO BASKETBALL GAME
	13 CLEAN ROOM

SET UP YOUR STUDY SCHEDULE

After you've determined what assignments you have to do, you need to think about when you're going to do them. To make the best use of your study time, you should begin to plan weekly or daily what you're going to do and when. Now that you know how long it takes to read ten pages in each of your textbooks, you can easily schedule all your reading assignments. You also should have a pretty good estimate of how long it will take to complete your writing, math, and study assignments. All these factors affect how efficiently you use your study time and how effectively you complete your assignments.

Assign Tasks to Available Study Time

To set up your study schedule, you need to refer to your Fixed Commitment Calendar to assign specific tasks to your available study time. Look back at Greg's Fixed Commitment Calendar in Figure 2.2; you'll notice that Greg has three one-hour time blocks and a four-hour time block on Wednesdays. Greg prefers to do his Algebra homework right after class when the information is still fresh. If he has a thirty-page chapter of History to read, for example, he could read the first ten pages before lunch, the next ten pages right after class, and the last ten pages from 7:00 to 8:00. Of course, Greg could have begun reading his History on Tuesday, too. Greg could then use his longer time block in the evening to work on an upcoming English paper. Assigning specific tasks to specific blocks of study time can help you complete your work on time.

Use One-Hour Time Blocks

Many students ignore one-hour blocks of time because they think that one hour is not long enough to really accomplish anything. In fact, one-hour blocks are the most important study blocks that you have. During a one-hour block of time, you can get a good start on a math assignment, complete a "chunk" of a reading assignment, complete a short writing assignment, or even review or expand on your lecture notes. If you've planned ahead, you'll find you can get a lot done in these short periods of time.

Use Your Daytime Study Hours

When you're planning your study schedule, don't forget to use your daytime study hours. In high school you may have been able to get all your homework done during the evening, but there aren't enough evening hours to complete all your study assignments in college. Look back at Greg's Fixed Commitment Calendar in Figure 2.2. Greg needed a minimum of thirty-two hours of study time per week to complete his assignments. If he used only his evening hours, he would be twelve hours short of his minimum. The fourteen hours that Greg has available during the day are necessary for him to do his work. Check your Fixed Commitment Calendar. Do you need your daytime study hours to complete your assignment, too?

Use Time Between Classes

You can also accomplish a lot by using the hours that you have between classes. Instead of going back to your room to drop off your books, find an empty classroom or sit in the hall and begin your next reading assignment. By getting a good solid start on the assignment, you increase your probability of completing it. You may also find that right after a class is the best time to edit your lecture notes (see Chapter 8). If you have a quiz scheduled or suspect that one will be given, you should use the time between classes to review your lecture notes and your highlighting or text notes before the quiz. Take a few minutes now to count how many hours you have between classes this semester. Using this time to accomplish some of your study goals is an important step in achieving good time management. Some additional tips for managing your time can be found in the Tip Block.

ACTIVITY 2.8 *Schedule Your Assignments*

Make a list of your study goals for tomorrow. Don't forget to break long assignments down into manageable units. Then refer to your Fixed Commitment Calendar and schedule your assignments into appropriate time blocks. Take your plan to class and discuss it with a group of your classmates. Did anyone have suggestions to improve your schedule?

TIP

MORE TIPS FOR MANAGING YOUR TIME

DEVELOP A SCHEDULE. Set up a schedule for both studying and completing your other responsibilities. Put your schedule in writing and stick to it. You may need to explain to your parents (or your children) that you need more time to study now that you are in college and won't be able to spend as much time doing household chores as you did before.

POST YOUR STUDY SCHEDULE. Put your list of study tasks on the bulletin board or on the refrigerator each week so that everyone in your family knows what you need to accomplish that week. This will help keep you more organized and let your family know what you need to do.

MAKE USE OF SMALL BLOCKS OF TIME. Many nontraditional students tend to study late at night after the children are asleep or all chores are completed. Instead of waiting for large blocks of time to do your work, break down your tasks and work on smaller portions of the assignment during fifteen-, thirty-, or even forty-five-minute time blocks throughout the day.

STUDY DURING BREAKS AT WORK. You'd be surprised at how much work you can do during breaks over a one-week period. You could read five pages of a chapter during lunch. You could review your word cards (flash cards for technical terminology) during a fifteen-minute break. You could even mentally review or quiz yourself on the material for an exam during a slow time at work.

PLAN TIME WITH YOUR FAMILY. Set aside time to spend with your family or friends each day or each week. Make this a regular part of your time-management schedule. During "slow" weeks or term breaks, plan special activities as a way of saying thank you for their support, patience, and help during the busier weeks.

DELEGATE SOME HOUSEHOLD TASKS. Unless you aren't planning to sleep, eat, or ever relax, you won't have time to do all your household chores when you're going to school. Do what you *have* to do and leave the rest for a slow week, day off, or even until term break. Ask your family to help out by doing some of the cooking, cleaning, or laundry. If each member of the family accepts just one task, you'll be amazed at the time you gain.

COOK AHEAD AND FREEZE MAIN COURSES. Instead of making one meat loaf for dinner tonight, make two and freeze one for the next week. You can also cook ahead during "light" weeks of the semester or during term breaks. Having dinner ready to pop in the microwave can be a real time-saver during busy weeks.

LEARN TO SAY NO. Believe it or not, I was a Girl Scout leader my first year in graduate school. As a mother, it was a great decision. As a returning student, it was a disaster. While you're attending college, you won't have time for many outside activities. When you do say no, explain that when you complete your education, you'll be happy to help out.

USE TIME-MANAGEMENT STRATEGIES TO STAY MOTIVATED

Organizing your work and scheduling your time can make a huge difference in how much time it takes to do your work. However, just planning to read twenty pages at 2:00 P.M. is no guarantee that you will get it done. Schedules are designed to organize your use of time, but they are not designed to make you do the work. *You* have to do that.

One thing that can make a difference in whether you accomplish your goals is your level of motivation. You can keep your motivation high by using some specific techniques.

STUDY IN ONE-HOUR BLOCKS

One effective strategy for keeping yourself motivated is to study in sixty-minute time blocks. As you schedule your study tasks, break them down so that they can be accomplished in one-hour blocks of time. Then plan to read, do problems, write, or study for fifty minutes. If you find that you can't concentrate on your work for the entire fifty minutes, work for thirty minutes and then take a five-minute break.

TAKE BREAKS

After each study block of fifty minutes, you should plan a ten-minute break. Be realistic about the kind of activity that you plan for a study break. Taking a ten-minute nap just will not work, and going out to play a quick game of basketball inevitably will lead to a longer game of basketball. What can you do in ten minutes? You can grab a snack, write a short letter, check on your kids, throw a load of laundry in the washer, or make a phone call. (Resist the temptation to call a good friend to chat—you won't be able to hang up in ten minutes.) Doing aerobics or just stretching is also a great activity for a break between study periods.

TACKLE DIFFICULT ASSIGNMENTS FIRST

Do the assignments for the course you dislike first and get them out of the way. You can easily complete the assignments for your favorite classes late in the day, even when you are feeling tired. Unfortunately, that usually is not true for those more difficult assignments. If you leave them until the wee hours of the morning, you may find instead that you don't do them at all.

Also, if you do the assignments that you like the most first, you have nothing to look forward to. It's kind of like eating dessert before you eat your meal. The best part is already over, and the rest is somewhat disappointing. You also may find that if you leave the more difficult tasks for the end of the day, you worry about them as you work on other tasks. A difficult assignment can feel like a heavy weight hanging over your head. Doing your least favorite or most difficult assignments first and your easiest or favorite assignments last will help you stay motivated throughout the day.

SWITCH SUBJECTS

Another good strategy for maintaining your motivation to study is to switch subjects. By alternating between reading psychology and working algebra problems, you can get more done without becoming bored and tired. If you have a long time block available for study (for instance, from 6:00 to 11:00), you should switch subjects every hour. Occasionally, you will find that you are really progressing on an assignment and, after the ten-minute break, want to continue working on it. In such cases, you should do so. However, most students find that after an hour they are only too willing to work on something else for a while.

BREAK TASKS DOWN

You may find that breaking down your tasks into manageable units will help you accomplish your goals. Which would you rather read, a fifty-page chapter or a ten-page chapter? Most people would agree that a ten-page chapter sounds much more appealing. If you have long reading assignments, break them down on your "To Do" list. You could divide that fifty-page chapter into five separate tasks. It may make your list a little longer, but it also will allow you to shorten it more rapidly. Once you complete the first ten-page chunk of reading, you will feel a sense of accomplishment and be motivated to read the next ten pages. Many of my students find that breaking down tasks reduces their tendency to procrastinate—perhaps you will, too.

PLAN REWARDS

In many ways, your ten-minute study break is a reward for having completed one block of study tasks. These short breaks, however, aren't always enough of a reward to keep you motivated. It's a good idea to get into the habit of rewarding yourself for completing difficult tasks or for completing all your work on a particular day. Rewards are whatever you can plan to do that will help keep you working when you want to stop. Students use many kinds of rewards to stay motivated. Ordering a pizza after finishing a tough assignment works for some students. Others work hard to complete their studying in time to watch a favorite television show. If you know that you want to watch "Monday Night Football," plan your work on Sunday and Monday so that you can be finished in time; then you'll be able to sit back and watch the game without feeling guilty. Going to a party or watching your favorite "soap" each day also can be used as a reward for completing one or two specific study goals. Using rewards can help keep you motivated to do your work.

WORK AHEAD

To be in control of your time, learn to work ahead on your assignments. You will find college much less stressful if you get out of the habit of doing Tuesday's assignments on Monday. Get into the habit of doing the work due for Tuesday on Sunday or even on Friday. Always being a little ahead of the game will give you a feeling of security. If something comes up (and something always does, at just the wrong time), you will still be prepared for class the next morning. There is no worse feeling than walking into class unprepared. It is incredible how professors always seem to call on students or give a quiz the one time that they didn't do the reading.

You should work ahead on long-range assignments, too. Schedule one to two hours each week to work on a term paper or project. By starting early in the semester, you can easily complete your term paper and still keep up with your regular assignments. Develop a list of tasks for your paper or project and decide when you will work on each task. Putting up a time line across the top of your bulletin board also may motivate you to work on completing your project.

ACTIVITY 2.9   *Schedule a Long-Range Assignment*

Choose one of your long-range assignments for the semester and list the steps you will have to accomplish in order to complete the project. Then set up a schedule for when you will complete each step. Write the week number or numbers next to each step, or develop a time line for your project. Be sure to include deadlines for the completion of each major part of the project. Check off each step as you complete it.

REDUCE PROCRASTINATION

Procrastination, putting things off, is a common behavior pattern for many students. According to Albert Ellis and William Knaus, the three main causes of procrastination are self-downing, low frustration tolerance, and hostility.[2] Self-downing refers to putting yourself down, telling yourself that you can't do it. If you don't really believe that you can successfully complete a task, you're more likely to put it off. If you are easily frustrated and tend to give up or have trouble starting a task because it appears to be difficult or too time consuming, you may have *low frustration tolerance*. Another common cause of procrastination is *hostility* toward the assignment, instructor, or the class. You may put off doing the task because you are angry with your professor. If you feel the assignment is unfair or that you were given too little time to complete it, your hostility can lead to procrastination. In the same way, if you think your professor grades too hard or embarrassed you in class, you may find it difficult to start the assignment.

Students procrastinate for many other reasons. Some students put off studying for exams until is almost too late. They may, in fact, be using procrastination to protect themselves from feelings of inadequacy. By not studying adequately, you can protect your ego because you can blame your failure on your lack of preparation rather than on your lack of ability. For example, a student might say, "Well, if I had studied, I would have gotten a B, but I just didn't have time." Poor time management can also lead to procrastination. Not planning ahead for long-range assignments leaves some students in a time crunch when they realize that a paper or project deadline is approaching. Instead of having six to eight weeks to prepare a term paper, procrastinators may find themselves with one week or less to complete it. Of course, this often leads to panic and poor performance. At times, students procrastinate on tasks because they just don't know how to get started. Many college freshmen have difficulty writing their first (or second) essay for Freshman Composition class. Although they aren't afraid of failure, they just can't figure out how to begin. Lack of motivation or interest can also contribute to procrastination. It's hard to get started if you aren't really interested in the task or don't feel that it is important to you.

Procrastination can become a habit—a way of life for some students. Procrastination leads to more procrastination. Once you start to put work off, things pile up. As your workload grows, it becomes even more difficult to get it all done. Because procrastination is such a common problem, many books, articles, and Web sites are devoted to the topic. Take a look at the strategies shown in the Tip Block. Many of them have been successful in helping my students break the procrastination habit. They can work for you, too.

ACTIVITY 2.10   *Check Your Procrastination Level*

Go to the *College Reading and Study Strategies* book-specific Web site and follow the link to the University of Texas Procrastination Quotient online evaluation tool. After answering each of the questions, score your responses.

---

[2]Albert Ellis and William J. Knaus, *Overcoming Procrastination* (New York: Signet, 1977), p. 16.

TIP

TEN TIPS FOR OVERCOMING PROCRASTINATION

JUST GET STARTED. The best way to overcome procrastination is simply to get started—to take action. Do anything. Tell yourself you only have to work for five or ten minutes. At the end of that time, you can decide whether you want to work for another ten minutes.

SET REALISTIC GOALS. If you set reasonable expectations for yourself, you are more likely to accomplish your goals and less likely to have negative feelings about your capabilities.

START WITH THE EASIEST PART OF THE TASK. You can avoid feeling overwhelmed if you start with the easiest part of the assignment or with only a small part of it. Once you start the assignment, you're more likely to continue working on it. Remember, getting started is the hardest part.

CREATE "TO DO" LISTS. Putting your tasks in writing helps you see exactly what you must accomplish and strengthens your commitment to complete your work. Adding a specific time to begin each task will help you organize your study time and avoid procrastination.

SET PRIORITIES. List all of the tasks that you need to accomplish each day. Include your school, work, and personal tasks on a "To Do" list. Then prioritize the tasks on your list so that you complete the most important ones first.

PLAN AHEAD FOR LONG-TERM ASSIGNMENTS. Set up a time plan to complete major papers and projects. If you set deadlines for each part of the task throughout the semester, you can avoid getting caught in a time crunch. The best time to start any long-range assignment is on the day it is assigned.

BREAK DOWN LARGE TASKS. Breaking down large tasks makes them appear less difficult and less time consuming. It is always easier to get yourself motivated to do a small task. When you feel more motivated, you're less likely to procrasinate.

RECOGNIZE THAT ALL ASSIGNMENTS ARE RELEVANT. Some students tend to procrastinate when they have to complete tasks that don't seem to be relevant to them. A college education will help prepare you for a career, but it is also your opportunity to become an educated person (something that will serve you well in any career).

USE POSITIVE SELF-TALK. Tell yourself that you can complete the task successfully, that you want to do it, and that it is important. Making excuses for not completing the task, such as it's too hard or it's just busywork, leads to procrastination. Using positive self-talk can get you started now.

IDENTIFY ESCAPIST TECHNIQUES. You can also avoid procrastination by figuring out what you do to keep from doing your work. Do you suddenly decide to clean the house, take a nap, check your e-mail, watch television, or chat with a friend when you should be doing assignments? Until you monitor your own escapist techniques, you may not even realize that you're using them.

ACTIVITY 2.11 *Describe Possible Strategies to Overcome Procrastination Problems*

List ten tasks that you put off in the last week or two. Identify the main reason that you procrastinated on each one. Work in a group to suggest strategies that you could have used to overcome your procrastination problems. Select five common procrastination problems to present to the class along with several of the coping strategies your group suggested.

REEVALUATE YOUR TIME PLAN

After you have used your time plan for a while, you may find that it's not working well for you. You may need more time for long-range assignments, or you may discover you need more time available for study than you thought. It's important to take a look periodically at how you are using your time during the semester.

A good time to reevaluate your time plan is after the fourth week of the semester; that's when the first round of exams usually occurs. One good way to determine whether you are putting in enough time studying is to consider the grades you received on your first set of exams. If your grades are in line with the goals you set, then your time plan is probably working effectively for you. You also can judge whether you are using your time efficiently by looking back at some of your calendars and "To Do" lists. Have you been accomplishing the study goals that you set each day? Are you moving many tasks to the next day? Are you leaving work undone? Did you have time to prepare adequately for your exams? By answering these questions, you can determine whether you need to change your time plan.

The second point at which you should evaluate your time plan is after midterm exams. By this time in the semester, you should be able to determine quite accurately which parts of your time plan work and which don't. This is the best time to make some changes that will help you improve your grades. Finally, you also should rethink your time plan about two weeks before final exams.

ACTIVITY 2.12   *Use PowerTrac to Locate Information on Time Management*

If you are using the InfoTrac College Edition, read the directions for doing a PowerTrac search, click on the search entry box, and do a key word search on the topic of *time management*. Experiment with several combinations of terms using the *and, not,* and *or* logical operators. You can learn more about how to use logical operators by following the link that appeared on the Searching PowerTrac screen.

If you get thousands of hits (articles containing the key words), you need to narrow the search more. Try using *time management and procrastination* "To-Do" lists or *study plans* this time. With fewer hits this time, click on the view button to explore what you found. Locate at least one article that includes information that you find useful and share it with the class.

ACTIVITY 2.13   *Where Are You Now?*

Now that you have completed Chapter 2, take a few minutes to repeat the "Where Are You Now?" activity, located on the *College Reading and Study Strategies* Web site. What changes did you make as a result of reading this chapter? How are you planning to apply what you've learned in this chapter?

SUMMARY

Good time-management strategies are crucial to your college success. Monitoring how you use your time now is the first step to achieving good time management. Keeping a time diary will help you get a better picture of any time-use problems that you have. Complete a Fixed Commitment Calendar to see how much time you actually have available for study tasks. Then set up an assignment calendar so that you get a semester view of your workload and important due dates for each of your courses. Preparing weekly task lists and daily "To Do" lists will keep you organized and up to date with your work. Make academics your number one priority when you decide how to use your *free* time. Taking breaks, switching subjects, and planning rewards are just a few of the strategies that will keep you motivated and on schedule. Many students fall into the procrastination trap. Understanding the real reasons for procrastination will help you learn why you may procrastinate in certain situations. By identifying your escapist techniques and making a decision to use more effective strategies, you can overcome this problem. Breaking down tasks, starting with the easiest part of the assignment, and setting specific goals are all good strategies for breaking the procrastination cycle. If you use good time-management techniques, you can stay up to date on your course assignments, have time for relaxation and other responsibilities, and eliminate the stress and panic that often result from not getting your work done.

Review Questions

Terms You Should Know: Make a flashcard for each term.

Escapist techniques	Procrastination	Semester calendar
Fixed commitment	Prospective	Study log
Fixed commitment calendar	Retrospective	Time diary
Hostility	Rewards	Time management
Low frustration tolerance	Self-downing	"To Do" list

Completion: Fill in the blank to complete each of the following statements.

1. The first step in good time management is _____ how you use your time now.

2. You need to spend almost one- _____ of your time each week on academic tasks if you are a full-time student.

3. The average student spends about _____ hours outside of class for every hour in class to complete assignments.

4. Completing a _____ calendar will help you determine how well you can stick to a schedule.

5. The best way to overcome problems with procrastination is simply to _____ _____.

Multiple Choice: Circle the letter of the best answer for each of the following questions. Be sure to underline key words and eliminate wrong answers.

6. You can determine your time available for study by completing a:
   A. time diary.
   B. fixed commitment calendar.
   C. semester calendar.
   D. prospective-retrospective calendar.

7. Which of the following is *not* one of the main causes of procrastination?
    A. Self-downing
    B. Low frustration tolerance
    C. Feelings of inadequacy
    D. Hostility

Short Answer–Essay: On a separate sheet, answer each of the following questions.

8. What are the five factors that influence how much time you need for study?

9. What are four strategies for scheduling study tasks?

10. What are five strategies that students can use to overcome problems with procrastination?

3 Introduction to College Reading Strategies

In this chapter you will learn more about:

➤ College reading tasks

➤ Reading texts in different disciplines

➤ Characteristics of successful reading

➤ Reading for different levels of comprehension

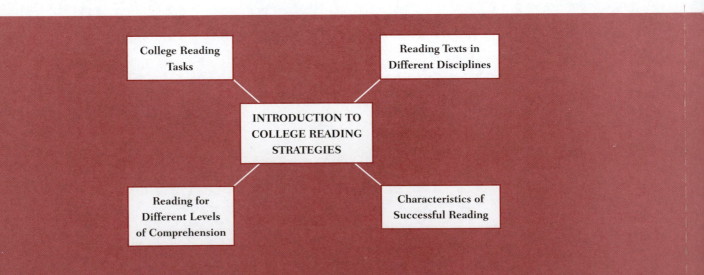

ACTIVITY 3.1 *Where Are You Now?*

Take a few minutes to answer *yes* or *no* to the following questions.

	YES	NO
1. Do you read all your text assignments at the same rate?	_____	_____
2. Do you know the expectations of your instructor about the text readings?	_____	_____
3. Do you read all your text assignments in the same way?	_____	_____
4. Do you plan out time for careful, close reading of text assignments?	_____	_____
5. When you read, do you tend to focus most of your attention on reading to figure out the words?	_____	_____
6. When you read, do you read to make sense of what you read?	_____	_____
7. Do you use the same strategies for reading literature as for reading science?	_____	_____
8. Do you have difficulty keeping up with all the text assignments?	_____	_____
9. When you read, do you try to connect the ideas in the text with what you already know?	_____	_____
10. When you read, do you try to think of how you could use the text information in new situations?	_____	_____

Total Points   _____

Score yourself 1 point for each *yes* answer to questions 2, 4, 6, 9, and 10. Score yourself 1 point for each *no* answer to questions 1, 3, 5, 7, and 8. Now total up your points. A low score indicates that you will need to readjust your approach for reading text assignments. A high score indicates that you know how to adjust your reading to different types of academic reading.

COLLEGE READING TASKS

Students beginning college, particularly if they have not been in academic settings for a while, typically feel overwhelmed by the amount of reading that they have to complete. This is a normal reaction, similar to the feeling of a couch potato who needs to get in shape to run in a race. With good training, an established routine of exercise, and daily perseverance, a nonathlete can get in shape. Similarly, an established routine for reading, a repertoire of comprehension strategies, and a positive attitude will help you get in shape for the amount and types of reading you need to complete in college. This section of this textbook will give you background ideas to help you become successful in completing college reading tasks. This chapter will provide a general introduction to college reading strategies, and the subsequent chapters in this textbook will help you develop those strategies.

READING COLLEGE-LEVEL MATERIALS

As a college student, the types of materials that you are expected to read are sophisticated, challenging, and content-rich. As your "tools" for the course, the readings provide important background for your class lectures and for your class activities. The readings that your course professors assign provide a critical foundation for your understanding of the course topics and help you make important connections between what you already know and what is relevant in the course.

Challenges of Reading College Material

Imagine that you have been assigned to read the following sentence:

Liffing brafnim is an enjoyable deglat when going to the plitra.

What made this sentence hard to read? The vocabulary? The number of nonsense words? The lack of prior information about the topic? If you answered "Yes" to any of these responses, then you are describing the typical factors that make this nonsense sentence difficult to read.

Yet you can understand this sentence if some background information is provided and a few of the nonsense words are translated into familiar words. For instance, let's assume that this sentence is about eating popcorn, noted in this sentence as "liffing brafnim." Now can you figure out the rest of the sentence? Another clue is provided by the phrase "going to." Where do you go and eat popcorn? That's right; you go to the movies. You can most likely determine the meaning of the sentence from these clues. Based on your prior knowledge about going to the movies and eating popcorn, you can generate a basic idea of the sentence. In order to figure out what the sentence meant, you can make some guesses about the meaning of the passage based on what you know and the information provided.[*]

Similarly, when you are reading challenging text, you can use good strategies, such as recalling what you know about the topic already, looking for author clues to determine the meanings of unknown words, and making inferences about the meaning of the passage. As you read, you can check your interpretation with new information that is presented and the information discussed in class.

Try the following activity so that you can identify some of the factors that make college-level reading material challenging to read.

---

[*]The translation of this sentence is: Eating popcorn is an enjoyable activity when going to the movies.

ACTIVITY 3.2 *What Makes College Materials Difficult to Read?*

Select a reading assignment from one of your classes. Now think of all of the factors that make this assignment difficult to read. Check all that apply. Be prepared to discuss your responses with your peers in a small group in class. Explain why you checked off the descriptors.

1. My reading assignment is from this textbook (name and page):

2. The factors that make the text difficult to understand are (check all that apply):

___ Difficult vocabulary   ___ Long sentences

___ Unfamiliar topic   ___ Unfamiliar symbols

___ Hard to follow the author's ideas   ___ Unfamiliar references to other topics

___ Topic seems irrelevant   ___ Other:

The Goals of Comprehending College-Level Texts

The fundamental goal of reading college texts is to comprehend what you read so that you will be able to use what you learn and understand the discipline you are studying. Comprehending text materials is a process of making meaning of what you read. This means that you may need to use a variety of strategies to determine what an author is communicating and to make meaningful connections of the author's ideas with your own experiences, beliefs, and background knowledge.[1]

Yet the goal of college-level reading is not just to comprehend the material; rather, the ultimate goal is to use the text ideas in meaningful ways. Often college texts present a variety of theories, principles, and terms that are common to a specific area, such as psychology, sociology, literature, or mathematics. College professors expect that you will not only read the material but that you will use the texts to become familiar with the principle ideas of the discipline, that you will think like someone in the field, and that you will understand and use the key principles.

ACADEMIC READING VERSUS NONACADEMIC READING

Although you may read several different types of text materials while you are in college, it is useful to remember that not all texts should be read in the same way. You may find it helpful to make a distinction between those texts that are required as part of your academic reading and those that are part of your nonacademic reading.

Academic Reading

As an adult student you have multiple types of texts to read. Your college instructor will most likely have a textbook that accompanies the class. Your instructor may have chosen not just one textbook but several for you to read and use. In addition, your college instructor may give you assignments in daily newspapers, weekly magazines, and professional journals. Your college instructor will most likely expect that you will read materials that you find through online sources, such as the Internet. These types of reading materials are described as "academic texts" because they are the materials you are reading for learning in college.

Nonacademic Reading

If you choose to live on campus, you will have information about the dormitories, a housing contract, the health benefits, and a variety of informational materials to help you get started. If you live off campus, you also encounter many reading materials through everyday tasks, such as reading a map and reading road signs when driving a car to get from one place to another. You encounter other types of reading material, too, such as tax forms, insurance forms, or even recipes for cooking. These types of reading materials are described as "nonacademic texts" because these texts are not required for academic work in college. Your nonacademic reading texts also include a variety of reading materials that you select for your own use; these texts help you learn more about certain topics, such as nutrition, physical fitness, or sports.

You can use some of the same strategies with both types of materials. For instance, when you begin to read an article, whether it is in your favorite sports magazine or in a science textbook, it is a good idea to ask yourself some questions about what you know

---

[1] D. E. Alvermann and S. F. Phelps, *Content Reading and Literacy: Succeeding in Today's Diverse Classrooms* (Boston, MA: Allyn & Bacon, 2002).

about the topic. You can think about other materials you have read about the topic, and you can recall other conversations you may have had about it. This strategy helps you make connections between what you know and what the author describes.

While you will be able to use some of the strategies described in this book with nonacademic texts, the focus of this book is primarily on reading academic texts. The major distinction is that academic texts are those required in a classroom setting for gathering materials for research, for understanding a discipline, or for gathering data to solve a problem. Your academic texts will be the primary tools for studying in preparation for your tests and for completing your course assignments.

ACTIVITY 3.3 *What Are Your Academic Reading Assignments?*

In the space below make a list of all your reading assignments from each of your classes for this week. This will help you see all the different types of reading assignments so that you will be able to plan out your study week. When you review your list, think about the topics that are already familiar to you and which ones are new to you.

Class	*Day and Time*	*Reading Assignments*	*Due Date*

EXPECTATIONS OF COLLEGE INSTRUCTORS

Each of your college instructors may have different expectations about how you are to complete your reading assignments. It's a good idea to find out what each of your instructors expects because those expectations will influence how you will be graded on tests and on course assignments. Your course syllabus and the specific directions your instructor gives you in class can tell you what you need to know. Generally, there are three different types of expectations college instructors hold requiring three different goals:

1. Complete certain reading assignments with a close, careful reading of the text.

In these cases the instructor regards the text as a primary tool for the class. For instance, when you study literature, you are expected to read the assigned selections very carefully, analyze them, and then be prepared to discuss the literary selections in class. In biology or economics classes, you may be expected to learn the meanings of new technical terms and use them to interpret information in charts or graphs. In fact, in courses requiring sophisticated analysis of the text, it is a good idea to read the assigned selections more than once. Your close, careful reading of the text will provide the background for participating in class discussions and in taking good class notes during lectures.

2. Complete certain reading assignments with a close, careful reading and then read the other text assignments to get a general idea.

In some cases the instructor has selected specific text readings as the primary assignments, but then the instructor may give a set of supplemental readings to provide general background about the topic. For instance, if you are reading a short story, the instructor may want you to read it carefully in order to analyze the way the author develops the characters. The instructor may also provide some supplemental readings that provide historical background about the time period when the author wrote the story. In this case you will need to allocate time for a careful reading of the short story and time to read for the general background about the story. Also, in some cases the instructor may provide a set of references for you to use for future research; if that is so, you are not expected to complete all these readings during the course. Therefore, it is important to know the extent and depth of reading the instructor expects for you to complete during the course so that you can manage your time effectively. (See Chapter 2.)

3. Complete supplemental reading assignments to gain background information about course activities.

In some cases the focus of the course is on a variety of activities that are not text-based, such as a Drawing class or perhaps a Physical Education class. In these cases the instructor expects you to complete a variety of assignments or activities that are evaluated according to your ability in relation to the performance standards. For instance, if you take a Tennis class you will be expected to hit the ball over the net and demonstrate specific swings. The text readings are to provide you with background knowledge, such as in this case about the game of tennis, so that you may use this information to be a better player.

ACTIVITY 3.4 *What Are Your Instructors' Expectations?*

Using the activities you listed in Activity 3.3, note your instructors' expectations about the extent and depth of reading expected. Be prepared to discuss your responses in class.

Instructor	*Reading Assignments*	*Your Instructors' Expectation of Extent & Depth of Reading*

READING TEXTS IN DIFFERENT DISCIPLINES

In the previous section you learned that there are differences in the types of college reading assignments because instructors use texts differently in their courses. It is also important to note that there are differences in the types of text from one discipline to another. These differences influence how you select and use comprehension strategies for understanding the text. In this section we will look at some representative college texts and see distinctions in the reading tasks you meet in college. Each of these disciplines has a unique vocabulary, uses certain types of texts, and uses texts with different types of organizational patterns. Knowing these distinctions can help you realistically set reading goals for comprehending the text. Therefore, in this section we will focus on the differences in types of academic text, and we will look at some of the strategies to help you comprehend those texts successfully. In subsequent chapters of this book we will take a closer look at those strategies and have multiple opportunities to practice those strategies.

READING TEXTS IN THE ARTS AND HUMANITIES

Similar to the types of readings that are typical in other academic areas, texts in the arts and humanities attempt to inform the reader of significant ideas, principles, and artistic themes. The author of texts in the arts and humanities, however, often has an additional goal; the author writes not only to inform the reader but also to describe the beauty, history, and significance of great works of art, forms of architecture, or other significant classical works in our cultural history. The purpose for reading involves reading to learn about them as well as to understand their aesthetic and cultural dimensions.

When you are reading texts in the arts and humanities, particularly in art history, you will be expected to pay close attention to pictures, photographs, charts, graphs, and other pictorial information. If you are assigned a research project, you will most likely conduct research that includes the traditional textbook sources and photographs and also newer textual sources that you can find through online resources, such as the Internet. Your instructor may expect you to give a presentation to the other class members after you have conducted your research. In all cases when you are reading texts in the arts and humanities, according to Roe, Stoodt-Hill, and Burns (2004), you are expected to be able to do each of the following:

1. Read for information and find main ideas and supporting details.

2. Read to follow directions, such as when reading about techniques.

3. Read to interpret charts, diagrams, and pictures.

4. Read critically.

5. Read to use the information.

6. Read in order to write reports.

7. Read to understand technical vocabulary.[2]

Each of these reading strategies will be discussed in the subsequent chapters in this textbook. You will find that these comprehension goals are important for understanding many different kinds of academic texts.

An example of a text in the area of the arts and humanities is in Figure 3.1. This excerpt from an art history textbook is typical of the types of texts you will encounter in the arts and humanities. As you read, note the artistic and historical descriptions that are im-

---

[2]B. D. Roe, B. C. Stoodt, and P. C. Burns, *Secondary School Literacy Instruction: The Content Areas,* 7th ed. (Boston: Houghton Mifflin, 2004), p. 372.

FIGURE 3.1
Stained Glass at Chartres

Source: From W. Fleming, *Arts & Ideas,* 9th ed. (New York: Harcourt Brace, 1995), p. 213.

Stained Glass at Chartres

Time has taken its inevitable toll of the exterior sculptures of Chartres. The flow of carved lines remains, and the varied play of light and shade relieves the present browns and grays. But only traces of the original colors and gilt are left to remind the observer that here was once a feast of color with an effect that can now only be imagined. In the interior, however, where the stained glass remains undimmed, the full color of medieval pageantry still exists. The wealth of pure color in the 175 surviving glass panels hypnotizes the senses. Through the medium of multicolored light something of the emotional exaltation that inspired medieval people to create such a temple to the Queen of Heaven can still be felt.

While Chartres must divide architectural and sculptural honors with its neighboring cities, the town was especially well known as the center of glass making. With the highest achievements of its glaziers exemplified in their own cathedral, Chartres is unsurpassed in this respect. The great variety of jewellike color was achieved chemically by the addition of certain minerals to the glass while it was in a molten state. When cool, the sheets were cut into smaller sections, and the designer fitted these into a previously prepared outline. Details, such as the features in the faces, were applied in the form of metal oxides and made permanent by firing in a kiln. Next, the glass pieces of various sizes were joined together by lead strips. Finally, the individual panels making up the pattern of the whole window were fastened to the iron bars already imbedded in the masonry. When seen against the light, the glass appears translucent, while the lead and iron become opaque black lines that outline the figures and separate the colors to prevent blurring at a distance.

portant for understanding the passage. Let us note that these paragraphs occur in a chapter about the Gothic style of medieval French architecture, notably in Chartres cathedral, an extraordinary example of striking Gothic beauty that survives to this day. (See the first through the second paragraphs in "Stained Glass at Chartres" in Figure 3.1.)

Let's take a closer look at the passage. Why is Chartres important? What point is the author trying to make? Read the paragraphs again. Can you imagine standing in this large cathedral and seeing the light shine through the large, beautiful panes of stained glass? Note the manner in which the author describes the beauty of the pattern, color, and style of the stained-glass windows. The author makes several references to the carefully designed artistic features of this cathedral and the reasons this cathedral was so beautiful. Note that the author states that Chartres was a town noted as a center of glass making. The author further describes the process of making the stained-glass windows and makes specific references how they looked like jewels when the sun shone through the panes.

Let us continue reading on to the next few paragraphs and note what the author says about the stained-glass windows in this exquisitely designed cathedral. (See the third through the fifth paragraphs under "Iconography and Donors" in Figure 3.2.) After you finish reading the passage, check your comprehension in Activity 3.5.

FIGURE 3.2
Iconography and Donors

Source: From W. Fleming, *Arts & Ideas,* 9th ed. (New York: Harcourt Brace, 1995), p. 213.

Iconography and Donors

The iconographical plan of the glass at Chartres, like that of the exterior sculptures, is held together mainly by the dedication of the church as a shrine of the Virgin. There is never any doubt on the part of those who enter that they are in the presence of the Queen of Heaven, who sits enthroned in majesty in the central panel of the apse over the high altar. Grouped around her in neighboring panels are the archangels, saints, and prophets, emblems of the noble donors, and symbols of the craftsmen and tradespeople, almost four thousand figures in all, who honor her and make up her court. Below, on her feast days, were the crowds of living pilgrims who gathered in the nave and chapels, aspiring to enter her eternal presence one day as they had entered her shrine.

An interesting commentary on the changing social conditions of the 13th century can be read in the records of the donors of the windows. In the lowest part of each one is a "signature" indicating the individual, family, or group who bore the expense of the glass. Only a royal purse was equal to a large rose window, as evidenced by the fleur-de-lys insignia so prominent in the north rose. Within the means of members of the aristocracy and the Church hierarchy, such as bishops and canons, were the lancet windows of the nave and choir. The status and prosperity of the guilds of craftsmen and merchants, however, was such that most of the windows were donated by them.

While the royal family of France and the Duke of Brittany were content with wndows in the transepts, the most prominent windows of all, the 47-foot (14.3-meter) high center lancets of the apse, were given by the guilds. The one over the high altar, toward which all eyes are drawn, was the gift of the bakers. Each guild had a patron saint, and a window under a guild's patronage was concerned with the life and miracles of its special saint. In the case of the nobility, the family coat of arms was sufficient to identify the donor; with a guild, the "signature" took the form of a craftsman engaged in some typical phase of work. In the windows of Chartres some nineteen different guilds are shown, including that of the bakers.

ACTIVITY 3.5 *Reading in the Arts and Humanities*

Read the selection in Figure 3.2 and then answer the following questions as true or false. Be prepared to discuss your responses in class.

_____ **1.** This passage notes that it was the practice of the medieval craftsmen and merchant guilds to donate the stained-glass windows in the Chartres cathedral.

_____ **2.** The stained-glass windows in the cathedral at Chartres are signed by the artist who made the window.

_____ **3.** The images in the stained-glass windows contain religious figures, symbols of craftsmen, and the insignia of royal families.

Check your work. Answers to this activity are found on the *College Reading and Study Strategies* book-specific Web site. It is important to check your work before continuing with the next section.

The sample passages in the previous activity showed typical examples of the types of college-level texts you will meet in classes in the arts and humanities. Subsequent chapters in this textbook will give you much practice in using the reading strategies important for understanding the reading materials in this area. Now let us turn to another type of college-level text.

READING LITERATURE

Reading texts in your literature classes can include many different forms. For instance, you may encounter informational text that provides background about a literary period, literary piece, or about an author. Or, you may read original literary texts, such as a short story, essay, poem, play, excerpt from a novel, or the lengthier complete work. When you are reading original literary works, you will most likely find that your instructor hopes you gain an appreciation of its literary merit as well as understand its literary components.

Much of the literary text that you will read is narrative text, that is, text that tells a story. When you read a short story, novel, or play, you will be expected to recall the significant characters, events, symbols, and themes. Readers are expected to interpret the text, make inferences, analyze aspects of the text, evaluate ideas in the text, make meaningful connections of the text with their own lives, and discover through the literary experience the complexities of human nature. Responding to literary texts by providing your own interpretation of the text is often an integral part of reading literature.

Characteristic of literary text is the manner in which authors use poetic devices, figurative language, symbols, and other literary tools. Good writers use these tools so that you can use your imagination, enjoy the artistic qualities of the literary work, and connect on an emotional level with the characters, events, and themes. Often a good story "moves" you because you can identify with someone in the story who faces problems similar to those in your own life, or because you can empathize with the crisis or tragedy presented in the story, or because the plot is so compelling you are intrigued by it. When you are reading literature from a different time period, you may initially find it difficult to understand the historical references or relate to the style of the author; however, when you gain the background for understanding the text, you will find universal themes that have stood the test of time and significant issues that have relevance even in today's society.

Most types of literature are characterized as *prose,* which means that it is written in the recognizable typical paragraph format (like this chapter). In contrast, *poetic* text does not use the same format as prose; rather, poets enjoy creating different line formats, different sounds, and different rhythms, typically to achieve a unique effect. Poets enjoy creating different images and often use figurative language to achieve special effects. Good writers of prose may also use several of the techniques that poets use, but as a reader you will most likely notice the unique qualities of poetry. In the following examples of poetry, look for the craft of the writer. (See "Facing West from California's Shores," in Figure 3.3, on the next page.)

What image do you see in this poem? The narrator, described through the first person "I," describes his journeys, his searching, his travels throughout the world, his quest. He finds himself facing home again. Can you think of a time in your own life during which you were searching for something? Can you relate to the narrator in the search for something? The narrator notes that now that he is returning home he is "very pleas'd and joyous." Can you recall a time when you were returning home after an extended absence? Note that the narrator uses the phrase "seeking what is yet unfound" and asks the ques-

FIGURE 3.3

Walt Whitman's "Facing West from California's Shores"

Source: **From C. R. Bogarad and J. Z. Schmidt,** *Legacies.* **(New York: Harcourt Brace, 1995), p. 1097.**

Facing West from California's Shores
Walt Whitman (1819–1892)

Facing west from California's shores,
Inquiring, tireless, seeking what is yet unfound,
I, a child, very old, over waves, towards the house of maternity,
   the land of migrations, look afar,
Look off the shores of my Western sea, the circle almost circled;
For starting westward from Hindustan, from the vales of Kashmere,
From Asia, from the north, from the God, the sage, and the
   hero,
From the south, from the flowery peninsulas and the spice islands,
Long having wander'd since, round the earth having wander'd,
Now I face home again, very pleas'd and joyous,
(But where is what I started for so long ago?
And why is it yet unfound?)

tion "why is it yet unfound?" Walt Whitman, noted as a great nineteenth-century American poet, poses this universal human condition of seeking for answers that are not easily found. Reread the poem and imagine standing on the same shore as the narrator. What would you say to him?

The theme of traveling on life's journey is echoed in the poem "Uphill." As you read this poem, think of the image of the inn for travelers as a metaphor for a final resting place of comfort. Then, reread the poem to see the effectiveness of this image throughout the entire poem. After you finish your reading, answer the questions in Activity 3.6. (See "Uphill," in Figure 3.4 on the following page.)

ACTIVITY 3.6   *Reading Literature*

Read the selection in Figure 3.4 and then answer the following questions as true or false. Be prepared to discuss your responses in class.

_____ **1.** Rossetti's imagery of traveling on an uphill road may be interpreted as the journey through life.

_____ **2.** When Rossetti refers to the "slow dark hours," she uses an image for death.

_____ **3.** Rossetti uses several stylistic effects in this poem, including using a rhyming pattern throughout the poem.

Check your work. Answers to this activity are found on the *College Reading and Study Strategies* book-specific Web site. It is important to check your work before continuing with the next section.

At this point in the chapter you have read some sample passages from textbooks in literature and in the arts and humanities. In passages from both of these two areas it has been important to look for textual information that encourages the reader to value the aesthetic qualities and to search for relevant cultural, historical, and literary information. Try one (or both) of the following activities to write about your reflections after reading literary text.

Uphill

Christina Rossetti (1830–1894)

Does the road wind uphill all the way?
    Yes, to the very end.
Will the day's journey take the whole long day?
    From morn to night, my friend.

But is there for the night a resting place?
    A roof for when the slow dark hours begin.
May not the darkness hide it from my face?
    You cannot miss that inn.

Shall I meet other wayfarers at night?
    Those who have gone before.
Then must I knock, or call when just in sight?
    They will not keep you standing at that door.

Shall I find comfort, travel-sore and weak?
    Of labor you shall find the sum.
Will there be beds for me and all who seek?
    Yea, beds for all who come.

FIGURE 3.4
Christina Rossetti's "Uphill"

Source: From C. R. Bogarad and J. Z. Schmidt, *Legacies.* (New York: Harcourt Brace, 1995), p. 1097.

ACTIVITY 3.7   *Writing in Response to Reading Literature*

Search for a contemporary short story. After reading it and using the Journal Entry Form that is located on the *College Reading and Study Strategies* Web site, reflect on one or more of the following statements by writing your response:

1. When I read this story, I liked/disliked it because:
2. My first response to this story was:
3. When I was reading this, I connected with this character because:
4. If I could talk to one of the main characters, I would say this:

ACTIVITY 3.8   *Responding to Literature or Art*

Artists and writers like to use imagery and symbolism to communicate to you important social and cultural themes. Choose a time period (such as the late twentieth century), and search for a favorite literary or artistic work. Then respond to these journal prompts:

1. A brief description of this work is:
2. I found these social and cultural messages in the work:
3. The image (or symbol) that meant the most to me was _____ because:

READING IN THE SOCIAL SCIENCES

The courses in the social sciences include courses in history, political science, economics, sociology, psychology, and/or anthropology. Social science texts are characterized by the presentation of facts, concepts, principles, and theories. Such texts are described as "expository" (that is, "informational") because they are used to explain ideas and topics and to inform the reader.

Comprehending texts in the social sciences involves much more than reading for facts and principles. According to Roe, Stoodt-Hill, and Burns (2004), you will find that in social science classes you will need to read for a variety of purposes, including the following:[3]

1. Understand the ideas and viewpoints of others.

2. Acquire and retain a body of relevant concepts and information.

3. Think critically and creatively, thus developing new attitudes and values and the ability to make decisions.

4. Consult a variety of sources, to develop more than one perspective regarding a topic.

5. Read critically about what has happened and *why* these events occurred.

Let's take a look at a sample text passage in the social sciences and see how these purposes apply. Let's start with the introduction to the Sapir-Whorf Hypothesis about how language influences culture. Read the two paragraphs in the passage entitled "How Language Influences Culture" in Figure 3.5.

Did you find the central question? Note that it is stated in the first sentence; we can rephrase the sentence to read, "Does language influence culture?" The author notes that there is not any agreement among the experts in the field about the answer to this question. One

---

[3]B. D. Roe, B. C. Stoodt, and P. C. Burns, *Secondary School Literacy Instruction: The Content Areas,* 7th ed. (Boston: Houghton Mifflin, 2004), p. 296.

FIGURE 3.5
How Language Influences Culture

Source: From G. Ferraro, *Cultural Anthropology, an Applied Perspective.* (Belmont, CA: Wadsworth, 2001), p. 119.

How Language Influences Culture

A major concern of linguistic anthropology since the 1930s has been the question of whether language influences or perhaps even determines culture. There is no consensus among ethnolinguists, but some have suggested that language is more than a symbolic inventory of experience and the physical world and that it actually shapes our thoughts and perceptions. This notion was stated in its most explicit form by Edward Sapir:

> The fact of the matter is that the real world is to a large extent unconsciously built up on the language habits of the group. No two languages are ever sufficiently similar to be considered as representing the same social reality. The worlds in which different societies live are distinct worlds, not merely the same world with different labels attached. (1929:214)

theory, held by Edward Sapir, proposes that language shapes our thoughts and perceptions. So far we have read to accomplish the first two purposes stated above. We have looked for the relevant concept in the paragraph. As we continue to read, we are trying to understand the perspective that Sapir proposed.

If we wished to continue our research about this topic, we could complete an Internet search to see if other linguists (those who study language) agree with the theory that Sapir proposed. Apparently, one of Sapir's students, Benjamin Whorf, agreed with Sapir's theory and found supporting evidence for it in his research in the field. Let's continue to read so that we will see a fuller description of the Sapir-Whorf Hypothesis, including examples in different cultures. After you finish reading, answer the questions in Activity 3.9. (See "The Sapir-Whorf Hypothesis" in Figure 3.6.)

FIGURE 3.6
The Sapir-Whorf Hypothesis

Source: **From G. Ferraro, *Cultural Anthropology, an Applied Perspective.* (Belmont, CA: Wadsworth, 2001), p. 119.**

The Sapir–Whorf Hypothesis

Drawing on Sapir's original formulation, Benjamin Lee Whorf, a student of Sapir, conducted ethnolinguistic research among the Hopi Indians to determine whether different linguistic structures produced different ways of viewing the world. Whorf's observations convinced him that linguistic structure was in fact the causal variable for different views of the world. This notion that different cultures see the word differently because of their different linguistic categories has come to be known as the Sapir–Whorf hypothesis.

Both Sapir and Whorf were suggesting that language does influence the way people see the world. That is, language is more than a vehicle for communication; it actually establishes mental categories that predispose people to see things in a certain way. For example, if my language has a single word—*aunt*—that refers to my mother's sister, my father's sister, my mother's brother's wife, and my father's brother's wife, it is likely that I will perceive all of these family members as genealogically equivalent and consequently will behave toward them in essentially the same way. Thus, Sapir and Whorf would suggest that both perception and the resulting behavior are determined by the linguistic categories we use to group some things under one heading and other things under another heading.

TESTING THE HYPOTHESIS Since Sapir and Whorf's original formulation, a number of ethnolinguists have attempted to test the hypothesis. One study (Ervin-Tripp 1964) concluded that the very content of what is said by bilingual people varies according to which language is being spoken. Working with bilingual Japanese American women in San Francisco, Ervin-Tripp (1964:96) found that the responses to the same question given at different times by the same women varied significantly depending on the language used. To illustrate, when asked in English to finish the statement "Real friends should . . . ," the respondent answered, "be very frank"; when asked the same question in Japanese at a different time, she answered "help each other." Or, when asked, "When my wishes conflict with my family . . . ," the response in English was "I do what I want"; but in Japanese, the response was, "It is a time of great unhappiness." In other words, when the question was asked in Japanese, the bilingual respondent was more likely to give a "typical" Japanese response, and when questioned in English, she was more likely to give a "typical" American response. This is the kind of evidence that has been presented to support the validity of the Sapir–Whorf hypothesis because it strongly suggests that the language influences or channels perceptions as well as the content of verbal utterances.

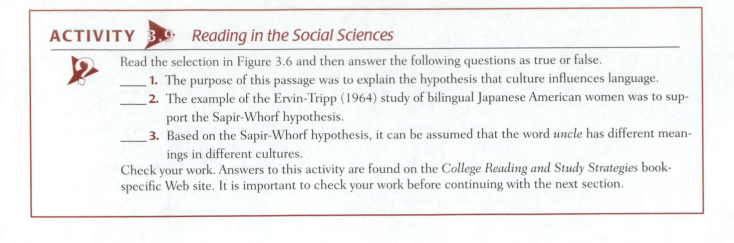

ACTIVITY 3.9 *Reading in the Social Sciences*

Read the selection in Figure 3.6 and then answer the following questions as true or false.

_____ **1.** The purpose of this passage was to explain the hypothesis that culture influences language.

_____ **2.** The example of the Ervin-Tripp (1964) study of bilingual Japanese American women was to support the Sapir-Whorf hypothesis.

_____ **3.** Based on the Sapir-Whorf hypothesis, it can be assumed that the word *uncle* has different meanings in different cultures.

Check your work. Answers to this activity are found on the *College Reading and Study Strategies* book-specific Web site. It is important to check your work before continuing with the next section.

The sample paragraphs we just completed are examples of typical texts in the social sciences. Note the presentation of theories and principles (i.e., the Sapir-Whorf Hypothesis), the examples from Japanese and American cultures, and the author's conclusion that such evidence does support the hypothesis. When you are reading, you can annotate your textbook according to "theories," "examples," and "conclusions" and use these annotations for studying for exams. You will learn more about these study strategies in Chapters 4 and 9.

It is important to note that when you are reading for different purposes in the social sciences, you will need to adjust your reading according to the different levels of comprehension. If your purpose is to learn more about the topic, then you can use the questions for literal and inferential comprehension. If your purpose is to read with a critical eye, then you can use the questions on the critical comprehension level. Often, reading text in the social sciences does involve reading with a critical eye, making good judgments about the worth of the information and the theories presented. We will be exploring the different levels of comprehension later in this chapter. In subsequent chapters of this textbook we will be looking at strategies for comprehending expository text and for working with unfamiliar vocabulary. These strategies will be important for understanding the texts you read in the social sciences.

READING TEXTS IN THE SCIENCES

Reading in the sciences includes reading texts in a variety of areas: biology, earth science, zoology, geology, physics, chemistry, and health, to name a few. When you read science texts, you will read explanations and definitions of concepts, theories, and principles. Many science texts also contain descriptions of experiments, including directions for you to follow to complete an experiment. Types of organizational patterns that you will find in science texts include classification, cause and effect, and problem-solution. Each of these types of organizational patterns is explained in this textbook in Chapter 12.

A typical science passage is contained in Figure 3.7. As you survey this textbook page, note that it has several words in boldfaced print, a schematic, and a series of photographs. From the title on the top of the page we see that the topic is about biological clocks. Next to the boldfaced print in the first paragraph, the author explains

FIGURE 3.7
Biological Clocks and Their Effects

Source: From C. Starr and R. Taggart, *Biology: The Unity and Diversity of Life*, 9th ed. (Belmont, CA: Brooks/Cole, 2001), p. 552.

Biological Clocks and Their Effects

Like other organisms, flowering plants have internal mechanisms that preset the time for recurring changes in biochemical events. These internal timing mechanisms—**biological clocks**—trigger shifts in daily activities. They also help induce seasonal adjustments in basic patterns of growth, development, and reproduction.

The alarm button for some biological clocks in plants is the blue-green pigment molecule **phytochrome.** This pigment can absorb both red and far-red wavelengths of light, with different results. At sunrise, red wavelengths dominate the sky, and phytochrome converts to Pfr, its active molecular form. Its activation may induce cells to take up free calcium ions (Ca^{++}) or induce certain plant organelles to release them. Either way, when the ions combine with calcium-binding proteins in cells, they initiate rhythmic movements of leaves and some other responses to light.

Phytochrome reverts to its inactive form (Pr) at sunset, at night, or in shaded areas. Then, far-red wavelengths predominate.

Rhythmic Leaf Movements

Each day, some plants position their leaves horizontally and then, at night, fold them closer to stems. Keep such a plant in full sunlight or darkness for a few days and it continues to move its leaves into and out of the "sleep" position!

Rhythmic leaf movements are one type of **circadian rhythm,** a biological activity that recurs in cycles, each of which lasts for about twenty-four hours. (*Circadian* means about a day.) Some experiments by Ruth Satter, Richard Crain, and their University of Connecticut colleagues demonstrated that the phytochrome molecule is part of controls over movements of leaves. Satter was a pioneer in studies of internal timing mechanisms, one of the first to correlate sleep movements of plants with "hands of a biological clock."

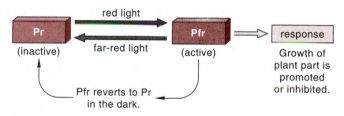
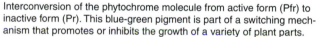

Interconversion of the phytochrome molecule from active form (Pfr) to inactive form (Pr). This blue-green pigment is part of a switching mechanism that promotes or inhibits the growth of a variety of plant parts.

what a "biological clock" is. The author also explains the function of the "phytochrome." Look for these explanations in the passage. (See Figure 3.7.)

Did you find the function of the biological clock? That's right. The biological clock functions as a timing mechanism. The passage describes how, when activated, the pigment molecule phytochrome initiates leaf movement. The schematic shows what happens when red light, present at sunrise, causes a biochemical change in plants. In the next activity, continue with your reading about circadian rhythms in "Rhythmic Leaf Movements" in the same textbook passage.

This passage is typical of the types of texts you will encounter in science classes. You will be able to apply many of the strategies described for expository texts. When you take a class in science, you will need to devote concentrated time in reading your texts, which may include not only a textbook but also supplemental course readings, journal articles,

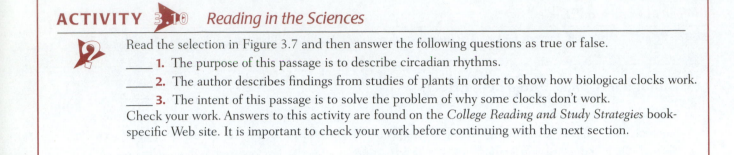

Check your work. Answers to this activity are found on the *College Reading and Study Strategies* book-specific Web site. It is important to check your work before continuing with the next section.

scientific reprints, experimental reports, and Internet sources. You will most likely be working with a variety of nonprint resources as well as your print sources. Your class instructor may provide you with study questions in order to focus your attention on the concepts that you need to know. Likewise, your textbook may contain a variety of study aids that will help you work with the vocabulary, essential concepts, and activities.

READING TEXTS IN MATHEMATICS

Reading to learn mathematics involves reading text quite differently than reading text in the sciences, social sciences, or arts and humanities. The typical mathematics text uses numerous symbols and examples in the place of prose passages to explain the material. Often, authors of mathematics texts explain mathematical concepts through both symbols and words. The typical mathematics text provides opportunities for problem solving and often gives numerous practice examples. When reading mathematics, you will find that you use several strategies for interpreting abstractions, apply what you read for solving new problems, and rely on your critical thinking and critical reading.

Reading texts in mathematics is characterized by slow, careful reading. You will find you need to translate the information and restate mathematical symbols and equations into your own words. You will need to interpret graphs, charts, and other pictorial information. When you read word problems, you will need to translate what the problem gives and what the problem is requesting. The goal of learning mathematics is often to apply the principles of mathematics to new situations.

The typical mathematics text contains verbal problems, explanations of new concepts, and mathematical formulas. Try using the following recommendations from Earle (1976) when you are reading verbal problems in mathematics:[4]

1. Read the problem quickly to obtain a general understanding of it. Visualize the problem. Do not be concerned with numbers.

2. Examine the problem again. Identify the question you are asked to answer.

3. Read the problem again to identify the information given.

---

[4]R. Earle, *Teaching Reading and Mathematics* (Newark, DE: International Reading Association). As cited in B. D. Roe, B. C. Stoodt, and P. C. Burns, *Secondary School Literacy Instruction: The Content Areas,* 7th ed. (Boston: Houghton Mifflin, 2004), pp. 319–320.

FIGURE 3.8
Absolute Value

Source: From T. W. Hungerford, *Contemporary College Algebra and Trigonometry: A Graphing Approach.* (New York: Harcourt, 2001).

Absolute Value

On an informal level most students think of absolute value like this:

The absolute value of a nonnegative number is the number itself.

The absolute value of a negative number is found by "erasing the minus sign."

If $|c|$ denotes the absolute value of c, then, for example, $|5| = 5$ and $|-4| = 4$.

This informal approach is inadequate, however, for finding the absolute value of a number such as $\pi - 6$. It doesn't make sense to "erase the minus sign" here. So we must develop a more precise definition. The statement $|5| = 5$ suggests that the absolute value of a positive number ought to be the number itself. For negative numbers, such as -4, note that $|-4| = 4 = -(-4)$, that is, the absolute value of the negative number -4 is the *negative* of -4. These facts are the basis of the formal definition:

Absolute Value ➤

The *absolute value* of a real number c is denoted $|c|$ and is defined as follows:
$$\text{If } c \geq 0, \text{ then } |c| = c.$$
$$\text{If } c < 0, \text{ then } |c| = -c.$$

Example 1

(a) $|3.5| = 3.5$ and $|-7/2| = -(-7/2) = 7/2$.

(b) To find $|\pi - 6|$ note that $\pi \approx 3.14$, so that $\pi - 6 < 0$. Hence, $|\pi - 6|$ is defined to be the *negative* of $\pi - 6$, that is,
$$|\pi - 6| = -(\pi - 6) = -\pi + 6.$$

(c) $\quad |5 - \sqrt{2}| = 5 - \sqrt{2}$ because $5 - \sqrt{2} \geq 0$. ∎

Here are the important facts about absolute value:

Properties of Absolute Value ➤

1. $|c| \geq 0$ and $|c| > 0$ when $c \neq 0$.
2. $|c| = |-c|$
3. $|cd| = |c| \cdot |d|$
4. $\left|\dfrac{c}{d}\right| = \dfrac{|c|}{|d|}$ $(d \neq 0)$

---

4. Analyze the problem to see how the information is related. Identify any missing information and any unnecessary information.

5. Compute your answer.

6. Examine your answer.

The passage in Figure 3.8 is a typical college reading passage from an algebra text. As you read this passage note the use of symbolic language. The author attempts to explain the symbols through definitions, examples, and prose language. After reading the passage, complete Activity 3.11.

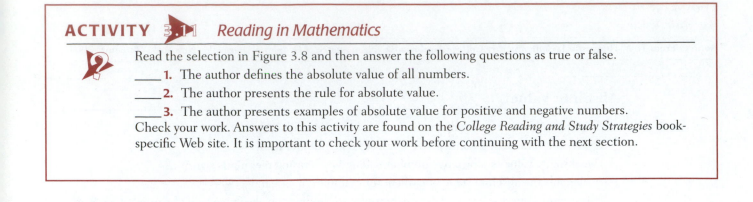

ACTIVITY 3.11 *Reading in Mathematics*

Read the selection in Figure 3.8 and then answer the following questions as true or false.

_____ **1.** The author defines the absolute value of all numbers.

_____ **2.** The author presents the rule for absolute value.

_____ **3.** The author presents examples of absolute value for positive and negative numbers.

Check your work. Answers to this activity are found on the *College Reading and Study Strategies* book-specific Web site. It is important to check your work before continuing with the next section.

Understanding the use of graphics, understanding vocabulary, and critical reading of the text are all important for reading mathematics text. Each of these topics will be explored more in depth in subsequent chapters.

CHARACTERISTICS OF SUCCESSFUL READING

Now that we have discussed important text characteristics for college reading, it is important to consider those characteristics that distinguish the successful reader from the unsuccessful reader. Successful readers read actively, read for meaning, and have clear goals that support good reading routines.

SUCCESSFUL READERS READ ACTIVELY

Reading your college text assignments is hard work. To be successful you need to read actively, not passively. To be an active reader you need to search for the information you need to understand; you can't expect that understanding your textbooks will just come to you easily all the time. Successful reading means that you need to stay focused, actively looking for concepts, principles, key ideas, and the details that support or explain them.

SUCCESSFUL READERS READ FOR MEANING

The main goal for successful reading is to read for meaning. Reading involves much more than figuring out the meanings of unfamiliar words. It involves looking for key ideas, making connections of those ideas with your background knowledge, evaluating the worth of those ideas, and applying those ideas to new situations. The successful reader uses inquiry processes and critical reading strategies.

Reading as Inquiry

The process of inquiry involves asking questions, exploring and gathering data to answer questions, examining data, organizing ideas, constructing a response using the data, and then evaluating the worth of the response. Inquiry learning is a process that uses what you are reading in the larger context of problem solving. College reading often involves using what you are reading to solve problems, to make new connections, and to read as part of the inquiry process.

Critical Reading

Examining and evaluating what you are reading is a key dimension of the reading process. Successful readers know the importance of taking a critical stance. Not everything you read is worthwhile. Good readers will take a few moments to check the credentials of the author, will critique the line of reasoning in a passage, and will evaluate the overall conclusions in a passage.

GOALS OF SUCCESSFUL READERS

Another distinction of successful readers is that they typically are strategic in their use of time and resources for studying and completing reading assignments. Successful readers often have several key goals. Let's take a look at the goals of successful readers.

Know What You Need to Know

Successful readers know what they need to know. Your class syllabus is a major resource for you in determining the types and amount of reading required by the class. When you have a clear idea about the instructor's expectations for completing the reading assignment, you will be able to determine the amount of time you will need to complete the assignment.

Understand the Reading Task

Successful readers understand the reading task. The reading task is defined by the type of reading required, the texts, and the reading purpose. For instance, do you need to read to prepare for a test? Or, do you need to prepare for a class discussion? Each of these situations requires different types of reading.

Construct Meaning

Successful readers focus on building meaning of what they read. In other words, as you read, the goal is to make sense of what you read. This goal of "making meaning" is at the heart of the comprehension process. This means that when you read you should be able to explain the text in your own words, draw conclusions from what you read, and use the new information in meaningful ways.

Relate Text Ideas with Your Background Knowledge

Successful readers relate the ideas presented in the text with their own background knowledge. In each of your classes you will be building a knowledge base that will grow as you become more familiar with the discipline. As you read, it is important to keep checking what you read with the ideas discussed in class. In some areas you may have had previous experience because of job training or other experiences outside of college. You can use those previous experiences to make connections between what you already know and what you are learning.

Monitor Reading

Successful readers monitor what and how they read. As you read it is important to check your comprehension. Are you using the most effective strategy? Do you need to select a different strategy? Monitoring your reading is similar to the way you drive a standard car. If you are driving up hill, you need to adjust your speed and your driving strategy; when you reach the top of the hill and begin to go down the hill, you also need to adjust your speed.

Adjusting Reading Rate

Successful readers adjust their reading rate according to their reading purpose and the difficulty of the text. Part of monitoring your reading includes adjusting how quickly or slowly you read. Some texts, such as mathematics texts, require a slow rate, particularly since you are working with symbols and formulas that need analysis. Other texts, such as reading the newspaper, may be read at a faster rate.

Understand Vocabulary

A critical goal for your college reading is for you to understand the vocabulary you meet. In Chapter 5 of this textbook you will have the opportunity to learn some strategies for improving your vocabulary.

Use Resources for Learning

A significant goal for succeeding in the classroom is using the variety of resources available to you for learning. These resources include the dictionary, subject-specific glossaries, the Internet, and professional journals.

ACTIVITY 3.12 *Reflecting About Reading Goals*

Reflect on one or more of the following statements. Be prepared to discuss your responses with a peer.
1. My most important reading goals are:

2. In my courses this semester, I plan to try the following so that I will be able to understand what I am reading:

3. So far, the questions that I have about becoming a successful college reader are the following:

4. The following resources usually help me understand what I am reading:

READING FOR DIFFERENT LEVELS OF COMPREHENSION

When your class instructor gives you a reading assignment either for homework or in class, you will discover new meanings of the text each time you read and reread the text passages. If they are available, it is a good idea to use the study guides the instructor or textbook provides. It's important to ask yourself questions to summarize what you are reading and to identify essential facts and ideas.

What you learn and remember in your text assignments depends on different reading goals, which reflect different levels of comprehension. If you can think of a stairway going from a ground floor to the second and then third level, you will be able to visualize the process of comprehension on different levels. On the ground floor you aim to read for literal comprehension, the next level up for inferential comprehension, and the third level up for critical comprehension. (See Figure 3.9.)

Each of these three levels of comprehension involves asking different kinds of questions. The next section describes these different levels and the types of questions on each level. In that section you will be able to read a short article from *Newsweek* and use

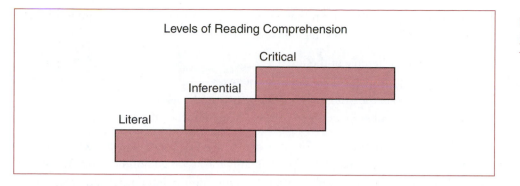

FIGURE 3.9
Levels of Comprehension

the questions from each of the different levels of comprehension in order to practice using the different levels of comprehension. The activities in the next three sections are ones that you will be able to use for any of your textbook reading assignments or for any other general print-based reading assignments. A summary of the questions that you can ask is in the Tip Block.

LITERAL COMPREHENSION

Reading for literal comprehension means that you "read the lines" in order to get the author's message.[5] When you are reading for literal comprehension, you are looking for the ideas, the facts, and the information that are explicitly stated in the text. You will be able

---

TIP

QUESTIONS TO ASK FOR COMPREHENDING A TEXT PASSAGE

When you read a text passage, use these questions as a guide.

LITERAL COMPREHENSION

➤ What is the main topic of the text?

➤ What are the key points mentioned in the text?

➤ Who (if any) are the primary people discussed in the text?

➤ If this text describes an event or a story, where and when did it occur?

INFERENTIAL COMPREHENSION

➤ What is the main point presented in the text?

➤ How do the details connect with the main point?

➤ What predictions can I make about the information presented?

CRITICAL COMPREHENSION

➤ What is significant about the topic?

➤ What is the author's opinion or point of view?

➤ What is the author's background and how does that relate to the topic?

➤ Are the author's points valid?

➤ How is the main topic presented?

➤ What textual information informs my own thinking about this topic?

---

[5]R. T. Vacca and J. L. Vacca, *Content Area Reading,* 7th ed. (Boston, MA: Allyn & Bacon, 2002), p. 325.

to underline the text information that answers the questions for literal comprehension. Some of the essential questions include the following:

What is the main topic of the text?

What are the key points mentioned in the text?

Who (if any) are the primary people discussed in the text?

If this text describes an event or a story, where and when did it occur?

Now read the short article from *Newsweek* about X-Treme Challenges. When you complete your reading, complete the questions for literal comprehension. You will be using the same article for completing the questions on the inferential and critical comprehension levels. As you progress through the different levels, note that you search for different kinds of information and use the results of your search in different ways. (See "For the Doers, Not the Viewers" in Figure 3.10.)

ACTIVITY 3.13   *Reading for Literal Comprehension*

Use the following questions to read and reread the article in Figure 3.10 entitled "For the Doers, Not the Viewers." Write your responses in your notebook.

Literal Comprehension

1. What is the main topic of the text?

2. What are the key points mentioned in the text?

3. Who are the primary people discussed in the text?

4. When and where did the events noted in the text occur?

INFERENTIAL COMPREHENSION

As noted previously, the primary aim of reading a text is to make sense of what it says. Part of this comprehension process is interpreting what is directly mentioned and using this information to figure out the meaning of the text.

Inferential comprehension requires the reader to make sense of the passage; the information will not be directly stated in the text, but good readers will use directly stated information to come up with a clear interpretation of the text. Inferential comprehension has often been called "reading between the lines"; although some of the information may not be directly stated, good readers can figure out what the text means.

Inferential comprehension is essential for understanding charts, maps, graphs, pictures, diagrams, and any other type of schematic. When reading these sources, good readers need to make inferences about relationships among data points. Sometimes these graphic aids are used to extrapolate future trends.

ACTIVITY 3.14   *Reading for Inferential Comprehension*

Use the following questions to read and reread the article in *Newsweek* entitled "For the Doers, Not the Viewers." Write your responses in your notebook.

1. Why did the author include the stories of the people in the article?

2. What is the main point presented in the text?

3. How do the details connect with the main point?

FIGURE 3.10
For the Doers, Not the Viewers

Source: From Debra A. Klein, "For the Doers, Not the Viewers," *Newsweek,* September 3, 2001. Reprinted by permission.

For the Doers, Not the Viewers

When Chicago attorney Tony McShane needed to escape his harried routine of career, commuting and coaching, he decided to lose himself in Virginia's Blue Ridge Mountains. And then navigate his way out. Hiking uphill and riding down on mountain bikes, McShane and his teammates (two men and a woman) covered nearly 70 miles in 24 hours of nonstop bushwhacking. The event was described as an "adventure race," and McShane's team finished 12th out of 22. But the participants were competing mostly against themselves. "It's a metaphor for my busy life," says McShane, 40. "You're exhausted, but you learn how far you can push yourself. You don't feel fatigued until you stop."

Inspired by "reality" television shows stressing survival in the wild, adventure racing is a holiday whose time has come. "We went from 50 races a year to over 300" since 1999, says Tony Farrar, president of the United States Adventure Racing Association. The races attract some hard-core athletes, veterans of triathlons and iron-man competitions. But most participants are just professionals looking for a type-A-plus vacation. That's too demanding for some, as it turns out; Farrar says about 15 percent of the racers fail to finish in one-day competitions, while the washout rate in the longest, toughest races is about 75 percent. But well-heeled thrill seekers aren't inhibited. "Doctors and lawyers who sit at a desk all day see exciting stuff on TV but not in their own lives," says Don Mann, a former Navy SEAL whose firm, Odyssey Adventure Racing, charges teams $750 and up to arrange wilderness competitions. "We have that instinct to push ourselves."

Pushing harder than most, Joseph Desena, a Wall Street trader, ran the grueling, 350-mile Iditasport race outside Anchorage, Alaska, last winter. He spent eight days traveling by foot, bicycle and cross-country skis over the same tough course used for the famous Iditarod dogsled race. "Everything else—losing money—is easy after that," says Desena.

Most competitors look for something a little less Darwinian. Jason Bagby, a Los Angeles salesman, says he shed his competitiveness during a weeklong Supreme Adventure Race through Idaho's Teton Valley this summer. "We saw bear, deer, sheep, sunsets, sunrises," he says. "We saw sides of each other our spouses have never seen." Bagby's team came in second out of 12, but he says, "It's more than just a race."

Sometimes much more. The Mild Seven Outdoor Quest charges competitors $2,900 each for a travel package that includes hotels, meals and airfare from Hong Kong to the race site in Li Jiang, China. The racers travel a 217-mile course by bike and by kayak on the Yangtze River. But instead of racing at night, as competitors do in many other events, they are tucked into bed at the end of each day. "We want to have fun and see a part of the world we would normally not see," says Lee Torbett, 57, a Realtor from Irving, Texas, who plans to take the trip with his wife, Gail, 51. They have done two previous races and are used to being the oldest couple in the field.

Some races are cushy to start with and then turn tough. Competitors in a two-day sprint across Grand Bahama Island organized by X-Treme Challenge Adventure Racing arrive on a cruise ship. They start the actual race with a round-trip, $1\frac{1}{2}$-mile swim to an offshore islet, wearing backpacks designed for swimming. After her swim in a race last June, Jessica Koelsch, a marine biologist from Sarasota, Fla., looked back across the water and saw shark fins. (Two shark attacks have been reported off Grand Bahama this summer, neither involving racers.) The rest of the race was equally arduous. "We had long periods without water and a blinding gale out of nowhere," Koelsch recalls. "You're asking yourself, 'How is this fun?' But 15 minutes later, you're having fun again." No pain, no gain, as the type-A mantra goes.

Often when making accurate inferences good readers will connect the ideas in the text with other ideas previously learned. When reading on an inferential level, good readers ask these questions: What is the main point presented in the text? How do the details connect with the main point? What predictions can I make about the information presented?

CRITICAL COMPREHENSION

Most college instructors believe that critical reading is the type of reading that students should do. It is not enough to read for specific information, but it is necessary to read for critical comprehension. This means that you need to use the text information, to analyze it, to critique it, and to evaluate the worth of it. When reading on a critical level, good readers ask the "hard" questions: Why? Why not? Is this a good idea? What's important? Why is it important? How can this be extended into a new situation? What's the author's point of view? How does my opinion compare with that of the author and others?

Critical reading involves many of the following processes and attitudes:

➤ Being open-minded and suspending judgment until adequate data is available, thus avoiding jumping to conclusions.

➤ Constantly questioning reading content.

➤ Having a problem-solving attitude.

➤ Being knowledgeable regarding the topic.

➤ Discerning the author's purpose.

➤ Evaluating the author's qualifications.

➤ Evaluating the validity of material.

➤ Evaluating the use of propaganda.

➤ Evaluating the author's logic.

➤ Evaluating the author's use of language.[6]

Reading at the critical level includes several different types of purposes for reading, such as reading to apply the ideas, analyze the text, synthesize the text ideas, critique those ideas, and judge their overall worth. Good readers will base their own judgments on the information in the text and on the reflection of their own ideas about the topic. At this level there is a close interaction between the reader's own background knowledge and the author's presentation of the topic. Some of the questions readers ask when they are reading critically include the following:

➤ What is significant about the topic?

➤ What is the author's opinion or point of view?

➤ What is the author's background and how does that relate to the topic?

➤ Are the author's points valid?

➤ How is the main topic presented?

➤ What textual information informs my own thinking about this topic?

In subsequent chapters there are discussions about each of these areas. You will have much opportunity to practice reading critically. Subsequent chapters will also focus on different strategies that authors use to present their ideas.

---

[6]B. D. Roe, B. C. Stoodt, and P. C. Burns, *Secondary School Literacy Instruction: The Content Areas,* 7th ed. (Boston: Houghton Mifflin, 2004), p. 128.

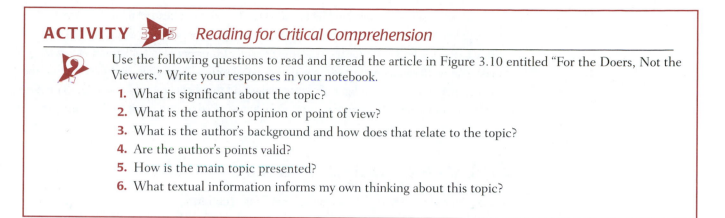

ACTIVITY 3.15   *Reading for Critical Comprehension*

Use the following questions to read and reread the article in Figure 3.10 entitled "For the Doers, Not the Viewers." Write your responses in your notebook.

1. What is significant about the topic?
2. What is the author's opinion or point of view?
3. What is the author's background and how does that relate to the topic?
4. Are the author's points valid?
5. How is the main topic presented?
6. What textual information informs my own thinking about this topic?

As you can surmise, reading comprehension is a complex process that does involve dedicated time, concentration, and effort. To perform well as a student it is important to manage your time well to keep up with the readings. However, just keeping up is not enough. You will need time to work with the ideas presented in your class and your text-books. Working with the text ideas will most likely include writing about what you are reading, researching the topics more deeply, discussing the topics with your class peers and the instructor, and using the information to solve problems, construct new meanings, and present it to others.

You will most likely work with multiple readings about a topic. This will give you the opportunity to summarize and synthesize ideas across multiple texts, critique those ideas, and construct your own interpretation. You will most likely use computer resources (such as the Internet) for researching your topic, as well as the specified texts. Your instructor will most likely expect you to use the text for problem solving, for inquiry, for research. You will most likely be expected to write about what you learn.

Depending on the complexity, depth, and extent of the course you may be asked to complete independent projects that reflect your own original thinking and creativity. As a result, it will be important to show how what you learn is meaningful and significant for others.

ACTIVITY 3.16   *Where Are You Now?*

Now that you have completed this chapter, take a few minutes to repeat Activity 3.1. What have you learned about your reading strategies in this chapter?

Summary

When reading college textbooks, the successful student considers the expectations of the college instructor, the types of assigned readings, the unique characteristics of the discipline, and the expected level and depth of comprehension. The types of reading texts and tasks in the sciences are different from the types and tasks of reading texts in the social sciences, the arts and humanities, mathematics, and in English literature classes. The successful reader reads for different levels of comprehension. When reading on the literal level, the reader focuses on the explicit textual material. When reading on the inferential level, the reader focuses on implied ideas. When reading on the critical level, the reader works with the text in order to analyze ideas, synthesize ideas, critique, and judge the way the author presents opinions and facts. Good readers also use textual material for research, for problem solving, and for generating unique perspectives about a discipline. In each of these cases it is important for the reader to consider his or her own background knowledge, make connections among text ideas with that background knowledge, and to reflect on the significance of the topic in light of text readings and that background knowledge. The ultimate goal of comprehending text is to make sense of what one reads and to apply those ideas in new situations.

REVIEW QUESTIONS

Terms You Should Know: Make a flash card for each term.

Academic reading	Informational text	Reading to learn
Analytic reading	Inquiry learning	Reading rate
Critical comprehension	Literal comprehension	
Inferential comprehension	Monitoring reading	

Completion: Fill in the blank to complete each of the following statements.

1. The goal of _____ is to read the text explicitly.

2. The goal of _____ is to read to look for main points and connections of ideas.

3. The goal of _____ is to use textual information for problem solving.

4. _____ describes the type of text found in science textbooks, lab manuals, literature anthologies, and mathematics texts, but not in popular magazines.

5. Close, careful reading in order to interpret the meaning of a passage is described as _____.

Multiple Choice: Circle the letter of the best answer for each of the following questions. Be sure to underline key words and eliminate wrong answers.

6. Of the following, which is the most important reading comprehension goal?
   A. Figure out the meaning of the words in a passage
   B. Construct a coherent interpretation of the passage
   C. Prepare study guides for what you read
   D. Determine the meanings of the vocabulary terms

7. Of the following types of text, which one requires reading it for its aesthetic qualities?
   A. Literature
   B. Science
   C. Mathematics
   D. Social Sciences

Short Answer–Essay: On a separate sheet, answer each of the following:

8. Describe at least three characteristics of successful readers.

9. Compare academic reading with nonacademic reading.

10. Compare and contrast what is important for reading text in the social sciences with reading text in the sciences.

4 General Reading Strategies for College Textbooks

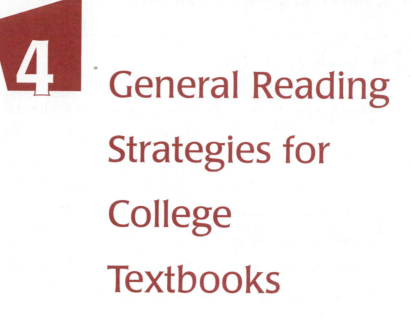

In this chapter you will learn about:

➤ Strategies you can use when you are getting ready to read

➤ Remembering, writing, and responding to text

➤ Using reading/study systems before, during, and after reading.

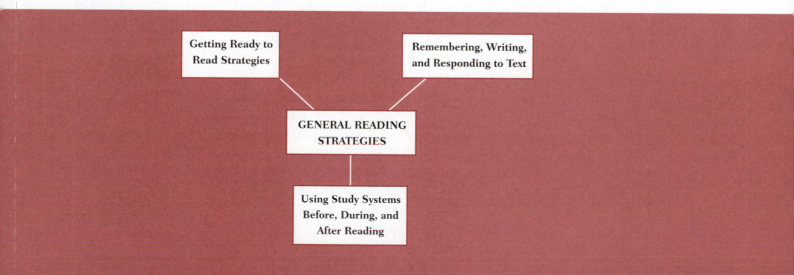

ACTIVITY 4.1 *Where Are You Now?*

Take a few minutes to answer *yes* or *no* to the following questions; choose "yes" if you do this most of the time; choose "no" if you do not consistently do it or if you are not sure.

	YES	NO
1. Before reading a text assignment, do you first preview it?	_____	_____
2. Do you adjust your reading rate depending on your purpose?	_____	_____
3. Do you use questions in the text to help you find key ideas?	_____	_____
4. Do you use textual features?	_____	_____
5. When you read, do you use graphic organizers?	_____	_____
6. When you read, do you make annotations to help you remember?	_____	_____
7. When you are reading to remember, do you highlight ideas?	_____	_____
8. When you read, do you have a clear purpose in mind?	_____	_____
9. When you read, do you write down what you wish to recall?	_____	_____
10. When you study, do you use a reading/study strategy?	_____	_____
Total Points		_____

Score yourself 1 point for each *yes* answer. Total up your points. A low score indicates that you will need to develop your reading strategies. A high score indicates that you have already developed many successful reading strategies.

GETTING READY TO READ STRATEGIES

The typical homework of a college student involves much academic reading. In other words, college students have reading assignments from course textbooks and supplemental readings from journals, periodicals, supplementary texts, and most likely, readings on the Internet. The successful student knows not only how to organize time and resources for learning and studying but also knows how and when to apply a variety of reading strategies. This chapter will provide you with a general background of worthwhile college reading strategies and will give you multiple opportunities to practice several strategies to help you keep on top of your reading assignments. You will find that these strategies will promote your academic and personal satisfaction.

This chapter will introduce you to a framework for college reading comprehension strategies, and subsequent chapters throughout this book will elaborate this framework and provide much more practice in specific reading comprehension strategies. The practice reading selections in this chapter are from typical college textbooks in the areas of psychology, sociology, political science, and biology. The reason these selections are included in this chapter is to demonstrate how you can apply the reading strategies to many different college disciplines.

Most successful college readers have well-developed reading strategies and very good prereading strategies. The prereading strategies discussed in the next sections show you how to be purposeful in your reading. The prereading strategies are organized into two main groups: previewing your text and making predictions about what you will be reading. Let us turn now to the first one.

PREVIEWING YOUR TEXT

When you need to read long sections of text, which may be a page with several paragraphs, a chapter, or even several chapters, you will find that previewing your text will help you comprehend what you are reading. Before you dig into the details and the task of studying, you can get a sneak preview of your reading assignment by taking a few minutes to see what the text contains. When you preview your text, your goal is to get a general idea about what you will be reading.

Previewing the chapter gives you some background about topics that may be new to you. When you preview a text, you read the introduction, the headings, and the summary in order to form a general understanding about what the chapter contains. You also gain an understanding of how the information is organized and presented. Both of these kinds of information can help you understand the text material better. Previewing before reading may increase your comprehension of the textbook chapter by 10 to 20 percent.

In many ways previewing a chapter before you read it is similar to checking the weather forecast before you venture on a trip. The weather forecast helps you make decisions about the type of clothes you should wear and plan out your route for traveling. If the forecast predicts bad weather and difficult driving conditions, and if you plan to drive, you can plan out your driving route to avoid treacherous places and give yourself enough time to deal with challenging road conditions. Similarly, if you are going to read a challenging chapter, you need to organize your resources for studying, choose the best strategies, and give yourself enough time to study.

Previewing your text gives you several advantages. First of all, previewing helps you answer the question: Am I familiar with this topic? If you are familiar with the topic, you have a storehouse of information that will help you make connections between what you already know and what you will be learning. When you read, you will want to search for the new information and add it to what you already know. The advantage of previewing is that you will quickly discover whether or not you will need to devote much time studying new information or to plan your time in a different way, such as thinking about ideas you had learned in the past and thinking about how the new ideas change and add to the "old" ideas.

Secondly, previewing will help you find out how long the chapter is; this will help you make decisions for managing your time, as described in Chapter 2. In other words if you are already familiar with many of the text ideas, if the new ideas do not seem to be too difficult to learn, and if the chapter is relatively short, you should be able to read the chapter in a short period of time. On the other hand, if the text ideas are not familiar to you, the vocabulary looks challenging, and the chapter is quite long, then you will need to devote a considerable amount of time reading and studying the chapter.

Third, previewing helps you find new vocabulary terms that will most likely be discussed in class and may appear on class tests. Depending on the book you are reading, you may find definitions and other study tips for remembering the most important concepts. In this chapter we will be discussing graphic organizers and text annotations; when you preview your text readings, you will be able to use the information in the graphic organizers and text annotations for studying and also recalling essential concepts.

Surveying the Text

One type of previewing strategy is surveying the text before you read it for comprehending and remembering. When you survey the text, you quickly look it over from the beginning to the end. Your goal is not to remember and study what you are reading but to get an overview of the whole chapter to see what it is generally about. It is important to look at the main heading, the introduction, the subheadings, the pictures and graphics, the conclusion and summary, as well as highlighted information in order to see what is presented in the text. For instance, if you had previewed this chapter and this textbook, you would have discovered that the introductory chapters in Part I are later elaborated in Part II and Part III of this textbook. See the Tip Block for some suggestions for surveying your text.

Surveying a text before you focus on slower, more careful reading is part of many different study methods; several of these will be described later in this chapter. To give you practice in surveying a text, read the text in Figure 4.1 and try Activity 4.2 on the following page.

TIP — SURVEYING YOUR TEXT

When you survey the text, first read the heading and subheadings, look at the accompanying figures, and quickly read over the whole passage for the general topics and ideas.

When you survey a text, look for the answers to these questions:

1. I think the text is about. . . .because the main headings, subheadings and accompanying graphics talk about. . . .

2. The topics mentioned in this chapter that are familiar to me are. . . .I already know this about them. . . .

3. The topics mentioned in this chapter that are not familiar to me are. . . .

4. After surveying the text, I have the following questions about the topic:

5. After surveying this text, I plan to do the following in order to understand it:

You will find that when you take a few minutes to survey your text, you will have a better sense of what the text contains. By previewing the text, you are able to form initial ideas about the text. The benefit is that you warm up to the text instead of jumping into it cold. As a result, you will have a clearer idea of what you need to do to comprehend the text.

FIGURE 4.1.
Erikson's Stage Theory

Source: From W. Weiten, *Psychology: Themes and Variations*, 6th ed. (Belmont, CA: Wadsworth/Thomson Learning, 2004), pp. 439–440.

Erikson's Stage Theory

Erikson partitioned the life span into eight stages, each of which brings a *psychosocial crisis* involving transitions in important social relationships. According to Erikson, personality is shaped by how individuals deal with these psychosocial crises. Each crisis involves a struggle between two opposing tendencies, such as trust versus mistrust or initiative versus guilt, both of which are experienced by the person. Erikson described the stages in terms of these antagonistic tendencies, which represent personality traits that people display in varying degrees over the remainder of their lives. Although the names for Erikson's stages suggest either-or outcomes, he viewed each stage as a tug of war that determined the subsequent *balance* between opposing polarities in personality. All eight stages in Erikson's theory are charted below. We describe the first four childhood stages here and discuss the remaining stages in the upcoming sections on adolescence and adulthood.

Trust Versus Mistrust. Erikson's first stage encompasses the first year of life, when an infant has to depend completely on adults to take care of its basic needs for such necessities as food, a warm blanket, and changed diapers. If an infant's basic biological needs are adequately met by his or her caregivers and sound attachments are formed, the child should develop an optimistic, trusting attitude toward the world. However, if the infant's basic needs are taken care of poorly, a more distrusting, pessimistic personality may result.

Autonomy Versus Shame and Doubt. Erikson's second stage unfolds during the second and third years of life, when parents begin toilet training and other efforts to regulate the child's behavior. The child must begin to take some personal responsibility for feeding, dressing, and bathing. If all goes well, he or she acquires a sense of self-sufficiency. But, if parents are never satisfied with the child's efforts and there are constant parent-child conflicts, the child may develop a sense of personal shame and self-doubt.

Initiative Versus Guilt. In Erikson's third stage, lasting roughly from ages 3 to 6, children experiment and take initiatives that may sometimes conflict with their parents' rules. Overcontrolling parents may begin to instill feelings of guilt, and self-esteem may suffer. Parents need to support their children's emerging independence while maintaining appropriate controls. In the ideal situation, children will retain their sense of initiative while learning to respect the rights and privileges of other family members.

Industry Versus Inferiority. In the fourth stage (age 6 through puberty), the challenge of learning to function socially is extended beyond the family to the broader social realm of the neighborhood and school. Children who are able to function effectively in this less nurturant social sphere where productivity is highly valued should learn to value achievement and to take pride in accomplishment, resulting in a sense of competence.

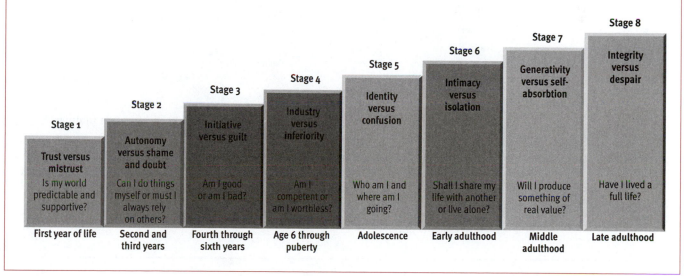

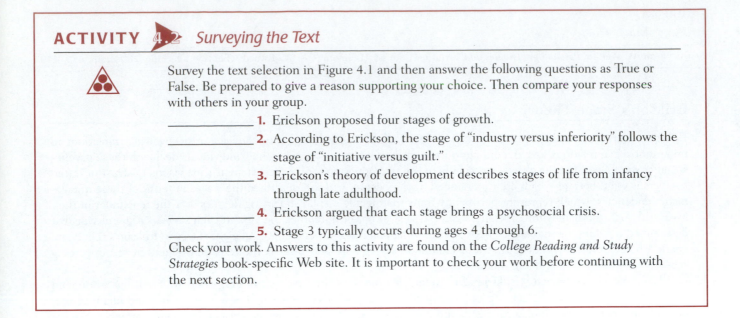

ACTIVITY 4.2 *Surveying the Text*

Survey the text selection in Figure 4.1 and then answer the following questions as True or False. Be prepared to give a reason supporting your choice. Then compare your responses with others in your group.

_____ **1.** Erickson proposed four stages of growth.

_____ **2.** According to Erickson, the stage of "industry versus inferiority" follows the stage of "initiative versus guilt."

_____ **3.** Erickson's theory of development describes stages of life from infancy through late adulthood.

_____ **4.** Erickson argued that each stage brings a psychosocial crisis.

_____ **5.** Stage 3 typically occurs during ages 4 through 6.

Check your work. Answers to this activity are found on the *College Reading and Study Strategies* book-specific Web site. It is important to check your work before continuing with the next section.

ACTIVITY 4.3 *Thinking About Previewing Strategies*

After previewing *Erickson's Stage Theory* (See Figure 4.1), write a response to the following statements. When you write your response, use information from the text to support your response.

1. When I previewed this selection, I found the description about Erickson's stages on the following page: _____. On this page I used the following text features to locate the description about Erickson's stages:_____.

2. When I looked at the names of Erikson's stages, I guessed that each of the stages meant the following:

Stage 1:

Stage 2:

Stage 3:

Stage 4:

3. When I previewed this selection about Erickson's Stage Theory, I was not familiar with the following vocabulary terms and concepts:

Did this strategy work for you? Reflect on how you can use previewing strategies with your college reading assignments.

When you tried these activities, did you quickly glance over all headings and sub-headings and the accompanying graphics? What do you know about this topic so far? After quickly surveying the text, do you have a general idea of what the text is about? If this was one of your reading assignments in a psychology class, how much time do you think you would need to read and study this section?

Skimming and Scanning

Another previewing strategy is to skim or scan a text. In contrast to a slow, careful reading of a text, skimming and scanning involve very fast reading. When you skim the text, you look over the whole text very quickly.[1] If you are searching for very specific information, you can use scanning as your strategy. When you scan, you quickly look over the text to search and locate specific information. For instance, what if you need the phone number of your dentist? You could quickly flip through the phone directory until you came to the section of the directory with your dentist's name, then skim and scan that section until you found it; you would slow down when you found your dentist's name and number. For practice in skimming and scanning return to the excerpt about Erikson's Stage Theory in Figure 4.1 and try Activity 4.4.

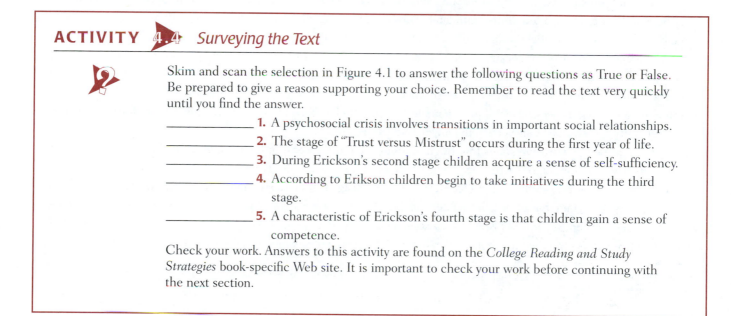

ACTIVITY 4.4   *Surveying the Text*

Skim and scan the selection in Figure 4.1 to answer the following questions as True or False. Be prepared to give a reason supporting your choice. Remember to read the text very quickly until you find the answer.

_____ **1.** A psychosocial crisis involves transitions in important social relationships.

_____ **2.** The stage of "Trust versus Mistrust" occurs during the first year of life.

_____ **3.** During Erickson's second stage children acquire a sense of self-sufficiency.

_____ **4.** According to Erickson children begin to take initiatives during the third stage.

_____ **5.** A characteristic of Erickson's fourth stage is that children gain a sense of competence.

Check your work. Answers to this activity are found on the *College Reading and Study Strategies* book-specific Web site. It is important to check your work before continuing with the next section.

In each of these examples you adjusted your reading rate depending on your purpose. In other words you read very quickly when you wanted to skim or scan the text. Knowing how and when to adjust your reading rate is an important choice in becoming a successful college reader.

---

[1]T. Harris and R. E. Hodges, *The Literacy Dictionary: The Vocabulary of Reading and Writing* (Newark, DE: International Reading Association, 1995).

FIGURE 4.2.
Who Can Become President?

Source: From S. W. Schmidt, M. C. Shelley, and B. A. Bardes, *American Government and Politics Today*, 2001–2002 ed. (Belmont, CA: Wadsworth/Thomson Learning, 2001), pp. 413–414.

Who Can Become President?

The requirements for becoming president, as outlined in Article II, Section 1, of the Constitution, are not overwhelmingly stringent:

> No person except a natural born Citizen, or a Citizen of the United States, at the time of the Adoption of this Constitution, shall be eligible to the Office of President; neither shall any Person be eligible to that Office who shall not have attained to the Age of thirty-five Years, and been fourteen Years a Resident within the United States.

The only question that arises about these qualifications relates to the term "natural born Citizen." Does that mean only citizens born in the United States and its territories? What about a child born to a U.S. citizen (or to a couple who are U.S. citizens) while visiting or living in another country? Although the question has not been dealt with directly by the Supreme Court, it is reasonable to expect that someone would be eligible if her or his parents were Americans. The first presidents, after all, were not even American citizens at birth, and others were born in areas that did not become part of the United States until later. These questions were debated when George Romney, who was born in Chihuahua, Mexico, made a serious bid for the Republican presidential nomination in the 1960s.[2]

The great American dream is symbolized by the statement that "anybody can become president of this country." It is true that in modern times, presidents have included a haberdasher (Harry Truman—for a short period of time), a peanut farmer (Jimmy Carter), and an actor (Ronald Reagan). But if you examine Appendix C, you will see that the most common previous occupation of presidents in this country has been the legal profession. Out of forty-three presidents, twenty-six have been lawyers, and many have been wealthy.

Although the Constitution states that the minimum-age requirement for the presidency is thirty-five years, most presidents have been much older than that when they assumed office. John F. Kennedy, at the age of forty-three, was the youngest elected president, and the oldest was Ronald Reagan, at age sixty-nine. The average age at inauguration has been fifty-four. There has clearly been a demographic bias in the selection of presidents. All have been male, white, and Protestant, except for John F. Kennedy, a Roman Catholic. Presidents have been men of great stature—such as George Washington—and men in whom leadership qualities were not so pronounced—such as Warren Harding.

[2] George Romney was governor of Michigan from 1963 to 1969. Romney was not nominated, and the issue remains unresolved.

Reading the Questions

A third previewing strategy is to look over the questions that the author poses. The questions may be at the beginning of a chapter, or they may be listed at the end for review. Or, questions may be part of subheadings and sprinkled throughout the chapter. Authors pose questions in order to guide the reader, to point to the most significant ideas in the text, and to challenge the reader to think more deeply about issues. When you preview the text, look for the questions: they will often lead you to the main points in the text. For instance, read the above excerpt from a political science textbook about American government entitled "Who Can Become President?" (see Figure 4.2) and look for the qualifications necessary to be an American president.

ACTIVITY 4.5   *Previewing for Questions*

Scan the selection in Figure 4.2 and look for the questions posed by the author. Then answer the following questions as True or False. Locate information in the text to support your response.

_____ **1.** The main question of the passage "Who Can Become President?" is answered in the United States Constitution.

_____ **2.** The author raises the issue of citizenship as a qualification for becoming an American president.

_____ **3.** The author poses a question about where someone is born as a criterion for becoming an American president.

_____ **4.** The Constitution states that if you were born outside the United States, even though are a citizen, you can still become an American president.

_____ **5.** The minimum age requirement to be a president is 35.

Check your work. Answers to this activity are found on the *College Reading and Study Strategies* book-specific Web site. It is important to check your work before continuing with the next section.

MAKING PREDICTIONS

When you use previewing strategies, you approach a text purposefully, actively, and expertly. It is the strategic reader who identifies key vocabulary, anticipates important ideas, and establishes purposes for reading.[2] In addition to using previewing strategies, the successful reader makes predictions about the text prior to a careful, close reading of it. In other words, when you make a prediction, you make a guess about what will be in the text. In order to do this the strategic reader uses several textual features, including headings and subheadings, graphics, and other graphic organizers. Let us turn our attention to these text features.

Reading the Headings

Although not all texts have headings and subheadings within a chapter, when you do have them, they are tremendous guides for helping you find the key concepts for a chapter. You can predict the main points in the text by reading the headings and subheadings. For instance, when you were previewing the psychology text example for Activity 4.2, you were able to use the subheadings for locating information and for predicting what the text contained. In this chapter you can use the headings and subheadings to locate different reading strategies. When you make a prediction about the text, read to see if your prediction is accurate.

Using the Text Features

In addition to headings and subheadings, authors and publishers like to give you other text features as guides for finding information. For instance, new vocabulary may be marked with italics when it is introduced in the text. Or, there may be a notation in the margin that explains new concepts. Textbooks often use introductory pages at the beginning of each

---

[2]B. D. Roe, B. C. Stoodt, and P. C. Burns, *Secondary School Literacy Instruction: The Content Areas,* 7th ed. (Boston: Houghton Mifflin, 2004).

chapter to introduce the key concepts that will be explained in the chapter. Furthermore, there are often summary boxes at the end of each chapter to highlight the main points of the chapter. Other text features may include graphics and pictures to illustrate the concepts presented in the text. In this textbook you will find at the beginning of each chapter an introductory page; you can use the bulleted lists at the beginning of the chapter as guides to make predictions about what you will be reading throughout the chapter. The wise student will use these text features before reading the chapter, will use them as guides while reading and studying, and will use them when studying for exams.

The next activity illustrates an example; the following excerpt from a political science textbook, entitled "Types of Federal Courts," uses a combination of text features, including a graphic showing the types of courts; the boldface print highlights the types of courts in the text.

Figure 4.3.
Types of Federal Courts

Source: **From S. W. Schmidt, M. C. Shelley, and B. A. Bardes,** *American Government and Politics Today,* **2001–2002 ed. (Belmont, CA: Wadsworth/Thomson Learning, 2001), pp. 481–483.**

Types of Federal Courts

Trial Court

The court in which most cases usually begin and in which questions of fact are examined.

General Jurisdiction

Exists when a court's authority to hear cases is not significantly restricted. A court of general jurisdiction normally can hear a broad range of cases.

Limited Jurisdiction

Exists when a court's authority to hear cases is restricted to certain types of claims, such as tax claims or bankruptcy petitions.

Appellate Court

A court having jurisdiction to review cases and issues that were originally tried in lower courts.

As you can see in the figure, the federal court system is basically a three-tiered model consisting of (1) U.S. district courts and various specialized courts of limited jurisdiction (not all of the latter are shown in the figure), (2) intermediate U.S. courts of appeals, and (3) the United States Supreme Court.

U.S. District Courts. The U.S. district courts are trial courts. **Trial courts** are what their name implies—courts in which trials are held and testimony is taken. The U.S. district courts are courts of **general jurisdiction,** meaning that they can hear cases involving a broad array of issues. Federal cases involving most matters typically are heard in district courts. (The other courts on the lower tier of the model shown in the figure are courts of **limited jurisdiction,** meaning that they can try cases involving only certain types of claims, such as tax claims or bankruptcy petitions.)

There is at least one federal district court in every state. The number of judicial districts can vary over time, primarily owing to population changes and corresponding case loads. Currently, there are ninety-four federal judicial districts. A party who is dissatisfied with the decision of a district court judge can appeal the case to the appropriate U.S. court of appeals, or federal **appellate court.** The figure shows the jurisdictional boundaries of the district courts (which are state boundaries, unless otherwise indicated by dotted lines within a state), as well as of the U.S. courts of appeals.

U.S. Courts of Appeals. There are thirteen U.S. courts of appeals—also referred to as U.S. circuit courts of appeals. Twelve of these courts, including the U.S. Court of Appeals for the District of Columbia, hear appeals from the federal district courts located within their respective judicial circuits (geographic areas over which they exercise jurisdiction). The Court of Appeals for the Thirteenth Circuit, called the Federal Circuit, has national appellate jurisdiction over certain types of cases, such as cases involving patent law and those in which the U.S. government is a defendant.

Note that when an appellate court reviews a case decided in a district court, the appellate court does not conduct another trial. Rather, a panel of three or more judges reviews the record of the case on appeal, which includes a transcript of the trial proceedings, and determines whether the trial court com-

Continued

Figure 4.3, *Continued*

Types of Federal Courts

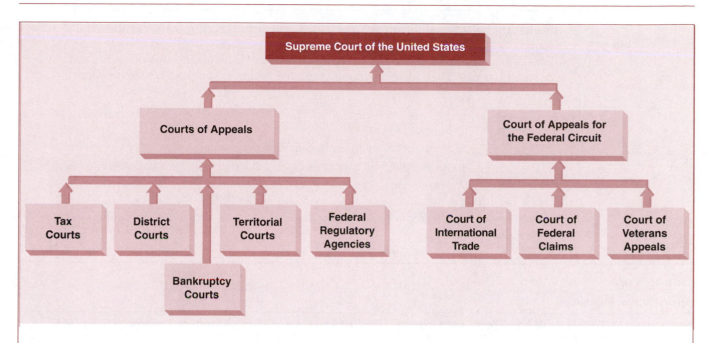

mitted an error. Usually, appellate courts do not look at questions of *fact* (such as whether a party did, in fact, commit a certain action, such as burning a flag) but at questions of *law* (such as whether the act of flag burning is a form of speech protected by the First Amendment to the Constitution). An appellate court will challenge a trial court's finding of fact only when the finding is clearly contrary to the evidence presented at trial or when there is no evidence to support the finding.

A party can petition the United States Supreme Court to review an appellate court's decision. The likelihood that the Supreme Court will grant the petition is slim, however, because the Court reviews only a very few of the cases decided by the appellate courts. This means that decisions made by appellate judges usually are final.

The United States Supreme Court. The highest level of the three-tiered model of the federal court system is the United States Supreme Court. When the Supreme Court came into existence in 1789, it had five justices. In the following years, more justices were added, and since 1837 there have been nine justices on the Court.

According to the language of Article III of the U.S. Constitution, there is only one national Supreme Court. All other courts in the federal system are considered "inferior." Congress is empowered to create other inferior courts as it deems necessary. The inferior courts that Congress has created include the federal courts of appeals and the district courts, as well as the federal courts of limited jurisdiction.

Although the Supreme Court can exercise original jurisdiction (that is, act as a trial court) in certain cases, such as those affecting foreign diplomats and those in which a state is a party, most of its work is as an appellate court. The Court hears appeals not only from the federal appellate courts but also from the highest state courts. Note, though, that the United States Supreme Court can review a state supreme court decision only if a federal question is involved. Because of its importance in the federal court system, we will look more closely at the Supreme Court in the next section.

ACTIVITY 4.6   *Using Text Features*

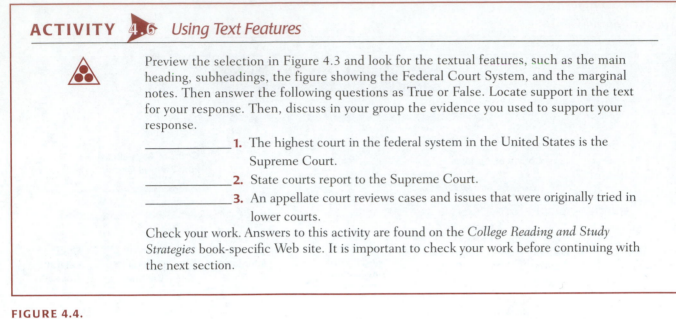

Preview the selection in Figure 4.3 and look for the textual features, such as the main heading, subheadings, the figure showing the Federal Court System, and the marginal notes. Then answer the following questions as True or False. Locate support in the text for your response. Then, discuss in your group the evidence you used to support your response.

_____ **1.** The highest court in the federal system in the United States is the Supreme Court.

_____ **2.** State courts report to the Supreme Court.

_____ **3.** An appellate court reviews cases and issues that were originally tried in lower courts.

Check your work. Answers to this activity are found on the *College Reading and Study Strategies* book-specific Web site. It is important to check your work before continuing with the next section.

FIGURE 4.4.

Adjusting to Marriage

Source: From W. Weiten, *Psychology: Themes and Variations*, 5th ed. (Belmont, CA: Wadsworth/Thomson Learning, 2001), p. 464.

Figure 11.22
Who does the housework?
Berardo, Shehan, and Leslie (1987) studied the proportion of housework done by husbands, wives, and other family members. As these pie charts show, wives continue to do a highly disproportionate share of the housework, even if they are employed.

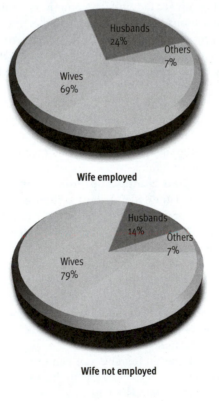

Wife employed

Wife not employed

Adjusting to Marriage

The newly married couple usually settle into their roles as husband and wife gradually. Difficulties with this transition are more likely when spouses come into a marriage with different expectations about marital roles (Kitson & Sussman, 1982; Lye & Biblarz, 1993). Unfortunately, substantial differences in role expectations seem particularly likely in this era of transition in gender roles. For instance, males differ from females in their view of what equality in marriage means. When the subjects in one survey were asked to define an egalitarian marriage, half the men could not (Machung, 1989). The other half defined it in purely psychological terms, saying a marriage is "equal" if it is based on mutual understanding and trust. The women were considerably more concrete and task oriented. They defined marital equality in terms of an equal sharing of chores and responsibilities. However, the evidence indicates that such equality is atypical. As Figure 11.22 shows, wives are still doing the bulk of the housework in America, even when they are employed outside the home (Berardo, Shehan, & Leslie, 1987; Blair & Johnson, 1992). Obviously, women's and men's marital role expectations often are at odds.

Using Graphics

Graphics visually present information and relate it in meaningful ways through figures, charts, or other such graphics. For instance, in the previous example, the relationship of the Supreme Court to the other courts was presented through a graphic called a hierarchical array, which helps the reader see the superordinate status of the Supreme Court as a higher court in relation to the lower courts.

There are several different types of graphics, including timelines, flowcharts, concept maps, pie charts, and bar graphs. Graphics are especially valuable for seeing how ideas are interconnected with each other. It is important to note that graphics are used throughout many textbooks to summarize key ideas. It is wise to study them carefully, especially in relation to the main points of the chapter. The main benefit of a graphic is that you can quickly see the key ideas and see their relationship to a central idea. In Part III of this book you will be reading graphics and interpreting other visuals when you practice reading for critical comprehension. (See Chapter 14, "Analyzing Key Points.") You may also wish to check the Web site for this textbook for additional examples of graphics and practice exercises for interpreting graphics.

For instance, let's see two additional examples of texts that use graphics. In each of these examples note how the graphic can direct your attention to the most important ideas in the text. The first example is entitled "Adjusting to Marriage" and uses pie charts to show the distinctions of husbands, wives, and "others" in doing housework. These graphics help you make predictions about what you will be reading in the text. (See Figure 4.4.)

ACTIVITY 4.7 *Using Graphics*

Preview the selection in Figure 4.4 and examine the accompanying graphics. Then answer the following questions as True or False. Support your response with evidence from the text. Discuss your responses with another member of your group. Compare and contrast your response with those of other group members.

_____ **1.** According to the pie charts there is an equal sharing between wives and husbands in doing the housework.

_____ **2.** Wives who are employed do the same amount of housework as wives who are not employed.

_____ **3.** When wives are employed, a greater number of "others" do the housework in comparison to "others" when wives are not employed.

Check your work. Answers to this activity are found on the *College Reading and Study Strategies* book-specific Web site. It is important to check your work before continuing with the next section.

How did you do with this activity? When you are reading graphics, look at the headings describing the information, then look to see what is being represented by the visual. It is a good idea to try to explain the graphic in your own words, noting any specific comparisons or links from one part of the graphic to another. For instance, in the pie charts for "Adjusting to Marriage" could you find the answer to the question "Who does the housework?" The pie charts show that in the study conducted by Berardo, Shehan, and Leslie (1987) wives did more of the housework than husbands in situations where both spouses worked and when the wife was not employed. The two pie charts help you visualize this

FIGURE 4.5.

How a Bill Becomes a Law

Source: From S. W. Schmidt, M. C. Shelley, and B. A. Bardes, *American Government and Politics Today,* 2001–2002 ed. (Belmont, CA: Wadsworth/Thomson Learning, 2001), p. 402.

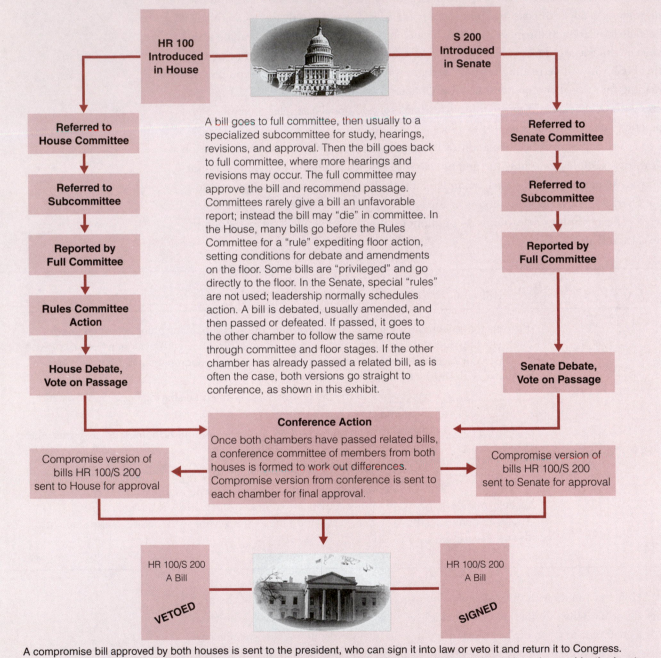

How a Bill Becomes Law

This illustration shows the most typical way in which proposed legislation is enacted into law. Most legislation begins as similar bills introduced into each chamber of Congress. The process is illustrated here with two hypothetical bills. House bill No. 100 (HR 100) and Senate bill No. 200 (S 200). The path of HR 100 is shown on the left and that of S 200, on the right.

HR 100 Introduced in House

S 200 Introduced in Senate

Referred to House Committee

Referred to Subcommittee

Reported by Full Committee

Rules Committee Action

House Debate, Vote on Passage

Referred to Senate Committee

Referred to Subcommittee

Reported by Full Committee

Senate Debate, Vote on Passage

A bill goes to full committee, then usually to a specialized subcommittee for study, hearings, revisions, and approval. Then the bill goes back to full committee, where more hearings and revisions may occur. The full committee may approve the bill and recommend passage. Committees rarely give a bill an unfavorable report; instead the bill may "die" in committee. In the House, many bills go before the Rules Committee for a "rule" expediting floor action, setting conditions for debate and amendments on the floor. Some bills are "privileged" and go directly to the floor. In the Senate, special "rules" are not used; leadership normally schedules action. A bill is debated, usually amended, and then passed or defeated. If passed, it goes to the other chamber to follow the same route through committee and floor stages. If the other chamber has already passed a related bill, as is often the case, both versions go straight to conference, as shown in this exhibit.

Conference Action

Once both chambers have passed related bills, a conference committee of members from both houses is formed to work out differences. Compromise version from conference is sent to each chamber for final approval.

Compromise version of bills HR 100/S 200 sent to House for approval

Compromise version of bills HR 100/S 200 sent to Senate for approval

HR 100/S 200 A Bill

VETOED

HR 100/S 200 A Bill

SIGNED

A compromise bill approved by both houses is sent to the president, who can sign it into law or veto it and return it to Congress. Congress may override a veto by a two-thirds majority vote in both houses; the bill then becomes law without the president's signature.

comparison. Note that the graphic explains a key idea in the paragraph about "Adjusting to Marriage." Therefore, when you preview a text, look at the graphic, and make a prediction about what you will be learning when you read the text passage. This will help you set a goal, a purpose for reading. Then, when you read, check to see if your prediction was accurate.

In the next activity you will see a flowchart for "How a Bill Becomes a Law." In this graphic you will be able to trace what happens after a bill is introduced in either the House or the Senate and follow its path through either the House or the Senate in becoming a law. Note that the explanation of the flowchart is included in the middle of the graphic.

ACTIVITY 4.8   *Using Graphics*

Preview the flowchart in Figure 4.5. Then answer the following questions as True or False. Discuss your responses with the other members in your group and use the flowchart to support your response.

_____ **1.** A bill can be introduced in either the House or the Senate.

_____ **2.** Before a bill is approved by either the House or the Senate, it typically is reviewed and revised in subcommittees.

_____ **3.** The President of the United States can veto a bill.

Check your work. Answers to this activity are found on the *College Reading and Study Strategies* book-specific Web site. It is important to check your work before continuing with the next section.

In sum, when you are getting ready for a close reading of the text, you can use many of the textual features to guide you. These include the headings, subheadings, graphic organizers, marginal notes, and introductory and concluding summaries. In this next section we will be looking at strategies for working with the text.

REMEMBERING, WRITING, AND RESPONDING TO TEXT

This section of the chapter will introduce you to several essential reading and study strategies. Each of these will be described in full throughout this textbook in subsequent sections. The intent of these strategies is for you to remember what you are reading, connect what you are reading to what you already know, and extend the text ideas to new situations. For most college courses the critical learning occurs when you are able to talk about the course ideas and extend those ideas, particularly in solving contemporary problems and seeing the connections with your own life and the lives of others.

ANNOTATING THE TEXT

Your textbook is a tool for helping you learn and remember essential ideas that are discussed in your course. If you personalize it with your own notes, then you will be more confident and prepared to discuss ideas in class and to take exams. In order to personalize your textbook with annotations, you make comments about what you read, typically next to the paragraph you are reading. You can also underline or highlight key concepts, ask questions, and include your own summary statements. Take a look at Figure 4.6 and see the annotations we have included for the section titled "Conifers Are Woody Plants that Produce Seeds in Cones."

Let's take an introductory look at some of the ways you can personalize your textbook by highlighting essential information, making marginal notes, and/or questioning the author.

Highlighting or Underlining

When you find an essential detail and/or a significant main idea directly stated in the text, you may wish to highlight it or underline it so that you can locate it again when you are studying. For instance, if you are reading an unfamiliar term, it is a good idea to highlight it. Essential definitions that are directly stated in the text should also be highlighted or underlined so that you will be able to find the definitions when you are studying. Remember that you should be selective when you highlight or underline. Research has indicated that underlining as a study strategy is more effective when combined with other strategies; in other words, underlining should not be used as your only strategy.[3] The more powerful reading and study strategy is to explain what you are reading in your own words. Making marginal notes will help you read more selectively and more meaningfully.

Making Marginal Notes

Marginal notes are text annotations in the form of short statements that you write next to the paragraph you are reading. Your annotations can be comments about main ideas and key points you want to remember, definitions of unfamiliar vocabulary words, notes about applying these ideas, and connections you make to other ideas. Sometimes marginal notes summarize key ideas that you infer after reading the text. Marginal notes may also be questions that you pose after thinking about the text ideas.

Questioning the Author

Good readers read actively. In other words, they read to understand what they are reading, and they also read with a critical stance. This means that you do not have to agree with everything you read. In fact, good readers argue with the author, pose "what if" questions, dialog with the author, sometimes disagree with the author, or sometimes agree with the author. Perhaps as you are reading this paragraph, you would like to ask us a question. Or, perhaps you are thinking of a question that you would like to ask your instructor and have discussed in class. These questions show that you are an active reader. So that you don't forget your questions, write them down. You could use a notebook for your comments and questions, or you could include them as text annotations next to the paragraph you are reading.

You will learn strategies for taking text notes and preparing for exams in Part II of this textbook, specifically in Chapter 9 ("Taking Text Notes") and Chapter 10 ("Preparing for

---

[3]D. C. Caverly, V. P. Orlando, and J. L. Mullen, "Textbook Study Reading," in R. F. Flippo and D. C. Caverly, eds., *Handbook of College Reading and Study Strategy Research* (Mahwah, NJ: Lawrence Erlbaum Associates, 2000), pp. 105–147.

FIGURE 4.6

Conifers Are Woody Plants that Produce Seeds in Cones

Source: From E. P. Solomon, L. R. Berg, and D. W. Martin, *Biology*, 5th ed. (Fort Worth, TX: Saunders, 1999), p. 571.

Marginal Notes & Questions	

Conifers Are Woody Plants that Produce Seeds in Cones

Examples of conifers: pines, spruces

The conifers (phylum Coniferophyra), which include pines, spruces, hemlocks, and firs, are the most familiar group of gymnosperms (Fig. 27–2). They are woody trees or shrubs that produce annual additions of secondary tissues (wood and bark; see Chapter 33); there are no herbaceous (nonwoody) conifers. The wood (secondary xylem) is composed of tracheids, which are long, tapering cells with pits through which water and dissolved minerals move from one cell to another.

"Woody" trees have tracheids.

Resin protects the trees.
Isn't resin sticky?

Many conifers produce resin, a viscous, clear or translucent substance consisting of seveal organic compounds that may protect the plant from attack by fungi or insects. The resin collects in resin ducts, tubelike cavities that extend throughout the roots, stems, and leaves. Resin is produced and secreted by cells lining the resin ducts.

Conifers have needles.
Typically they stay green all year.
Most are not deciduous and keep their needles.

Most conifers have leaves (megaphylls; see Chapter 26) called needles that are commonly long and narrow, tough, and leathery. Pines bear clusters of two to five needles, depending on the species. In a few conifers such as American arborvitae (*Thuja occidentalis*), however, the leaves are scalelike and cover the stem. Most conifers are evergreen and bear their leaves throughout the year. Only a few, such as the dawn redwood, larch, and bald cypress, are deciduous and shed their needles at the end of the growing season.

Monoecious means there are separate male & female reproductive parts on the same plant.
Conifer: "bears cones"

Most conifers are monoecious, which means that they have separate male and female reproductive parts in different locations on the same plant. These reproductive parts are generally borne in strobili that are commonly called cones, hence the name conifer, which means "bears cones."

They are found throughout the world.

The approximately 550 species of conifers occupy extensive areas, ranging from the Artic to the tropics, and are the dominant vegetation in the forested regions of Alaska, Canada, northern Europe, and Siberia. In addition, they are important in the Southern Hemisphere, particularly in wet, mountainous areas of temperature and tropical regions in South America, Australia, New Zealand, and Malaysia. Southwestern China, with more than 60 species of conifers, has the greatest regional diversity of conifer species on Earth. California, New Caledonia (an island west of Australia), southeastern China, and Japan also have considerable diversity of conifer species.

They are useful for humans and animals.
Christmas trees are conifers.
How do you care for conifers?

Ecologically, conifers contribute food and shelter to animals and other organisms, and their roots hold the soil in place and help prevent soil erosion. Humans use conifers for their wood (for building materials as well as paper products), medicine (for example, the anticancer drug taxol from the Pacific yew), turpentine, and resins. Because of their attractive appearance, conifers are grown for landscape design and Christmas trees.

FIGURE 4.7.
Learned Preferences and Habits

From: W. Weiten, *Psychology: Themes and variations*, 6th ed. (Belmont, CA: Wadsworth/Thomson Learning, 2004), p. 387.

Learned Preferences and Habits

Are you fond of eating calves' brains? How about eels or snakes? Could I interest you in a grasshopper or some dog meat? Probably not, but these are delicacies in some regions of the world. Arctic Eskimos like to eat maggots! You probably prefer chicken, apples, eggs, lettuce, potato chips, pizza, cornflakes, or ice cream. These preferences are acquired through learning. People from different cultures display very different patterns of food consumption (Kittler & Sucher, 1998). If you doubt this fact, just visit a grocery store in an ethnic neighborhood (not your own, of course). As Paul Rozin (1996) points out, immigrant groups "seem to retain their ethnic identity through food long after they have become assimilated in most other ways" (p. 20).

Humans do have some innate taste preferences of a general sort. For example, our preference for high-fat foods appears to be at least partly genetic in origin (Schiffman et al., 1998). Nonetheless, learning wields a great deal of influence over *what* people prefer to eat (Booth, 1991, 1994). Taste preferences are partly a function of learned associations formed through classical conditioning. For example, youngsters can be conditioned to prefer flavors paired with high caloric intake or pleasant social interactions (Logue, 1991). Of course, as we learned in Chapter 6, taste aversions can also be acquired through conditioning when foods are followed by nausea (Bernstein & Meachum, 1990).

Exams"). You may also wish to look at the Web site for this textbook for additional practice exercises making text annotations. In the meantime, as you are learning strategies for reading and studying, practice using the three strategies discussed above: selective highlighting, marginal notes, and questions for the author. As a practice activity, try marking the text in Figure 4.7 with your annotations, marginal notes, underlining or highlighting, and questions for the author; the text entitled "Learned Preferences and Habits" is an excerpt from a typical introductory-level Psychology college textbook.

ACTIVITY 4.9 *Annotating the Text*

First skim the textbook passage entitled "Learned Preferences and Habits" in Figure 4.7 to get an overall idea of the topic. Next, read the passage again, underlining essential vocabulary terms. Now reread the passage again and add your own marginal notes, questions, and comments. As you make your text annotations, you may include notes about your own taste preferences or taste aversions. What types of text annotations best help *you* understand and remember?

DETERMINING READER PURPOSES

What do you want to learn when you read? In other words, why are you reading the text? We have heard some students say, "I'm reading it because it was assigned to me" or "I need to learn what the instructor says I need to know." However, we are hoping that you as an active, critical, strategic reader will respond differently and say, "It depends on my

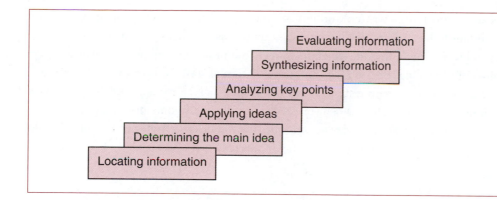

FIGURE 4.8
Reader Purposes

reading purpose." We are hoping that as a successful student you know that you need to have clear reading purposes and that you select the appropriate comprehension strategies for each of your reading purposes. In this section we will introduce you to the framework of reader purposes; this is the framework that forms the organization of Part III in this textbook. Our assumption is that you will learn how to be a successful reader by determining your reading purposes and selecting the strategies appropriate for each of these purposes (Figure 4.8).

Locating Information

When your reading purpose is to locate explicitly stated textual information, this means that you are looking for specific details and directly stated explanations. Typically these details answer the questions Who? What? Where? When? Your purpose may be to locate specific terminology, definitions of these terms, or explanations of concepts that you need to learn and remember. You will learn more about locating information in Chapter 13, "Locating Specific Details."

Determining the Main Idea

Learning about specific details and vocabulary terms is not the main purpose of your college study. When you read, you also need to look for the main points, some of which may not be explicitly stated. In other words the reader purpose that will often guide your reading is to determine the answer to this essential question: "What's the point of this?" You will most likely need to look for organizational patterns within the text passages to see how ideas are related to each other. You will learn more about determining main ideas in Chapter 12.

Applying Ideas

When asked to describe what college students need to know in their courses, most college instructors say that college students should be able to apply the main ideas to current events, to other relevant time periods, and to situations and issues within their own lives. Making personal connections that show the relevancy and criticality of the course ideas enhances your learning. Whenever you see why ideas in your reading assignments are important to your own life, you will find it enjoyable and intriguing to read and learn.

Analyzing Key Points

Essential to your success as an active, strategic reader is carefully reading the text and asking questions, such as Why? Why not? Is this a fact or opinion? Does the author present biased information? What types of assumptions does the author hold? What was the social context for the written work? When you work with your college assignments, it is important to be a critical reader and to ask questions that help you analyze the work on several levels, including its social, historical, and philosophical perspectives. Current thinking in reading research focuses on the notion of "critical literacy" and the importance of readers asking questions about the deeper social meanings and connections to their own lives.[4] Therefore, when you read your college assignments, read to analyze the ideas of the text and to include your critique. We will discuss strategies for critical analysis in Chapter 14, "Analyzing Key Points," in this textbook.

---

[4]H. Fehring and P. Green, *Critical Literacy* (Newark, DE: International Reading Association, 2001).

FIGURE 4.9.

The Judiciary: Issues for the Twenty-First Century

Source: From S. W. Schmidt, M. C. Shelley, and B. A. Bardes, *American Government and Politics Today,* 2001–2002 ed. (Belmont, CA: Wadsworth/Thomson Learning, 2001), p. 504.

The Judiciary: Issues for the Twenty-First Century

The judiciary remains one of the most active and important institutions in American political life. Particularly at the federal level, judicial decision making through the years has affected the way all of us live and work. As the ultimate decision maker on constitutional issues, the Supreme Court will continue to play a significant policy-making role in American government. Whether the policymaking powers of the Supreme Court and other courts in the federal judiciary are too extensive and should be curbed, as some scholars and politicians suggest, remains a controversial issue.

Since the 1980s, there has been a trend toward a noticeably more conservative federal judiciary. Some have argued that this "conservative" legacy of the Reagan-Bush years will remain effective for years to come. The judicial appointments of Bill Clinton, however, may have a significant effect on the ideological leanings of the federal judiciary. When he took office, over one hundred judicial openings in the lower federal courts existed. By the time he left office, he had appointed more than two hundred federal court judges, including two Supreme Court justices. Consequently, some argue that the direction of the federal judiciary will not necessarily continue to be in a conservative direction.

Given the possible retirement of some of the Supreme Court justices in the next few years (three of them are over seventy years old), the composition of the Court may change. Few believe, however, that the change will be radical. As mentioned in the *Critical Perspective* earlier in this chapter, a Senate so strongly divided in terms of partisanship will not likely confirm the appointment of any judicial appointee with strong ideological leanings.

A number of key constitutional issues will continue to be brought before the federal judiciary. These issues include affirmative action programs, congressional redistricting to maximize minority representation, indecent speech on the Internet, privacy rights, and a variety of other civil rights issues, as well as questions involving states' rights. The work of the judiciary in this sense will always remain unfinished. Even when an issue seems to be "resolved," it may come up again many years later. After all, the Supreme Court decision in *Roe v. Wade* appeared to have put an end to discussion about restrictions on abortion. Yet the issue continues to come before the courts and is currently being settled there, as well as through decisions and movements in public opinion. In a dynamic nation with a changing population, we can never expect issues to be resolved once and for all.

Synthesizing Information

When you synthesize information from your text readings, your reading purpose requires that you work with the texts in a different way; you step back from the texts and work to integrate the ideas you have read into a summary that captures the key points of your readings. Your reading task may require that you read multiple text sources and look for themes common to all of the texts. Your main goal is to pull together ideas from several sources so that you will have a crystallized, well-articulated summary of the essential points you wish to remember. This reading purpose often requires that you communicate your summary to someone else. Therefore, you will find that you must sharpen your written and oral communication skills in order to share your synthesis with an audience. Chapter 15, "Synthesizing Information," in this textbook will give you practice in reading and writing in order to synthesize information.

Evaluating Information

When you read to evaluate information, you work with the text in order to analyze, critique, and judge the worth of it. As discussed in Chapter 16, "Evaluating Information," you will read to determine the types of arguments that are presented in a text, the types of evidence presented, and the sources for the ideas that are presented. You will find that when your reader purpose is to read to evaluate information, you will read with a keen eye. Not only will you find the main points in a text, but you will also determine if the logic the author uses is sound.

You will have much practice in reading for each of these different purposes. However, to note the distinctions among the different reader purposes, try Activity 4.10 "Determining Reader Purposes" after reading "The Judiciary: Issues for the Twenty-First Century" in Figure 4.9. Use this same text for the journal activity in Activity 4.11.

ACTIVITY 4.10   *Determining Reader Purposes*

First skim the textbook excerpt entitled "The Judiciary: Issues for the Twenty-First Century" in Figure 4.9. Then read question 1 and then read the passage to answer the question; determine the reader purpose for question 1. Check your response and be prepared to discuss your response. Then read question 2 and read the passage to answer question 2; determine the reader purpose for question 2. Try question 3 in the same manner. When you finish this activity, think of how you changed your reading approach depending on your purpose. Be prepared to discuss your responses with a peer in class.

_____ **1.** Since the 1980s what has been the trend in the federal judiciary? (What is your reader purpose?)

_____ **2.** In the first paragraph the author raises a controversial issue for the twenty-first century. Explain it in your own words. (What is your reader purpose?)

_____ **3.** Of the constitutional issues that are mentioned in the text, which do you believe will be the most important in the twenty-first century? (What is your reader purpose?)

Check your work. Answers to this activity are found on the *College Reading and Study Strategies* book-specific Web site. It is important to check your work before continuing with the next section.

REMEMBERING AND REFLECTING

When you are assigned readings for class discussion or for preparation for an exam, you will find that you will be working with the text in a variety of ways. Most of the time you will want to both remember and reflect on what you read. Just as it is important to be clear about your reading purpose (i.e., Why are you reading it?), it is also important to know that you have several reading and study strategies available to you. The following are a few of the most widely used strategies for working with college reading assignments so that you can remember what you read.

Recalling Text Information

When you wish to remember key ideas, vocabulary, and significant details, you will want to work with the text for recalling essential information. In this textbook Chapter 7, "Improving Memory," provides you with specific strategies for helping you recall information. It is important to note that the process of recalling text information is actually a three-step process:

1. Depending on your reading purpose, identify in your text passages what you want to recall. You may also include information that you write in your marginal notes, text annotations, and questions for the author.

2. Choose a memory strategy (see Chapter 7). For instance, a popular strategy is to create an acronym (word) to help you remember a long list. For instance, to recall Erikson's Stage Theory (Figure 4.1), can you think of a word associated with the beginning letters of each of the first four stages?

3. Practice. Practice. Practice. You will need to give yourself enough time to practice recalling what you have identified. One strategy is to practice aloud. Another strategy is to recall what you have read by discussing it with a peer. Another strategy is to write down what you recall and check yourself by comparing your notes with your response.

Outlining the Text

Many students are familiar with outlining text material. You probably did some outlining in junior or senior high school. If you find that outlining helps you read and understand your textbook, go ahead and use this strategy. Make each heading a main point in your outline and be sure to include some details from the material under each heading. However, watch out for one-word outlines; they don't provide enough information for later review. Outlining also will be described in more detail in Chapter 9.

Writing Summaries

When you write a summary, you make a compacted version of the text that contains the key ideas. For an example of a summary see the end of this chapter. When you write a summary, you record the highlights of what you read. Typically a summary is written in full paragraph form. Some students prefer to outline what they read; other students prefer to write out their thoughts so that they can explain how ideas are connected. Other students like to use graphic organizers, or visuals, to write down the essential ideas of what they read. In Chapters 9 and 15 you will have the opportunity to practice writing summaries.

Making Graphic Organizers

There are many different types of graphics, including timelines, flowcharts, concept maps, pie charts, and bar graphs. Additional ways of visually representing the ideas of the text are through concept maps, hierarchical arrays, and semantic feature matrices. These graphic organizers are very important tools for learning vocabulary (as noted in Chapter 5), for remembering text notes (as noted in Chapter 9), and for comprehending what you read (as noted in Part III of this textbook).

Graphic organizers help you consolidate what you read so you can remember essential ideas. The following descriptions of three widely used graphic organizers have an accompanying figure that you may copy and use for your lecture notetaking and your reading assignments. The purpose of introducing these to you here is to provide you with some initial tools that you can use now in your college classes. When you read about these tools in subsequent chapters, you will be able to refine your use of them, adding more elaborate features.

➤ **Concept Maps**

Concept maps visually represent significant ideas and details. When you look at a concept map, you can get a quick overview of the main ideas. In this textbook we use concept maps to introduce each of the chapters. The concept map will give you a quick overview of the chapter before you read it. Figure 4.10 is a simple concept map that you may use for your text readings.

Note that in this figure the main point is in the middle and that the supporting details extend out from the middle. More complex concept maps include additional supporting details that show connections from one detail to another. When you read Chapter 5, "Using Vocabulary Strategies," you will gain more practice using concept maps in order to think of the meaning of a concept. You will also gain experience reading and interpreting concept maps and other types of graphic organizers in Chapter 14.

➤ **Hierarchical Arrays**

A hierarchical array (sometimes called a *hierarchical map*) looks like a family tree. You place your main idea at the top of the tree and list the supporting ideas underneath. If you wish to make this more complex, you can include another layer of supporting details underneath the first layer. Note that when you are making a hierarchical array you are moving from the top down to the bottom. On the other hand when you make a concept map

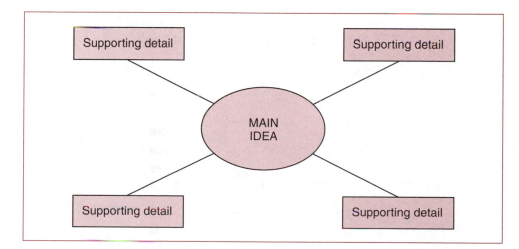

FIGURE 4.10.
Concept Map

(semantic web), you start in the center and radiate out, like the spokes on a wheel. It typically is a matter of personal choice to use either a concept map or a hierarchical array to make a graphic organizer of what you read. Figure 4.11 is an example of a hierarchical array that you may use for your study reading.

➤ Semantic Feature Matrix

A semantic feature matrix is a chart that shows the descriptions (features) of a set of similar ideas. This type of graphic organizer shows you each of the main topics and a description. For instance, when you are studying about different authors during a literary era, you can make a semantic feature matrix to list the name of each author, their characteristics, and examples of what they wrote. The chart helps you compare and contrast each of the topics.

When you are working with longer pieces of text, such as a whole chapter or section of a chapter, you will find that a semantic feature matrix helps you organize your study reading so that you will be able to recall essential ideas in the future. Figure 4.12 is a sample semantic feature matrix that you can use for your study reading.

Note the example of a semantic feature matrix in Figure 4.13 about "Types of Societies." This graphic organizer shows you how each of the types of societies are characterized by its economic base and social organization. The graphic also includes examples of each of the different types of societies.

FIGURE 4.11.
Hierarchical Array

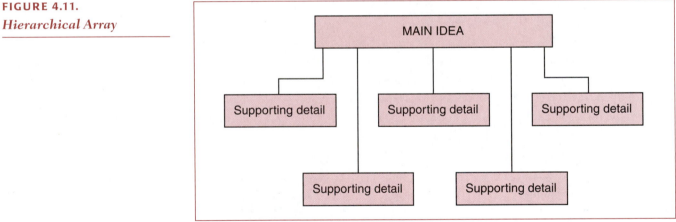

FIGURE 4.12.
Semantic Feature Matrix

	Feature 1	Feature 2	Example
Name A			
Name B			
Name C			

Figure 4.13.

Types of Societies

Source: From M. L. Andersen and H. F. Taylor, *Sociology: Understanding a Diverse Society*, 3d ed. (Belmont, CA: Wadsworth/Thomson Learning, 2004), p. 139.

TYPES OF SOCIETIES

	Economic base	Social organization	Examples
Foraging societies	economic sustenance dependent on hunting and foraging	gender is basis for social organization, although division of labor is not rigid; little accumulation of wealth	Pygmies of Central Africa
Pastoral societies	nomadic societies, with substantial dependence on domesticated animals for economic production	complex social system with an elite upper class and greater gender role differentiation than in foraging societies	Bedouins of Africa and Middle East
Horticultural societies	society marked by relatively permanent settlement and production of domesticated crops	accumulation of wealth and elaboration of the division of labor, with different occupational roles (farmers, traders, craftspeople, etc.)	Aztecs of Mexico; Incan empire of Peru
Agricultural societies	livelihood dependent on elaborate and large-scale patterns of agriculture and increased use of technology in agricultural production	caste system develops that differentiates the elite and agricultural laborers; may include system of slavery	American South, pre-Civil War
Industrial societies	economic system based on the development of elaborate machinery and a factory system; economy based on cash and wages	highly differentiated labor force with a complex division of labor and large formal organizations	19th- and 20th-century United States and western Europe
Postindustrial societies	information-based societies in which technology plays a vital role in social organization	education increasingly important to the division of labor	contemporary United States, Japan, and others

---

ACTIVITY 4.11   *Making Graphic Organizers*

Revisit "Erikson's Stage Theory" in Figure 4.1. Then choose a graphic organizer to visually represent the main topic and each of the four stages. You may use the examples in Figures 4.10, 4.11, or 4.12 as your guide. After making your graphic organizer, explain it to the other members of your group. Which of your choices helped you the most?

Reflecting on Your Reading

Depending on the course, your study reading may also include taking a few minutes after reading and writing down your thoughts, your questions, your connections to your own life. Your reflections can answer the questions: What did I learn? What was most valuable to me? What questions do I have after reading this? In classes where you are expected to participate in discussions, these written reflections will help you prepare for class. You may also find these reflections valuable if you need to write course papers or if you need to research a topic. Some students prefer keeping their own Reading Journal apart from their notes so that they can record their thoughts. Other students reserve a section of their notebook for these reflections. If you are faithful in writing down your reflections, you will find that you will be actively interested in your courses and in your text readings; consequently, you will be motivated and interested in your college learning and chosen academic path.

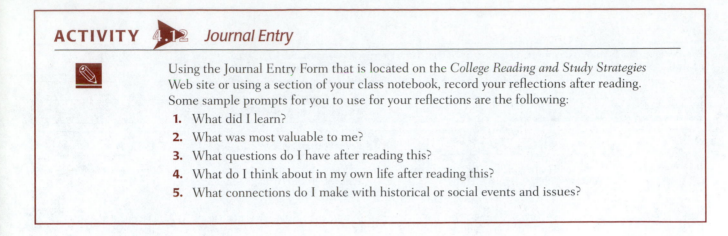

ACTIVITY 4.12   *Journal Entry*

Using the Journal Entry Form that is located on the *College Reading and Study Strategies*
Web site or using a section of your class notebook, record your reflections after reading.
Some sample prompts for you to use for your reflections are the following:

1. What did I learn?

2. What was most valuable to me?

3. What questions do I have after reading this?

4. What do I think about in my own life after reading this?

5. What connections do I make with historical or social events and issues?

USING READING/STUDY SYSTEMS BEFORE, DURING, AND AFTER READING

Many study skills instructors no longer teach students to use long, complicated
reading/study systems. Even though these systems do work, too many of their students don't use them. Some students have trouble learning all the various steps in the
systems, and many others feel that they simply take too much time to use. You can get
more out of the time you spend reading your textbook by using an easy, three-step
approach.

P2R

The P2R reading/study system is designed for textbooks that are from easy to average
level in difficulty. We recommend that you use P2R on the entire chapter or on ten-
page chunks. The overall strategy is as follows: First, preview the chapter. Next, read
actively by highlighting or taking notes as you read. Finally, review using an active
strategy such as reciting, answering questions, or creating a recall column. Each of
these steps will be described below with additional strategies from which you may
choose.

> ### Preview

You should always preview a chapter before you read it. Previewing takes very little
time and effort. Most students can preview a text chapter in two to five minutes. As
noted previously, the first thing to do is read the title of the chapter. Then read the introduction, outline, or structured overview (a visual display of key information) at the beginning of the chapter. If your text does not begin with an introduction, outline, or structured overview, read the first two paragraphs. As you turn the pages of the chapter, read
the headings in bold print and glance at any pictures, tables, or graphs. Don't stop to
read any of the text along the way. At the end of the chapter, read the summary or the
last two paragraphs. If your text contains an extensive summary (a page or more in
length), you may want to read only the first and last sentence of each of the paragraphs
in the summary.

➤ Read Actively

The second step of the P2R system is to read actively. This is the step when you mark your text as you read. In recent years there has been a great deal of discussion about the value of marking your textbook as you read. One view suggests that marking your textbook is a way to avoid learning the material as you read it. In some ways this is true. However, if you have already started college, you probably realize that you just don't have time to learn the material *well* the first time you read. Highlighting or notetaking allows you to keep up with your class assignments and at the same time identify and mark that material that you will need to study further.

After previewing, read and mark the first ten-page chunk of your chapter. One method of marking is to highlight the text. After you have read a paragraph or headed section of text, pause to think about what you have read. Go back and use a highlighter to mark any material that you think you will want to review again before the exam. By highlighting the text, you are actively involved in thinking about the material, and you are condensing what you will need to review at a later time.

Another method of text marking is notetaking. Taking notes on a text is a lot like taking notes on lectures. Write the heading in your notebook and then jot down the important details. Another way to take notes on your text is to write recall words or questions in the margin. You can also write brief summary statements in the margin of your text.

The main reason for marking your text is to condense the text material so that you never have to read the entire chapter again. Some students are responsible for more than 2,000 pages of text material during a semester. It certainly is not unusual to have 300 pages of text to review for just one exam.

➤ Review

After you complete a ten-page chunk of reading, you need to review the important information. There are a number of ways that you can review the text material, but here are four of the most common ones. First, you may want to summarize the key points that the author made. Try to write three or four statements that you think summarize the key points made in the reading selection. Second, you can recite the information. Using the headings as a guide, cover the page of text and try to recite the key information under each heading. You also may want to recite from recall questions that you wrote in the margin or from your notes. Third, you can do the test at the end of the chapter or any study guide material. Finally, you can review your text chapter by predicting and answering questions that may be on a quiz or test. Don't try to use all of these strategies at the same time. Test them as you read assignments in several of your courses. Then choose the one that works best for you.

SQ4R

This reading/study system extends the work of Robinson,[5] who created SQ3R: Survey, Question, Read, Recite, and Review. The fourth R in SQ3R stands for wRite, which occurs along with Read. This popular system, which has been in use for over half a century, utilizes many of the beneficial strategies discussed so far: previewing your text, activating your prior knowledge about the text, establishing purposes for reading, monitoring your reading, summarizing what you know, and recalling and reviewing what you have studied. The steps in this system occur as follows:

[5]F. P. Robinson, *Effective Study*, 2nd ed. (New York: Harper & Row, 1946).

➤ **Survey**

To begin, preview your reading assignment, being sure to read the headings, introductory paragraphs and summaries. Look over the graphics, illustrations, and other visually represented information. Check the boldfaced or italicized vocabulary terms. The point in this step is to think about what you already know, think about what you need to know, and set your reading purposes. In this step you need to get an overall sense of the text and be clear about your reading goals.

➤ **Question**

In this step you form the questions that will guide your reading. When you look at the headings, subheadings, and graphics, ask yourself "What do I need to know about the topic?" Your class assignments may give you some direct clues for developing the questions. Also, your reading purpose will guide you in deciding the depth of reading that could be required.

➤ **Read**

In this step you read to answer your questions. Your reading purpose should also guide you in this step. During this stage your reading should involve close, careful reading of the text.

➤ **wRite**

While you are reading, write your text annotations, marginal notes, questions for the author, and reflections. Usually, students read a substantial segment of text, then write down what they need to remember. As you are reading and writing, check to see whether or not you are answering all your questions.

➤ **Recite**

After reading a section of your text assignment and after writing down your text notations, it is important to step away from the text and to try to recall what you have read. Your recitation can be aloud; you can share your recollections with a peer; they could also be written down and checked.

➤ **Review**

At this step you review what you have read. Your focus is to recall what you have read without returning to the text. If you find that you can't remember what you had read, you can return to the text, but try to recall what you had read without any extra guides. When you review what was read, it is a good idea to reflect on what you had read, elaborate what you had read, and make connections with ideas and events in your own life.

There are numerous adaptations to this reading/study system. However, the essential steps of previewing, actively reading, and working to remember provide the basic foundation for this study system. The mnemonic of SQ4R helps you remember what you need to do next. You may find that the adaptations of this system help you with more ease. The following is an example of this adaptation.

ACTIVITY 4.13   *SQ3R Adaptations*

There are many different adaptations of SQ3R, as originally introduced by Robinson. Search the Web for one other adaptation, try it, and reflect on it as a strategy for your own use. Use the journal prompts from Activity 4.12 for your reflections.

S-RUN-R

Because of its simplicity, one variation that may be very useful for college students is Bailey's *S-RUN* (*S*urvey, *R*ead, *U*nderline, *N*otetaking) reading method.[6] Bailey's students were reluctant to use SQ3R because it seemed like too much work; however, they used S-RUN with great success.

The S-RUN-R reading/study system combines Bailey's system with a review step to better meet the needs of college students. Because students are asked to focus on the text one headed section at a time, it does take longer than P2R, which is done on the entire chapter (or ten-page chunks). Therefore, S-RUN-R should be used with more difficult text material.

➤ **Survey**

The first step in the S-RUN-R reading/study system is to survey the entire chapter. Read the title, introduction, headings, subheadings, and summaries (and glance at pictures, charts, and graphs). Like P2R, this survey provides a quick overview of the chapter. You should spend about two to five minutes completing the survey.

➤ **Read**

Before reading the first headed section, write the heading on a piece of notebook paper next to the left margin. Just copying the heading helps you pay more attention to it and may help focus your reading. Then read the section as you would any text material, thinking critically about the material.

➤ **Underline**

After you finish reading each paragraph, think about what was important in the paragraph and underline or highlight the important information. Because highlighting is faster and easier to do, feel free to substitute it for underlining.

➤ **Notetake**

As soon as you complete all of the highlighting for the entire headed section, stop and turn back to your notebook page. Now take notes on the key information. Briefly summarize the underlined or highlighted information under the previously written heading. Indent slightly and write the notes using meaningful phrases as you do when taking lecture notes. Taking text notes helps you get a better understanding of the information and helps you condense it even more. By putting the information in your own words, you will increase your comprehension. Continue jotting down each heading, reading, underlining (or highlighting), and taking notes for each remaining headed section.

➤ **Review**

When you have completed the entire chapter, review to reinforce the important information. You can recite the key information that you wrote under each heading. Doing the end-of-chapter questions (if there are any) may also help you review the key information in the chapter. Some students find that predicting questions and creating self-tests helps them identify and practice the main points in the chapter. You may also create a recall column in your textbook or for your text notes. Writing recall questions in the margin can help you prompt your memory of the key points you underlined or included in your text notes. You can use the review step to simply get more repetition on the material or to actually check your understanding or memory of it.

---

[6]N. Bailey, "S-RUN: Beyond SQ3R," *Journal of Reading* 32 (1988): p. 170.

Creating a recall column in your textbook or notebook provides you with repetition on the material, but actually using the recall column to prompt your memory will let you know whether or not you really have learned it.

Now that you have learned about three reading/study systems for reading college textbooks, it is important to be comfortable with using the system that best fits your own study style and your reading purposes. For you to use these systems confidently, you need to practice, practice, practice. It will most likely take more time in the beginning to learn the systems, but once you have practiced using them, you will find that it actually takes less time to study because you have a strategy for reading and studying. Activity 4.14 gives you an opportunity to practice using a reading/study system.

ACTIVITY 4.14   *Using Reading/Study Systems*

Choose a chapter from one of your courses that is assigned for study reading. Choose one of the reading/study systems: P2R, SQ4R, S-RUN-R. Use the reading/study system you select to read the chapter. Write down your reflections about what you learned. (You may use the prompts from Activity 4.12.) Be prepared to share your reflections.

ACTIVITY 4.15   *Using Infotrac College Edition to Locate Information About Reading/Study Systems*

A variety of reading/study systems have been developed for specific disciplines, such as mathematics or literature. Search InfoTrac College Edition for these alternative reading/study systems. Pick one or two that you could use this semester. Try them out. Compare and contrast these alternative systems with the ones mentioned in this chapter.

ACTIVITY 4.16   *Where Are You Now?*

Now that you have completed this chapter, take a few minutes to return to the beginning of this chapter and repeat Activity 4.1, Where Are You Now? What have you learned about your reading and study strategies in this chapter? What are you going to do differently now? How are you going to change your study reading strategies?

Summary

Active, critical reading, which is required for success in college classrooms, involves previewing your text and making predictions about what you will be reading. When you preview your text, you get an overview of the text. This helps you think about the topic and recall what you know already about it. Textual information such as the chapter headings, questions, and graphics help you find essential main ideas and details and help you preview and make predictions.

However, in order to be a strategic, successful reader, you need to be clear about your reading purpose. Your reading purpose could be to locate specific textual information that is explicitly stated. Or, you may need to read to determine the main idea of the passage. Typically, you need to read for several purposes, such as determining both the main idea and to locate specific details. Additional reader purposes include reading to apply what you read, analyze what you read, synthesize what you've read, and evaluate what you've read.

The task of study reading often requires recalling what you've read and using a variety of tools to help you organize, elaborate, and reflect on what you've read. Successful students use a variety of approaches, including outlining, highlighting, making graphic organizers, writing summaries, and creating text annotations. Furthermore, successful students reflect on what they read, dialogue with the author, and question the author. Many students prefer to use a reading/study system. In this chapter we discussed three of those systems: P2R, SQ4R, and S-RUN-R.

Review Questions

Terms You Should Know: Make a flash card for each term.

Active reading	Reader purposes	Reading to synthesize
Concept map	Reading to analyze	information
Graphic organizers	information	Scanning
Hierarchical array	Reading to apply	Semantic feature matrix
Highlighting	information	Skimming
Main ideas	Reading to determine the	SQ4R
Making predictions	main idea	S-RUN-R
Marginal notes	Reading to evaluate	Summary writing
Outlining	information	Surveying
P2R	Reading to locate	Text annotations
Previewing	information	

Completion: Fill in the blank to complete each of the following statements.

1. Reading/study systems such as the following help you remember what you read: _____, _____, and _____.

2. When your reader purpose is _____, then you look for explicitly stated details in the text.

3. When your reader purpose is _____, then you read to make connections between what is in the text and current issues.

4. These graphic organizers help you visually represent main ideas and details: _____, _____, and _____.

5. Reading very quickly to locate specific information is called _____.

Multiple Choice: Circle the letter of the best answer for each of the following questions. Be sure to underline key words and eliminate wrong answers.

6. Which of these best promotes critical reading and a deep understanding of text?
    A. Underlining vocabulary words you don't know
    B. Highlighting details you think you will need to remember
    C. Outlining the main ideas and details
    D. Writing a summary of the text using your own words to explain the ideas

7. Which of the following reader purposes is best met when you use a semantic feature matrix to compare and contrast ideas in a text passage?
    A. Reading to evaluate information
    B. Reading to apply information
    C. Reading to analyze information
    D. Reading to synthesize information

Short Answer–Essay: On a separate sheet answer each of the following questions.

8. Explain how you would use P2R to read the assignments in one of your courses.

9. Describe three types of information that you could include in marginal notes.

10. Compare and contrast how you use a concept map, a hierarchical array, and an outline.

5 Using Vocabulary Strategies

In this chapter you will learn more about:

➤ General vocabulary goals

➤ Context clues for determining the meaning of a word

➤ Four approaches for vocabulary development

➤ Resources for vocabulary development

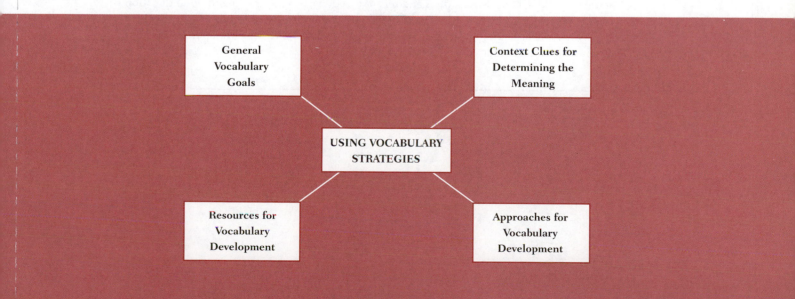

ACTIVITY 5.1   *Where Are You Now?*

Take a few minutes to answer *yes* or *no* to the following questions; choose "yes" if you do this most of the time; choose "no" if you do not consistently do it or if you are not sure.

	YES	NO
1. When you read, do you have a strategy for determining the meaning of unfamiliar concepts?	_____	_____
2. Do you use the glossary in your textbook to look up words that are unfamiliar to you?	_____	_____
3. When reading unfamiliar words, do you look for familiar prefixes and roots to figure out the definitions?	_____	_____
4. When you try to remember the definition of a word, do you use mental images?	_____	_____
5. When studying for a test, do you have a strategy for remembering new concepts?	_____	_____
6. When trying to remember the meanings of new words, do you primarily use repetition as your study strategy?	_____	_____
7. When you do not know the meaning of a word in a text passage, do you look for clues elsewhere in the text about the meaning?	_____	_____
8. When trying to remember the meaning of a word, do you think of a sentence containing the word?	_____	_____
9. Do you write down unfamiliar words in a vocabulary notebook or on study cards?	_____	_____
10. Do you read for at least thirty minutes every day?	_____	_____

Total Points   _____

Score yourself 1 point for each *yes* answer to questions 1–5 and 7–10 and *no* to question 6. Total up your points. A low score indicates that you will need to develop your strategies for improving vocabulary. A high score indicates that you have already developed many successful strategies for vocabulary development.

GENERAL VOCABULARY GOALS

The general focus of this chapter is for you to use strategies for developing your *Reading* vocabulary, that is, the concepts that you meet in printed text. Read the following poem and see if you can figure out the meanings of the words:

'Twas brillig, and the slithy toves
Did gyre and gimble in the wabe:
All mimsy were the borogroves,
And the mome raths outgrabe.[1]

When you are reading unfamiliar text, does it sound like these lines from *Jabberwocky*, Lewis Carroll's famous poem? The poem is from *Through the Looking Glass*, and Alice (the same one from *Alice in Wonderland*) says that the text is "rather hard to understand!" Alice says, "Somehow it seems to fill my head with ideas—only I don't exactly know what they are!"[2] Perhaps you can empathize with Alice and can describe similar experiences reading texts that contain very difficult vocabulary. It is only after Alice meets Humpty Dumpty on one of her adventures that she learns what the passage means. Humpty Dumpty explains that the words mean: "Well, *'slithy'* means 'lithe and slimy.' 'Lithe' is the same as 'active.' You see it's like a portmanteau—there are two meanings packed up into one word." (You can read the rest of the translation by reading *Through the Looking Glass*.) Like Alice, you can also unlock the meanings of words when you learn a strategy for figuring out the meanings.

Your vocabulary knowledge actually includes four areas: your *Listening, Speaking, Reading,* and *Writing vocabularies.* Do you ever find yourself trying to recall a word on the "tip of your tongue"? You may have seen the word or heard someone else say the word, but you may have had difficulty expressing the word. Generally, your *Speaking* and *Writing vocabularies* are smaller than the others because for the *productive vocabularies* you need not only to recognize the meaning of the word but to be able to use it appropriately in speech or written text. On the other hand, for your *receptive vocabularies*, developed through listening and reading, you need to be able to associate the meaning of a word with its printed or spoken form. In conversation you also have the added advantage of asking the speaker to clarify the meaning of a word if you are not familiar with it.

The purpose of this chapter is to introduce you to a variety of strategies that will help you be more effective in understanding the unfamiliar concepts in your college reading assignments. As in the development of any skill, it will be important to practice using these strategies and apply them in your college courses with multiple texts.

---

[1]L. Carroll, *Jabberwocky* (Cleveland, OH: Modern Curriculum Press, 1987).
[2]L. Carroll, *Through the Looking Glass* (New York: Crown, n.d.).

BUILD BACKGROUND KNOWLEDGE
ABOUT WORD MEANINGS

Children learn on average the meanings of about 3,000 new words per year.[3] By the time students reach college their vocabularies have grown to 40,000 to 50,000 words.[4] Estimates of the vocabulary size of university graduates range up to 200,000 words.[5] Yet, huge differences can exist between poor and good readers; the range of learning new words can vary from 1,000 words to 5,000 words per year.[6] According to Stahl and Shiel (1992) a key discrepancy between good and poor readers is the sheer amount of text they read each year.[7] Therefore, the most highly recommended approach for improving one's vocabulary is to *read widely*. In other words, if you set aside thirty minutes each day for your own independent reading, you will have the exposure to text that is requisite for vocabulary growth. The purpose of establishing a habit of reading for thirty minutes a day for your own recreational reading is to build fluency in reading and to read about a wide variety of topics, thereby building your own background knowledge.

When you read widely, you meet both familiar and unfamiliar words. If you have a hobby or are interested in a sport, you will learn about the special vocabulary in that area. For instance, if you are a baseball fan, you know the meanings of *dugout*, *slide*, *line drive*, *center field*, *bullpen*, *shortstop*, and *grand slam*. If you like to cook, you know the meanings of *mousse*, *stroganoff*, *pasta*, *score*, *fricassee*, and *bisque*. When you read materials related to your own interests, you will find that you are comfortable with the vocabulary and that you develop an expertise in it. When you maintain a steady routine of recreational reading, you also find your own interests expand, and as a result your vocabulary increases in other interest areas.

Perhaps you enjoy reading about a favorite topic. Or, perhaps you enjoy reading books by a favorite author. In addition to favorite books, newspapers and magazines are a good source of materials for recreational reading. One of the benefits of having a good routine for recreational reading is that you can enjoy reading for the intrinsic pleasure of learning without the worry of studying for a test.

The following activity is designed to be a daily activity. (See Activity 5.2 on the next page.) To improve your vocabulary you will need to meet many new and challenging words through repeated practice. Therefore, use this activity as a daily routine. The activity is not designed as a test but as an activity to help you develop your vocabulary through your own recreational reading.

When you are reading, a key goal is to connect what you already know with what you don't know. In other words, when you are reading new information, try to think first of what you already know about the topic. College textbook publishers provide you

[3]W. Nagy and P. Herman, "Breadth and Depth of Vocabulary Knowledge: Implications for Acquisition and Instruction," in M. McKeown and M. Curtis, eds., *The Nature of Vocabulary Acquisition* (Hillsdale, NJ: Erlbaum, 1987), pp. 19–35.
[4]M. W. Olson and S. P. Homan, *Teacher to Teacher* (Newark, DE: International Reading Association, 1993).
[5]M. F. Graves, "Vocabulary Learning and Instruction," in E. Z. Rothkopf, ed., *Review of Research in Education*, vol. 13 (Washington, DC: American Educational Research Association, 1986), pp. 49–89.
[6]T. G. White, M. F. Graves, and W. H. Slater, "Growth of Reading Vocabulary in Diverse Elementary Schools: Decoding and Word Meaning," *Journal of Educational Psychology*, 82 (1990): pp. 281–290.
[7]S. A. Stahl and T. G. Shiel, "Teaching Meaning Vocabulary: Productive Approaches for Poor Readers," *Reading and Writing Quarterly*, 8 (1992): pp. 223–241.

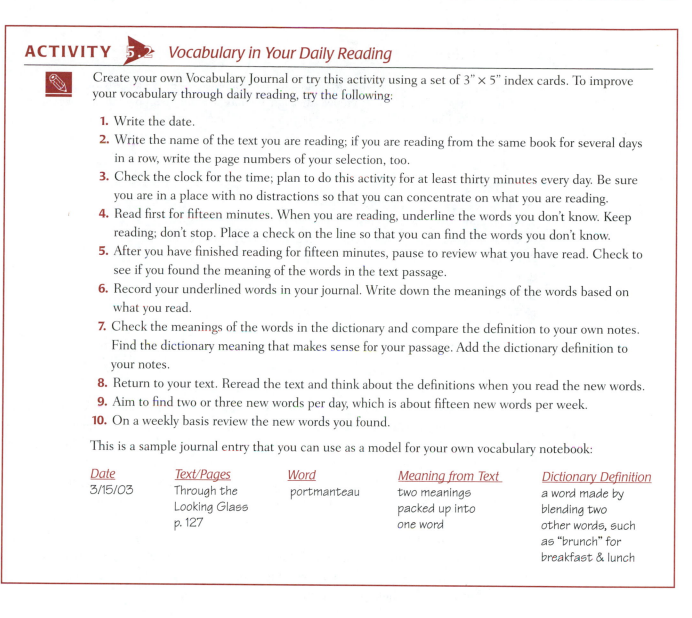

ACTIVITY 5.2 *Vocabulary in Your Daily Reading*

Create your own Vocabulary Journal or try this activity using a set of 3" × 5" index cards. To improve your vocabulary through daily reading, try the following:

1. Write the date.
2. Write the name of the text you are reading; if you are reading from the same book for several days in a row, write the page numbers of your selection, too.
3. Check the clock for the time; plan to do this activity for at least thirty minutes every day. Be sure you are in a place with no distractions so that you can concentrate on what you are reading.
4. Read first for fifteen minutes. When you are reading, underline the words you don't know. Keep reading; don't stop. Place a check on the line so that you can find the words you don't know.
5. After you have finished reading for fifteen minutes, pause to review what you have read. Check to see if you found the meaning of the words in the text passage.
6. Record your underlined words in your journal. Write down the meanings of the words based on what you read.
7. Check the meanings of the words in the dictionary and compare the definition to your own notes. Find the dictionary meaning that makes sense for your passage. Add the dictionary definition to your notes.
8. Return to your text. Reread the text and think about the definitions when you read the new words.
9. Aim to find two or three new words per day, which is about fifteen new words per week.
10. On a weekly basis review the new words you found.

This is a sample journal entry that you can use as a model for your own vocabulary notebook:

Date	Text/Pages	Word	Meaning from Text	Dictionary Definition
3/15/03	Through the Looking Glass p. 127	portmanteau	two meanings packed up into one word	a word made by blending two other words, such as "brunch" for breakfast & lunch

with a variety of textual aids to help you orient yourself to the topic. Let us turn our attention now to look at them.

LOOK FOR TEXTUAL AIDS

As we have noted in our previous chapters, a key goal of successful readers is to connect what you have learned in the past with the new information. College readers are faced with the task of learning much new information, and for this reason current textbook publishers provide many text features that can help you as a college reader make connections between the new information and the old, find definitions and explanations of new concepts, and review ideas during your study reading. In the following activity use your college textbooks to orient yourself to the features of the text.

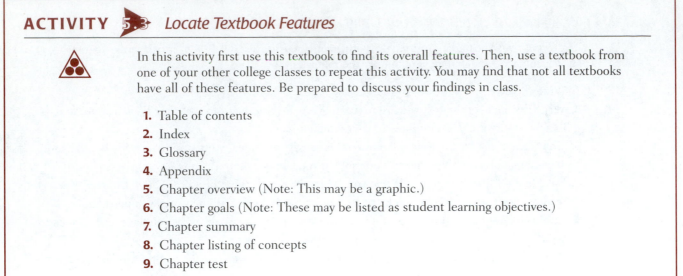

ACTIVITY 5.3   *Locate Textbook Features*

In this activity first use this textbook to find its overall features. Then, use a textbook from one of your other college classes to repeat this activity. You may find that not all textbooks have all of these features. Be prepared to discuss your findings in class.

1. Table of contents
2. Index
3. Glossary
4. Appendix
5. Chapter overview (Note: This may be a graphic.)
6. Chapter goals (Note: These may be listed as student learning objectives.)
7. Chapter summary
8. Chapter listing of concepts
9. Chapter test
10. Supplemental resources (including the Internet)

Now that you have found these textual features, which of these give you introductory information? Which summarize the major concepts you need to know and remember? Which help you during your reading to keep track of ideas? Which help you understand new concepts? Which help you find terms that you need to know?

Within each chapter you will also find textual features that help you locate important terminology, locate definitions, and understand how concepts are related. In this next activity use one chapter from one of your college classes to explore the text features.

You will find that these text features help to build your background knowledge, or help you determine the meaning of a concept, or help you with a summary of the major concepts. When a professor assigns a text reading, it is important to read and use all the text features to help you understand the major concepts.

ACTIVITY 5.4   *Locate Chapter Features*

Choose at least two textbooks from your other college classes to find the chapter features. You will find that not all textbook chapters have all of these features. Be prepared to discuss your findings in class.

1. Boldfaced print for terminology
2. Tables, charts, or graphs
3. Pictures, photographs, or drawings
4. Historical notes
5. Maps
6. Timelines
7. Anecdotes (short stories)

When you are assigned textbook reading in your college classes, you will find that when you don't understand a word, it is best to use the chapter and text features. Why? You will find that authors have precise meanings for the terms in specific content areas. These precise definitions are specific to a discipline, and college professors expect their students to be fluent in using these precise terms in class and on exams. Simpson and Randall (2000) note the demands for understanding college-level vocabulary: "College students must understand the discipline-specific, general, and technical words in their assigned texts and heard in lectures or discussions if they hope to succeed. They also need extensive and varied expressive vocabularies in order to write essays and research papers and deliver oral presentations during class" (p. 43).[8] Therefore, as you complete your text readings and listen to the professor during lectures, use a notetaking strategy to locate and use key vocabulary terms. (See Chapter 8 and Chapter 9 in this textbook for strategies that you can use.)

USE THE WORD IN MULTIPLE WAYS

When you meet a new word, it truly does not become a word you know until you can use it when speaking with others or when using it in written context, such as in a summary, a research paper, a letter, or other longer, connected text. When you can talk about what the word means, give examples about it, and respond to other people's questions about it, then you are showing that you understand what the word means. Simply giving a memorized definition of a word does not show that you know what a word means. Each person typically has a set of words that are known in depth; these typically are the words you can remember and use with ease. There are some words that are partially known; you may know something about the meaning, but you may not know all the meanings of the word. Then there are words for which you can recite the definition, but you have trouble using the word. We all have vocabularies like this. With more experience and with more in-depth reading and studying we can increase not only the words we know but also increase our understanding of what these words mean.

As summarized by Nagy and Scott (2000) there are different stages of knowing a word;[9] Dale (1965) proposed the first four and Partibakht and Wesche (1997) proposed the fifth:

1. Never saw it before;

2. Heard it but don't know what it means;

3. Recognize it in context as having something to do with . . .

4. Know it well;[10]

5. Can use the word in a sentence.[11]

---

[8]M. L. Simpson and S. N. Randall, "Vocabulary Development at the College Level," in R. Flippo and D. C. Caverly, eds., *Handbook of College Reading and Study Strategy Research* (Mahwah, NJ: Lawrence Erlbaum, 2000), pp. 43–73.

[9]W. E. Nagy and J. A. Scott, "Vocabulary Processes," in M. L. Kamil, P. B. Mosenthal, P. D. Pearson, and R. Barr, eds., *Handbook of Reading Research,* vol. III (Mahwah, NJ: Lawrence Erlbaum Associates, 2000), pp. 269–284.

[10]E. Dale, "Vocabulary Measurement: Techniques and Major Findings," *Elementary English,* 42 (1965): pp. 82–88.

[11]T. S. Paribakht and M. Wesche, "Vocabulary Enhancement Activities and Reading for Meaning in Second Language Vocabulary Acquisition," in J. Coady and T. Huckin, eds., *Second Language Acquisition* (Cambridge: Cambridge University Press, 1997), pp. 174–200.

In the following activity, rate the words you know in one of your college-level classes.

ACTIVITY 5.5 *Rate How Well You Know a Word*

Write down ten words from one of your college class lectures or from one of your textbook readings. Then rate each of the words, using the following scale: (1) Never saw it before; (2) Heard it but don't know what it means; (3) Recognize it in context as having something to do with . . .; (4) Know it well; (5) Can use the word in a sentence.

Word   *Rating*

1.

2.

3.

4.

5.

6.

7.

8.

9.

10.

Your goals, then, are to learn the meanings of these words, be able to use these terms in both speech and in written contexts, and be able to give examples of what these terms mean. When you own the word, you will be able to claim it as part of your listening, speaking, reading, and writing vocabularies.

When learning a word, keep in mind these five key points: (1) Determine the meaning of the word; (2) write the definition in your own words; (3) make an association; (4) distinguish the denotation of the word from its connotation; and (5) check the meaning of the word. Let's talk about what each of these means and try out some practice activities.

➤ **Determine the Meaning of the Word Using Information in the Text**

As you find a new word in either your assigned readings or your lectures, write the word in your vocabulary journal. Some students prefer to keep the last few pages of the their notebooks as their vocabulary journal so they can keep the words in a notebook connected to their lecture notes and their textbook notes. Then, check to see if there is a glossary in your textbook or a glossary of terminology at the end of your chapter. It is also a good idea to check your lecture notes for the instructor's definitions. When you find the meaning of the word, write it in your vocabulary journal.

If you do not find the definition in a glossary or your instructor's notes, then return to the text passage for context clues for the meaning of the word. We shall talk about using context clues in the next section of this chapter as one of the approaches for vocabulary development. Some textbooks also provide annotations (short notes) in the margins that will give definitions of key terms you need to know.

If you still cannot find the definition of a word, consult a good dictionary, preferably one that specializes in terminology for that field. For instance, when this author is looking for the precise definition for a word about reading processes, this author consults a dictionary that specializes in terminology in reading processes. A good college dictionary can also provide you with the definition, but you will need to check to see which definition you need for a specialized field. Another recommendation is to ask the instructor in class for clarification about the meaning of a word.

The purpose of determining the meaning of a word is to be sure you have a good, clear working definition of the concepts you need to know. If you are not sure what the words in your assigned readings mean, then make the effort to seek clarification about their meanings.

To practice determining the meanings of words, read the excerpt from a political science text in Figure 5.1. This passage discusses the importance of primary elections in the process of nominating a presidential candidate. As you read this passage, use the textbook annotations on the left side of the text for understanding the terminology in the passage.

You may use these annotations for recording the definitions in your own vocabulary journal.

FIGURE 5.1
The Primary as a Springboard to the White House

Source: From S. W. Schmidt, M. C. Shelley, and B. A. Bardes, *American Government and Politics Today,* 2001–2002 ed. (Belmont, CA: Wadsworth/Thomson Learning, 2001), p. 323.

The Primary as a Springboard to the White House

Caucus

A closed meeting of party leaders to select party candidates or to decide on policy; also, a meeting of party members designed to select candidates and propose policies.

Front-Runner

The presidential candidate who appears to have the most momentum at a given time in the primary season.

Super Tuesday

The date on which a number of presidential primaries are held, including those of most of the southern states.

Front-Loading

The practice of moving presidential primary elections to the early part of the campaign, to maximize the impact of certain states or regions on the nomination.

As soon as politicians and potential presidential candidates realized that winning as many primary elections as possible guaranteed the party's nomination for president, their tactics changed dramatically. Candidates running in the 2000 primaries, such as John McCain, concentrated on building organizations in states that held early, important primary elections. Candidates realized that winning early primaries, such as the New Hampshire election in February, or finishing first in the Iowa **caucus** meant that the media instantly would label the winner as the **front-runner**, thus increasing the candidate's media exposure and increasing the pace of contributions to his or her campaign fund.

The states and state political parties began to see that early primaries had a much greater effect on the outcome of the presidential election and, accordingly, began to hold their primaries earlier in the season to secure that advantage. While New Hampshire held on to its claim as the "first" primary, other states moved to the next week. The southern states decided to hold their primaries on the same date, known as **Super Tuesday,** in the hopes of nominating a moderate southerner at the Democratic convention. When California, which had held the last primary (in June), moved its primary to March, the primary season was curtailed drastically. Due to this process of **front-loading** the primaries, in 2000 the presidential nominating process was over in March, with both George W. Bush and Al Gore having enough convention delegate votes to win their respective nominations. This meant that the campaign was essentially without news until the conventions in August, a gap that did not appeal to the politicians or the media. Both parties discussed whether more changes in the primary process were necessary.

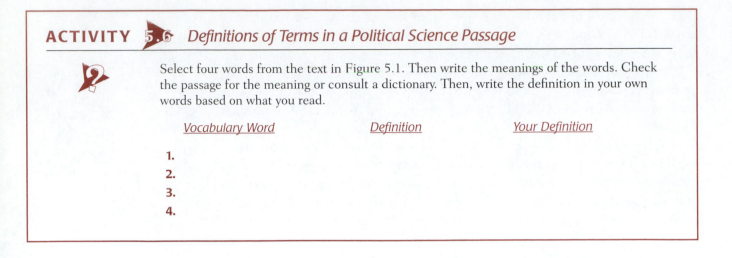

ACTIVITY 5.6   *Definitions of Terms in a Political Science Passage*

Select four words from the text in Figure 5.1. Then write the meanings of the words. Check the passage for the meaning or consult a dictionary. Then, write the definition in your own words based on what you read.

Vocabulary Word	*Definition*	*Your Definition*
1.		
2.		
3.		
4.		

> **Write the Definition in Your Own Words**

On your journey to "know" a word the most important step is for you to interpret the definition and put it into your own words. Why is this important? When you put the definition into your own words, you think deeply about the meaning of the word and connect it with your own background knowledge and experiences. It is this process of integrating the new ideas with your own prior knowledge that is a powerful factor in learning new vocabulary.[12] In the previous activity you could first copy the word and its definition and record them in your vocabulary journal. However, in the next step you needed to think of a meaningful definition and connect this definition with what you had previously learned.

You may find that is it difficult to generate a definition on your own. If you do, listen for multiple uses of the term in class lectures and discussions and look to see how the author is using the term in printed text. You may find that you need to ask your instructor for alternative definitions and for examples of the concept.

> **Make an Association**

In this step you use the definitions and your own paraphrases to think of connections among the new word, its meaning, and your own prior experiences. There are a variety of ways to make these associations. These associations include using mental imagery, making picture cues, using examples, using mnemonics, and using sound cues. Perhaps you have already used some of these strategies in studying for tests and trying to remember other items, such as grocery lists or phone numbers. Although we will be exploring memory strategies in Chapter 7, try the suggestions in the Tip Block.

> **Distinguish the Denotation from Connotation**

As you work with words and their meanings, you will find two levels of definitions: the denotation and the connotation. The *denotation* of a word is the definition you will find in the dictionary or a glossary. On the other hand, the richer meanings of words are found in their *connotations*, which are the implied meanings of words. Some words have certain meanings in certain contexts, particularly in everyday speech; such connotations are not captured in a dictionary definition. Likewise, some words may be appropriate in

---

[12]W. Nagy, *Teaching Vocabulary to Improve Reading Comprehension* (Newark, DE: International Reading Association, 1988).

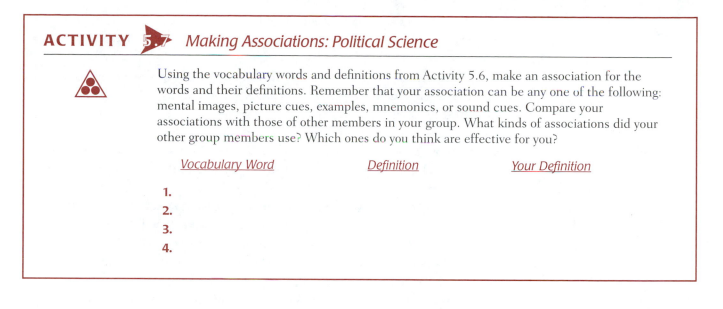

ACTIVITY 5.7   *Making Associations: Political Science*

Using the vocabulary words and definitions from Activity 5.6, make an association for the words and their definitions. Remember that your association can be any one of the following: mental images, picture cues, examples, mnemonics, or sound cues. Compare your associations with those of other members in your group. What kinds of associations did your other group members use? Which ones do you think are effective for you?

Vocabulary Word	Definition	Your Definition
1.		
2.		
3.		
4.		

MAKING ASSOCIATIONS AS A STRATEGY TO REMEMBER WORD DEFINITIONS

Are you looking for strategies for remembering the meanings of words? As a strategic reader, your goal is to understand and remember the meaning of the words you are learning. To reach that goal many students like to use the strategy of making associations between the word and its definition. As a step toward that goal, here are some suggestions:

USE MENTAL IMAGERY. Create a mental image. Visualization is a powerful memory strategy and will help you "see" the connections.

MAKE PICTURE CUES. Make a drawing of the concept and its definition and characteristics. Whereas you use your imagination to create a mental image for the first tip, in this one you make a picture, even if you use stick figures to illustrate the concept. Remember, it is not important that you make a beautiful drawing; however, it is important that you carefully think about the meaning of the term, then show it in some way on paper through a basic drawing.

USE EXAMPLES. Think of real-life examples to illustrate the concepts you are studying.

USE MNEMONICS. Use "memory aids." Perhaps you remember the mnemonic for the colors of the spectrum: ROY G BIV (red, orange, yellow, green, blue, indigo, violet). If you have a group of related terms, you may want to use an acronym, that is, a word made of the initial letters in a list of words. Or, perhaps you may want to use an acrostic, that is, a sentence in which the initial letters of the words in the sentence correspond to the initial letters of the words in a list. For instance, "Every good boy does fine" corresponds to EGBDF, which is the musical notation for the lines of the staff.

USE SOUND CUES. Associate the definition and the word with the sound of another word, using sound cues. Although sound cues do not focus on the meaning of a word, they may help you recall a word when you are searching for it from memory. To use sound clues you say, "This word/definition sounds like. . ." You may want to use a favorite song or rhythm to help you recall the definition of a word.

only certain contexts, restricted by levels of formality and style. Other words evoke certain images and feelings, which may be used with the poetry of language to create a certain mood.

For instance, if you were to look up definitions for the word *yellow* you might find the words *color, afraid,* or *aged.* For instance, you could say, "The curtains yellowed with time," meaning that over the years the curtains lost their brightness. This definition applies typically to fabrics. You could describe cheese as "aged" but not as "yellowed." Another meaning of *yellow* is "afraid"; but that term is not used in formal conversation and could not be a substitute in the sentence "The child is afraid of thunderstorms."

When you look up a word in the dictionary or a glossary, return to the text to see the intended meaning of the word in the passage. It may be that the fuller definition of the word is not captured in the dictionary definition. For instance, what comes to mind when you hear the words *college, money,* or *exam*? Chances are, your images are much richer and more elaborate than the dictionary definitions. Therefore, as you read, check the implied meanings of words, particularly on how they influence your thinking about a topic. Likewise, when you are writing about a topic and you select a synonym from the dictionary or a thesaurus, consider the connotations of the term as well. The following activity will help you explore the distinctions between denotations and connotations.

ACTIVITY 5.8 *Distinguishing Denotation From Connotation*

Write down the following group of words. Then, using a thesaurus, dictionary, or glossary, find three related words (synonyms). Finally, write a note beside each related term regarding its meaning and when you would use the term. Compare your responses to those of the other group members. What did you find about the meanings of these words?

Term		Related Term	Meaning of Term	Suggested Context
became unemployed		fired	let go	told to leave
1. run	a.			
	b.			
	c.			
2. face	a.			
	b.			
	c.			
3. place	a.			
	b.			
	c.			

➤ **Check the Meaning of a Word in Context**

Our English language has numerous examples of a word spelled the same but having different meanings, particularly in specialized fields. You may be familiar with the definition of a word in one context, but you may not be familiar with the specialized use of it in a specific field. The last point related to using words in multiple ways is to check for multiple meanings of the same word.

For instance, do you know the meaning of *score* when it is used in cooking? Do you know that potters also use the word *score* in preparing clay? Likewise, the word *score* is used in the field of music, as in a "musical score." On the other hand, if you play sports, then you are familiar with the rules of the game in order to *score* points. In each of these examples there are multiple meanings of words that at first glance may seem easy to know but have very precise meanings in specific fields. Therefore, the final recommendation is to check the meaning of the word in context. We shall turn our attention to that topic in the section that follows.

CONTEXT CLUES FOR DETERMINING THE MEANING

When you are studying a specific content area, such as psychology, art history, biology, mathematics, or business, you will meet terminology that is specific to that area. In order to understand the concepts in that content area, you will need to know the precise meanings of those terms, to be able to give examples to illustrate the concepts, and to be able to compare and contrast those concepts with other ones. Most textbook authors provide you with the meanings of those terms. However, to be skilled in recognizing those definitions requires that you are skilled in using context clues, that is, the clues for the definitions that are found right in the passage itself. You will find that when you effectively use context clues, you can also check the meaning of a word that you look up in a dictionary or glossary.

Generally speaking, authors use a common set of context clues. Once you are familiar with these, you can look for the definitions directly in the passage. The most commonly used context clues are stated definitions, appositives and synonyms, repetition, comparisons and contrasts, and analogies. An author may not use all of these for stylistics reasons, but if you are familiar with these different types of context clues, then you will be more accurate and precise in determining the meaning of specific vocabulary words.

STATED DEFINITIONS

The author directly gives you the definition of the word. Included in the definition may be full descriptions, characteristics, examples, and non-examples. If the textbook uses boldfaced print to point out the major concepts you need to know, also look for the definitions of these terms directly stated in the text.

For instance, when you were reading the selection about primaries in Figure 5.1, would you have liked a good definition of a primary? When you read the passage in Figure 5.2, notice how the author gives you the definition of the different types of primaries. Read to find the definitions of closed primary, open primary, blanket primary, and run-off primary. Notice how the author gives a stated definition directly in the text by saying "an *open primary* is . . ." For the last definition notice how the author gives you the definition first then says that it is ". . . called a *run-off primary*." These are different styles that author uses to give stated definitions in the text.

FIGURE 5.2

Types of Primaries

Source: From S. W. Schmidt, M. C. Shelley, and B. A. Bardes, *American Government and Politics Today,* 2001–2002 ed. (Belmont, CA: Wadsworth/Thomson Learning, 2001), pp. 322–323.

Types of Primaries

Not only do the states and state parties use different devices for nominations, but they also may hold different types of primary elections. Among the most likely to be seen are those discussed here.

Closed Primary. In a *closed primary,* the selection of a party's candidates in an election is limited to avowed or declared party members. In other words, voters must declare their party affiliation, either when they register to vote or at the primary election. A closed-primary system tries to make sure that registered voters cannot cross over into the other party's primary in order to nominate the weakest candidate of the opposing party or to affect the ideological direction of that party.

Open Primary. An *open primary* is a primary in which voters can vote in either party primary without disclosing their party affiliation. Basically, the voter makes the choice in the privacy of the voting booth. The voter must, however, choose one party's list from which to select candidates. Open primaries place no restrictions on independent voters.

Blanket Primary. A *blanket primary* is one in which the voter may vote for candidates of more than one party. Alaska, Louisiana, and Washington all have blanket primaries. Blanket-primary campaigns may be much more costly because each candidate for every office is trying to influence all the voters, not just those in his or her party.

In 2000, the United States Supreme Court issued a decision that will alter significantly the use of the blanket primary. The case arose when political parties in California challenged the constitutionality of a 1996 ballot initiative authorizing the use of the blanket primary in that state. The parties contended that the blanket primary violated their First Amendment right of association. Because the nominees represent the party, they argued, party members—not the general electorate—should have the right to choose the party's nominee. The Supreme Court ruled in favor of the parties, holding that the blanket primary violated parties' First Amendment associational rights.[9]

The Court's ruling called into question the constitutional validity of blanket primaries in other states as well. The question before these states now is how to devise a primary election system that will both comply with the Supreme Court's ruling yet offer independent voters a chance to participate in the primary elections.

Run-off Primary. Some states have a two-primary system. If no candidate receives a majority of the votes in the first primary, the top two candidates must compete in another primary, called a *run-off primary.*

---

[9]California Democratic Party v. Jones, 120 S. Ct. 2402 (2000).

APPOSITIVES AND SYNONYMS

Another commonly used type of context clue is an appositive or a synonym. This type of context clue is usually a short phrase or word directly following the new word, which may be in boldfaced print or italics. An appositive renames the new word; a synonym provides a word similar in meaning. The author often uses a pair of commas or parentheses when starting an appositive or synonym. The author may also give the definition using the phrases "which is . . .," "or . . .," "meaning . . .," or "called." Note how the author uses appositives and synonyms in the passage in Figure 5.3.

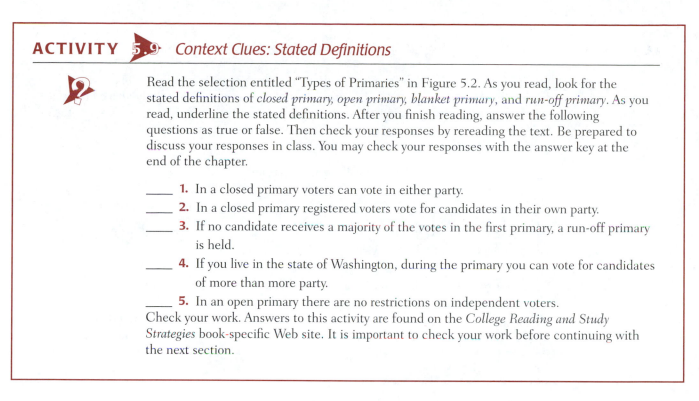

ACTIVITY 5.9 *Context Clues: Stated Definitions*

Read the selection entitled "Types of Primaries" in Figure 5.2. As you read, look for the stated definitions of *closed primary, open primary, blanket primary,* and *run-off primary.* As you read, underline the stated definitions. After you finish reading, answer the following questions as true or false. Then check your responses by rereading the text. Be prepared to discuss your responses in class. You may check your responses with the answer key at the end of the chapter.

_____ **1.** In a closed primary voters can vote in either party.

_____ **2.** In a closed primary registered voters vote for candidates in their own party.

_____ **3.** If no candidate receives a majority of the votes in the first primary, a run-off primary is held.

_____ **4.** If you live in the state of Washington, during the primary you can vote for candidates of more than more party.

_____ **5.** In an open primary there are no restrictions on independent voters.

Check your work. Answers to this activity are found on the *College Reading and Study Strategies* book-specific Web site. It is important to check your work before continuing with the next section.

FIGURE 5.3

Amphibians Were the First Successful Land Vertebrates

Source: **From E. P. Solomon, L. R. Berg, and D. W. Martin,** *Biology,* **5th ed. (Fort Worth, TX: Saunders, 1999), pp. 652–653.**

Amphibians Were the First Successful Land Vertebrates

The first successful **tetrapods,** or land vertebrates, were the **labyrinthodonts,** clumsy, salamander-like animals with short necks and heavy, muscular tails. These ancient members of class Amphibia somewhat resembled their ancestors, the lobe-finned fishes. However, they had limbs strong enough to support the weight of their bodies on land. The largest labyrinthodonts were the size of crocodiles. They flourished during the late Paleozoic and early Mesozoic eras, then became extinct. It is probable that the labyrinthodonts gave rise to other primitive amphibians, to frogs and salamanders, and to the earliest reptiles, the **cotylosaurs.**

Modern amphibians are classified in three orders: order **Urodela** ("visible tail") includes the salamanders, mudpuppies, and newts, all animals with long tails; order **Anura** ("no tail") is made up of the frogs and toads, with legs adapted for hopping; and order **Apoda** ("no feet") contains the wormlike caecilians. Although some adult amphibians are quite successful as land animals and can live in dry environments, most return to the water to reproduce. Eggs and sperm are generally released in the water.

The embryos of frogs and toads develop into larvae called **tadpoles.** These larvae have tails and gills, and most feed on aquatic plants. After a time, the tadpole undergoes metamorphosis. The gills and gill slits disappear, the tail is resorbed, and limbs emerge. The digestive tract shortens, and food preference shifts from plant material to a carnivorous diet; the mouth widens; a tongue develops; the tympanic membrane (ear drum) and eyelids appear; and the eye lens changes shape. Many biochemical changes also accompany the transformation from a completely aquatic life to an amphibious one.

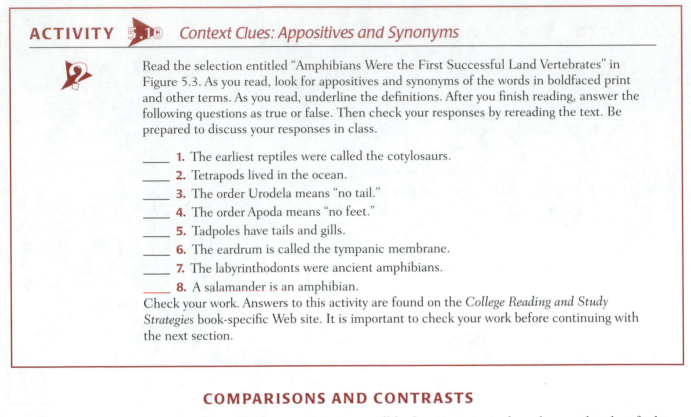

ACTIVITY 5.10   *Context Clues: Appositives and Synonyms*

Read the selection entitled "Amphibians Were the First Successful Land Vertebrates" in Figure 5.3. As you read, look for appositives and synonyms of the words in boldfaced print and other terms. As you read, underline the definitions. After you finish reading, answer the following questions as true or false. Then check your responses by rereading the text. Be prepared to discuss your responses in class.

_____ **1.** The earliest reptiles were called the cotylosaurs.
_____ **2.** Tetrapods lived in the ocean.
_____ **3.** The order Urodela means "no tail."
_____ **4.** The order Apoda means "no feet."
_____ **5.** Tadpoles have tails and gills.
_____ **6.** The eardrum is called the tympanic membrane.
_____ **7.** The labyrinthodonts were ancient amphibians.
_____ **8.** A salamander is an amphibian.

Check your work. Answers to this activity are found on the *College Reading and Study Strategies* book-specific Web site. It is important to check your work before continuing with the next section.

COMPARISONS AND CONTRASTS

In many of your courses you will be learning terminology that can be classified into groups or sets. Many of the vocabulary words that you meet are related to other key words; therefore, you will find that you will learn not only a series of single words but also a group of concepts. It will be important to learn distinctions among those concepts and how they are related to each other. Therefore, another typical way of learning new words in context is to learn how concepts are compared and contrasted. The author may

FIGURE 5.4
Conditioned Reinforcement

Source: **From W. Weiten,** *Psychology: Themes and Variations,* **6th ed. (Belmont, CA: Wadsworth/Thomson Learning, 2004), p. 235.**

Conditioned Reinforcement

Operant theorists make a distinction between unlearned, or primary, reinforcers as opposed to conditioned, or secondary, reinforcers. *Primary reinforcers* are events that are inherently reinforcing because they satisfy biological needs. A given species has a limited number of primary reinforcers because they are closely tied to physiological needs. In humans, primary reinforcers include food, water, warmth, sex, and perhaps affection expressed through hugging and close bodily contact.

Secondary, or *conditioned, reinforcers* are events that acquire reinforcing qualities by being associated with primary reinforcers. The events that function as secondary reinforcers vary among members of a species because they depend on learning. Examples of common secondary reinforcers in humans include money, good grades, attention, flattery, praise, and applause. Most of the material things that people work hard to earn are secondary reinforcers. For example, people learn to find stylish clothes, sports cars, fine jewelry, elegant china, and state-of-the-art stereos reinforcing.

ACTIVITY 5.11   *Context Clues: Comparisons and Contrast*

Read the selection entitled "Conditioned Reinforcement" in Figure 5.4. As you read, look for the comparison and contrast of *primary reinforcers* and *secondary reinforcers*. As you read, underline the definitions and the examples. After you finish reading, answer the following questions as true or false. Then check your responses by rereading the text. Be prepared to discuss your responses in class. When you are checking your responses, discuss in your group how you used context clues to determine the meaning of the concepts.

_____ **1.** Secondary reinforcers satisfy biological needs.

_____ **2.** Money is a primary reinforcer.

_____ **3.** Food is a primary reinforcer.

_____ **4.** Music is a primary reinforcer.

_____ **5.** A new, expensive car is a primary reinforcer.

_____ **6.** Primary reinforcers are learned.

_____ **7.** Secondary reinforcers are the same for all cultures throughout the world.

_____ **8.** Secondary reinforcers of people in the nineteenth century are the same for people in the twenty-first century.

Check your work. Answers to this activity are found on the *College Reading and Study Strategies* book-specific Web site. It is important to check your work before continuing with the next section.

use examples to show how the concepts are similar or different. Some of the signal words to look for include words and phrases such as "similar to," "like," "unlike," "in contrast," "distinctions," "compared to," or "opposed to." Notice how the author describes *primary reinforcers* in contrast to *secondary reinforcers* in Figure 5.4.

REPETITION

An author explaining a new concept will often use repetition to highlight key ideas, to emphasize what is important, and to summarize examples that are used to illustrate the concept. Repetition can occur on the word level; that is, the author may decide to repeat the same word or group of words. Or, the author may decide to repeat the same idea using a series of synonyms. Notice in Figure 5.5 how the author describes Van Gogh's *The Starry Night*. As you are reading, look for the descriptors of the energy portrayed in this classic painting.

FIGURE 5.5
Van Gogh: **The Starry Night**

Source: **From J. Canaday,** *Mainstreams of Modern Art.* **(Fort Worth, TX: Harcourt Brace Jovanovich, 1987), pp. 344–346.**

Van Gogh: "*The Starry Night*"

Modern expressionism stems directly from the tragic Dutchman Vincent van Gogh (1853–1890), a man a little older than Seurat, who died a year before Seurat did. Both stemming from impressionism, these contemporaries could hardly be more unlike—Seurat with his calculation, his method, his deliberation, van Gogh with

Continued

FIGURE 5.5, *Continued*

his passion, his shattering vehemence. Instead of *La Grande Jatte,* so cool, so defined, so self-contained, van Gogh gives us *The Starry Night* [405], where a whirling force catapults across the sky and writhes upward from the earth, where planets burst with their own energy and all the universe surges and pulsates in a release of intolerable vitality.

Like all the most affecting expressionist creations, *The Starry Night* seems to have welled forth onto the canvas spontaneously, as if the creative act were a compulsive physical one beyond the artist's power to restrain. "Inspiration" as a kind of frenzied enchantment visited upon a painter, a paroxysm calling forth images only half-willed, is a justifiable concept in van Gogh's case if it is ever justifiable at all. *The Starry Night* implies that it was executed in a fever of creation, as if it had to be set down somehow on canvas in an instant, as if a pause for calculation would check the gush, the momentum, of a brush guided by a mysterious spiritual force rather than by knowledge and experience. And to a certain extent this was so. Van Goh's letters tell of days when his painting went well, when he would work into the night without stopping to eat. In some instances, the paint is squeezed onto the canvas straight from the tube, as if to reduce to a minimum the obstructions between conception and execution. Yet all this is misleading. His letters also speak of his studies for a picture that obsesses him, a picture of a starry night. There is a full preliminary drawing.

If *The Starry Night* seems to burst, to explode, to race, it does not run away. It is built on a great rushing movement from left to right; this movement courses upward through the landscape, into the hills and on into the sky, and floods into the picture like a swollen river in the galaxy beginning at the border on the upper left. But this movement curls back on itself in the center of the picture, then rushes forward again at a reduced pace, and finally curls back once more to join other rhythms instead of running out of the picture. In the rest of the sky, the moon and stars are whirlpools meshing with these major movements. The cypresses rise abruptly and lean slightly in the opposite direction as a brake; their own motion, spiraling upward, is another check to the horizontal lunge of earth and sky; a church steeple cuts less conspicuously across the sweep of a hill on the horizon, to the same effect. The moon, largest of the whirlpools of light, is itself a force that sucks the current back into the picture at a point where it would otherwise rush beyond the frame and be lost.

ACTIVITY 5.12   *Context Clues: Comparisons and Contrast*

Read the selection entitled "Van Gogh: *The Starry Night*" in Figure 5.5. As you read, look for the words that describe movement and energy. As you read, underline these descriptors. On a separate piece of paper write down as many words as possible that the writer uses to describe the energy of this painting. Be prepared to discuss your responses in class.

In the passage above did you see how the author captured the movement in *The Starry Night*? Notice how the phrases "whirling force," "catapults across the sky," "burst with their own energy," "momentum," "burst," "explode," "movement courses upward," as well as many others repeat the idea that the painting shows great energy. Most likely, you found many other examples in the passage as well.

ANALOGIES

Another type of context clue that will help you find the meaning of a word is the use of analogies. To illustrate a concept an author may describe how the concept is *like* something. This comparison may continue through several paragraphs. The use of analogies is particularly effective throughout explanations of abstract principles or ideas. When you are reading the analogy, consider the characteristics of the object used to explain the characteristics of the abstract idea. In Figure 5.6, an excerpt from an article about human memory, find the analogies used to describe human memory.

FIGURE 5.6

Storage: Maintaining Information in Memory

Source: From W. Weiten, *Psychology: Themes and Variations,* 6th ed. (Belmont, CA: Wadsworth/Thomson Learning, 2004), p. 266.

Storage: Maintaining Information in Memory

In their efforts to understand memory storage, theorists have historically related it to the technologies of their age (Roediger, 1980). One of the earliest models used to explain memory storage was the wax tablet. Both Aristotle and Plato compared memory to a block of wax that differed in size and hardness for various individuals. Remembering, according to this analogy, was like stamping an impression into the wax. As long as the image remained in the wax, the memory would remain intact.

Modern theories of memory reflect the technological advances of the 20th century. For example, many theories formulated at the dawn of the computer age drew an analogy between information storage by computers and information storage in human memory (Atkinson & Shiffrin, 1968, 1971; Broadbent, 1958; Waugh & Norman, 1965). The main contribution of these *information-processing theories* was to subdivide memory into three separate memory stores (Estes, 1999; Pashler & Carrier, 1996). The names for these stores and their exact characteristics varied some from one theory to the next. For purposes of simplicity, we'll organize our discussion around the model devised by Atkinson and Shiffrin, which proved to be the most influential of the information-processing theories. According to their model, incoming information passes through two temporary storage buffers—the sensory store and short-term store—before it is transferred into a long-term store. Like the wax tablet before it, the information-processing model of memory is a metaphor; the three memory stores are not viewed as anatomical structures in the brain, but rather as functionally distinct types of memory.

ACTIVITY 5.13   *Context Clues: Analogies*

Read the selection entitled "Storage: Maintaining Information in Memory" in Figure 5.6. As you read, look for the analogies used to describe human memory throughout the ages. On a separate piece of paper write down these analogies. Do you find this a useful strategy for understanding and remembering the text?

FOUR APPROACHES FOR VOCABULARY DEVELOPMENT

In this next section of the chapter you will learn four different approaches for improving your vocabulary: (1) utilizing Greek and Latin word prefixes and roots, (2) generating vocabulary study cards, (3) connecting concepts through graphic organizers, and (4) reflecting on the meaning of the concept. Although each of these approaches is an independent approach for improving your vocabulary, the versatile student often uses a combination of these approaches for textbook reading and for studying for course exams. For each of these approaches it is important to use the same vocabulary goals and use the same vocabulary strategies discussed in the previous sections of this chapter, particularly in (1) determining the meaning the word, (2) writing the definition in your own words, (3) making an association, (4) distinguishing the denotation of the word from its connotation, and (5) checking the meaning of the word.

UTILIZING GREEK AND LATIN WORD PREFIXES AND ROOTS

Among college courses in vocabulary improvement there is wide appeal in teaching students many of the commonly occurring Greek and Latin prefixes and roots that appear in the English language, though the efficacy of using such an approach is not validated with much empirical evidence.[13] However, when you attend to the meanings of groups of words related by a common prefix or root, you see the relationships and verbal associations among the groups of words; this is a significant step in understanding new vocabulary.

In the content areas, particularly in science, you will find a basic knowledge of commonly occurring Greek and Latin word parts a valuable tool in determining the meanings of unfamiliar words. For instance, you will find that the biological sciences typically name many of the organisms, parts of the human body, and biological processes with words that have Greek or Latin word roots. As you read, look for words that are part of a family of words, then look for defining distinctions among the words.

Let's try an example. Perhaps you are familiar with the word *dermatologist,* that is, a doctor who specializes in caring for the skin. The name *dermatologist* is from the Greek root "derma," meaning skin. This same Greek root is used in describing the three layers of the skin: ectoderm, mesoderm, and endoderm. When you read the passage in Figure 5.7, read to identify these three layers; an additional tip is that *ecto* is a Greek root for "outside"; *meso* is from the Greek root "mesos," meaning "middle"; and *endo* is from the Greek root "endon," meaning "within."

When you come across an unfamiliar word, look for a familiar part of the word and think of the definition of the familiar word. You will still need to check the meaning of the word in context or a glossary to verify the precise meaning of the word for a specific content area. However, you will be able to use your knowledge of the roots and prefixes to build "word families," that is, words that have the same common roots. For instance, the root "phon" means "sound." Can you think of words with "phon" in them? Do microphone,

---

[13]M. L. Simpson and S. N. Randall, "Vocabulary Development at the College Level," in R. Flippo and D. C. Caverly, eds., *Handbook of College Reading and Study Strategy Research* (Mahwah, NJ: Lawrence Erlbaum, 2000), pp. 43–73.

FIGURE 5.7
Tissue and Organ Formation

Source: From C. Starr and R. Taggart, *Biology: The Unity and Diversity of Life,* 9th ed. (Belmont, CA: Brooks/Cole, 2001), p. 569.

Tissue and Organ Formation

Where do tissues of organ systems come from? To get a sense of how they originate, start with sperm and eggs. (These form from *germ* cells, or immature reproductive cells. All other cells in the body are *somatic,* after a Greek word for body.) A zygote forms after a sperm fertilizes an egg, then mitotic cell divisions form an early embryo. In vertebrates, cells become arranged as three primary tissues—ectoderm, mesoderm, and endoderm. These three are embryonic forerunners of all tissues in an adult. **Ectoderm** gives rise to skin's outer layer and to tissues of a nervous system. **Mesoderm** gives rise to tissues of muscle, bone, and most of the circulatory, reproductive, and urinary systems. **Endoderm** gives rise to the lining of the digestive tract and to organs derived from it.

ACTIVITY 5.14   *Using Greek Roots*

Read the selection entitled "Tissue and Organ Formation" in Figure 5.7. As you read, use the definitions of *ecto, meso, endo,* and *derm* to define "ectoderm," "mesoderm," and "endoderm." Then, write a short definition of each of these terms. Reread the text using your definition to check the meaning of the passage.

Ectoderm:

Mesoderm:

Endoderm:

ACTIVITY 5.15   *Building Word Families*

For each of the following roots, write at least five words containing the root. You may use a dictionary, if you wish. Then, compare your list to the words generated by the other members of your group. You can add to your list the other words from the other group members. How many different words did you find?

1. *chron* meaning "time"
2. *gen* meaning "birth"
3. *graph* meaning "to write"
4. *meter* meaning "measure"
5. *nov* meaning "new"
6. *ped* meaning "foot"
7. *spec(t)* meaning "to look"
8. *vers* or *vert* meaning "to turn"
9. *voc* meaning "voice"
10. *viv* meaning "life"

telephone, and saxophone come to mind? Other related words include cacophony, phonics, and megaphone. It is often a fun and challenging exercise to see how far you can extend your word families. Try building a few word families in Activity 5.15.

It is also useful to be familiar with the common prefixes that are used in our English language. White, Sowell, and Yanagihara (1989) identified the twenty prefixes that are used in 97% of prefixed words of printed school English; these twenty are listed below in Activity 5.16.[14] If you are familiar with these twenty prefixes, then when you see a word containing the prefix, you will be able to make a good guess about the meaning of the word. Most likely, you are familiar with many of these prefixes already. Note that for the third one on the list, *in* (meaning "not"), the *n* changes to either *m, l,* or *r* depending on the consonant next to the prefix. For instance, *illegal* means "not legal" and *irregular* means "not regular"; the spelling changes so that the word is easier to pronounce.

ACTIVITY 5.16 *Using Prefixes*

Work with a partner to write a short definition of each of the following prefixes, then find a word that contains the prefix. Compare your responses with other those of another group of two.

Prefix	Meaning	Example
un		
re		
in/im/il/ir		
dis		
en/em		
non		
in/im		
over		
mis		
sub		
pre		
inter		
fore		
de		
trans		
super		
semi		
anti		
mid		
under		

Another group of prefixes that is particularly important to know are the prefixes that designate numbers. For instance, a unicycle has one wheel, a bicycle has two wheels, and a tricycle has three wheels. In Activity 5.17, try to think of words that contain these common prefixes.

---

[14]T. G. White, J. Sowell, and A. Yanagihara, "Teaching Elementary Students to Use Word-Part Clues," *The Reading Teacher,* 42 (1989): pp. 302–309.

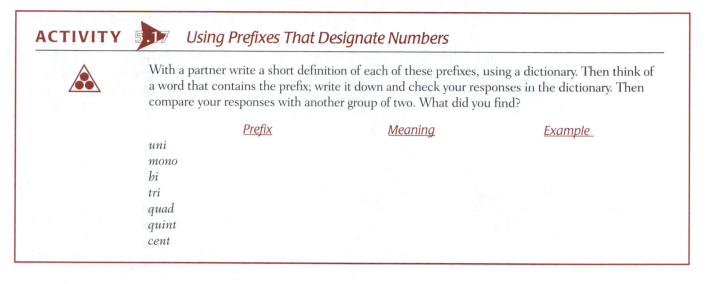

ACTIVITY 5.17 *Using Prefixes That Designate Numbers*

With a partner write a short definition of each of these prefixes, using a dictionary. Then think of a word that contains the prefix; write it down and check your responses in the dictionary. Then compare your responses with another group of two. What did you find?

Prefix	*Meaning*	*Example*
uni		
mono		
bi		
tri		
quad		
quint		
cent		

GENERATING VOCABULARY STUDY CARDS

As you encounter new words in your textbook readings and in your lectures, you may begin to feel overwhelmed with the sheer quantity of new words that you need to know. However, if you have a study strategy for recording and remembering the new words that you meet, then you will feel confident about using the words in class in oral and written work, and you will feel confident while taking tests. The key in using this strategy, though, is practice, practice, practice. On a regular basis you will need to review the meanings of the words that you generate for your study cards. Figure 5.8 gives you one idea how you can create vocabulary cards. You will learn additional strategies in Chapter 10.

FIGURE 5.8
Vocabulary Study Card

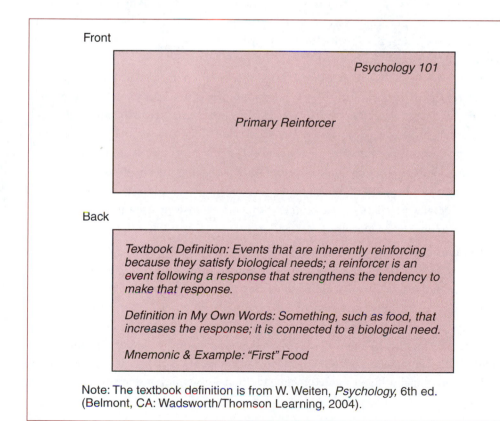

Front

Psychology 101

Primary Reinforcer

Back

Textbook Definition: Events that are inherently reinforcing because they satisfy biological needs; a reinforcer is an event following a response that strengthens the tendency to make that response.

Definition in My Own Words: Something, such as food, that increases the response; it is connected to a biological need.

Mnemonic & Example: "First" Food

Note: The textbook definition is from W. Weiten, *Psychology,* 6th ed. (Belmont, CA: Wadsworth/Thomson Learning, 2004).

The basic assumption behind this approach is that you will build a bank of study cards for the words you need to know, remember, and use. If you use a vocabulary journal (highly recommended!) to record the new words you meet, then the study cards give you the opportunity to review their meanings in multiple ways. Study cards give you the flexibility of carrying them to different places, so that when you have a few minutes here and there, you can pull out your vocabulary cards and review them.

ACTIVITY 5.18   *Creating and Using Vocabulary Cards*

Find at least twenty vocabulary words (particularly those you need to know for a test) in your other classes. Create a set of at least twenty vocabulary cards, using Figure 5.8 as your guide. After you have created your cards, pretest your knowledge of those words, then provide for practice for the words you need to study. Be sure to retest yourself after you have learned all twenty words.

CONNECTING CONCEPTS THROUGH GRAPHIC ORGANIZERS

Although students often think that learning new vocabulary means learning new words, the truer picture is that learning new vocabulary means learning new concepts; these concepts are related to other groups of concepts and to truly understand the meanings of new vocabulary words, you need to understand the associations that exist among the concepts. For instance, in the passage in Figure 5.7 the overall concept was "Layers of Skin"; the specific terms described what was the outer, the middle, or the layer underneath.

Rarely does a course professor present a single, isolated concept for you to know. Therefore, the main goal of this vocabulary approach is to organize related terms in a meaningful, visual schematic so that you can see how terms are associated with each other. Although there are many different tools available for you to do this, the most common graphic organizers are semantic (or concept) maps, hierarchical arrays, and semantic feature matrices. These graphic organizers group together meaningfully related ideas. For instance in Chapter 4 and Chapter 13 you use graphic organizers to see how main ideas and details are related to each other. Students extensively use these same graphic organizers to illustrate concepts.

➤ **Semantic Map**

A semantic map can illustrate the definition of a word, an example, essential features, non-features, and words related to it. (See the model in Figure 5.9 and the example in Figure 5.10.) To create a semantic map, you place the vocabulary word in the center of the page; then radiating out from the center you place your descriptors. For instance, in Figure 5.10 you can see the characteristics of the concept "primary reinforcers." The benefit of a semantic map is that all of these critical characteristics can be displayed graphically. If you wanted to add additional examples or items to it, you could do so.

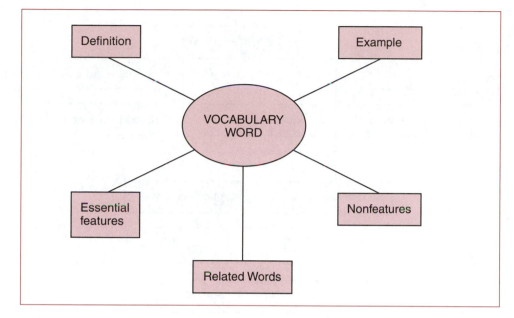

FIGURE 5.9
Semantic Map

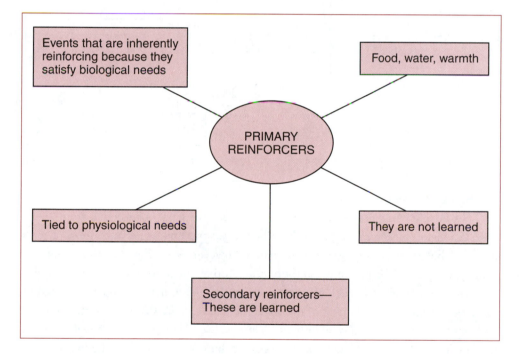

FIGURE 5.10
Semantic Map of "Primary Reinforcers"

➤ Hierarchical Array

You are probably familiar with the diagram of a family tree; at the top of the tree you would place your grandparents, then branching down would be your parents, then the next level branching down would be you and any of your siblings. Similarly, a hierarchical array is useful when you have a group of concepts that have superordinate and subordinate relationships. The superordinate concepts are placed at the top of the graph, and the subordinate relationships branch underneath them. (See Figures 5.11 and 5.12 on the next page.) For instance, Figure 5.12 shows the different elements of drama: character, plot, setting, symbolism, and theme.

FIGURE 5.11
Hierarchical Array

FIGURE 5.12
Hierarchical Array of "Elements of Drama"

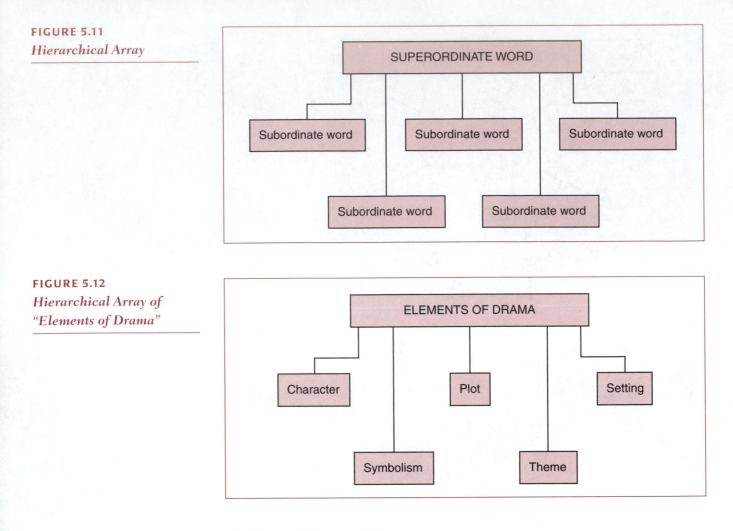

> ➤ **Semantic Feature Matrix**

The benefit of a hierarchical array is that you can see what belongs in a group. However, the hierarchical array does not describe the positive and negative features of those items in the group. A semantic feature matrix, however, does show you those features. This type of graphic is useful when there is a group of concepts and you wish to delineate the characteristics of each of them. A semantic feature matrix condenses much information in one table; a benefit of the semantic feature matrix is that you can compare and contrast concepts on several different features. (See Figures 5.13 below and 5.14 on the next page.) You can add additional rows and columns, as needed, in the matrix.

FIGURE 5.13
Semantic Feature Matrix

	Feature 1	Feature 2	Feature 3
Word 1			
Word 2			
Word 3			

FIGURE 5.14

Example of Semantic Feature Matrix: Psychoactive Drugs

Source: From W. Weiten, *Psychology: Themes and Variations*, 6th ed. (Belmont, CA: Wadsworth/Thomson Learning, 2004), p. 203.

Psychoactive Drugs: Methods of Ingestion, Medical Uses, and Effects

Drugs	Methods of Ingestion	Principal Medical Uses	Desired Effects	Short-Term Side Effects
Narcotics (opiates) Morphine Heroin	Injected, smoked, oral	Pain relief	Euphoria, relaxation, anxiety reduction, pain relief	Lethargy, drowsiness, nausea, impaired coordination, impaired mental functioning, constipation
Sedatives Barbiturates (e.g., Seconal) Nonbarbiturates (e.g., Quaalude)	Oral, injected	Sleeping pill, anticonvulsant	Euphoria, relaxation, anxiety reduction, reduced inhibitions	Lethargy, drowsiness, severely impaired coordination, impaired mental functioning, emotional swings, dejection
Stimulants Amphetamines Cocaine	Oral, sniffed, injected, freebased, smoked	Treatment of hyperactivity and narcolepsy, local anesthetic (cocaine only)	Elation, excitement, increased alertness, increased energy, reduced fatigue	Increased blood pressure and heart rate, increased talkativeness, restlessness, irritability, insomnia, reduced appetite, increased sweating and urination, anxiety, paranoia, increased aggressiveness, panic
Hallucinogens LSD Mescaline Psilocybin	Oral	None	Increased sensory awareness, euphoria, altered perceptions, hallucinations, insightful experiences	Dilated pupils, nausea, emotional swings, paranoia, jumbled thought processes, impaired judgment, anxiety, panic reaction
Cannabis Marijuana Hashish THC	Smoked, oral	Treatment of glaucoma; other uses under study	Mild euphoria, relaxation, altered perceptions, enhanced awareness	Bloodshot eyes, dry mouth, reduced short-term memory, sluggish motor coordination, sluggish mental functioning, anxiety
Alcohol	Drinking	None	Mild euphoria, relaxation, anxiety reduction, reduced inhibitions	Severely impaired coordination, impaired mental functioning, increased urination, emotional swings, depression, quarrelsomeness, hangover

You may find several examples of semantic feature matrices in your college textbooks because they often summarize much information in a chapter. For instance, in the table entitled "Psychoactive Drugs: Methods of Ingestion, Medical Uses, and Effects" (in Figure 5.14) you can see the distinctions among a variety of drugs; if you wished to compare the effects of sedatives and stimulants, you would be able to find the information in this table.

These three are only a few examples of graphic organizers for you to use for learning the meanings of concepts. We will be discussing how graphic organizers can help you remember main ideas and supporting details in future chapters. These three graphic organizers can serve you well in your toolbox of strategies for improving your vocabulary. To gain more practice using graphic organizers, try the following activity. You will meet a passage from a psychology textbook that describes classic terminology in the field of behaviorism. (See Figure 5.15.) Read the passage through completely to get an overall sense of the ideas, then return to the passage to construct your own graphic organizer describing the terms in boldfaced print.

FIGURE 5.15
Operant Conditioning, Reinforcement, and Punishment

Source: From R. Sternberg, *Psychology: In Search of the Human Mind*, 3d ed. (Fort Worth, TX: Harcourt, 2001), pp. 212–213.

Operant Conditioning, Reinforcement, and Punishment

Operant conditioning is of great importance in our lives, literally from the day we are born. Parents reward some actions and punish others, exploiting the laws of operant conditioning to socialize their children. In this way, parents hope to strengthen their children's adaptive behavior and to weaken the children's maladaptive behavior. The same mechanisms are used in school. Some kinds of behavior are rewarded by nods, approbation, or good grades, whereas other kinds of behavior result in isolation from other students, trips to the principal's office, and so on. Operant conditioning, like classical conditioning, can be sensitive to the context in which it takes place. It is also subject to the kind of occasion setting described earlier for classical conditioning (Colwill & Delameter, 1995). Next we examine these mechanisms in more detail.

Reinforcement

In the study of operant conditioning, the term *operant* refers to a kind of behavior that operates on or has some effect on the world. Asking for help, drinking a glass of water, threatening to hurt someone, kissing your lover—all of these are operants. Operant conditioning results in either an increase or a decrease in the probability that these operant behaviors will be performed again.

A reinforcer is a *stimulus* that increases the probability that a given operant behavior associated with the stimulus (which usually has occurred immediately or almost immediately before the reinforcing stimulus) will be repeated. Reinforcers can be either positive or negative.

A **positive reinforcer** is a reward, a pleasant stimulus that follows an operant and strengthens the associated response. Examples of positive reinforcers (for most of us) are a smile or a compliment from a teacher following a correct answer or a candy bar released by a vending machine after we put in the required change. When a positive reinforcer occurs soon after an operant response, we refer to the pairing of the positive reinforcer with the response as positive reinforcement.

Continued

FIGURE 5.15, *Continued*

A **negative reinforcer** is a (usually unpleasant) stimulus whose removal or cessation increases the probability that the type of behavior that preceded it will be repeated in the same type of situation. Negative reinforcement refers to the process whereby the removal of the unpleasant stimulus results in an increased probability of response. For example, the removal of electric shock would serve as a negative reinforcement if the reward of its removal increased the probability that the type of behavior that preceded it would be repeated in the same type of situation. If putting up an umbrella stops cold rainwater from trickling down the back of your neck, you might be more likely to open your umbrella in the future because you have been negatively reinforced for doing so.

Punishment

Do not call to a dog with a whip in your hand.

—Zulu proverb

Unlike the various forms of reinforcement, which increase the probability of an operant response, punishment is a process that *decreases* the probability of an operant response. (It should not be confused with negative reinforcement, despite its somewhat unpleasant-sounding name and associations with aversive stimuli, which *increases* the likelihood of a response.) **Positive punishment** is the application of an unpleasant stimulus. Examples of positive punishment include being hit, humiliated, or laughed at, or receiving a failing grade in a course or a negative evaluation from a work supervisor. **Negative punishment** (also sometimes called a *penalty*) is the removal of a pleasant stimulus. Being restricted from enjoyable activities such as television viewing or social interactions with friends are examples of negative punishment.

One way of looking at the difference between reinforcement and punishment is that reinforcement captures and to some extent controls behavior, whereas punishment blocks behavior. Reinforcement has fairly predictable consequences and punishment does not. Punishment is thus a less effective way of controlling behavior than is reinforcement.

ACTIVITY 5.19   *Creating Your Graphic Organizer*

Read the text passage in Figure 5.15 about operant conditioning and reinforcement. After you have finished reading the passage, return to the text and find the terms in boldfaced print. Then, choose one of the graphic organizers in Figures 5.9, 5.11, or 5.13. Complete your graphic organizer using definitions, examples, descriptions of critical features, and non-features. Why did you select the graphic organizer you picked? Does it help you remember all the ideas you need to know?

The textbook author summarizes this passage in a table that describes the "Stimulus Presented in the Environment as an Outcome of Operant Behavior" as one feature and the "Effect of Stimulus on Operant Behavior" as another critical feature. This table is presented in Figure 5.16. Compare the information you selected in your graphic organizer with the information in this table. Then try Activity 5.20 to test your vocabulary knowledge about the terms in this passage.

FIGURE 5.16

Summary of Operant Conditioning

Source: From R. Sternberg, *Psychology: In Search of the Human Mind,* 3d ed. (Fort Worth, TX: Harcourt, 2001), p. 214.

Summary of Operant Conditioning

For a given operant behavior, reinforcement increases the probability of its future recurrence, whereas punishment reduces the likelihood that it will be repeated in the future. How might you use these principles to shape the behavior of persons in your environment?

Operant-Conditioning Technique	Stimulus Presented in the Environment as an Outcome of Operant Behavior	Effect of Stimulus on Operant Behavior
Positive reinforcement	Presentation of *positive reinforcer*— Pleasant stimulus that is introduced follows desired behavior	Strengthens and increases the likelihood of the operant behavior
Negative reinforcement	Presentation of *negative reinforcer*— Unpleasant stimulus that is removed following desired behavior	Strengthens and increases the likelihood of the operant behavior
Positive punishment	Presentation of unpleasant stimulus	Weakens and decreases the likelihood of the operant behavior
Negative punishment (penalty)	Removal of pleasant stimulus	Weakens and decreases the likelihood of the operant behavior

---

ACTIVITY 5.20 *Using Your Graphic Organizers*

Read the selection about operant conditioning in Figure 5.15 and the table in Figure 5.16. As you read, look for the definitions and examples of *positive reinforcement, negative reinforcement, positive punishment,* and *negative punishment.* After you finish reading, answer the following questions as true or false. Then check your responses by rereading the text and the table. Be prepared to discuss your responses in class.

_____ **1.** If a child receives candy after good behavior, then the candy is used as a positive reinforcer.

_____ **2.** If a child is not permitted to watch TV after behaving poorly, then "not watching TV" is a negative reinforcer.

_____ **3.** According to psychologists who use operant conditioning, punishment is not as effective as other ways to control behavior.

_____ **4.** A reinforcer strengthens behavior.

_____ **5.** The intention of the use of punishment is to weaken the likelihood of a specific behavior.

Check your work. Answers to this activity are found on the *College Reading and Study Strategies* book-specific Web site. It is important to check your work before continuing with the next section. How did you do? How can you use this strategy in your own classes?

REFLECTING ON THE MEANING OF THE CONCEPT

To truly know the meaning of a concept you need to do much more than look up a word in the dictionary or a glossary. Simpson and Randall (2000) summarized the research about "knowing a word" as follows:

Students should be able to:

1. Recognize and generate critical attributes, examples, nonexamples of a concept;

2. Sense and infer relationships between concepts and their own backgrounds;

3. Recognize and apply the concept to a variety of contexts;

4. Generate novel contexts for the targeted concept.[15]

In the activities in this chapter you have found the meanings of words in context and have written about the meanings of many concepts in your vocabulary journal. What you have not had the opportunity to do is to make applications of these concepts to your life and to extend those applications to new situations.

For instance, if you take an introductory psychology course, you will learn about the principles of behaviorism, including operant conditioning. However, can you think of instances in your own life in which your own behavior was changed as a result of a reinforcer or punishment? Can you think of examples in our society that use reinforcers or punishment to shape behavior? For instance, if you get a parking ticket for parking illegally, is that *positive reinforcement, negative reinforcement, positive punishment,* or *negative punishment?* Can you think of other examples? Here are a few more examples: a raise or a promotion for a job, getting free tickets to go to a concert for listening to a radio station, or losing one's driving license because of a DUI (Driving Under the Influence) offense. As you take your own classes, reflect on the meanings of the concepts you learn, think of examples, and think of associations in your own life.

RESOURCES FOR VOCABULARY DEVELOPMENT

As you use strategies for improving your vocabulary, you will also need a variety of resources to help you look up unfamiliar words, check multiple meanings of words, or think of synonyms (similar words) or antonyms (opposite words). Some of these resources are print-based, and others are electronic tools. They typically include dictionaries and glossaries, thesauri, the Internet, and other technological resources. It is important, however, to be familiar with the types of information you can find in each of these resources so that you can best choose your resource to find the information you need.

DICTIONARIES AND GLOSSARIES

For many of the mainstream words you meet in everyday texts, such as the newspaper or a popular magazine, the dictionary is a good resource for helping you determine the meaning of a word. To help you improve your vocabulary through general reading, it is

---

[15]M. L. Simpson and S. N. Randall, "Vocabulary Development at the College Level," in R. Flippo and D. C. Caverly, eds., *Handbook of College Reading and Study Strategy Research* (Mahwah, NJ: Lawrence Erlbaum, 2000), p. 45.

FIGURE 5.17

Glossary Page from a Psychology Textbook

Source: From W. Weiten, *Psychology: Themes and Variations*, 6th ed. (Belmont, CA: Wadsworth/Thomson Learning, 2004), p. G-9.

Somnambulism (sleepwalking)   Arising and wandering about while remaining asleep.

Source   The person who sends a communication.

Source monitoring   The process of making attributions about the origins of memories.

Source-monitoring error   An error that occurs when a memory derived from one source is misattributed to another source.

Split-brain surgery   A procedure in which the bundle of fibers that connects the cerebral hemispheres (the corpus callosum) is cut to reduce the severity of epileptic seizures.

Spontaneous recovery   In classical conditioning, the reappearance of an extinguished response after a period of nonexposure to the conditioned stimulus.

Spontaneous remission   Recovery from a disorder without formal treatment.

SQ3R   A study system designed to promote effective reading by means of five steps: survey, question, read, recite, and review.

Stage   A developmental period during which characteristic patterns of behavior are exhibited and certain capacities become established.

Standard deviation   An index of the amount of variability in a set of data.

Standardization   The uniform procedures used in the administration and scoring of a test.

---

highly recommended that you have a good college-level dictionary. Or, if you have a computer, access to online dictionaries and glossaries are highly desirable.

However, as noted above in the discussion of context clues, when you use a dictionary, you need to select the appropriate definition from the definitions in an entry. A textbook glossary, on the other hand, will give you the specific meaning of a word for the content discipline you are studying. For instance, if you are reading a biology textbook, then the glossary in that biology book will give you the precise meanings of terms as they are used in biology. Let's look at an example. Let's take a look at an excerpt from a glossary from a psychology textbook (see Figure 5.17) and a dictionary entry (see Figure 5.18).

As you can see from these examples, this glossary gives you only one definition following the term. On the other hand, the dictionary definition provides multiple meanings of the same term and indicates the part of speech, that is, if it is used as a noun or verb. The dictionary entry notes how the word is pronounced and notes its root words. Note the definition of *stage* in the psychology glossary in Figure 5-17. Now compare that definition with the definitions of *stage* in the dictionary entry in Figure 5-18. Did you find the dictionary definition that corresponds to the glossary definition?

When you look up a word in the dictionary, think of the contextual use of the word. Think of a sentence. After you check the meaning in the dictionary, recheck the meaning of the word in context. If you have a glossary available to you that matches the content discipline you are studying, use the glossary to determine how that word is used in specific discipline contexts.

FIGURE 5.18
Dictionary Entry

Source: From *The American Heritage Dictionary,* 2nd college edition, 1982, Boston, MA: Houghton Mifflin. Reprinted by permission.

stage (stāj) *n.* **1.** A raised and level floor or platform. **2.** A platform on a microscope on which slides to be viewed are mounted. **3.** A worker's scaffold. **4. a.** The raised platform upon which theatrical performances are presented. **b.** An area in which actors perform. **c.** The acting profession. **d.** Dramatic literature or performance; the theater. **5.** The scene or setting of an event or series of events. **6.** A resting place on a journey, esp. one providing overnight accommodations. **7.** The distance between stopping places on a journey. **8.** A stagecoach. **9.** A level or story of a building. **10.** The level of the surface of a river or other fluctuating body of water in relation to some datum: *at flood stage.* **11.** A level, degree, or period of time in the course of a process; step. **12.** One of two or more successive propulsion units of a rocket vehicle that fires after the preceding one has been jettisoned. **13.** *Geol.* A subdivision in the classification of stratified rocks, ranking just below a series and representing rock formed during a chronological age. **14.** *Electronics.* An element or group of elements in a complex arrangement of parts, esp. a single tube or transistor and its accessory components in an amplifier. —*v.* **staged, stag·ing, stag·es.** —*tr.* **1.** To exhibit, present, or perform on or as if on a stage: *stage a boxing match.* **2.** To produce or direct (a theatrical performance). **3.** To arrange and carry out: *stage an invasion.* —*intr.* To be adaptable to or suitable for theatrical presentation. [ME , < OFr. *estage* < VLat. **staticum* < Lat. *stare,* to stand.]

FIGURE 5.19
Thesaurus Entry

Source: From *Roget's II, The New Thesaurus,* 1980, Boston, MA: Houghton Mifflin. Reprinted by permission.

stage *noun*
1. A temporary framework with a floor, used by workmen: *a window-washing stage.*
2. The raised platform on which theatrical performances are given: *the stage in Lincoln Center.*
3. The art and occupation of an actor.
4. One of the units in a course, as on an ascending or descending scale.
5. An interval regarded as a distinct evolutionary or developmental unit.
6. The place where an action or event occurs.

stage *verb*
1. To produce on the stage: *staged a new performance every month.*
2. To organize and carry out (an activity).

1. **Syns:** platform, scaffold, scaffolding.
2. **Syns:** the boards, proscenium.
3. ACTING *noun.*
4. DEGREE.
5. PERIOD.
6. SCENE.

1. **Syns:** act (out), do, dramatize, enact, give, perform, present², put on.
2. HAVE.

THESAURUS

If you are looking for alternate words that mean the same (i.e., synonyms) or for words that are opposite in meaning (i.e., antonyms), a thesaurus (plural: *thesauri*) is the best resource. Let's take a look at the entry for stage in a thesaurus, shown in Figure 5.19.

Note that synonyms for *stage* include platform, scaffold, scaffolding, the boards, proscenium, as well as others. *Stage* can also be a verb; note the different synonyms for stage as a verb. Therefore, when you are writing your academic papers and find that you are lost for words or feel that the word is "on the tip of your tongue," use a thesaurus to locate the best meaning of the word you wish to use. Try the following activity to try out using these three different sources.

ACTIVITY 5.21   *Using a Dictionary, Glossary, and Thesarus*

Use Figures 5.17, 5.18, and 5.19 for this exercise. Answer the questions as true or false. Then check your responses by rereading those figures. Be prepared to discuss your responses in class.

_____ **1.** The definition of *stage* in the glossary in the psychology textbook is the same one as the item 5 synonym in the thesaurus.

_____ **2.** The definition of *stage* in the psychological glossary is also in the dictionary entry.

_____ **3.** The meaning of "stage" in Shakespeare's phrase "All the world is a stage" can be found in the dictionary definition.

_____ **4.** Both the fields of psychology and geology use the concept of "stage" similarly.

_____ **5.** A synonym of the word *stage* is "perform."

Check your work. Answers to this activity are found on the *College Reading and Study Strategies* book-specific Web site. It is important to check your work before continuing with the next section.

INTERNET AND TECHNOLOGICAL RESOURCES

The Internet, dictionary CDs, and other technological resources provide you with electronic avenues for finding the meanings of concepts. Instead of relying on printed text forms, you are able to locate and retrieve definitions literally at your fingertips. However, as vast as the choices are for you, the process of checking the meaning and its appropriateness in a specific context is the same. For instance, many word-processing programs include (typically under "tools") a thesaurus; in this feature you have the option of finding synonyms for the words in your document. The beauty of these features is that looking up a word and its meaning is done very quickly.

For instance, what if you were interested in the history of our English language. Have you ever wondered why we have so many variations for spelling words in our language? Do you know from where certain words in our English language come? Do you know how English was spoken five hundred or a thousand years ago? You can find the answers to these questions by searching the Internet and finding different Web sites about the English language and its history. In the following activity you can explore the Internet for an article about the English language.

ACTIVITY 5.22 Explore the English Language Using InfoTrac College Edition

The English language has changed in many ways during the past fifteen hundred years. Use InfoTrac College Edition to search and select an article about the English language. For instance, you could choose an article about the English language during the Middle Ages. Then highlight or underline any of the terms that are unfamiliar to you. Use one of the strategies described in this chapter to determine the meaning of the term. Try this activity with at least ten unfamiliar words. Be prepared to discuss what you found in class.

ACTIVITY 5.23 Using the Internet

Select a concept that you are studying in one of your college classes. Then use the Internet to search for articles about that topic. What did you find?

ACTIVITY 5.24 Using Vocabulary Strategies

Reflect on your use of the vocabulary strategies described in this chapter. Respond to the following prompts in your own journal notebook:

1. The strategy that works best for me is . . . because:
2. When I come across an unfamiliar word, I am going to use these strategies:

ACTIVITY 5.25 Where Are You Now?

Now that you have completed this chapter, take a few minutes to repeat the "Where Are You Now?" activity at the beginning of this chapter and on the *College Reading and Study Strategies* Web site. What have you learned about using vocabulary strategies? What are you going to do differently now? How are you going to change your study strategies?

Summary

Essential for building your vocabulary throughout your adult life is recreational reading, during which you read for at least thirty minutes a day; this helps you build your general vocabulary knowledge and provides you with background knowledge for making connections with what you read in your college textbooks. How do you effectively develop your college-level vocabulary? To begin, your textbooks provide you with a variety of features that will help you find the meanings of new terminology; these features include annotations, chapter overviews and summaries, and glossaries, just to name a few.

When you meet new terminology in your college readings, it is important to understand the multiple meanings of words; depending on the content discipline you are studying, there are precise meanings for how the words are defined in a specific discipline. To understand a new word, it is important to determine the meaning of the word, write the definition in your own words, make an association of the meaning of the word with your own background knowledge, distinguish the shades of meaning of the word, and check how the word is used in context. To make an association that will help you remember the word, you can use imagery, picture cues, examples, sound cues, and other mnemonics.

Using context clues is another key strategy for determining the meaning of a word. Context clues can include stated definitions, appositives, synonyms, comparisons and contrasts, repeated words, and analogies. Other strategies for learning and remembering the meanings of new vocabulary words include using Greek and Latin prefixes and roots, generating vocabulary study cards, and using graphic organizers, such as semantic maps, hierarchical arrays, and semantic feature matrices. Essential for learning vocabulary in most content disciplines is reflecting on how concepts in a content discipline apply to one's own life and extending those concepts to new situations. Finally, while learning new vocabulary words in college, it is helpful to be familiar with the distinctions and the types of information available in a college dictionary, the textbook glossary, a thesaurus, and other nonprint resources, such as the Internet.

Review Questions

Terms You Should Know: Make a flash card for each term.

Analogy	Denotation	Productive vocabulary
Annotations	Dictionary entry	Receptive vocabulary
Antonym	Glossary	Recreational reading
Appendix	Graphic organizer	Repetition
Appositive	Hierarchical array	Root words
Chapter listing of	Imagery	Semantic feature matrix
concepts	Implied meaning	Semantic map
Chapter overview	Index	Sound cue
Chapter summary	Internet	Synonym
Comparison and contrast	Mnemonics	Table of contents
Connotation	Picture cue	Thesaurus
Context clue	Prefixes	Vocabulary study cards

Completion: Fill in the blank to complete each of the following statements.

1. Your _____ vocabulary includes the words you know while listening and reading, while your _____ vocabulary includes the words you know while speaking and writing.

2. Three textbook features that help you find the meaning of new terminology include the _____, _____, and _____.

3. A context clue that compares one object to another is a(n) _____.

4. A context clue that provides you with a word that is the same in meaning is a(n) _____; if the context clue provides you with a word that is opposite in meaning, it is called a(n) _____.

5. Three strategies for making an association between a word and its definition include
_____ _____, _____ _____, and _____ _____.

Multiple Choice: Circle the letter of the best answer for each of the following questions. Be sure to underline key words and eliminate wrong answers.

6. The best way to improve one's general vocabulary knowledge is to:
   A. read widely on a daily basis for at least thirty minutes a day.
   B. identify the Greek and Latin prefixes and roots in unfamiliar words.
   C. memorize the meanings of new words.
   D. check the spelling of words that are unfamiliar to you.

7. A graphic organizer that shows the distinctive characteristics among several concepts is a:
   A. semantic map.
   B. timeline.
   C. hierarchical array.
   D. semantic feature matrix.

Short Answer–Essay: On a separate sheet, answer each of the following questions.

8. Describe three strategies for making an association between the words you need to learn and their meaning.

9. Describe the difference between the denotation of a word and its connotation.

10. Think of a word and its meaning; create a vocabulary study card for them.

College

Study

Strategies

6 Improving Concentration

In this chapter you will learn more about:

➤ Different levels and types of concentration

➤ Causes of concentration problems

➤ Strategies for improving your concentration

➤ Benefits of improved concentration

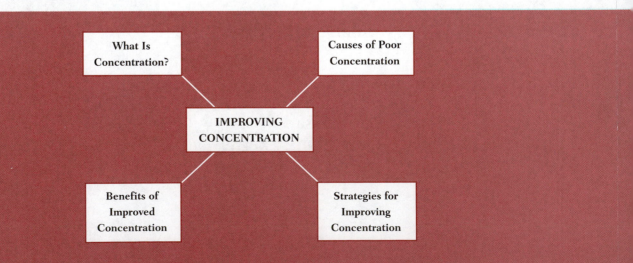

ACTIVITY 6.1 *Where Are You Now?*

Take a few minutes to answer *yes* or *no* to the following questions.

	YES	NO
1. Do you have trouble getting back into your work after you've been interrupted?	___	___
2. Do you read and study in a noisy, cluttered room?	___	___
3. Do you find that even though you schedule study time, you don't actually accomplish very much?	___	___
4. Do you use any strategies to help increase your ability to concentrate?	___	___
5. Can you concentrate on your work even if the subject doesn't interest you?	___	___
6. Do you use your preferred learning style when completing assignments?	___	___
7. Do you tend to think about personal plans or problems when you are reading and studying?	___	___
8. Do you find that when you finish reading your textbook assignment, you don't really remember what you read?	___	___
9. Do you get totally engrossed in the material when you read and study?	___	___
10. Do you daydream a lot when you are listening to lectures?	___	___

Total Points ___

Give yourself 1 point for each *yes* answer to questions 4, 5, 6, and 9, and 1 point for each *no* answer to questions 1, 2, 3, 7, 8, and 10. Now total up your points. A low score indicates that you need some help improving your concentration. A high score indicates that you are already using many good concentration strategies.

WHAT IS CONCENTRATION?

Concentration is focusing your attention on what you are doing. Concentration is important in just about anything you do, but in this chapter we'll focus on improving concentration during reading, listening, and studying. It's hard to describe what concentration is, but it's easy to explain what it isn't. Consider the following example. If you're reading a chapter in your sociology text, you're concentrating on it only as long as you're thinking of nothing else. As soon as you think about how many pages you have left to read, what time you're going to eat dinner, or what the professor will discuss in class, you're experiencing a lack of concentration. If you think about the fact that you *should* be concentrating on the assignment, that means you have in fact lost your concentration. Let's look at another example. If, during a lecture class, you become interested in the conversation going on in the row behind you, you've lost your concentration. You may even find that you've missed several new points that your professor just introduced.

Being distracted interferes with your ability to attend to or focus on the task at hand. In each of the above examples, you were actually concentrating on something. The problem is that you were concentrating on something other than the lecture or the reading material—you were concentrating on the distractions.

Difficulty with concentration is a common problem for college students. Every semester, I ask students to look over the syllabus and mark the three topics that they think will help them the most. Improving concentration is one of the most common choices.

THE THREE LEVELS OF CONCENTRATION

As you read one of your text assignments, ask someone to time you for about twenty minutes. Each time you think of something else or even look up from your reading, put a check mark in the margin of your book. You may have found that you were not always concentrating at the same level. At some points during the twenty-minute period, you may have noticed that you were more focused on the material than at other times. Look back at the check marks you made in your book. Were more of them located in the early pages of the assignment? Why does this happen?

To understand why students are less distracted toward the end of a twenty-minute reading period, let's take a better look at how concentration works. Anne Bradley has divided concentration into three levels: light, moderate, and deep.[1] Look at the diagram in Figure 6.1.

---

[1]Adapted from Anne Bradley, *Take Note of College Study Skills* (Glenview, IL: Scott, Foresman, 1983), pp. 41–42.

FIGURE 6.1
The Concentration Cycle

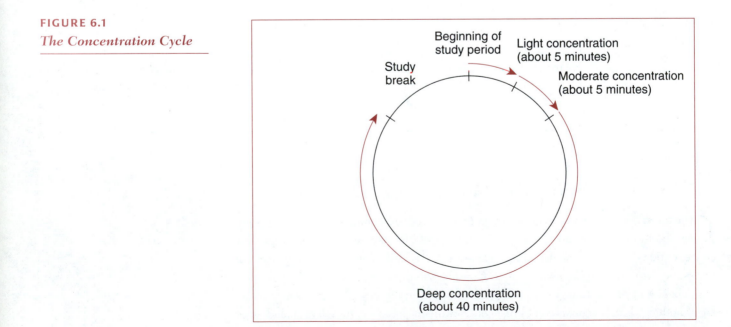

Light Concentration

When you first sit down to read or study, you are in a state of light concentration. This stage of concentration continues for about the first five minutes of study. At this point, you're just getting settled into your reading, listening, or studying. Students in light concentration can be seen wiggling around in their chairs, twisting their hair, or pulling out study supplies. When you are in light concentration, you are easily distracted. You may hear people talking down the hall, notice other students walking into the room, be annoyed by any noise occurring around you, or find yourself thinking about other things. You don't accomplish much during this stage, and very little learning actually occurs.

Moderate Concentration

During the next five minutes or so, you move into moderate concentration. At this point you begin to pay attention to the material that you are reading, hearing, or studying. You may find that you are actually getting interested in the lecture or text material. In this stage you'll probably find that you're not as easily distracted. Although you may lose your concentration if someone talks directly to you, you may not notice the voices of people talking down the hall or even someone coughing in the same room. Some learning occurs in this stage.

Deep Concentration

Once you move into deep concentration, you aren't thinking about anything except what you are hearing, writing, or reading. At this point, you are totally engrossed in the material. Have you ever jumped when someone came up behind you and touched your arm? Because you were in deep concentration, you may not have even noticed that person enter the room or call your name. When you are in deep concentration, you are not aware of the clock ticking, the door opening, or the things that you normally would find rather distracting. It is at this stage in the concentration cycle that you are working most effectively. You learn the most and can complete more work in less time in deep concentration.

THE CONCENTRATION CYCLE

You may be thinking that it sounds fairly easy to reach a high level of concentration—that after an initial ten minutes or so, you can expect to remain at a level of deep concentration. Unfortunately, this is not the way it really works for many students. Instead, they move in and out of the three stages of concentration.

Look at the diagram of the ideal study session in Figure 6.2A. In this situation, you would be able to work in deep concentration for forty minutes during a fifty minute study session. You can learn the most during this type of study session because when you are in deep concentration, you are working at your highest level of comprehension and learning.

Unfortunately, some students never get into deep concentration. They move back and forth between light and moderate concentration because they are distracted constantly (Figure 6.2B). Every time you're distracted, you move back to the stage of light concentration. If you stop to check how many more pages you still have to read, you've been distracted. If you look up when someone walks past you in the library, you've been distracted. If a family member asks you a question, you've been distracted. Each time

FIGURE 6.2
*Study Sessions and Levels
of Concentration*

A. The Ideal Study Session: Good Concentration

| 5 min. | 5 min. | 40 min. | 10 min. |
| B LC | MC | Deep concentration | Study break |

B. A Common Study Session: Poor Concentration

| 5 min. | 5 min. | | | | | | | | | | |
| B LC | MC I | LC   MC   I | LC   MC   I | LC   I | LC   MC   I | Break or "I give up" |

B: Beginning of study session
LC: Light concentration
MC: Moderate concentration
I: Interruption

you're interrupted while you're listening to a lecture, working on a homework assignment, or studying for a test, you move out of deep concentration.

You may find it doesn't take you quite as long to get interested in the material on your second or third try. However, you will still have to move through the "warming up" stages again before you can reach a state of deep concentration. If you tend to study in places where you're interrupted a lot, your study session may more closely resemble the concentration cycle in Figure 6.2B. Without strategies that will improve your ability to concentrate, you may have difficulty concentrating on a lecture, or you may spend a lot of time reading or studying yet accomplish very little.

You may also find that your ability to concentrate varies from text to text (what you study), place to place (where you study), and time to time (when you study). You may have to use more active strategies or different strategies in order to increase your ability to concentrate when you're working on material that doesn't interest you, in noisy or distracting study areas, or even at different times of the day.

ACTIVITY 6.2 *Evaluate Your Last Study Session*

Use the following time line to evaluate your last fifty-minute study session. Plot the interruptions that you experienced and how much time you spent in each of the three levels of concentration. What did you discover?

*Beginning of
Study session*

*Study
Break*

|←——————————————— 50 minutes ———————————————→|

CONCENTRATION COMPONENTS

Most students have concentration problems, but not all students actually have the same problems concentrating. Concentration involves three basic components: the ability to focus at will, the ability to sustain focus over a period of time, and the ability to limit focus to one task at a time.[2]

The Ability to Focus at Will

Have you ever noticed that you have difficulty concentrating when the professor begins to lecture? You may find yourself looking around the room, pulling out your notebook and pen, or even thinking about whether you'll get out of class early. If you have trouble focusing your attention on the lecture, you may have difficulty focusing at will—being able to turn your attention to the task of listening to a lecture at the moment the professor begins to speak.

Why can some students concentrate immediately while others find it difficult to focus their attention? Many students have developed techniques to focus their attention on the task. Have you ever competed in a sporting event? Picture yourself at that critical moment when you are about to "make your move." Do you go through a ritual designed to calm yourself, to focus your attention, to remove all other distractions? Ball players, bowlers, tennis players, and runners (just to name a few) all have strategies for focusing their attention just as they shoot a foul shot, attempt a difficult split, serve, or begin a race. Of course, listening to a lecture, writing a paper, and reading a text chapter aren't exactly the same as sporting events, but you can use the same techniques to focus your attention.

Many students use self-talk to focus at will. You may say things like: pay attention; okay, I need to do this; let's get going now! However, creating a verbal prompt is only one way to help you focus at will. Other students find that creating physical prompts are just as effective. Sitting down in your seat and pulling out your notebook and pen may be enough to focus your attention. Some students can instantly begin to concentrate when they sit down at a table or desk, pick up a special pen or highlighter, or put on a special hat or study slippers. Anything that you associate with concentrating on your work can help you learn to focus at will.

Sustaining Focus Over a Period of Time

Although learning to focus your concentration immediately is important, it's also important to sustain your focus. As you learned in the previous section, the concentration cycle, this is not always as easy as it sounds. Some students have difficulty maintaining their concentration no matter what the task. Other students, however, can concentrate for long periods of time when reading their text assignments, but are constantly distracted when doing their math and vice versa. What makes the difference? The difficulty level of the task, the student's interest in the material, and the student's level of motivation all could be factors. In the next two sections, you'll learn more about the causes of poor concentration and some suggestions for improving concentration. Many of the strategies described will help you sustain your concentration for a longer period of time.

---

[2]Becky Patterson, *Concentration: Strategies for Attaining Focus* (Dubuque, IA: Kendall Hunt, 1993).

Limiting Your Focus to One Task at a Time

The final component of concentration is limiting your focus to one task at a time. You may find this to be especially difficult during high-pressure weeks. You need to learn to focus your attention on one page in your text (without looking over at the English paper you must do for tomorrow), one math problem (without thinking about how many others are on the page), or studying for one exam (without thinking about the other two you have this week). Many of the strategies that involve creating a good study environment can help you avoid distractions around you. The strategies that you learned for managing your time and establishing priorities will also help you focus on one task at a time.

CAUSES OF POOR CONCENTRATION

The two main causes of poor concentration are external and internal distractions. A distraction is anything that diverts your focus (attention) from the task at hand. External distractions include things like noise, an uncomfortable study area, and, of course, other people. If you try to study in a noisy place, you may find that you're constantly distracted and interrupted. Dorm rooms and the kitchen table at home are not always good places to do your work. The phone rings, people stop by, and TVs and stereos are on all the time.

Although you can walk away from noisy study areas, you can't escape internal distractions; they go with you wherever you go. Internal distractions are things that you think about or worry about. Common internal distractions are anxiety caused by a certain course, the feeling that study won't help, worry over personal problems, indecision about what to do next, and so on. Many students even worry about the fact that they can't concentrate, and *that* worry interferes further with their ability to concentrate on their work.

Although it's easy to blame all concentration problems on internal and external distractions, the real causes of most concentration problems are lack of attention, lack of interest, and lack of motivation.[3] By identifying the real reason for your concentration problems, you'll be able to select the appropriate strategy to overcome each of your concentration problems.

The internal and external distractions that were discussed earlier often stem from a lack of attention to the task at hand. When you find yourself thinking of other things, staring out the window, or being distracted by noises around you, you may not be focusing your attention. You may be having difficulty focusing your attention at will, sustaining your attention, or limiting your attention to only one thing.

You've probably already found that it's easy to concentrate when you're interested in what you're doing. Do you find that you can concentrate well in some lecture classes but not in others? Is it easy to stay involved in your reading in some texts but not in others? If you answered yes to either of these questions, your level of interest in the course or in the material may be the reason for your concentration success in one course and difficulty in the other. Without a high level of interest, it's easy to lose concentration, especially when you're surrounded by distractions.

Lack of motivation is another cause of poor concentration. If you really don't care about getting a college degree, it's hard to go to class, read your text assignments, take

---

[3]Based on ideas from "AIM to Listen," from *The Secretary* magazine, reprinted in *Communication Briefings,* 1991.

lecture notes, and prepare for exams. If you don't see the relevance of the course or the assignment, it's hard to exert the effort to do it well. If you don't really care about making the grade, it's going to be very difficult to concentrate on your work. If you ever find yourself asking, "Why am I even trying to do this assignment?" "Why am I sitting in this class?" or "Why am I in college?" you may have a motivation problem. To improve your ability to concentrate, you need to be motivated to succeed. We can refer to these three causes of concentration problems as AIM (attention, interest, and motivation). They are often the real reasons that internal and external distractions disrupt your concentration.

ACTIVITY 6.3   *Identify Concentration Problems*

List ten concentration problems that you've had during the last week. Try to focus on academic tasks like taking lecture notes, reading text assignments, writing papers, or preparing for exams as you develop your list. Next, list the distraction that interfered with your concentration. Consider the underlying cause of your concentration problem and label it as A (attention), I (interest), or M (motivation). What was the most common cause of your concentration problems?

	Task	Distraction	Cause (A, I, or M?)
1.			
2.			
3.			
4.			
5.			
6.			
7.			
8.			
9.			
10.			

CONCENTRATION PROBLEMS DURING LECTURE CLASSES

Many students experience problems with concentration when they are trying to listen and learn in class. Do you ever have trouble concentrating on the lecture your professor is presenting? What gets in your way? One of the more common problems is distractions caused by other students. It's hard to concentrate on what your professor is saying when the person sitting next to you is constantly talking to you or to someone near you. Even a conversation two or three rows behind you can interfere with your ability to stay focused on the lecture. Noises outside the lecture room also can be distracting and can interfere with your ability to stay focused.

Internal distractions are another cause of difficulty during lecture classes. Worrying about personal problems and thinking about what you have to do after the class are common internal distractions. Feeling hungry or tired is another common internal distraction.

A number of students indicate that they can't concentrate on a lecture if they are not actively involved in the class; they have difficulty playing the role of a passive observer. Other students complain that it is impossible to stay involved and focused on a lecture when the professor always mumbles or speaks in a quiet voice. Still others have problems when the professor doesn't ask questions or interact with students during the lecture.

Finally, some students have concentration problems during lecture classes because of their attitude toward the class or the material. Many students have more trouble concentrating when they place a low value on the material or the course. Moreover, they experience more difficulty paying attention to the lecture when the topic is uninteresting or difficult to understand. In situations like this, some students begin to daydream, think about more interesting things, or even doze off.

ACTIVITY 6.4 *Evaluate Your Concentration During Lecture Classes*

Make a list of the problems or difficulties that you experience in at least two of your lecture classes. What differences did you notice in your ability to concentrate in each class? What were the causes of your concentration problems?

CONCENTRATION PROBLEMS WHEN YOU READ YOUR TEXT

Many students have difficulty concentrating when they read textbook assignments. Unlike lecture classes, where the professor may help keep you focused by varying his or her tone of voice or by asking questions, you alone are responsible for concentrating on your reading assignments. Do you have trouble concentrating when you read some or all of your text assignments? If you think that you're the only student with this problem, you're wrong. Many students indicate that they have more trouble concentrating when they read than at any other time.

External distractions such as a cluttered or uncomfortable study environment, noise, and other people are common causes of poor concentration when reading. How many times this week were you interrupted as you tried to read your text assignment? Many students need complete silence in order to concentrate on reading assignments. If you live in a dormitory, finding a quiet study place can be quite a problem. However, students who live at home find that a family can be just as distracting.

The time of day that you tackle your reading assignments also can affect your ability to concentrate. If you try to do your reading late at night, you may experience more difficulty staying focused because you're tired. Concentration requires effort, and it's harder to make that effort when you're tired. Have you noticed that it's more difficult to concentrate on the road when you're driving late at night and feel tired? For the same reason, many students have more difficulty maintaining their concentration when they try to read for long periods of time without a break.

Although most students indicate that their problems with concentration stem from external distractions or from internal distractions such as the interest they have in the material or the value they place on the course, other internal distractions can also be a factor. Personal problems, concerns about grades or progress in the course, and fear of not knowing the answer or how to do the problems in class can all interfere with a student's ability to focus on the material. Many students find that when they have difficulty concentrating (for any of the above reasons), they tend to think about other things. Sometimes they worry about both academic and personal problems. At other times, they tend to use escapist techniques and daydream about something that they would rather be doing—something that would be a lot more interesting or a lot more fun than reading a textbook.

ACTIVITY 6.5 *List Your Distractions as You Read*

Choose one of your texts and read a section that you haven't already read. After you finish reading, make a list of the distractions you experienced. Repeat the task using another text or do it at a different time of day. What differences do you notice in your lists or in your ability to concentrate on the two reading assignments? What was the main cause of your concentration problems?

CONCENTRATION PROBLEMS WHEN YOU STUDY FOR EXAMS

Some students have a lot of trouble concentrating when they are preparing for exams. Aside from the usual external distractions, they often experience special problems. Some students may not be as motivated to focus on the task of test preparation early in the semester because they don't put as much value on the first exam. It's more difficult to concentrate when you're studying for a test on which you place little value. Other students get distracted when they study because the material is difficult or uninteresting. Some students have concentration problems because studying is not a specific assignment like "reading pages 186 to 201." Any time your goals are vague or you're not sure what to do, it's more difficult to stay focused.

A common complaint from students is that they get tired of studying and begin to think of other things. Some think about things they would rather be doing or things that their friends, who don't have exams, are doing. Worrying about what the test will be like, what questions will be on it, and how well you will do are all common internal distractions.

Another problem that leads to poor concentration when preparing for exams is passive study techniques. Most students still study for college exams by simply reading over the text and lecture material. When students use passive strategies, they are more susceptible to internal and external distractions.

Procrastination can also lead to poor concentration. When you leave your test preparation to the last minute, you may feel overwhelmed by having too much to learn in too little time. In situations like this, students generally try to cram for the exam, which often results in passive study and increased worry about the results.

ACTIVITY 6.6 *Evaluate Your Concentration While You Study*

Make a list of the problems or difficulties you experience the next time you prepare for an exam. If you have several exams in the next few weeks, evaluate your preparation for one class that you are very interested in or place a high value on and one that you don't. What differences do you notice in your lists or in your ability to concentrate as you prepared for different exams? Share your findings with a group of your classmates. What were the most common problems faced by your group?

STRATEGIES FOR IMPROVING CONCENTRATION

By now you probably realize that problems with concentration are fairly common for college students. Although it may make you feel better to know you aren't the only person in the world who can't concentrate, it doesn't help you correct the problem. Many students indicate that they have few, if any, strategies for improving their concentration; they have a problem concentrating, but they don't know how to correct it. You can improve your ability to concentrate by using motivational and organizational strategies, by creating a good learning environment, by dealing promptly with internal distractions, by using active learning strategies, by matching your learning style to the task, and by monitoring your concentration.

USE MOTIVATIONAL AND ORGANIZATIONAL STRATEGIES

You can improve your concentration by using many of the motivational and organizational strategies that you learned in Chapters 1 and 2. Several of the most helpful strategies are having a positive attitude, setting goals, and scheduling your assignments.

Develop a Positive Attitude Toward Your Work

Having a positive attitude toward your assignments is critical to focusing at will—concentrating on the task the minute you begin to work. First, you must *want* to do the assignment. You need to see the relevance, value, and importance of the task. If you aren't interested in completing the task, you'll also have difficulty concentrating. You need to find ways to make the material more interesting—you can generate interest. Second, you must believe that you *can* do the assignment. You need to have confidence in your ability to successfully complete the task. If you have self doubts or feelings of anger or frustration about the task, they will interfere with your concentration. Having a positive attitude will help you focus as you begin to study and will help sustain your focus as you work.

Use Goal-Setting Strategies

Setting clear goals can also help you achieve better concentration. If you know exactly what you want to accomplish when you begin an assignment, you'll be able to limit your focus to the task at hand. Setting learning goals can help you determine what you need to learn or accomplish during a specific study session. It's equally important to know exactly what you need to do to complete the assignment—you need to understand what the professor expects from you and what the grading criteria will be. If you aren't sure about how to do the assignment, check with a classmate or the professor. If you don't, you may find that you will have problems concentrating on the task because you will be worrying about whether you are doing it correctly. Having a clear purpose in mind can help you limit distractions as you complete your work.

Use Time-Management Strategies

Almost any of the time-management strategies that you learned in Chapter 2 will help you improve your concentration. Using "To Do" lists and planning calendars are critical to good concentration. One of the most common internal distractions among college students is the worry that they won't get their work done. Many students report that they're constantly thinking of other assignments when they try to concentrate on their work. Do you? If you develop a study schedule each day and assign each of your study tasks to a specific study time, you won't have to worry about getting your work done. You'll be able to focus completely on each task as you work on it, knowing that you have already scheduled all of the others. By organizing your study time, you can better focus your attention on one task at a time.

CREATE A POSITIVE LEARNING ENVIRONMENT

You can dramatically improve your ability to concentrate by creating a positive learning environment. The first step is to control external distractions, and the best way to control external distractions is simply to eliminate them.

Strategies for Lecture Classes

In lecture classes, you can avoid most external distractions by moving to the front of the room. Fortunately, most students who chat during class tend to sit in the back. However, you still occasionally may find yourself sitting near some noisy students. If the students sitting near you keep you from concentrating on the lecture, get up and move! You also can be distracted by things going on around you. If you find yourself looking out the window or watching what goes on in the hall, find a seat where you can't see out the window or the door. Make the professor the center of your line of vision.

Strategies for Studying

Finding a good place to read and study may require some experimentation. Try working in different places at different times of the day to see which study area works best for you. The library, study rooms, and empty classrooms are usually good study areas. If you're living at home, you may find that setting up a table or desk in the basement or the attic is the only way you can avoid constant interruptions. Once you find a good place to work, establish a regular routine. Studying in the same place at the same time each day helps you get down to work. It may even help to use special objects that you associate with study. By sitting in a special chair, wearing your "study" slippers, or even using a special pen or clipboard, you'll help yourself get into a study mode, and this will help you improve your concentration. The Tip Block includes some additional suggestions for creating a better study environment.

TIP

TEN TIPS FOR SETTING UP A GOOD STUDY ENVIRONMENT

FIND A QUIET STUDY SPACE. Find a place to study that is away from the "center" of dormitory or household activities. It is almost impossible to concentrate if you are surrounded by distractions. A card table in the basement may not look pretty, but the quiet will make up for it. If you can't study at home, try the library or a quiet study room.

LIMIT YOUR DISTRACTIONS. Put your desk against the wall and remove all photos, mementos, and decorations. When you look up from your work, you won't be distracted by reminders of your friends or family or other responsibilities.

USE YOUR DESK FOR STUDYING ONLY. If you use your desk only for studying, you will automatically think about studying when you sit down.

STUDY IN A NOT-TOO-COMFORTABLE CHAIR. Sitting in a chair that is *too* comfortable, though, may lead to passive reading. Completing assignments is hard work, so you need to study in a semitense position.

NEVER STUDY LYING DOWN IN BED. You'll have trouble concentrating and may get so comfortable that you fall asleep.

SCREEN YOUR CALLS. If you're constantly interrupted by phone calls, take the phone off the hook or let an answering machine screen your calls. Turn off instant messenging, too.

TURN OFF THE TELEVISION, STEREO, AND RADIO. If you need some sound to serve as a "white noise" to block out the other noises around you, use soft, familiar music. Save that new CD as a reward for completing your work.

DO YOUR WORK WHEN YOUR HOUSE IS QUIET. Study when family members are asleep or out. Schedule study hours before your children get up and after they go to bed. If you get home from work or school an hour before they do, use that time to do course work.

CONSIDER STUDYING AT SCHOOL. If you can't concentrate at home, you may have to do your work at school, before or after class. You can often find an empty classroom, quiet corner in the library, or study area in the student union. Compare your distractions when studying on campus and at home.

GET HELP WHEN YOU NEED IT. Ask a family member or friend to stay with your children when you are trying to study for exams or complete major assignments. If necessary, hire a sitter or a mother's helper to entertain or care for your children.

ACTIVITY 6.7 *Describe Your Study Environment*

Use the Journal Entry Form on the *College Reading and Study Strategies* Web site to describe your current study environment. Where do you read and study? What types of distractions surround you? What changes could be made that would help you study more effectively? What plans are you making (or have you made) to create a more positive learning environment?

DEAL WITH INTERNAL DISTRACTIONS

Once you set up a quiet study environment, you should see a big difference in your ability to concentrate. However, just eliminating external distractions doesn't guarantee that you'll be able to focus on your work. Many students find that after they eliminate the external noises around them, they notice the internal "noises" even more. Although you can't really eliminate internal distractions, you can take steps to keep them from interfering with your work.

Deal with Competing Activities

No matter how focused you are when studying, it's not unusual to think about other things. If you think of something that you want or need to do or if you come up with an idea for another assignment, jot it down or plan a time to do it, and then continue with your work. The key is to minimize the distraction—to keep it as short as possible. Then you can move back to deep concentration more quickly. If you don't write it down, you'll probably continue thinking about it or even begin to worry that you may forget it. In either case, you'll be concentrating more on the internal distraction than on your assignment.

Deal with Academic Problems

Worrying about academic problems is a common internal distraction. Instead of worrying, do something! Go see your professor and share your concerns about the course. Get a tutor or have a talk with yourself about what you need to do to meet your goals. Remind yourself that getting down to work and doing your best are steps in the right direction. Then, if you still don't understand the material or can't do the problems, ask for help. Remember, it's easier to block out internal distractions when you have confidence in yourself as a student. You'll gain this confidence by learning that you can be successful in college, not by worrying about it.

Deal with Personal Problems

Personal worries and concerns are common internal distractions. Many students allow an argument with a boyfriend or girlfriend or family problems to interfere with their concentration. Make a decision to do something about your problem as soon as you complete your work. Write down exactly what you plan to do and return immediately to your study tasks. Calling a friend and talking honestly about your problem, or scheduling an appointment at your campus counseling center are good strategies for dealing with personal problems. Some students find that writing about whatever is bothering them in a journal or talking it out with friends helps them experience a feeling of closure about the problem.

ACTIVITY 6.8 *Find Tips for Dealing with Internal Distractions*

Go to Google.com and type in "Internal Distractions." You'll find a long list of links to college Web sites as well as those from other sources. Select four or five and check them out.

Copy the best tips for dealing with internal distractions (and the Web addresses) to share with your class.

USE ACTIVE LEARNING STRATEGIES

One of the best ways to keep external and internal distractions from interfering with your concentration is to become more involved in the lecture, the text, or your test preparation. You can generate this high level of involvement by using active learning strategies.

You may have noticed that you concentrate better when you do math problems and grammar exercises or complete a study guide for your Psychology textbook. Why does this happen? One possible reason is that you like those classes or assignments more than some of your other classes. However, another reason may be that you need to use active learning strategies to complete those tasks. Solving problems, correcting grammatical errors in sentences, and looking for answers to study guide questions are all active strategies that get you involved in and help you focus your attention on each of the tasks. Because you are actively involved in working on the material, you can concentrate more on your assignments. When you're attending lectures, reading course assignments, and preparing for exams, you can dramatically improve your concentration by using active study strategies.

Strategies for Lecture Classes

Taking notes during lecture classes helps you focus on what the professor is saying. If you know that you're going to have to write something, you'll be more motivated to pay attention. Many students actually find that lecture classes become more interesting and go much faster when they take notes. Because they are actively involved, they have reached a state of deep concentration.

Many students have trouble concentrating during lecture classes simply because they're not actively involved in what's going on in the class. Asking and answering questions, predicting what the professor will say next, and taking notes are all ways of becoming more involved during lecture classes. Becoming a more active participant in class is one of the keys to eliminating internal and external distractions and increasing concentration.

You may also find that you can increase your concentration in lecture classes by sitting directly in your professor's line of vision. You're more likely to pay attention if you feel as if you're on the spot. It's pretty hard to fall asleep or look out the window when your professor is standing right in front of you. If you focus your attention on the professor and keep him or her directly in your line of vision, you'll be able to block out distractions more easily, too.

Strategies for Reading Text Assignments

Becoming an active reader will significantly improve your ability to concentrate when you read your textbook assignments. Reading with your eyes but not your brain leads to daydreaming and other concentration problems. Have you ever read a paragraph or even an entire page of text and then realized that you had no idea what you had just read? Even though your eyes did "look at the words," your mind was somewhere else. Using a reading/study system, previewing, highlighting, and taking notes are all active strategies that can improve your concentration.

Strategies for Test Preparation

How can you maintain your concentration as you prepare for exams? Jennifer sums it up pretty well: "When studying for a test, I'm active. I don't just reread my notes and the chapter. I write down what I need to know from the text and then I rewrite my notes."

Just reading over the textbook and your lecture notes isn't a very effective way to improve your concentration when you study. When you prepare for an exam, dig through the material, looking for important information. Taking notes, developing study sheets, and creating graphic displays will help you become totally engrossed in the material. Reciting the key information out loud and self-testing are just two of many rehearsal strategies that also can help you learn. We'll talk more about them in Chapters 7 and 10. For now, however, remember that the more actively involved you are in studying the material, the easier it will be to maintain your concentration.

You can also increase your concentration by using motivational strategies. Jennifer motivates herself to study by thinking about getting a good grade. She says, "You just need to make the decision that you want to succeed." Taking breaks, switching subjects, and planning rewards are helpful in increasing your motivation, and they also can help increase your concentration. It's much harder to stay focused on your work when you become tired or bored. When you just can't concentrate anymore, stop and take a break. Then switch to a different subject to eliminate feelings of boredom and frustration. Setting deadlines and limiting the amount of time that you allow for each of your study tasks also can motivate you to use your time more effectively. Deadlines make you feel rushed, so you actually force yourself to concentrate better (unless you've left yourself too little time—in that case, your level of anxiety increases and the number of your internal distractions may increase as well).

MATCH YOUR LEARNING STYLE TO THE TASK

You learned in Chapter 1 that you can maximize your time and effort by working in your preferred learning style or using the learning style that best suits the task you need to complete. You may have also discovered that matching your learning style to the task helps you improve your concentration, too. If you learn best in the morning, you'll also find it easier to concentrate in the morning. If you tend to work best with quiet music playing in the background, you may discover that music helps you concentrate by blocking out other noises that might actually distract you. Approaching a task from your preferred style results in a better fit or match—studying feels right. However, using a style that is inappropriate to the task or to the material you want to learn (even if it is the style you prefer) can itself become distracting and interfere with your ability to concentrate. When you use the appropriate learning style for each task during a study session, you'll probably be less distracted and move into deep concentration more easily.

ACTIVITY 6.9 *Work Together to Solve Concentration Problems*

Write three concentration problems that you experienced during the past week on each of three index cards. Put the last four digits of your Social Security number at the top right corner of the back of the card (do not use your name). After the cards are shuffled and distributed to various groups within the class, discuss each of the problems assigned to your group. Discuss possible solutions to the problem and write several of the best on the back of the card. Select one or two of the most common (or most interesting) to describe to the class. At the end of the class period, each student can claim his or her card (by Social Security number) and make use of the suggestions that were offered.

MONITOR YOUR CONCENTRATION

Monitoring how often you lose your concentration can be very helpful in learning how to improve your concentration. Put a check mark or write the time in the margin of your book or your lecture notes every time you're distracted. At the end of your class or study session, count the number of interruptions. Make a commitment to reduce that number the next time you read or go to your lecture. Setting goals, changing your learning environment or strategies, or using positive self-talk all can help you improve your concentration. In a few weeks, you may find that your ability to concentrate improves dramatically.

When you notice that you're daydreaming or thinking about other things, try to figure out what actually triggered your loss in concentration. If you can pinpoint the cause of your distraction, you're only one step away from the solution. Hold yourself accountable for your lapses in concentration—find a way to overcome them. Remember, you can improve your ability to concentrate, but it is you who must take the responsibility for doing so.

ACTIVITY 6.10 *Monitor Your Concentration*

On a separate sheet of paper, create a chart using the following headings. Record up to ten of the concentration problems that you encounter over a one-week period. Include one or more strategies that you used or should have used to improve your concentration. Then indicate how well your strategy worked.

DATE   STUDY TASK   CONCENTRATION PROBLEM   CAUSE   STRATEGY   EVALUATION

BENEFITS OF IMPROVED CONCENTRATION

There are many benefits to improved concentration. One of the most obvious is that you'll be able to make better use of your time. You'll find that when you spend the majority of your time in deep concentration, you get more done during a study session. In addition, because you're operating in deep concentration for a longer period of time, you'll gain a better understanding of what you have read. It stands to reason that if you spend most of your time focused on the course material, you'll understand it better than if you are constantly distracted.

Improved concentration during lecture classes can help you take better lecture notes. If you're focused on the information your professor is presenting rather than on other people, negative thoughts about the course, or personal plans, you'll be able to take better notes. In addition, you may find that you become more involved in the lecture and gain a better understanding of the material. You'll be able to form connections between the material being presented and the material you already know. This helps you learn and understand what you're hearing.

You may also notice that once you set up a better study environment, you're better able to prepare for quizzes and exams. Working in a quiet, nondistracting study area can have a positive effect on what you study and learn. Setting goals and using active study strategies will not only improve your concentration but also your mastery of the material.

After concentrating on your studies for one or two hours, you will be pleased by what you were able to accomplish. You may even experience increased self-confidence and higher self-esteem.

ACTIVITY 6.11 *Use InfoTrac College Edition to Locate Information on Concentration*

If you're using InfoTrac College Edition, access it and search for articles related to concentration. Although you won't find a huge number on this topic, there are several that will provide you with additional information and new perspectives on how some researchers look at concentration and learning. Locate one article and read it. Print both the article and the list of references and go to the library and locate one additional article from the list of references or request it through interlibrary loan. (InfoTrac College Edition can help you locate library references on various topics if you note the references used in recent articles.) Write a paragraph or two describing what you learned about how to improve your concentration.

ACTIVITY 6.12 *Where Are You Now?*

Now that you have completed Chapter 6, take a few minutes to repeat the "Where Are You Now?" activity, located on the *College Reading and Study* *Strategies* Web site. What changes did you make as a result of reading this chapter? How are you planning to apply what you've learned in this chapter?

Summary

Most college students have problems with concentration, often defined as focused attention. Unfortunately, if you're focusing on the conversations going on out in the hall, instead of on your professor's lecture, you're concentrating on the wrong thing. During an ideal study session, students move from light, to moderate, to deep concentration—the level where most learning occurs. During a typical study session, however, students move in and out of these stages of concentration because of interruptions or distractions. Some students never even reach deep concentration.

The most common causes of poor concentration are external and internal distractions. By monitoring your distractions, you can hold yourself more accountable during lecture classes, as you do your day-to-day assignments, and when you prepare for exams. Avoiding common distractions and using active study strategies can help you increase your concentration. Creating a positive learning environment is critical to good concentration. It's easy to blame all concentration problems on a noisy room or a cluttered desk, but many times the real culprits are lack of attention, lack of interest, and lack of motivation. By analyzing the real cause of your external and internal distractions, you may be able to identify the real cause of your concentration problems. If you set goals, focus your attention, increase your interest, and improve your motivation, your ability to concentrate will improve. If you find that you're putting a lot of time into your studies but not getting much accomplished, you may have a concentration problem.

Review Questions

Terms You Should Know: Make a flash card for each term.

Concentration	Focusing at will	Moderate concentration
Deep concentration	Internal distraction	Sustaining your focus
Distraction	Light concentration	
External distraction	Limiting your focus	

Completion: Fill in the blank to complete each of the following statements.

1. _____ college freshmen experience concentration problems.

2. Some students never get into _____ concentration.

3. Use _____ study strategies to improve your concentration when studying for exams.

4. Both _____ and _____ distractions affect your ability to concentrate during lectures.

5. Having difficulty concentrating at the beginning of a task is referred to as a problem focusing at _____.

Multiple Choice: Circle the letter of the best answer for each of the following questions. Be sure to underline key words and eliminate wrong answers.

6. Which of the following is *not* one of the real causes of poor concentration?
   A. Lack of interest
   B. Lack of attention
   C. Lack of motivation
   D. Lack of self-efficacy

7. You can reduce your distractions by:
   A. studying in an empty classroom.
   B. using your desk only for study.
   C. screening your phone calls.
   D. all of the above are good strategies.

Short Answer–Essay: On a separate sheet, answer each of the following questions.

8. Describe the characteristics of each of the three stages of the concentration cycle.

9. How should students overcome problems with internal and external distractions?

10. How will improving your concentration benefit you in college?

Improving Memory

In this chapter you will learn more about:

➤ How information is processed in memory

➤ Why you need memory strategies

➤ General strategies to improve your memory

➤ Specific strategies to improve your memory

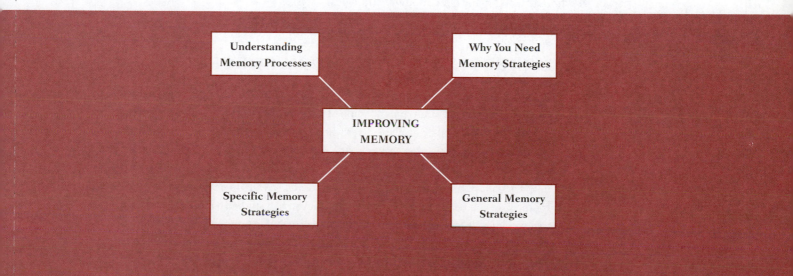

ACTIVITY 7.1 *Where Are You Now?*

Take a few minutes to answer *yes* or *no* to the following questions.

	YES	NO
1. Do you often know the answer to a question but find that you can't think of it?	_____	_____
2. Do you organize or group information to help you remember it?	_____	_____
3. After you study, do you go back and test yourself to monitor your learning?	_____	_____
4. Do you make up rhymes or words to help you remember some information?	_____	_____
5. Do you space your practice when reviewing information?	_____	_____
6. Do you try to memorize all the information that you need to know for an exam?	_____	_____
7. Do you often find that you get confused by closely related information?	_____	_____
8. Do you often forget a lot of the information that you studied by the time you take the test?	_____	_____
9. Is the TV or stereo on while you study?	_____	_____
10. Can you learn and remember information just by making up a rhyme, word, or other memory aid?	_____	_____
Total Points		_____

Give yourself 1 point for each *yes* answer to questions 2, 3, 4, and 5 and 1 point for each *no* answer to questions 1, 6, 7, 8, 9, and 10. Now total up your points. A low score indicates that you need to improve your memory skills. A high score indicates that you are already using many good memory strategies.

UNDERSTANDING MEMORY PROCESSES

Doing well on exams requires an effective study plan, active study strategies, and a good memory. What you typically think of as learning involves storing information in your memory so that it will be available later when you need it. In this chapter, you'll gain a better understanding of how information is stored in memory. This will help you understand why you need to be actively involved to learn and retain course material. "Having a good memory" involves both putting information into memory *and getting it back out*—both storage and retrieval. Can you recall a time when you thought you had studied a particular topic well enough that you knew it for the exam, only to find that you couldn't remember the information during the test? Perhaps you never really got the information into your long-term memory, or perhaps you simply were unable to recall it when you needed to. Why do we forget? How do we learn?

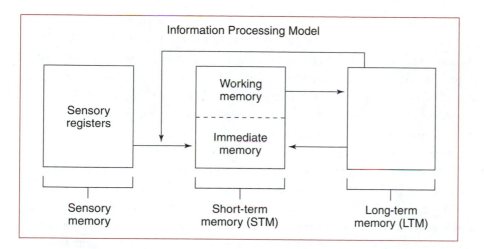

FIGURE 7.1
*Information Processing
Model*

Many students really don't understand how memory works. Do you? Learning about how we store and retrieve information will help you understand why some study strategies work and others don't. Over the years, psychologists have tried to develop theories to explain how memory works. One of the most useful of these is the Information Processing Model.

INFORMATION PROCESSING MODEL

The Information Processing Model suggests that memory is complex and consists of various processes and stages. For example, there are at least three types of memory: sensory memory, short-term memory (STM), and long-term memory (LTM). In addition, there are three important memory processes: encoding, storage, and retrieval. Figure 7.1, which was adapted from a model developed by Bourne, Dominowski, Loftus, and Healy,[1] shows the three types of memory (represented as boxes) and the memory processes (represented as arrows).

To learn and remember, we must encode, store, and retrieve information. The first step in this process is encoding—interpreting information in a meaningful way. Suppose you want to remember what a cloud looks like. Clouds are amorphous (without a definite shape) and lack any clear structure. You might find it difficult to remember exactly how a cloud looks after observing it briefly. However, if you notice that the cloud looks somewhat like an elephant, you'll be better able to remember its shape later simply by picturing an elephant. To be remembered, information must be encoded; it must be interpreted in a meaningful way. The second step in the memory process, storage, involves working on (for example, repeating and organizing) information so that it can be placed into LTM. Information doesn't automatically move into LTM unless we work to store it there. Much of what we think of as studying involves storage processes. The third step, retrieval, involves getting information out of LTM. As you'll see, retrieving a memory is very much like going into your basement to find the badminton set that you know is there, somewhere—you may have to hunt for a while, but eventually you'll find a clue that will lead you to it.

Sensory Memory

You probably have heard about short-term and long-term memory. However, sensory memory, also known as the sensory registers, may be new to you. Essentially, our senses (vision, hearing, smell, taste, and touch) are always very busy. We hear, see, smell, taste, and touch

---

[1]L. E. Bourne, R. L. Dominowski, E. F. Loftus, and A. F. Healy, *Cognitive Processes,* 2d. ed. (Englewood Cliffs, NJ: Prentice Hall, 1986).

hundreds of stimuli each moment. Most of these stimuli are unimportant and are therefore quickly forgotten. However, some stimuli are important to us and worth remembering.

At one time scientists believed that we remembered, somewhere in our brain, everything that we ever saw, heard, smelled, tasted, or touched. We now realize that such a feat would be nearly impossible; our memories quickly would fill up with billions upon billions of bits of useless information. Instead, we remember only those stimuli that we decide are important, those to which we attend.

When we see something, even if only for a split second, we hold onto an "afterimage" of the stimulus for between one-half and one second. Although one second isn't a very long time, it gives our memory system plenty of time to decide whether the material is important and whether we want to remember it and to pick out details.

There also is a sensory register for hearing. After hearing a sound, we hold onto an afterimage, or "echo," of that sound for between two and four seconds. Again, this gives our memory system enough time to decide whether we need to remember the stimulus and to pick out details.

Short-Term Memory

Once we decide to remember material, we immediately have to move it into short-term memory. This process is represented by the arrow (in Figure 7.1) that goes from the sensory registers to the immediate memory. However, for us to do this, the material must be encoded—we must make it meaningful. Short-term memory has two components: immediate memory and working memory. Immediate memory is related to the concept of consciousness. Whatever we currently are thinking about is in our immediate memory. Think of your immediate memory as being similar to a small desk. In a two-hour study session you may work on several tasks at your desk. However, because your desk is very small, you can place only a limited amount of material on it at any one time. If you want to work on something new, you need to move aside the material on which you were just working. Immediate memory is similar to this because you can remember only the material that is "sitting on your desk" at any one time. Because immediate memory is very limited, we typically can retain only about seven (plus or minus two) chunks of information on our "desk." Furthermore, without continual rehearsal, those seven chunks can stay on the "desk" for only twenty to thirty seconds before they slip away.

To hold on to information and get it into your long-term memory, you must first move the material into the other part of your short-term memory, the working memory. This part of the memory system is aptly named because you really have to "work" on the material to make it meaningful, memorable, and easy to retrieve. You can use a variety of strategies to move information into your working memory, but all have one thing in common. The harder you work on the material, the greater the probability that you'll put the material into LTM in a place where you can find it again.

The strategies that we use in our working memory all are geared toward making material more memorable. Some strategies require us to organize material in a way that's logical for each of us, whereas other strategies require us to make material meaningful, to relate it to ideas we already remember well.[2] In the remainder of this chapter and in later chapters, you'll learn many new strategies that you can use in working memory.

[2]C.F. Weinstein and R. F. Mayer, "The Teaching of Learning Strategies," in M. C. Wittrock, ed., *Handbook of Research on Teaching* (New York: Macmillan, 1986).

Long-Term Memory

Once material has been processed in working memory, it can be moved into long-term memory (represented by the arrow going from the working memory to the long-term memory). Long-term memory has an almost unlimited capacity. In fact, the more we learn, the more capacity for learning we appear to have. Building long-term memories appears to provide a structure for adding new memories. LTM also is remarkable because we appear to hold on to most of our memories indefinitely. We also rely on our LTM to encode new information. For example, we use our memory of an elephant (stored in LTM) to identify and describe a cloud shape. The arrow in Figure 7.1, which starts at the LTM and points to the encoding arrow, represents this process.

Long-term memory can be compared to a warehouse full of filing cabinets. The cabinets in the warehouse and the material within the cabinets are arranged in a logical order; each cabinet drawer is labeled, and there are dividers within each drawer. Materials (memories) are placed in specific folders, in specific sections, in specific drawers, in specific file cabinets, in specific sections of the warehouse. However, the warehouse (your LTM) is enormous. Unless the material is carefully classified, labeled, and placed in the correct file, it can easily be misfiled. Once material is misfiled, or just poorly labeled, classified, and filed, it's much more difficult to retrieve. Only when we really work to appropriately classify and label it are we able to retrieve it easily. When material isn't well classified, we must resort to searching through all of the various files where we might have stored the material. In that case we would be very lucky to find it quickly, and it's just as likely that it could take a considerable amount of searching before we find it. If you need to remember important information for an exam, you'll be much better off if the information has been carefully "filed" in your LTM for easy retrieval.

ACTIVITY 7.2 *Take Two Memory Tests*

Go to the *College Reading and Study Strategies* book-specific Web site and follow the link in Chapter 7 to the QueenDom.com Web site to take a visual memory test. Then take the Short-Term Memory Test by clicking on the University of Washington link. Be prepared to discuss the results.

WHY YOU NEED MEMORY STRATEGIES

Now that you understand how information is encoded, stored, and retrieved, you may wonder why you need to learn specific strategies to aid your memory. According to Donald Norman, "To remember is to have managed three things successfully: the acquisition, retention, and retrieval of information. Failure to remember means failure at managing one of those steps."[3] To perform well in college courses, you need to use strategies that aid the storage, retention, and retrieval of the information that you want to learn. In college, learning to get information out of memory is just as important as learning to put that information into memory.

---

[3]D. A. Norman, *Learning and Memory* (New York: Freeman, 1982), p. 2.

EVALUATE YOUR MEMORY STRATEGIES

Let's try an experiment to find out what kinds of strategies you already use. Be sure to complete Activity 7.3 before you continue reading.

ACTIVITY 7.3   *Test Your Memory*

Can you name all fifty states? Write down the first ten that you can remember in the margin of your text, then read the remainder of this page.

How did you remember the states that you wrote down in Activity 7.3? What method did you use to remember them? Look at the first couple of states that you wrote down. Do they follow some type of order? Some students use alphabetical order to list the states. Is that what you did? Others use a geographic order like Maine, New Hampshire, Vermont or Washington, Oregon, California. Although these are the two most common ways that students tend to remember the states, many students use other strategies. What strategies did you use?

How you remembered the states for Activity 7.3 really isn't important. The important thing is that most of you used some strategy to recall information that you probably learned many years ago.

If you learned the states in alphabetical order, it's easier for you to retrieve that information alphabetically than geographically. On the other hand, if you learned the information geographically, by doing maps or by travel, you may find it difficult to list the states alphabetically. From this exercise, you should have learned that the method you use to organize information during study will in some way determine how effectively you can retrieve that information. In addition, the more associations you develop for particular information, the easier it will be to retrieve. In the next two sections, you'll learn some general and specific strategies that will help improve your ability to learn and retrieve information.

ACTIVITY 7.4   *Describe Your Memory Strategies*

Use the Journal Form available on the *College Reading and Study Strategies* Web site to describe your strategies for storing and retrieving information. Think of the last test you took and discuss your preparation strategies. Then describe several of the strategies you used during the exam to recall that information. Did you use effective methods?

RETRIEVAL AND FORGETTING

If we can hold on to memories indefinitely, why do we forget? As you might guess, there are a number of reasons for forgetting, some of which are related to retrieval (pulling information back out of long-term memory). At times, we think that we've forgotten information, but in fact we never really got it into LTM at all. Either we worked on it too little to store it or we did such a poor job of organizing it that, although it is in LTM, it's in a form that's unrecognizable and unusable.

Many memories are available to us in our long-term memory; however, they aren't all accessible. To access a memory, we need to know *how* to find it. Many times we need a key term, or what psychologists call a *cue,* a label, hook, or link to the information, to unlock the memory. Memories that we use frequently typically are stored with a number of cues, thus making them easier to remember. However, at times we store memories with only one or two cues. Unless we use those cues, we can't retrieve those memories. Clearly, the more ways we devise for material to be remembered, the more cues we develop that make the material more accessible to us. For example, creating study sheets (see Chapter 10) with a specific topic and a series of specific headings helps integrate the material better than just learning lists of facts, details, and definitions in isolation because more associations (more cues) are formed with the material.

Other processes also affect retrieval. For example, organization affects retrieval. Material that is well organized is easier to retrieve than material that is not well organized. Anxiety also affects retrieval. When we're anxious, it's more difficult to recall cues and retrieve important information because anxiety affects our ability to focus and concentrate. Many of us have had the experience of being unable to retrieve an answer during an examination and then remembering the material once the exam is over and our anxiety is reduced.

Interference theory, another memory model, also is important to the concept of forgetting. Interference theory states that memories can interfere with one another during the retrieval process. Over the years we tend to learn many things that are similar to one another. Unless we make each of these memories distinctive, there's a strong likelihood that one memory will interfere with another. It's well worth the effort to develop some unique cues that will help make each memory distinctive.

Due to a combination of failing to store information properly in long-term memory, using too few cues, and interference, we tend to forget newly learned material rapidly if we don't continue to rehearse it. The remainder of this chapter will discuss strategies you can use to improve your memory.

GENERAL MEMORY STRATEGIES

The following general strategies can help you acquire, retain, and retrieve course information.

SPACED PRACTICE

There are many benefits to using spaced practice instead of massed practice. Massed practice, like cramming, involves studying all the material at one time. Spaced practice, on the other hand, involves spacing your study time over a longer period, with breaks between practice sessions. Studying for short periods of time, such as one fifty-minute session, prevents boredom, helps avoid fatigue, and improves motivation. If you space out your study over a period of days (see the Five-Day Study Plan in Chapter 10 for more information on how to space your study), you gain additional benefits. First of all, you delay forgetting. As pointed out earlier, even when you think you've learned the information, some information usually is forgotten. By reviewing the same material the next day, you have a chance to find out what you've forgotten and work on it again. In addition, you benefit by reviewing and reinforcing the information that you previously studied.

Spaced practice—or distributed practice, as it is also known—allows time for the information to consolidate or jell in long-term memory. During consolidation, information is organized and stored in LTM. If you try to shove too much information into memory at one time, you won't be able to retrieve very much of it. One explanation for this is that the longer you study, the more inhibitions you develop (feeling tired, bored, and so on) that decrease your efficiency for storing the material in LTM. With massed practice, you may get to the point where you're just reading over the material rather than "working on it" to learn it.

Another problem that may occur with massed practice is that you don't organize the information well enough to store it in a way that allows you to find it again in your LTM. Allowing breaks between learning sessions gives you time to think about what you've been studying and to structure or organize it according to what you already know about the topic.

BREAK DOWN TASKS

By spacing out your learning, you can also focus your study. Instead of trying to learn all of the material for your exam at one time (cramming), study only one or two chapters (and the accompanying lecture material) each day. When you study small chunks of material at one time, you can do a better job of getting it into long-term memory. It's easier to stay focused and actively involved in your learning when you don't feel as if you have to learn it all at one time. You'll be more willing to take the time to create study sheets, create word and question cards, or recite or self-test yourself on the material. By breaking down study tasks and organizing and storing small units of material, you increase the likelihood that you'll efficiently and effectively store the material in your long-term memory.

REPETITION

Spaced learning also works because it involves repeating the material. Each time you write or recite the same information (especially if you do it in a slightly different way), you strengthen your memory of it. An early theory of how memory works described traces or pathways in the brain. Although developing a memory really is not like wearing a path in the brain, you may find that this analogy helps you understand how learning and retrieval occur. Each time you work on the material (by writing, reciting, or even thinking about it), you strengthen the path to the material in LTM. Here's another way to look at it. Imagine that each time you practice the same piece of information, you open a particular file in one of the drawers of your LTM filing cabinet. The more times that you open that same drawer and pull out that same file, the easier it is to do it the next time; you know just where to go in LTM and exactly where in the filing cabinet to look. Repetition, especially spaced over several hours or days, can help you strengthen and maintain your memory of important material.

OVERLEARNING

Overlearning is an important strategy for test preparation. Overlearning involves continuing to work on material even after it's learned. This practice is very helpful in improving your memory. Each time you review the material, you reduce forgetting and strengthen the path to your LTM. Overlearning may provide additional benefits. It may lead you to review the material in other ways so you may form different cues for, or associations with, the material. You may even find that as you continue to work on the material, you gain a better understanding of it.

Overlearning also can help you cope with test anxiety, which interferes with your ability to retrieve information from LTM. If you're worrying about an exam, you may have difficulty identifying or remembering the cues that you need to locate the information that you stored. Overlearned material is less susceptible to the debilitating effects of anxiety because it is so firmly embedded in LTM. You can count on overlearned information to help you get started during the exam. Answering questions that cover overlearned information is a good way to use your test time efficiently until you calm down.

SPECIFIC MEMORY STRATEGIES

Besides the general strategies described earlier, many specific learning strategies are effective in developing your memory processes. Weinstein and Mayer describe five groups of learning strategies: rehearsal strategies, elaboration strategies, organizational strategies, comprehension monitoring strategies, and affective and motivational strategies.[4] Each category includes a variety of learning strategies that can be used to improve the various memory processes. Let's look at some of them.

REHEARSAL STRATEGIES

Rehearsal strategies involve repeating the material until it is learned. How did you study your spelling and vocabulary word lists in elementary school and junior high? If you wrote them ten times or recited them over and over again, you were using low-level rehearsal strategies. You may have studied for many of your high school exams by simply reading over the material two or three times until you felt that you knew it. Here again, you were using low-level rehearsal strategies. Although these rehearsal strategies are quite effective for learning simple lists or remembering easy-to-recall information, they aren't as well suited to some of the more complex learning tasks that you need to use for college classes.

High-level rehearsal strategies such as outlining, predicting quiz questions, and creating charts and concept maps all help you rehearse the information (you're still going over it) as you organize and condense it for later review. When you use higher-level rehearsal strategies, you're operating on the material—you may be adding information that you already know, organizing the material in a way that's more memorable to you, creating additional cues to help you locate and recall the material in long-term memory. To make up even one test question about some information you recently read, you would have to reread your highlighting, transform the important information into a question, write the question, think about the answer, and write the answer—providing you with a significant amount of rehearsal. You're also using high-level rehearsal strategies when you recite information from word or question cards, explain information in your own words, answer review questions, or take self-tests.

---

[4]Weinstein and Mayer.

In Chapter 10, you'll learn other high-level rehearsal strategies, such as creating study sheets and making self-tests. Just about any strategy that you use to prepare for a quiz or test involves rehearsal. The key, though, to effective rehearsal is combining your review of the material with one or more of the organizational, elaboration, comprehension monitoring, or motivational strategies that are presented in the remainder of this chapter.

ELABORATION STRATEGIES

Elaboration strategies involve expanding on the information, forming associations, or determining how new information relates to what you already know. Paraphrasing, summarizing, explaining, answering questions, forming mental images, and using mnemonics ("ni-mon-iks") are all elaboration strategies. Effective note taking requires you to embellish or refine what the professor or the author has said. When you take notes in your own words and add comments or make connections, you're using an elaboration strategy. One of the chief advantages of elaboration strategies is that they help you create more associations with the material to be learned, thereby providing you with more routes or cues for getting to the information during retrieval. Explaining the material out loud, creating questions in the margin, and making maps also are examples of elaboration strategies that you may already be using. You'll learn more about how to use those strategies in Chapters 9 and 10. In this section we'll discuss some other elaboration techniques, including the use of mnemonics.

Mnemonic devices or techniques often are referred to as memory tricks. However, many of these techniques aren't tricks at all. They are, instead, techniques that can help you remember things when you can't seem to remember them any other way. The advantage of mnemonic devices is that they form an association with the material, so if you remember the mnemonic, you remember the material. Mnemonics provide an organizational framework or structure for remembering information that may not appear to have a structure of its own.

This brings up a very important point. Mnemonic devices are aids to retrieval, but they do *not* guarantee that you will learn the material. You can't just decide that you're going to remember Weinstein and Mayer's five categories of learning strategies by remembering the word REOCA (Rehearsal, Elaboration, Organizational, Comprehension monitoring, Affective and Motivational). Before you can use "REOCA" to help you list or discuss these strategies, you have to practice the connection between the mnemonic and the information to be learned. Although this section focuses on the use of mnemonics, it's important to remember that you must use the other high-level rehearsal strategies to learn the information in the first place. You can then use mnemonics to retrieve what you have learned.

According to Kenneth Higbee, "A mnemonic system may help you in at least three ways when you're trying to find items in your memory: (1) It will give you a place to start your search, a way to locate the first item. (2) It will give you a way of proceeding systematically from one item to the next. (3) It will let you know when your recall is finished, when you have reached the last item."[5] You'll learn more about how to make those connections and use mnemonics as retrieval aids as you examine the use of acronyms, acrostics, and other mnemonic aids.

---

[5]K. Higbee, *Your Memory: How It Works and How to Improve It* (Englewood Cliffs, NJ: Prentice Hall, 1977), p. 78.

ACTIVITY 7.5   *List the Associations You Use*

During the next week, make a list of at least ten associations that you use to help you remember information both in and out of the classroom. Which of the associations were helpful? Why? Discuss your responses with other members of your group.

Acronyms, or Catchwords

Acronyms are "words" that are made up of the first letters of other words. Acronyms are so commonly used today that most of us don't even realize that some aren't real words. SCUBA, NASA, FBI, and COD are all quite familiar. We don't even think of them as standing for self-contained underwater breathing apparatus, National Aeronautics and Space Administration, Federal Bureau of Investigation, and cash on delivery; they all are well understood in their abbreviated form.

John Langan used the term *catchword* to describe an acronym.[6] In a sense, acronyms do help us catch or hold on to the information that we have learned. Catchwords, or acronyms, can be real words or nonsense words designed to aid recall. You probably can name all the colors in the spectrum because someone taught you to use the catchword "ROY G. BIV" (red, orange, yellow, green, blue, indigo, violet). "REOCA" also is an example of a catchword; each letter stands for the first letter in a list of other words. Can you say them now? Try it.

How to Create Catchwords.   Catchwords are useful for remembering lists of information. Look at the five general principles of nonverbal communication that are listed below. Try to create a catchword to remember them.

1. Nonverbal communication is multichanneled.

2. Nonverbal communication conveys emotions.

3. Nonverbal communication is ambiguous.

4. Nonverbal communication may contradict verbal messages.

5. Nonverbal communication is culture-bound.[7]

To make an acronym or catchword, you first have to identify a key word in each statement. Go back and underline the following words: *multichanneled, emotions, ambiguous, contradict,* and *culture-bound.* These words should work well as hooks or tags to help you remember the entire list of principles. Next, list (or underline) the first letter of each word: M, E, A, C, C. "MEACC" doesn't sound as though it will be very memorable, but

---

[6]J. Langan, *Reading and Study Skills,* 4th ed. (New York: McGraw-Hill, 1989), p.207.
[7]From W. Weiten and M. A. Lloyd, *Psychology Applied to Modern Life,* 6th ed. (Belmont, CA: Wadsworth, 2000), p. 189. Used with permission.

FIGURE 7.2

Student Examples of Catchwords

Swinburne's and Aquinas's Views

Swinburne—SWOMP		Aquinas—ICON	
S	simultaneously	I	immutable
W	within time	C	continuum
O	own actions	O	omniscient
M	mutable	N	not in time
P	personable		

Kwan's Catchwords

FASCISM

1. Authoritarian governments
2. Masses are incapable of governing themselves (democratically)
3. State terrorism is used
4. Hierarchically structured organic society
5. Elites govern

A M S H E = **SHAME**

Heather's Catchword

---

by simply rearranging the letters you could form the catchword "MECCA" or "CAMEC." Both of these are fairly easy to recall.

Your work's not done, though. Can you list the five general principles of nonverbal communication? Just creating the catchwords doesn't mean that you've learned the material. To strengthen the associations and learn the material, you need to practice connecting the catchword to the key word and then the key word to the entire phrase. Reciting or writing will help you form the connections. If I were going to use the catchword "MECCA," I would rehearse the information this way: "M" stands for "multichanneled," and "multichanneled" stands for "nonverbal communication is multichanneled." "E" stands for "emotions," and "emotions" stands for "nonverbal communication conveys emotions" (and so on). You may need to practice this connection several times. Of course, you still have to be sure that you understand what the terms *multichanneled* and *emotions* mean in this context. Students who say that mnemonics don't work for them often think that simply constructing the mnemonic should firmly embed the information in long-term memory. Unfortunately, the mere construction of a word or phrase doesn't replace learning the information. Your catchword will help you retrieve the information from memory *only after the information is learned*. Take a look at how two students used catchwords to remember course material (Figure 7.2).

ACTIVITY 7.6 *Create Catchwords*

Make up a catchword that will help you remember each of the following lists of information. Put your catchword on an index card and exchange your card with another classmate. Could your classmate retrieve the information using your catchword? Compare the catchwords you made to those of others in your group.

1. The five great lakes: Superior, Michigan, Huron, Erie, Ontario.

2. Freud's five stages of psychosexual development: oral, anal, phallic, latency, and genital.

3. Refer back to Chapter 6 and create a catchword to remember the four benefits of improved concentration.

Acrostics, or Catchphrases

Acrostics, or catchphrases as Langan called them, are phrases or sentences that are made up of words beginning with the first letters of other words. Just as the catchword "FACE" helped most of us remember the names of the spaces in music class, the catchphrase "Every Good Boy Does Fine" worked to recall the names of the lines. Did you remember learning "My Very Educated Mother Just Served Us Nine Pies" to remember the nine planets in order? If you did, you used an acrostic, or catchphrase, to remember the information. Catchphrases worked in junior high, and they can work in college, too. The difference, though, is that you need to create your own catchphrases in college to help you remember the information that you want to learn for your exams.

When to Use Catchphrases. Catchphrases are especially useful if you have to remember the information in a special order or if you can't form an easy-to-remember word from the letters available to you (for instance, you may have all consonants but no vowels). You can create catchphrases to recall all kinds of course material. Remembering lists of names, steps in a process, causes and effects, and key points for essay answers are just a few ways that students use catchphrases.

How to Create Catchphrases. You can create catchphrases in much the same way you created catchwords. If you had to learn the five principles of nonverbal behavior in order, you might find that "Mary Ellen Answered Conrad Curtly," is more memorable than "MEACC." This example can provide us with some additional tips for creating acrostics, or catchphrases. You may have noticed that in the example ("Mary Ellen Answered Conrad Curtly"), the two *c* words have the same second letters (the vowels *o* and *u*) as the original key words (*contradict* and *culture-bound*). When you have two key words that start with the same letter, it's helpful to use the second letter to show which one comes first. You may also find that making your mnemonic sentences outrageous, silly, or humorous helps you remember them. We tend to remember

FIGURE 7.3
*Student Examples
of Catchphrases*

Four Classes of Heterotrophic Organisms

<u>C</u>arnivores—animal eaters

<u>H</u>erbivores—plant eaters

<u>O</u>mnivores—animal and plant eaters

<u>D</u>ecomposers—eat decaying organisms

"<u>C</u>an <u>H</u>enry <u>O</u>mit <u>D</u>ents"

Terri's Catchphrase

Five Building Blocks of Structure

1. <u>J</u>ob design
2. <u>D</u>epartmentalization
3. <u>C</u>oordinating mechanisms
4. <u>S</u>pan of management
5. <u>D</u>elegation

"<u>J</u>eff is <u>d</u>epressed about <u>c</u>oming to <u>s</u>ee <u>D</u>avid"

Todd's Catchphrase

FOUR KINDS OF LOVE

1. <u>P</u>assionate love
2. <u>C</u>ompassionate love
3. <u>F</u>atuous love
4. <u>C</u>onsummate love

<u>P</u>eggy <u>c</u>ounted <u>f</u>our <u>c</u>hickens   *Peggy's Catchphrase*

<u>P</u>laying <u>c</u>ards <u>f</u>or <u>c</u>ash   *Mathew's Catchphrase*

funny or outrageous catchphrases better than dull and boring ones. Whenever you're using catchphrases to help you learn and remember text material, consider the following five steps:

1. Select a key word to represent each piece of information.

2. Underline or write down the first letter of each key word.

3. Form a catchphrase from words beginning with the first letter of each word.

4. Practice associating the new word to the key word and then the key word to the actual information that you need to know.

5. Use the mnemonic to test your memory—to retrieve the original information.

After a little practice, you'll find that you can use catchphrases to help you recall information for many of your college courses. Figure 7.3 includes several examples of acrostics, or catchphrases, that students used when preparing for essay exams.

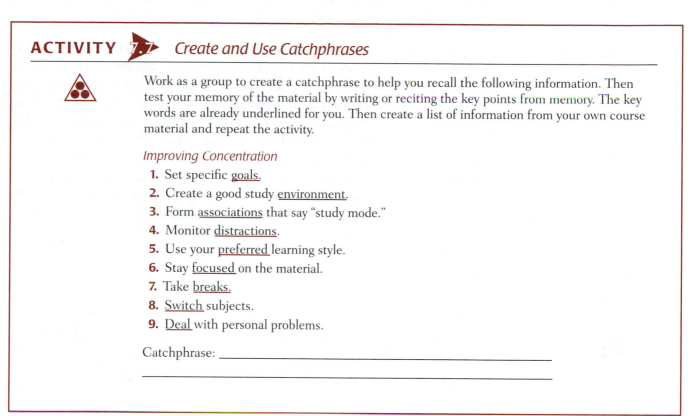

ACTIVITY 7.7 *Create and Use Catchphrases*

Work as a group to create a catchphrase to help you recall the following information. Then test your memory of the material by writing or reciting the key points from memory. The key words are already underlined for you. Then create a list of information from your own course material and repeat the activity.

Improving Concentration

1. Set specific <u>goals</u>.
2. Create a good study <u>environment</u>.
3. Form <u>associations</u> that say "study mode."
4. Monitor <u>distractions</u>.
5. Use your <u>preferred</u> learning style.
6. Stay <u>focused</u> on the material.
7. Take <u>breaks</u>.
8. <u>Switch</u> subjects.
9. <u>Deal</u> with personal problems.

Catchphrase: _____

_____

Imagery

You've already seen how effective visual imagery can be in helping you remember catchphrases. However, you can create visual images to remember course material without writing catchwords or catchphrases. Concept maps can be used to present a visual display of material that you need to remember. After developing and practicing a map, you may be able to recall much of the information by visualizing the map itself.

You also can paint visual pictures in your mind to remember main points and supporting information. If you were studying the Boston Tea Party, for example, you could remember many of the details about this historic event just by visualizing what happened. By incorporating names, places, dates, and so on in your visual image, you can recall a great deal of information about your topic.

Another mnemonic device that uses imagery is known as the method of place or the method of loci ("lo-sigh," meaning locations). Here you form an association between something you want to remember and a particular location on a familiar walk. Let's say that you have to present a speech about healthy eating habits in one of your classes and that your speech consists of seven main ideas. You simply imagine yourself taking a very familiar walk. As you pass the first familiar landmark on that walk, you develop an image that somehow connects that familiar landmark to the first point in your speech. For example, let's say you're giving a speech on developing a healthier lifestyle. If your first main point is to eat more fruits and vegetables, you might picture yourself buying fruits and vegetables at the farmer's market in the park.

ORGANIZATIONAL STRATEGIES

Organizational strategies allow you to organize the information to make it easier to learn and recall. Tasks such as listing, ordering, grouping, outlining, mapping, and diagramming are all examples of organizational strategies. In each of these activities, you act on the material that is to be mastered. With outlining or mapping, for example, you organize the material in a way that shows how each component is related to the others. In Chapter 9, you'll use both outlining and mapping techniques. One of the advantages of organizational strategies is that by structuring the material, you provide yourself with new ways to remember many of the details. If you can remember the structure—the main headings of the outline or the web strands of your map, for example—you will be able to remember many of the details. Before you continue reading, complete Activity 7.8.

ACTIVITY 7.8 *Try Some Organizational Strategies*

Look at the following list of words for sixty seconds; then cover it with your hand or a piece of paper and try to write the words in the margin.

Newspaper, pencil, bus, automobile, book, pen, boat, magazine, comic book, chalk, crayon, train

You may have found that it was difficult to remember all twelve of the items. Do you know why? Earlier you learned about the capacity of short-term memory. If you recall, you can remember only about seven pieces of information at one time. You can, however, increase this capacity by chunking (grouping) the information. You probably will be able to remember all twelve items if you group them as follows:

Things You Read	Things You Write With	Things You Ride In
newspaper	pencil	bus
book	pen	automobile
magazine	chalk	boat
comic book	crayon	train

With this grouping, you have three pieces or chunks of information to remember instead of twelve. It's easy to remember three things, right? You also can remember the four items in each category quite easily because the headings help trigger your memory. Now look at the three groups for sixty seconds and try to write down as many of the items as you can in the margin.

Did you find that grouping made it easier to remember the words in Activity 7.8? Did you use any other strategies for remembering? You may have used some rehearsal and elaboration strategies. You may have used a catchword such as "BABT" to help you remember *bus, auto, boat,* and *train.* Did you notice that the second column contains two words that start with *p* and two words that start with *c*? Can you think of a catchphrase that would help you remember the four "things you read"? You might find that you could learn and recall the fifty states more easily if you classified or grouped them into categories such as New England, Mid-Atlantic, Southern, Midwestern, Western, and so on.

Organize Material by Grouping

You can improve your ability to learn and recall a large amount of material by grouping or chunking it. However, you should follow some basic guidelines when setting up your groups. First, never set up more than seven groups. Why? If you make up ten or fifteen groups, you won't be able to remember all the group headings. For the same reason, limit the number of items in each group to seven. Second, be sure you use a simple system. If your plan for remembering the information is extremely complex, you won't be able to remember it (the plan), and then you won't be able to remember the information itself. Third, you can't learn the information just by looking at it. You need to write or recite the lists and then test yourself. Finally, there is a tendency to forget the items in the middle of the list more quickly than those that are first or last. Did you have that problem earlier? You can avoid this problem by practicing the items in different orders or by using some of the elaboration strategies previously described. Remember, the more organized the information is when you put it into LTM, the more easily you'll be able to retrieve it later.

ACTIVITY 7.9 *Organize Information*

After you read and mark the text selection "Defining Global Media Systems," available on the *College Reading and Study Strategies* Web site, organize the information that you need to learn. Group, outline, or map the information to make it more meaningful. Then devise a strategy for remembering the main points that you included. Compare your organizational structure and any mnemonics you create with those of your group.

COMPREHENSION MONITORING STRATEGIES

Comprehension monitoring strategies allow us to keep tabs on our learning. They help us monitor our progress in mastering the material and allow us to evaluate the effectiveness of the strategies that we use to gain that mastery. Setting goals and then assessing your progress, reciting from recall columns or question cards, taking self-tests, replicating study sheets, and even just asking yourself whether you understand something are all examples of comprehension monitoring strategies.

All these activities involve metacognition—the ability to think about and control one's learning.[8] Metacognition involves three types of awareness on the part of the learner. First, students must learn *task awareness*—they must learn to identify what information they have to study and learn in a particular situation. Second, students must learn *strategy awareness*—they need to determine which strategy will be most effective for learning specific information, for preparing for different types of exams, and for using with different types of course material. Finally, students must learn *performance awareness*—they must learn to determine whether they have mastered the material that they previously identified as important, and how well it has been learned.[9]

---

[8]L. Baker and A. L. Brown, "Metacognitive Skills and Reading," in P. D. Pearson, ed., *Handbook of Reading Research* (New York: Longman, 1984).

[9]S. E. Wade and R. E. Reynolds, "Developing Metacognitive Awareness," *Journal of Reading*, 33 (1989): 6–14.

When to Use Comprehension Monitoring Strategies

Comprehension monitoring strategies help us determine when learning or understanding breaks down. For example, you may find, as you read and take notes on one of your textbooks, that you can't figure out how to formulate questions about the information under one of the headings. At that point, you should realize that you did not comprehend or understand that section of the text.

When you use self-testing activities, you're monitoring your learning. If you find that you don't really know the information as well as you thought you did, you can review it again. Self-testing also allows you to practice retrieving the information from LTM in a testlike situation. Some students become frustrated when they take exams because they spend hours and hours studying but can't seem to recall the information during the exam. Although they may have worked on acquisition and retention, they probably didn't spend much time working on retrieval of the information. Each time you self-test, you practice getting the information back out of memory. This provides you with an opportunity to practice the cues and strategies that you intend to use during the exam and to monitor their effectiveness.

Comprehension monitoring strategies also help us examine and evaluate the strategies that we're using to acquire, retain, and retrieve information. By taking a self-test, for example, you may discover that you don't really know as much as you thought you did about a particular section of the text and lecture material. Again, your discovery that you haven't learned that material provides you with some feedback on your progress in preparing for an exam. However, it also may allow you to evaluate the strategy that you originally used to "learn" that material. You may realize, for example, that just reading over the material was not very effective for getting it into LTM or that just reciting the information from your notes did not prepare you to write an essay about it. Once you determine that your study strategies aren't effective, you can modify the way you learn and select more effective strategies to use.

ACTIVITY 7.10 *Monitor Your Learning*

Use the Journal Entry form on the *College Reading and Study Strategies* Web site to describe your use of memory strategies. Which of the memory strategies did you find most effective for helping you learn and retrieve information? Describe how you used each one and explain why it worked for you.

AFFECTIVE AND MOTIVATIONAL STRATEGIES

Affective and motivational strategies are strategies that relate to your attitude, interest, and motivation toward learning. They can influence how effectively you learn and remember information. Many of the strategies that you used for setting goals, managing time, and improving concentration are examples of affective and motivational strategies. These strategies help prepare us mentally for studying and create a positive learning environment. Setting realistic, moderately challenging goals helps get you motivated to study and learn. Using "To Do" lists, planning rewards, and taking breaks are just a few of the motivational strategies that you probably are using on a regular basis. They help you keep up with your daily assignments and give you a sense of accomplishment at the end of the day. When you have a long-range project that requires more time and effort, such as writing a term paper or studying for an exam, get started on it quickly, even if you don't have time to do much right away.

Your attitude about learning the material can influence how well you will attend to it, organize it, and store it. If you're trying to prepare for an exam, it's important that you feel interested in the material and motivated to learn and remember. Establishing a purpose for studying, seeing the relevance of the course, and using active learning strategies can all help increase your motivation. If you think studying won't help, you won't be very motivated to study. In Chapter 10, you'll learn a number of active learning strategies that will help you learn and remember the material. Using strategies that are both effective and interesting can make learning fun. Many students actually enjoy studying for a test using these strategies because they end each study session feeling good about what they have accomplished.

Monitoring your learning also can be an effective motivational device. If you test your learning by covering the material and trying to recite the information, you'll be able to evaluate your storage and retrieval processes. You also can accomplish this by reciting from a recall column, taking self-tests, reproducing maps or charts, and so on. One advantage of reciting is that it allows you to test your memory. If you're able to remember the information that you're reviewing, you feel good—you know you are learning. Successful recitations motivate you to continue to study and to continue to use that learning strategy because it worked. Changing to a different learning strategy or studying for a longer period of time may be necessary to successfully store the "missed" information in LTM memory. When you know that you know the important information for a test, you develop more confidence in yourself as a student, and this can affect your performance on the exam.

Your state of mind during the exam also affects how well you're able to retrieve the information. If you experience test anxiety, you may not be able to concentrate on the exam questions. You may find that you're so upset that you can't think of the answers. Knowing you're well prepared for an exam reduces and, in some cases, eliminates feelings of test anxiety. Not knowing the material well enough or not being sure that you know the material well enough can lead to even more test anxiety. Spacing your study, using active learning strategies, and practicing retrieval all help you prepare well for the exam. If you begin the exam with positive feelings about your preparation and expect to do well, you can increase your probability for success.

When you get your test back, use it to evaluate how well your study plan and strategies worked for you. Go over all of the test items, both the correct and incorrect ones, to examine your preparation and test-taking skills. Instead of being discouraged by a poor test grade, find out why you made the mistakes you made. Plan ways to avoid making the same mistakes again. You'll find some additional tips for improving your memory in the Tip Block.

TIP

MORE TIPS FOR IMPROVING YOUR MEMORY

DON'T ASSUME THAT YOU WILL REMEMBER. Many students think they will remember everything they read in their textbooks and hear in their class lectures. However, even if it worked for you in high school, it won't in college because college tests are spaced further apart, allowing us to forget much of the information. Take good class notes and highlight or take notes as you read and then work hard to learn the information.

REVIEW REGULARLY. Review your text and lecture information on a daily or weekly basis to keep the information fresh in your memory. Doing an end-of-week review also allows you to integrate text and lecture material and organize it in long-term memory.

ORGANIZE THE INFORMATION LOGICALLY. The more logically you organize the information you need to remember, the easier it will be to learn it and retrieve it from memory. Restructuring the information so that it's more meaningful to you aids your memory of it.

FORM ASSOCIATIONS TO INCREASE MEMORY CUES. Don't study information in isolation. It's very difficult to recall information when you learn it as an isolated piece of information. By developing study sheets, explaining the material, or making maps, you form associations with and among the material that add a variety of cues that will help you remember it for an exam.

ORGANIZE THE INFORMATION IN YOUR STUDY SHEETS. The more organized the information is when you put it into long-term memory, the more easily you'll be able to find it when you're taking an exam. Creating titles, headings, and main points in your study sheets helps you organize the information and provides you with cues to aid retrieval.

USE YOUR OWN EXPERTISE TO AID MEMORY. When information is meaningful, it's easier to remember. Think of how what you are learning connects with your own life and work experiences. Create examples from your own experiences to help you remember the information you're learning in your college classes.

USE RHYMES, STORIES, OR SONGS TO HELP YOU REMEMBER. If you're good at writing or remembering songs, rhymes, or stories, use those methods to help improve your memory. Words that rhyme, the details of a story, or even the melody of a song add additional cues that may help you remember information for your exam.

MONITOR YOUR MEMORY. Many students are frustrated when they can't remember information during an exam. If this has happened to you, you may not have *learned* the information (at least not at the recall level). Check your memory of the information before the exam by self-testing on paper or by reciting. If you can't say the answer out loud without peeking, you don't really know it.

ACTIVITY 7.11 *List Affective and Motivational Strategies That You Use*

List in the margin five affective and motivational strategies that you used during the past week. Were they effective in improving your learning and memory? What other strategies do you plan to use in the future?

ACTIVITY 7.12   *Monitor How You Learn and Remember*

Choose a chapter or part of a chapter in one of your textbooks, select the material that you think you need to learn for an exam, and organize it on a separate sheet of paper. Then determine how you could learn the material. Work on it until you think you know it.

Finally, test yourself to monitor your learning. Write a paragraph or two describing the process that you used to learn the material and how you decided to monitor your learning. Describe your results.

ACTIVITY 7.13   *Use InfoTrac College Edition to Locate an Article on Memory Techniques*

If you are using InfoTrac College Edition, find an article that contains information on memory techniques. Print the article and make a list of the key points for two topics presented

in the article. Then develop at least two mnemonics that will help you remember the key points in the article. Share the information with other members of your class.

ACTIVITY 7.14   *Where Are You Now?*

Now that you have completed Chapter 7, take a few minutes to repeat the "Where Are You Now?" activity, located on the *College Reading and Study Strategies* Web site. What changes

did you make as a result of reading this chapter? How are you planning to apply what you've learned in this chapter?

Summary

Learning how information is stored and retrieved in the human brain—learning how memory works—may help you better understand why you need to be actively involved with your course material as you complete day-to-day assignments and prepare for exams. To learn anything, we must encode it—make it meaningful. At that point, we must rehearse the material in some way to move it from short-term to long-term memory. The more organized the information is as we store it, the more easily we'll be able to locate it later—retrieve it. By working on the material in different ways, we can form many associations or cues to help us retrieve the information when we need it. However, interference, anxiety, improper encoding, and passive study can all lead to poor retrieval and what we call forgetting.

Learning to use general and specific memory strategies can help you improve your ability to encode, store, and retrieve information. Strategies such as spaced practice, breaking down tasks, repetition, and overlearning are the cornerstones of improving your memory. Specific memory strategies can also be used effectively to increase your ability to store and retrieve information. Rehearsal strategies help you store course information in long-term memory. Elaboration strategies such as forming associations, creating acronyms and acrostics, and using visual imagery are mnemonic devices (memory tricks) that can help you more easily retrieve the information that you've already learned. You can also improve your memory by using organizational strategies like grouping, outlining, mapping, and charting. Through comprehension monitoring strategies such as recitation, self-testing, and evaluating your progress in learning, you can keep tabs on how well you're learning the material and how effective your strategies are. As you've probably discovered, many of these strategies work best when you use them together. Affective and motivational strategies help keep you on task, encourage you to work hard, and reward you when your efforts pay off. A good memory is not something most people are born with, but anyone can develop a good memory by working hard and becoming a strategic learner.

Review Questions

Terms You Should Know: Make a flash card for each term.

Acronyms	Encoding	Overlearning
Acrostics	Immediate memory	Rehearsal strategies
Affective and motivational	Information Processing	Retrieval
strategies	Model	Sensory memory
Comprehension monitoring	Massed practice	Sensory registers
strategies	Metacognition	Spaced practice
Consolidation	Method of loci	Storage
Cue	Mnemonic devices	Working memory
Elaboration strategies	Organizational strategies	

Completion: Fill in the blank to complete each of the following statements.

1. _____ memory is very susceptible to interference.

2. If information is well _____, it is easier to learn and recall.

3. Another term for spaced practice is _____ practice.

4. Mnemonic devices are designed to aid _____, not _____.

5. _____-level rehearsal strategies are more effective in getting information into long-term memory.

Multiple Choice: Circle the letter of the best answer for each of the following questions. Be sure to underline key words and eliminate wrong answers.

6. _____ occurs when we make things meaningful.
   A. Encoding
   B. Storage
   C. Retrieval
   D. Memory

7. Which of the following is not an advantage of overlearning?

    A. It helps you organize the information you need to learn.

    B. It reduces test anxiety.

    C. It prevents forgetting.

    D. It helps you understand the material better.

Short Answer–Essay: On a separate sheet, answer each of the following questions.

8. Compare and contrast short-term and long-term memory.

9. Why do some students have difficulty retrieving information? What should they do differently?

10. Describe Weinstein and Mayer's Five Groups of Learning Strategies.

8 Taking Lecture Notes

In this chapter you will learn more about:

➤ Why to take lecture notes

➤ How to take lecture notes

➤ Effective note-taking systems

➤ How to edit your notes

➤ How to review your notes

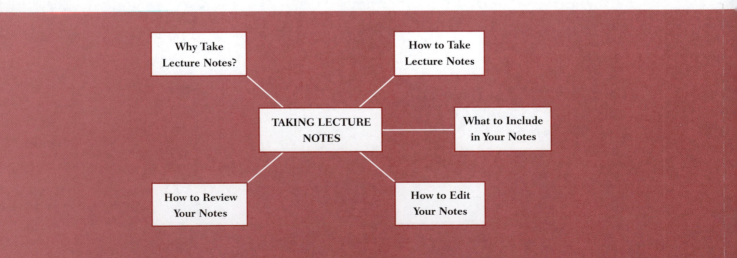

ACTIVITY 8.1   *Where Are You Now?*

Take a few minutes to answer *yes* or *no* to the following questions.

	YES	NO
1. Do you review and edit your notes within twenty-four hours after each of your classes?	_____	_____
2. Do you try to write down exactly what your professor says in class?	_____	_____
3. Do you separate the main points from supporting information in your notes?	_____	_____
4. Are you able to read and understand your notes when you study for your exam?	_____	_____
5. Do you sometimes find that your notes don't make sense when you review them before an exam?	_____	_____
6. Do you tend to write down only important or key words when you take notes?	_____	_____
7. Do you review your notes by reciting them out loud?	_____	_____
8. Do you tend to miss a lot of information when you take notes?	_____	_____
9. Are you actively involved in the lecture?	_____	_____
10. Do you read your textbook assignment before you go to your lecture class?	_____	_____
Total Points	_____	

Give yourself 1 point for each *yes* answer to questions 1, 3, 4, 7, 9, and 10 and 1 point for each *no* answer to questions 2, 5, 6, and 8. Now total up your points. A low score indicates that you need some help in note taking. A high score indicates that you are already using many good note-taking strategies.

WHY TAKE LECTURE NOTES?

Other than attending class every day, taking good lecture notes is probably the single most important activity for college students. Taking notes during college lectures is a difficult task for most entering college students because little or no real practice in note taking occurred when they were in high school. There, note taking involved copying the information off the chalkboard as the teacher talked and wrote. In college, however, most professors don't do the job of note taking for you. Instead, you must listen, select the appropriate information, paraphrase it, condense it, and then write it down with few (if any) clues from the professor. Developing good note-taking skills takes both time and practice. Taking lecture notes promotes active listening, provides an accurate record of information, provides an opportunity to interpret, condense, and organize the information, and provides an opportunity for repetition of the material. Learning and practicing effective strategies for how to take lecture notes will help you become a more successful student.

PROMOTES ACTIVE LISTENING

Taking notes in class promotes active listening by helping you concentrate on the lecture. Have you ever sat in class and realized that you had no idea what the professor just said? This is a very common experience for many students. Even though everyone gets distracted once in a while, it becomes a real problem if you daydream so much that you miss what your professor is saying. By taking notes, you can improve your concentration because you're focusing your attention on what's being said; you have a purpose—listening for the next point that the professor will make so that you can write it down.

Some students find sitting in lecture classes very boring; they prefer classes where they are more actively involved in the learning experience. Taking notes, however, is a very active process. You can generate a high level of involvement in your own learning by taking notes. Note taking involves more than just writing down what the instructor is saying. It includes thinking about what has been said, determining what is important, recognizing how different points relate to others, anticipating what will be said next, putting the information into your own words, and organizing the information in your notes. The process of taking good lecture notes can help you become both an active listener and an active participant in your classes.

PROVIDES AN ACCURATE RECORD OF INFORMATION

The most important reason for taking notes in college is to get an accurate record of the information that was presented in class. Taking notes can actually help you learn and remember the information. Even if you learn some of the information during the lecture class, you probably won't remember it by the time you take your exam. In college, exams are given after four, seven, or even fifteen weeks; you won't remember all the lecture material by the time you take a test. Research studies indicate that without rehearsal, you may forget 50 percent of what you hear in a lecture within twenty-four hours and 80 percent in just two weeks.[1] In fact, you may forget 95 percent within one month. This comes as a big shock to most college students; however, it explains why some students have difficulty on exams. If you don't leave a lecture class with a good set of notes, an accurate record of information, you won't have the opportunity to review that material again before the exam. You can't just rely on your memory of the lecture; you need your notes,

---

[1]H. Spitzer, "Studies in Retention," *Journal of Educational Psychology* 30 (1939): 641–656.

ACTIVITY 8.2 *Test Your Notes*

A good set of notes should stand up to the test of time. Try the following exercise several times during the semester. Be sure to test the notes from each of your classes. Go back to the notes that you took yesterday in one of your classes and read them. Do they make sense to you? Do you feel as though you are sitting in the lecture and hearing your professor talk about the topic? Now go back to the notes that you took at the beginning of the semester. Do they still make sense? Did they contain all of the information presented in the lecture? Do you feel as though you understand and recall all the information from the lecture?

too! Why? In many classes the majority of the exam questions come from the lecture material. Without a good set of notes, you won't be able to prepare for the exam.

HOW TO TAKE LECTURE NOTES

Learning to take notes effectively and efficiently takes time. You can begin to improve your note-taking skills rapidly, however, if you learn to use some basic strategies. One of the first things you need to do is learn to become an active listener. Although there's no one correct way to take notes, some methods or systems work better than others. In this section, you'll learn a number of basic strategies to help improve your note taking, as well as several options for form and format. Instead of just selecting one method to use, you may find it beneficial to try all the techniques and then decide which ones work best for you.

PREPARE BEFORE TAKING NOTES

Before you ever walk into a lecture class, you need to prepare to take notes. The best way to prepare for your note-taking activity is to read the text assignment before class. Much of the material that's presented in college lectures will be new to you. By reading the text assignment before the lecture, you build up some background about the topic. If you have some idea what the lecture is about, it will be easier for you to understand the presentation and take good notes. Reading before the lecture also will give you the opportunity to become familiar with the main topics or ideas that will be presented. You'll find it easier to identify main ideas and organize your notes as the professor delivers the lecture. Finally, you'll be somewhat familiar with key terms and names after reading the text. This will help you keep up with the lecturer and avoid making content errors in your notes. If you have been having difficulty understanding the lecture or taking notes, try reading your text assignment before the next lecture. Remember, you only get one chance to listen to the lecture, but you can read the text as many times as you want.

As you walk into the lecture classroom, get ready to take notes. If you sit near the front, you'll be able to see and hear better. You'll probably find that other interested and motivated students also tend to sit in the first few rows of the class. By avoiding the back of the room, you'll avoid those students who tend to chat and walk in late. While you're waiting for class to begin, review the notes that you took during the last class meeting. Many professors pick up where they left off in the last lecture. Your review will remind you of the main topics and the general organization of the lecture and will prepare you for the next point that will be made.

BECOME AN ACTIVE LISTENER

Although reading your text assignment helps you build some background for understanding the lecture, it doesn't guarantee that you'll take good notes. Researchers have discovered that we ignore, misunderstand, or forget about 75 percent of what we hear.[2] As you may have discovered earlier, note taking is an active process that involves paying attention to the information that the lecturer is presenting, interpreting it (so you can understand and remember it), condensing it, and writing it down in an organized manner. To achieve this goal, students must first become active and effective listeners.

---

[2]Diane Bone, *The Business of Listening* (Los Altos, CA: Crisp Publications, 1988), p. 5.

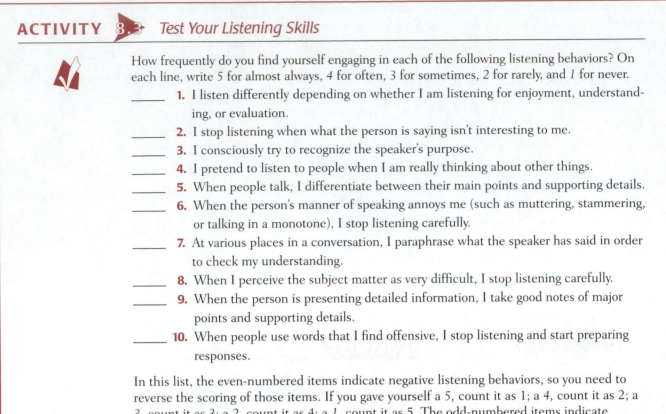

ACTIVITY 8.3 *Test Your Listening Skills*

How frequently do you find yourself engaging in each of the following listening behaviors? On each line, write 5 for almost always, *4* for often, *3* for sometimes, *2* for rarely, and *1* for never.

_____ **1.** I listen differently depending on whether I am listening for enjoyment, understanding, or evaluation.

_____ **2.** I stop listening when what the person is saying isn't interesting to me.

_____ **3.** I consciously try to recognize the speaker's purpose.

_____ **4.** I pretend to listen to people when I am really thinking about other things.

_____ **5.** When people talk, I differentiate between their main points and supporting details.

_____ **6.** When the person's manner of speaking annoys me (such as muttering, stammering, or talking in a monotone), I stop listening carefully.

_____ **7.** At various places in a conversation, I paraphrase what the speaker has said in order to check my understanding.

_____ **8.** When I perceive the subject matter as very difficult, I stop listening carefully.

_____ **9.** When the person is presenting detailed information, I take good notes of major points and supporting details.

_____ **10.** When people use words that I find offensive, I stop listening and start preparing responses.

In this list, the even-numbered items indicate negative listening behaviors, so you need to reverse the scoring of those items. If you gave yourself a 5, count it as 1; a *4*, count it as 2; a *3*, count it as 3; a *2*, count it as 4; a *1*, count it as 5. The odd-numbered items indicate positive listening behaviors. Count each as given. Sum all your scores. There are 50 points possible. If you score over 40, you are effective in your listening. If you score below 40, identify which questions seemed to cause your lowest scores.[3]

Active Versus Passive Listening

Many students confuse hearing and listening. Our ears may receive sounds during a lecture, or we may listen by watching a sign language interpreter or real-time reporter, but that doesn't mean that we're listening—paying attention to and interpreting what we're hearing. As you learned in Chapter 7, we only remember a small proportion of all sounds that we hear because we don't attend to (pay attention to) most of them.

Characteristics of Active Listeners

Active listeners are physically and mentally focused on the lecture. They sit up straight, lean forward slightly (indicating interest), and make the lecturer the center of their attention by making eye contact or sitting directly in the lecturer's line of vision. Active listeners often sit near the front of the classroom to avoid external distractions. They eliminate internal distractions, too, by pushing other thoughts out and focusing all their

[3]Listening test from Rudolph F. Verderber and Kathleen S. Verderber, *Inter-Act*, 8th ed. (Belmont, CA: Wadsworth, 1998), p. 213. Used with permission.

FIGURE 8.1

Strategies to Improve Your Listening Skills

- Read the text assignment before the lecture to build background on the topic.

- Review your last set of notes prior to the lecture.

- Sit in the professor's direct line of vision (first row across or middle row from the front to the back of the room).

- Decide that you want to listen.

- Focus your attention physically by sitting up and making eye contact with the speaker.

- Focus your attention mentally by eliminating or avoiding distractions.

- Listen with an open mind, setting aside your own biases.

- Control your emotional responses.

- Listen for the main points and related details and take notes.

- Ask and answer questions during the lecture.

- Monitor your listening. Edit your notes for accuracy and completeness.

- Hold yourself accountable for the material presented.

attention on the information being presented. They're open minded and willing to listen to the lecture, putting aside their own biases. Students who are actively involved in the lecture ask questions, answer questions, and take notes. They evaluate what they are hearing and often consider how this information connects to their prior knowledge of the subject. Professors often can identify students who are actively involved in the lecture by their body language, too. They may nod or smile in agreement, look amazed or confused at times, and pull back or frown when they disagree with what is being said. Active listeners are physically, intellectually, and emotionally involved in the lecture.

Factors That Interfere with Effective Listening

Both internal and external distractions can interfere with a student's ability to concentrate during a lecture. Not attending to the lecture can lead to uncertainty about what was said, difficulty understanding the information, or missed information. Many students also either stop listening or become less involved in the presentation when they're angry or offended by the speaker or the message. They react emotionally to the situation and blame the speaker and often stop paying attention to what he or she is saying as a way of retaliating. Some students become angry or closed minded when the lecturer discusses controversial material that is in direct opposition to their own personal point of view. Similarly, some students are "turned off" by language or gestures that they consider inappropriate. They allow their personal sense of propriety to interfere with their listening.

Strategies to Improve Your Listening Skills

Figure 8.1 includes a number of effective strategies that will help you become a better listener. Pick two or three to try during your next class. Then add more.

USE AN EFFECTIVE NOTE-TAKING SYSTEM

Dozens of systems have been developed to help students become effective note takers. Some of them are quite complex and provide explicit details on every step of the process. Unfortunately, a number of these systems involve so many steps and so much work that many students resort to their old methods or just don't take notes at all. Other systems are rather simple and provide only a few basic guidelines. For the new college student, they may not provide enough structure about how to get the information on paper.

The Cornell note-taking system (developed at Cornell University) includes an excellent format for setting up your notes. A sample note page using the Cornell system is shown in Figure 8.2. To set up your page, use a ruler to create a new margin line that is $2\frac{1}{2}$ to $3\frac{1}{2}$ inches from the edge or purchase a summary margin notebook available in some college bookstores. Most notebooks give you a one-inch margin, which doesn't allow enough space to write recall questions that will help you prompt your memory as you review your notes (you'll learn more about this later in the chapter). At the end of each page, leave a two-inch margin so that you can write a summary of the important points as you review your notes. In the large six-inch space to the right of the margin, write down as much information about the lecture as you can. You can use a variety of methods to take your notes, but the outline, block, and modified-block styles have proven to be effective for most college lectures.

The Outline Method

Many students use the outline method to take notes in lecture classes. Outlining involves indenting each level of supporting details under the preceding heading, subheading, or detail. One of the reasons this style is so popular is that it's familiar to many students. Is this the style that you're using now? Some students use outlines because their professors provide them with some form of outline at the beginning of the lecture. Even the four- or five-point outline written on the board can set the pattern that you use for taking notes. Outlines work, however, only when the lecturer is well organized and proceeds in an orderly manner from main points to supporting points.

You can effectively use an outline style of note taking as long as you are careful not to fall into several traps. Don't get distracted by the "rules" of formal outlining. You could spend too much time thinking about how you should label or designate the next point in your notes. You may find yourself thinking about whether to write a "B" or a "2" in your notes instead of concentrating on the content of the lecture.

Too often, students equate outlining with just writing down key words. One-word outlines contain too little of the content of the lecture to provide an accurate record of information. You may not realize how little information you have in your notes until you look at another student's notes. Look at the sample notes in Figure 8.3, which were taken by two students in the same Economics class. Gary simply wrote down key words. His notes look well organized and effective until you compare them to the notes taken by Bryan. Bryan's notes contain much more information about the topics presented in the lecture. When it's time to prepare for exams, students with "one-word notes" simply don't have enough information from which to study. Which set of notes would you rather have before the exam?

FIGURE 8.2
Cornell Note Page

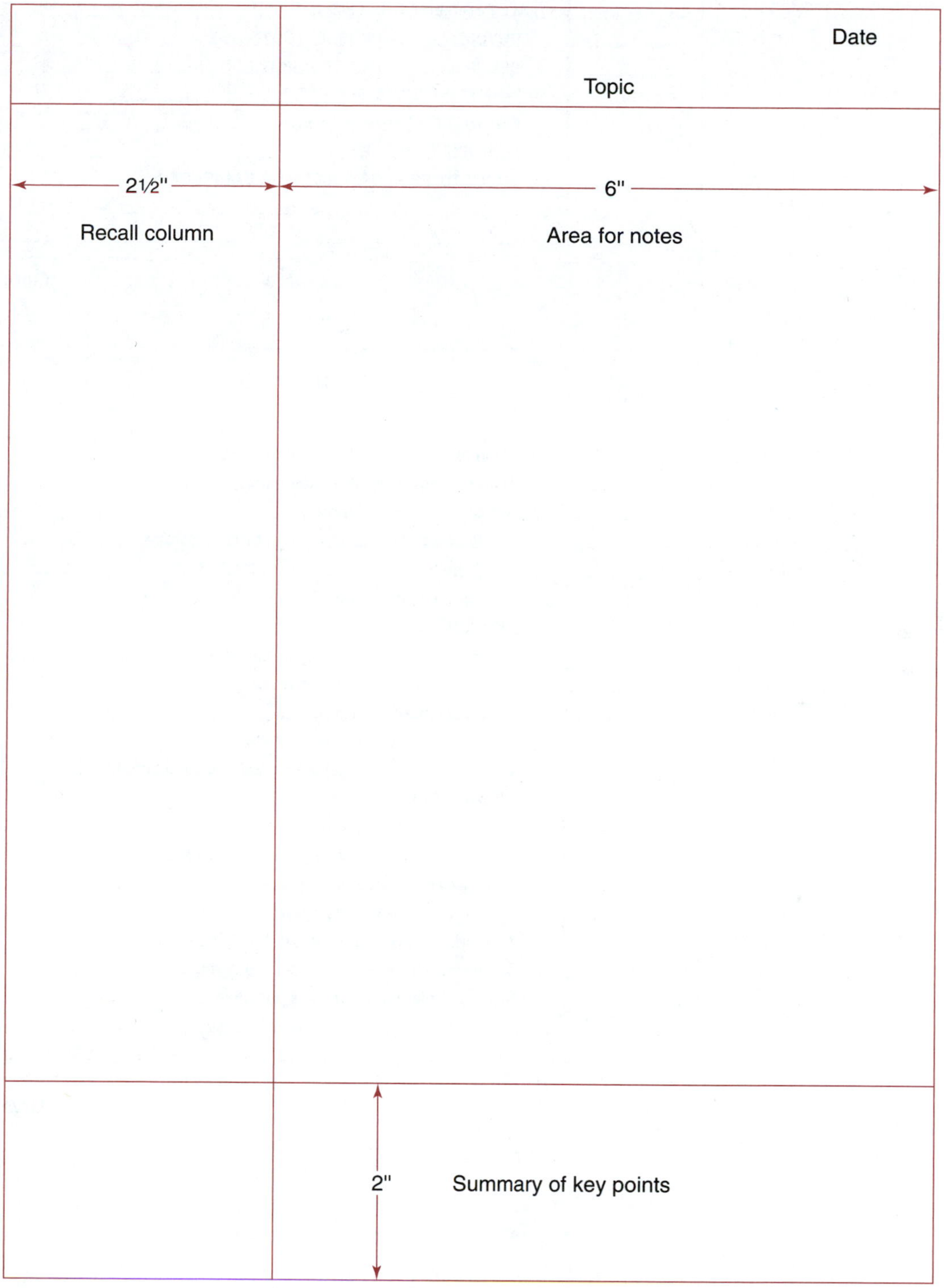

Date

Topic

2½"   Recall column

6"   Area for notes

2"   Summary of key points

FIGURE 8.3

Two Examples from the Same Economics Lecture

1) ALL PEOPLE ACT "SELFISHLY"
    BUYING   PRODUCT (OUTPUTS)
    SELLING   FACTOR (INPUTS)
2) "MANY" BUYERS & SELLERS
    PRODUCT MARKETS: SELLERS
    MONOPOLY: 1 SELLER
    SUBSTITUTES - FOR SUCCESSFUL MARKET

Gary's Notes

Starting pts. for an economic system
    All people act selfishly (economically)
    Two Broad Types of Markets
        Product Markets (output) Market Activity
        Selfish
        Factor Market (input)
    Product Market
        Seller → firms (bus organ.) such as corporations
            → Maximize profits
        Consumers → buyers
            – Maximize utility
            – as prices increase, less is bought
    Factor Market
        Sellers – laborers, workers
            – maximize wages, minimize effort
        Buyers – firms (bus organ.)
            – maximize profits
    All markets structural – great #'s of buyers
    & sellers. Market is competitive – no single
    buyer or seller influences the outcome

Bryan's Notes

FIGURE 8.4
Sample Block Notes

Piaget – Intellectual Development 9/17

Development of perception

knowledge of infants limited – 60s – no visual or hearing
ability – difficult to test – infants do have percep
abilities at birth – even prenatally – can hear

Vision

visual acuity poor 20/600 at birth – see 20 ft what we
see 600 ft away – 1 mo. 20/150 = someone with
glasses – 12 mo. 20/20 – abilities improve as does
ability to use them – newborns – only fixed focus – 9" –
same distance as mom to baby's eyes when fed – eye
muscles weak – lack coordination = normal

Abilities at birth

can see – follow a bright light – have preferences – peep
board experiment – infant in seat – 2 panels – objects
on each – experimenter watch infant's pupils – see obj in
eye – now TV camera & computer – prefer complex
pattern to simple – bk/w checkerboard to bright red
patch – most preferred at 2 mo – simple human face
☺ – inborn pref for human face – smile first

The Block Method

The block style of note taking is another very simple system to learn. After noting the topic of the lecture and the date, write the first heading (main point the professor makes; for example, "Depth Perception" or "What About Depth Perception?") starting at the lefthand margin of your notebook. Indent a few spaces on the next line and then begin to write your notes in block form. Listen for what the lecturer has to say about the heading and write down as many of the details as you can. Block notes are written continuously across the line, separating the details by dashes (—) or slashes (/). Demonstrating the block form, Figure 8.4 contains a set of notes from a lecture on Intellectual Development. The headings from the lecture stand out because they're next to the margin, whereas the details are clustered together in a block indented slightly under each heading. Remember, you don't have to write complete sentences just because your notes are shaped like a paragraph; you still want to concentrate on using *meaningful phrases*. By skipping a line or two between each main heading, you can organize your notes and leave room to add something later in the lecture.

The Modified-Block Method

Some students are uncomfortable putting all their notes in block form. If you like the idea of having all information grouped under a heading without showing various levels of support as in an outline, you may prefer to use a modified-block format. To use the modified block method, you would simply indent about one-half inch and list all related details straight down the page under each heading. You would take each of the details clustered under the heading, "Development of Perception" and list them individually, one statement per line (Figure 8.5). Having each detail on a separate line makes it easy to take notes, organize them, and review for the exam.

FIGURE 8.5
*Sample Modified-Block
Notes*

Piaget – Intellectual Development 9/17

Development of perception

knowledge of infants limited in 1960s

believed no visual or hearing ability

difficult to test

now know infants do have percep abilities at birth

prenatally can hear

Vision

visual acuity poor at birth 20/600

see at 20 ft what we see 600 ft away

1 mo   20/150 = someone w glasses

12 mo 20/20

abilities improve as does ability to use them

newborns have a fixed focus – 9"

same distance as mom to baby's eyes when being fed

eye muscles weak

lack coordination = normal

Abilities at birth

can see

follow a bright light

have preferences

peep board experiment

exper infant in seat

2 panels w objects on each

watch infant's pupils

see preferred obj in infant's eye

computer experiment

now use TV camera connected to computer

prefer complex pattern to simple

bk/w checkerboard to bright red patch

most preferred at 2 mo is simple human face

inborn preference for human face

smile first for faces ☺

The block and modified-block methods allow you to take notes efficiently and effectively because you have to concentrate on only two things: (1) writing down the main points (headings) and (2) writing down any details about them. You don't have to spend a lot of time trying to figure out where to place or how to label each new piece of information. Look at the Tip Block, which includes some additional tips for taking lecture notes.

TIP

MORE TIPS FOR TAKING LECTURE NOTES

DON'T RELY ON YOUR MEMORY ALONE.
Many students think that they should be able to re-member the information presented in a lecture if they pay careful attention. Unfortunately, we forget rapidly. With four to seven weeks between most exams, taking good lecture notes is critical to college success.

USE A FULL-SIZE NOTEBOOK. Use a sepa-rate $8\frac{1}{2} \times 11$-inch notebook for each of your classes. Using smaller notebooks can unconsciously lead to writing fewer notes. You need a full-size note page to take your notes and still have room for recall questions.

ADD THE DATE AND TOPIC TO YOUR NOTES. Be sure to add the date to each page of notes, especially if you're using a loose-leaf notebook. Follow that by the topic; it will help you organize your mind for listening and your notes for later review.

LEAVE SPACE BEFORE STARTING A NEW HEADING. Leave two or three lines before you write in the next heading in case the professor adds information about that topic later in the lecture.

USE FAMILIAR ABBREVIATIONS. By using some familiar abbreviations, you can get the informa-tion down more quickly. Don't try to learn and use more than two or three new abbreviations at a time. You may find that you're trying to think of how to abbreviate the word instead of getting down the next point the professor makes.

LEAVE ROOM IF YOU MISS INFORMATION.
Skip a line or two if you realize that you just missed something in the lecture and go on to the next point. If you try to recall the missed information, you'll miss the next couple of points. If you miss one key word (in a definition, for example), draw a line and just keep writing. After class ask a classmate or your professor what you missed.

USE A TAPE RECORDER WITH A COUNTER. If you need to use a tape recorder at the beginning of the semester, get one with a counter on it. When you can't keep up with the lecturer and miss information, jot down the number on the counter in the margin of your notebook and leave some space in your notes. After class, fast-forward using the counter numbers and fill in the missing information.

PLAY TAPED LECTURES WHILE YOU COMMUTE. If you have a long commute to and from school, you may want to tape the lectures of your most difficult classes (but take notes during class). Then play the tape while you drive or ride the bus or train. The additional review may help you improve your understanding of the material.

FIND A NOTE-TAKING BUDDY. You may miss a class because of illness, car trouble, or an emer-gency. Set up a plan with one of your classmates to let you copy his or her notes in case you're absent. Ex-change phone numbers or e-mail addresses to check on any upcoming assignments or scheduled exams.

ACTIVITY 8.4   *Practice Different Note-Taking Methods*

Develop a set of notes from the following material on cells, using the block, modified block, or outline method. Exchange notes with a classmate and compare your content and organization.

Today we are going to discuss the basic aspects of cell structure and function. Cells differ greatly in size, shape, and activities, as you might gather by comparing a tiny bacterium with one of your relatively giant liver cells. Yet they are alike in three respects. All cells start out life with a plasma membrane, a region of DNA, and a region of cytoplasm.

The plasma membrane, the cell's outermost membrane, maintains the cell as a distinct entity, apart from the environment, and allows metabolic events to proceed in organized, controlled ways. The plasma membrane does not *isolate* the cell interior; substances and signals continually move across it.

The DNA-containing region, the nucleus, contains DNA, which occupies part of the cell interior, along with molecules that can copy or read its hereditary instructions.

The cytoplasm is everything between the plasma membrane and the region of DNA. It consists of a semifluid matrix and other components, such as ribosomes (structures on which proteins are built).[4]

WHAT TO INCLUDE IN YOUR NOTES

Although some general rules will help you figure out what to include in your notes, there's no simple answer to the question "What should I write down?" Some students are so afraid that they'll miss even one point during the lecture that they try to write down every word the professor says. This is both impractical and ineffective. You can't write as fast as your professor can talk. A good general rule is to treat a lecture class like a lab class. You should be an active participant during the entire period. The best thing to do is to take as many notes as you can in a well-organized format. As soon as you pick out the heading, listen carefully for any information that explains or expands upon it, and add that information to your notes. Have you ever caught yourself thinking, "I wonder if I should write that down?" Anytime you think about whether to write something down, go ahead and write it down. You may even find that your hand hurts at the end of the period; that's fine. *Remember: When in doubt, write it out.*

HEADINGS

Always note all headings—the main points—that are made during a lecture. You may find that sometimes you have no trouble at all identifying the main points, and other times you have a lot of trouble. Main points appear to be obvious during some lectures because the lecturer states them in an easily recognizable manner. Introductions such

---

[4]Adapted from C. Starr and R. Taggart, *Biology: The Unity and Diversity of Life,* 9th ed. (Belmont, CA: Wadsworth, 2001), p. 54.

as: "The next thing we're going to talk about is . . . ," "Another reason is . . . ," "What about vision?" and "First of all, . . ." make main points easy to pick out. Listen during your next lecture and see how your professor introduces each main topic. If your professor puts an outline on the board, you may want to copy it into your notebook right away. However, as each main topic comes up during the actual lecture, write it down again in your notes.

DETAILS

After you write the heading in your notes, listen for all details, the points that support each heading the professor presents about that topic. Until you develop more sophisticated note-taking skills, you may want to rely on some of the following tips in deciding which details to include.

➤ Details, facts, or explanations that expand or explain the main points that are mentioned.

➤ Definitions, word for word, especially if your professor repeats them several times.

➤ Enumerations or lists of things that are discussed.

➤ Examples; you don't need to note all details for each example, but you do need to know to which general topic (heading) each example relates.

➤ Anything that is written on the chalkboard, powerpoint slide, or on a transparency (on an overhead projector).

➤ Anything that is repeated or spelled out.

DISCUSSION CLASSES

Most students don't take notes during discussion classes or during those portions of a lecture class that are devoted to discussion. This is a big mistake. Many professors prefer the discussion format when teaching. They could very easily just "tell" students the information, but they prefer to allow the information to emerge through a guided discussion. Even though the material is presented in a different format, however, the information often will still appear on tests.

You can easily take notes on a discussion. Instead of writing down the main heading, write down the question that is posed. Then jot down the various points that are made during the discussion. Remember, it is very important to indicate who made which point in the discussion. The easiest method is to simply write "P" in front of any statement made by the professor and "S" in front of any statement made by a student.

MATH AND SCIENCE CLASSES

Taking notes in math and science classes requires special strategies. The modified-block method probably will be more effective than the outline method because you'll need to include many problems and drawings that are written on the board. You may not think that you need to write down all problems that the professor puts on the board, but you should. Even more important, however, you need to write down what the professor says *about* the problems. Get into the habit of writing the name or type of problem first. Then copy down the problem and take notes on steps to follow, tricky areas, what to do first, and even why you should do it. Think of the explanations about a particular problem or model as minilectures. You may find it helpful to write the problem on the left side of the note page and anything the professor says about it directly across from each step. Listen carefully for the main points and the important details and put them in your notes.

POWERPOINT PRESENTATIONS

Many professors are now using PowerPoint presentations (which incorporate a series of "slides" containing main points, details, diagrams, and examples) to enhance their lectures. In addition to showing each "slide" on a large screen, many of them pass out a paper copy with space for notes to their students. However, there isn't enough space on them to get down all the details. Instead of taking notes on the handout sheet, use it to organize your notes by copying the headings and subheadings into your notes as the professor refers to them. Then listen to what the professor says about the "slide" and take notes. Leave space in your notes to tape in the "slides" showing diagrams or problems (make a note with the name for each).

ACTIVITY 8.5   *Practice Taking Notes*

Go to the Piaget lecture on the *College Reading and Study Strategies* Web site, which includes the first ten minutes of an actual lecture from an Introductory Psychology class. As you read the lecture, take notes as you usually do. Pretend that it's a real lecture and take the best notes you can. Compare your notes to those of the other members in your group. After you complete this activity, evaluate the quality of your notes.

HOW TO EDIT YOUR NOTES

Taking good lecture notes is only the first step in the note-taking process. After you leave the classroom, you need to edit, revise your notes to correct errors, clarify meaning, make additions, and improve organization. Editing is a fairly easy process once you know how to do it. Early in the semester you may spend a lot of time making corrections or additions to your notes. You may need to reorganize your notes or rewrite them to make them useful. You'll soon benefit from these editing experiences, however, and your ability to take good notes will improve. You'll probably find that by the second half of the semester, you won't need to spend nearly as much time editing, and you can instead devote this time to more active review of your notes.

Editing your notes helps you become a better note taker because you get feedback on the quality of your lecture notes. As you go through your notes to check for accuracy, fill in gaps in information, and improve the organization, you can see where you made mistakes. Without knowing what types of errors you tend to make, you may not make changes in your preparation, attention, or note-taking style. Editing can also benefit you later in the semester. Because most test questions tend to come from lecture notes, it's important that you have a complete, accurate, and well-organized set of notes. Finally, editing provides you with an active review of all of the important information in both your text and notes. This additional repetition (which requires both critical thinking and an active restructuring of the material) helps you reinforce what you read and heard, leading to a better understanding of the material.

Edit your lecture notes within twenty-four hours after the lecture. If you wait much longer, you won't remember the lecture well enough to make any necessary additions or corrections in your notes. Look back at your Fixed Commitment Calendar and set aside a certain time each day to edit and review your lecture notes. In as little as half an hour, you can turn "so-so" notes into excellent notes.

FILL IN THE GAPS

The first thing you should do is read through your notes and fill in any missing information that you can recall from memory. As you read your notes, the lecture will "come back" to you. You may be able to add a few words to further clarify a point, fill in additional details, or even add information that you didn't have time to record during the lecture. Look at Nikki's edited Life Science notes and Todd's edited Accounting notes in Figures 8.6 and 8.7. Both Nikki and Todd added some additional information (shown in

FIGURE 8.6
Nikki's Revised Notes for Life Science

1/22

What are decomposers?

(3) Decomposers
– heterotrophs
– get nourishment from other organisms
– do not have digestive tracts

What are scavengers?

(4) Scavengers
– let something else kill organism
– bacteria that break down dead tissue

What are waste feeders?

(5) Waste feeders
– feed on dung, feces, undigested food
– type of scavenger

What do they feed on?

– have digestive systems
– eat food
   Ex: Egyptian scarab beetles

What is detritus?

detritus – miscellaneous organic material passing by
– mixture of decaying organisms + dung w/partially
   digested food
   Land – mixes w/soil – earthworms/soil insects eat
– May float or settle on bottom

How do filter feeders eat?

(6) Filter feeders
– pass water thru comb-like feeders
– take things floating in water
– may use mouth parts, gills, special limbs

Four types of consumers are decomposers/scavengers, waste feeders, and filter feeders. Detritus is a mixture of decaying organisms + dung along with partially digested food.

FIGURE 8.7

Todd's Edited Notes for Accounting

What are corporations?	Corporations- legal entity having an existence separate and distinct from that of its owners
What rights does an artificial person have?	- Artificial person - same legal rights as a person - can be sued, can sue
Who owns the assets of a corporation?	- assets of corporation belong to a corporation itself, not to stockholders.
What are 5 advantages of a corporation?	Why have a corporation? (Advantages) 1. No personal liability for stockholders 2. Ease of accumulating capital 3. Ownership shares are readily transferable 4. Continuous existence - lives on forever 5. Professional management
What are the limits of risk for stockholders?	- amount of money stockholders risk is limited to the amount of their investment
What are the 3 disadvantages of a corporation?	Disadvantages of having a corporation 1. Heavy taxation - tax twice, when they earn and pay income- double taxation
What is the role of the owner of a corp.?	2. Greater regulation 3. Separation of ownership and control -guy who owns corporation doesn't run it
What is double taxation?	Double taxation - First taxing corporate income and then taxing distributions of that income to stockholders

red) after the lecture. Nikki also added a brief summary of the key information in the bottom margin of her notes.

You also can refer to your textbook to help fill in gaps in your notes. If you still feel your notes are incomplete, you may need to use a friend's notes to expand on the ones you took in class. If you taped the lecture, listen to the recording and fill in the information you weren't able to write down during the lecture.

CHECK FOR ACCURACY

As you go through your notes, you also need to check for accuracy. If you notice some incorrect information in your notes or if you're unsure of the accuracy of some points, check with the professor or a friend or use your textbook to verify whether the information is correct. If you find that some of your information is incorrect, change it. Some students lose points on exams because they have incorrect information in their notes.

Even though they study for the exam, they still get questions wrong because they have been rehearsing inaccurate information.

CLARIFY MEANING

You may find that some of your notes are cryptic or hard to understand. To make your notes more readable and understandable, you may need to expand some abbreviations, finish some words, or correct spelling errors. If you use a lot of abbreviations or shortcuts in note taking, you should try to clarify some of them while you still know what words they represent. For example, if you wrote "priv" in your notes, you may want to add on "ileged" after class, because "priv" is not a common abbreviation and you may become confused about what you meant when you review your notes at a later time.

REWRITE TO IMPROVE ORGANIZATION

You may need to rewrite your notes in order to improve the organization of the information. If you took notes on a lecture that was poorly organized, your notes may be disorganized, too. Even though you may have an accurate record of the information, you may find it difficult to study. By reorganizing the information in your notes, you can clarify the relationship between the main points and the supporting details. You may need to add headings or make the headings that you have in your notes stand out. You can do that by writing the headings next to the margin and then indenting the subordinate points. You also may need to reorganize your notes in order to group together related information. If your professor tends to jump from point to point during the lecture, you may find that information on the same topic is scattered over several pages in your notes. As you rewrite your notes, group these points together under the appropriate heading. Reorganizing and editing your notes will make your notes more useful when you are ready to study for the exam.

ACTIVITY 8.6 *Work Together to Edit Lecture Notes*

Make a copy of the lecture notes that you took earlier this week. Exchange your notes with another member of your group. Ask your classmate to explain the course information to you. How similar was this explanation to the original lecture? What information in your notes needs to be expanded or clarified? Edit your notes. What changes will you make the next time you take notes?

DEVELOP RECALL QUESTIONS

Adding recall questions in the margin helps increase the value of your notes. The process of making up these questions forces you to identify the most important information and later serves as cues to prompt your memory. Recall questions have been added in the margin for the notes in Figure 8.8. Write your question directly across from its "answer." Developing both broad and specific questions will help you learn the information in different ways. Of course, the more questions you write, the more effectively you can use them to study the information in your lecture notes. If you'd like, you can highlight or underline the answer to each question.

ACTIVITY   8.7   *Develop Recall Questions*

Download and print the enlarged copy of the lecture notes from the lecture on Intellectual Development from the *College Reading and Study Strategies* Web site. After you review the notes, write as many recall questions for the important information as space permits. Compare your questions with those of the other members of your group.

FIGURE 8.8

Example Using Recall Questions

	Impact of Computers on Society	9/14
What are the four ways computers extend the mind and body?	Extends capacity of human body & mind — Thru imaging, robotics, processing, memory.	
What is Feasibly Finite?	Extends the boundaries of "Feasibly Finite" — Limits of what we can do — Acceleration in the rate of change	
Who wrote Future Shock?	— Alvin Toffler "Future Shock"	
How do computers work with the global village?	The Global Village – Marshall McLuhan — Extends communication around globe — World conflict awareness – stock market – business & trade – advances in research	

Explain "High Tech-High Touch"
What are five ways computers bring us closer to others?
	Emphasis on education in an info. age
	— "High tech – high touch" — John Naisbitt
	— tech brings us closer to others
	    communication – medicine – retail – manufacturing –
	    home shopping	

What are some computing inequities?	Computing Inequities — women & minorities get less opportun to work w/computers.	

What are some computing crimes?	Concepts & Crime
	— Theft
	    phone fraud – credit cards
	— privacy invasion
	— software piracy
	    hacking & cracking	

HOW TO REVIEW YOUR NOTES

Reviewing your notes is the final step in the note-taking process. Even though editing your notes provides you with a review of the lecture material, reviewing daily, weekly, and before an exam all help you master the information in your notes and prepare for exams. After you edit your notes and complete the recall column, you're ready to review. You can't learn all the information in your notes just by editing or reading over them. You also need to study the information in your notes using more active methods. How you review your notes often determines how much of the information you learn.

WHEN AND WHY YOU SHOULD REVIEW

As you learned in the last chapter, you need to review your lecture notes in order to store the information in your long-term memory. Even though you may have an accurate record of the information presented, you still need to learn it. The best time to review and edit your notes is immediately after the lecture, when the material is still fresh in your mind. You also can review your notes when you're waiting for your next class to begin. You may want to set aside an hour or two each weekend to review the notes that you took in all of your classes during the week. If you've been reviewing daily, you'll need only to test your memory (using the recall questions) during your weekly review. Reviewing your notes frequently during the semester will keep you actively involved in the learning process and will reduce the amount of time you need to study before exams.

THREE WAYS TO REVIEW

The best way to review your notes is to recite the information—to say it out loud. Just reading over your notes is a very passive activity. Reciting also helps because you may learn more by *hearing* information than just by seeing it. Use the recall questions that you created or the headings in your notes to test your memory of the information. This self-testing will let you know whether you really do know the information in your notes.

Recite from the Recall Column

When you think that you know the information in your notes, use the recall questions to test your memory of the main points and supporting details. Put your hand or a piece of paper over your notes so that you can see only the recall questions. Then recite the answers to the questions. If you can't say the answers out loud, you don't really know the material. Use this technique to review the information in your notes on a regular basis. You should perform this kind of active review immediately following the lecture, at the end of the week, and again before the exam.

Recite from the Headings

You also can review your notes by using the headings or topics to prompt your memory. After you review your notes by reciting them aloud, cover the information under each heading and try to recall all points relating to that topic. Try to explain or recite aloud all details you can remember about each of the main topics in your notes. Then check your notes to see whether you missed anything. If you study in a place where you can't recite out loud, you can accomplish the same thing by mumbling quietly to yourself or by writing out the information from memory. Repeat this process until you know all the information in your notes.

Talk About the Information with Others

Another way to study the information in your notes is simply to talk about it. Putting the information in your own words and explaining it to others is an excellent way to move it into long-term memory. Get together with your note-taking buddy or a study group to edit and review your notes. You can take turns discussing the information (be sure you do some of the explaining), predicting test questions, and quizzing each other on the information.

ACTIVITY 8.8   *Recite to Review Your Notes*

Select a set of your notes for review. Recite the information in your notes in order to learn it. Then cover the supporting points with your hand and try to recite them using only the headings as cues. Work on one section until you know it; then go on to the next. Halfway through your notes, switch and use the recall questions to review. Which strategy worked best for you? Why?

ACTIVITY 8.9   *Edit and Review Your Notes*

Choose a set of lecture notes that you took within the last twenty-four hours. Edit them, making any necessary changes or corrections. Also, write down any additional information that you remember. If you know that you are missing specific information, refer to your text or to someone else's notes in order to complete your notes. Finally, add recall questions in the margin and then review your notes. Write a paragraph describing the changes that you made, the type of recall cues that you used, and the method of review that you found most effective. Attach a copy of your original notes and your edited notes.

ACTIVITY 8.10   *Use InfoTrac College Edition to Locate Lecture Information*

Pretend you are preparing a lecture on a topic that you recently studied in one of your classes. If you are using InfoTrac College Edition, locate information on the topic. Since you are planning to locate information on a particular subject, do a subject search in PowerTrac. Change the index to *subject search* and type in your topic after the two-letter index abbreviation. For more information on how to use index abbreviations, use the Help Index on the bar at the top of your screen. Click on the View button to display the list of articles. Locate one or two articles to "write" your lecture. Instead, take notes on the material in an informal outline, block, or modified-block format. Be sure to include meaningful phrases so that you could deliver the lecture using only your notes.

ACTIVITY 8.11   *Where Are You Now?*

Now that you have completed Chapter 8, take a few minutes to repeat the "Where Are You Now?" activity, located on the *College Reading and Study Strategies* Web site. What changes did you make as a result of reading this chapter? How are you planning to apply what you've learned in this chapter?

Summary

Taking good lecture notes in college is critical to your success because the primary mode of instruction for most college professors is the formal lecture. Without an accurate record of information from the lecture, you won't have good information to review before the exam. However, just taking notes doesn't mean that you took good notes. The two most important criteria in evaluating the quality of your notes are the content and the organization. You can improve your note-taking skills by reading the text chapter prior to the lecture. Not only will you pick up background information about the topic but you will also get a sense of how the information is organized. To take good notes, you have to be actively involved in the lecture; you need to be an active listener. Unless you focus your attention on the professor and get actively involved in the lecture, you may miss a great deal of information. Many students get caught up in fancy note-taking systems. Using a simple system such as the informal outline, block, or modified-block will help you focus on the lecture material. These systems involve writing down the main topic (the heading) and then jotting down any information the professor provides about that topic (the details).

After the lecture, edit your notes within twenty-four hours. Recopying your notes to clean them up or make them look nicer is often a waste of time. Unless you're actively involved in evaluating and restructuring your notes, you won't benefit from the editing process. Checking the accuracy of your notes, filling in gaps, creating recall questions, and improving the organization of your notes are all active editing processes. Then review your notes daily, weekly, and before the exam in order to learn the information. Passive studying, like reading over your notes, doesn't help much. Instead, study your notes by reciting out loud from the recall column or from the headings. Talk about the material, explain key points to a friend, or try to reconstruct the lecture from your headings or recall questions.

Review Questions

Terms You Should Know: Make a flash card for each term.

Active listener	Details	Organization
Block method	Edit	Outline method
Content	Headings	Recall questions
Cornell system	Modified-block method	

Completion: Fill in the blank to complete each of the following statements.

1. The most important reason to take lecture notes is to get a(n) _____ record of information.

2. _____ is an active, selective process.

3. Take notes in _____ _____; don't write whole sentences.

4. Writing questions in the _____ provides you with an opportunity to test your memory of your notes.

5. You should edit your notes within _____ _____ of the lecture.

Multiple Choice: Circle the letter of the best answer for each of the following questions. Be sure to underline key words and eliminate wrong answers.

6. You can improve your listening skills in all of the following ways except:
    A. reading along in the text as the professor gives the lecture.
    B. deciding that you want to listen.
    C. controlling your emotional response.
    D. holding yourself accountable for the material presented.

7. Which of the following is not a way to edit your notes?
    A. Recopy your notes to improve the appearance.
    B. Rewrite your notes to fill in missing information.
    C. Rewrite your notes to improve the organization.
    D. Add a recall column to your notes.

Short Answer–Essay: On a separate sheet, answer each of the following questions.

8. What are the key features of the outline, block, and modified-block methods of taking notes?

9. How do students benefit from taking notes?

10. How should students review their lecture notes?

9 Taking Text Notes

In this chapter you will learn more about:

- ➤ Why to take text notes

- ➤ When to take text notes

- ➤ How to take text notes

- ➤ How to review your notes

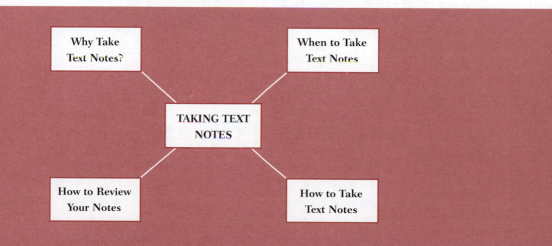

ACTIVITY 9.1   *Where Are You Now?*

Take a few minutes to answer *yes* or *no* to the following questions.

		YES	NO
1.	Do you take notes on textbook material after you've highlighted the chapter or section?	_____	_____
2.	Do you take text notes when you read the chapter for the first time?	_____	_____
3.	Do you read the whole paragraph before you begin to take notes?	_____	_____
4.	Do you evaluate your text notes after an exam?	_____	_____
5.	Do you usually copy information from the text in the same wording that the author used in the book?	_____	_____
6.	Do you recite your text notes when you review for an exam?	_____	_____
7.	Do you create concept maps when you take notes on the textbook material?	_____	_____
8.	Are your text notes a good summary of the text material?	_____	_____
9.	Do you tend to write down only key words when you take notes?	_____	_____
10.	Do you predict questions about the important information in your text?	_____	_____

Total Points   _____

Give yourself 1 point for each *yes* answer to questions 1, 3, 4, 6, 7, 8, and 10 and 1 point for each *no* answer to questions 2, 5, and 9. Now total up your points. A low score indicates that you need some help in taking notes on text material. A high score indicates that you are already using many good note-taking strategies.

WHY TAKE TEXT NOTES?

Taking notes on text material is the most effective method for becoming an active reader. Note taking keeps you actively involved in the text material. It also helps you condense the information that you'll need to review before the exam. Finally, taking text notes allows you to develop a system of organization that is distinctly yours—a system that you design and that makes sense to you. This activity helps you clarify the meaning of the material and aids in your retention and retrieval of information.

PROMOTES ACTIVE READING

Taking text notes keeps you actively involved as you read because you know you'll have to write something down. This can help keep you alert and focused on the material. Note taking keeps you involved in what the author is saying because you have to make decisions about what's important—you need to identify both the main points and the supporting details. One of the keys to taking good text notes is writing the information in your own words (as much as possible) in a format that's easy to study and remember. You have to think about the material, decide what's important, "translate" what the author is saying into words that make sense to you, and restructure the information in a new, easier-to-learn format. As you take text notes you increase your involvement with the text material and strengthen your memory of it.

IMPROVES YOUR COMPREHENSION

Note taking also improves your comprehension of the material. To write the information in your own words, you have to analyze what the author has said and relate it to what you already know about the topic. This interaction with the text increases your level of comprehension of the material and your understanding of the concepts and ideas that are presented. Reading, thinking about the material, and then writing it in your own words also gives you more repetition on the material. This built-in review of the important information helps you understand it better. If you've already used the S-RUN-R reading/study system, which was described in Chapter 4, you know that the note-taking step helps to reinforce the important information in the material.

MONITORS YOUR COMPREHENSION

Note taking can also serve as an excellent comprehension monitoring system. Note taking provides you with feedback about how well you're concentrating on and understanding what you're reading. If you can't recall the important points to write down, you may not have been reading actively—you may have been daydreaming or thinking about something else. In addition, if you can't put the information into your own words, it could be a signal that you didn't really understand what you just read. You may need to reread the material or ask your professor, teaching assistant, or tutor to explain the information in that section. Keeping tabs on your reading can help you stay focused on the material as you read and can let you know when comprehension has broken down.

CONDENSES THE INFORMATION

Another reason for taking notes on textbook material is to condense the information for later review. You can condense the text material by writing the material in meaningful phrases or by creating a visual display of the information. If you take text notes, you won't have to read the chapter again when you prepare for an exam. As you condense the material, you also have an opportunity to organize it in a way that makes sense to you. Your text notes, like your edited lecture notes, will provide you with a condensed version of the important information that you need to learn.

ORGANIZES THE INFORMATION

Unlike highlighting or underlining, taking text notes allows you to restructure and organize the information in a way that makes sense to you. When you highlight or underline your textbook, you're still operating inside the author's organizational structure. When you take notes, however, you can create an organizational structure of your own. Some note-taking strategies also force you to restructure the material in ways that show the relationships within the material. If you use some of the concept mapping and charting techniques described later in the chapter, you can organize the information into a visual display that clearly shows how the information is connected. This adds additional cues that can lead to improved memory of the material.

ACTIVITY 9.2   *Why Do You Take Text Notes?*

Think about why you take text notes. Do you take notes in all of your texts or just in certain ones? How does taking text notes help you the most? Jot your responses in the margin or on notebook paper.

WHEN TO TAKE TEXT NOTES

There are benefits to taking notes at different points in your reading and study of the textbook. You can take notes when you first read the chapter, after the lecture, at the end of the week, or before the exam.

AS YOU READ THE CHAPTER

Some students take notes as they read the chapter instead of highlighting or underlining. Although it's a more active method, note taking is very time-consuming. If you try to take notes the first time you read the chapter, you may find that you write down more information than you'll need. After all, all the information will be new to you, and everything may seem important. If you highlight the text when you first read it and then take notes afterward, you'll save time and have a better set of text notes. If you're using the S-RUN-R reading/study system, for example, you already may have discovered that taking notes after highlighting or underlining helps you condense the information even more.

AFTER THE LECTURE

Taking text notes right after the lecture has several advantages. You can condense the information in the text while editing your lecture notes. If your professor's lectures follow the text fairly closely, you can fill in information that you may have missed during the lecture and at the same time note important points that were never touched on in class. Taking notes after the lecture saves you time, since you don't have to write down all the material that also appears in your lecture notes. It's not a good idea, though, to add all the additional text information to your lecture notes. If your professor tests mainly on lecture material, you want to spend more time studying that material. Instead, write your text notes in another notebook or on looseleaf notebook paper so that you can lay your text notes and your lecture notes out side by side when you're studying.

AT THE END OF THE WEEK

You may find that taking text notes at the end of the week serves as a good way of reviewing the information that you read (and marked) and that you took notes on during the lecture. At the end of the week, the material probably will be more familiar to you because you've had a chance to read, listen, discuss, edit your lecture notes, and think about the information. At that point, you should be able to take more selective and more organized notes on the text material.

WHEN YOU PREPARE FOR THE EXAM

Another good time to take your text notes is when you're preparing for your exam. Instead of just reading over the highlighted or underlined text material, take notes on it. As you know, just reading without some form of marking is a passive activity that results in little actual learning. By the time you're ready to prepare for the exam, you already may have learned a lot of the information that you originally highlighted or underlined. Not only will you save time by waiting to take notes, but you'll also benefit from the active review that requires you to determine what you still need to learn. Writing down this information will help you learn it, and allows you to condense what you need to study for the exam. Of course, you still need to practice the information in your notes to learn it.

ACTIVITY 9.3 *Take Notes at Different Times*

During the next week of classes, experiment with taking notes at different times. Try taking notes on one part of a text chapter as you first read the chapter. Then take notes on a different part of the chapter after the lecture.

Finally, wait until the end of the week and take notes on another section of the chapter. Note the time it took you to complete each task. What did you find? Which set of notes do you think is most useful? Why?

HOW TO TAKE TEXT NOTES

There are many different ways to take notes on text material. Some of the more useful methods are annotating the text, outlining, and taking block or modified-block notes. You may also find that mapping and charting text material helps you learn and recall it more effectively than written notes. In this section, you'll learn how to use each of these note-taking techniques. Try each method as you do your own reading. Then decide which one works best for you.

ANNOTATE THE TEXT

If you have wide margins in your textbook, you may find that annotating (adding comments or summary notes) your text may help you improve your comprehension as you read and prepare your text for later study. Some students like to make notes in the margin as they read. These marginal notes help you focus your reading and can serve as recall cues for your highlighting. Other students prefer to predict questions (formulate questions about the important information that they highlighted). These questions can also help you improve your comprehension of the text material and, at the same time, prepare the text for later review.

Make Marginal Notes

As you mark, you also may want to add marginal notes, summary statements in the margin of the text. These notes can summarize information presented in the selection. You can also make notes to indicate that you agree or disagree with a point that the author made. You can put a question mark in the margin to indicate that you don't understand something or would like to

FIGURE 9.1

Example of Highlighted Text with Marginal Notes

WHY ARE THE OCEANS IMPORTANT?

Earth = "Ocean"

As landlubbers, we tend to think of Earth in terms of land, but Earth is largely a water planet. A more accurate name for the planet would be Ocean, because salt-water oceans cover more than 71 percent of its surface.

"O" → survival of all life

The oceans play key roles in the survival of virtually all life on Earth. Because of their size and currents, the oceans mix and dilute many human-produced wastes flowing or dumped into them to less harmful or even harmless levels, as long as they are not overloaded. Oceans also play a major role in regulating Earth's climate by distributing solar heat through ocean currents and by evaporation as part of the global hydrologic cycle. They also partic-ipate in other important nutrient cycles.

1. dilute waste

2. regulate climate

3. regulate temp

By serving as a gigantic reservoir for carbon dioxide, oceans help regulate the temperature of the troposphere. Oceans provide habitats for about 250,000 species of marine plants and animals, which are food for many organisms, including human beings. They also supply us with iron, sand, gravel, phosphates, magnesium, oil, natural gas, and many other valuable resources.

4. habitat ≈ 250,000 species

5. source nat. resources

---

ask about it in class, or use a star to indicate that the professor hinted that something would be on the test. Making brief notes in the margin will help increase your level of interaction with the text. However, don't overdo it. If you try to copy all the important information in the margin, you're defeating the purpose of marking. The marginal notes in Figure 9.1 summarize the main points made in the selection.

ACTIVITY 9.4 *Annotate Your Text*

Go back to the section on When to Take Text Notes that you just read and make marginal notes in the margin of the text. Then go to the *College Reading and Study Strategies* book-specific Web site and download the sample marginal notes. Compare your notes with the sample notes. Did you have the same information?

Predict Quiz Questions

After you finish reading and marking your text chapter, you can go back and review the important information by predicting and writing quiz questions in the margin. You can use these same questions to review for exams, of course, but they will provide you with an excellent way to reinforce and learn the information before you even walk into class for the lecture or for a quiz.

FIGURE 9.2

Example of Predicted Questions

STEP 2: Write question

What are the six characteristics of goals?

STEP 3: Underline answer

Why should goals be self chosen?

What happens if goals are too challenging?

What factor can help you determine how challenging to make your goals?

What are moderately challenging goals?

What is another word for realistic?

What is an example of an unrealistic goal?

STEP 1: Identify information

CHARACTERISTICS OF GOALS

To be both useful and motivating, the goals you set must have some important characteristics. Your goals should be self-chosen, moderately challenging, realistic, measurable, specific, and positive.

1. **Goals should be self-chosen.** Goals that are set by your parents, teachers, or friends may not always work for you. You need to determine or choose your own goals; *you* need to decide what you want to accomplish. If you set your own goals, you will be more motivated to achieve them.

2. **Goals should be moderately challenging.** You probably were told to set high or even exceptionally high goals for yourself in college; you may have been told to "shoot for the stars" or "go for straight As." In fact, this may not be the best advice. If your goal is to achieve all As during your first semester in college, you may be disappointed. As soon as you "lose your A" in one class, you may feel that you failed to achieve your goal, and you may be tempted to give up.

   One way to set moderately challenging goals is to consider what you have done in the past. Of course, everyone is different, but high school grades are fairly good predictors of college success. Why were you successful in some classes yet unsuccessful in others? You may have been more motivated, so you may have worked harder. Of course, if you didn't work very hard in high school, you can do better in college if you choose to apply yourself; study skills can make a big difference. Even so, you should set goals that are moderately challenging—goals that will require you to achieve more than you did before but will not place undue pressure on you. Goals can always be revised if you discover you can achieve more than you originally set out to accomplish.

3. **Goals should be realistic.** Think about whether your goals are attainable. It would be unrealistic to expect to get a B or better in Calculus if your math background is very weak and your high school grades in math were never higher than a C. To set realistic goals, you must carefully evaluate your chances of achieving each goal. Using the five-step approach to setting goals (discussed later in this chapter) can help you make this decision.

There are three basic steps involved in predicting quiz questions. First, go back and reread the highlighted material for the first paragraph and identify an important point that you want to remember. (See Step 1 in Figure 9.2.) Next, turn it into a question and write it directly across from the information, in the margin of the textbook (see Step 2). Be sure you write questions that have stated answers in the text and not *yes* or *no* answers. Next, underline the answer to the question in your text (see Step 3). After you finish reading, go back and quiz yourself by covering the text material and reciting the answers from memory (Step 4).

The more questions that you write, the more repetition you get on the material and the more you can test your learning. It's a good idea to write both broad and narrow questions. Write a broad question for each heading or subheading and then as many specific questions as you can in the space available. If your text doesn't have wide margins, you can still use this strategy. Write the questions on a long strip of paper (about 3 inches wide), which you can line up with the top of the text page. Keep the question strip in the text on that page for later review (note the page number on each strip). You can also write each question on the front of an index card and the answer on the back (note the page number on the back, too).

Predicting quiz questions in the margin of your text provides you with at least three more interactions with the text material. You reread the highlighted material, think about its importance, turn it into a question, and then underline the answer. Of course, when you use the questions to check your learning, you're getting even more practice with the material. When I ask my students at the end of the semester to list the one strategy that they think has helped them the most, more than twenty-five percent list predicting quiz questions.

ACTIVITY 9.5 *Predict Quiz Questions*

Read and highlight the text material in Figure 9.3 from a Political science textbook. Predict and write quiz questions in the margin of the text and then underline the answer to each. Compare your marking, questions, and underlined answers to those of others in your group. How closely did your marking match that of the others in the group? How many of your questions were the same or similar to those of the others in the group? Did you understand and remember the information better than the material that you marked in one of your own textbooks? Take turns quizzing each other on the material. Did you know most of the answers to your questions?

FIGURE 9.3
Political Science Excerpt

Source: From S. Schmidt, M. Shelley, and B. Bardes, *American Government and Politics Today,* 2001–2002 ed. (Belmont, CA: Wadsworth, 2001), pp. 326–328.

The Electors' Commitment

If a plurality of voters in a state chooses one slate of electors, then those elec-tors are pledged to cast their ballots on the first Monday after the second Wednesday in December in the state capital for the presidential and vice presidential candidates for the winning party. The Constitution does not, however, require the electors to cast their ballots for the candidate of their party.

The ballots are counted and certified before a joint session of Congress early in January. The candidates who receive a majority of the electoral votes (270) are certified as president-elect and vice president–elect. According to the Constitution, in cases in which no candidate receives a majority of the electoral votes, the election of the president is decided in the House from among the candidates with the three highest number of votes (decided by a plurality of each state delegation), each state having one vote. The selection of the vice president is determined by the Senate in a choice between the two highest candidates, each senator having one vote. Congress was required to choose the president and vice president in 1801 (Thomas Jefferson and Aaron Burr), and the House chose the president in 1825 (John Quincy Adams).

Continued

It is possible for a candidate to become president without obtaining a majority of the popular vote. There have been numerous minority presidents in our history, including Abraham Lincoln, Woodrow Wilson, Harry Truman, John F. Kennedy, Richard Nixon (in 1968), and Bill Clinton. Such an event can always occur when there are third-party candidates.

Perhaps more distressing is the possibility of a candidate's being elected when the opposing candidate receives a larger share of the popular vote. This occurred on three occasions—in the elections of John Quincy Adams in 1824, Rutherford B. Hayes in 1876, and Benjamin Harrison in 1888, all of whom won elections without obtaining a plurality of the popular vote.

Criticisms of the Electoral College

Besides the possibility of a candidate's becoming president even though his or her major opponent obtains more popular votes, there are other complaints about the electoral college. The idea of the Constitution's framers was to have electors use their own discretion to decide who would make the best president. But electors no longer perform the selecting function envisioned by the founders, because they are committed to the candidate who has a plurality of popular votes in their state in the general election.

One can also argue that the current system, which gives all of the electoral votes to the candidate who has a statewide plurality, is unfair to other candidates and their supporters. The current system of voting also means that presidential campaigning will be concentrated in those states that have the largest number of electoral votes and in those states in which the outcome is likely to be close. All of the other states generally get second-class treatment during the presidential campaign.

It can also be argued that there is something of a less-populous-state bias in the electoral college, because including Senate seats in the electoral vote total partly offsets the edge of the more populous states in the House. A state such as Alaska (with two senators and one representative) gets an electoral vote for roughly each 183,000 people (based on the 1990 census), whereas Iowa gets one vote for each 397,000 people, and New York has a vote for every 545,000 inhabitants.

Proposed Reforms

Many proposals for reform of the electoral college system have been advanced. The most obvious is to get rid of it completely and simply allow candidates to be elected on a popular-vote basis; in other words, have a direct election, by the people, for president and vice president. This was proposed as a constitutional amendment by President Jimmy Carter in 1977, but it failed to achieve the required two-thirds majority in the Senate in a 1979 vote. An earlier effort in 1969 passed the House but was defeated in the Senate due to the efforts of senators from less populous states and the South.

A less radical reform is a federal law that would require each elector to vote for the candidate who has a plurality in the state. Another system would eliminate the electors but retain the electoral vote, which would be given on a proportional basis rather than on a unit (winner-take-all) basis. This method was endorsed by President Richard Nixon in 1969.

The major parties are not in favor of eliminating the electoral college, fearing that it would give minor parties a more influential role. Also, less populous states are not in favor of direct election of the president, because they feel they would be overwhelmed by the large urban vote.

TAKE WRITTEN NOTES

Taking written notes is probably the most common method that students use for taking notes on text material. If you don't have wide margins or if you like to organize text information in ways that make it easier for you to learn and remember, you may find that taking notes outside of the textbook works best for you. You can take your notes on sheets of paper or on index cards—some students prefer one instead of the other. Like lecture notes, you may find that the outline method or the modified-block method works well for you. Since you have the time to read, highlight, think, and then take notes, you could also summarize some types of information. You'll learn more about how to write summaries in chapter 15.

ACTIVITY ▶ 9.6 *Take Written Text Notes*

Refer to the text excerpt "Understanding Job Satisfaction," available on the *College Reading and Study Strategies* Web site. Take written notes on the first two pages on notebook paper. Then compare your notes with those of one or two of your classmates. What do you think of the notes you took? Do they contain the important information? Are they well organized? Are they easy to study from?

Outlining

One popular method of taking notes on text material is outlining. If you want to use formal outlining to take your notes, you can use the author's organization to structure your notes. Refer to the table of contents at the beginning of the book to find the main headings to use in your outline. These may be the chapter subdivisions or the main headings. Use Roman numerals (I, II, III, IV, and so on) for them in your outline.

Read and mark the first section in the chapter. Then write down the heading and use a capital letter (A, B, C, D) to indicate that it's a main point in your outline. Go back and jot down any other important information that you want to include. Number these points using Arabic numerals (1, 2, 3, and so on). If you wish, you can further break down your outline and indicate subpoints with lowercase letters (a, b, c).

Although formal outlining is useful, informal outlining is more efficient for taking notes (Figure 9.4). If you've been using the outline method for taking lecture notes, you already are familiar with the basic format for informally outlining text material. When you take notes on your text, you can rely on the author's organization or you can create your own. You can use the chapter subdivisions as your main points. You don't have to use every heading as a main point; some of them may be combined or omitted. Write the heading next to the left margin, go to the next line, and then indent to indicate supporting information. You don't need to use any numbers or letters in your informal outline. Don't forget, your outline will be much more helpful if you write meaningful phrases instead of copying entire sentences.

FIGURE 9.4
*Sample Notes in Informal
Outline Form*

```
                    Benthic Communities
    Rocky Intertidal Communities
            Intertidal zone
                    land between highest and lowest marshes
                    hundreds of species
            Problems living there
                    wave shock — force of crashing waves
                    temperature change
                    ice grinding against shoreline
                        higher altitudes
                    intense sunlight
                        in tropics
            Reasons for diversity
                    large quantities of food available
                        strong currents keep nutrients stirred
                    large number of habitats available
                        high, salty splash pools
                    cool, dark crevices
                    provide hiding places
                        rest places
                        attachment sites
                        mating nooks
```

ACTIVITY 9.7 *Take Notes in Outline Form*

Work as a group to take notes. Use the remaining pages of the text excerpt from Activity 9.6 to generate a set of text notes using either formal or informal outlining. What differences do you notice in your notes this time?

Block Notes

Some students prefer using the block method described earlier in Chapter 8 for taking text notes. If you already are using the block method to take lecture notes, you may want to use it to take your text notes. The block method, however, may not be the best method for taking text notes. It works well for lecture notes because it is fast. But speed is not an issue when taking text notes. If you're a visual learner, you may have difficulty picturing the information in your notes because the information is crowded together, rather than spaced out in an easy-to-recall format.

Modified-Block Notes

The modified-block method may be even more effective because you list all the important details directly under each other. Some students put a dash in front of each meaningful phrase, whereas others simply indent the list slightly. Look at the sample of modified-block notes in Figure 9.5. The information is well organized and includes sufficient detail to make it useful for later study. If there are too many details to list under just one heading, you can create additional headings or subheadings to organize the material in a way that makes it easier to study and learn.

FIGURE 9.5
Sample Notes in Modified-Block Form

Levels of Depression

Depressive Episodes
— mildest form
— lasts several weeks or several months
— little pleasure — feel empty or worthless
— headaches, difficulty sleeping
— comes & goes without warning
— triggered by death or simple things
   (schedule change)
Dysthymic Disorder
— psychotic depression
— thought disorder
— more severe — can last a year or more
— occasional delusions
— psychomotor skills very slow
— no energy — want to stay in bed
— low risk of suicide but can be dangerous
— few friends, lonely, alone at home
Bipolar Disorder
— manic depression
— fluctuate back and forth
— similar to dysthymic but with manic
   episodes that alternate with depression
— manic episodes cause high energy
— thoughts flow quickly, get confused
— disappears (seems to) periodically

ACTIVITY **9.8** *Take Written Text Notes*

Refer to the text selection "The Code of Hammurabi" in Figure 9.6. Ask each member of your group to take text notes using one of the following formats: outline, block, or modified-block. Then compare the information in your notes. Which method do you prefer?

FIGURE 9.6

Excerpt from a History Text

Text material from W. Duiker and J. Spielvogel, *World History,* 3d ed. (Comprehensive Volume). (Belmont, CA: Wadsworth, 2001), pp. 11–12.

THE CODE OF HAMMURABI

Hammurabi is best remembered for his law code, a collection of 282 laws (see the box on p. 12). For centuries, laws had regulated people's relationships with one another in the lands of Mesopotamia, but only fragments of these earlier codes survive. Hammurabi's collection provides considerable insight into almost every aspect of everyday life there and provides us a priceless glimpse of the values of this early society.

The Code of Hammurabi reveals a society with a system of strict justice. Penalties for criminal offenses were severe and varied according to the social class of the victim. A crime against a member of the upper class (a noble) by a member of the lower class (a commoner) was punished more severely than the same offense against a member of the lower class. Moreover, the principle of retaliation ("an eye for an eye, a tooth for a tooth") was fundamental to this system of justice. It was applied in cases where members of the upper class committed crimes against their social equals. For crimes against members of the lower classes, a money payment was made instead.

Hammurabi's code took seriously the responsibilities of public officials. The governor of an area and city officials were expected to catch burglars. If they failed to do so, officials in the district where the crime was committed had to replace the lost property. If murderers were not found, the officials had to pay a fine to the relatives of the victim. Soldiers were likewise expected to fulfill their duties and responsibilities for the order and maintenance of the state. If a soldier hired a substitute to fight for him, he was put to death, and the substitute was given control of his estate.

The law code also furthered the proper performance of work with what virtually amounted to consumer protection laws. Builders were held responsible for the buildings they constructed. If a house collapsed and caused the death of the owner, the builder was put to death. If the collapse caused the death of the son of the owner, the son of the builder was put to death. If goods were destroyed by the collapse, they had to be replaced and the house itself reconstructed at the builder's expense.

The number of laws in Hammurabi's code dedicated to land tenure and commerce reveals the importance of agriculture and trade in the Mesopotamian economy. Numerous laws dealt with questions of landholding, such as the establishment of conditions for renting farmland and the division of produce between tenants and their landlords. Laws concerning land use and irrigation were especially strict, an indication of the danger of declining crop yields if the lands were used incompetently. Commercial activity was also carefully regulated. Rates of interest on loans were watched closely. If the lender raised his rate of interest after a loan was made, he lost the entire amount of the loan. The Code of Hammurabi even specified the precise wages of laborers and artisans, such as brick makers and jewelers.

The largest category of laws in the Code of Hammurabi focused on marriage and the family. Parents arranged marriages for their children. After marriage, the parties involved signed a marriage contract; without it, no one was considered legally married. While the husband provided a bridal payment, the woman's parents were responsible for a dowry to the new husband.

As in many patriarchal societies, women possessed far fewer privileges and rights in the married relationship than men. A woman's place was in the home, and failure to fulfill her expected duties was grounds for divorce. If she was not able to bear children, her husband could divorce her, but he did have to return the dowry to her family. If a wife tried to leave home to engage in business, thus neglecting her house, her husband could divorce her and did not have to repay the dowry. Furthermore, a wife who was a "gad-about,...neglecting her house [and] humiliating her husband" could be drowned. We do know that in practice not all women remained at home. Some worked in business and were especially prominent in the running of taverns.

Women were guaranteed some rights, however. If a woman was divorced without good reason, she received the dowry back. A woman could seek divorce and get her dowry back if her husband was unable to show that she had done anything wrong. In theory, a wife was guaranteed use of her husband's legal property in the event of his death. The mother could also decide which of her sons would receive an inheritance.

Sexual relations were strictly regulated as well. Husbands, but not wives, were permitted sexual activity outside marriage. A wife caught committing adultery was pitched into the river, although her husband could ask the king to pardon her. Incest was strictly forbidden. If a father had incestuous relations with his daughter, he would be banished. Incest between a son and mother resulted in both being burned.

Fathers ruled their children as well as their wives. Obedience was duly expected: "If a son has struck his father, they shall cut off his hand." If a son committed a serious enough offense, his father could disinherit him, although fathers were not permitted to disinherit their sons arbitrarily.

Use Note Cards to Organize Your Text Notes

Some students prefer to take notes on index cards rather than on notebook paper. As you'll see in later chapters, note cards or index cards can be used for many study techniques. They're especially effective for taking notes, though, because they make it easy to organize information and they are so easy to carry around. You can use note cards to organize all the important information on one particular heading or topic.

Write the heading at the top of the card and then jot down any important supporting information that you want to review. You may want to write a summary of the text material or take notes in outline or modified-block format. Look at the sample note card in Figure 9.7, which contains modified-block notes.

If you do take notes on index cards, you may also find it helpful to write recall questions on the back of each note card. By doing this, you're reinforcing the important information and, at the same time, creating a set of self-test question cards for later review.

CREATE CONCEPT MAPS

Maps are visual displays of text information. They are a way of organizing the key information in the text into easy-to-read and easy-to-remember pictures or diagrams. Although there are many different types of concept maps, only *line maps, hierarchical maps,* and *semantic webs* will be described in this chapter. You may find that mapping is a great way to take notes. When you take exams, this strategy may help you recall the information that you learned because of the way you organized it. You may also find you see a picture of it in your mind or remember how you set it up.

Line or Wheel Maps

One of the easiest types of maps to create is the line or wheel map. A line map is a visual display of information drawn by adding lines or spokes that radiate out from a central hub. You already may be familiar with time lines from history class. To create a line map for other types of text material, write the topic in the center of the paper and then add subordinate points on lines that radiate up, down, or out from it. Add supporting details by inserting lines that extend out from the previous lines. Many students like using line maps because they provide more space to write meaningful phrases.

FIGURE 9.7
Sample Note Card

Further Evolution

Paleozoic Period
- Major geologic events
- Led to effects on evolution of life
- Gondwana & Laurasia → Pangea
- Rest of surface covered by Tethys Sea

Collision of landmasses
- habitats lost
- diversity of life declined
- reduced # species of marine animals by 96% (240 m yrs ago)
- led to changes in climate & currents, which affected all lifeforms

Although they seem easy to create, it's also easy to make mistakes when designing your line map. First, don't turn the paper as you draw the lines. You want the information to be written horizontally across the paper so that you can easily study and learn it. If you turn the paper, you may find that half of your information is upside down when you're ready to study. There's also a tendency to simply list all of the details on individual lines that extend directly from the heading. For texts that contain only a few details this is fine. However, some text material is so detailed that you could have fifteen or twenty lines all connected to one heading.

Instead, you need to create subheadings as you map the text information. The subheadings organize the information, separate the details into easier-to-remember chunks, and serve as additional cues to help you learn and retrieve the information. Christy created her own subheadings to better organize the text material (Figure 9.8). Take a few minutes and read a portion of the text excerpt "Gender stratification," available on the *College Reading and Study Strategies* Web site that Christy used to create her map. As you will see, the author did not include the subheadings food source, social practices, and technology. You may have also noticed that Christy made some notes on the introductory material from the text at the top of her map. As you create your own line maps to take notes on text material, feel free to move outside of the author's organizational structure and create one that will make your map a well-organized study tool.

Hierarchical Maps

One of the most common forms of maps is the hierarchical map. Hierarchical maps or arrays (that you read about in Chapter 4) provide a top-down display of information. You often see this form of map in science texts in the form of flowcharts or process charts. To create a hierarchical map, write the topic at the top of the page and put a box around it. Then draw lines to indicate the subdivisions (the headings) and write and box each of them. You can then further divide each of these points into one or more subheadings and then add supporting details. Look at Figure 9.9, the hierarchical map that Wendy developed from the text material from a Special Education textbook. Look for the excerpt entitled "Chemically Dependent Youth" on the *College Reading and Study Strategies* Web site. You can see the natural progression from the main topic of the selection down to the supporting details.

Semantic Webs

One of the newest styles of mapping is the Semantic Web. Instead of using a top-down display, as in the hierarchical map, Semantic Webs radiate from a central focal point. There are four main components in a semantic web: the Core Question or Concept, the Web Strands, the Strand Supports, and the Strand Ties. The Core Question or Concept is the main focus of the text chapter or section. It may be the title of an article or chapter or the heading of the section that you decide to map. To start your web, write this word, phrase, or question in the center of a piece of paper and draw a circle or oval around it. The second component, the Web Strands, show the main ideas that describe the Core Concept. They are the main points that the author makes about the topic. In written notes, they would be the headings. They are joined to the Core Concept by lines that radiate from it. Circle each main point as well. The Strand Supports do just what their title implies; they support the Web Strands. They include the details that support the Web Strands. Finally, the Strand Ties are words or phrases that are written on the lines that

FIGURE 9.8

Christy's Line Map

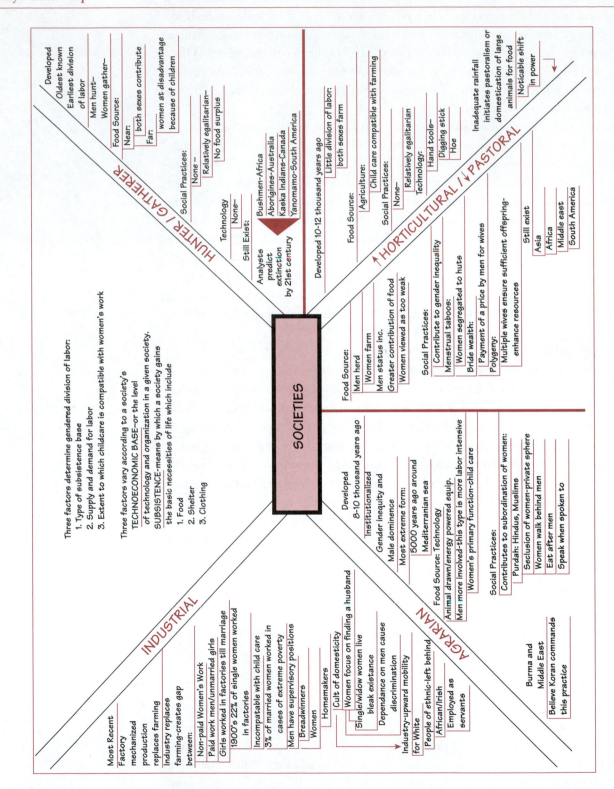

FIGURE 9.9
Wendy's Hierarchical Map

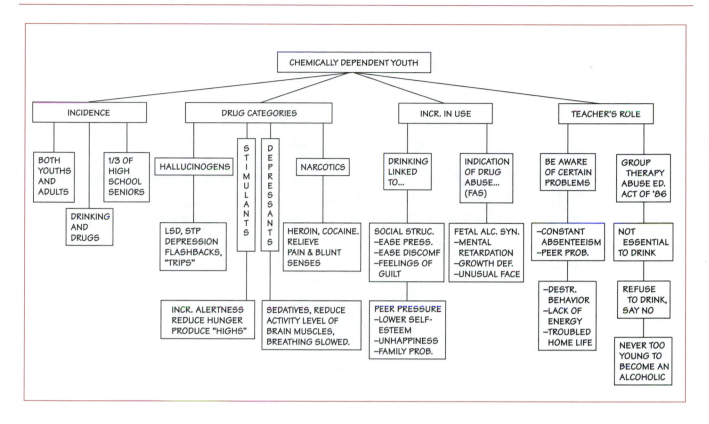

connect some of the information. They define the relationships between some of the Web Strands or Strand Supports.[1]

Look at Figure 9.10, the Semantic Web that Kelly produced for the "Chemically Dependent Youth" selection. Can you locate each of the components mentioned above? First, what is the Core Concept? If you look at the center of Kelly's web, you'll see that she used the phrase "Drug Categories." It also is easy to find the four Web Strands because Kelly used double lines to connect them to the center focal point. You may have noticed that Kelly used several levels of Strand Supports. She moved from "Narcotics" (a Web Strand) to "Examples" (a Strand Support) to "marijuana" (a detail supporting the Strand Support). Even though this last level of support was not in the "rules" for how to construct a semantic web, Kelly felt that the text information demanded further division. Don't leave out information you think is important just because it doesn't fit the formula for a particular type of map. Instead, adapt the mapping technique to fit your text material. You can have second-level, third-level, and fourth-level strand supports if the text demands it. You may have noticed that Kelly didn't add Strand Ties to her map. She could have written "used to" on the line between "Narcotics" and "relieve pain," or "leads to" on the line that connects "Narcotics" to "blunt senses."

You may also find that color coding your maps can help you recall the information. Color coding will work on any type of map, but it's especially effective for Semantic Webs

---

[1]Adapted from G. Freeman and E. G. Reynolds, "Enriching Basal Reader Lessons with Semantic Webbing," *The Reading Teacher* 33 (1980): 677–684.

FIGURE 9.10
Kelly's Semantic Map

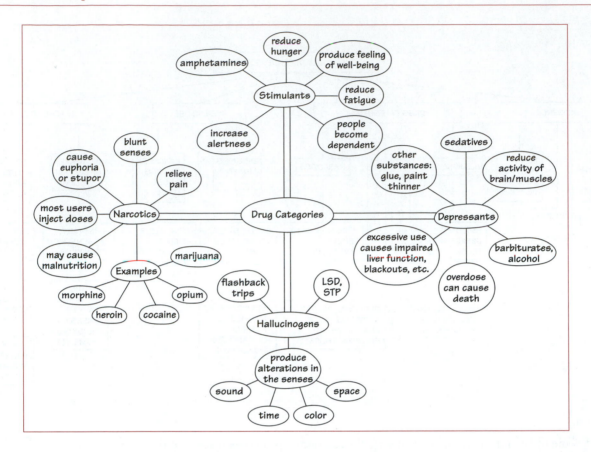

because you create "clusters" of information for each of the main ideas in the text material. You can either draw the ovals in color or use a highlighter or colored pencil to fill in each portion of the map. For example, you could color code all of the information related to narcotics orange, stimulants red, depressants blue, and hallucinogens green. Using a different color for each of the clusters in your map helps separate the details and provides you with an additional cue to trigger your memory of the material. It's important to use light colors if you're going to shade the information that you write—you still want to be able to read it clearly. For some material, you may find that the colors you choose are related to the material itself, providing even more associations with it.

ACTIVITY 9.9 *Experiment with Mapping Techniques*

Using the text material on Desert Biomes in Figure 9.11, work as a group to take text notes. First, highlight the text material and decide which type of map you plan to use. Then decide which important points you should include in the map. Also, create a set of headings and subheadings to better organize the material. Once you know what you want to include in your map, ask each group member to create a line map, a Semantic Web, or a hierarchical map. Compare your map to the others to evaluate the organizational structure and the content you included. Which method do you think will work best for you?

FIGURE 9.11

Excerpt from an Environmental Science Text

Text material from: G. Tyler Miller, Jr., *Living in the Environment,* 11th ed. (Pacific Grove, CA: Brooks/Cole, 2000). pp. 168–171.

7-3   Desert Biomes

What Are the Major Types of Deserts? A **desert** is an area where evaporation exceeds precipitation. Precipitation is typically less than 25 centimeters (10 inches) a year and is often scattered unevenly throughout the year. Deserts have sparse, widely spaced, mostly low vegetation, with the density of plants determined primarily by the frequency and amount of precipitation.

Deserts cover about 30% of the earth's land, and are situated mainly between tropical and subtropical regions north and south of the equator, at about 30° north and 30° south latitude (Figure 7-11). In these areas, air that has lost its moisture over the tropics falls back toward the earth (Figure 7-6). The largest deserts are in the interiors of continents, far from moist sea air and moisture-bearing winds. Other, more local deserts form on the downwind sides of mountain ranges because of the rain shadow effect (Figure 7-10).

The baking sun warms the ground in the desert during the day. At night, however, most of this heat quickly escapes because desert soils (Figure 5-16) have little vegetation and moisture and the skies are usually clear. This explains why in a desert you may roast during the day but shiver at night.

Low rainfall combined with different average temperatures creates tropical, temperate, and cold deserts (Figures 7-12 and 7-14). In *tropical deserts,* such as the southern Sahara (Arabic for "the desert") in Africa, temperatures are usually high year-round. Average annual rainfall is less than 2 centimeters (0.8 inch), and rain typically falls during only one or two months of the year, if at all (Figure 7-14, left). Chile's Atacama tropical desert has had no measurable precipitation in over 28 years. These driest places on earth typically have few plants and a hard, windblown surface strewn with rocks and some sand.

Daytime temperatures in *temperate deserts* are hot in summer and cool in winter, and these deserts have more precipitation than tropical deserts (Figure 7-14, center). Examples are the Mojave, Sonoran, and Chihuahuan deserts, which occupy much of the American southwest and northern and western Mexico. The vegetation is sparse, consisting mostly of widely dispersed, drought-resistant shrubs and cacti or other succulents. Animals are adapted to the lack of water and temperature variations (Figure 7-15). In *cold deserts,* such as the Gobi Desert in China, winters are cold and summers are warm or hot; precipitation is low (Figure 7-14, right).

In the semiarid zones between deserts and grasslands, we find *semidesert.* This biome is dominated by thorn trees and shrubs adapted to long dry spells followed by brief, sometimes heavy rains.

How Do Desert Plants and Animals Survive? Adaptations for survival in the desert have two themes: "Beat the heat" and "Every drop of water counts." Desert stoneplants avoid predators by looking like stones, and their light coloration also reflects heat. Some desert plants are evergreens with wax-coated leaves (creosote bush) that minimize transpiration. Most desert perennials tend to have small leaves (coachman's whip) or no leaves (cacti), which helps them conserve water. Perennial shrubs such as mesquite and creosote plants grow deep roots to tap into groundwater, and they drop their leaves to survive in a dormant state during long dry spells.

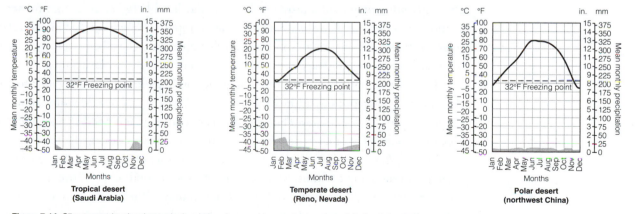

Figure 7-14 Climate graphs showing typical variations in annual temperature and precipitation in tropical, temperate, and polar (cold) deserts.

Continued

Other perennials such as short (prickly pear; Figure 7-15) and tall (saguaro) cacti spread their shallow roots wide to quickly collect water after brief showers; they then store it in their spongy tissues. Most of these succulents are armed with sharp spines to discourage herbivores from feeding on their water-storing fleshy tissue. The spines also reduce overheating by reflecting some sunlight and by providing shade and insulation. Some desert plants, such as the creosote bush and sagebrush, also secrete toxins in the soil. This reduces competition for water and soil nutrients from nearby plants of other species.

Many desert plants are annual wildflowers and grasses that store much of their biomass in seeds during dry periods and remain inactive (sometimes for years) until they receive enough water to germinate. Shortly after a rain, in a frenzy of biological activity, the seeds germinate, grow, carpet the desert with a dazzling array of colorful flowers, produce new seed, and die—all in only a few weeks.

Other, less visible desert plants are mosses and lichens, which can tolerate extremely high temperatures, dry out completely, and become dormant until the next rain falls. In museums, some desert moss specimens have been known to recover and grow after 250 years without water.

If you visit a desert during the daytime you may see only a few lizards, a bird or two, and some insects. However, deserts have a surprisingly large number of animal inhabitants that come out mostly in the cool of night. Most desert animals are small. They beat the heat and reduce water loss by evaporative cooling. They hide in cool burrows or rocky crevices by day and come out at night or in the early morning. Birds, ants, rodents, and other seed-eating herbivores are common, feeding on the multitudes of seeds produced by the desert's annual plants. Some deserts have a few large grazing animals such as gazelle and the endangered Arabian oryx.

Major carnivores in temperate North American deserts are coyotes, kit and gray foxes, and various species of snakes and owls that come out mainly at night to prey on the desert's many rodent species. The few daytime animals, such as fast-moving lizards and some snake species, are preyed upon mostly in the early morning and late afternoon by hawks and roadrunners.

Desert animals have physical adaptations for conserving water (Spotlight, right). Insects and reptiles have thick outer coverings to minimize water loss through evaporation. They also reduce water loss by having dry feces and by excreting a dried concentrate of urine. Some of the smallest desert animals, such as spiders and insects, get their water only from dew or from the food they eat. Some desert animals become dormant during periods of extreme heat or drought and are active only during the cooler months of the year. Arabian oryxes survive by licking the dew that accumulates at night on rocks and on one another's hair.

DEVELOP CHARTS

Another interesting method of note taking is charting. A chart is a graphic display of information that shows the similarities and differences of related information. You can't chart an entire chapter of a textbook, but you may be able to create a chart for several sections of a chapter. If you have a collection of topics or headings that are all related (types or forms of something), you may find that creating a chart helps you organize the information while noting the distinct similarities and differences of each topic.

To create a chart, first determine categories and headings. If you decided to chart the four drug categories from the excerpt on the Web site, you would write them along the left margin of your paper. The next step is not so easy. You need to read and think about the material in order to determine any areas of similarity among the topics.

Look at the example in Figure 9.12, which shows a portion of a matrix, a chart designed with rows and columns. Melissa listed the four periods of cognitive development down the left side of her chart and then looked carefully at the information in her text before determining the names of the categories. Since the text included information about the age, definition, development of skills and abilities, and key concepts or flaws for each period of cognitive development, she used those as the headings for the categories. If you were taking notes using written or mapping formats, these categories would be equivalent to subheadings that you would have created.

FIGURE 9.12
Melissa's Chart

Overview of Piaget's Stage Theory

Period	Age	Definition	Development	Key Concept or Flaw
Sensorimotor	birth to age 2	Ability to coordinate sensory Inputs with motor actions	Symbolic thought Behavior dominated by innate reflexes	Key concept: *Object permanence* Recognizing that object continues to exist even when no longer visible
Preoperational	age 2 to age 7	Improve use of mental images Preoperational because of all the weaknesses	Development of symbolic thinking Not yet grasped concept of conservation: quantities remain constant regardless of shape or appearance	Key flaws: Centration: Focus on one part of problem Irreversibility: Inability to undo an action Egocentrism: Inability to share other's viewpoints Animism: Believe all things are living

---

ACTIVITY 9.10   *Complete the Chart*

Read the excerpt "Chemically Dependent Youth" on the *College Reading and Study Strategies* book-specific Web site and complete the matrix also available on the Web site by filling in each of the squares with the relevant information. Compare your chart with those of at least two of your classmates.

HOW TO REVIEW YOUR NOTES

There are three main ways to review text notes, but simply "reading over them" is not one of them. Try reciting your notes, replicating your notes, and creating recall questions.

RECITE YOUR NOTES

One way to transfer the information in your notes into your long-term memory is to recite it. First, practice the information by reviewing the main and supporting points. Try to recall and recite the headings that you used to set up the information in your notes. Then recite the details under each heading. Look back at your notes to see whether you're correct. Then cover your notes and practice again. If you made note cards, carry them with you. Review them whenever you have a few minutes to spare. Then look away and try to recite (or mumble) the information. Try taping your notes to a mirror, or tack them to a bulletin board. Review them in the morning and then try to recite them as you walk to class.

REPLICATE YOUR NOTES

Another way to review text notes is to replicate them. Take a blank sheet of paper and try to reconstruct your notes. If you mapped the information in the text, you probably will find that it's fairly easy to recall the visual image that you created; try to remember the map and also how you set it up. If you made a detailed map, practice drawing it one section at a time. You also can practice writing out your modified-block notes, outlines, or charts. When you review charts or matrixes, don't try to learn all the information at once. Work on one column or row at a time. Practice matrixes by starting with a blank sheet of paper. Write in the headings and the categories. Then try to fill in one column across or one row down. Keep working on the matrix until you can write it from memory.

ADD RECALL QUESTIONS

If you took written notes on notebook paper or index cards, you can also write questions in the margin as a way of reviewing your notes. Be sure you create both general and specific questions in the recall column so that you can test yourself on all of the important information. You

FIGURE 9.13

Text Notes with Recall Questions

	Types of Political Organizations
	Band Societies
What are the characteristics of band societies?	Characteristics
	• Least complex
What is the occupation of bands?	• small, nomadic groups of food collectors
How large are the groups?	• can range from 20 to several hundred
	• members share all belongings
How much role specialization is there?	• very little role specializations
What is egalitarian?	• egalitarian—few differences in status and wealth
	Political Integration
How much political integration occurs?	• have least —bands are independent
What is the political integration based on?	• based on kinship and marriage
What ties members of bands together?	• bound together by language and culture
What type of leadership occurs in bands?	Leadership roles
	• informal—no designated authority
Who serves as leader? Why?	• older men are leaders—respected for their wisdom and experience
Who makes decisions?	• decisions made by adult men
What are the powers of a head man?	• head man advises—has no power
	Example
What is an example of a band society?	! Kung of the Kalahari
	Tribal Societies
What are the characteristics of tribal societies?	Characteristics
What is their occupation?	• food producers
What are pop. like?	• populations—large, dense, sedentary

can develop the recall column when you first take notes or when you review for your exam. Just developing the questions requires you to go back and review the notes you took. Then you get another review of the material each time you test yourself. If you've already predicted quiz questions in the margin of your text or written your recall questions in the margin of your text notes, review by covering your notes and writing or reciting the answers to the questions. Gavin, Beth, Chris, and Sara developed a set of notes and recall questions on text material from an anthropology textbook. A portion of those notes is shown in Figure 9.13. Did you notice that both general and specific questions are included? Some additional tips for taking notes and reviewing them can be found in the Tip Block.

TIP

MORE TIPS FOR TAKING TEXT NOTES

CREATE WORD CARDS. As you read (or even before you read) the chapter, make out a set of word cards for all of the new technical terminology. Write the word on the front of the card and the definition on the back (one per card). This will help improve your understanding of the terms and the text material. You can also begin working on learning the definitions immediately.

TAKE NOTES ON DIFFICULT MATERIAL ON NOTE CARDS. Writing your notes on index cards serves two purposes. First, you organize the information from one headed section (or one specific topic) on each card. This may make the information easier for you to learn and remember. Second, you can carry your cards with you for quick reviews during work breaks, while commuting, or even before class begins.

ADD QUESTIONS TO YOUR NOTE CARDS. If you take notes only on the front of each card, you can write recall questions on the back. You can study the material on the front of the card and then check your learning by answering the questions on the back. Feel free to shuffle the cards to make sure you aren't learning the information in order.

TAKE NOTES ON LITERARY ASSIGNMENTS. Use a separate index card for each play, short story, or novel you read. Develop a list of categories of information that you want to record for each work. You may want to include the title, author, setting, theme, main characters, symbolism, and a brief summary or diagram of the plot line. Jot down any

other important information that stands out and include your own reaction to what you read.

CREATE A TEMPLATE ON YOUR COMPUTER. You can take notes on the computer, too. Set up a template for a note card (2 or 3 per page) and simply type in the notes and print them out.

TAKE NOTES ON OUTSIDE READING ASSIGNMENTS. Use note cards to take notes on any outside reading material. Include the title of the article and the author at the top of the card and then jot down the important material using any of the note-taking methods.

EXPAND CONCEPT MAPS. Many textbooks, like this one, have concept maps at the beginning of every chapter. They serve as an overview of what the chapter is about. In most cases these maps include only the topics and main points that you will be reading about. Copy the map onto your own paper so that you can add details to it as you read.

COMPARE YOUR TEXT NOTES WITH THOSE OF ANOTHER CLASSMATE. Until you feel more confident about the content and organization of your text notes, get together with a classmate or study group to compare notes.

GET HELP FROM YOUR PROFESSOR OR LEARNING ASSISTANCE CENTER. If you haven't taken text notes before, ask your professor or someone in your college learning center to evaluate your text notes. The feedback you get can help you take better notes in the future.

ACTIVITY 9.11   *Review Your Text Notes*

Select a set of text notes that you took recently. Then divide the notes into three sections. Review the first section by reciting the information using the headings to prompt your memory. Review the second section by replicating your notes—rewriting them from memory. Finally, review the last section of notes by creating recall questions in the margin and reciting the answers from memory. Which review strategy was the most effective in learning the information? Why?

ACTIVITY 9.12   *Use InfoTrac College Edition to Locate Articles on Taking Text Notes*

If you're using InfoTrac College Edition, locate two articles on taking text notes using *written,* or *mapping,* techniques. Take notes on the articles using the informal outline or modified-block method. Then list three strategies that you plan to use. Be prepared to describe the process you used to locate the information and how you plan to use the strategies that you selected.

ACTIVITY 9.13   *Where Are You Now?*

Now that you have completed Chapter 9, take a few minutes to repeat the "Where Are You Now?" activity, located on the *College Reading and Study Strategies* Web site. What changes did you make as a result of reading this chapter? How are you planning to apply what you've learned in this chapter?

Summary

Taking text notes is an active and effective method of condensing your text. When done properly, taking text notes improves your comprehension, organizes the information, and condenses the material for later review. Although many students take notes as they read the chapter for the first time, that's not the most efficient way to take notes on your text. Since everything seems important during a first reading, students tend to write down much more information than they would after hearing the lecture, during a weekly review of material, or while reviewing to prepare for an exam. Taking written notes using the outline or modified-block methods, predicting quiz questions, or making marginal notes are effective ways to take text notes. Concept maps are especially effective for some students and some types of material. Creating hierarchical maps, Semantic Webs, and line maps allows you to organize material in ways that can more easily be recalled for later use. Just taking written notes or creating maps doesn't automatically mean that you've learned the information, though. Review your notes on a regular basis by reciting them, writing them from memory, or creating a recall column. Then test your notes for completeness, accuracy, and clarity after the exam.

Review Questions

Terms You Should Know: Make a flash card for each term.

Annotate

Block method

Comprehension monitoring
  system

Core Concept

Formal outlining

Hierarchical map

Informal outlining

Line map

Maps

Marginal notes

Modified-block method

Semantic Web

Strand Supports

Strand Ties

Web Strands

Wheel map

Completion: Fill in the blank to complete each of the following statements.

1. You may not want to take text notes as you read the chapter for the first time because everything seems _____.

2. You can edit your _____ notes as you take your text notes.

3. Some students like to take text notes on _____ _____ because they can carry them around to review when they have a few extra minutes.

4. _____ _____ show the supporting details in a Semantic Web.

5. _____ cannot be used to take notes on entire chapters.

Multiple Choice: Circle the letter of the best answer for each of the following questions. Be sure to underline key words and eliminate wrong answers.

6. When you annotate your notes, be sure to
   A. write whole sentences.
   B. use the outline method.
   C. focus only on key points.
   D. use your own words.

7. Which of the following is a top-down method of taking text notes?
   A. Recall columns
   B. Hierarchical maps
   C. Semantic Webs
   D. Charts

Short Answer–Essay: On a separate sheet, answer each of the following questions.

8. Why is note taking more effective than highlighting or underlining?

9. Why do some students have difficulty taking text notes? What should they do differently?

10. How should students review their text notes?

10 Preparing for Exams

In this chapter you will learn more about:

➤ How to gather information about an exam

➤ The Five-Day Study Plan

➤ Specific strategies for objective exams

➤ Specific strategies for essay exams

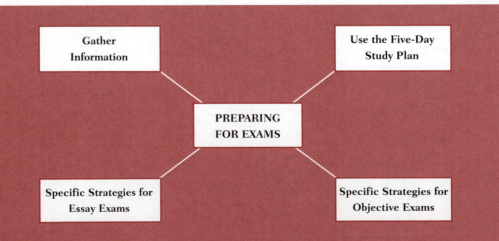

ACTIVITY 10.1   *Where Are You Now?*

Take a few minutes to answer *yes* or *no* to the following questions.

	YES	NO
1. When preparing for exams, is your primary study method to read over the material?	_____	_____
2. Do you study differently for essay and objective tests?	_____	_____
3. After an exam are you unsure of how well you did?	_____	_____
4. Do you make up self-tests as a way of studying for exams?	_____	_____
5. Do you predict possible essay questions before an exam?	_____	_____
6. Do you tend to study only the day or night before the exam?	_____	_____
7. Do you review your lecture notes and text material together according to the topic?	_____	_____
8. Do you often know the answers to multiple-choice questions even before you look at the alternatives?	_____	_____
9. Do you review by reciting out loud or by making up study sheets?	_____	_____
10. Do you space your study time over several days?	_____	_____
Total Points		_____

Give yourself 1 point for each *yes* answer to questions 2, 4, 5, 7, 8, 9, and 10 and 1 point for each *no* answer to questions 1, 3, and 6. Now total up your points. A low score indicates that you need to learn how to study for college exams. A high score indicates that you are already using many good test preparation strategies.

GATHER INFORMATION BEFORE YOU STUDY

Before you begin to study for an exam, gather information about both the test and yourself. Learning about the type of test that will be given will help you know how best to prepare for it. In addition, knowing how you learn best can help you choose the most effective ways to prepare for an exam. Together, this information can lead to better grades.

LEARN ABOUT THE EXAM

The first thing to do in preparing for an exam is find out what the exam will be like. If your professor has not already discussed the exam, ask about it. Don't feel afraid or foolish; the more you know, the better you can prepare. You need to know what types of questions you will be expected to answer. Ask whether the exam is objective or essay or both. If the exam is an objective one, find out if all questions will be multiple choice or if some will be true/false, matching, or completion.

LEVELS OF QUESTIONS

Many college students don't realize that professors test their understanding of the material at many different levels. Although most of the questions on your high school tests depended only on your ability to memorize, six different levels of questions are often found on college exams. Take a look at each of them in Figure 10.1.

LEARN ABOUT YOURSELF

As you decide which strategies to use when you prepare for an exam, you should also consider how you learn best. Refer to the section on learning styles in Chapter 1. Using your preferred learning style as you prepare for exams may help you stay more focused on the material and may make your study sessions more productive. Don't forget, though, that using a combination of learning styles is often most effective when you're dealing with a new type of course, a professor who doesn't teach to your style, or a type of test that you've had difficulty with in the past.

FIGURE 10.1
Levels of Questions

Based on Bloom's Taxonomy in B. S. Bloom, ed., *Taxonomy of Educational Objectives: The Classification of Educational Goals. Handbook 1. Cognitive Domain* **(New York: McKay, 1956).**

1. **Knowledge-level questions** require only rote memory; they're the easiest type of question to answer. They include remembering terms, facts, dates, lists, and so on. To answer this type of question, you need only to recognize or recall the information as it was written in the text or spoken in the lecture.
2. **Comprehension-level questions** require you to understand the material well enough to be able to identify concepts and issues even when they are phrased differently from the way you read them or heard them presented.
3. **Application-level questions** require you to apply the information that you learned to a new situation. Application questions are common in math and science courses, but may appear on any exam.
4. **Analysis-level questions** require you to break down a complex concept into its components or parts. Many essay questions involve analysis.
5. **Synthesis-level questions** require you to bring information together into a single unit or whole. Many essay questions involve synthesis.
6. **Evaluation-level questions** require you to make judgments about the value or worth of an idea. In most cases, both analysis and synthesis are required to answer an evaluation-level question. They are the most difficult type of question to answer and require the highest-level thinking skills.

ACTIVITY ▶ **10.2**   *List Test-Preparation Strategies of Successful Students*

Make a list of what successful students do when preparing for exams. Then compare your responses with other members of your group. Select the twenty best exam preparation strategies and create a list. Then make a list of the strategies you use now. How many of your strategies appeared on the group list?

USE THE FIVE-DAY STUDY PLAN

Once you find out what the exam will be like, you should organize your study time. The Five-Day Study Plan provides you with a structure to plan and organize your learning. It's a well-structured plan that puts into practice what we know about how people learn and remember.

SPACE YOUR STUDY

One reason many new college students get poor grades on exams is that they don't put enough time into studying. How much time do you think you should spend studying for a four-chapter exam? How much time did you study for your last exam? You need to spend about eight to ten hours studying to get an A or B on a college exam. Of course, this is only a general guideline. Some students constantly review material (daily and weekly) so that they don't need to put in quite as much time just before the exam. Other students may need to study even more.

If you're trying to figure out when you can find time to study eight to ten hours for one exam, don't panic. You don't need or really want to put in all of your study time on one day. It's much more effective to study over several days than to cram one day before an exam. Research studies have demonstrated that we learn better by spacing out our study over time. Instead of trying to study for ten hours the night before an exam, try studying for two hours each day for five days before the exam (Figure 10.2). If you need to put in more time, add more time to each day's study session or add more days to your study plan.

FIGURE 10.2
Five-Day Study Plan
Overview

Tuesday			
	Prepare	CH 1	2 hrs
Wednesday			
	Prepare	CH 2	2 hrs
	Review	CH 1	30 min
Thursday			
	Prepare	CH 3	1-1/2 hrs
	Review	CH 2	30 min
	Review	CH 1	15 min
Friday			
	Prepare	CH 4	1 hr
	Review	CH 3	30 min
	Review	CH 2	15 min
	Review	CH 1	10 min
Sunday			
	Review	CH 4	30 min
	Review	CH 3	20 min
	Review	CH 2	10 min
	Review	CH 1	10 min
	Self-test		1 hr

DIVIDE THE MATERIAL

The next step is to divide the material that will be on the exam. If your exam will cover four chapters, you can divide the material into four chunks, focusing on one chapter per day and then conducting a final review on the last day. How would you divide the material if your test covered only two chapters? You could study the first half of Chapter 1 on day 1, the second half of Chapter 1 on day 2, and so on. If you only had three chapters on the exam, you could use a four-day plan instead, or you could divide the oldest (or most difficult) chapter in half. How would you set up a plan for six chapters or eight chapters? Working on smaller units of material each day allows you to work on it more actively and concentrate all of your effort on it.

When you set up your five-day plan, be sure to start with the oldest chapter first. When you look carefully at the overview of the Five-Day Study Plan, you'll notice that the oldest chapters are given the most preparation time and the most review time. You need to spend more time on the old material because it's not as fresh in your mind. If you covered Chapter 1 four weeks ago, you won't remember very much of it. In Figure 10.2, Chapters 3 and 4 are more familiar and therefore may require less preparation time and review. However, if Chapter 3 or 4 happens to be an especially difficult chapter, you may need to modify the plan and add some additional time for preparation and review.

PLAN ACTIVE STUDY TASKS

Look again at the sample Five-Day Study Plan in Figure 10.2. This plan includes both time to prepare a chapter and time to review that chapter several times before the exam. (Remember that "CH 1" means the text chapter, the lecture notes, and any other related materials.) The Five-Day Study Plan is a task-oriented plan. In many ways, it's like creating a "To Do" list for your study plan. If you've been rereading your text and lecture notes for hours before an exam and still not getting the grades you want, you need to change your strategy. Unlike reading over the material, writing and reciting strategies are excellent ways of putting information into long-term memory. In Figure 10.3 you can see some suggested preparation and review tasks for Wednesday and Thursday, the second and third days of this Five-Day Study Plan. To effectively learn information, you need to use a variety of active strategies.

Use Active Preparation Strategies

Preparation strategies help you identify what you need to learn, condense it, organize it, and write it. You can use the mnemonic ICOW to help you remember the role of preparation strategies. Preparation strategies are primarily writing strategies. If you're a kinesthetic or visual learner, preparation strategies will help you learn the material. Using at least three different preparation strategies allows you to work on the material different ways. You can make word or question cards to learn key terms, facts, and details. You may also take notes on your text marking or even condense your lecture notes further as you reread them. Although these are all good preparation strategies, you should also include at least one integrated study strategy in your plan. Making study sheets or planning possible essay questions allows you to study and learn the material in a more integrated manner. As you gather and organize the information on one topic or one question, you form many additional associations with the material. This helps you create additional cues to long-term memory, which makes it easier to retrieve the information during the

FIGURE 10.3
*Actual Tasks for Five-Day
Study Plan*

```
Wednesday
    Prepare CH 2          1.  Re-mark highlighting
                          2.  Make study sheets
                          3.  Make word cards
                          4.  Make question cards

    Review CH 1           1.  Recite rehighlighted material
                              *unknowns (recite main points)
                          2.  Mark and recite study sheets
                          3.  Recite word cards
                          4.  Recite question cards
Thursday
    Prepare CH 3          1.  Re-mark highlighting
                          2.  Make study sheets
                          3.  Make word cards
                          4.  Make question cards

    Review CH 2           1.  Recite rehighlighted material
                              *unknowns (recite main points)
                          2.  Mark and recite study sheets
                          3.  Recite word cards
                          4.  Recite question cards

    Review CH 1           1.  Make a list of information still not
                              known from text or study
                              sheets—recite
                          2.  Recite cards still not known
                          3.  Make self-test questions
```

exam. Preparation strategies are effective learning strategies because they force you to condense, organize, and write the material.

Use Active Review Strategies

During the review stage, you need to practice the material that you prepared each day in your study plan. Review strategies are mainly recitation strategies that help you practice, extend, and monitor your learning. They force you to recite the information out loud, so they're especially effective for auditory learners. You could get the same level of practice by writing the material again, but that's a bit more time-consuming. By reciting the information in your predicted questions, word cards, and study sheets, for example, from the previous chapters each day, you can continue working on the material (often forming additional cues), keep it fresh in long-term memory, and monitor your learning. Each day, as you review the material, you continue to condense what you still don't know.

Since you will be reviewing some of the material three or four times, it's also a good idea to vary your review strategies. Although you should use the same three or four strategies to prepare each chapter and to review each chapter the first time, you need to select different strategies to review the chapter the second, third, and fourth time. By working on the material different ways, you can create more new connections to it, use the learning style that may be the most effective, and make studying fun and interesting.

The tasks listed in Figure 10.3 are just a few examples of the types of tasks that you could use to study for an exam. The menu of active preparation and review strategies includes many other excellent strategies you can use in your study plan (Figure 10.4). You also may develop some excellent strategies of your own. Varying the activities you

FIGURE 10.4
Menu of Active Study Tasks

PREPARATION STRATEGIES	REVIEW STRATEGIES
develop study sheets	recite study sheets
develop concept maps	replicate concept maps
make word cards	recite word cards
make question cards	recite question cards
make formula cards	practice writing formulas
make problem cards	work problems
make self-tests	take self-tests
do study guides	practice study guide info out loud
re-mark text material	take notes on re-marked text
do problems	make a list of 20 (30 or 40)
outline	recite list of 20 (30 or 40)
take notes	do "missed" problems
predict questions in the margin	recite main points from outline
chart related material	recite notes from recall cues
list steps in the process	recite out loud
predict essay questions	re-create chart from memory
plan essay answers	recite steps from memory
write essay answers	answer essay questions
answer end-of-chapter questions	practice reciting main points
prepare material for study group	write essay answers from memory
	recite answers
	explain material to group members

use when you study can keep you from feeling bored. You also may discover that many of these active strategies are fun and make learning interesting and exciting.

MONITOR YOUR LEARNING

One reason the Five-Day Study Plan is so effective is the built-in self-testing. As you review the old material each day, you are really testing your mastery of it. If you can't say it out loud or write it from memory, you don't really know it. You may be able to recognize the correct answer if it appeared on the exam (recognition learning), but you won't be able to recall it if it is rephrased or if you need to answer completion, short answer, or essay questions. Each time you recite your flash cards or practice the main points in your essay answer, you're checking to see what you do know and what you don't know. Although you may be disappointed that you don't get all the question cards correct the first time you review them, you will get some right. That tells you that you are learning the material and lets you know the strategy you're using is working. Have you ever tried to check your learning after just reading over the material? You may find that you don't really know very much of it.

Many students create their self-tests as a review strategy on day 2 or day 3 of the plan. Then they can take the test several times before the real exam. Self-testing gives you a feeling of accomplishment—makes you feel like all the hard work is paying off. That motivates you to keep going. You also will find that as you test your learning, you won't know some of the material. Identifying what you still don't know allows you to focus your efforts the next day on that material. Self-testing also allows you to practice retrieving information from your long-term memory. Since that's exactly what you'll have to do on the exam, the retrieval practice better prepares you for the test. Finally, taking a self-test on the last day of your study plan can help reduce any anxiety that you may be feeling about the exam. After all, if you take your test and do well, you *know* that you know the material.

ACTIVITY 10.3   *Set Up a Five-Day Study Plan*

Set up a Five-Day Study Plan for an exam that you have coming up in the next few weeks. Decide when you're going to study; then divide up the material into four chunks. Select active study tasks to add to your study plan from the menu in Figure 10.4. This list is not exhaustive, so use some preparation and review strategies from the list but feel free to create other strategies of your own. Exchange plans with another member of your group. What are the strengths and weaknesses of each plan? Discuss your responses with other members of your group.

STRATEGIES FOR OBJECTIVE EXAMS

In this section, you'll learn about a variety of active study strategies. Some of these strategies lend themselves to the preparation stage and others lend themselves to the review stage. You won't use all of these strategies to study for one exam; there are just too many of them. What you should do, however, is try each of them as you prepare for different exams during the semester. You probably will find that some strategies work better for you than others. You also may find that certain strategies work well for one type of exam or course material but others are better for another. As you read about how to use these strategies, think about which ones you would use to prepare for exams in each of your courses this semester.

REREAD AND RE-MARK YOUR TEXT AND NOTES

Many students start preparing for a test by rereading their highlighting. You'll stay actively involved in your reading if you re-mark the text as you read it. You can further condense the material that you will need to review again by determining what you do know and what you don't know.

Mark the important information in your lecture notes as you reread them, too. You can condense them just as you did your text material. You may want to go through the chapter and your notes and reread the newly marked information the next day, too. This time, use another one of the methods to again condense what you need to learn. Create questions, take notes, prepare study sheets, or talk about the material with someone else. Remember, you need to write and recite to get the information into long-term memory—to learn it at the recall level of learning. At this level, you'll be able to recall the information without any additional cues.

If your professor tends to ask picky questions on small details, you may benefit from one quick rereading of your highlighting. This can be especially helpful if your exam is a multiple-choice test. To answer multiple-choice questions correctly, you often can rely on recognition-level learning. That means you don't need to recall the actual answer; you need only to *recognize* it from among the answers listed on the exam. If you've recently read that material, the answer may stand out or seem familiar to you. However, many professors rephrase the information on multiple-choice tests. Of course, if your exam is completion, short answer, or essay in design, that quick rereading won't help at all.

PREPARE WORD CARDS

Think back to the last objective test that you took. How many of the questions on the test required you to know the meaning of a word that was part of the specialized vocabulary for that unit of material? You may have been surprised to find a technical term somewhere in the question or in at least one of the possible answers. Many students don't spend much time on technical terminology because they know that they won't have to actually write out the definitions for an exam. What they don't realize, though, is that they're expected to know the meanings of those terms, and this understanding is necessary for answering many of the questions on the exam.

How do you learn all those terms? One way is to make word cards. By going through the chapter and writing out word cards, you're actively involved with the material. Just the process of writing them will help you learn them. Put the word on the front of a three-by-five card and then write a brief definition on the back. Put only one word on a card. You want to use them like flash cards, so they shouldn't be cluttered with information. If you're trying to save money, cut your cards in half.

Use Word Cards for Any Subject

You can make word cards for just about any subject. If you're in a Psychology class, you may have forty or fifty technical terms for just one chapter. In addition, you may want to make cards for famous psychologists and what they did, theories, or even research studies that were emphasized by your professor. In History, put people, dates, events, treaties, or anything else you need to learn on the cards. Make formula cards for math and science classes. Put the formula on one side and the name of the formula or when it's used on the other side. Of course, word cards are a great way to learn foreign-language vocabulary terms. Some students even put diagrams or sketches of things that they will have to identify on the front of the card and the explanations on the back. Look at the examples of word cards from History, Biology, and Psychology in Figure 10.5. Word cards are easy to make, and they're quite effective in getting information into long-term memory.

Practice Your Word Cards

After you make your word cards, you need to learn them. Although you'll learn some of them just from writing them out, you won't learn all of them that way. Study them by practicing ten or fifteen at a time. Carry them around with you and recite or mumble the definitions whenever you have a few minutes to spare. After you know that group, start on the next pack of fifteen.

FIGURE 10.5
Examples of Word Cards

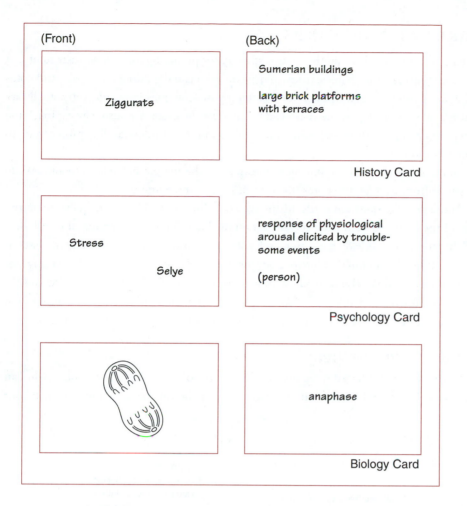

(Front)

(Back)

Ziggurats

Sumerian buildings

large brick platforms
with terraces

History Card

Stress

Selye

response of physiological
arousal elicited by troublesome events

(person)

Psychology Card

anaphase

Biology Card

Hold the stack of cards in your hand and look at the first term. Try to recite the definition out loud. Turn the card over to check your answer. If you were right, set that card aside. If you couldn't think of the answer or were not completely correct, read the definition out loud. Then put it on the bottom of the pile. Continue practicing the cards until you have none left in your hand. After you know all the terms, shuffle the cards to check your learning. If you also include the word card information in your maps, charts, study sheets, or outlines, you will find that you can tie the information to a major concept. This will help reduce the effects of learning the information in isolation.

ACTIVITY **10.4** *Learn Technical Vocabulary*

Prepare a set of word cards for all the technical terms from one chapter in any of your texts. Practice reviewing the cards using the reciting and writing methods described previously. Then try to write or recite the definitions. How many did you get right? How many times did you need to practice the terms? Which strategy worked best for you?

MAKE QUESTION CARDS

Making question cards is another active strategy for preparing for exams. Instead of just concentrating on terms, names, dates, and events, you can dig through your text and notes and write questions on all types of information. By making question cards, you actually are focusing on specific details you may need to know for the exam. You also may approach the material in a slightly different manner and focus more on understanding rather than on simple memorization.

Some students prefer to put their questions in the margin of their textbooks. Write questions from your lecture notes, too (on cards or in the margin).

You can make question cards on any type of information. Write the question on the front of the card and then write the answer on the back. Make a minimum of twenty-five per chapter. If you already have prepared a stack of word cards for the chapter, concentrate on different information for your question cards. Focus on lists or on how things relate or how they differ. Look at the sample question cards for Business, History, and Biology in Figure 10.6. These questions emphasize steps in a process, lists of things, and causes and effects. You can also create problem cards for math and science classes.

Practice Your Questions

If you've already predicted questions in the margin of your text and/or notes, you can begin learning the information immediately. Cover the text or note material with your

FIGURE 10.6
Sample Question Cards

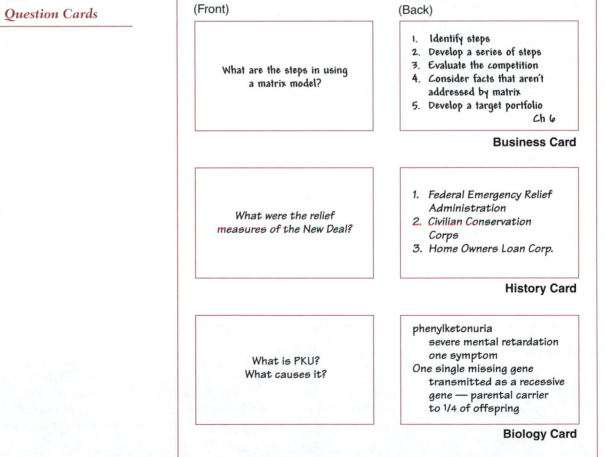

(Front)

What are the steps in using a matrix model?

(Back)

1. Identify steps
2. Develop a series of steps
3. Evaluate the competition
4. Consider facts that aren't addressed by matrix
5. Develop a target portfolio
Ch 6

Business Card

What were the relief *measures of the New Deal?*

1. Federal Emergency Relief Administration
2. Civilian Conservation Corps
3. Home Owners Loan Corp.

History Card

What is PKU? What causes it?

phenylketonuria
 severe mental retardation
 one symptom
One single missing gene
 transmitted as a recessive
 gene — parental carrier
 to 1/4 of offspring

Biology Card

hand or a piece of paper and recite each answer out loud from memory. Slide your hand or the paper down the page to check your answers. Continue to practice your predicted questions until you know them all.

Use your question cards as you would flash cards. Practice answering the questions aloud until you know them all. You can use your question cards if you work in groups or with a study partner. If both you and your partner make question cards on the chapters, you will be able to test each other on the material. You may be surprised because each of you will write different questions on the same material. Although you may have questions on the same information, each of you may approach it from a different angle. This can be helpful in preparing for the exam because you can test your learning in several ways. Your question cards are in fact another form of a self-test. Each time you recite the answer, you're prompting your memory for the information—you're practicing retrieval.

CREATE STUDY SHEETS

Developing study sheets is one of the best ways to prepare for an exam. A study sheet is a one-page compilation of all the important information on a particular topic. The sample study sheet on Mesopotamia in Figure 10.7 is the first of four study sheets prepared for the first chapter of a Western Civilization exam.

It's easy to make study sheets. Put a specific topic at the top of the sheet of paper and go through your text and lecture notes looking for all of the important information

FIGURE 10.7
Sample Study Sheet

Mesopotamia

I.   Sumer (3500—2350 BC)
   agricultural settlements T & E valley formed towns
   first system of writing
      (signs on clay tablets – cuneiform)
   led to trade → cities
   center of life – temple
      religion – seasons – fertility   Great Mother
      ex. Lady of Warka
   govern – priests

Epic of Gilgamesh (most famous ruler) fiction
   pessimistic (life struggle against disaster –
      no afterlife)
   1. quest — human is a questioner (ultimacy)
   2. death — pos & neg moments
   3. story — human is a mythmaker

II. Akkad
   Semitic King Sargon ruled (2350 to 2150)
      art – bronze head of Nineveh
         Stele of Naram – Sim
      buildings – ziggurats

about that topic. Then combine the information in an organized manner. Creating a study sheet requires you to identify, condense, organize, and integrate the important information from both the text and your lecture notes into a single study sheet. By the way, this is an excellent way to prepare for an open-book exam. When you create study sheets, include both the material you already know and the material you need to learn. The already learned information will help you learn and remember the new information because it will serve as hooks and cues to help you store and retrieve the new information. Study sheets allow you to work on information using high-level rehearsal strategies combined with organizational and elaboration strategies.

You can use a variety of formats for study sheets. You can use written formats, maps, or charts. If you're using one of the written formats, it's important to include headings and subheadings in your study sheet. The headings help you break up the information into manageable units and serve as cues to help you learn and remember the main points and details in your study sheet. How many study sheets you prepare depends a lot on how you organize or divide the information you need to learn. If you are preparing for a History exam, for example, you can make a study sheet on each main topic that was covered in lecture or each main subdivision of the chapter. You might have four study sheets for one chapter, or you could have six or seven.

ACTIVITY 10.5 *Work Together to Prepare a Study Sheet*

Work together to prepare a study sheet on the Five-Day Study Plan. Be sure that you combine the information from your text and your lecture notes. Share your study sheet with other members of the class. Did you include the same topics? Did you include the same details? Which format did you use? What changes would you make the next time?

MAKE SELF-TESTS

Making self-tests is another active way to prepare for an exam. To make a self-test, you have to decide what information you need to know for the exam and then formulate questions about it. Although you may have already developed questions in the margin or question cards, you can benefit even more from your self-tests if they're composed of the same types of questions that will be on the exam. For example, if you're going to have a Psychology exam that is fifty multiple-choice questions, you may be able to improve your score by writing multiple-choice test items rather than completion items. One advantage of actually making up multiple-choice items is that you have to generate three or four wrong answers in addition to the right answer. This can help you improve your score on the exam because you're learning to distinguish between the correct answer and several possible but incorrect answers. In a sense you are predicting the incorrect answers or distractors that your professor may also use. If you choose the same ones that are on the actual test, you'll be able to eliminate them immediately.

In the same way, writing your own true/false items can help you tune in to key words that can be used or changed to make a statement false. Making up matching tests helps you make fine distinctions among terms, concepts, people, and so on. If you'll have to answer essay questions, you need to prepare by predicting and practicing possible essay test questions, which will be discussed later in the chapter.

Use Your Self-Test to Monitor Your Learning

Use your self-test to monitor your learning. One benefit of making self-tests is that you can use them over and over again to test your knowledge of the information. Write the answers on another sheet of paper or on the back of your self-test. Once you mark the answers on the test, you've changed the test into a review sheet. As you prepare the chapter, make a self-test and then take the test as a way of reviewing what you've learned. Some students like to make up test questions as they prepare each chapter and then answer all of them the night before the test. This can provide an effective final review. Be sure, however, to leave some time to learn those items that you don't get right. Then test yourself again just to be sure. Some additional study strategies are described in the Tip Block.

TIP — MORE ACTIVE STUDY STRATEGIES

PREPARE REVIEW CARDS. In some classes, students are permitted to take one index card to the exam with anything on it they wish. Even if you aren't permitted to do so, creating a review card may be an excellent final review strategy. To do it you need to identify those key pieces of information that are the most critical or that you still don't know. Writing and organizing the information on the card are active ways to review for your exam.

TURN DIAGRAMS INTO A SELF-TEST. Photocopy or trace any important diagrams that may be on the exam and label them with numbers instead of the names. Then use them to test your learning by reciting or writing the actual names of the bones, structures, or muscles for example. Then you can use your labeled version as your answer key.

TEACH THE INFORMATION TO SOMEONE OR SOMETHING ELSE. When you explain material to someone else or even to the lamp in the corner, you have to organize the information and put it into your own words. Explaining it out loud also helps you better understand the material.

FORM A STUDY GROUP. Many students benefit from working with a study group throughout the semester. You can share study materials, quiz each other, take turns explaining the material, or even share predictions about what will be on the exam. Study groups work the best if all members are committed to working hard.

USE STUDY GUIDES TO TEST YOUR LEARNING. Many textbooks come with a study guide (often on a Web site) that includes word lists, questions, and practice tests. Don't actually fill in your study guide as you read the chapter. Instead, answer the questions and take the tests on notebook paper. That way you can use the study guide to test your learning again before the exam.

USE OLD EXAMS AS A RESOURCE. Use copies of old exams to get more information about what the test will be like. You can get an idea about the kinds of questions the instructor uses, the topics that were emphasized, and the level of detail of questions. If the tests closely parallel your current material, take them for extra practice

PREPARE TAPED SELF-TESTS. Read your test questions into a tape recorder, pause after each question while letting the tape run, and then read the answer. As you commute to school or work, you can take your tests. Try to answer the question out loud during the paused portion of the tape, listen to the answer, and check your learning.

GET YOUR FAMILY AND FRIENDS INVOLVED. Your family and friends can be a great resource to you as you prepare for tests. Ask a family member to help you with your word or question cards. Teach the material to your friends, parents, or older children. Ask someone to quiz you by asking you questions from the study guide, the end of the chapter, or from the study sheets or self-test that you prepared.

ACTIVITY 10.6 *Create a Taped Self-Test*

Develop a self-test on a cassette tape to play as you commute to and from school or work. Be sure to let the tape run for a few seconds after you record your question. Then record the correct answer. As you listen to the tape, recite the answer to each question out loud and then check it against the correct answer that you recorded. How did making the tape help you learn the information? How often were you able to play the tape and take your own self-test? How effective was this strategy in preparing you for the exam? Would you use this strategy again? Why, or why not?

STRATEGIES FOR ESSAY EXAMS

Essay tests are more difficult than objective tests for many students because they require recall learning. You need to know what you're writing about. An essay test requires you to write paragraph-style answers to the questions. Sometimes you'll be asked to write about topics that were presented either in the lecture or in the text. Other times, you will be required to pull together bits and pieces of information from one or more lectures, several sections of your text, or even information from both lectures and the text in order to answer the question. Essay tests may require you to focus on rather specific information or to synthesize a large body of information.

PREDICT QUESTIONS

The first step in preparing for an essay exam is to predict questions. A good rule of thumb is to predict four to five times the number of questions that will be on the exam. If you will have to answer two essay questions on the exam, then you should predict eight to ten questions. Another approach is to predict three or four questions from each chapter. This is especially effective if you have only one essay question to answer. The more questions you predict, the greater your chances of accurately predicting the questions that the professor will put on the exam. Also, even if you don't predict the exact questions, you may find that you have predicted a question similar to the one on the test. In the process of studying to answer your question, you may learn the information that you need to answer the question that the professor asks. The more questions that you predict and prepare, the better you will do on the test.

You should predict broad, challenging questions if the exam will cover large amounts of material. If the essay test will include ten questions on only two chapters of text, however, the questions may be more specific and require more detail about a topic. Predicting broad questions helps prepare you for either type of question.

Narrow questions that focus on why or how something happened often are too limited in scope. Most essay questions ask you to discuss causes and effects, compare and contrast, explain the steps in a process, and so on.

ACTIVITY 10.7 *Read and Predict Essay Questions*

Read and mark the text excerpt "Types of Political Organization," located on the *College Reading and Study Strategies* Web site and then predict three essay questions. Include at least one broad question. Use the chart of frequently used terms for essay exams (also available on the Web site) to start your questions.

GATHER INFORMATION

Predicting essay questions is not the end of your preparation for an essay exam; it's just the beginning. The next step is to gather information. You need to find the main and supporting points required to answer the questions. This process is valuable because it forces you to dig through the text and your lecture notes looking for relevant information. This active study technique may help you learn some of the other text information at the same time.

An easy way to gather information is to treat each question separately. Write each question across the top of a large piece of paper. Then open your text and your notes to that section of the material. Start to look for information that you would use if you had to answer that question. Pretend that it's an open-book exam and you have the opportunity to look for the material that you are going to use. As you locate important points and details that would be useful in answering the question, write them down on your sheet of paper. Don't copy the information; rather, write it in meaningful phrases. If you use a two-column format, you'll be forced to condense the material.

ORGANIZE INFORMATION

After gathering information for a number of questions, you may find that you have a huge amount of information to remember. By organizing the information and creating an outline for each question, you'll find it is easier to learn and remember the points you want to make for each question.

You can organize your gathered information by *labeling* each point. Look at each piece of information that you wrote down and decide where it should go in your essay. Find the point that you want to make first and label it 1. Any points that support it should be marked 1A, 1B, and so on. Creating an informal outline will help you remember the points that you want to make in an essay answer. The easiest way to outline your answer is simply to list the main points (most important points) next to the margin and then list the supporting details indented slightly underneath. Try to limit your main points to seven or fewer so that you can remember them. Three or four main points with good support for each should be sufficient for most answers. Of course, if you need to know the five causes of something, then you'll have five main points.

Take a look at Lisa's essay plan in Figure 10.8. Lisa created the catchphrase, "Nancy sells every car for parts," to help her remember the six main points for her sociology answer. If you're taking an open-book exam, your essay plans should help you write the answers to a wide variety of exam questions.

ACTIVITY    *Gather and Organize the Information*

Work as a group to gather, organize, and outline the information that you read on "Types of Political Organization." What were your main points? Did you have supporting details or examples for each?

FIGURE 10.8

Lisa's Gathered Information and Outline with Mnemonic Cues

Explain the view Thomas Hobbes took on the problem of order and the social contract.

1 social order is political natural law	3 equality among people
2 state of nature	4 people form a social contract
2A people are selfish and violent	4A agreement b/w societies
2C people become power hungry	4B people give up natural liberty
2B central concept is power	4C laws tell us how to act
3A state of nature is condition of war	5 if break laws we are denied
3B common fear of power	freedom
	6 power of state is order

TS Thomas Hobbes viewed order in society as a hunger for power among people.

1. Social order is political natural law

2. State of nature
   A. people are selfish & violent
   B. central concept is power
   C. people become power hungry

3. Equality among people
   A. State of nature is condition of war
   B. Common fear of power

4. People form a social contract
   A. agreement b/w societies
   B. people give up natural liberty
   C. laws tell us how to act

5. If we break laws, we are deprived of freedom

6. Power of state is order

1. Natural
2. State
3. Equality
4. Contract
5. Freedom
6. Power

(Nancy sells every car for parts.)

LEARN THE INFORMATION

Gathering and outlining the information that you would use to answer a question doesn't guarantee that you'll be able to replicate the answer on the test. The next step is to learn the information. It's not necessary to memorize your outline word for word. Reciting the main points and then practicing the details that you wish to add should enable you to remember the material for your exam. The best way to remember key points is to practice them over and over. Cover everything except the question with your hand or another sheet of paper. Ask yourself, "What are the points that I want to make about this question?" Even better, try to write your outline without looking back. Practicing (reciting and writing) the information over a period of days will help you remember it during the exam. Once you know the key points, practice the details in your outline. Each of the main points can then serve as a cue to help you recall the details. More tips for how to prepare for essay tests can be found in the Tip Block.

TIP

TIPS FOR PREPARING FOR ESSAY TESTS

PREDICT BROAD, GENERAL QUESTIONS. Predict broad questions that cover major topics that were covered. The information that you learn for your questions can then help you answer more specific questions as well as a closely related question.

REVIEW OLD EXAMS. Use old exams to get ideas for the types of questions your professor uses. Don't just rely on those questions, though, because few professors use the same essay questions semester after semester. Predict your own questions, too.

PREPARE ALL SAMPLE QUESTIONS. If your instructor gives you sample essay questions, prepare an essay plan for each one. Often the same, or very similar, questions are used on the exam. By preparing each of those answers, you will also cover most of the major topics on the exam. Don't forget to predict your own questions, too.

SET UP A STUDY GROUP. Some students find that working in a group is quite effective when preparing for essay exams. Compare your questions with those of the members of your study group or predict questions as a group. Other members of the group may find connections in the material that you hadn't considered. Then exchange outlines or essay answers with the other members of your group. Compare the content and organization of the answers.

USE MNEMONICS TO AID YOUR RETENTION. Developing catchwords and catchphrases can help you recall the main points in your sample essay answers (in your outline). Remember, mnemonics don't replace learning the information; they just help you get it back out of memory after you have learned it.

PRACTICE WRITING OUT THE ANSWERS TO THE MOST DIFFICULT QUESTIONS. Getting what you know on paper is often the hardest part of taking an essay exam. By writing out several of your most difficult planned answers, you have the opportunity to practice connecting the information together. Try doing it with your outline in front of you and then do it again without your outline. If you can write out the hardest answers, you'll have no problem with the easy ones.

GET SOME FEEDBACK BEFORE THE TEST. If you really aren't sure about the quality of your essay answers, ask your professor to take a look at one or two of them. Your professor can give you valuable feedback on how well you are preparing for the exam and how well you are able to communicate what you know.

ACTIVITY 10.9   *Practice Learning Information*

Make up a mnemonic to help you remember the main points that you selected for the question on "Types of Political Organization" in Activity 10.8 or for some other question that you've planned. Practice learning the main points out loud. Then review out loud, or write the supporting points that you would like to add. Then use your mnemonic to replicate the main points in your outline. Which strategy was the most useful? How many times did you practice before you could replicate your outline?

ACTIVITY 10.10   *Work as a Group to Predict Essay Questions*

Work as a group to develop a list of predicted essay questions for the material in Chapter 9 of this text. Use the chart of frequently used terms in essay questions (available on the Web site) to help you develop a variety of broad general questions. Then choose one question and gather information for the answer individually. Work together to develop a group essay plan, including an outline. Then write the answer from the outline that you developed.

ACTIVITY 10.11   *Evaluate Your Exam-Preparation Strategies*

Evaluate the preparation strategies that you used to prepare for one of your exams. Consider the following questions as you analyze your study plan.

1. What study strategies did you use to prepare for the exam?

2. How effective were each of the strategies that you used?

3. After you finished taking your exam, how did you feel about your preparation?

4. When your exam was returned, did you feel that you used effective strategies?

5. What changes do you plan to make when you prepare for your next exam?

ACTIVITY 10.12   *Use InfoTrac College Edition to Locate Articles on Test Preparation*

If you are using InfoTrac College Edition, use PowerTrac to locate a list of articles on test preparation. Test a number of key-word combinations until you narrow the hits to those that contain useful information on active test-preparation strategies. Make a list of the five best test-preparation strategies that you found. Why did you choose these strategies? What changes do you plan to make in how you study for your next exam?

ACTIVITY 10.13   *Where Are You Now?*

Now that you have completed Chapter 10, take a few minutes to repeat the "Where Are You Now?" activity, located on the *College Reading and Study Strategies* Web site. What changes did you make as a result of reading this chapter? How are you planning to apply what you've learned in this chapter?

Summary

Preparing for exams requires you to be a strategic learner. If you prepare the same way that you did for high school tests, use the same strategies for all of your courses, or prepare the same way as your friends or classmates do, you may not get the grades you want or deserve. Before you prepare for an exam, you need to learn as much about the exam as you can. That way, you can design your study plan correctly. You need to plan what to study, when to study, and how to study. You may decide to study with a group for a math exam but study alone for your history exam. That's fine; you need to consider your learning style as well as the type of exam you will have to determine how you can learn best. In any case, you should set up a Five-Day Study Plan to organize your study efforts and space out your learning over several days. Divide the material into smaller units so that you can concentrate your efforts and incorporate daily reviews to keep the material fresh in your memory. Use active study strategies as you prepare and review each of the chapters or units of material. You shouldn't study for every exam the same way. Choose the strategies and techniques that you think will work the best for you. To be properly prepared for essay exams, you need to predict broad, challenging questions—questions that cover the main topics presented in the course. Then gather, organize, and learn the information that you'll need to answer each question. Write out some of the more difficult questions to get comfortable with putting the answers on paper. Then self-test to monitor your learning.

Review Questions

Terms You Should Know: Make a flash card for each term.

Broad questions	Main points	Recognition-level learning
Distractors	Mnemonic devices	Review strategies
Five-Day Study Plan	Narrow questions	Self-test
Gather information	Preparation strategies	Study sheet
Integrated study	Question cards	Supporting details
Isolated study	Recall-level learning	Word cards

Completion: Fill in the blank to complete each of the following statements.

1. You should study the _____ chapter on day 1 of the Five-Day Study Plan.

2. You should study for _____ to _____ hours for a college exam.

3. Studying your text and lecture material together is known as _____ study.

4. If you only have one essay question on an exam, you should predict _____ or _____ questions from every chapter.

5. After you create an outline for your answer, you must _____ the information.

Multiple Choice: Circle the letter of the best answer for each of the following questions. Be sure to underline key words and eliminate wrong answers.

6. _____-level questions require you to understand the information so you can select the answer even when it is phrased differently on the exam.
   A. Knowledge
   B. Comprehension
   C. Application
   D. Analysis

7. Which of the following is not a good source for predicted essay questions?
   A. Main headings in the textbook
   B. Main topics from your lecture notes
   C. Recall questions in your text and notes
   D. Old exams

Short Answer–Essay: On a separate sheet, answer each of the following questions.

8. How should you prepare for an exam that contains both objective and essay questions?

9. Why do some students have difficulty preparing for essay exams? What should they do differently?

10. Why is the Five-Day Study Plan so effective?

11 Taking Exams

In this chapter you will learn more about:

- ➤ How to reduce test anxiety

- ➤ General test-taking strategies

- ➤ Specific test-taking strategies

- ➤ Learning from exams

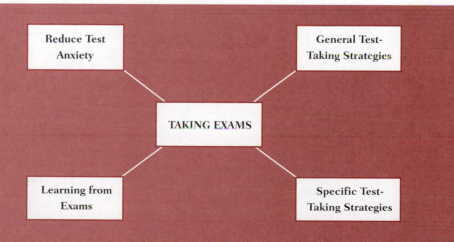

ACTIVITY 11.1   *Where Are You Now?*

Take a few minutes to answer *yes* or *no* to the following questions.

	YES	NO
1. Do you always read the directions before you begin to answer the questions on an exam?	_____	_____
2. Do you eliminate wrong answers on multiple-choice exams?	_____	_____
3. Does test anxiety interfere with your performance on exams?	_____	_____
4. Do you ever leave blanks on exams?	_____	_____
5. Do you use strategies to help you figure out the correct answer when you are unsure of it?	_____	_____
6. Do you ever find that you are unable to finish an exam before time runs out?	_____	_____
7. Do you go back over the entire exam before you turn it in?	_____	_____
8. After your exam is returned, do you go over it to evaluate your preparation and clarify your errors?	_____	_____
9. When you get your exam back, are you often surprised by the grade that you received?	_____	_____
10. Do you organize your answer before you begin to write on essay exams?	_____	_____

Total Points   _____

Give yourself 1 point for each *yes* answer to questions 1, 2, 5, 7, 8, and 10 and 1 point for each *no* answer to questions 3, 4, 6, and 9. Now total up your points. A low score indicates that you need to develop some new skills for taking objective tests. A high score indicates that you are already using many good strategies.

REDUCE TEST ANXIETY

To perform well on tests, you have to be well prepared. However, several other factors also may contribute to your success or failure. One of these factors often is referred to as your "test-taking ability." Some students are more skilled at taking tests than others. They have learned strategies and techniques that improve their performance on exams. Another factor that can affect test performance is your level of comfort when you take an exam. Some students view exams as everyday events, whereas other students consider them to be monumental obstacles that must be overcome. These different attitudes toward exams may be, in part, a result of students' varying levels of test anxiety.

All students experience a certain level of test anxiety at one time or another, but some students experience high levels of anxiety, fear, and frustration before, during, and after taking exams. Understanding the real causes of test anxiety and developing coping techniques can help students reduce the amount of test anxiety they experience.

WHAT IS TEST ANXIETY?

Some students come into an exam feeling well prepared, well rested, and highly motivated. Other students, however, feel uncertain about their level of preparation and anxious about their performance on the test. We could say that they are experiencing test anxiety. Test anxiety involves both physical responses, such as headaches, nausea, rapid heart beat, and shallow breathing, and emotional responses, such as worry and negative thoughts.

Although many students experience test anxiety, we don't know for sure whether test anxiety really causes some students to perform less well on exams. The connection between test anxiety and poor test performance still is being investigated by many researchers. However, test anxiety does appear to be related to poor test performance in students who exhibit very high levels of anxiety. For most of us, though, test anxiety alone does not cause test failure. Instead, lack of preparation (which can contribute to test anxiety) is the real cause of test failure.

WHAT CAUSES TEST ANXIETY?

What causes some students to experience test anxiety while others appear calm and collected on exams? Although there is no real answer to this question, several possible explanations may help us understand the problem. For some students, past experiences during exams lead to anxious feelings about subsequent exams. Failure accompanied by embarrassment and frustration in one testing situation can lead to anxiety in the next. Failure, by the way, doesn't mean the same thing for every student. When most people talk about failing an exam, they mean getting a grade that's below passing. For some students, however, getting a C or even a B is like failing; they fail to get the grade they wanted or needed. Excellent students often exhibit high levels of test anxiety because of the pressure they (or others) put on themselves to be the best.

The amount or level of anxiety that you experience also may depend on the value that you place on the exam. If doing well in the course is very important to you personally or professionally, you may view the exam as a critical or "must win" situation. On the other hand, if you see the class as having little value or being unimportant to your future, you may experience little anxiety. This may explain why some students suffer from test anxiety in one class but not in others.

Sometimes the type of test being given can lead to test anxiety. Some students panic when they find that they have to take essay tests. Others become anxious over oral exams. And, some, like me, hate true/false tests. Different types of tests cause feelings of anxiety for different people. The added pressure of having to complete an exam within a limited time period also creates feelings of anxiety for many students.

IS TEST ANXIETY NORMAL?

With all of these factors contributing to test anxiety, it's hard to believe that any student doesn't feel some level of anxiety. Actually, just about everyone does. It's perfectly normal to be anxious about an exam. If you weren't a little anxious about your performance, you probably wouldn't study at all. A small amount of test anxiety is good. We can describe this state of anxiety as facilitating test anxiety—anxiety that facilitates or helps motivate us to prepare before and work hard during the exam. On the other hand, a high level of test anxiety can interfere with your performance on an exam. We call this type of anxiety debilitating test anxiety. Like a debilitating illness, it prevents us from functioning in a normal way. High levels of test anxiety may interfere with your ability to concentrate on the exam, take the exam, or even to prepare for it. If you are out in the hall throwing up, you're losing time you could have spent completing the exam.

Some students find that they really can't prepare for exams because they are so anxious about them. When they begin to study, they start to think about the exam, and they experience some of the physical and emotional symptoms that we've discussed. They have difficulty concentrating on the material during the study session in much the same way that they do during the exam. This leads to poor preparation, which then leads to a poor test grade, and so the cycle begins (Figure 11.1).

COPING WITH TEST ANXIETY

There are a number of ways that you can learn to cope with test anxiety. First of all, remember that some test anxiety is good, so your goal should be to reduce higher levels of anxiety to a level that becomes facilitating. Look again at the test-anxiety cycle in Figure 11.1. There really is only one point at which a test-anxious student could interrupt the cycle and therefore change the outcome. Where is it? If you said, "can't study effectively," you were correct. This is the only point at which you can effectively change the outcome of your next exam.

There are a number of strategies that can help you reduce your test anxiety.

1. **Prepare Well.** By using active study strategies like writing and reciting, you can master the material for your exam.

2. **Self-Test.** By monitoring your learning through self-tests, you can feel confident about your preparation.

3. **Use Relaxation Strategies.** Use breathing or muscle-relaxing techniques to calm yourself. Just taking a few deep breaths can help you calm down. If that doesn't work, try taking a breath and then blowing it out very slowly a few times until you find that you're able to control your breathing.

4. **Avoid Negative Thoughts.** Negative thoughts about failing the test, whether you studied the right material, or that you don't belong in school interfere with your ability to concentrate on the test itself. Negative thoughts compete with and distract you from concentrating on the exam.

5. **Recite a Positive Mental Script.** After you study for the test, prepare a positive statement or script. As soon as you begin to think any negative thoughts during the exam, yell "STOP" or "STOP IT" in your mind and then immediately start to repeat your positive script.

6. **Use Visualization.** Try to imagine the professor walking in with the exam, giving directions, and passing out the tests. Picture yourself starting the exam. As you go through this role playing, monitor your level of anxiety. If you begin to feel anxious, use one of the stress-reduction activities to calm yourself.

FIGURE 11.1
Test-Anxiety Cycle

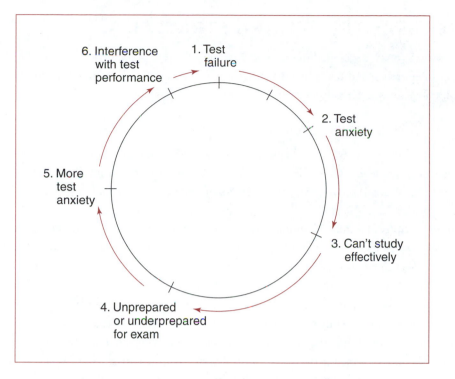

7. **Don't Arrive Too Early.** Enter the classroom about five minutes before the exam is to start. You'll have time to settle in and do a quick review but not enough time to allow yourself or others to make you nervous.

8. **Identify Your Triggers.** Identifying what triggers your feelings of anxiety can help you cope with them. If essay questions are your troublesome area, do the objective part of the test first. If your instructor makes you nervous by announcing the time every five minutes, tell him or her about your problem.

9. **Answer the Questions You Know First.** Test anxiety doesn't last forever; for most students the symptoms subside after about fifteen or twenty minutes. If you use strategies to help reduce your anxiety and at the same time answer the ones you know, your anxiety need not affect your grade.

10. **Don't Let Test Anxiety Become an Excuse.** Some students blame test anxiety instead of themselves when things aren't going well. They blame their test failure on their anxiety rather than on their lack of preparation, poor class attendance, or poor preparation in high school. After all, that's easier than having to work hard and face the results of their efforts. Be sure you don't fall into that trap.

ACTIVITY 11.2 *Check Your Test Anxiety Level*

Go to the *College Reading and Study Strategies* Web site and follow the link to the Test Anxiety Scale. Answer each of the questions online or by printing a copy of the questionnaire. Then follow the scoring instructions to determine your test anxiety level. What did you find?

GENERAL TEST-TAKING STRATEGIES

Now that you've developed many good strategies for test preparation, you need to learn how to approach and take objective and essay tests. Learning how to approach tests in a calm, logical way can help you increase your score.

FOLLOW DIRECTIONS

Reading the directions before beginning an exam can make the difference between getting a good grade and failing the exam. The directions give you information on how many questions to answer, what form the answers must take, and special directions for some parts of the test. The directions for all parts of an exam are not necessarily the same. Some sections of a multiple-choice exam, for example, may ask you to choose the best answer. Other sections may ask you to select all the correct answers or the only incorrect answer. Marking only the best answer when all correct choices are required may cost you 2 or 3 points per question.

On an essay exam, be sure that you look to see *how many* questions you're expected to answer. On many essay exams, you're given a choice of questions to answer. Consider the following set of directions: 1. *Answer two of the following questions.* (Six questions are given in total.) 2. *Answer two questions from set A and two questions from set B.* (Three questions are included in set A, and three questions are included in set B.) In each of these cases you are being limited to a certain number of questions and, in the latter case, to a certain number of questions from two different sets. The test directions also may include information about how the essay is to be formatted. The directions also may tell you to write on every other line, to include an example, or to include a brief outline.

BUDGET YOUR TIME

If you budget your time during a test, you should be able to complete the entire test before time runs out. If you lose track of time or spend too much time on one part of the exam, you may end up leaving some questions undone. Being unable to finish even five (two-point) questions on a test can mean the difference of one letter grade.

Consider Point Values

Previewing the exam gives you an idea of what you need to accomplish during the test period. Count the total number of questions that you have to answer. Then look at each section of the exam and check the point value for each question. Some students ignore the differences in point values among questions and treat all questions as if they were of equal weight. Occasionally, this has disastrous effects. If you use the following rule, you always will be able to determine how much time to spend on each question or section of the test:

> **Rule:** Percentage of the total points = Percentage of total time

Pace Yourself During the Exam

Even if your exam is all multiple-choice questions, you still need to budget your time. You want to complete the entire test and still have time to go back over it. Divide the time you have by the total number of questions and then shave off some for your review. You may have forty questions to answer in a fifty-minute period. If you allow ten minutes for review, you can spend one minute on each question. Pacing yourself during the exam—by dividing up the test and setting time goals for each third, fourth, or fifth of the exam—can help you complete the entire exam. For example, if you had forty questions to answer in forty minutes, you might divide the test at the end of each ten-question chunk. If your exam started at 2:00, you might jot 2:10 in the margin next to question 10, 2:20 in the margin next to 20, and 2:30 in the margin next to question 30. Each time you moved to the next chunk of questions, you could check the time and monitor your progress. If you were working slowly, you would realize it early enough to speed up. If you realized that you were racing through the questions, you could slow down and spend more time on each question.

What to Do If Time Runs Out

If you have one or two questions left to do when time runs out, ask the professor for a few more minutes. Even though some professors are sticklers about time, they may allow you to finish the exam while they gather up their materials. If you only have a few minutes left, you can still pick up most of the points on an essay answer. Let's say you have started writing your last essay answer out in paragraph form. When you have only about five minutes left, simply list the remaining points that you wanted to make. Add a little note to the professor that says something like, "I'm sorry that I didn't have time to finish my essay. These are the additional points that I wanted to make." Some professors will give you full credit for your answer, assuming it is a good one, even though you didn't write all of it out. This is a better strategy than just writing until time runs out and answering only half of the question.

ACTIVITY 11.3   *Budget Your Time*

Work as a group to determine how much time you should spend on each section in the following practice tests. (For this exercise, don't allow time to review the entire test.)

Practice Test A:

	Case 1	Case 2
10 multiple-choice items worth 20 points	_____	_____
20 identification items worth 40 points	_____	_____
2 essay questions worth 40 points	_____	_____

(Case 1: You have 100 minutes for the test.)

(Case 2: You have 50 minutes for the test.)

Practice Test B:

	Case 1	Case 2
30 multiple-choice items worth 2 points each	_____	_____
10 completion items worth 2 points each	_____	_____
1 essay worth 10 points	_____	_____

(Case 1: You have 80 minutes for the test.)

(Case 2: You have 50 minutes for the test.)

WORK LOGICALLY THROUGH THE EXAM

You can improve your score on both objective and essay exams by working logically and methodically through the exam. To maximize your score, you should answer the easiest questions first, use strategies to figure out the correct answer when you don't know it immediately, and answer all questions.

Answer the Easiest Questions First

Another strategy for improving your grade on an exam is to answer the easiest questions first. By immediately answering all questions that you know, you can maximize your score on the test. If you do run out of time, you'll be sure to receive points for the questions that you did know. In addition, you can reduce your test anxiety by answering the easiest questions first. By the time you go back to work on the more difficult questions, you'll feel more relaxed. This is because you build up your confidence as you complete the easy questions; you know that you know at least some or even many of the answers. One student reported that she used this strategy on an algebra exam. By the time she went back to the "difficult" questions, they didn't seem nearly as hard. Because she was more relaxed, she was able to think through the problems more logically and solve them correctly.

Some students panic if they read the first question on the test and realize they don't know the answer. Instead of allowing yourself to start thinking negative thoughts, just tell yourself "This is a hard question—I'll come back to it later." This type of positive thinking allows you to focus on the rest of the test.

Work Strategically to Answer All Questions

As you move through the exam, skip the questions you aren't sure of and go on to the easier questions. If you know that you don't know an answer, don't spend a lot of time on the question. Think through each question. Underline key words in the question to help you focus your thinking. Eliminate any answer that you know is wrong and then try to figure out the correct answer. Do a memory search to try to retrieve the information about the topic. Ask yourself questions about the material. Try to determine whether the answer came from the lecture or from the text. Try to remember where you saw it on the page, where it was written in your notes, or what the professor was talking about just before or after that topic was presented. By searching your memory, you can often find a clue or cue that helps you recall the information.

Look for Clues in Other Questions

You may find the answer to an early question in one of the possible answers to a question three pages away. Even if you don't find the answer itself, you may find a clue or cue to help you answer the question. You may read a word in another question or in another possible answer that triggers your memory and helps you retrieve the information that you need. You also can use the objective part of an exam to give you ideas or gather details for essay exams. Professors often test on the same topic in both objective and essay formats. Even if you pick up a clue to only one or two questions as you move through the test, that can often make a difference in your grade.

GUESSING STRATEGIES

Even if you are well prepared for a test and use good test-taking strategies, you still may find that you can't answer some questions. When none of your test-taking strategies work, then you should guess. Strategic guessing does not guarantee that you will get all of the questions right, but it certainly improves your odds of getting some of them right.

What is a guess anyway? Some students describe a guess as just putting down any letter they can think of to fill the slot. They choose randomly from among the alternatives. However, strategic guessing involves more active processes. There are a number of strategies that you can use to pick up a few more points on a test even when you don't know the correct answer.

Look for Patterns

Pretend that you answered all of the easy questions on an exam and then went back and used problem-solving strategies to figure out the answers for a few more. Rather than just guessing randomly, look for patterns in the answers. Many professors never use the same letter more than two or three times in a row before shifting to a different response. So if you know that B is the correct response for the three previous questions and you eliminated C and D, A would be a more strategic guess than B. Go back and look at some of your old exams to see what types of patterns your professors use. By using that strategy, you should be able to get at least a few of the answers right—adding several points to your total test score.

ACTIVITY 11.4 *Guess at True/False Questions*

Pretend that you answered all the easy questions on an exam and then went back and figured out a few more by using problem-solving strategies. There are still seven items on the following answer sheet that you can't answer. In the empty spaces below, write T for true or F for false for each of the unanswered questions. Although you don't have the actual questions, try to guess the actual answers from a real exam.

1. __T__	6. __F__	11. __T__	16. _____	21. __F__
2. _____	7. __T__	12. __T__	17. __F__	22. __F__
3. __F__	8. _____	13. __F__	18. __F__	23. __T__
4. __F__	9. __T__	14. _____	19. __F__	24. _____
5. _____	10. __F__	15. __T__	20. _____	25. __T__

List any strategies that you used to figure out the correct answers. Jot them in the margin. Check the answers on the *College Reading and Study Strategies* Web site.

ACTIVITY 11.5 *Guess at Multiple-Choice Questions*

Pretend that you answered all the easy questions on a multiple-choice exam and then went back and figured out a few more by using problem-solving strategies. There are still fourteen items on the following answer sheet that are blank. In the empty spaces below, write A, B, C, or D for each of the unanswered questions. Although you don't have the actual questions, try to guess the actual answers from a real exam.

1. __A__	11. __B__	21. __D__	31. _____	41. _____
2. _____	12. __A__	22. __D__	32. __B__	42. __C__
3. __C__	13. __C__	23. __A__	33. _____	43. _____
4. __C__	14. _____	24. _____	34. __B__	44. __D__
5. __B__	15. __B__	25. __A__	35. __D__	45. __A__
6. __D__	16. _____	26. __C__	36. _____	46. __B__
7. __C__	17. __C__	27. __A__	37. _____	47. __A__
8. _____	18. __C__	28. __B__	38. __D__	48. _____
9. __B__	19. __D__	29. __D__	39. __A__	49. __D__
10. __D__	20. __A__	30. _____	40. _____	50. __C__

List any strategies that you used to figure out the correct answers. Jot them in the margin. Check the answers on the *College Reading and Study Strategies* Web site.

Check for Balanced Answer Keys

Some professors always have balanced answer keys; they use exactly the same number of As, Bs, Cs, and Ds. If you find that there are three or four questions that you can't answer, count how many of each letter you have already used. You may find that you have fewer As than any other letter. By marking your remaining answers "A," you probably will get some right. Although this sounds like a great strategy, it works only if you are well enough prepared to get most of the other answers right.

Guessing Doesn't Replace Proper Preparation

Remember, guessing strategies are designed to help you pick up a few additional points when you absolutely can't figure out the correct answer any other way. They are *not* designed to replace proper preparation or substitute for more active problem-solving strategies that can lead you to the correct answer by providing you with clues or aiding your recall of the answer. Use them *only* after all other attempts to figure out the correct answer have failed. In fact, the students who are the best prepared to take an exam can benefit the most since they have only a small number of unanswered questions.

SPECIFIC TEST-TAKING STRATEGIES

If you prepare well, reduce test anxiety, read and follow directions, pace yourself, and answer the easiest question first, you should do well on exams. However, some students still have trouble on objective and essay exams because they lack test-taking skills. There are a number of specific strategies that can help you maximize your score on exams.

STRATEGIES FOR MULTIPLE-CHOICE EXAMS

The most common type of objective test is the multiple-choice test. Multiple-choice tests allow instructors to test students' knowledge of the course material at various levels of understanding. Many new college students have difficulty in these exams because they expect all questions to be at the knowledge level. They prepare by memorizing the material and often do not take the time to really learn and understand it. If you're able to recall the correct answers from memory without cues, multiple-choice exams will be easy for you. Most multiple-choice exams contain a stem, which is composed of a question or an incomplete sentence, and several alternatives or possible answers.

Many strategies are effective for taking multiple-choice exams; however, these strategies come in two different forms. The first group includes problem-solving strategies that can help you figure out the correct answer from the various distractors or decoys. The other group involves test-wise strategies that should be used only after you have tried all the logical strategies first.

Problem-Solving Strategies

Problem-solving strategies can help you logically and methodically identify the correct answer even if you don't know it when you first read the question.

1. **Read the question and all answers before you select the "correct" answer.** Some students lose points on multiple-choice exams because they do not read all possible answers before selecting the one that they think is correct. In most multiple-choice tests, you generally are asked to select the best answer. In that case, several of the choices may be correct or good answers, but only one answer is the "best" answer.

2. **Underline key words.** By underlining key words in the question, you can better focus your attention on what's being asked. In addition, you may find that underlining key words helps you identify a cue that triggers your long-term memory. Finally, taking the time to underline key words in both the question and the possible answers forces you to slow down and read the question and answers more carefully. Many students rush when they take exams and misread questions or answers. They make careless errors that cost them points they should have had. If you can't write on the exam, use your finger to underline the key words.

3. **Work to eliminate incorrect alternatives rather than looking for the "right" answer.** After reading the question and all alternatives, begin looking for those that you know are wrong. When you're sure that one possible answer is a distractor (incorrect answer designed to appear correct), cross it off. Continue eliminating choices until only one answer remains. If you can eliminate all alternatives except one, you know you have found the correct answer.

4. **Connect the stem of the question to each alternative answer; then treat each statement as a true/false item.** If you're good at taking true/false tests, use the same strategies that work for you on the true/false items for the multiple-choice items. Identify key words, underline words or phrases that make the statement false, and watch for absolute, qualifying, and negative words.

5. **Read the question, cover the alternatives, and think of the answer.** Some students find multiple-choice tests difficult because they allow the alternative answers to confuse them. To avoid this problem, read the question and think of the answer. Then read each alternative and ask yourself, "Does this mean the same thing as the answer that I know is correct?"

6. **Use caution when "all of the above" and "none of the above" are included as choices.** If you can eliminate even *one* alternative, you can eliminate "all of the above" as the correct answer. Similarly, if you are sure that at least one choice is correct, you can eliminate "none of the above." If you have three alternatives and you know that two of them are correct but aren't sure of the third, "all of the above" must be correct (assuming you can choose only one answer). If "all of the above" and "none of the above" are used only occasionally on the test, they are probably the correct choices. Watch for patterns like this on each exam.

Test-Wise Strategies

Use test-wise strategies to help you determine the correct choice when you can't figure it out. Many courses that are designed to prepare students to take the SATs or other standardized tests seem to specialize in these "test-smart" strategies. Some of them are very helpful; others are not so useful. The key to using these tricks or clues is to use them sparingly. Never follow a test-wise strategy that would require you to select one alternative when you are fairly sure that another alternative is the correct answer. Use these strategies only when you can't determine the correct answer by using the more conventional strategies.

Some of the more effective and useful test-wise strategies are listed below.

1. **An answer that contains more specific, detailed information probably is correct. Vague or general alternatives are often used as distractors.**

2. **An answer that contains the most words, especially if it also contains the most specific information, probably is correct.**

3. **An answer that is in the middle probably is correct, especially if it has the most words.**

4. **An answer that is about in the middle numerically probably is correct.**

5. **An answer that contains an unfamiliar term probably is wrong.**

6. **An answer that contains a "typo," especially if there are very few typos in the test, probably is wrong.**

7. **An answer that is grammatically correct probably is right if the other choices are not grammatically correct.**

8. **An answer that contains a form of the word or a word similar to one in the stem of the question is probably correct.**

9. **If a question contains two opposite alternatives, one of them is probably correct.**

10. **If a question contains two alternatives that are almost identical (perhaps only one word is different), then one of them is probably correct.**

ACTIVITY 11.6   *Take a Multiple-Choice Test*

Without looking back at Chapter 7, circle the best answer for each of the following questions. Use both conventional problem-solving strategies and test-wise clues to arrive at the correct choices. The answers are available on the *College Reading and Study Strategies* Web Site. What strategies did you use to answer each question?

1. Which memory theory is concerned with how old memories affect newer memories?

   a. Decay theory

   b. Interference theory

   c. Reconstructive theory

   d. Schema theory

2. According to the Information Processing Model, the process of finding material in long-term memory is known as

   a. encoding.

   b. mnemonics.

   c. retrieval.

   d. storage.

3. According to the Information Processing Model, we are able to pay attention to about _____ thing(s) at any one time.

   a. one

   b. two

   c. three

   d. several

4. Bonnie, a waitress, takes the order from a table of eight customers. She must remember the order until she gets to the kitchen where she can write it down. This whole process takes about five minutes. How might she accomplish this feat?

   a. Iconic memory will do the trick.

   b. Immediate memory will do the job for her.

   c. She can rely on her sensory registers.

   d. She will need to move that material into long-term memory.

STRATEGIES FOR TRUE/FALSE EXAMS

Many students like true/false exams because they provide excellent odds for guessing correctly. However, some students have difficulty dealing with this type of test because the statements can be tricky. To make a statement incorrect, professors may change key words, omit key words, add absolute or qualifying words, add negative words, add extraneous information, and so on. Because there are so many ways to make a statement "false," students must consider all of them as they examine each statement.

Use the following basic guidelines when taking true/false tests:

1. **Always read the directions before beginning a true/false test.** Some instructors are very particular about how they expect students to mark true/false items. If you don't complete the exam according to the directions, you may not get credit for your answers.

2. **For a statement to be true, it must be all true.** If any part of the statement is false, the entire statement is false.

3. **True/false items are not all tricky.** Some students start to look for "tricks" or read too much into the question when a true/false item seems "too easy." If you're properly prepared for a test, some true/false items should appear to be easy.

4. **Identify the key words or phrases.** Many professors make a statement false by substituting another word or phrase for the correct one. By identifying and verifying the accuracy of key words, you can more easily decide whether a statement is true or false.

5. **Statements that contain absolute words are usually false.** Words like *always, all, none, never, only, every,* and *no* are examples of absolute words. Each of these words implies that there are no exceptions. Although the inclusion of these words in a true/false item doesn't guarantee that it's false, it usually indicates a false statement.

6. **Statements that contain qualifying words are usually true statements.** Words like *usually, often, may, can, sometimes, frequently, rarely, most, some, many, few,* and *generally* are examples of qualifying words. These words qualify or "temper" the statement to allow for exceptions and are generally associated with true statements. However, if you know that a statement is false, mark it *false,* even though it contains a qualifying word.

7. **Statements that contain negative words often are tricky and require careful attention.** Double negatives, which generally include the word *not* plus another word that contains a negative prefix often confuse students. If a statement contains a double negative, cross off the word *not* and the negative prefix (*in, il, ir,* or *un*) and then reread the statement in order to determine whether it's true or false.

8. **Always underline the word or words that make a statement false.** If you can't identify and mark the actual key words, absolute words, negative words, and so on that cause the statement to be incorrect, assume that it's correct and mark it true. There is one exception, however. If you know that a statement is false by

omission (because a key word or phrase has been left out), mark the statement *false* even though you can't actually underline the words that make it false.

9. **Correct all false items on the exam if you have time to do so.** By correcting the statement, you show the professor and remind yourself what you were thinking during the exam. (By the time you get the exam back, you may not remember why you thought the item was false.)

10. **Professors usually include more true items than false items on an exam.** Many professors use tests to reinforce the main ideas that were presented in the course. If you absolutely can't figure out whether a statement is true or false, mark it true. Watch for patterns on each test.

ACTIVITY **11.7** *Take a True/False Test*

Work with a partner to indicate whether each item in the following section is true or false. If it is false, underline the word or words that make it false and then correct the statement. Circle any absolute words. Compare your responses to those in another group. Check the answers on the *College Reading and Study Strategies* Web site.

_____ 1. Reading and active reading involve exactly the same processes.

_____ 2. You should always make maps when studying for exams.

_____ 3. You may find it helpful to read the summary before reading the chapter.

_____ 4. Sitting in the front of the room will assure you of getting a good grade.

_____ 5. When skimming a chapter, you should have complete comprehension.

_____ 6. Once you learn something, you never have to review it again.

_____ 7. Some students use recall columns when they take lecture notes.

_____ 8. Recopying notes verbatim is an active study strategy.

_____ 9. All students should take self-tests to reduce test anxiety.

_____ 10. All students who fail exams have high levels of test anxiety.

STRATEGIES FOR MATCHING EXAMS

With proper preparation and test-taking strategies, you should be able to get top scores on matching tests. Matching tests require you to recognize the correct answer from a list of alternatives. The answers to all questions are given; you do not have to "pull" the answer from memory. Before beginning a matching test, be sure that you read the directions. Usually, you are instructed to use each letter only once, but some matching tests allow for or require the repeated use of some letters. Although you probably aren't familiar with the terms and definitions in the matching test in Activity 11.8, try it now. By taking the test and then reading about how to figure out many of the answers, you can learn a number of test-taking strategies.

ACTIVITY 11.8   *Practice Answering Matching Questions*

Match the terms and definitions from a psychology chapter on the biological basis of behavior.[1] Write the letter of the correct definition on the line in front of each term. Each letter is used only once. How many were you able to get correct? What strategies did you use?

TERMS

_____   **1.** ablation

_____   **2.** action potential

_____   **3.** aphasia

_____   **4.** cerebral cortex

_____   **5.** endorphins

_____   **6.** genotype

_____   **7.** myelin sheath

_____   **8.** neurons

_____   **9.** soma

_____   **10.** thalamus

DEFINITIONS

A. a disorder characterized by language and speech disorders attributed to brain damage

B. individual cells of the nervous system

C. a person's genetic makeup

D. surgical removal of a piece of the brain

E. the convoluted outer layer of the cerebrum

F. a structure in the forebrain through which all sensory information must pass

G. insulating material that encases some axons

H. the family of internally produced chemicals that resemble opiates in structure and effects

I. the body of a cell, which contains the nucleus

J. a brief change in a neuron's electrical charge that travels along the axon

Work from One Side

Matching tests often include a list of names or terms in one column and then a list of identifications, accomplishments, or definitions in the other column. When you take a matching test like the one in Activity 11.8, always work from one side only. Crossing off items in both columns leads to confusion and often results in careless errors or wasted time. From which side did you work in that test? You should always work from the column that has the most words. In the sample test, there are thirteen words in the term column and over eighty words in the definition column. If you worked from the term column, you would have to scan more than eighty words in the definition column to find a correct match. If, instead, you worked from the definition column, you would have to scan only thirteen words on each pass—saving you time for other parts of the exam.

Answer the Questions You're Sure of First

Earlier in the chapter you read about the advantages of answering the easiest questions first. When taking a matching test, it's crucial that you answer the questions or make the matches that you are absolutely sure of first. By eliminating all choices that

---

[1]Test items prepared by Dr. Malcolm Van Blerkom based on information from W. Weiten, *Psychology: Themes and Variations* (Pacific Grove, CA: Brooks/Cole, 1989). Used with permission.

you are sure of, you can narrow the alternatives for the remaining choices. When I took the test in Activity 11.8, I hadn't studied or prepared for it. Even though I didn't prepare, I still was able to make all matches correctly. In the next three sections, I'll tell you how I figured out each match.

Eliminate and Cross Off Alternatives

As you go through the list of definitions, cross off the letter (not the word) of the ones that you use. Just put one diagonal line through the letter so that you can recheck your matches later. If you can eliminate five of the ten alternatives on your first pass through the list, you've improved your chances of getting the others right. The first time I read through the definitions in Activity 11.8, I was able to make only three matches. I knew that aphasia was "A," a disorder that caused speech problems. I knew that endorphins had to match with "H" because I learned that the good feeling I get from exercise is caused by the release of a chemical, endorphins. I also figured out that myelin sheath had to be "G" because a sheath is a covering, so it *encases* or covers something, and the word *encases* is used in answer "G."

After you match all items you're sure of, start with the first unmatched definition that you have and try to match it with each remaining term. If you're sure of a match, make it; if not, skip over that definition and go on to the next one. Continue down the list until you can make one more match. Then go back through the list again. Having eliminated one more alternative, you may find that only one other term could possibly be correct for one of the definitions. Through the process of elimination, you should be able to make all the matches.

On my second pass through Activity 11.8, I matched "C" with *genotype* because *genetic makeup* had *gene* in it, as did *genotype*. I also matched "E" with *cerebral cortex* because I knew it was a part of the brain and it had a similar word part in it, too (*cerebrum*). I also matched "D" with *ablation* because I had never heard of the word *ablation* and no other term appeared to fit the definition. I had some idea about the meaning of most of the other terms. I matched "J" with *action potential* because the definition involved a change in the charge, and change to me seemed to fit with *action*. Also, it didn't seem to fit well with any of the other choices.

Jot Down Alternatives That You're Sure Don't Match

Sometimes you actually can figure out a correct choice by making notes about which terms are definitely wrong for each definition. For example, after my second pass through the test in Activity 11.8, I had three items left to match (8, 9, and 10) and three definitions ("B," "F," and "I"). I knew that *thalamus* was a part of the brain and not a cell, so it couldn't be matched with "B" or "I." Therefore, "F" had to match with number 10. I also knew that "B" and "I" had to match with *neurons* and *soma*. It was difficult to determine which was correct because I had not prepared for this test; however, I vaguely remembered that neurons were like connections in the brain, so I matched "B" with neurons. Also "B" contained a plural noun, cells, and *neurons* was also plural. The only remaining alternative was to match "I" with *soma*.

Although I didn't expect to get them all right, I did. Did you use any of these strategies to figure out the correct matches? If you prepare properly for an exam, you should be able to match most of the items without difficulty. Then, by using some of the previous strategies, you should be able to figure out the other matches. Don't be afraid to draw on information from other courses and your own experiences to help you figure out correct answers, just as I did.

Recheck Your Work

After you've matched all items on the list, go back and check to be sure that you haven't accidentally used the same letter or number twice. Going through the letters or numbers and crossing off each one again can help you avoid careless errors. If you do find that you

---

TIP

END-OF-EXAM STRATEGIES

DON'T LEAVE THE EXAM EARLY. Some students rush through the exam just to get out of class early. Others begin to panic as soon as the first student turns in his or her paper. You need to use all of the exam time to get the best grade you can. You may be able to pick up a few more points by using the strategies you learned in this chapter.

GO BACK OVER DIFFICULT QUESTIONS. Use any additional time to rethink difficult questions on the exam. Underline key words in the question and in the alternatives. Eliminate wrong answers. Look for clues in other questions. Rephrase the question or the alternatives.

REDO PROBLEMS TO CHECK YOUR WORK. Some students lose points on exams because of careless errors. If you have time, cover the problem with your hand and rework it. Then compare your answers. If they differ, check your work line by line until you locate your mistake.

PROOFREAD YOUR ESSAY ANSWER. If you take just a few additional minutes to reread your answer, you may catch careless errors in sentence construction, grammar, or mechanics. You might even think of additional points to make or a better way to phrase the information.

USE CAUTION WHEN CHANGING ANSWERS. During a final review of the test, many students change answers because they start to have doubts about their original choices. This strategy often leads to changing correct answers to incorrect ones. Instead use this rule: Don't change an answer unless you find that you misread the question or actually find the correct answer or a clue to it somewhere else on the exam.

REVIEW THE ENTIRE EXAM. When you complete the exam, take a few minutes to go back over it and check your answers. Some students make careless errors when they begin the exam because they are anxious; others do the same toward the end of the exam when they think they're running out of time. You may be able to correct some careless mistakes that would have cost you valuable points.

CODE YOUR TEST IF YOU HAVE EXTRA TIME. Put a line through the letters of answers that you eliminate. Circle the letter of the answer that you select and leave blank the letters of any answers that you aren't sure about. After the exam is over, you can see how effectively you were able to eliminate wrong answers. You should also put a dot next to the answer when you guess. You can monitor your guessing ability after the exam, too.

CHECK YOUR ANSWER SHEET AGAINST YOUR EXAM. Before you turn in your test paper, take a minute or two to check to be sure that you marked the correct answers on your answer sheet. It's easy to make mistakes when you're nervous or in a hurry. You want to get the points for all of your correct answers.

have one term left and one definition left, and you know that they do not match, you need to go back and recheck your work, especially because it is unlikely that this is your only error. Go back through the list looking for any term that could fit the remaining definition. If necessary, rewrite the letters or numbers next to the original list and cross them off again. A number of other end-of-exam strategies are shown in the Tip Block.

STRATEGIES FOR ESSAY EXAMS

There are a number of strategies for taking essay exams that can help you retrieve, relate, and organize the information that you learned. After you read the directions, you should plan before you write and organize your answer to be more successful on essay exams.

Plan Before You Write

If you take a few minutes to plan your answers before you write them, you'll find that you write better essay answers in a shorter period of time. When you first look at the essay test, read *all* essay questions before you decide which ones you want to answer.

As you read each question, make notes in the margin as the ideas for an answer pop into your mind. If you predicted one or more of the questions, jot down your mnemonic device, the key words, or the main points from the outline that you planned. You'll be able to make a better decision about which question or questions you should answer after you look at your notes.

Making notes as you read the questions can be very helpful. Sometimes it's hard to remember what you wanted to say about a particular question when you're ready to answer it. Reading the other questions and thinking about whether you should answer them can cause interference. The notes you jot in the margin also serve as additional cues to long-term memory. Each of the words you write down can later help you retrieve even more details for your answer. In addition to aiding your memory, making notes in the margin helps relieve test anxiety. Once you know that you can answer the question, you can relax and feel more comfortable about the exam.

After you have chosen to answer a question and have jotted your ideas in the margin, you should reread the question to make sure that your notes reflect all parts of the question.

Organize Your Ideas Before Writing

After jotting down your ideas in the margin, you can organize your essay in just a few seconds. Simply number your ideas in the margin as Kesha did in Figure 11.2. Look at the ideas that you jotted down and ask yourself, "What's the first thing that I want to talk about?" After that, you can decide what to put second, third, and so on. You also may decide that some of your ideas actually support some of the others. You can indicate that some of your ideas are supporting points by marking them with an "A" or a "B" after the number.

Some students don't feel that they can take the time to plan their answers in the margin because they feel pressured for time during exams. However, you should be able to plan and organize an answer in just one or two minutes. For a longer essay, you can organize your ideas even more by writing a brief outline in the margin.

FIGURE 11.2
Kesha's Organized
Marginal Notes

Question: What general and specific strategies should a student follow
when taking a matching test?

Notes in margin:

③ – work from one side to other   ⑥ – do the ones you know 1st
④ – usually longest first   ⑦ – do not guess right away
⑤ – do not work from side to side   ① – read directions
   – cross off answer if you use it   ② – read through all choices

---

ACTIVITY ▶ 11.9 *Organize Your Answers*

Jot down your ideas in the margin as you read each of the following questions. Then work
with a group to organize them by creating an informal outline.

1. Why should students answer the easiest questions first when taking objective exams?

2. What general and specific strategies should a student use when taking a true/false exam?

3. Compare and contrast short-term and long-term memory.

Write Your Answer

Getting started is often the hardest part of writing an essay answer. So, start with the easiest question first. Write your essay answer as you would write an essay for one of your English classes.

Begin your essay with a topic sentence that states the central idea of your paragraph. After the topic sentence, state your first main point. After stating your first main point, back it up with one or more supporting sentences. Each of these sentences may include details, facts, or examples that further explain your main point. Next, state your second main point, followed by a sentence or two of support. Your third main point should be made next, followed by relevant support. Additional main points and secondary supporting information also can be included here. Finally, end your paragraph with a concluding sentence.

Not all essays can be answered in only one paragraph. You may be expected to write several paragraphs or several pages in order to answer a question properly. In that case, instead of having a topic sentence followed by several main points, each paragraph in your essay would focus on one of these main points. A one-paragraph answer can easily be expanded to a four- or five-paragraph answer simply by developing each point more fully. The topic sentence would be expanded to an introductory paragraph containing a thesis statement, each main-point sentence would be expanded to form a supporting paragraph, and the concluding sentence would become a concluding paragraph.

Finally, you should end your paragraph or essay with a conclusion, a concluding sentence or paragraph that reminds your professor of the main points that you made. Professors form opinions of essays as they read, but they don't assign an actual grade until after they have read the entire answer. If you have made some of your best points early in your answer, it helps remind your professor of them just before he or she assigns a grade. Also, the concluding sentence or paragraph helps bring the answer to a logical ending, making

FIGURE 11.3
Sample Essay

	Question: How did Greek ①architecture and ②sculpture reflect the Greeks' concern for ᵃ·order, ᵇ·reason, and the ᶜ·ideal? What rules did they follow? (30 points)
1 rules of proportion 3 Parthenon 2 human-ideal 4 perfect image 5 virtual image	Answer:

The Greeks valued architecture and sculpture and tried to make them reflect their concern for order, reason, and the ideal. First, the Greeks followed very careful rules of proportion in creating their sculptures of gods and heroes. Every human figure was seven and one-half heads tall. The distances from the head to the chest, the chest to the groin, and the ankle to the foot all followed exact proportional measurements that had previously been determined. Also, the Greeks followed careful "rules" in the way they portrayed man and the gods in their sculpture. All works were idealized. They showed only the best human features. Second, the Greeks used the rules of proportion and measurement in creating their works of architecture. The Parthenon provides an excellent example of this order. The columns were spaced in proportion to the others in order to create a "perfect" image for the viewer. The number of columns across the side was equal to twice the number across the front plus one. This provided a sense of balance to the Greeks. Also, all of the columns leaned inward in order to maintain the illusion that they were exactly parallel and vertical. They were also thicker in the middle so that from the bottom of the hill, they appeared to be perfectly straight. Other similar "corrections" were made to the floor and the decorations in the frieze in order to maintain that "virtual image" that was so important to the Greeks. Both sculpture and architecture reflected the Greeks' concern for order, reason, and the ideal.

the entire essay appear well thought out. Look at the sample essay in Figure 11.3. Which sentence is the topic sentence? Which sentences present the main points? Which sentences provide the secondary support? Which sentence presents the conclusion? Are transitions used? Which ones?

LEARNING FROM EXAMS

Many students think that once an exam is over, the only thing that matters is the grade. However, exams are learning opportunities. Professors often use them to help reinforce the critical concepts that they are trying to present. Reviewing an exam after it's returned can help you learn more about the course content and clarify any errors that you made. You also can learn a great deal about your professor's testing methods and about your own test-taking skills.

EVALUATE YOUR PREPARATION

Your graded exam can be used to help you evaluate your preparation. By finding out where each question came from (the lecture or the textbook), you can determine whether you're focusing on the same topics and ideas as your professor. You also can check how well you mark and take notes by scanning the text or your text notes and looking for questions that were on the test. If you find that few of the test questions came from the material that you highlighted or noted, you can adjust for the next test. Determining how many of the questions came from the text and how many came from the lecture can help you decide how much time to spend on each type of material the next time you prepare.

One of the most important things you'll learn from your returned essay exam is how closely your answer matched what the professor wanted. If you got a good grade on the exam, you probably are doing a good job of presenting the information that the professor wanted. If, on the other hand, your grade was lower than you expected, you need to find out where you went astray. It's important to understand why you got the grade that you did.

LEARN FROM YOUR MISTAKES

Understanding why you were wrong about a particular answer can be critical to your success on the next exam. In some cases, you may need to clarify or correct some of the information that you learned. By discussing your mistakes with your professor, you may find that you hadn't really understood the material after all. By examining your errors, you also can determine whether they resulted from poor preparation or from carelessness or poor test-taking strategies.

If you don't understand why you got a poor grade on your esssay exam, set up an appointment to discuss your test with your professor. Don't go into the meeting with the expectation of getting extra points. Instead, focus on finding out how you should have answered the question in order to gain the maximum number of points. In this way, you and the professor are on the same side; you are working toward the same goal. Often, when you "fight" for additional points, you and the professor may find yourselves acting as opponents or adversaries. If that type of atmosphere is generated, you may gain a point or two on the exam, but you'll probably lose the opportunity to learn how to write a better answer.

ACTIVITY   11.10   *Learn from Your Exam*

Review one of the exams that recently was returned to you. Write a paragraph or two discussing what you were able to learn from the exam. Include information about how the test was designed, your preparation, and your test-taking skills. What changes do you plan to make for your next exam?

ACTIVITY 11.11   *Evaluate Sample Essay Answers*

Take a few minutes and answer the following essay question: *Compare and contrast a catchword and a catchphrase.* Then read each of the essay answers available on the *College Reading and Study Strategies* Web site, and evaluate them using the criteria that were discussed in this chapter. Evaluate each answer and assign a grade from 1 to 10 points (no grade is used more than once). Jot down a few notes to justify your decision. Which are the three best essays, in order? _____ _____ _____. Which are the three worst essays, in order? _____ _____ _____. Be prepared to defend your choices with your group.

ACTIVITY 11.12   *Use InfoTrac College Edition to Locate Articles on Test Anxiety*

If you are using InfoTrac College Edition, use PowerTrac to locate a recent article or research study on how test anxiety affects test performance. Describe the study and any suggestions that were included on how to cope with anxiety before and during college tests. List three strategies that you can use to reduce your own test anxiety. After using them before or during your next exam, describe any changes you noted in your performance or your ability to concentrate. Be prepared to present the information in class.

ACTIVITY 11.13   *Where Are You Now?*

Now that you have completed Chapter 11, take a few minutes to repeat the "Where Are You Now?" activity, located on the *College Reading and Study Strategies* Web site. What changes did you make as a result of reading this chapter? How are you planning to apply what you've learned in this chapter?

Summary

Your preparation for exams is only one factor that influences your final grade. Some students appear to be good test takers and others don't. Why? One explanation involves how effectively they can handle the stress of taking exams. Test anxiety can have a major impact on your ability to prepare for and take exams. Some students get queasy, feel faint, worry, or even "go blank" during exams. Because of test anxiety, they can't completely focus on the exam questions and their grades suffer. Coping techniques such as doing relaxation exercises, visualizing, using positive self-scripts, and identifying anxiety triggers can help reduce your test anxiety. However, the most effective way to reduce test anxiety is being well prepared.

Following directions carefully is crucial during any testing situation. Too often, though, students skip this important step in order to save time or because of high levels of test anxiety. Budgeting your time during exams is also important so that you can complete all questions and still have time for a final review of the test. You can maximize your test score and pick up clues to more difficult questions by answering the easiest questions first. Using both problem-solving strategies and test-wise clues will help you gain points on matching, true/false, completion, and multiple-choice exams.

Doing memory searches, eliminating wrong answers, and underlining key words are just a few ways to "figure out" the correct answer when you're not sure of it. However, when you still can't come up with the right choice, you should use strategic guessing. If you've taken the time to prepare properly for your exam, take the time to "take" it, too. Use the full amount of time that's been allotted for the exam. Students who persevere—continue to work on difficult questions, think through confusing items, look for clues in other questions, and use problem-solving and test-wise strategies—do better on exams.

If you're well prepared, essay tests can be even easier than objective tests. Some students lose points on essay tests, not because they don't know the material, but because they don't know how to take essay tests. First, read the directions to determine how many questions to answer, their point values, and any special limitations or formatting requirements. Most professors give students a choice of questions to answer, so consider them all before you decide which ones to answer. As you read each question, though, jot down any ideas that pop into your head. Then, organize the material before you begin to write. Turn the question into a thesis statement or topic sentence (for one-paragraph answers) and then write your first main point. Be sure to back it up with reasons, details, facts, and examples. Continue in the same manner until you've included all the relevant information that you know. Take a few minutes to sum up your main points and then proofread your answer.

When you get your test back, evaluate your preparation and performance. You *can* learn how to improve your grade on the next exam.

Review Questions

Terms You Should Know: Make a flash card for each term.

Absolute words	Main point	Supporting point
Balanced answer keys	Marginal notes	Test anxiety
Debilitating test anxiety	Problem-solving strategies	Test-wise strategies
Distractors	Qualifying words	Thesis statement
Facilitating test anxiety	Strategic guessing	Topic sentence

Completion: Fill in the blank to complete each of the following statements.

1. The real cause of test anxiety is _____ _____.

2. Doing an informal outline in the margin can help you _____ your essay answer before you begin to write.

3. The most important factor in determining how much time to spend on a test question is the _____ _____.

4. On a matching test, you should always work from the side with the _____ words.

5. Unless you _____ the question or find the correct answer (or a clue to it) somewhere else on the test, you shouldn't change your answer.

Multiple Choice: Circle the letter of the best answer for each of the following questions. Be sure to underline key words and eliminate wrong answers.

6. A good _____ tells the professor you know the answer to the question.
   A. outline
   B. paragraph
   C. thesis statement
   D. transition

7. _____ words generally make a statement false.
   A. Negative
   B. Absolute
   C. Qualifying
   D. Italicized

Short Answer–Essay: On a separate sheet, answer each of the following questions.

8. Why should students answer the easiest questions first?

9. How should students cope with test anxiety in order to improve their performance on exams?

10. What strategies should students use to maximize their scores on objective and essay exams?

College

Reading

Strategies

12 Comprehending Main Ideas

In this chapter you will learn how to:

- ➤ Determine main ideas

- ➤ Find stated and implied main ideas in paragraphs

- ➤ Use signal words to determine main ideas

- ➤ Find main ideas in different ways paragraphs are organized

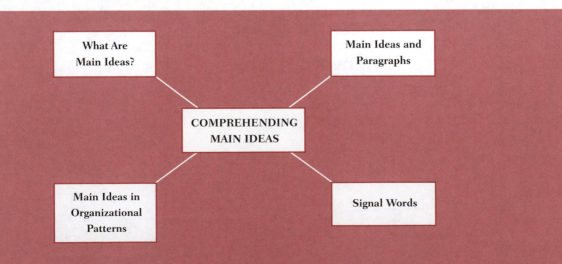

What Are Main Ideas?

Main Ideas and Paragraphs

COMPREHENDING MAIN IDEAS

Main Ideas in Organizational Patterns

Signal Words

ACTIVITY 12.1   *Where Are You Now?*

Take a few minutes to answer *yes* or *no* to the following questions; choose *yes* if you do this most of the time; choose *no* if you do not consistently do it or if you are not sure.

	YES	NO
1. When you read an assigned textbook section, can you determine the main point of it?	_____	_____
2. When a main idea is not directly stated in a paragraph can you determine the main point of it?	_____	_____
3. Do you use clues in a paragraph to figure out the main idea?	_____	_____
4. Do you use signal words to determine the main point in a series of paragraphs?	_____	_____
5. Can you think of at least two transition words between paragraphs that show comparison and contrast?	_____	_____
6. Can you think of at least two transition words between paragraphs that show causes and effects?	_____	_____
7. Can you think of at least two transition words between paragraphs that show problems and solutions?	_____	_____
8. When you read a narrative, do you summarize the main point of it?	_____	_____
9. When you read text selections in psychology or sociology, do you summarize the main points ?	_____	_____
10. Do you use textbook cues, such as boldface print, to locate the main points?	_____	_____
Total Points	_____	

Score yourself 1 point for each *yes* answer. Total up your points. A low score indicates that you will need to develop your reading strategies to comprehend the main idea. A high score indicates that you have already developed many successful reading strategies for determining the main ideas in text selections.

WHAT ARE MAIN IDEAS?

If someone asked you, "Why are you here in college? What's the point of taking college classes?" you most likely would give a one-line response, such as "I want to further my education so that I can get a good job," or perhaps "I want to learn more about my chosen field of study," or "I want to get a degree in my chosen area." In a short statement you would articulate your overall goal, your main point of pursuing college study. You would be able to respond in a short statement that summarizes the "essential idea" of why you are going to college.

In this chapter you will learn about the "Main Idea" of a reading selection. You will learn about the "essential idea" of what you are reading, particularly in your college reading assignments. More importantly, you will practice determining the main idea of a reading selection so that in your college classes you will be successful in comprehending your reading textbooks and related materials.

Reading researchers Harris and Sipay (1990) define the term *main idea* as "a single word or a statement that summarizes or tells all about the other information in that unit of text."[1] Main ideas may be explicitly mentioned in the text; however, sometimes main ideas are not mentioned in the text and, as a result, are implied, requiring the reader to generate a summary sentence that encapsulates the main idea. *The Literacy Dictionary* (Harris & Hodges, 1995) defines the term *main idea* as:

1. The gist of a passage; central thought.

2. The chief topic of a passage expressed or implied in a word or phrase.

3. The topic sentence of a paragraph.

4. "A statement in sentence form which gives the stated or implied major topic of a passage and the specific way in which the passage is limited in content or reference" (Harris, 1981).[2]

As noted in these definitions, the main idea points to a central idea. This central idea summarizes the point of the details in the passage. If you can imagine a bicycle wheel, the spokes of the wheel are like the supporting details; the center of the wheel is like the main idea. All the details (the spokes) are linked to the main idea (the center).

DETAILS AND MAIN IDEAS

Most likely, when you engage in a close reading of a text, you are looking for specific types of information. You may be looking for facts, unfamiliar vocabulary terms, names, dates, and definitions; these are all details that you underline, notate, or write down in your notebook. When you finish reading a section of text, such as a paragraph or several related paragraphs, you will need to step away from the text for a minute and ask, "What's the essential point?" The details give you the clues about the topic. The main idea tells you the point of the topic. Let's investigate this further.

Paragraph Topics

As noted in Chapter 4, textbooks contain many clues about the main topics. You can look for clues in the headings, introductions, conclusions, and graphic aids. If someone says to you, "What's the text about?" you might respond with a short phrase or even a word: "It's about. . . ." Let's look at a sample selection and think about a short phrase or word that describes what the selection is about. (See "Interference" in Figure 12.1.) After you read the paragraph, look for clues to respond to the statements in Activity 12.2.

---

[1]A. J. Harris and E. R. Sipay, *How to Increase Reading Ability: A Guide to Developmental and Remedial Methods,* 9th ed. (New York: Longman, 1990), p. 589.
[2]T. L. Harris and R. E. Hodges, *The Literacy Dictionary: The Vocabulary of Reading and Writing* (Newark, DE: International Reading Association, 1995), p. 148.

FIGURE 12.1
Interference

Source: From W. Weiten, *Psychology: Themes and Variations*, 6th ed. (Belmont, CA: Wadsworth/Thomson Learning, 2004), p. 281.

Interference

Interference theory proposes that people forget information because of competition from other material. Although demonstrations of decay in long-term memory have remained elusive, hundreds of studies have shown that interference influences forgetting (Anderson & Neely, 1996; Bjork, 1992). In many of these studies, researchers have controlled interference by varying the *similarity* between the original material given to subjects (the test material) and the material studied in the intervening period.

Interference is assumed to be greatest when intervening material is most similar to the test material. Decreasing the similarity should reduce interference and cause less forgetting. This is exactly what McGeoch and McDonald (1931) found in an influential study. They had subjects memorize test material that consisted of a list of two-syllable adjectives. They varied the similarity of intervening learning by having subjects then memorize one of five lists. In order of decreasing similarity to the test material, they were synonyms of the test words, antonyms of the test words, unrelated adjectives, nonsense syllables, and numbers. Later, subjects' recall of the test material was measured. Figure 7.20 shows that as the similarity of the intervening material decreased, the amount of forgetting also decreased—because of reduced interference.

Figure 7.20

Effects of interference. According to interference theory, more interference from competing information should produce more forgetting. McGeoch and McDonald (1931) controlled the amount of interference with a learning task by varying the similarity of an intervening task. The results were consistent with interference theory. The amount of interference is greatest at the left of the graph, as is the amount of forgetting. As interference decreases (moving to the right on the graph), retention improves. (Data from McGeoch & McDonald, 1931)

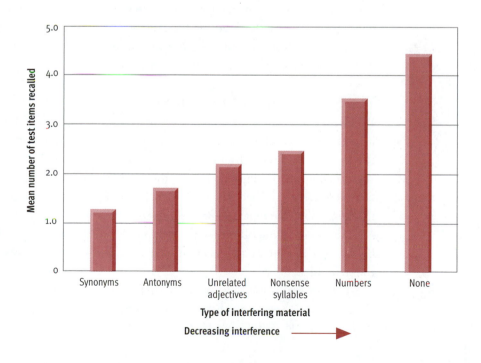

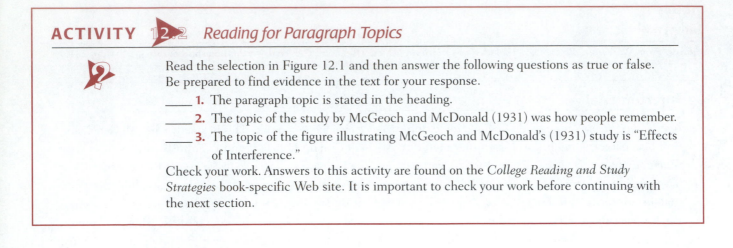

ACTIVITY 12.2 *Reading for Paragraph Topics*

Read the selection in Figure 12.1 and then answer the following questions as true or false. Be prepared to find evidence in the text for your response.

_____ **1.** The paragraph topic is stated in the heading.

_____ **2.** The topic of the study by McGeoch and McDonald (1931) was how people remember.

_____ **3.** The topic of the figure illustrating McGeoch and McDonald's (1931) study is "Effects of Interference."

Check your work. Answers to this activity are found on the *College Reading and Study Strategies* book-specific Web site. It is important to check your work before continuing with the next section.

When you were responding to the statements in Activity 12.2, did you look for clues in the heading, the introductory sentence, and the title of the figure? Yes, the topic of the paragraph is "Interference," which is noted in the heading, introductory sentence, figure title, and illustrated by the figure listing the types of interfering material. Notice how the author uses the McGeoch and McDonald (1931) study, which focused on the topic of interference.

Now for the tough question: What does interference theory say? Note that the author answers that question in the first sentence: "Interference theory proposes that people forget information because of competition from other material." The focus of this paragraph, then, is not on how people remember. Notice that the first sentence not only describes the topic of the paragraph but also states the main point of the topic: "Interference theory proposes that people forget information because of competition from other material." In other words, it describes why people forget information, that is, why other material interferes when people try to remember.

The Main Point of a Main Idea

In the previous activity, you found the topic of the paragraph. When you find the main idea of the paragraph, you make a statement about the topic. In other words, you tell the main point about the topic. When you state the main idea of a paragraph, you state a complete thought about the topic. This means you should be able to write a complete sentence about the topic. The point of stating the main idea is to focus your thinking about the topic to one essential point. When you find the main idea, you will see that most (if not all) sentences support the main idea. The other sentences may be examples to illustrate the main idea and often include many details that support the main idea.

Let's try another activity in which you find the topic; however, this time try to state a complete sentence about the topic. That sentence is the main idea of the paragraph. (See "Brown Algae" in Figure 12.2.)

FIGURE 12.2
Brown Algae

Source: From E. P. Solomon, L. R. Berg, and D. W. Martin, *Biology*, 5th ed. (Fort Worth, TX: Saunders, 1999), p. 517.

Brown Algae

Brown algae are commercially important for several reasons. Their cell walls contain a polysaccharide called algin that possibly helps cement the cell walls of adjacent cells together. Algin is used as a thickening and stabilizing agent in ice creams, marshmallows, toothpastes, shaving creams, hair sprays, and hand lotions. Brown algae are an important human food, particularly in East Asian countries, and they are rich sources of certain vitamins and of minerals such as iodine. Brown algae are one source of the antiseptic tincture of iodine.

ACTIVITY 12.3   *Reading for Paragraph Topics and Main Ideas*

Read the selection in Figure 12.2 and then complete the following statements. Be prepared to find evidence in the text for your response and to discuss your responses in a small group.

1. The paragraph topic is: (Hint: Write two words.)

2. The main idea of this paragraph is: (Hint: Write one complete sentence.)

3. One example that supports this main idea is: (Hint: Find one complete sentence in the paragraph.)

4. Another example that supports the main idea is: (Hint: Find another complete sentence in the paragraph.)

Check your work. Answers to this activity are found on the *College Reading and Study Strategies* book-specific Web site. It is important to check your work before continuing with the next section.

Did you note that the main idea is the first sentence? Notice that all the remaining sentences support this main idea by giving examples of how brown algae (the topic) is commercially important. Was this a difficult activity? It should be easy because the main idea was directly stated. However, sometimes the main idea is not directly stated; it is implied. In other words, when a main idea is implied, you will need to generalize what the point is. Let's look at the distinctions between stated and implied main ideas in the next two sections.

STATED MAIN IDEAS

You can locate a stated main idea directly in the text. When you are reading your textbooks and find clearly stated main ideas, you may wish to use a notation system that designates a main idea; one suggestion is to use brackets at the beginning and at the end of the sentence and make a short marginal note about the content of the main idea. Read the following paragraph about green algae and locate a sentence that directly states the main idea; remember that the remaining sentences should provide support for the main idea. (See "Green Algae" in Figure 12.3.)

FIGURE 12.3
Green Algae

Source: **From E. P. Solomon, L. R. Berg, and D. W. Martin, *Biology*, 5th ed. (Fort Worth, TX: Saunders, 1999), p. 519.**

Green Algae

Green algae can be found in both aquatic and terrestrial environments. Aquatic green algae primarily inhabit fresh water, although there are a number of marine species. Terrestrial green algae are restricted to damp soil, cracks in tree bark, and other moist places. Many of the green algae are symbionts with other organisms; some live as endosymbionts in body cells of invertebrates, and a few grow together with fungi as "dual organisms" called lichens. Regardless of where they live, green algae are ecologically important as the base of the food web.

ACTIVITY 12.4   *Reading for Stated Main Ideas*

Read the selection in Figure 12.3 and then complete the following statements. Be prepared to find evidence in the text for your response and to discuss your responses in a small group.

1. The paragraph topic is: (Hint: Write two words.)

2. The main idea of this paragraph is: (Hint: Write one complete sentence.)

3. One example that supports this main idea is: (Hint: Find one complete sentence in the paragraph.)

4. Another example that supports the main idea is: (Hint: Find another complete sentence in the paragraph.)

Check your work. Answers to this activity are found on the *College Reading and Study Strategies* book-specific Web site. It is important to check your work before continuing with the next section.

Did you find the main idea in the first sentence? Did you notice that the next three sentences in the paragraph are examples that show that green algae can be found both in the ocean and on land? You may have found the vocabulary more difficult in this paragraph; however, notice that there are several verbs that show that the main idea is about where green algae live; the author uses verbs such as *inhabit, live,* and *grow together.* These verbs point to the paragraph's main idea that "green algae can be found in both aquatic and terrestrial environments."

IMPLIED MAIN IDEAS

Many authors, however, do not directly state the main idea. They imply the main idea and expect that the reader will generate a sentence that states a main idea. In order to determine the main idea, you need to read the entire paragraph, ask "What is the topic?" and then ask "What is the author saying about the topic?" When the main idea is not directly stated, you will need to step back from the text and ask the question, "What's the point?" You will need to generalize from the details. Try the following activity to determine an implied main idea. (See "Viruses" in Figure 12.4.)

FIGURE 12.4
Viruses

From: **E. P. Solomon, L. R. Berg, and D. W. Martin,** *Biology,* **5th ed. (Fort Worth, TX: Saunders, 1999), p. 482.**

Viruses Are Infectious Agents That Are Not Assigned to Any of the Six Kingdoms

During the late 1800s, botanists searched for the cause of tobacco mosaic disease, which stunts the growth of tobacco plants and gives the infected tobacco leaves a spotted, mosaic appearance. They found that the disease could be transmitted to healthy plants by daubing their leaves with the sap of diseased plants. In 1892 Dmitrii Ivanowsky, a Russian botanist, showed that the sap was infective even after it had been passed through filters fine enough to remove particles the size of all known bacteria. A few years later his work was expanded by Martinus Beijerinck who provided evidence that the agent that caused tobacco mosaic disease had many characteristics of a living organism. He hypothesized that the agent could only reproduce within a living cell.

Early in the 20th century, scientists discovered infectious agents that could cause disease in animals or kill bacteria. Like the agents that cause tobacco mosaic disease, these pathogens passed through filters that removed known bacteria and were so small that they could not be seen with the light microscope. Curiously, they could not be grown in laboratory cultures unless living cells were present. These pathogens that infected plants or animals came to be known as viruses. Those that killed bacteria were called **bacteriophages** ("bacteria eaters"), or **phages.**

ACTIVITY 12.5 *Reading for Implied Main Ideas*

Read the selection in Figure 12.4 and then complete the following statements. Be prepared to find evidence in the text for your response.

1. The paragraph topic is: (Hint: Write a phrase.)

2. The main idea of this paragraph is: (Hint: Write one complete sentence.)

3. One example that supports this main idea is: (Hint: Find one complete sentence in the paragraph.)

4. Another example that supports the main idea is: (Hint: Find another complete sentence in the paragraph.)

Check your work. Answers to this activity are found on the *College Reading and Study Strategies* book-specific Web site. It is important to check your work before continuing with the next section.

This example shows that you can generalize the main point when you read the sequence of sentences describing the history behind the discovery of viruses. The writer uses a short chronological history that explains what a virus is. As a reader, you can ask, "What's the point of reading this?" Your answer will help formulate the main idea.

MAIN IDEAS AND PARAGRAPHS

As we discovered in the previous section, you can find the main idea in longer connected text comprised of several paragraphs. Short paragraphs, too, have main ideas. To help you find the main idea in either short or long text, you can use clues for finding it. For instance, many times the main idea will be located at the beginning of the paragraph as the introduction to the topic. Another frequent location of the main idea is at the end as a summarizing or concluding sentence.

There are many ways an author points to the main idea. Let's turn our attention to these. As you read the description of these, look at their symbols to help you remember where the main idea is placed in a paragraph. (When you are reading your textbooks, you can also use these symbols as marginal notes to show the location of the main idea.)

STATED MAIN IDEAS AS INTRODUCTIONS

When you are reading your textbooks, perhaps the most common place where you can find the main idea is the first sentence (or first two sentences) of the paragraph, as shown by Figure 12.5. This paragraph pattern shows that there is an introduction, fol-

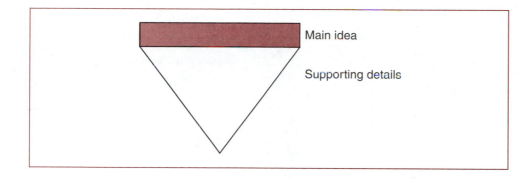

FIGURE 12.5
Introductory Stated Main Idea

lowed by specific examples throughout the remainder of the selection. This paragraph pattern follows a "deductive" organizational pattern, which means that the general statement occurs first and related specific details follow. Notice the first two sentences in the following selection. After reading the first two sentences, look for examples as support when you read the remaining sentences. (See "The Social Construction of Gender" in Figure 12.6.)

In this selection note that the author defines the topic of "gender socialization" in several ways. The first sentence defines "socialization," then the second sentence defines "gender socialization." The remaining sentences in the paragraph extend the conversation about the importance and effects of gender socialization; these remaining sentences support the topic introduced at the beginning of the paragraph. One clue that the author uses to tell you that the remaining sentences provide support for the introductory main idea is the use of the phrase "for example" followed by two examples; the last sentence, then, is a supporting detail.

FIGURE 12.6
The Social Construction of Gender

Source: From M. L. Andersen and H. F. Taylor, *Sociology: Understanding a Diverse Society,* 3d ed. (Belmont, CA: Wadsworth/Thomson Learning, 2004), p. 349.

The Social Construction of Gender

Socialization is the process by which social expectations are taught and learned. Through gender socialization, men and women learn the expectations associated with their sex. The rules of gender extend to all aspects of society and daily life. Gender socialization affects the self-concepts of women and men, their social and political attitudes, their perceptions about other people, and their feelings about relationships with others. Although not everyone is perfectly socialized to conform to gender expectations, socialization is a powerful force directing the behavior of men and women in gender-typical ways. For example, men who believe that the role of women is to act as wife and mother are not likely to share housework; women who believe they are incomplete unless they are attached to men are not likely to be very independent.

FIGURE 12.7

Main Idea as Conclusion

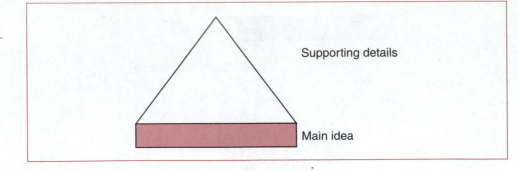

STATED MAIN IDEAS AS CONCLUSIONS

Some authors prefer to give you a series of facts, supporting details, and examples first, then lead you to a conclusion at the end of the paragraph. In this type of paragraph pattern, as shown by Figure 12.7, the stated main idea occurs last. This type of paragraph is "inductively" organized, which means that the supporting details occur first and the generalization about those details occurs last. In this type of paragraph pattern the author gives you a clue that the last sentence is the conclusion and uses signal words such as "in conclusion," "in summary," "thus," "as a result," or "consequently." In the following activity look for the stated main ideas in each paragraph. As you are reading, use the author's clues to point to the main ideas. (See "Implicit and Explicit Memory" and "Declarative Versus Procedural Memory" in Figure 12.8.)

ACTIVITY   12.6   *Reading for Main Ideas as Introductions and Conclusions*

Read the selection in Figure 12.8 and then identify the location of the stated main idea for each paragraph. Be prepared to discuss your responses in class.

Paragraph 1:

Paragraph 2:

Paragraph 3:

Paragraph 4:

Check your work. Answers to this activity are found on the *College Reading and Study Strategies* book-specific Web site. It is important to check your work before continuing with the next section.

FIGURE 12.8

Implicit and Explicit Memory

Source: From W. Weiten, *Psychology: Themes and Variations*, 6th ed. (Belmont, CA: Wadsworth/Thomson Learning, 2004), pp. 290–291.

Implicit and Explicit Memory

Research has uncovered many interesting differences between implicit and explicit memory (Roediger, 1990; Tulving & Schacter, 1990). Explicit memory is conscious, is accessed directly, and can be best assessed with recall or recognition measures of retention. Implicit memory is unconscious, must be accessed indirectly, and can be best assessed with variations on relearning (savings) measures of retention. Implicit memory is largely unaffected by amnesia, age, the administration of certain drugs (such as alcohol), the length of the retention interval, and manipulations of interference. In contrast, explicit memory is affected very much by all these factors.

Some theorists think these differences are found because implicit and explicit memory rely on *different cognitive processes* in encoding and retrieval (Graf & Gallie, 1992; Jacoby, 1988; Roediger, 1990). However, many other theorists argue that the differences exist because implicit and explicit memory are handled by *independent memory systems* (Schacter, 1992, 1994; Squire, 1994). These independent systems are referred to as declarative and procedural memory.

Declarative Versus Procedural Memory

Many theorists have suggested that people have separate memory systems for different kinds of information (see Figure 7.27). The most basic division of memory into distinct systems contrasts *declarative memory* with *nondeclarative* or *procedural memory* (Squire & Zola, 1996; Winograd, 1975). **The *declarative memory system* handles factual information.** It contains recollections of words, definitions, names, dates, faces, events, concepts, and ideas. **The *nondeclarative* or *procedural memory system* houses memory for actions, skills, operations, and conditioned responses.** It contains memories of how to execute such actions as riding a bike, typing, and tying one's shoes. To illustrate the distinction, if you know the rules of tennis (the number of games in a set, scoring, and such), this factual information is stored in declarative memory. If you remember how to hit a serve and swing through a backhand, these perceptual-motor skills are stored in procedural memory.

Some theorists believe that an association exists between implicit memory and the procedural memory system (Squire, Knowlton, & Musen, 1993). Why? Because memory for skills is largely unconscious. People execute perceptual-motor tasks such as playing the piano or typing with little conscious awareness of what they're doing. In fact, performance on such tasks often deteriorates if people think too much about what they're doing. Another parallel with implicit memory is that the memory for skills (such as typing and bike riding) doesn't decline much over long retention intervals. Thus, the procedural memory system may handle implicit remembering, while the declarative memory system handles explicit remembering.

Figure 7.27

Theories of independent memory systems. There is some evidence that different types of information are stored in separate memory systems, which may have distinct physiological bases. The diagram shown here, which blends the ideas of several theorists, is an adaptation of Larry Squire's (1987) scheme. Note that implicit and explicit memory are not memory systems. They are observed behavioral phenomena that appear to be handled by different hypothetical memory systems (the procedural and declarative memory systems), which cannot be observed directly.

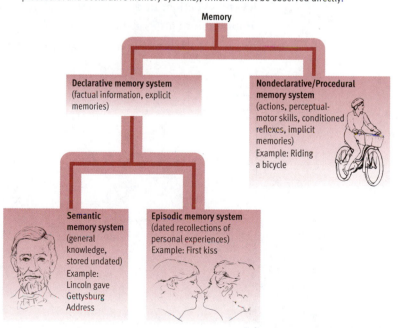

Memory

Declarative memory system (factual information, explicit memories)

Nondeclarative/Procedural memory system (actions, perceptual-motor skills, conditioned reflexes, implicit memories) Example: Riding a bicycle

Semantic memory system (general knowledge, stored undated) Example: Lincoln gave Gettysburg Address

Episodic memory system (dated recollections of personal experiences) Example: First kiss

ACTIVITY 12.7 *Reading and Remembering Main Ideas as Introductions and Conclusions*

Reread the selection in Figure 12.8; close your book. Using a section of your class notebook, record what you remember and note your reflections after reading. Use the following prompts. As you are writing, do not look back at the text.

1. The main ideas of this passage are the following. . . .

2. The main points about declarative and procedural memory systems are. . . .

3. When I read the passage I thought of the following examples. . . .

4. If I could ask the author a question, I would ask. . . .

After you finish writing, return to the text and check your responses. What did you remember? What did you forget? Did you find it easier to remember main ideas that were at the beginning? the end?

STATED MAIN IDEAS EMBEDDED IN A PARAGRAPH

As noted in Figure 12.9, sometimes the main idea is embedded in the middle of a paragraph. The author typically does this to give you some background information first, then gives you the main point, then elaborates the main point with more details. Read the following selection. In the first paragraph note how the author first gives you some background information about placebos, then gives you the main definition of placebo effects, then describes placebo effects in medicine. All of these descriptions point to the

Figure 12.9
Embedded Stated Main Idea

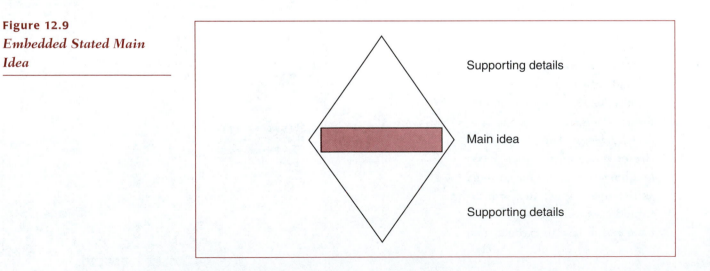

FIGURE 12.10
Placebo Effects

Source: From W. Weiten, *Psychology: Themes and Variations*, 6th ed. (Belmont, CA: Wadsworth/Thomson Learning, 2004), p. 59.

Placebo Effects

In pharmacology, a *placebo* is a substance that resembles a drug but has no actual pharmacological effect. In studies that assess the effectiveness of medications, placebos are given to some subjects to control for the effects of a treacherous extraneous variable: participants' expectations. Placebos are used because researchers know that participants' expectations can influence their feelings, reactions, and behavior. **Thus, *placebo effects* occur when participants' expectations lead them to experience some change even though they receive empty, fake, or ineffectual treatment.** In medicine, placebo effects are well documented (Quitkin, 1999). Many physicians tell of patients being "cured" by prescriptions of sugar pills. Similarly, psychologists have found that participants' expectations can be powerful determinants of their perceptions and behavior when they are under the microscope in an empirical study.

For example, placebo effects have been seen in research on meditation. A number of studies have found that meditation can improve people's energy level, mental and physical health, and happiness (Alexander et al., 1990; Carrington, 1987). However, in many of the early studies of meditation, researchers assembled their experimental groups with volunteer subjects eager to learn meditation. Most of these subjects *wanted* and *expected* meditation to have beneficial effects. Their positive expectations may have colored their subsequent ratings of their energy level, happiness, and so on. Better-designed studies have shown that meditation can be beneficial. However, placebo effects have probably exaggerated these benefits in some studies (Shapiro, 1987).

Researchers should guard against placebo effects whenever subjects are likely to have expectations that a treatment will affect them in a certain way. The possible role of placebo effects can be assessed by including a fake version of the experimental treatment (a placebo condition) in a study. We saw the value of this approach in the Greenwald et al. (1991) study on the effects of subliminal self-help tapes. The mislabeled tapes served as a placebo treatment that allowed the researchers to control for the effects of participants' positive expectations about the subliminal audiotapes.

main point about placebo effects in the middle of the first paragraph—the sentence that the author has placed in bold lettering. The second and third paragraphs provide an extended description about placebo effects, providing further support for the main idea. (See "Placebo Effects," in Figure 12.10.)

IMPLIED MAIN IDEAS IN A PARAGRAPH

Unlike the previous paragraph patterns, when the main idea is not explicitly stated but is implied (see Figure 12.11), you will need to generalize from the information given to you. When you were reading the selection about placebo effects in Figure 12.10, did you return to the first paragraph for the definition of placebo effects? Without the first paragraph, the second and third paragraphs are more difficult to understand. Reread the second paragraph. What is the main point of the second paragraph? This paragraph gives an example of a placebo effect. The author describes how meditation might be a placebo because participants expect beneficial change. The author, however, does indicate that other studies have shown that meditation is not a placebo.

When you are reading literature, poems, or other literary works, you will need to look for literary themes, symbols, and figurative language. In these works the main idea

FIGURE 12.11
Implied Main Idea

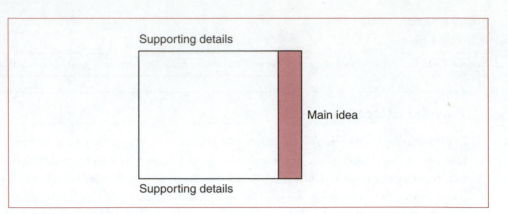

is often implied. In addition, when an author uses examples, anecdotes, or short stories, think about the author's point. In these cases you will need to step back from the text and ask the key question, "What's the point?"

When the main idea is not directly stated, you will need to summarize the main idea in your own words. To do so, ask yourself the question, "What's the point about the details?" Imagine a bicycle wheel, as shown in Figure 12.12.

When you are summarizing the point of the passage, you write a sentence about the topic; this sentence will be at the center of the wheel. The supporting details radiate out of the center, like the spokes on the bicycle wheel. Let's take a look at the article entitled "Tomb Raiders, Beware"; as you read this article, think of the main idea of the passage. (See Figure 12.13.)

FIGURE 12.12
Graphic Organizer for a Main Idea and Supporting Details

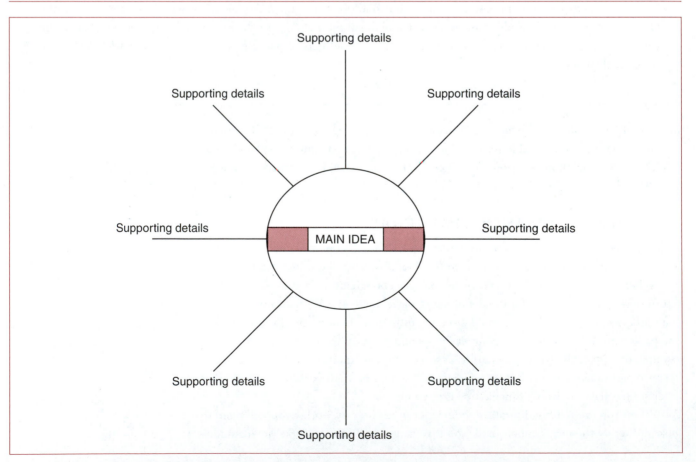

FIGURE 12.13
Tomb Raiders, Beware!

Source: From "Tomb Raiders, Beware!" *Newsweek,* September 2, 2002. Reprinted by permission.

Archeology
Tomb Raiders, Beware!

The 'curse of the mummies' has a new way to strike

By Gretel C. Kovach

The assistant's hand trembles as he slices open the two twine-wrapped cardboard boxes. In the dusty silence of Cairo's Egyptian Museum he painstakingly unrolls the bubble wrap, then steps aside to let Zahi Hawass, 55, the mediagenic director of Egypt's Supreme Council of Antiquities, examine the contents. Each box holds a 2,000-year-old burial mask, made from powdered gypsum and adorned with dancing cobras. The pair was confiscated two years ago in a police raid on the home of a Florida arms trader. Now both masks have been returned to Egypt, cleaned and restored. Hawass emits an audible sigh of satisfaction. "Very nice," he says.

But no more than a start, he hopes. Since taking the post of antiquities czar earlier this year, Hawass has launched a high-profile campaign to take back the ancient treasures he considers the rightful property of the Egyptian people—in particular, those items that have been plundered since UNESCO's 1970 decree to prevent illicit trafficking in cultural artifacts. Egypt itself has often been lax about guarding its heritage. Not until 1983 did new finds legally become government property. But Hawass insists he means business. To get the word out, he's using the connections and world-wide reputation he enjoys as one of Egypt's leading archeologists. He has taught at UCLA, authored several internationally successful books on Egyptology, overseen the excavation of the Valley of the Golden Mummies after its discovery in 1996 and guided visitors like Princess Diana and Bill Clinton to the temples.

One thing he knows is the power of publicity. His staff has barraged museums around the world with announcements of Egypt's readiness to make "the most strenuous efforts" to reclaim illegally exported antiquities. He has created a special investigative team to seek out such artifacts in museum catalogs, auction listings and Web postings. And he's aiming also to stop the trade at its source. Last week authorities made a long-delayed sweep of private dealers' Egyptian storerooms, seizing items discovered since 1983. One trader in Luxor alone is giving up 17,000 artifacts.

The attention Hawass commands is paying off. This June a French Egyptologist noticed a granite relief in a Christie's New York auction catalog. She was sure the carving had been plundered no more than eight years ago from the Temple of Isis at Behbeit Al Hagara, in the Nile delta. There used to be little she could do to stop such a sale. But now she contacted Hawass and his team, and as soon as they heard from her, they fired off a two-line e-mail to info@christies.com. The auction house immediately pulled the item, and Hawass is expecting to receive it within the next week or two. When it arrives, he's going to unveil plans to rebuild the ruined temple. He plans a similar announcement when Emory University returns fragments of the Temple of Seti it obtained—unaware they were stolen—a few years ago. Hawass hopes to lure home other pieces of the temple from museums in Europe—including the Louvre itself. "When they know that I am serious, that I plan to rebuild the temples *in situ,* how could they refuse?"

What about institutions that won't cooperate? "I'll post their names on the Internet!" Hawass says. "I'll take them to court! No scientific cooperation!" That's the kind of threat that gets a museum director's attention. Hawass has permanently barred two Western archeologists, one British, one American, from working in Egypt. They had dared to defend Frederick Schultz, a New York dealer who was convicted in June of conspiring to receive stolen Egyptian artifacts (Schultz is appealing the decision).

Retrieving recently taken artifacts is what Hawass calls only "phase one." In three years he plans to expand his efforts—exactly how, he's not saying. He says museums should be allowed to keep most items that left Egypt before its independence in 1952, but he's not sure there should be any statute of limitations for what he calls stolen masterpieces. "I don't want to scare anyone," says Hawass, "but phase two will surprise everyone." One treasure particularly haunts him: a limestone bust of Queen Nefertiti unearthed by a German archeologist in 1911. It has stood in a Berlin museum since 1924. Hawass dreams of bringing her home to Cairo. "I want to open my eyes and see her standing in the Egyptian Museum," says Hawass. "Then I can retire." For now, he has just one regret: "Unfortunately, there's no 'curse of the mummies'," he says. Hawass is doing his best to fill that role himself.

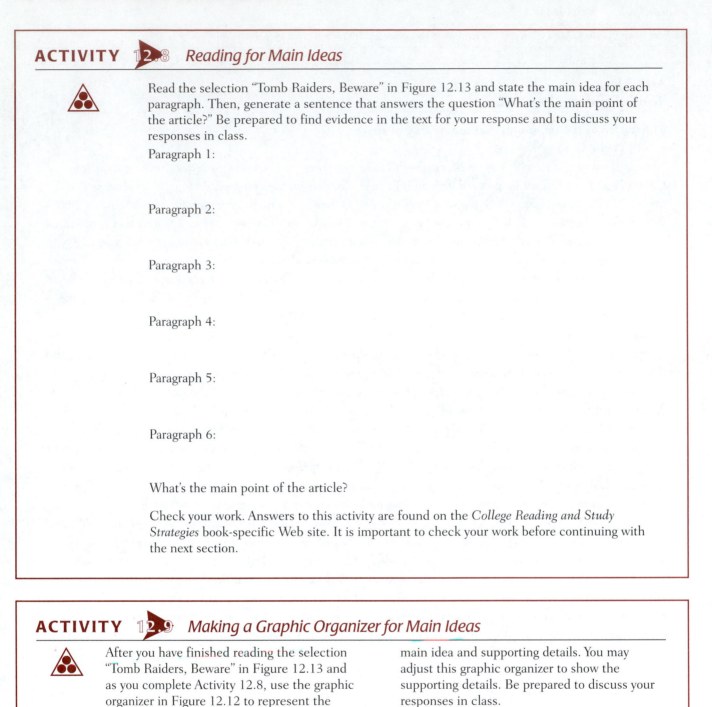

ACTIVITY 12.8 *Reading for Main Ideas*

Read the selection "Tomb Raiders, Beware" in Figure 12.13 and state the main idea for each paragraph. Then, generate a sentence that answers the question "What's the main point of the article?" Be prepared to find evidence in the text for your response and to discuss your responses in class.

Paragraph 1:

Paragraph 2:

Paragraph 3:

Paragraph 4:

Paragraph 5:

Paragraph 6:

What's the main point of the article?

Check your work. Answers to this activity are found on the *College Reading and Study Strategies* book-specific Web site. It is important to check your work before continuing with the next section.

ACTIVITY 12.9 *Making a Graphic Organizer for Main Ideas*

After you have finished reading the selection "Tomb Raiders, Beware" in Figure 12.13 and as you complete Activity 12.8, use the graphic organizer in Figure 12.12 to represent the main idea and supporting details. You may adjust this graphic organizer to show the supporting details. Be prepared to discuss your responses in class.

SIGNAL WORDS FOR FINDING THE MAIN IDEA

When you were looking for the main idea in the previous activities, you used clues in the paragraphs that signal the location of the main idea. Good writers use these signal words to call attention to key points in a passage, to help the reader stay on track, and to indicate a logical pattern of ideas, in other words, the organizational pattern. As you read, look for these signal words; they are important words for guiding your comprehension.

Likewise, when you write, use these signal words to inform your audience about your main points and supporting details.

REPETITION

One of the more obvious indicators of the topic of a selection is the repetition of a word, typically a noun. In other words, the word that is repeated most often typically points to the topic. Then, after finding the topic, as a reader you would ask yourself the question, "What main point is the author making about this topic?" For instance, in the following selection underline the term that is repeated throughout the passage; if you have difficulty finding it, read the passage aloud and find the term you say most often. (See "Labeling Effect," in Figure 12.14.)

FIGURE 12.14
Labeling Effect

Source: From M. L. Andersen and H. F. Taylor, *Sociology: Understanding a Diverse Society,* 3d ed. (Belmont, CA: Wadsworth/Thomson Learning, 2004), p. 451.

Labeling Effect

Both high- and low-track students are subject to a **labeling effect:** Once a student is assigned to a particular track and is thereby labeled, the label has a tendency to stick, whether or not it is accurate. Once a student is labeled "gifted" or "high ability," other people—students, teachers, administrators—tend to react in accordance with that label. One is regarded as "smart" and high achieving. Students labeled "slow" or "low ability" encounter a negative reaction from the same people, including the expectation of low achievement. Even when a student is transferred from one track into another—for example, from a lower track to a higher one as the result of a recent cognitive ability test—the prior perceptions tend to persist; teachers and students still think of the youngster as "lower track," and even the recently promoted student may retain the self-perception developed in response to the prior track assignment.

ACTIVITY 12.10   *Using Repetition to Locate Topics*

Read the selection in Figure 12.14 either aloud or silently. Then complete the following statements.

1. The term that is repeated throughout this paragraph is . . .

2. The main idea is located in the following sentence . . .

3. The author uses this example to support the main idea . . .

Check your work. Answers to this activity are found on the *College Reading and Study Strategies* book-specific Web site. It is important to check your work before continuing with the next section.

FIGURE 12.15
Signal Words Indicating Conclusions

> thus
> in conclusion
> therefore
> in summary
> as a result
> consequently

SIGNAL WORDS

When you are looking for a main idea, look for the one word or two-word phrase that shows the author's line of thinking. In our previous examples we found the main idea after the signal word "thus." Other signal words that give you a clue about the location of the main idea are "in conclusion," "therefore," "in summary," "as a result," or "consequently." (See Figure 12.15.)

In the next section of this chapter we will be discussing different organizational patterns; each of these patterns has typical transition words that will help you determine the author's line of thinking and will help you locate the main idea. These signal words are powerful cues that help you not only as a reader but also as a writer. When you are writing your responses to the text, practice using the transition words as well as the organizational patterns so that the reader will be able to follow your line of thinking.

MAIN IDEAS IN ORGANIZATIONAL PATTERNS

The organizational pattern of a text passage is similar to the framework of a house. How you build that framework will determine the final overall result of the house. Similarly, the text structure determines how the author organizes the main ideas and supporting details. Learning to recognize the text structure will help you determine what's most important in a paragraph and will help you determine the main idea.

There has been much research related to text structure in reading comprehension, rhetorical theory, communication, and, in general, the field of English language arts. Depending on the area of research, a variety of terms related to the same concept are used. The term "organizational pattern" is synonymous with the terms "text structure," "paragraph pattern," "rhetorical pattern," "rhetorical structure," and "text frame." As a whole, the research indicates that well-written paragraphs are carefully constructed, contain a logical organization, and use transition words indicative of the text structure. According to research about text structure, good readers use text cues and their knowledge of text structure when comprehending a passage.[3]

Text patterns and cues are important for good comprehension. Text patterns indicate that some sentences are general statements and other sentences are specific points; furthermore, all of the sentences cohere, or "stick together," according to the unique organizational pattern. As a reader, once you are tuned into the ways the author uses organiza-

---

[3]S. Goldman and J. A. Rakestraw, "Structural Aspects of Constructing Meaning from Text," in M. L. Kamil, P. B. Mosenthal, P. D. Pearson, and R. Barr, eds., *Handbook of Reading Research, Volume III* (Mahwah, NJ: Lawrence Erlbaum, 2000), pp. 311–335.

TEXT ORGANIZATIONAL PATTERNS

The five text structures described by Meyer (1985)—description, collection, comparison, causation, and response—correspond to the classic rhetorical text patterns commonly taught in college freshman writing courses. Good writers use these text organizational patterns to communicate their ideas. Good readers can likewise use these patterns for finding the main idea in a passage. Essential to all of these patterns is the answer to the question: "What's the point?" With practice you can use these patterns for finding the main idea in the texts you are reading.

Description
- **Definition**
- **Explanation**

Collection
- **Enumeration**
- **Sequence**
- **Classification**

Comparison
- **Comparison and Contrast**

Causation
- **Cause and Effect**

Response
- **Problem and Solution**

Narration

tional patterns, you will find that your comprehension of the text selection increases. The text patterns introduced to you in the following sections are guides to help you determine the main idea about a passage and related significant details in that passage. Note that in some of the text selections the main idea is explicitly stated; in others, the main idea is implied. However, you will be able to generate a main idea based on the organizational pattern.

These patterns are based on the classic text structures of Meyer (1985), who noted five structures for expository text: description, collection, comparison, causation, and response.[4] Each of these is elaborated with the organizational patterns typically found in a college composition course and in many college reading courses. The last pattern, "narration," which is not an expository text pattern, is included because it describes the pattern most often found in literature. To see a list of these text patterns, see the Tip Block.

---

[4]B. J. F. Meyer, "Prose Analysis: Purposes, Procedures, and Problems," in B. K. Britton and J. B. Black, eds., *Understanding Expository Text* (Hillsdale, NJ: Lawrence Erlbaum, 1985), pp. 11–64.

FIGURE 12.16
Signal Words Indicating
Description

for example
to illustrate
for instance

DESCRIPTION: DEFINITION AND EXPLANATION

A "descriptive" text provides much detail *about* something. College textbook authors use description to define and explain new concepts, particularly since much of the new vocabulary introduced to you needs much explanation. When you read descriptive text, look for attributes, characteristics, and other information that identifies. Examples of transition words that will help you find descriptive text are included in Figure 12.16.

Let's look at an example of a descriptive passage. In the following selection note how the first three sentences in the first paragraph define "the Exclusionary Rule." The remaining paragraphs provide a rationale for the rule and explain its application by citing Supreme Court decisions using the rule. (See "The Exclusionary Rule" in Figure 12.17.)

FIGURE 12.17
The Exclusionary Rule

Source: From S. W. Schmidt, M. C. Shelley, and B. A. Bardes, *American Government and Politics Today,* 2001–2002 ed. (Belmont, CA: Wadsworth/Thomson Learning, 2001), p. 143.

The Exclusionary Rule

At least since 1914, judicial policy has prohibited the admission of illegally seized evidence at trials in federal courts. This is the so-called **exclusionary rule.** Improperly obtained evidence, no matter how telling, cannot be used by prosecutors. This includes evidence obtained by police in violation of a suspect's *Miranda* rights or of the Fourth Amendment. The Fourth Amendment protects against unreasonable searches and seizures and provides that a judge may issue a search warrant to a police officer only on probable cause (a demonstration of facts that permit a reasonable belief that a crime has been committed). The question that must be determined by the courts is what constitutes an "unreasonable" search and seizure.

The reasoning behind the exclusionary rule is that it forces police officers to gather evidence properly, in which case their due diligence will be rewarded by a conviction. The exclusionary rule has always had critics who argue that it permits guilty persons to be freed because of innocent errors.

This rule was first extended to state court proceedings in a 1961 Supreme Court decision, *Mapp v. Ohio.*[66] In this case, the Court overturned the conviction of Dollree Mapp for the possession of obscene materials. Police found pornographic books in her apartment after searching it without a search warrant and despite her refusal to let them in.

Over the last several decades, however, the Supreme Court has diminished the scope of the exclusionary rule by creating some exceptions to its applicability. For example, in 1984 the Supreme Court held that illegally obtained evidence could be ad-

Exclusionary Rule
A policy forbidding the admission at trial of illegally seized evidence.

[66]367 U.S. 643 (1961).

Continued

FIGURE 12.17, *Continued*
The Exclusionary Rule

---

mitted at trial if law enforcement personnel could prove that they would have obtained the evidence legally anyway.[67] In another case decided in the same year, the Court held that a police officer who used a technically incorrect search warrant form to obtain evidence had acted in good faith and therefore the evidence was admissible at trial. The Court thus created the "good faith" exception to the exclusionary rule.[68]

---

[67]*Nix v. Williams,* 467 U.S. 431 (1984).
[68]*Massachusetts v. Sheppard,* 468 U.S. 981 (1984).

ACTIVITY 12.11   *Locating the Main Idea in Descriptive Text*

Read the selection in Figure 12.17 and then answer the following questions as true or false. Be prepared to discuss your responses in class.

_____ **1.** The main idea of the first paragraph is in its third sentence.

_____ **2.** According to this selection, the Supreme Court has always upheld the exclusionary rule because of the Fourth Amendment.

_____ **3.** The last paragraph of this text selection provides examples that show that the Supreme Court is redefining the parameters of the exclusionary rule.

Check your work. Answers to this activity are found on the *College Reading and Study Strategies* book-specific Web site. It is important to check your work before continuing with the next section.

ACTIVITY 12.12   *Using InfoTrac College Edition to Read Definition Paragraphs*

As indicated in the selection about "The Exclusionary Rule," recent Supreme Court rulings are redefining this rule. Use InfoTrac College Edition to locate a recent application or modification of this rule. Then, using a section of your class notebook, record this definition. Write a short comment about the text clues that helped you determine the definition.

COLLECTION: GROUPING THROUGH ENUMERATION, SEQUENCE, OR CLASSIFICATION

When you have a collection of items, you have a group of them. Three common organizational patterns found in texts show a grouping of items: enumeration, sequence, and classification. The first one, enumeration, means a listing of items; in this pattern it does not matter which is first or last. An example of enumeration is a grocery list or the names of the people in your class. You may find that in some textbooks the author uses bulleted lists instead of numbers to show a listing.

FIGURE 12.18
*Signal Words Indicating
Grouping*

Listing or Sequence
  first, second, third . . .
  a, b, c . . .
  to begin
  to end
  finally

Classification
  similar to
  like
  part of
  type of
  member
  group
  class

On the other hand, if you have a sequence, the order of which is first, second, and third does matter. For instance, you could alphabetize the names of the people in your class; in this example your sequence would be according to *A, B, C,* and so on. Another example of a sequence is a chronology of events. For instance, if you were describing the events that led up to a car accident, you would place the events in a time order. Similarly, if you were describing the events that led to the American Revolution, you would use a chronology. When you are reading a passage that uses enumeration (a listing) or sequence (such as a chronology), look for signal words such as *first, to begin, second, third, next,* and *finally.* In historical passages the author often uses dates to signal the sequence of events. When you are reading history, look for timelines; a timeline visually shows you the information arranged sequentially according to the dates the events occurred.

One of the most widely used organizational patterns is classification. This pattern is particularly popular in the biological sciences. As its name suggests, the purpose of classification is to group items together according to common characteristics. Signal words that mark a classification pattern include words such as *similar to* and *like.* In classification patterns look for words (particularly in the headings) such as *type, classification, class, is part of this group,* or *member of.* As discussed in Chapter 4, when you are reading to remember the information in this organizational pattern, a hierarchical array or a semantic feature matrix helps you sort out the general information from the specific details. See Figure 12.18 for a list of these signal words.

In Figure 12.19, you will see how the author explains the "McDonaldization of Society." As you read, note the author's use of text clues and the clear organizational structure. After you read this selection, read the next selection entitled "Types of Interest Groups," in Figure 12.20. Both of these selections use an organizational text structure that groups ideas together. How each author uses a classification text structure is quite different.

FIGURE 12.19
The McDonaldization of Society

Source: From M. L. Andersen and H. F. Taylor, *Sociology: Understanding a Diverse Society,* 3d ed. (Belmont, CA: Wadsworth/Thomson Learning, 2004), pp. 161–162.

The McDonaldization of Society

Sometimes the problems and peculiarities of bureaucracy can affect the total society. Such has been the case with what George Ritzer (2002) has called the *McDonaldization of society,* a term coined from the well-known fast-food chain. In fact, one study (Schlosser 2001) concludes that each month, 90 percent of the children between ages 3 and 9 visit McDonald's! Ritzer noticed that the principles that characterize fast-food organizations are increasingly dominating more and more aspects of U.S. society and societies around the world. "McDonaldization" refers to the increasing and ubiquitous presence of the fast-food model in most organizations that shape daily life. Work, travel, leisure, shopping, health care, education, and politics have all become subject to McDonaldization. Each industry is based on a principle of high and efficient productivity, which translates into a highly rational social organization, with workers employed at low pay, and customers experiencing ease, convenience, and familiarity.

Ritzer argues that McDonald's has been such a successful business model that other industries have adopted the same organizational characteristics. Some have nicknames that associate them with the McDonald's chain: McPaper for *USA Today,* McChild for child-care chains such as Kinder-Care, and McDoctor for the drive-in clinics that deal quickly and efficiently with minor health and dental problems.

Ritzer identifies four dimensions of the McDonaldization process: efficiency, calculability, predictability, and control. These characteristics, Ritzer notes, were anticipated long ago by theorist Max Weber:

1. **Efficiency** means that things move from start to completion in a streamlined path. Steps in the production of a hamburger are regulated so that each hamburger is made exactly the same way—hardly characteristic of a home-cooked meal. Business can be even more efficient if the customer does the work once done by an employee, such as using automated teller machines without the personal contact.

2. **Calculability** means there is an emphasis on the quantitative aspects of products sold—size, cost, and the time it takes to get the product. At McDonald's, branch managers must account for the number of cubic inches of ketchup used per day. Sensors on drink machines can cut off the liquid flow to ensure that each drink is exactly the same size. Workers are monitored to determine how long it takes them to complete a transaction. Every bit of food and drink is closely monitored by computer, and everything has to be accounted for.

3. **Predictability** is the assurance that products will be exactly the same, no matter when or where they are purchased. Eat an Egg McMuffin in New York, and it will taste just the same as an Egg McMuffin in Los Angeles or Paris!

4. **Control** is the primary organizational principle that lies behind McDonaldization. Behavior of the customers and workers is reduced to a series of machine-like actions. Ultimately, efficient technologies replace much of the work that humans once did. People are also carefully monitored and watched in these organizations, given that uncertainty in human behavior will produce inefficiency and unpredictability.

Continued

FIGURE 12.19, *Continued*

The McDonaldization of Society

McDonaldization clearly brings many benefits. There is a greater availability of goods and services to a wide proportion of the population, instantaneous service and convenience to a public with less free time, predictability and familiarity in the goods bought and sold, and standardization of pricing and uniform quality of goods sold, to name a few. However, this increasingly rational system of goods and services also spawns irrationalities. For example, the majority of workers at McDonald's lack full-time employment, have no worker benefits, have no control over the workplace, and quit on average after four to five months (Schlosser 2001). Ritzer argues that, as we become more dependent on what is familiar and expected, the danger of dehumanization arises.

FIGURE 12.20

Types of Interest Groups

Source: **From S. W. Schmidt, M. C. Shelley, and B. A. Bardes,** *American Government and Politics Today,* **2001–2002 ed. (Belmont, CA: Wadsworth/Thomson Learning, 2001), p. 253.**

Types of Interest Groups

Thousands of groups exist to influence government. Among the major types of interest groups are those that represent the main sectors of the economy—business, agricultural, government, and labor groups. In more recent years, a number of "public-interest" organizations have been formed to represent the needs of the general citizenry, including some "single-issue" groups. The interests of foreign governments and foreign businesses are also represented in the American political arena.

Economic Interest Groups

Numerous interest groups have been formed to promote economic interests. These groups include business, agricultural, labor, public employee, and professional organizations.

Business Interest Groups. Thousands of trade and business organizations attempt to influence government policies. Some groups target a single regulatory unit, whereas others try to effect major policy changes. Three large business groups are consistently effective: (1) the National Association of Manufacturers (NAM), (2) the U.S. Chamber of Commerce, and (3) the Business Roundtable. The annual budget of the NAM is more than $22 million, which it collects in dues from about 14,000 relatively large corporations. Sometimes called the National Chamber, the U.S. Chamber of Commerce represents nearly 200,000 companies. Dues from its members, which include about 3,000 state and local chambers of commerce, exceed $30 million a year. Separately, two hundred of the largest corporations in the United States send their chief executive officers to the Business Roundtable. This organization is based in New York, but it does its lobbying in Washington, D.C.

ACTIVITY 12.13 *Organizational Patterns of Grouping*

Read the selections in Figure 12.19 and Figure 12.20 and then answer the following questions with a short response. Be prepared to find evidence in the text for your response and to discuss your responses in class.

1. Which of the two selections contains a classification organizational pattern?

2. What signal words in that selection indicate a classification pattern?

3. Which of the two selections contains an enumeration organizational pattern?

4. What signal words in that selection indicate an enumeration?

5. In your own words state the main idea of "The McDonaldization of Society" in Figure 12.19.

6. In your own words state the main idea of "Types of Interest Groups" in Figure 12.20.

Check your work. Answers to this activity are found on the *College Reading and Study Strategies* book-specific Web site. It is important to check your work before continuing with the next section.

COMPARISON AND CONTRAST

This text pattern reveals not only the similarities of items in a group but also the distinctions among them. Signal words (See Figure 12.21) in this text pattern often point to a change, to the contrasting characteristics; examples of these signal words are *but, however, on the other hand, in contrast to, although,* and *unlike.* Typically this pattern is used to compare and contrast two items. In the following selection note how the author compares and contrasts an "industrial society" with an "agricultural society." (See "Industrial Societies" in Figure 12.22.)

FIGURE 12.21
Signal Words Indicating Comparison and Contrast

```
similar . . . different
in contrast to
like . . . unlike
however
although
but
on the other hand
```

FIGURE 12.22
Industrial Societies

Source: From M. L. Andersen and H. F. Taylor, *Sociology: Understanding a Diverse Society,* 3d ed. (Belmont, CA: Wadsworth/Thomson Learning, 2004), p. 139.

Industrial Societies

An *industrial society* is one that uses machines and other advanced technologies to produce and distribute goods and services. The Industrial Revolution began only 200 years ago when the steam engine was invented in England, delivering previously unattainable amounts of mechanical power for the performance of work. Steam engines powered locomotives, factories, and dynamos, transforming societies as the Industrial Revolution spread. The growth of science led to advances in farming techniques such as crop rotation, harvesting, and ginning cotton, as well as huge industrial-scale projects such as dams for hydroelectric power. Joining these advances were developments in medicine, new techniques to prolong and improve life, and the emergence of birth control to limit population growth.

Unlike agricultural societies, industrial societies rely upon a highly differentiated labor force and the intensive use of capital and technology. Large formal organizations are common. The task of holding society together, falling more on institutions such as religion in preindustrial societies, now falls more on the high division-of-labor institutions such as the economy and work, government and politics, and large bureaucracies.

ACTIVITY   12.14   *Organizational Patterns of Comparison and Contrast*

Read the selection in Figure 12.22 and then answer the following questions with a short statement. Be prepared to find evidence in the text for your response and to discuss your responses in class.

1. What two ideas does the author contrast in this selection?

2. Which transition word in the second paragraph signals comparison and contrast?

3. The purpose of this selection is to:

Check your work. Answers to this activity are found on the *College Reading and Study Strategies* book-specific Web site. It is important to check your work before continuing with the next section.

ACTIVITY   12.15   *Read Comparison and Contrast Paragraphs*

Although English is spoken in many different countries, there are differences in the meanings of certain words depending on the geographical location. Pick two countries that speak English, such as England and the United States, or Canada and the United States. Search for a short article that describes similarities and differences in how people from these two countries speak English. Then, using the Journal Entry Form located on the *College Reading and Study Strategies* Web site or using a section of your class notebook, record those similarities and differences. Write a short comment about any text clues that helped you locate the comparisons in your text passages.

CAUSE AND EFFECT

A "cause and effect" organizational pattern shows a causal relationship that explains "why" something occurs. Signal words (see Figure 12.23) such as *because, as a result, thus,* and *consequently* and other words such as *cause, influence,* and *effect* indicate a causal relationship. As you are reading this next selection, note the author's use of "why" questions, the attempt to explain why there could be a cause-effect relationship, and the explanations that show there is not a cause-effect relationship. As you are reading, look for the author's line of reasoning and pay attention to the signal words that give you clues about the organizational pattern. (See "Causes of World Poverty" in Figure 12.24.)

why
because
cause
effect
influence
as a result
thus
consequently

FIGURE 12.23
Signal Words Indicating Cause and Effect

FIGURE 12.24
Causes of World Poverty

Source: From M. L. Andersen and H. F. Taylor, *Sociology: Understanding a Diverse Society,* 3d ed. (Belmont, CA: Wadsworth/Thomson Learning, 2004), pp. 306–307.

Causes of World Poverty

What causes world poverty, and why are so many people so desperately poor and starving? Poverty is not necessarily caused by rapid population growth, although high fertility rates and poverty are related. Many of the world's most populous countries, India and China, for instance, have large segments of their population that are poor, but these countries have reduced poverty levels, even with very big populations. Poverty is also not caused by people being lazy or uninterested in working. People in extreme poverty work tremendously hard just to survive, and they would work hard at a job if they had one. It is not that they are lazy; it is that there are no jobs for them.

Poverty is caused by a number of factors. The areas where poverty is increasing have a history of unstable governments or, in some cases, virtually no effective government to coordinate national development or plans that might alleviate extreme poverty and starvation. World relief agencies are reluctant to work in, or send food to, countries where the national governments cannot guarantee the safety of relief workers or the delivery of food and aid to where it should go. Food convoys may be hijacked or roads blocked by bandits or warlords.

In many countries with high proportions of poverty, the economies have collapsed and the governments have borrowed heavily to remain in operation. As a condition of these international loans, lenders, including the World Bank and the International Monetary Fund, have demanded harsh economic restructuring to increase capital markets and industrial efficiency. These economic reforms may make good sense for some and may lead these coun-

Continued

FIGURE 12.24, *Continued*
Causes of World Poverty

tries out of economic ruin over time, but in the short run, these imposed reforms have placed the poor in a precarious position because the reforms also called for drastically reduced government spending on human services.

Poverty is also caused by changes in the world economic system. Increases in poverty and starvation in Africa and Latin America can be attributed in part to the changes in world markets that favored Asia economically but put sub-Saharan Africa and Latin America at a disadvantage. As the price of products declined with more industrialization in places like India, China, Indonesia, South Korea, Malaysia, and Thailand, commodity-producing nations in Africa and Latin America suffered. In Latin America, the poor have flooded to the cities, hoping to find work, whereas in Africa, they did the opposite, fleeing to the countryside hoping to be able to grow subsistence crops. Governments often had to borrow to provide help to their citizens. Many governments collapsed or found themselves in such great debt that they were unable to help their own people, creating massive amounts of poverty and starvation.

In sum, poverty has many causes. It is now a major global problem that not only affects the billions of people who are living in poverty, but also affects all people on Earth in one way or another. In some areas, poverty rates are declining as some countries begin to improve their economic situation. However, in other areas of the world, poverty is increasing, and countries are sinking into financial, political, and social chaos.

ACTIVITY 12.16   *Organizational Patterns of Cause and Effect*

Read the selection in Figure 12.24 and then answer the following questions with a short statement. Be prepared to discuss your responses in class.

1. What key questions does the author pose in this selection?

2. What conditions are *not* causes of poverty? Cite the paragraph where you found your evidence.

3. What conditions does the author note contribute to poverty? Cite the paragraphs where you found your evidence.

4. Review this text selection. Circle signal words that indicate that this text selection uses cause-effect relationships. Write the signal words here:

Check your work. Answers to this activity are found on the *College Reading and Study Strategies* book-specific Web site. It is important to check your work before continuing with the next section.

ACTIVITY 12.17   *Using InfoTrac College Edition to Read Cause and Effect Paragraphs*

Environmental issues are often explained through causes and effects. Pick one environmental issue and use InfoTrac College Edition to find an example of a cause-and-effect text passage. Then, using the Journal Entry Form located on the *College Reading and Study Strategies* Web site or using a section of your class notebook, record what you found about the environmental issue, including the causes and effects. Write a short comment about any text clues that helped you locate the causes and effects.

RESPONSE: PROBLEM AND SOLUTION

When you read your college textbooks, you will find a mix of organizational patterns, especially in longer connected text. Many authors use a variety of organizational patterns, yet most authors present a central theme, an overarching question, or a unifying goal. Longer passages often contain a mix of the organizational patterns previously discussed. However, when you step back from the text and ask the question, "What's the point of this passage?" you will be able to see that the overarching purpose of the passage is to do more than explain, compare and contrast, or describe causes and effects. The author's goal may be to respond to a question, explore a problem, or present and explore solutions.

In some passages, the overall purpose is to present a problem and solution. (We will discuss "problems and solutions" in more detail in Chapter 15.) In a problem-solution passage the author describes the problem, then explores possible solutions to it. The organizational framework of a problem-solution passage is to (1) present the problem, (2) define and explain the problem, (3) explore possible solutions, and (4) present a conclusion. Most likely, the author will use the same signal words previously discussed because the author will be explaining causes and effects or making comparisons to explain a solution.

When reading problem-solution passages, look for the topic and the intent of the author. You might find more substance or more explanation in one area and not much in other areas. The solutions to some problems are very complex. You may also feel inclined to add your own opinion because the topics may be controversial. When reading for the main idea, however, try to be objective and find the author's key points. When we discuss responding to text in Chapters 15 and 16 of this textbook, you will be able to add your own opinion to the issues. For instance, in the following passage, entitled "The Question of Animal Research," note the controversy and the resulting opinions. Also, note the resulting action of the American Psychological Association to address the problem. (See "The Question of Animal Research" in Figure 12.25.)

FIGURE 12.25

The Question of Animal Research

Source: From W. Weiten, *Psychology: Themes and Variations,* 6th ed. (Belmont, CA: Wadsworth/Thomson Learning, 2004), pp. 62–64.

The Question of Animal Research

Psychology's other major ethics controversy concerns the use of animals in research. Psychologists use animals as research subjects for several reasons. Sometimes they simply want to know more about the behavior of a specific type of animal. In other instances, they want to see whether certain laws of behavior apply to both humans and animals. Finally, in some cases psychologists use animals because they can expose them to treatments that clearly would be unacceptable with human subjects. For example, most of the research on the relationship between deficient maternal nutrition during pregnancy and the incidence of birth defects has been done with animals.

It's this third reason for using animals that has generated most of the controversy. Some people maintain that it is wrong to subject animals to harm or pain for research purposes. Essentially, they argue that animals are entitled to the same rights as humans (Regan, 1997). They accuse researchers of violating these rights by subjecting animals to unnecessary cruelty in many "trivial" studies (Bowd & Shapiro, 1993; Hollands, 1989). They also assert that most animal studies are a waste of time because the results may not even apply to humans (Millstone, 1989). For example, Ulrich (1991) argues that "pigeons kept confined at 80% body weight in home cages that don't allow them ever to spread their wings, take a bath, or relate socially to other birds provide questionable models for humans" (pp. 200–201).

Although some animal rights activists simply advocate more humane treatment of research animals, a survey of 402 activists questioned at a Washington, D.C. rally found that 85% wanted to eliminate *all* research with animals (Plous, 1991). Some of the more militant animal rights activists have broken into laboratories, destroyed scientists' equipment and research records, and stolen experimental animals. According to David Johnson (1990), the animal rights movement has enjoyed considerable success. He notes that "the single issue citizens write about most often to their congresspersons and the President is not homelessness, not the drug problem, not crime. It is animal welfare" (p. 214).

In spite of the great furor, only 7%–8% of all psychological studies involve animals (mostly rodents and birds). Relatively few of these studies require subjecting the animals to painful or harmful manipulations (American Psychological Association, 1984). Psychologists who defend animal research point to the major advances attributable to psychological research on animals, which many people are unaware of (Baldwin, 1993; Compton, Dietrich, & Smith, 1995). Among them are advances in the treatment of mental disorders, neuromuscular disorders, strokes, brain injuries, visual defects, headaches, memory defects, high blood pressure, and problems with pain (Carroll & Overmier, 2001; Domjan & Purdy, 1995). To put the problem in context, Neal Miller (1985), a prominent psychologist who has done pioneering work in several areas, noted the following:

At least 20 million dogs and cats are abandoned each year in the United States; half of them are killed in pounds and shelters, and the rest are hit by cars or die of neglect. Less than 1/10,000 as many dogs and cats were used in psychological laboratories. . . . Is it worth sacrificing the lives of our children in order to stop experiments, most of which involve no pain, on a vastly smaller number of mice, rats, dogs, and cats? (p. 427)

Continued

Figure **2.18**

Ethics in research. Key ethical principles in psychological research, as set forth by the American Psychological Association (1992), are summarized here. These principles are meant to ensure the welfare of both human and animal subjects.

APA Ethical Guidelines for Research

1 A subject's participation in research should be voluntary and based on informed consent. Subjects should never be coerced into participating in research. They should be informed in advance about any aspects of the study that might be expected to influence their willingness to cooperate. Furthermore, they should be permitted to withdraw from a study at any time if they so desire.

2 Participants should not be exposed to harmful or dangerous research procedures. This guideline is intended to protect subjects from psychological as well as physical harm. Thus, even stressful procedures that might cause emotional discomfort are largely prohibited. However, procedures that carry a modest risk of moderate mental discomfort may be acceptable.

3 If an investigation requires some deception of participants (about matters that do not involve risks), the researcher is required to explain and correct any misunderstandings as soon as possible. The deception must be disclosed to subjects in "debriefing" sessions as soon as it is practical to do so without compromising the goals of the study.

4 Subjects' rights to privacy should never be violated. Information about a subject that might be acquired during a study must be treated as highly confidential and should never be made available to others without the consent of the participant.

5 Harmful or painful procedures imposed upon animals must be thoroughly justified in terms of the knowledge to be gained from the study. Furthermore, laboratory animals are entitled to decent living conditions that are spelled out in detailed rules that relate to their housing, cleaning, feeding, and so forth.

6 Prior to conducting studies, approval should be obtained from host institutions and their research review committees. Research results should be reported fully and accurately, and raw data should be promptly shared with other professionals who seek to verify substantive claims. Retractions should be made if significant errors are found in a study subsequent to its publication.

Far more compelling than Miller are the advocates for disabled people who have entered the fray to campaign against the animal rights movement in recent years. For example, Dennis Feeney (1987), a psychologist disabled by paraplegia, quotes a newsletter from an organization called The Incurably Ill for Animal Research:

No one has stopped to think about those of us who are incurably ill and are desperately waiting for new research results that can only be obtained through the use of animals. We have seen successful advances toward other diseases, such as polio, diphtheria, mumps, measles, and hepatitis through animal research. We want the same chance for a cure, but animal rights groups would deny us this chance. (p. 595)

As you can see, the manner in which animals can ethically be used for research is a highly charged controversy. Psychologists are becoming increasingly sensitive to this issue. Although animals continue to be used in research, psychologists are taking greater pains to justify their use in relation to the potential benefits of the research. They are also striving to ensure that laboratory animals receive humane care.

The ethics issues that we have discussed in this section have led the APA to develop a set of ethical standards for researchers (American Psychological Association, 1992). Although most psychological studies are fairly benign, these ethical principles are intended to ensure that both human and animal subjects are treated with dignity. Some of the key guidelines in these ethical principles are summarized in Figure 2.18.

ACTIVITY 12.18   *Organizational Patterns of Problem and Solution*

Read the selection in Figure 12.25 and then answer the following questions with a short statement. Be prepared to discuss your responses in class.

1. What controversy does the author pose in this selection?

2. The author cites three reasons for the use of animals as research. Cite the paragraph that states these reasons.

3. The author explores the background of the controversy. Cite the paragraphs that do this.

4. What solution is presented in response to the problem? Cite the paragraph that contains the response.

Check your work. Answers to this activity are found on the *College Reading and Study Strategies* book-specific Web site. It is important to check your work before continuing with the next section.

NARRATION

All the previous organizational patterns characterize expository text, that is, text that informs you about something. This last organizational pattern, "narration," does not characterize expository text, but "narrative" text. A narrative tells a story. Narrative text has people in it, a setting (i.e., place), a series of events related to a central conflict or goal, and a final outcome. Good writers use narration to provide background material, to illustrate an example, to show the human dimension for abstract concepts, to personalize information, or to describe historical events. After reading a narrative, it is a good idea to take a step away from the text and ask a key question: "What's the point of the story?" Your response should inform you about the main idea of the passage.

ACTIVITY 12.19   *Journal Activity*

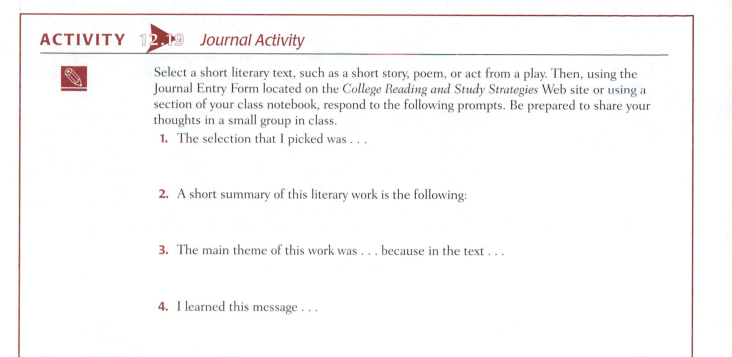

Select a short literary text, such as a short story, poem, or act from a play. Then, using the Journal Entry Form located on the *College Reading and Study Strategies* Web site or using a section of your class notebook, respond to the following prompts. Be prepared to share your thoughts in a small group in class.

1. The selection that I picked was . . .

2. A short summary of this literary work is the following:

3. The main theme of this work was . . . because in the text . . .

4. I learned this message . . .

ACTIVITY 12.20   *Where Are You Now?*

Now that you have completed this chapter, take a few minutes to return to the beginning of this chapter and repeat Activity 12.1, Where Are You Now? What have you learned about reading for the main idea? What are you going to do differently now? How are you going to change your study reading strategies?

Summary

When you are reading for the main idea, you look for the point of the passage. Generally, if it is not directly stated, you can generate the main idea by identifying the topic of the passage and then creating a sentence about the topic that summarizes a central idea. A well-written passage contains supporting details for a main idea; these details can include examples, elaborations, and descriptions that explain the main idea.

The experienced reader knows how to identify the main idea by looking for it in the introductions and conclusions. Many authors directly state the main idea, often in the first and last sentence of a passage. Main ideas may also be located in the middle of the passage. Some main ideas, though, are implied; in this case the reader generalizes from the details.

Good writers use organizational patterns as frameworks to discuss central ideas and related details. These organizational patterns include five classic structures for expository text: description, collection, comparison, causation, and response. These text structures may be further delineated with the organizational frameworks of definition and explanation, enumeration, sequence, classification, and problem solution. An additional organizational framework, narration, applies specifically to stories. For each of these organizational frameworks authors use signal words to help the reader locate significant details.

R eview Questions

Terms You Should Know: Make a flash card for each term.

Cause-effect	Enumeration	Sequence
Central idea	Examples	Signal word
Classification	Implied main idea	Stated main idea
Comparison-contrast	Introduction	Supporting detail
Conclusion	Narration	Text structure
Definition	Problem-solution	Topic
Description	Repetition	

Completion: Fill in the blank to complete each of the following statements.

1. The main idea of the passage summarizes the _____.

2. Stated main ideas are often found in a passage's _____.

3. These signal words indicate an organizational framework for a_____ pattern: similar, different, like, on the other hand.

4. These signal words indicate an organizational framework for a _____ pattern: result, because, why, consequently.

5. The organizational framework that is a listing is _____.

Multiple Choice: Circle the letter of the best answer for each of the following questions. Be sure to underline key words and eliminate wrong answers.

6. This picture shows that the main idea is located:
    A.   As an introduction.
    B.   As a conclusion.
    C.   Embedded within the passage.
    D.   As an implied statement.

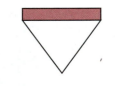

7. When the author poses a question and then responds with the answer, this passage
   is characterized as a:
   A. Cause-effect passage.
   B. Classification passage.
   C. Problem-solution passage.
   D. Narrative passage.

Short Answer–Essay: On a separate sheet answer each of the following questions.

8. Describe three graphic organizers that you could use for reading and remembering a
   passage that classifies items.

9. State three signal words that will help you read and recall a passage that contains
   enumeration.

10. Describe the organizational framework of a problem-solution passage.

13 Locating Specific Details

In this chapter you will learn how to:

➤ Find stated and implied details

➤ Locate details as evidence for main ideas

➤ Use signal words to locate details

➤ Generate a paraphrase using details and inferences

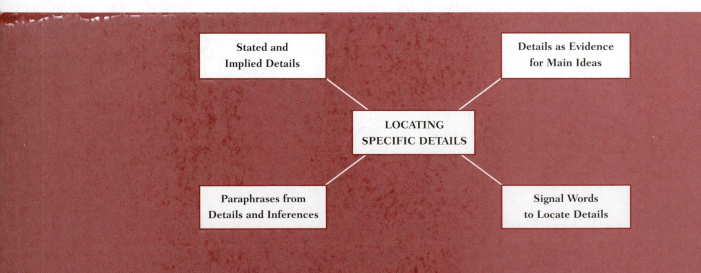

Stated and
Implied Details

Details as Evidence
for Main Ideas

**LOCATING
SPECIFIC DETAILS**

Paraphrases from
Details and Inferences

Signal Words
to Locate Details

ACTIVITY 13.1   *Where Are You Now?*

Take a few minutes to answer *yes* or *no* to the following questions; choose *yes* if you do this most of the time; choose *no* if you do not consistently do it or if you are not sure.

	YES	NO
1. When you read an assigned textbook section, do you usually find important details?	_____	_____
2. When looking for specific details, do you use a strategy for finding details?	_____	_____
3. Do you use text clues in a paragraph to locate details?	_____	_____
4. Do you make good inferences about the details you read?	_____	_____
5. Do you know the difference between details and main ideas?	_____	_____
6. Can you think of a question that would help you find details?	_____	_____
7. Can you think of a question that would help you find the definition of a word you don't understand?	_____	_____
8. When you paraphrase a passage, do you use author's clues?	_____	_____
9. When you make an inference, do you add your opinion?	_____	_____
10. Are implied details directly stated in a passage?	_____	_____
Total Points	_____	

Score yourself 1 point for each *yes* answer to questions 1–8 and *no* to questions 9 and 10. Total up your points. A low score indicates that you will need to develop your reading strategies to locate and use details. A high score indicates that you have already developed many successful reading strategies for working with details in text selections.

WHAT IS A SPECIFIC DETAIL?

Do you like solving mysteries? You will find in this chapter that locating details is like being a detective. Some details are easy to find, while others involve looking for clues to figure out the important details. In some cases you will need to make inferences, that is, good guesses, to find the information you need.

You will find that writers give details to provide you with specific information. Good writers like to provide rich descriptions to make people, places, and actions come alive. For instance, if you are reading about a historical event, the details will help paint a picture so that the people, places, things, and actions will seem real to you. On the other hand, if you are reading about an organism in biology, you will find that the details provide the specific descriptors that will help you make distinctions between one organism and another. So, as you are reading this chapter, practice building your comprehension strategies so that you will be able to locate details and use them effectively for understanding your college-level readings.

You will find that the strategies in this chapter are fundamental for your college success. As you are reading this chapter, think of the details as all the small dots on a page that, when connected together, form a picture. If you are missing some of the details, the picture is not complete. However, the more details you have, the more elaborate and complete picture you will see.

THE FIVE W'S

Let's imagine that you have been assigned the job to be a reporter to cover the following story: A whale helplessly beaches on the shores of Cape Cod. What would be some of the questions you could ask? Reporters like to find answers to the "Five W's," which are Who? What? Where? When? Why? Reporters may also ask a sixth question: How? These questions lead you to the essential details in a story.

Now, use the Five W's to guide your reading of the article "Death on the Sand," the story of the whales that had beached. As you read, look for the details that answer the questions Who? What? Where? When? and Why? When you find the answer to one of these questions, underline the text. You can record in your notebook each of the details you underlined.

FIGURE 13.1
Death on the Sand

Source: From "Death on the Sand," *Time*, August 12, 2002, pp. 52–53. Reprinted by permission of Time, Inc.

Death on the Sand

Whales beach on Cape Cod all the time. What made this pod different?

By Frederic Golden

It was a summertime saga that gripped the nation, for its poignancy and the troubling mystery it posed. Just as the sun rose over the languid beaches in the crook of the elbow-shaped playland of Cape Cod, early-morning strollers were astonished by surprise visitors. Lying helplessly in shallows near the town of Dennis, Mass., like so many black boulders, were 55 grounded pilot whales. Although nine of the whales soon died or had to be put down (with lethal injections of sodium pentothal), rescuers managed to push 46 others out to sea.

But this feel-good story quickly turned bad. During the night, the whales, all dutifully tagged in the morning, beached themselves again, in a salt marsh 25 miles away. By the time good *sea*maritans got to them, six of the whales were dead and nine others had such weak heartbeats that scientists knew they would not make it. Even those that could be refloated soon returned to shore, oblivious to the frantically splashing rescuers trying to shoo them off. By evening, all the whales—mostly females, some of them pregnant—were dead.

With its shallow waters and shifting sands, Cape Cod has long been a graveyard for both man and whale, especially pilot whales. In this treacherous terrain, the whales' critical echolocation system—those telltale clicks whales depend on for everything from avoiding predators to finding a mate—can easily become confused. Yet even after years of studying these big-brained creatures, scientists admit that's only an informed guess and doesn't explain groundings elsewhere. "I could give you an unlimited number of scenarios," says veteran Smithsonian cetologist James Mead, "and because we know so little about whale biology, any of them is possible."

These possibilities include fatal illnesses, perhaps contracted from eating poisoned fish. Or startled reactions to the cacophony of a ship's engine. Or the sudden appearance of a predator. Some scientists have even linked whale groundings to magnetic anomalies that can play havoc with the internal compasses on which whales seem to depend for navigation. One scenario, however, has been pretty much dismissed in this case: disruption by underwater sonic booms from the powerful new U.S. Navy submarine-hunting sonar that recently inflicted fatal hearing damage on beaked whales in the Bahamas—and prompted an outcry from environmentalists when the Bush Administration allowed these exercises to continue. "Extremely unlikely," says Woods Hole Oceanographic Institution's Darlene Ketten, an expert on marine-mammal hearing who found hemorrhaging and other signs of trauma in the beaked whales and is now examining tissue from the grounded pilots.

Continued

FIGURE 13.1, *Continued*
Death on the Sand

What is known for certain is that pilot whales (which are actually large dolphins) are highly social creatures. They travel in pods that can be several hundred strong, usually led by a dominant male. If the leader loses his way while hunting a favorite food like squid, the rest of the pod will follow, even onto a beach. The closely knit whales will also converge on a calf that has accidentally grounded and is clicking and squeaking in anguish. In neither case, however, do scientists regard the whales' behavior as a suicide impulse. "That's old folklore," insists Joseph Geraci of the National Aquarium in Baltimore, Md., "and should be forgotten."

Yet once they are grounded, the plight of the whales quickly becomes desperate. Under their crushing weight—1,800 lbs. for an adult—organs break down and blood circulation slows, impairing cooling and putting the animals in a state of shock. Unless rescuers can push the whales back out to sea almost immediately, the animals are usually doomed by their injuries. Explains Geraci: "They have no other way to survive except to return to the shore, which, at least, keeps them from drowning."

Human activities, though, may be part of this fatal mix. Some scientists, Geraci among them, connect a rise in marine-mammal deaths to a sharp increase in toxic plankton blooms—great eruptions of poisonous algae in the sea. As the toxins from these tiny plants pass up the food chain, they become increasingly concentrated until they contaminate the fish on which seals, sea lions and whales feed. Suspected causes of the blooms: the inadvertent fertilization of coastal waters by agriculture runoffs and most alarmingly, the rise in seawater temperatures from global warming. If so, the death of the whales last week off Cape Cod could be a warning to us all.

ACTIVITY   13.2   *Using the Five W's to Locate Details*

Read the selection entitled "Death on the Sand" in Figure 13.1, and then answer the Five W's in a short response. Find evidence in the article to prove your response; mark the text so that you will be able to find the details. Be prepared to discuss your responses in class.

1. Who were the animals mentioned in the article?

2. Who are the people mentioned in the article?

3. What was the plight of the animals?

4. Where did this story take place?

5. When did this story take place?

6. Why was this happening, according to Geraci?

Check your work. Answers to this activity are found on the *College Reading and Study Strategies* book-specific Web site. It is important to check your work before continuing with the next section.

ACTIVITY 13.3   *Using the Five W's to Determine Details*

Now that you have read the selection in Figure 13.1, use the Five W's to create questions on your own. Imagine that you are the reporter assigned to cover the story about the whales. Think of some other questions that you could answer with specific details. Write your questions in the spaces for questions below:

1. Question 1:

   Response:

2. Question 2:

   Response:

3. Question 3:

   Response:

4. Question 4:

   Response:

5. Question 5:

   Response:

Now, swap your questions with a partner in a small group. Try to answer your partner's questions and record your responses next to the questions. Then, reread the article to check your responses.

When you read the article on your own, did you make a question for each of the Five W's? Check each kind of question you made for each of the following:

Who?
What?
Where?
When?
Why?

The responses to those questions are the significant details that lead you to the most memorable information. When you locate the significant details, you find the information that supports the main idea and provides much description about the topic. At times these significant details are directly stated; at other times you will need to make inferences about the details. In the next two sections we will discuss reading for directly stated and implied details. As you are reading about these two topics, use the Five W's to help you locate the details.

DIRECTLY STATED DETAILS

When you are reading a passage, look for the details that inform you about what is important. Directly stated details are right in the text; when you find them, you should underline them and use a text notation strategy to remember them. (See Chapter 9 for text notation strategies.) In addition to details that answer the Five W's, other important details are new vocabulary words, their definitions, and descriptions about the topic. When you are reading for details, also look for facts, statistics, and explanations, especially those that support a main point.

It is often a temptation when you are reading difficult material to underline and notate many details. If you find yourself getting lost in the details, ask yourself the question "What's the main topic?" As a clue, look at the headings and subheadings, any marginal notes, any italicized or boldfaced print, or key words noted in the chapter introduction or summary. A college instructor often expects that you will use the details to make important connections of the text ideas and to use the information in some meaningful way, not just to memorize details.

IMPLIED DETAILS

Good readers make inferences about the stated details and answer questions about what is implied. Not every detail is stated; however, from the information that is given, you can accurately read "between the lines." Although details may not be directly stated, you can paraphrase the information and make accurate generalizations from the information given to you.

For instance, let's assume you are planning a trip and call ahead for a hotel reservation. The hotel reservation desk clerk might say that the room rate is $95 plus 11% tax, plus a $2 occupancy tax. If you were planning to stay at that hotel for three nights, would $300 cover the cost of the room? Before you read the next paragraph, see if you can figure out the answer.

From the details that are stated you can figure out the answer. You can infer that the rate for the room each night is $95 plus $10.45 tax and an extra $2 occupancy tax for a total of $107.45 each night. The total for the three nights would be $322.35; therefore, $300 would not be enough money to pay for the room for three nights.

When you are reading for implied details, look for stated details and make inferences that bridge the ideas to the main topic. As you are reading, ask yourself the questions, "What is the concept the author is describing to me? What explanations and details help support or prove this concept?"

For instance, if you see a list of temperatures (Fahrenheit) that are 10 degrees, 25 degrees, and 5 degrees, you could ask yourself the question "What do they all have in common?" You could generalize that they are all below freezing. You can make this generalization because you have the background experience that tells you that temperatures below 32 degrees are freezing temperatures. If you don't have the background experience that helps you make this conclusion, then ask questions that help you see patterns or connections among the details. In our example, these three details all designate temperature readings. Then, as you are reading, look for the author's conclusions. Once again, you are the detective in trying to find out how the details are linked together.

The article in Figure 13.2 will give you practice in looking for stated and implied details. As you are reading, consider details that relate to the title "Age Discrimination in Employment." Look for both stated and implied details that point to the controversy in age discrimination.

FIGURE 13.2

Age Discrimination in Employment

Source: **From S. W. Schmidt, M. C. Shelley, and B. A. Bardes,** *American Government and Politics Today,* **2001–2002 ed. (Belmont, CA: Wadsworth/Thomson Learning, 2001), pp. 196–197.**

Age Discrimination in Employment

Age discrimination is potentially the most widespread form of discrimination, because anyone—regardless of race, color, national origin, or gender—could be a victim at some point in life. The unstated policies of some companies not to hire or to demote or dismiss people they feel are "too old" have made it difficult for some older workers to succeed in their jobs or continue with their careers. Additionally, older workers have fallen victim at times to cost-cutting efforts by employers. To reduce operational costs, companies may replace older, higher-salaried workers with younger, lower-salaried workers.

The Age Discrimination in Employment Act of 1967. In an attempt to protect older employees from such discriminatory practices, Congress passed the Age Discrimination in Employment Act (ADEA) in 1967. The act, which applies to employers, employment agencies, and labor organizations and covers individuals over the age of forty, prohibits discrimination against individuals on the basis of age unless age is shown to be a bona fide occupational qualification reasonably necessary to the normal operation of the particular business.

Specifically, it is against the law to discriminate by age in wages, benefits, hours worked, or availability of overtime. Employers and unions may not discriminate in providing fringe benefits, such as education or training programs, career development, sick leave, and vacations. It is a violation of the act to publish notices or advertisements indicating an age-preference limitation or discrimination based on age. Even advertisements that imply a preference for youthful workers over older workers are in violation of the law. Requesting age on an application is not illegal but may be closely scrutinized in light of the employer's hiring practices.

To succeed in a suit for age discrimination, an employee must prove that the employer's action, such as a decision to fire the employee, was motivated, at least in part, by age bias. Proof that qualified older employees are generally discharged before younger employees or that co-workers continually made unflattering age-related comments about the discharged worker may be enough. In 1996, the Supreme Court held that even if an older worker is replaced by a younger worker falling under the protection of the ADEA—that is, by a younger worker who is also over the age of forty—the older worker is entitled to bring a suit under the ADEA. The Court stated that the issue in all ADEA cases is whether age discrimination has in fact occurred, regardless of the age of the replacement worker.[5]

---

[5] *O'Connor v. Consolidated Coil Caterers Corp.,* 517 U.S. 308 (1996).

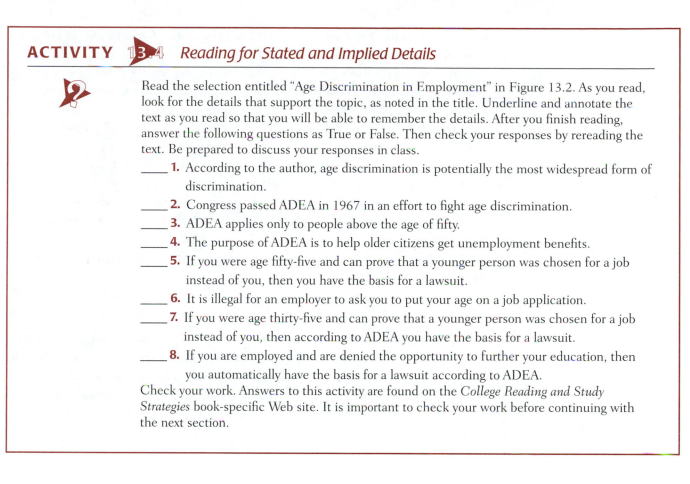

ACTIVITY 13.4 *Reading for Stated and Implied Details*

Read the selection entitled "Age Discrimination in Employment" in Figure 13.2. As you read, look for the details that support the topic, as noted in the title. Underline and annotate the text as you read so that you will be able to remember the details. After you finish reading, answer the following questions as True or False. Then check your responses by rereading the text. Be prepared to discuss your responses in class.

_____ **1.** According to the author, age discrimination is potentially the most widespread form of discrimination.

_____ **2.** Congress passed ADEA in 1967 in an effort to fight age discrimination.

_____ **3.** ADEA applies only to people above the age of fifty.

_____ **4.** The purpose of ADEA is to help older citizens get unemployment benefits.

_____ **5.** If you were age fifty-five and can prove that a younger person was chosen for a job instead of you, then you have the basis for a lawsuit.

_____ **6.** It is illegal for an employer to ask you to put your age on a job application.

_____ **7.** If you were age thirty-five and can prove that a younger person was chosen for a job instead of you, then according to ADEA you have the basis for a lawsuit.

_____ **8.** If you are employed and are denied the opportunity to further your education, then you automatically have the basis for a lawsuit according to ADEA.

Check your work. Answers to this activity are found on the *College Reading and Study Strategies* book-specific Web site. It is important to check your work before continuing with the next section.

Did you find the details? Return to the text and note where you found your answers. For instance, the first sentence was an important one because it pointed to the significance of the topic of age discrimination. Notice the boldfaced print in the next paragraph. The second paragraph gives you the definition of ADEA; this definition is an important detail. The third paragraph gives you a supporting clarification of the law. Then, the fourth paragraph gives you an explanation of the main ingredients for a lawsuit using age discrimination as a basis. We will continue our study of locating specific details in the next sections.

SPECIFIC DETAILS AND TOPICS

Do you remember our discussion of main ideas? When we were looking for the main ideas, we were looking for statements that summarized ideas about topics. Generally, we needed to read several sentences to find the main point. On the other hand, when we read for details, we typically are reading for words or phrases that provide supporting information about a topic. The details give you many specific descriptors that bring a topic to life.

TOPICS AS THE OVERALL IDEA

Perhaps the following analogy will help you see the differences among details, topics, and main ideas: Let's imagine that you decide to go get an ice cream sundae. You step inside the ice cream store and see that you can choose among forty different flavors. You narrow your choice to one scoop of chocolate ice cream with hot fudge, whipped cream, and a cherry on top. Satisfied, you enjoy the luxurious taste of your sundae and leave the store as one satisfied customer.

In this example our topic is "ice cream sundae" because all the details—that is, chocolate ice cream, hot fudge, whipped cream, and the cherry—are describing the choice of sundae you made. The main point at the end was that you were happy with your choice. If we could make a picture of the relationship of details with topics and main ideas, our picture could look like the diagram in Figure 13.3.

When you look at this diagram, you can see that the topic is the key word at the center. The main idea makes a statement about the topic. The details provide the substance for proving the main idea. Good writers use details as examples, or elaborations, or descriptions that support the main idea. Or, sometimes the details show comparisons or contrasts that will prove the main idea. Therefore, as you are reading, look for the connections of the details and see how they relate to the topic and the main idea.

DETAILS AS EVIDENCE

Let's continue our discussion about the link between the details and the main idea. When you are reading college-level text, you will find that authors like to support the main idea with details as evidence. Authors often cite notable studies that provide research evidence for the claims in the main idea. Authors use facts, statistics, and data as evidence. Let's take a look at the article in Figure 13.4 to see how the author uses research evidence to prove a point.

FIGURE 13.3
Topics, Details, and Main Ideas

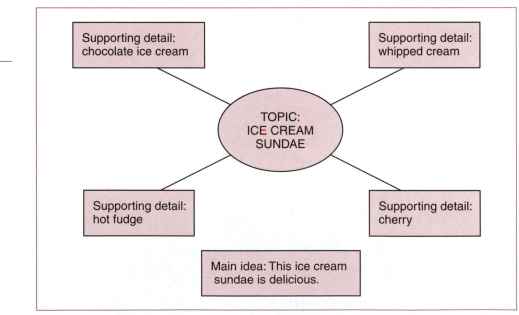

FIGURE 13.4
Cross-Cultural Similarities in Emotional Experience

Source: From W. Weiten, *Psychology: Themes and Variations*, 6th ed. (Belmont, CA: Wadsworth/Thomson Learning, 2004), pp. 409–411.

Cross-Cultural Similarities in Emotional Experience

After demonstrating that Western subjects could discern specific emotions from facial expressions, Ekman and Friesen (1975) took their facial-cue photographs on the road to other societies to see whether nonverbal expressions of emotion transcend cultural boundaries. Testing subjects in Argentina, Spain, Japan, and other countries, they found considerable cross-cultural agreement in the identification of happiness, sadness, anger, fear, surprise, and disgust based on facial expressions (see Figure 10.23). Still, Ekman and Friesen wondered whether this agreement might be the result of learning rather than biology, given that people in different cultures often share considerable exposure to Western mass media (magazines, newspapers, television, and so forth), which provide many visual depictions of people's emotional reactions. To rule out this possibility, they took their photos to a remote area in New Guinea and showed them to a group of natives (the Fore) who had had virtually no contact with Western culture. Even the people from this preliterate culture did a fair job of identifying the emotions portrayed in the pictures (see the data in the bottom row of Figure 10.23). Subsequent comparisons of many other societies have also shown considerable cross-cultural congruence in the judgment of facial expressions (Biehl et al., 1997; Ekman, 1992, 1993). Although some theorists disagree (Russell, 1994, 1995), there is reasonably convincing evidence that people in widely disparate cultures express their emotions and interpret those expressions in much the same way (Izard, 1994; Matsumoto, 2001).

Cross-cultural similarities have also been found in the cognitive and physiological elements of emotional experience (Schere & Wallbott, 1994). For example, in making cognitive appraisals of events that might elicit emotional reactions, people from different cultures generally think along the same lines (Mauro, Sato, & Tucker, 1992; Mesquita & Frijda, 1992). That is, they evaluate situations along the same dimensions (pleasant versus unpleasant, expected versus unexpected, fair versus unfair, and so on). Understandably, then, the types of events that trigger specific emotions are fairly similar across cultures (Frijda, 1999; Scherer, 1997). Around the globe, achievements lead to joy, injustices lead to anger, and risky situations lead to fear. Finally, as one might expect, the physiological arousal that accompanies emotion also appears to be largely invariant across cultures (Wallbott & Scherer, 1988). Thus, researchers have found a great deal of cross-cultural continuity and uniformity in the cognitive, physiological, and behavioral (expressive) elements of emotional experience.

Figure 10.23

Cross-cultural comparisons of people's ability to recognize emotions from facial expressions. Ekman and Friesen (1975) found that people in highly disparate cultures showed fair agreement on the emotions portrayed in photos. This consensus across cultures suggests that facial expressions of emotions may be universal and that they have a strong biological basis.

SOURCE: Data from Ekman, P., & Friesen, W.V. (1975). *Unmasking the face.* Englewood Cliffs, NJ: Prentice-Hall.

Agreement in judging photos (%)

Country	Fear	Disgust	Happiness	Anger
United States	85	92	97	67
Brazil	67	97	95	90
Chile	68	92	95	94
Argentina	54	92	98	90
Japan	66	90	100	90
New Guinea	54	44	82	50

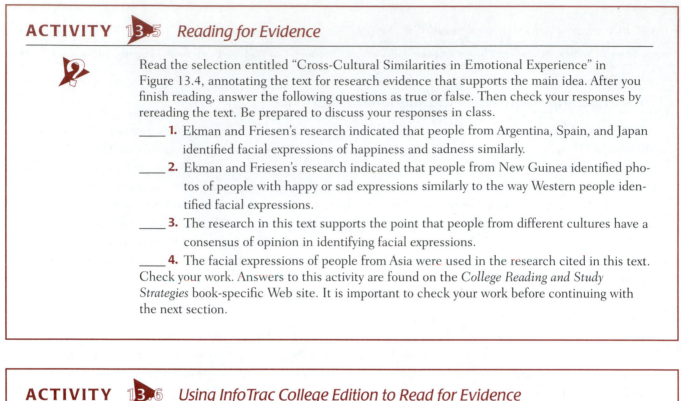

ACTIVITY ▶13.5   *Reading for Evidence*

Read the selection entitled "Cross-Cultural Similarities in Emotional Experience" in Figure 13.4, annotating the text for research evidence that supports the main idea. After you finish reading, answer the following questions as true or false. Then check your responses by rereading the text. Be prepared to discuss your responses in class.

_____ **1.** Ekman and Friesen's research indicated that people from Argentina, Spain, and Japan identified facial expressions of happiness and sadness similarly.

_____ **2.** Ekman and Friesen's research indicated that people from New Guinea identified photos of people with happy or sad expressions similarly to the way Western people identified facial expressions.

_____ **3.** The research in this text supports the point that people from different cultures have a consensus of opinion in identifying facial expressions.

_____ **4.** The facial expressions of people from Asia were used in the research cited in this text.

Check your work. Answers to this activity are found on the *College Reading and Study Strategies* book-specific Web site. It is important to check your work before continuing with the next section.

ACTIVITY ▶13.6   *Using InfoTrac College Edition to Read for Evidence*

Do you think people from other cultures have the same perspectives as you do about showing happiness, sadness, fear, or anger? Use InfoTrac College Edition to locate research describing how different cultures express emotion. Then, using the Journal Entry Form located on the *College Reading and Study Strategies* Web site or using a section of your class notebook, write down the names of the researchers you find along with a short statement describing their research findings. Pay particular notice to the way authors use research studies as evidence to support their point. Be prepared to present your response in class.

GENERAL VERSUS SPECIFIC IDEAS

When you look for details, you look for specific information that provides support for a general idea. As noted above, the main idea, which tells you something about a topic, is best explained when the author gives you rich description, facts, examples, and other details as evidence. It is sometimes helpful to think of the distinction between main ideas and details as the difference between the name of a group and the members of a group; in other words, the specific idea is "part of" or a "type of" the general idea. To see some examples of the distinctions between general and specific ideas, try the following activity to sort out the members of a group with the name of a group; in other words, distinguish the "general" ideas from the "specific" ones.

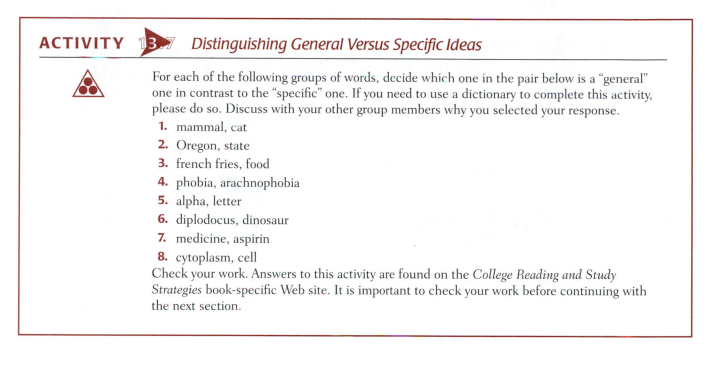

ACTIVITY 13.7 *Distinguishing General Versus Specific Ideas*

For each of the following groups of words, decide which one in the pair below is a "general" one in contrast to the "specific" one. If you need to use a dictionary to complete this activity, please do so. Discuss with your other group members why you selected your response.

1. mammal, cat
2. Oregon, state
3. french fries, food
4. phobia, arachnophobia
5. alpha, letter
6. diplodocus, dinosaur
7. medicine, aspirin
8. cytoplasm, cell

Check your work. Answers to this activity are found on the *College Reading and Study Strategies* book-specific Web site. It is important to check your work before continuing with the next section.

MAJOR AND MINOR DETAILS

When you read for details, you find that some details are more important to remember than other ones. When you read descriptive text, you find that some details help bring the text alive with sights, sounds, smells, tastes, and textures. Passages containing rich detail help you make distinctions among different topics, or things, or events. It is important to note that you do not need to read to remember all the details you read.

How do you know which details are the ones you need to remember? Strategic readers look for text cues, such as signal words (which we will discuss in the next section, and which are listed in the Tip Block). As a student taking a specific course, you can also try the direct approach: Ask your instructor. In addition, use any study guides that the instructor distributes to the class, as well as any study hints for exams.

It is also important to ask yourself questions as you read, such as the following:
What is my topic? Which details describe it?
Which details provide evidence to prove the point in my text passage?
In order to summarize the main point, what details should I select?

Let's practice using these questions in the following activity.

ACTIVITY 13.8 *Distinguishing Major Versus Minor Ideas*

Read the text entitled "The Somatic Nervous System" in Figure 13.5. While you are reading ask yourself the questions:

1. What is my topic? Which details describe it? (Hint: Think of a sentence.)

2. Which details provide evidence to prove the point in my text passage?

3. In order to summarize the main point what details should I select?

Reread the text in Figure 13.5, looking for the topic, at least two major details, and a minor detail. Write them in the appropriate columns below or in your notebook:

Topic	Major Detail	Minor Detail
(Write a sentence.)	*(Write two.)*	*(Write one.)*

Check your work. Answers to this activity are found on the *College Reading and Study Strategies* book-specific Web site. It is important to check your work before continuing with the next section.

FIGURE 13.5
The Somatic Nervous System

Source: From W. Weiten, *Psychology: Themes and Variations*, 6th ed. (Belmont, CA: Wadsworth/Thomson Learning, 2004), pp. 84–85.

The Somatic Nervous System

The *somatic nervous system* is made up of nerves that connect to voluntary skeletal muscles and to sensory receptors. These nerves are the cables that carry information from receptors in the skin, muscles, and joints to the central nervous system and that carry commands from the CNS to the muscles. These functions require two kinds of nerve fibers. *Afferent nerve fibers* are axons that carry information inward to the central nervous system from the periphery of the body. *Efferent nerve fibers* are axons that carry information outward from the central nervous system to the periphery of the body. Each body nerve contains many axons of each type. Thus, somatic nerves are "two-way streets" with incoming (afferent) and outgoing (efferent) lanes. The somatic nervous system lets you feel the world and move around in it.

SIGNAL WORDS

Do you remember the signal words in Chapter 12? These signal words helped you locate the main idea. In this section we are looking for specific details. You can use these signal words to locate essential details as well. As you are looking for these signal words, remember that when you are looking for details, you are also looking for their connection to the main idea.

REPETITION LEADING TO KEY DETAILS

One of the most common writing techniques that authors use to signal key details is repetition. When you are reading about a topic, look for ideas that are repeated throughout a section; the author will provide support for those ideas with key details. Sometimes the key ideas are repeated throughout a passage with the use of synonyms or antonyms so that the passage is stylistically interesting; therefore, look for key details when you see related synonyms or antonyms. Remember that what counts is the repetition of the key idea throughout the passage. Sometimes this repetition occurs over several sentences in a paragraph, or many even occur over several paragraphs. For practice read the text passage in Figure 13.6; the passage describes leisure in the nineteenth century and illustrates how people in the nineteenth century enjoyed themselves.

FIGURE 13.6
Leisure in an Age of Mass Society

Source: From W. J. Duiker and J. J. Spielvogel, *World History,* 3d ed. (Belmont, CA: Wadsworth, 2001), p. 641.

Leisure in an Age of Mass Society

In the preindustrial centuries, play or leisure activities had been closely connected to work patterns based on the seasonal or daily cycles typical of agricultural and even artisanal life. The process of industrialization in the nineteenth century had an enormous impact on that traditional pattern. The factory imposed new work patterns that were determined by the rhythms of machines and clocks and removed work time completely from the family environment of farms and workshops. Work and leisure became opposites as leisure was viewed as what people did for fun after work. In fact, the new leisure hours created by the industrial system—evening hours after work, weekends, and later a week or two in the summer—largely determined the contours of the new mass leisure.

New technology also determined the forms of the new mass leisure. The new technology created novel experiences for leisure, such as the Ferris wheel at amusement parks, while the mechanized urban transportation systems of the 1880s meant that even the working classes were no longer dependent on neighborhood bars, but could make their way to athletic games, amusement parks, and dance halls. Likewise, railroads could take people to the beaches on weekends.

The upper and middle classes had created the first market for tourism, but as wages increased and workers were given paid vacations, tourism, too, became another form of mass leisure. Thomas Cook (1808–1892) was a British pioneer of mass tourism. Secretary to a British temperance group, Cook had accepted responsibility for organizing a railroad trip to temperance gatherings in 1841. This experience led him to offer trips on a regular basis after he found that he could make substantial profits by renting special trains, lowering prices, and increasing the number of passengers.

By the late nineteenth century, team sports had also developed into yet another important form of mass leisure. Unlike the old rural games, they were no longer chaotic and spontaneous activities, but became strictly organized with sets of rules and officials to enforce them. These rules were the products of organized athletic groups, such as the English Football Association (1863) and the American Bowling Congress (1895).

The new team sports rapidly became professionalized. In Britain, soccer had its Football Association in 1863 and rugby its Rugby Football Union in 1871. In the United States, the first National Association to recognize professional baseball players was formed in 1863. By 1900, the National League and American League had a monopoly over professional baseball. The development of urban transportation systems made possible the construction of stadiums where thousands could attend, making mass spectator sports into a big business.

Continued

FIGURE 13.6, *Continued*
Leisure in an Age of Mass Society

The new forms of popular leisure were standardized amusements that drew mass audiences. Although some argued that they were important for improving people, in truth, they mostly served to provide entertainment and distract people from the realities of their work lives. The new mass leisure also represented a significant change from earlier forms of popular culture. Festivals and fairs had been based on an ethos of active community participation, whereas the new forms of mass leisure were standardized for largely passive mass audiences. Amusement parks and professional sport teams were, after all, big businesses organized to make profits.

ACTIVITY 13.9 *Using Repetition to Locate Details*

In this activity you are asked to read the passage several times, then write about the details you find. The passage is entitled "Leisure in an Age of Mass Society," and as noted by the title, the passage describes the types of activities people did for amusement.

1. Each time you read the passage, circle the word *leisure* each time you see it.
2. What are some synonyms for the word *leisure*? What are some other words for leisure? Here are some: *play, fun, activities, trips, amusement, tourism, athletics, games, team sports.* Reread the text passage and circle these words when you find them. You may find some additional synonyms; circle those words, too.
3. Think of some antonyms for the word *leisure*. For instance, an antonym for *leisure* is the word *work*. Reread the text passage and underline any antonyms.
4. Reread the text in its entirety.

Then using the Journal Entry Form located on the *College Reading and Study Strategies* Web site, make a two-column page. At the top of the left column write the word *Leisure* and at the top of the right column write *Detail*. Under the "Leisure" column write any of the synonyms or antonyms that you circle. Under the "Detail" column write any of the details that describe leisure in the nineteenth century.

TRANSITIONS POINTING TO DIRECTLY STATED DETAILS

The signal words that are noted in the Tip Block will help you locate significant details. When you use these signal words, think of the author's purpose. For instance, if the author intends to *explain* a key point, look for transition words that help you find explanations; some examples of these transition words are *such as, for example,* and *for instance.* If the author intends to *compare and contrast* key points, look for transitions that help you find comparisons and contrasts, such as *similarly, in contrast,* and *on the other hand.*

If you need to review the different text patterns, return to Chapter 12 for their descriptions. You will find that as you use the signal words to identify the text pattern, then you can use these same signal words to locate the details that support the main idea. In the next sections you will have more practice in finding details using signal words.

TIP

TRANSITION WORDS

When you are looking for significant details related to a main point, you can use transition words that signal the text pattern. The transition words in the right-hand column point to the text pattern listed in the left-hand column. As signals, these words help you find the details that support a main point. You can also use these transition words in your own writing to create clear, readable text.

TEXT PATTERN	TRANSITIONS
Listing, Sequence, Chronology	A, B, C First, Second, Third In addition Next Last Finally
Description	For example To illustrate For instance Such as
Classification	Similar to Like
Comparison and Contrast	Similar . . . different In contrast to Like . . . unlike However Although But On the other hand
Cause and Effect	As a result Consequently Why Because
Conclusion	Thus In conclusion Therefore In summary

TRANSITIONS LEADING TO IMPLIED DETAILS

As you read for details, you can use transition words to help you determine implied details; these are details that are not directly stated in the text. Using the stated information and the signal words in the passage, you can find good evidence about your topic and main idea. With enough good evidence, you can arrive at appropriate conclusions and make good inferences about the details. Let's take a look in the text passage in Figure 13.7 for how the author uses repetition and transitions that signal both the stated and implied details.

FIGURE 13.7

Norms

Source: From M. L. Andersen and H. F. Taylor, *Sociology: Understanding a Diverse Society,* 3d ed. (Belmont, CA: Wadsworth/Thomson Learning, 2004), p. 66.

Norms

Norms are the specific cultural expectations for how to behave in a given situation. A society without norms would be in chaos; with established norms, people know how to act, and social interactions are consistent, predictable, and learnable. Norms govern every situation. Sometimes they are *implicit;* that is, they need not be stated for people to understand what they are. For example, when waiting in line, an implicit norm is that you should not barge in front of those ahead of you. Implicit norms may not be formal rules, but violation of these norms may produce a harsh response. Implicit norms may be learned through specific instruction or by observation of the culture. They are part of a society's or group's customs. Norms are *explicit* when the rules governing behavior are written down or formally communicated and specific sanctions are imposed for violating explicit norms.

In the early years of sociology, William Graham Sumner (1906) identified two types of norms: folkways and mores. **Folkways** are the general standards of behavior adhered to by a group. You might think of folkways as the ordinary customs of different group cultures. Men wearing pants and not skirts is an example of a cultural folkway. Other examples are the ways that people greet each other, decorate their homes, and prepare their food. Folkways may be loosely defined and loosely adhered to, but they nevertheless structure group customs and implicitly govern much social behavior.

Mores (pronounced "more-ays") are stricter norms than folkways that control moral and ethical behavior such as the injunctions, legal and religious, against killing others and committing adultery. The mores are often upheld through rules or laws, the written set of guidelines that define right and wrong in society. Laws are formalized mores and violating mores can bring serious repercussions.

When any social norm is violated, sanctions are typically meted out against the violator. **Social sanctions** are mechanisms of social control that enforce norms. The seriousness of a sanction depends on how strictly the norm is held. Violations of folkways carry lighter sanctions than violations of mores. Dressing in an unusual way that violates the cultural folkways of dress may bring ridicule, but is usually not seriously punished. In some cultures the rules of dress are strictly interpreted, such as among fundamentalist Islams requiring women who appear in public to have their bodies cloaked and faces veiled. The sanctions for violating mores can be as severe as whipping, branding, banishment, even death.

ACTIVITY 13.10   *Using Signal Words to Locate Details*

In this activity you are asked to read to locate details, using signal words, in the passage in Figure 13.7 entitled "Norms." As you read the passage, circle each of the signal words. Look for details that explain norms, folkways, and mores. After you finish reading, answer the following questions as true or false. Then check your responses by rereading the text. Be prepared to discuss your responses in class.

_____ **1.** Norms may be explicit or implicit.

_____ **2.** Folkways and mores govern behavior on both group and personal levels.

_____ **3.** If you violate the norms of your culture, then you most likely will face unpleasant consequences, some of which may be severely punitive.

_____ **4.** Norms dictate how you should dress.

_____ **5.** In a society mores are often upheld as laws.

_____ **6.** Examples of mores are the rules for playing sports, such as basketball and football.

_____ **7.** Driving a car is governed by the norms of the country where you live.

_____ **8.** The consequences for violating folkways are more severe than violating mores.

Check your work. Answers to this activity are found on the *College Reading and Study Strategies* book-specific Web site. It is important to check your work before continuing with the next section.

As you were completing this activity, did you note the signal words? Did you note how the author gave you an example of a norm in the first paragraph? Did you find the examples of folkways in the second paragraph? Did you find the example of mores in the third paragraph? The author gave you these examples to clarify the definitions of norms, folkways, and mores. Can you think of other examples, too? Since the author's intent in these paragraphs is to define each of the concepts of "norms," "folkways," and "mores," a good study strategy is to write down the definition and an example to help you remember the distinctions among each of the three concepts.

PARAPHRASING TEXT

You will find that locating details is an essential strategy for comprehending your college textbooks. However, in most of your college classes, you will need to generate your own summary after you find the significant details. Generating your own summary will help you think about the key details and main points and write down ideas that are meaningful to you. In the following sections you will need to paraphrase the important point of a passage using the details. As you are practicing the activities in the following sections, notate the sample texts and write down the significant points.

STATING IMPORTANT DETAILS

As noted in the previous section of this chapter, when you read, you are looking for both explicit and implicit details that support a main point about a topic. As noted in Chapter 12, look for text clues that will help you focus on the main point. Typically, the

TIP

DECISION GUIDE FOR A GRAPHIC ORGANIZER

When you are reading, look for details that provide support for a main point. To decide which graphic organizer to use, look for the text pattern and signal words. A graphic organizer visually represents the details, main point, and connections between them.

IF YOU SEE A:	THEN USE:
Listing *Sample key words:* *A, B, C*	**Concept map**
Description *Sample key words:* *For example*	**Concept map**
Classification *Sample key words:* *Member of*	**Hierarchical array**
Classification with Description *Sample key words:* *Characteristics of this Class Member*	**Semantic feature matrix**
Comparison and Contrast *Sample key words:* *Similar . . . different*	**Venn diagram**
Sequence or Chronology *Sample key words:* *First, Second, Third*	**Timeline**
Cause and Effect *Sample key words:* *As a result*	**Fishbone map**

author provides you with a statement that indicates the main idea, signaling the intent of the passage; the details then provide support for the main idea. Therefore, as you read, write down the details that provide support for a main point.

Many students find that it's useful to use a graphic organizer to state the important details. Although the most popular graphic organizer is a concept map, such as the one in Figure 13.3, you may use any graphic organizer that shows the connection between the main point and the supporting evidence. To help you decide which of the graphic organizers will help you state the main ideas, use the decision guide in the Tip Block. Once you decide which graphic organizer you would like to use, either make a sketch of it or use one from the *College Reading and Study Strategies* Web site.

As you are reading, look for both stated and implied details that provide the support for your main point. When stating the important details, closely read the text passage and pull

FIGURE 13.8
Erikson's View of Adulthood

Source: From W. Weiten, *Psychology: Themes and Variations*, 6th ed. (Belmont, CA: Wadsworth/Thomson Learning, 2004), pp. 456–457.

Erikson's View of Adulthood

Insofar as personality changes during the adult years, Erik Erikson's (1963) theory offers some clues about the nature of changes people can expect. In his eight-stage model of development over the life span, Erikson divided adulthood into three stages.

Intimacy Versus Isolation. In early adulthood, the key concern is whether one can develop the capacity to share intimacy with others. Successful resolution of the challenges in this stage should promote empathy and openness, rather than shrewdness and manipulativeness.

Generativity Versus Self-Absorption. In middle adulthood, the key challenge is to acquire a genuine concern for the welfare of future generations, which results in providing unselfish guidance to younger people and concern with one's legacy. Self-absorption is characterized by self-indulgent concerns with meeting one's own needs and desires.

Integrity Versus Despair. During the retirement years, the challenge is to avoid the tendency to dwell on the mistakes of the past and on one's imminent death. People need to find meaning and satisfaction in their lives, rather than wallow in bitterness and resentment.

Empirical research on the adult stages in Erikson's theory has been sparse, but generally supportive of the theory. For example, research by Susan Whitbourne and her colleagues (1992) suggests that personality development proceeds in an orderly sequence of stages and that favorable resolutions of psychosocial crises in earlier stages lead to more favorable outcomes in later stages. And *generativity* has proven to be a measurable trait that increases between young adulthood and middle-age as originally envisioned by Erikson (McAdams, de St. Aubin, & Logan, 1993).

out the words and phrases that support the author's point. If you directly quote a sentence or key phrase from the text, use quotation marks and note the page number of the quote.

Although it is highly recommended that you use a graphic organizer to state important details (because it shows the connections of ideas in a visual format), you also have the option of making a list or outline of the important details. If you choose to write out the details in this format, after listing the details write a heading for your list, noting the major topic or point. The following activity will give you practice in selecting and stating the important details. Read the text passage entitled "Erikson's View of Adulthood" in Figure 13.8 and then complete the activity.

ACTIVITY 13.11 *Stating Important Details*

In your notebook state the important details for the passage entitled "Erikson's View of Adulthood" in Figure 13.8. As you read, use the heading, subheadings, and the author's description of the key challenges and concerns for each stage. Include in your statement of the details a short comparison and contrast of each stage. Be prepared to discuss your responses in class.

As you read the passage, did you use the subheadings "Intimacy versus Isolation," "Generativity versus Self-Absorption," and "Integrity versus Despair" to find the important details? Did you read the text closely and notate the descriptions of each stage? If your answer to these questions is "yes," then you are a careful reader. The next challenge is to make inferences based on what you read.

MAKING INFERENCES

Perhaps the most active job you have as a reader is to make inferences about what you read. This means that you need to make good guesses about the details that are not supplied to you. Based on the information you do have, you can make "bridging inferences" from ideas in the text to ideas outside of the text. When you make inferences, you base your "good guess" on information directly stated in the text. An inference is not your opinion; however, when we work on critical reading comprehension strategies in subsequent sections of this textbook, you may use your opinions to agree or disagree with what the author is saying. At this point, however, it is important to carefully and closely read the text so that you understand what the author is saying.

Here is an example of an inference. If I said, "The snow from yesterday's storm is melting," then asked you the question "What is the temperature outside?" you would be able to say, "It's above freezing; it's more than 32 degrees Fahrenheit." Even though the text did not state the temperature, you can infer what the temperature is based on the available information.

In the following activity reread "Erikson's View of Adulthood" in order to make inferences about the text. You will not find the information directly stated in the text; however, you will be able to use the explicit details you have already located to make good guesses that are supported by the text.

ACTIVITY 13.12 *Making Inferences*

In this activity you are asked to read to make inferences, based on the evidence in the text. Reread the text passage in Figure 13.8. Reexamine the details that you located for your graphic organizer or outline. Now use those details for making good inferences. If a statement is "true," mark it as true. Then check your responses by rereading the text. Be prepared to discuss your responses in class.

_____ **1.** During the stage of "Intimacy versus Isolation" the key challenge is to seek and show the capacity to care for a mate.

_____ **2.** People who are over sixty-five are in the stage "integrity versus despair."

_____ **3.** According to Erikson adults who are manipulative face isolation.

_____ **4.** According to Erikson one of the challenges of adulthood is to create a future legacy for the generations to come.

_____ **5.** Erikson discusses the need to plan for the future through retirement plans.

_____ **6.** Erikson's theory is well supported with much research.

Check your work. Answers to this activity are found on the *College Reading and Study Strategies* book-specific Web site. It is important to check your work before continuing with the next section.

How did you do? Did you find evidence in the text to support each of your responses? While you were reading for evidence, did you write down the significant details? When you are creating your own notes from your readings, it is also a good idea to write down the page number so that you can return to the text for the full text explanation. Your notes and graphic organizers provide a good sketch of the details and points you wish to remember. Now, you are ready to create paraphrases of the text that provide a good summary of what you read.

GENERATING PARAPHRASES

When you generate a paraphrase, you state in your own words the main idea and supporting details. To do so, summarize the author's main point and then use your notes and/or graphic organizer to state the supporting evidence. Let's revisit the text passage in Figure 13.8 describing Erikson's view of adulthood. Do you remember the three stages that were listed in this passage? There are six key terms in this text; as pairs they describe, compare, and contrast the three stages. In the following activity, write a short description about each of the six key terms, then about each of the three stages. You may use your notes from the previous activities for this activity.

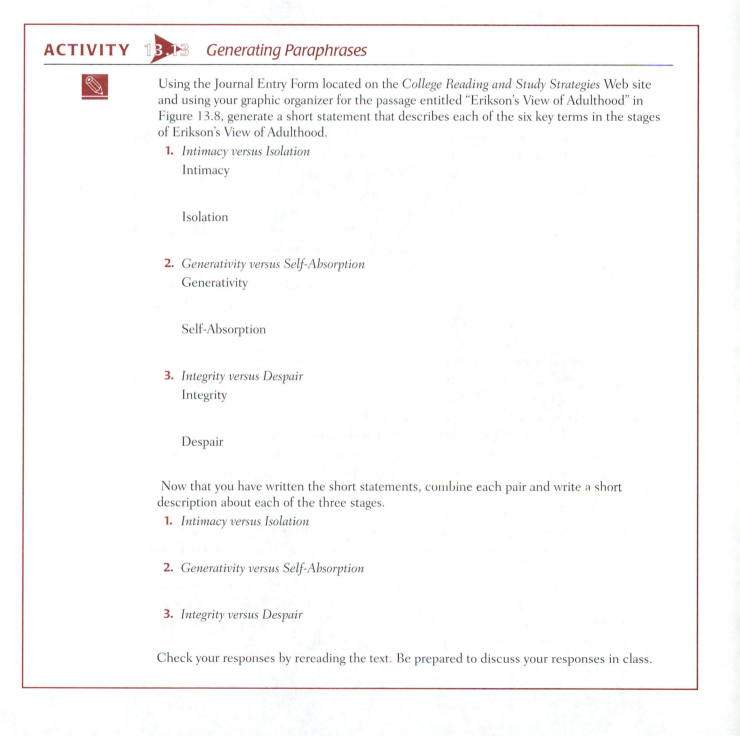

ACTIVITY 13.13   *Generating Paraphrases*

Using the Journal Entry Form located on the *College Reading and Study Strategies* Web site and using your graphic organizer for the passage entitled "Erikson's View of Adulthood" in Figure 13.8, generate a short statement that describes each of the six key terms in the stages of Erikson's View of Adulthood.

  1. *Intimacy versus Isolation*
   Intimacy

   Isolation

  2. *Generativity versus Self-Absorption*
   Generativity

   Self-Absorption

  3. *Integrity versus Despair*
   Integrity

   Despair

 Now that you have written the short statements, combine each pair and write a short description about each of the three stages.

  1. *Intimacy versus Isolation*

  2. *Generativity versus Self-Absorption*

  3. *Integrity versus Despair*

Check your responses by rereading the text. Be prepared to discuss your responses in class.

Did you see how your paraphrase was based on your notes? Did you see how your paraphrase was based on a close reading of the text? Did you use your graphic organizer? The following activities are designed to give you additional practice in locating significant details and generating paraphrases.

FIGURE 13.9
A Golden Age of Literature: England and Spain

Source: From W. J. Duiker and J. J. Spielvogel, *World History*, 3d ed. (Belmont, CA: Wadsworth, 2001), p. 456.

A Golden Age of Literature: England and Spain

Periods of crisis often produce great writing, and this period, which was characterized by a golden age of theater, was no exception. In both England and Spain, writing for the stage reached new heights between 1580 and 1640. The golden age of English literature is often called the Elizabethan Era because much of the English cultural flowering of the late sixteenth and early seventeenth centuries occurred during her reign. Elizabethan literature exhibits the exuberance and pride associated with English exploits under Queen Elizabeth. Of all the forms of Elizabethan literature, none expressed the energy and intellectual versatility of the era better than drama. Of all the dramatists, none is more famous than William Shakespeare (1564–1614).

Shakespeare was the son of a prosperous glover from Stratford-upon-Avon. When he appeared in London in 1592, Elizabethans were already addicted to the stage. By 1576, two professional theaters run by actors' companies were in existence. Elizabethan theater became a tremendously successful business. Soon at least four to six theaters were open six afternoons a week in or near London. They ranged from the Globe, which was a circular unroofed structure holding 3,000, to the Blackfriars, which was roofed and held only 500. In the former, an admission charge of one or two pennies enabled even the lower classes to attend, while the higher prices in the latter ensured an audience of the well-to-do. Elizabethan audiences varied greatly, putting pressure on playwrights to write works that pleased nobles, lawyers, merchants, and even vagabonds.

William Shakespeare was a "complete man of the theater." Although best known for writing plays, he was also an actor and shareholder in the chief company of the time, the Lord Chamberlains' Company, which played in theaters as diverse as the Globe and the Blackfriars. Shakespeare has long been recognized as a universal genius. A master of the English language, he was instrumental in transforming a language that was still in a period of transition. His technical proficiency, however, was matched by an incredible insight into human psychology. Whether in his tragedies or comedies, Shakespeare exhibited a remarkable understanding of the human condition.

The theater was one of the most creative forms of expression during Spain's golden century. The first professional theaters established in Seville and Madrid in the 1570s were run by actors' companies as in England. Soon, every large town had a public playhouse, including Mexico City in the New World. Touring companies brought the latest Spanish plays to all parts of the Spanish empire. Beginning in the 1580s, the agenda for playwrights was set by Lope de Vega (1562–1635). Like Shakespeare, he was from a middle-class background. He was an incredibly prolific writer; almost 500 of his 1,500 plays survive. They have been characterized as witty, charming, action-packed and realistic. Lope de Vega made no apologies for the fact that he wrote his plays to please his audiences. In a treatise on drama written in 1609, he stated that the foremost duty of the playwright was to satisfy public demand. He remarked that if anyone thought he had written his plays for fame, "undeceive him and tell him that I wrote them for money."

Continued

FIGURE 13.9, *Continued*

A Golden Age of Literature: England and Spain

One of the crowning achievements of the golden age of Spanish literature was the work of Miguel de Cervantes (1547–1616), whose *Don Quixote* has been acclaimed as one of the greatest literary works of all time. In the two main figures of his famous work, Cervantes presented the dual nature of the Spanish character. The knight Don Quixote from La Mancha is the visionary who is so involved in his lofty ideals that he is oblivious to the hard realities around him. To him, for example, windmills appear as four-armed giants. In contrast, the knight's fat and earthy squire, Sancho Panza, is the realist who cannot get his master to see the realities in front of him. But after adventures that took them to all parts of Spain, each came to see the value of the other's perspective. We are left with Cervantes's conviction that both visionary dreams and the hard work of reality are necessary to the human condition.

ACTIVITY   13.14   *Locating Details and Generating Paraphrases*

In this activity you are asked to generate a paraphrase of the text entitled "A Golden Age of Literature: England and Spain" in Figure 13.9. As you are reading, make notes of the significant details; you may use a graphic organizer. Second, generate a short statement about each of the details you selected. Third, write a paraphrase that summarizes the main idea and uses the details you selected. As you read, look for text clues, including the heading and signal words. Then, after you have written your paraphrase, check your responses by rereading the text. Discuss your responses with your group members.

ACTIVITY   13.15   *Read for Details and Generating Paraphrases*

Much is written about William Shakespeare and about Miguel de Cervantes. Search the Web for an article about either of these two writers. Then, select a text passage about three to four paragraphs in length. Next, write down the significant details; you may use a graphic organizer. Next, generate a short statement about each of the details you selected. Finally, write a paraphrase that summarizes the main idea and uses the details you selected. As you read, look for text clues, including the heading and signal words.

ACTIVITY   13.16   *Locating Significant Details and Generating Paraphrases*

In this activity you are asked to find a text passage from your own college textbooks and apply what you have learned in this chapter. First, select a text passage about three to four paragraphs in length from one of your college textbooks. Then, state the important details for the passage; you may use a graphic organizer. Next, generate a short statement about each of the details you selected. Finally, write a paraphrase that summarizes the main idea and uses the details you selected. As you read, look for text clues, including the heading and signal words. After you have written your paraphrase, check your responses by rereading the text. How did you do? Could you pick out key details? Did you generate a paraphrase of the text? What worked? What do you still want to know about selecting details?

ACTIVITY 13.17 *Where Are You Now?*

Now that you've completed Chapter 13, take a few minutes to return to the beginning of this chapter and repeat Activity 13.1, Where Are You Now? What have you learned about locating details? What are your perspectives now about what you will need to do when reading your text assignments?

Summary

Locating details, a fundamental strategy for your success as a college reader, involves close, careful reading of text. It is helpful to use the "5W's" to locate significant details, in other words, answering the questions Who? What? Where? When? Why? You may find that some of the details that you need to know are directly stated in the text; other details are implied.

Good readers make inferences about significant details and ideas in the text. Good readers also make distinctions between major and minor details; the major details are significant as support for the main point of the passage. When looking for significant details, good readers use a variety of text clues, including headings, subheadings, repetition, and transition words. Often, good writers use transition words to signal the text pattern, which describes how the writer logically explains important ideas. Common text patterns include listing, sequence, chronology, description and explanation, classification, comparison and contrast, and cause and effect. When locating and stating details, a reader strategy is to use a graphic organizer to visually show the details, main idea, topic, and connections among the details. The choice of graphic organizer depends on the author's text pattern.

A reader strategy for remembering details in a text passage is to make a short statement about each of the details selected. A paraphrase of the text passage includes a statement of the main idea and this set of short statements about the details. Thus, through the combined use of detailed graphic organizers and written paraphrases of the text, a reader has a solid foundation for remembering text ideas, discussing text ideas, and using details as evidence in support of key text ideas.

Review Questions

Terms You Should Know: Make a flash card for each term.

Cause/effect	Graphic organizer	Semantic feature
Chronology	Hierarchical array	matrix
Classification	Implied detail	Sequence
Comparison/contrast	Inference	Stated detail
Concept map	Listing	Text patterns
Description	Main idea	Timeline
Fishbone map	Major versus minor	Transition words
Five W's	details	Venn diagram
General versus	Paraphrase	
specific ideas		

Completion: Fill in the blank to complete each of the following statements.

1. When you use the 5 W's to locate details, you ask these questions: _____, _____, _____, _____, and _____.

2. When you make a good guess, using information stated in the text, you make a(n) _____.

3. Main ideas are best supported with _____ details.

4. Words such as *for example, in comparison to,* and *finally* are called _____ _____ because they point to significant details.

5. When you summarize the essential ideas and details in the text in your own words, you generate a(n) _____.

Multiple Choice: Circle the letter of the best answer for each of the following questions. Be sure to underline key words and eliminate wrong answers.

6. In the following sets of words, which has the *general* word stated first and a *related specific* word stated second?
A. 32 degrees, freezing temperature
B. Clothes, shirt
C. Apple, fruit
D. Emotion, generosity

7. In a psychology textbook, you read definitions about the ego, superego, and id. You come to the conclusion that the purpose of this passage is to explain Freud's theory of the personality. Which of the following graphic organizers would help you locate and state the significant details about Freud's theory?
A. Timeline
B. Venn diagram
C. Concept map
D. Hierarchical array

Short Answer–Essay: On a separate sheet answer each of the following:

8. Describe a reader strategy for locating major details.

9. Explain the distinctions among major details, minor details, and main ideas.

10. Explain how you could use a concept map for stating and remembering major details in a text passage.

14 Analyzing Key Points

In this chapter you will learn how to:

➤ Read for critical comprehension

➤ Analyze the author's perspective

➤ Analyze the text for bias, fact, and opinion

➤ Analyze graphs, charts, and diagrams to find critical information

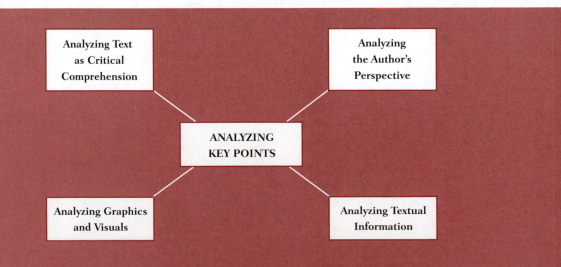

ACTIVITY 14.1   *Where Are You Now?*

Take a few minutes to answer *yes* or *no* to the following questions; choose "yes" if you do this most of the time; choose "no" if you do not consistently do it or if you are not sure.

	YES	NO
1. When you read your college textbooks, do you read for critical comprehension?	_____	_____
2. When you read about current events, do you read just for the facts and main ideas?	_____	_____
3. When you read an article in the newspaper or in a popular magazine about a controversial topic, do you recognize the author's point of view?	_____	_____
4. When you read a passage from a college text in the social sciences, such as history or political science, do you analyze the social contexts of the passage?	_____	_____
5. When you read a passage from a college text in the social sciences, such as history or political science, do you recognize the author's tone?	_____	_____
6. When you read, do you recognize an author's biases?	_____	_____
7. When you read, do you distinguish the facts from the opinions?	_____	_____
8. When you look at a graph, such as a chart or table, do you recognize what is compared?	_____	_____
9. When you look at a graph, such as a chart or table, do you extrapolate information?	_____	_____
10. Do you understand the charts and tables in your textbooks?	_____	_____

Total Points   _____

Score yourself 1 point for each *yes* answer to questions 1 and 3–10 and *no* to question 2. Total up your points. A low score indicates that you will need to develop your strategies for analyzing the text. A high score indicates that you have already developed many successful strategies for critical comprehension.

ANALYZING TEXT AS CRITICAL COMPREHENSION

What do you think is important for comprehending college-level texts? Is it understanding the vocabulary? Is it understanding the main ideas and supporting points? Is it understanding important facts, principles, and concepts? Hopefully, you have answered these questions as "yes." However, there is more to the process of comprehension than understanding main ideas and important details. You also need to read for critical comprehension.

FIGURE 14.1

Levels of Comprehension

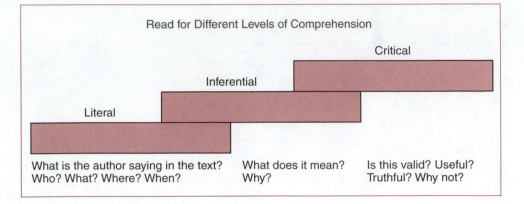

READING CRITICALLY FOR COMPREHENSION

Reading for critical comprehension means that you sharpen your analytical skills to look deeper at the ideas presented in the text; in other words, you don't have to accept everything that you read at face value. Being a critical reader does not mean that you read to criticize or discount the ideas of the author. Rather, it means that you carefully weigh those ideas and consider the merits of them. As a critical reader you not only look at the details, the main points, the examples, the word choices, but also analyze the logic of the conclusions, the importance of the evidence, and the significance of the ideas.

In this chapter you will be able to extend what you have learned about reading for details, main ideas, and essential concepts, and learn to sharpen your analytical skills for comprehension as a critical reader. As you read this chapter, think of how you can apply the ideas to your college textbook readings and to your general everyday reading.

Do you remember the discussion of reading for different levels of comprehension in Chapter 3? We discussed the importance of reading for comprehension on the literal level for finding the basic details, then reading on the inferential level to determine main points. Then, we discussed extending our comprehension goals to read on a critical level, asking questions about the validity, usefulness, or truthfulness of what we read. (See Figure 14.1.)

You have already learned how to read for literal and inferential comprehension. In Chapters 12 and 13 you learned how to locate details and how to generalize main ideas from those details. You are ready for the next step. As a reader, it is important to apply the ideas you learn to new situations and to make connections of those ideas with your own life and the world we live in. While reading critically, it is important to reflect about what you read and ask the "why" questions: Why is this important? Why is it important for me and for the world we live in? These questions are part of the process of critical comprehension.

In this textbook we view critical comprehension in three areas: analysis, synthesis, and evaluation. (See Figure 14.2.) Therefore, in the remaining three chapters of this textbook we will focus on each of those processes so that you will be able to sharpen your skills as a critical reader. This chapter will focus more deeply on the process of analyzing key points in text. Then, in Chapters 15 and 16 you will learn how to synthesize and evaluate text information.

When you read critically for comprehension, you not only look for important details and main ideas, you also ask questions that point to the integrity of the ideas. Reading critically for comprehension means that you analyze the text with the intent of making an informed judgment about the worth of those ideas. According to *The Literacy Dictionary* (Harris & Hodges, 1995) *critical reading* is defined as:

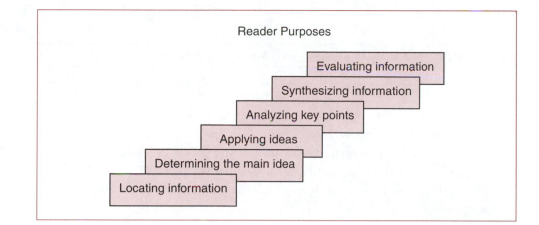

Figure 14.2
Reader Purposes

reading in which a questioning attitude, logical analysis, and inference are used to judge the worth of text according to an established standard. . . . Among the skills of critical reading are those having to do with ascertaining the author's credibility, intent, or purpose; assessing the accuracy, logic, reliability, and authenticity of the writing; and identifying literary forms, components, and devices through literary analysis.[1]

When you read this definition, note that critical comprehension involves combination processes of analysis, synthesis, and evaluation. It is also important to note that when you are a *critical reader* you are also a *critical thinker* because you will need to step back from the text and think deeply about what you are reading; you will also sharpen your skills of thinking more inquisitively about what you are learning in college.

To be a critical reader, then, you need to use processes of inferencing, questioning, reflection, and problem solving. When you are reading for critical comprehension, you are engaged in an active, dynamic dialogue with the author, which most likely will be reflected in your classroom discussions with your professor and classmates. You will most likely be involved in discussions that are lively, perhaps heated, and perhaps controversial. Reading for critical comprehension is certainly not boring.

Current perspectives of reading critically also include reading for critical literacy, which is defined as "literacy that begins with a rising consciousness of not merely the functionality of print but also the power or language to both silence and give voice to instances of oppression in issues of socially determined disparities" (Lesley, 2001, p. 184).[2] What this means is that as you read, it is important to reflect on the issues of power, social conditions, and the social relationships described in the text. As you discuss the text passages in class, reflect on the differences in interpretations you and your classmates may have, particularly in the analysis of power relationships and belief systems.

Let's try an activity to illustrate this point. Let's try the following example: read the passage in Figure 14.3 and then try Activity 14.2. You may need to read this passage multiple times in order to analyze the key points.

---

[1]T. L. Harris and R. E. Hodges, *The Literacy Dictionary: The Vocabulary of Reading and Writing* (Newark, DE: International Reading Association, 1995), p. 49.
[2]M. Lesley, "Exploring the Links between Critical Literacy and Developmental Reading," *Journal of Adolescent & Adult Literacy, 45,* no. 3 (2001), pp. 180–189.

FIGURE 14.3
Until Dust Do Us Part

Source: From Dirk Johnson, "Until Dust Do Us Part," *Newsweek,* March 25, 2002, p. 41. Reprinted by permission.

Until Dust Do Us Part

In a new study the dirty truth is revealed about men, women and housework: nobody really wants to do it.

ONCE UPON A TIME, men were treated like indulged children in the house, as women bustled about cleaning, sweeping, cooking. That was 50 years ago, some men say. That was this morning, some women say.

Want to start a fight? Ask about housework and the division of labor. For that matter, ask what housework means. Does gardening count? How about running a snow blower?

To settle the score, a new study from the University of Michigan examines how the housework burden is shared by women and men. The results: women still do much more than men, though men are getting better (actually, men were getting better until about 1985, and then stalled out). But the real news stood out like a streak of clean glass on a grimy window: nobody really cares that much about housework at all anymore. In 1965 women did 40 hours of housework a week, men a mere 12. Nowadays women are averaging 27 hours; men, closing the gap, average 16. That means housework has decreased even as average house size has ballooned.

None of this comes as a shock to Gale Zemel's 73-year-old mother, Lita. She simply won't visit her daughter— they go to mom's place or meet at a restaurant. "The clutter drives her nuts," said Gale, a 48-year-old office manager in Oak Park, Ill. "And it's true, the place is a mess."

For millions of Americans, it comes down to math. He works. She works. The kids need to be transported all

16 HOURS	**70%**	**51** HOURS	**50%**
Today, men average 16 hours of housework each week, up from an average of 12 hours in 1965	Though they do a third less housework than in 1965, women do 70 percent more than men	Women average a total of 51 hours on the job and doing housework. Men average 53.	Swedish men average 24 hours of housework a week, 50 percent more than American men

over creation for soccer and piano lessons. People are too pooped to mop. "Who's got time to clean?" says Hiromi Ono, an author of the report by the Institute for Social Research at Ann Arbor, Mich.

Each of the 6,000 people in the study—from the United States and around the world—kept a daily record of the work they did around the house, from sweeping the kitchen floor to changing the oil. As it turned out, American men were much more helpful than Japanese men (four hours a week), but slackers compared to the Swedes (24 hours a week).

When it comes to thankless chores, of course, everyone thinks they're doing too much already and that their other half could be doing just a little bit more. "Every time my husband gets a raise," one suburban Chicago woman bristles, "he starts throwing his clothes all over the floor." Zemel's husband, David Mausner, will tell you he's a pretty helpful mate, a virtue he attributes to "having my consciousness raised in the '70s by a succession of girlfriends." Mausner says he's setting tables, clearing them, washing dishes and fixing whatever needs fixing. "When there's something that requires a tool, I'm the guy for the job." His wife sees it somewhat differently. "He does the dishes. Period."

Neither claims to be a fanatic about cleaning. Zemel acknowledges: "I don't even know where the iron is." Mausner says simply, "I guess I could do more."

People are working hard—just not at hunting dust bunnies. The Michigan researchers credit a strong job market in the 1990s for the phenomenon they term "vanishing housework." Women in their study averaged 24 hours of

Continued

FIGURE 14.3

Until Dust Do Us Part, Continued

paid work outside the home, while men averaged 37. (For those keeping score, men total 53 combined hours of job and housework; women 51.)

Everybody is simply trying to do too much, says Cheryl Mendelson, the author of the surprise best-seller "Home Comforts: The Art and Science of Keeping House." With families on the run, she says, the home has been reduced to a changing station, a pit-stop between wind sprints.

It's a question of priorities, and some things matter more than others. For all the demands on their time, most parents are not shirking when it comes to the kids. Another recent study from the University of Michigan found that most parents—working and stay-at-home—spend more time with the children than parents did 20 years ago. Linda Rufer, a doctor in suburban Milwaukee, said housecleaning ranked a distant second to taking her three children to the Wisconsin Dells last weekend. "Either the house is clean or I see my kids," she said. "And as a pediatrician, it's bad form not to see the kids." For Rufer and plenty of others, the mess will be still there when they get home. The kids, on the other hand, grow up fast. And then they'll be gone.

ACTIVITY 14.2 *Reading for Critical Comprehension*

Read the article "Until Dust Do Us Part" in Figure 14.3. As you are reading, annotate the article and underline key points. Reread the article. Then, respond to each of the following and be prepared to discuss them in a small group.

1. Write a short response to these questions:
   a. What situation does this writer describe?

   b. What is compared and contrasted?

   c. What statistics does the writer give?

   d. What are the writer's key points?

2. Write at least four questions to ask another classmate.

READING AND QUESTIONING FOR CRITICAL COMPREHENSION

At the heart of critical comprehension are the twin processes of questioning and reflection. In other words, as you read, it is important to ask many questions, then reflect on your responses to those questions. Your questions can occur on many levels, but particularly on the level that moves you beyond the text so that you think about what the text means to you as well as the social influences and beliefs that shape the writing of the text. As you read for critical comprehension, it is a good idea to write down your questions, to make notes in the text, and to record your reflections in a notebook.

Fundamental to critical comprehension is asking questions of analysis. This means that when you analyze the text, you look for evidence and examples that prove a key point. This includes looking at the facts that are presented. (Later in this chapter we will discuss the importance of distinguishing facts from opinions and seeing how the writer proves a key point.) When you analyze the text, look to see what type of information is described and what is compared (and contrasted). If the author presents a problem, look for the solutions that the author presents. In addition, look for cause-effect relationships and note how the author is describing those causes and effects. Therefore, some questions you can ask are the following: What is the key point? What information or situation is being compared? What cause-effect relationships are present? What evidence does the author present? If there is a problem, what solution is presented?

When you read for critical comprehension, you engage in a dialogue with the author and ask the "hard" questions; you ask "why?" and "why not?" Asking "why" and "why not" questions point to the significance of what you are reading and studying. In addition to these questions, look for the context of the writing. For instance, the following questions help you read at an analytical level: What social conditions exist? What belief systems exist? How do the social conditions influence the belief systems? Do unequal power relationships exist; if so, what are they and why? What is your belief about the topic and why? You will find that these questions are particularly important as you read texts in the social sciences, in literature, and about current events.

ACTIVITY 14.3 *Reading and Reflecting for Critical Comprehension*

Reread the article "Until Dust Do Us Part" in Figure 14.3. Then write a short response to each of the following questions:

1. Why do you think this article was written?

2. What is the social condition described by the article?

3. Do unequal power relationships exist? If so, what are they? Why?

4. What is your belief about this topic? Why?

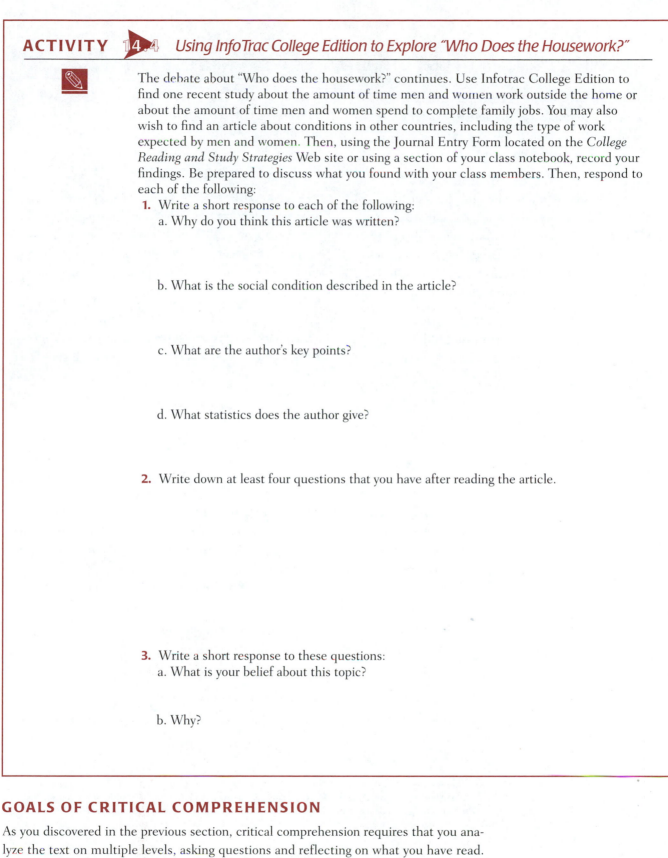

ACTIVITY 14.4   *Using InfoTrac College Edition to Explore "Who Does the Housework?"*

The debate about "Who does the housework?" continues. Use Infotrac College Edition to find one recent study about the amount of time men and women work outside the home or about the amount of time men and women spend to complete family jobs. You may also wish to find an article about conditions in other countries, including the type of work expected by men and women. Then, using the Journal Entry Form located on the *College Reading and Study Strategies* Web site or using a section of your class notebook, record your findings. Be prepared to discuss what you found with your class members. Then, respond to each of the following:

1. Write a short response to each of the following:
 a. Why do you think this article was written?

 b. What is the social condition described in the article?

 c. What are the author's key points?

 d. What statistics does the author give?

2. Write down at least four questions that you have after reading the article.

3. Write a short response to these questions:
 a. What is your belief about this topic?

 b. Why?

GOALS OF CRITICAL COMPREHENSION

As you discovered in the previous section, critical comprehension requires that you analyze the text on multiple levels, asking questions and reflecting on what you have read. As a college student, you are expected to be able to read a variety of textbook and journal article passages and be proficient in interpreting them, analyzing them, discussing them,

TIPS FOR READING FOR CRITICAL COMPREHENSION

DETERMINE THE AUTHOR'S PURPOSE. As you read, determine why the author wrote the text passage. Is the author trying to inform you about something? Persuade you? Entertain you?

DETERMINE THE AUTHOR'S POINT OF VIEW. As you are reading, look for clues, such as word choices and examples, that reveal the author's point of view. Then, ask yourself these questions: What is the author's point of view about the topic? Is the author's perspective favorable about the topic? Unfavorable? What are the author's biases towards the topic?

THINK ABOUT YOUR OWN PERSPECTIVES AND BELIEFS. As you are reading, think about your own point of view about the topic. Is your perspective the same as the author's?

DETERMINE THE EXISTING SOCIAL CONTEXTS AND POWER RELATIONSHIPS. If the author describes a social or historical condition, carefully look for descriptions of power relationships. Whose perspective is presented?

DISTINGUISH FACTS FROM OPINIONS. A good sign of critical comprehension is distinguishing facts from opinions. The author may present an opinion to prove a point. Therefore, it is important to differentiate opinions and facts used to prove a main point.

EVALUATE THE VALIDITY AND WORTH OF THE AUTHOR'S ARGUMENT. Carefully read the author's conclusions. What is the main argument? What type of evidence does the author use? Is the argument valid?

and applying the principles and ideas. Key strategies for you to use include reading the text multiple times, annotating the text, formulating questions, and summarizing what you have read; according to Maloney (2003), these are the critical inquiry techniques that every college student needs to know.[3]

When you read for critical comprehension, you read to analyze and interpret the text to meet the following goals:

➤ Determine the author's purpose, point of view, and tone

➤ Determine existing belief systems

➤ Detect bias

➤ Determine the existing social contexts and power relationships

➤ Reflect on your own perspectives, biases, and beliefs in relation to the text

---

[3] W. H. Maloney, "Connecting the Texts of Their Lives to Academic Literacy: Creating Success for At-risk First-Year College Students," *Journal of Adolescent & Adult Literacy, 46*, no. 8 (2003), pp. 664–673.

➤ Distinguish facts from opinions

➤ Evaluate the author's evidence for proving the main point

➤ Evaluate the validity and worth of the author's argument

In the next section of this chapter, we will discuss the first six goals. The remaining two goals will be discussed in Chapter 16. These goals are also described in the accompanying "Tips for Reading for Critical Comprehension."

ANALYZING THE AUTHOR'S PERSPECTIVE

If you receive a letter from a friend and read about a personal situation, you most likely are able to hear your friend's voice, picture what your friend looks like, and think of your friend's personal life, interests, and background. What if you read a letter in the "Letters to the Editor" section of the newspaper? Most likely you will be able to determine the writer's perspective because the writer will express an opinion about an issue. The writer may also give some background knowledge about his or her age, interests, and life experiences. Therefore, for some texts that you read, it is easy to determine the author's perspective.

On the other hand, for much of the college-level text that you read (particularly in textbook assignments), the author is much less obvious. When you read your textbooks, can you describe the authors' ages? interests? backgrounds? Can you make a mental picture of the authors and then carry on a conversation with them? Most likely, the answer is "no" because many textbook authors try to be much more distant and to keep a low profile in terms of their own personal life, interests, and background. However, it is important to know that even when you cannot clearly identify the author, a certain perspective or bias may be presented to you.

When a reader reads for critical comprehension, whether the passage is from a letter from a friend, a letter in the editorial section of the newspaper, or a college textbook, the critical reader considers the author's perspective. Why? The author's perspective influences not only what he or she discusses but also influences the type of evidence, facts, examples, statistics, and even word choices that the author uses. Depending on the author's perspective, information may be omitted. Therefore, even when the text appears to be "objective," the text, because it is written from the author's perspective, reflects the author's stance, background knowledge, and bias. In other words, it is truly difficult to find text passages that are purely objective. This does not mean that authors intentionally try to mislead readers, or to lie, or to give a one-sided picture. However, what this does mean is that as critical readers we need to consider the historical, philosophical, scientific, and social perspectives that situate the text in a certain time period and social context.

Let's consider an example. Figures 14.4, 14.5, and 14.6 describe a situation. The information is revealed to you in sequence. As you look at the figures, think of what each means to you and how your interpretation changes as you are given additional information.

Figure 14.4
Sequence 1[*]

Figure 14.5
Sequence 2[*]

Figure 14.6
Sequence 3[*]

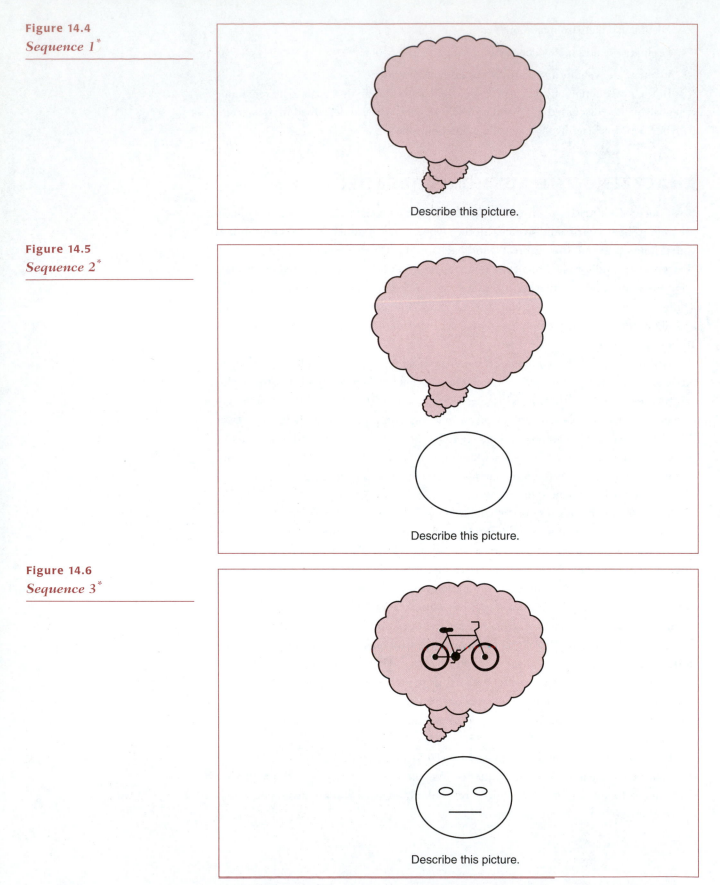

Describe this picture.

Describe this picture.

Describe this picture.

*Note: Look at each picture one at a time in sequence. Think about how your interpretation changes with new information.

ACTIVITY   14.5   *Reading and Questioning for Critical Comprehension*

Look at Figures 14.4, 14.5, and 14.6 one at a time. After you view the first one, write a short response before you view the next one. Be prepared to discuss your responses with a partner in class.

1. Figure 14.4 looks like:

2. Figure 14.5 looks like:

3. Figure 14.6 looks like:

What did you think about when you saw the first figure? How did your interpretation change when you looked at the second figure? How did it change when you saw the third one? What did you learn about how perspectives can change when additional information is given?

Reading for critical comprehension is similar to interpreting this series of figures. When you saw the first figure, could you anticipate what would happen next? When you saw the second figure, did you make a guess about the third figure? As you looked at these figures in sequence, did you notice how your interpretation changed as you had more information? Similarly, when you read information in a newspaper or your textbook, you try to put the pieces together to make a coherent explanation of the ideas in the text. The more information you have, the better you will be able to form a more complete picture. When reading critically, it is wise to evaluate the new information you receive.

Much of what you read in your college textbooks is from the perspective of an expert in the field. It is wise to check the credentials of the author(s). Many textbooks include a section describing their background, credentials, work experience, and activity in the field. Why would this be important? The author communicates a situation or set of ideas from his or her own perspective. As you read, you can learn about their perspectives, what they value, and how those in the field think. Then, as a critical reader, think about this perspective.

DETERMINING THE AUTHOR'S PURPOSE FOR WRITING

For much of the material you read in your college classes, you will find that the main purpose of the author is "to inform" you about the major ideas, principles, and issues in that field of study. Most authors who are writing in the sciences, mathematics, business, or social sciences write "to inform" you about the generally accepted ideas in that field. This means that the author tries to stay close to the facts and to stay objective.

While the author's purpose for most of the text you will be reading is "to inform," there are other purposes typically used in college writing. Brewer (1980) described text that is written "to entertain," "to persuade," and "to provide an aesthetic experience for

Figure 14.7
Learning from Conflict-Management Failures

Source: From K. S. Verderber and R. F. Verderber, "Learning from Conflict-Management Failures," in *Inter-Act: Interpersonal Communication Concepts, Skills, and Contexts* (Belmont, CA: Wadsworth/Thomson Learning, 2001), p. 334.

Learning from Conflict-Management Failures

Ideally, you want to resolve conflicts as they occur. The biblical admonishment "Never let the sun set on your anger" is sage advice. Nevertheless, there will be times when no matter how hard both persons try, they will not be able to resolve the conflict. Sillars and Weisberg (1987, p. 143) have pointed out that conflict can be an extremely complex process and that some conflicts may not be resolvable even with improved communication.

Especially when the relationship is important to you, take time to analyze your inability to resolve the conflict. Ask yourself questions such as the following: Where did things go wrong? Did one or more of us become competitive? Or defensive? Did I use a style that was inappropriate to the situation? Did we fail to implement the problem-solving method adequately? Were the vested interests in the outcome too great? Did I initiate or respond inappropriately? Am I failing to use such basic communication skills as paraphrasing, describing feelings, and perception checking? When I become angry, do I fall back on what Turk and Monahan (1999) label "repetitive non-optimal behaviors"—behaviors such as verbal abuse, dishonest replies, or sarcasm (p. 232)?

By taking time to analyze your behavior, you put yourself in a better position to act more successfully in the next conflict episode you experience. And since conflict is inevitable, you can count on using this knowledge again.

the reader."[4] This classification shows that some authors will attempt to persuade you to agree to something or to take sides with a certain point of view. Texts that have a persuasive intent speak to social issues and current events. Other texts (those with an aesthetic purpose) are meant for you purely to enjoy. Some texts are written artistically, and like any other piece of art, these texts should be appreciated for their literary and artistic value. You will find texts with literary and artistic merit in your literature classes.

Depending on the author's purpose (inform, entertain, persuade, or provide an aesthetic experience), the author will either be objective or subjective about the topic. You will be able to tell the difference because an author who chooses to be objective tries to stick to the facts, avoid bias, and present a logical, unemotional, and detached treatment of the topic. On the other hand, an author who chooses to be subjective uses emotional language, reveals opinions, and tries to personalize the topic. For instance, if the author's purpose is to persuade you to do something, the author will most likely give you not only many facts but will also voice an opinion about why or why not you should act.

The text excerpt in Figure 14.7 is from a textbook chapter about communication. As you read this text, note that the authors aim to inform you about strategies about managing conflict and and to persuade you to use them. As you read this passage, look for the authors' perspective about what works best and the recommendations for learning from conflicts.

[4] W. F. Brewer, "Literary Theory, Rhetoric, and Stylistics: Implications for Psychology." In R. J. Spiro, B. C. Bruce, and W. F. Brewer, eds., *Theoretical Issues in Reading Comprehension* (Hillsdale, NJ: Lawrence Erlbaum, 1980), pp. 221–239.

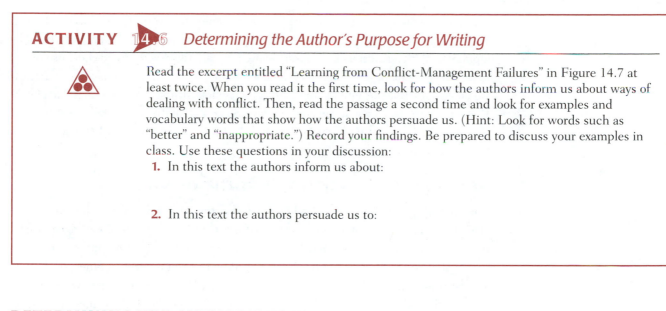

ACTIVITY 14.6   *Determining the Author's Purpose for Writing*

Read the excerpt entitled "Learning from Conflict-Management Failures" in Figure 14.7 at least twice. When you read it the first time, look for how the authors inform us about ways of dealing with conflict. Then, read the passage a second time and look for examples and vocabulary words that show how the authors persuade us. (Hint: Look for words such as "better" and "inappropriate.") Record your findings. Be prepared to discuss your examples in class. Use these questions in your discussion:

1. In this text the authors inform us about:

2. In this text the authors persuade us to:

DETERMINING THE AUTHOR'S TONE

When you were reading the passage in Figure 14.7, did you note the authors' tone? If the authors read this passage aloud, what tone of voice would they use? Would they be excited? Calm? Sarcastic? Sad? How would you describe the emotional level? What words could you pick out that show this level?

The author's tone can help you determine the author's perspective. An author who intends to be objective and to inform you about a topic will try to be calm, distant, and impersonal. On the other hand, if the author intends to be persuasive, the author's voice becomes more emotional, involved with the topic, personal, and opinionated.

Let's look at an example. Look at the title and first two paragraphs of the article "Stop Calling Us" in Figure 14.8. Note the emotional impact of the title. The situation in

FIGURE 14.8
Stop Calling Us

Source: From Perry Bacon, Jr., and Eric Roston, "Stop Calling Us," *Time,* April 28, 2003, pp. 56–58. Reprinted by permission of Time, Inc.

STOP Calling Us

Afraid of your phone? You're not alone. But new gadgets and laws can help fend off telemarketers

SIX-THIRTY P.M. IS A SACRED TIME IN American life, but one also often filled with dread. Mom and Dad are home from work, Junior's back from piano and Sis from soccer, and everyone's washed up and ready to eat. We count on dinner as the family hour yet know that at any moment it could be punctured by a phone call from some scripted stranger hawking island vacations or aluminum siding.

If the number of intrusive sales calls you receive seems to be on the rise, that's because it is. Revenue from telemarketing pitches increased 250% from 1990 to 2002, to $295 billion, and is growing today even amid an economy that's flat. Salespeople this year will place 100 million calls daily to homes and businesses, and those who get on hot-prospect lists—usually by buying something—can easily get half a dozen calls a day. The greater call volume means higher blood pressure for most Americans and more bitterly clever responses to the question, "May I speak with [*your mispronounced name here*], please?"

the first paragraph is one in which many of us can empathize with "Mom," "Dad," "Junior," and "Sis." Notice how the authors describe suppertime as "sacred," but now "punctured by a phone call." The authors also describe the time as "filled with dread" because of the intrusion of telemarketers. Can you find other examples that have an impact on you? How would you describe the authors' tone? Don't they sound frustrated? angry? upset? annoyed? Do you feel the same when you have a telemarketer call in the middle of your supper? If you were reading the title of this article and the first two paragraphs, what would be the tone of your voice?

DETERMINE THE AUTHOR'S POINT OF VIEW

The author's point of view is the perspective that the author holds. In other words, if a side or position is presented in the text, what is the author's position? Once again, to determine the author's point of view, look at the author's choice of words and examples.

In the article "Stop Calling Us," note the authors' point of view. In other words, look at their perspective and opinions. Do they like telemarketers? Are they annoyed by them? Do they think that it is a good idea that telemarketing is on the rise? Do they sympathize with "Mom" and "Dad" who have their supper interrupted by telemarketers? As you read, pay specific attention to the words and examples that indicate how the authors voice their perspectives.

FIGURE 14.9
Stop Calling Us

Source: From Perry Bacon, Jr., and Eric Roston, "Stop Calling Us," *Time*, April 28, 2003, pp. 56–58. Reprinted by permission of Time, Inc.

STOP Calling Us

Afraid of your phone? You're not alone. But new gadgets and laws can help fend off telemarketers

SIX-THIRTY P.M. IS A SACRED TIME IN American life, but one also often filled with dread. Mom and Dad are home from work, Junior's back from piano and Sis from soccer, and everyone's washed up and ready to eat. We count on dinner as the family hour yet know that at any moment it could be punctured by a phone call from some scripted stranger hawking island vacations or aluminum siding.

If the number of intrusive sales calls you receive seems to be on the rise, that's because it is. Revenue from telemarketing pitches increased 250% from 1990 to 2002, to $295 billion, and is growing today even amid an economy that's flat. Salespeople this year will place 100 million calls daily to homes and businesses, and those who get on hot-prospect lists—usually by buying something—can easily get half a dozen calls a day. The greater call volume means higher blood pressure for most Americans and more bitterly clever responses to the question, "May I speak with [*your mispronounced name here*], please?"

Consumers are buying gadgets with names like Phone Butler and TeleZapper to help keep unwanted salespeople at bay. But the callers keep developing new technologies to defeat the gadgets. Federal and state legislators are passing laws to tighten regulation of telemarketers. President Bush recently signed a bill authorizing the Federal Trade Commission (FTC) to create a national do-not-call registry, which anyone can sign up for online beginning July 1 and by phone soon thereafter. Eventually the list will be merged with similar lists maintained by 30 states—a chore that may take up to two years. Companies must begin using the list by Oct. 1. But there are big asterisks in the federal law, which, for instance, exempts from regulation telemarketers for charities and political

Continued

candidates. And those can be among the most aggressive callers. Last month Amnesty International and Doctors Without Borders were dialing for contributions to aid victims of the Iraq war as soon as President Bush finished his prewar address.

You may pride yourself on never buying anything from a telemarketer—or even letting one finish a sentence. But enough of your neighbors and colleagues respond to phone pitches to make it a lucrative business. Home repairers, mortgage refinancers, long-distance providers and, we should point out, popular magazines like this one have found phone pitches to be among their most cost-effective sales tools. U.S. consumers also unwittingly hand over as much as $50 billion a year to fraudulent callers, who make pleas for phony charities or offer prizes with strings attached or cheap vacations with hidden fees.

Telemarketing has been around almost as long as the telephone, but it didn't take off until the 1980s brought a decline in long-distance prices, along with a powerful technology called the automatic dialer. This device can call hundreds of homes at the same time and then immediately route the unwitting customer to a live telemarketer. When you answer your phone at home and hear nothing but light static, it's often because an automatic dialer has reached you but no agent was free to take the call. An unlisted number used to provide protection, until digital technology allowed marketers to easily gather lists of consumers who have given their numbers to credit-card companies or others with which they do business.

While technology has greatly expanded the telemarketers' reach, it has also given consumers weapons to fight back. Caller ID—which is used by 38% of U.S. households today, up from 30% in 1998—at first allowed users to detect calls from salespeople and other pests. But telemarketers learned to mask their numbers so that they read as UNAVAILABLE or OUT OF AREA on caller-ID displays, and users often answer because they think the call might be an urgent one from a friend or colleague—an impulse that's especially prevalent in these days of orange alerts.

Major phone companies offer services like SBC's Privacy Manager, which for $5 a month screens calls that don't register on caller ID. Anyone with an anonymous phone number is required to identify herself, and if she's a telemarketer, you can press a button to activate a prerecorded message telling her not to call again—a request that telemarketers are required under federal law to respect (but one that many nonetheless ignore). "Clearly this is a privacy war, and many times the phone companies are the arms dealers," says Robert Bulmash of Private Citizen Inc., based in Naperville, Ill., which campaigns against telemarketing. Like many arms dealers, the phone companies work both sides of the conflict: they avidly sell their services by phone and also peddle their customers' phone numbers to other telemarketers.

The phone companies face growing competition, though, from products like the $30 Phone Butler, sold by Morgan-Francis Inc., based in Fort Myers, Fla., which performs a function similar to that of the Privacy Manager. A more aggressive approach is touted by Privacy Technologies, based in Glenwillow, Ohio, which developed the TeleZapper. A small black box that connects to any phone, the $40 TeleZapper greets each incoming call with shrill tones that resemble the sound of a disconnected phone. When automatic dialers detect this sound, they often interpret it to mean the number is disconnected and hang up. A downside of this device, though, is that it might cause your mom to do the same. Another problem: some telemarketers have either changed their software or bought new dialers that stay on the line even when they hear the zapper's tones.

You might think—or hope—that telemarketers would eventually run out of workers willing to endure constant rejection and abuse. Think again. Expanding global trade, combined with falling prices for international calls, has allowed telemarketers to move call centers to countries where more pliant employees line up for such work. "In the U.S., to work in a call center is not a very glorifying job," but in countries such as India and Mexico, the white-collar environment and relatively high wages have job applicants lining up, says Robert

Continued

FIGURE 14.9, *Continued*
Stop Calling Us

Fabro, president of Hispanic Call Centers, which oversees phone banks in 62 countries and specializes in reaching immigrant populations in the U.S.

Overbuilding in the telecommunications sector has slashed overseas cable costs as much as 80% since 1999, encouraging the flight overseas. Derek Holley, president of eTelecare, which owns call centers in the Philippines, says international lines that cost $40,000 a month in 1999 can be leased for about $7,000 today. The line quality has improved so much that his company can pack twice as many digitized calls, with better sound, into the same number of circuits. "Suddenly price wasn't a huge obstacle," he says, "and the world really was open."

Lately, the fight against telemarketers has shifted toward Washington and the state capitals, inspired by not only constituent complaints but also the personal experiences of lawmakers like Carl Carpenter. Back in 1987, Carpenter's mother Ruth suffered a stroke, making it almost impossible for her to talk. But she always wanted to hear from her adult children and excitedly answered when the phone rang in her small apartment in Plant City, Fla., east of Tampa. Trouble was, most of the calls were from telemarketers. She was finally driven to create a code for her family: whenever they called, they should let the phone ring three times, hang up and then call back.

Carpenter, then a member of the Florida house of representatives, led his state's 1989 adoption of a do-not-call plan in which phone companies were required to put an asterisk in the phone book beside the names of people who did not want to hear from telemarketers. This law was soon modified into a formal do-not-call list. But the law didn't completely shield Floridians because out-of-state telemarketers, often unaware of the list, continued to call. And Florida-based firms started annoying residents of neighboring Georgia—and helped inspire Georgians to pass their do-not-call law.

Politicians in other states have begun to realize how much voters hate telemarketing. In Indiana, attorney general Stephen Carter was elected with help from an ad that showed his daughter spilling milk on the dinner table as Carter is saying, "Not interested" to a sales caller. Carter pushed the state legislature to adopt a do-not-call list, for which more than a million Hoosiers have signed up. And he has aggressively prosecuted companies that call people on that list. Overall, states have collected more than $3 million in fines against telemarketers over the past four years.

Almost all the 20 states that don't have do-not-call laws are considering them. More than 15 million Americans have signed up for the lists, and states that have lists are seeking to strengthen them. Some, like Indiana, ban almost all telemarketing calls, but in most states, certain big industries, such as insurers, have been exempted. One idea being considered in the state legislatures and Congress is a so-called dinner-hour ban that would preclude any telemarketing calls in the early evening, even to people not on do-not-call lists. That includes the usual exemptions, such as the one for politicians, whose solicitations are protected by the First Amendment.

The law President Bush signed in March allots $16 million to set up a national do-not-call list. The law also instructs the Federal Communications Commission (FCC) to adopt similar rules and make industries that the FCC regulates—banking, telecommunications and media—subscribe to the national list. The new federal rules, which took effect March 31, require telemarketers to display their phone numbers on caller-ID devices beginning early next year and also combat dead-air calls from autodialers.

One silver lining in the current economic slump is that it has forced some firms to cut back on telemarketing, just as they have on advertising. Jack Keenan, CEO of Tele Resources in Duluth, Minn., has seen a 40% drop in clients' call-volume requests and has had to cut his staff from 225 to 150 since the end of 2002. Unfortunately, though, fewer cold calls may not mean a reduction in sales pitches. Some firms offer more goods and services when *you* call *them*, be it for plane tickets, banking or Internet service.

Lawsuits filed in Colorado and Oklahoma by telemarketing firms are challenging the FTC's jurisdiction in maintaining a do-not-call registry. But telemarketers might not find much luck in court. In 1986, before the days

Continued

FIGURE 14.9, *Continued*
Stop Calling Us

of antitelemarketing laws and TeleZappers, Bulmash of Private Citizen won a suit he filed against a persistent telemarketer, which was forced to pay court fees and the 97¢ it would cost Bulmash to have his number unlisted for a month. "The judge pointed at the defendant," Bulmash recalls, "and said, 'I was called twice last night during the football game by guys like you. Mr. Bulmash, you win.'"

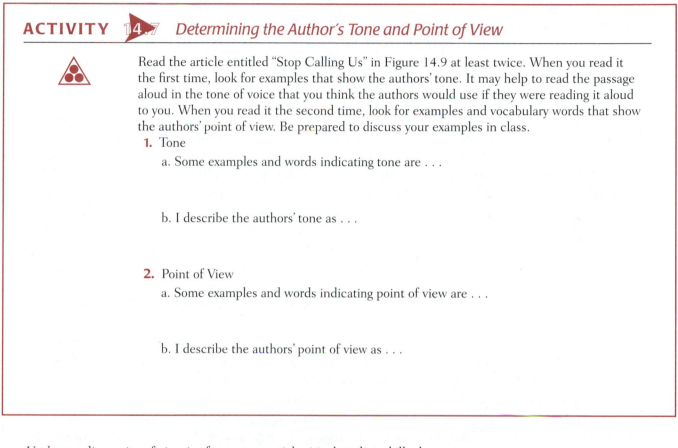

ACTIVITY 14.7   *Determining the Author's Tone and Point of View*

Read the article entitled "Stop Calling Us" in Figure 14.9 at least twice. When you read it the first time, look for examples that show the authors' tone. It may help to read the passage aloud in the tone of voice that you think the authors would use if they were reading it aloud to you. When you read it the second time, look for examples and vocabulary words that show the authors' point of view. Be prepared to discuss your examples in class.

1. Tone
   a. Some examples and words indicating tone are . . .

   b. I describe the authors' tone as . . .

2. Point of View
   a. Some examples and words indicating point of view are . . .

   b. I describe the authors' point of view as . . .

Understanding point of view is often an essential critical reading skill when you are reading literature. "Point of view" refers to the perspective of the narrator, that is, the one telling the story. In some cases, the story is told with the "I" first-person narration in which the reader learns about the events from the eyes, heart, mind, and soul of the person telling the story. Other literary works are written from a third-person point of view in which the story is told from a third-person narration; the author describes the events about what "he" or "she" did. This gives you, the reader, the ability to see into the hearts and minds of several different characters.

In the following passage you will read an excerpt from an autobiography written by Harriet Jacobs, who was born a slave in North Carolina and orphaned as a child. In this passage she describes her escape to her grandmother's house, where she hid for seven years. As you read the passage, consider the historical and social contexts, as well as the perspectives of those in the passage. It is important to note that you are reading from the perspective of someone in the twenty-first century; therefore, as you read, consider your own opinion about the author and her situation.

FIGURE 14.10

The Loophole of Retreat

Source: From H. Jacobs, "Incidents in the Life of a Slave Girl," in C. R. Bogarad and J. Z. Schmidt, eds., *Legacies* (Fort Worth: Harcourt Brace, 1995), pp. 941–942.

The Loophole of Retreat
(Linda Brent Escapes)

A small shed had been added to my grandmother's house years ago. Some boards were laid across the joists at the top, and between these boards and the roof was a very small garret, never occupied by any thing but rats and mice. It was a pent roof, covered with nothing but shingles, according to the southern custom for such buildings. The garret was only nine feet long and seven wide. The highest part was three feet high, and sloped down abruptly to the loose board floor. There was no admission for either light or air. My uncle Phillip, who was a carpenter, had very skillfully made a concealed trapdoor, which communicated with the storeroom. He had been doing this while I was waiting in the swamp. The storeroom opened upon a piazza. To this hole I was conveyed as soon as I entered the house. The air was stifling; the darkness total. A bed had been spread on the floor. I could sleep quite comfortably on one side; but the slope was so sudden that I could not turn on the other without hitting the roof. The rats and mice ran over my bed; but I was weary, and I slept such sleep as the wretched may, when a tempest has passed over them. Morning came. I knew it only by the noises I heard; for in my small den day and night were all the same. I suffered for air even more than for light. But I was not comfortless. I heard the voices of my children. There was joy and there was sadness in the sound. It made my tears flow. How I longed to speak to them! I was eager to look on their faces; but there was no hole, no crack, through which I could peep. This continued darkness was oppressive. It seemed horrible to sit or lie in a cramped position day after day, without one gleam of light. Yet I would have chosen this, rather than my lot as a slave, though white people considered it an easy one; and it was so compared with the fate of others. I was never cruelly overworked; I was never lacerated with the whip from head to foot; I was never so beaten and bruised that I could not turn from one side to the other; I never had my heel-strings cut to prevent my running away; I was never chained to a log and forced to drag it about, while I toiled in the fields from morning till night; I was never branded with hot iron, or torn by bloodhounds. On the contrary, I had always been kindly treated, and tenderly cared for, until I came into the hands of Dr. Flint. I had never wished for freedom till then. But though my life in slavery was comparatively devoid of hardships, God pity the woman who is compelled to lead such a life! My food was passed up to me through the trap-door my uncle had contrived; and my grandmother, my uncle Phillip, and aunt Nancy would seize such opportunities as they could, to mount up there and chat with me at the opening. But of course this was not safe in the daytime. It must all be done in darkness. It was impossible for me to move in an erect position, but I crawled about my den for exercise. One day I hit my head against something, and found it was a gimlet. My uncle had left it sticking there when he made the trap-door. I was as rejoiced as Robinson Crusoe could have been at finding such a treasure. It put a lucky thought into my head. I said to myself, "Now I will have some light. Now I will see my children." I did not dare to begin my work during the daytime, for fear of attracting attention. But I groped round; and having found the side next the street, where I could frequently see my children, I stuck the gimlet in and waited for evening. I bored three rows of holes, one above another; then I bored out the interstices between. I thus succeeded in making one hole about an inch long and an inch broad. I sat by it till late into the night, to enjoy the little whiff of air that floated in. In the morning I watched for my children. The first person I saw in the street was Dr. Flint. I had a shuddering, superstitious feeling that it was a bad omen. Several familiar faces passed by. At last I heard the merry laugh of children, and presently two sweet little faces were looking up at me, as though they knew I was there, and were conscious of the joy they imparted. How I longed to *tell* them I was there!

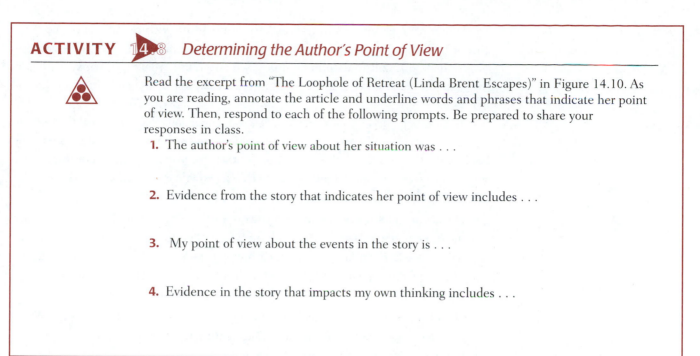

ANALYZING TEXTUAL INFORMATION

The texts that you read reflect not only the author's perspective but also the philosophical, historical, scientific, religious, and social beliefs of the time the work was written. Likewise, your own perspectives are grounded in beliefs influenced by your own background experiences and knowledge base. Sometimes when you are reading a text, it is difficult to spot the beliefs of the authors; at other times they are crystal clear. In this section of this chapter we will explore how you can read to determine bias and to distinguish facts from opinions; these are important for critical comprehension.

DETERMINING BIAS

According to the dictionary, the term *bias* refers to "a particular tendency or inclination, especially one which prevents unprejudiced consideration of a question."[5] A bias can be favorable or unfavorable. In other words, a person may be inclined toward a person, thing, or idea, or a person may be against a person, thing, or idea. In most cases, whether it is apparent or not, the author holds certain beliefs and biases toward the subject he or she is describing. For instance, as authors about college reading and study strategies, we hold a bias: We believe in the importance of lifelong learning and the importance of a solid foundation in reading strategies. We would not be able to write this book unless we believed passionately about the importance of critical literacy in college, the workplace, and our personal lives.

When we look for bias in the texts we are reading, we are looking to see if the author holds specific beliefs that influence the presentation of facts and examples. This may be difficult to determine unless you are familiar with the wider context of the text you are reading. Or, the author may clearly spell out the context and his or her beliefs.

To determine bias, you may ask yourself some questions that will reveal the underlying historical, scientific, religious, philosophical, and social beliefs and perspectives. Each of these contexts is influenced by each other; for instance, when and where a person lives (historical context) influences to a considerable extent his or her religious beliefs and social norms. Here are some examples:

➤ Historical context: When was the text written? What beliefs did people hold during that time period that differ from current beliefs? For example, if you read about the Salem Witchcraft trials, consider the historical context of life in Plymouth Colony in 1692, including how people lived their lives, who governed them, what they believed, how they communicated with others, and what they valued.

➤ Scientific context: Which scientific theories do the authors believe to be true? For instance, an example of a controversial scientific theory is evolution. Many textbooks use an evolutionary perspective in the discussion of the origins and development of different species. When you read texts in the biological sciences, look for assumptions about scientific theories. Another example was the belief during the Middle Ages that the world was flat, a belief discounted with new scientific discoveries.

➤ Religious context: Is a certain religious doctrine used as an underlying belief system? Is a certain religious doctrine assumed to be true, and others assumed to be false? Does the author use evidence that reflects a belief grounded in a specific religion? For instance, if the author discusses matters such as "after death" or "before birth," does the author operate from a specific religious belief system? For example, why did the Egyptians prepare their dead as mummies? Do all cultures believe in an afterlife? Why do some cultures celebrate Halloween? Why do some cultures believe in a God?

➤ Philosophical context: Does the author hold assumptions about what is considered truth? About what is false? About what is right? About what is wrong? For instance, in the field of education there are those who believe in giving standardized tests, such as the SAT (Scholastic Aptitude Test) or GRE (Graduate Record Exam), to students as a prerequisite for college admission. On the other hand, there are those who hold the philosophy that it is more important to consider a student's past performance, such as grade point average, as a predictor of future success. What do you think?

➤ Social context: Each society holds strong and powerful expectations about the way humans should behave in groups, with each other, and on their own. The norms of our society govern much of what we do, particularly in the contexts of families, schools, businesses, government, religion, and other group settings such as sports and recreation. These norms are influenced by the culture in which we live. For instance, consider the norms and expectations we have related to dating and marriage. When should parents give their daughter or son permission to date? At what age should people marry? How many partners should a person have? As you are reading these questions, you most likely have strong opinions about these matters.

ACTIVITY 14.9 *Using the Internet to Analyze Historical Perspectives*

Search the Web to find an article about the historical, social, and religious contexts of the Salem Witchcraft trials. For instance, find the writings of Cotton Mather, who influenced the thinking of the people in the Plymouth Colony in 1692. Be prepared to share your article with other members of your group. In your discussion, describe the opinions and perspectives of the colonists during that time period that differ with the opinions and perspectives of people in the twenty-first century. Use these questions as your guide:

1. What notable historical events predated the Salem Witchcraft trials?

2. What religious beliefs did the colonists hold?

3. What social beliefs and perspectives did the colonists hold?

4. How are your beliefs and perspectives different from those of the colonists?

When you are reading critically, it is important to be aware of the perspectives and opinions of the author. However, it is also important to be aware of your own perspectives and opinions, particularly if you are in disagreement. It is not necessary for you to agree with everything you read; in fact, disagreement is a healthy sign that you are reading with a critical eye. On the other hand, you may find yourself in agreement with the author, even though the author presents information that does not show the whole picture or consider the perspectives of others. What is important is that you are able to spot the author's opinion. In the text excerpt in Figure 14.11, the author introduces the term *proxemics* and shows a very specific perspective.

FIGURE 14.11
Proximity and Personal Space

Source: From J. T. Wood, *Gendered Lives: Communication, Gender, and Culture*, 4th ed. (Belmont, CA: Wadsworth, 2001), pp. 146–147.

Proximity and Personal Space

In 1968, Edward T. Hall coined the word proxemics to refer to space and our use of it. As researchers began studying space, they realized it is a primary means through which cultures express values and shape patterns of interaction (Hall, 1959, 1966; Sommer, 1959, 1969). Early work revealed that different cultures have different norms for how much space people need and how closely they interact. For instance, in Latin American countries, people interact at closer distances than in reserved societies like the United States (Hall, 1959, 1966). Different cultures also have distinct understandings of personal space. In some countries, houses for big families are no larger than small apartments in the United States, and the idea of private rooms for individual members of families is unheard of. As these examples indicate, cultural views are evident in proxemic behavior.

Proxemics offers keen insight into the relative power and status accorded to various groups in society. Space is a primary means by which a culture designates who is important, who has privilege. In societies that have been slow to recognize women's value, women may not be allowed to own property. Thus, women are literally denied space. Only in the mid-1990s did India's legislature pass a measure that allows daughters to inherit property in the same manner that sons have always enjoyed.

Consider who gets space in our society. You'll notice that executives have large offices, although there is little functional need for so much room. Secretaries, however, are crowded into cubbyholes that overflow with file cabinets and computers. Generally there is a close correlation between status and the size of a person's home, car, office, and so forth. Who gets space and how much space they get indicate power. In fact, both Daphne Spain (1992) and Leslie Weisman (1992) have shown in detail how the use of space in the United States designates lesser status for women and minorities. Now think about the amount of space women and men typically have in our society. As we have seen, early socialization encourages boys to go out on their own and girls to stay closer to adults and home. From these patterns, boys come to expect space for themselves, whereas girls learn to share space with others (Evans & Howard, 1973; Harper & Sanders, 1975; Lewis, 1972).

Gender-differentiated use of space continues in adult life. Think about your family. Did your father have his own room, space, or chair? Did your mother? Some researchers (Frieze & Ramsey, 1976) report that many men have private studies, workshops, or other spaces that others do not enter freely, but few women with families have such spaces. My students initially disagreed with this report and informed me their mothers had spaces. When we discussed this, however, it turned out mothers' spaces were kitchens and sewing rooms—places they do things for other people! Years ago, Virginia Woolf gave a famous lecture titled "A Room of One's Own," in which she argued that women's ability to develop and engage in creative, independent work is hampered by not having an inviolate space for themselves. A century later, most women still do not have a room of their own.

Proxemics also concerns how space is used. Again, think of your family. Who sat at the head of the table—the place reserved for a leader? In most two-parent families, that position belongs to the man and symbolizes his leadership of the family. Now consider the extent to which men's and women's spaces are invaded by others. We have already seen that men are more likely than women to have spaces that are off-limits to others. Yet this is not the only way in which men's territory is more respected than that of women.

ACTIVITY 14.10   *Determining Bias*

Read the passage entitled "Proximity and Personal Space" in Figure 14.11. As you read, annotate the article and underline words, phrases, and examples that indicate the author's point of view. Look for specific evidence of bias. Then respond to each of the following questions in your notebook and be prepared to discuss your responses in class.

1. Describe the social context of this passage.

2. Describe the main point of the passage and evidence in support of that point.

3. Describe the author's perspective about the differences between men and women in our culture regarding personal space.

4. Comment on whether you agree or disagree with the author.

DISTINGUISHING FACT FROM OPINION

Essential to your work as a critical reader is the job of separating the facts from the opinions in the texts you read. To prove a main point an author may attempt to convince you with emotional language or with the author's own interpretation of the facts. However, as a critical reader, your work is to find the facts and evaluate the evidence as appropriate for proving the main point.

What are the facts you need to find? As you read, look for details that answer the who, what, where, when questions. Names, dates, places, data, research, terminology with accepted definitions, listings of events, and objective reporting of a story may be used as factual evidence. On the other hand, opinions typically include judgments, emotional appeals, colorful words, "I" statements, and subjective interpretations; opinions should not be used as hard evidence to prove a point.

It is not wrong for an author to use opinions; in fact, you will find that subjective language makes a passage come alive and reveals the author's voice. However, when you are asked to agree with the author's conclusions, it is important to see the basis for those conclusions. An example of text that includes a mix of facts and opinions is the following passage from an art history textbook. As you read this passage about Art Deco, note which statements are based on fact and which are based on opinion.

FIGURE 14.12
Art Deco

Source: From A. Fleming, *Art & Ideas*, 9th ed. (Forth Worth, TX: Harcourt Brace, 1995), p. 621.

Art Deco

Art deco was a reflection of the jazz age of the roaring 1920s and the more sober 1930s when it was the popular style, particularly in the United States. This was an art glorifying the machine and inspired by the speed of the automobile and airplane. It found expression in everything from soaring skyscrapers and luxury ocean liners to streamlined statuettes, overstuffed furniture, jukebox designs, radio cabinets, toasters, and other kitchen gadgetry. Art deco was motivated by the vibrant energy released at the end of World War I, a faith in mechanized modernity, and a joy in such new materials as glass, aluminum, polished steel, and chrome.

The most extravagant forms of art deco were found in the department stores and particularly in the movie houses of the period. These "people's palaces" were the stuff dreams were made of. Here one found release from drudgery, boredom, and the humdrum activities of daily life. Audiences could revel in romances played by beautiful screen idols, hear the peals from the mighty Wurlitzer organs, and relax to the luxuriant sound of real symphony orchestras that rose up on stage elevators as they played hit tunes from Broadway musicals.

The architecture of these theaters was eclecticism gone wild—fantastic mixtures inspired by the *Arabian Nights,* Persian gardens, Egyptian temples, and Chinese pagodas. There were imaginary recreations of King Solomon's temple, Babylonian towers, Muslim mosques with minarets, and Mayan jungle pyramids. All were designed for spectacular entertainment in delightfully gaudy interiors complete with spacious lobbies, winding staircases, grandiose murals, glittering chandeliers, banks of organ pipes, and a general profusion of ornamentation defying description.

There were also such less ornate and more enduring architectural masterpieces as the Chrysler Building, long the symbol of New York City before the Empire State Building (also in art deco style) eclipsed it in height and size. It was finished in 1930 by its designer, William van Alen, who was called the "Ziegfeld of architecture." As the structure rises well over 1,000 feet (305 meters), there is a pause at the thirtieth floor for a brick frieze featuring an abstract pattern that suggests automobiles with decorative hubcaps and huge winged radiator caps serving as gargoyles. The culmination of the structure is the familiar stainless steel sunburst tower, with its overlapping projections pierced by sharply pointed triangular windows, which terminates in a soaring cadmium-plated spire.

The rich art deco interior is equally remarkable with its three-story entrance hall leading to a triangular lobby of African marble with stainless steel trim. Each detail participates in this exuberant design from the elevator doors to the marble floors. Even the elevator cabs with their inlaid wood and intricately detailed geometric patterns become perfectly appointed small art deco rooms.

ACTIVITY 14.11 *Determining Facts from Opinions*

Read the passage about art deco in Figure 14.12. As you read, annotate the article and underline words, phrases, and examples that are factual. Then, reread the text and look for the author's opinions. Then respond to each of the following prompts:

1. Facts used in this passage include . . .

2. Words that show the author's opinion are . . .

3. The author's main point about art deco is . . .

What did you pick as fact? You could choose as factual the time period of the 1920s and 1930s. You could list the places where art deco was found. You could describe the characteristics of art deco as a style of art. What did you pick as opinion? The author inserts phrases such as "eclecticism gone wild," "fantastic mixtures," and "delightfully gaudy" in his description of art deco; the adjectives provide a spirit, an emotional flair, and a window into the author's own enjoyment of this artistic style.

ANALYZING GRAPHICS AND VISUALS

Although many of the reading assignments you have in college are printed passages in word form, you will also be expected to interpret and analyze text in graphic form, such as charts and tables. Most of the time you will find that the charts and tables are explained in the chapter readings; likewise, the chapter readings refer you to the graphics as a summary of the main points and statistics. When reading critically, it is important to analyze the information presented in the accompanying graphics. Your goal, then, is twofold: first, determine what is represented in the graphic, and second, determine what is compared. When you are comfortable with interpreting the information in charts and tables, then you will be able to use the information, evaluate it, and make judgments based on the available data.

DETERMINING WHAT IS REPRESENTED IN THE GRAPHIC

The first goal when reading graphics is to determine what is represented. In other words, what data does the graphic summarize? You can determine this by looking at all the headings, including any descriptions of the graphic. For example, when you read the text excerpt in Chapter 12 about interference theory and viewed the accompanying graph, did you read all the headings? Let's take a look at this graphic again, which describes McGeoch and McDonald's (1931) study about what people remember when there is interference. (See Figure 14.13.)

FIGURE 14.13
Interference

Source: From W. Weiten, *Psychology: Themes and Variations,* 6th ed. (Belmont, CA: Wadsworth/Thomson Learning, 2004), p. 281.

Interference

Interference theory proposes that people forget information because of competition from other material. Although demonstrations of decay in long-term memory have remained elusive, hundreds of studies have shown that interference influences forgetting (Anderson & Neely, 1996; Bjork, 1992). In many of these studies, researchers have controlled interference by varying the *similarity* between the original material given to subjects (the test material) and the material studied in the intervening period.

Interference is assumed to be greatest when intervening material is most similar to the test material. Decreasing the similarity should reduce interference and cause less forgetting. This is exactly what McGeoch and McDonald (1931) found in an influential study. They had subjects memorize test material that consisted of a list of two-syllable adjectives. They varied the similarity of intervening learning by having subjects then memorize one of five lists. In order of decreasing similarity to the test material, they were synonyms of the test words, antonyms of the

Continued

FIGURE 14.13, *Continued*
Interference

test words, unrelated adjectives, nonsense syllables, and numbers. Later, subjects' recall of the test material was measured. Figure 7.20 shows that as the similarity of the intervening material decreased, the amount of forgetting also decreased—because of reduced interference

Figure

Effects of interference. According to interference theory, more interference from competing information should produce more forgetting. McGeoch and McDonald (1931) controlled the amount of interference with a learning task by varying the similarity of an intervening task. The results were consistent with interference theory. The amount of interference is greatest at the left of the graph, as is the amount of forgetting. As interference decreases (moving to the right on the graph), retention improves. (Data from McGeoch & McDonald, 1931)

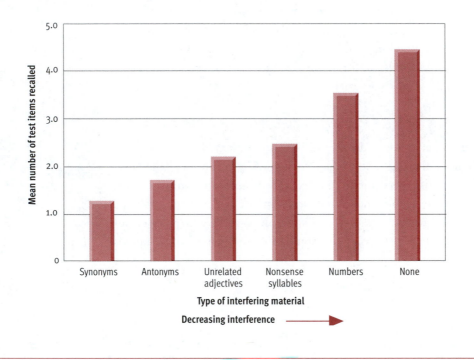

Notice that at the bottom of the graph there are labels for the type of interfering material, that is, "synonyms," "antonyms," "unrelated adjectives," "nonsense syllables," "numbers," and "none." Notice that at the bottom of the graphic there is an additional label: "decreasing interference." Now notice that as you move from left to right on the graph, the columns in the graph get higher. Now notice the left side of the graph, which is labeled with the "mean number of test items recalled" along with the range of numbers from 0 (at the bottom) to 5.0 (at the top). So what does this graph tell us? When you read the graph from left to right, you can see an increase in what is recalled. As noted in the description of the graph, you can remember more items when you have less interference from other items.

You will find many similar type graphs in your textbooks because such visuals help to summarize research studies and other pertinent data; these visuals show you trends that

FIGURE 14.14

Twin Studies of Personality

Source: From W. Weiten, *Psychology: Themes and Variations*, 6th ed. (Belmont, CA: Wadsworth/Thomson Learning, 2004), p. 501.

Behavioral Genetics and Personality

Recent research in behavioral genetics has provided impressive support for the idea that many personality traits are largely inherited (Plomin & Caspi, 1999; Rowe, 1997). For instance, Figure 12.14 shows the mean correlations observed for identical and fraternal twins in studies of the Big Five personality traits summarized by Loehlin (1992). Higher correlations are indicative of greater similarity on a trait. On all five traits, identical twins have been found to be much more similar than fraternal twins. Based on these and many other data, Loehlin (1992) concludes that genetic factors exert considerable influence over personality.

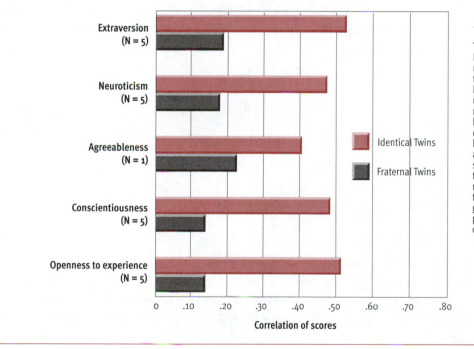

Figure **12.14**

Twin studies of personality. Loehlin (1992) has summarized the results of twin studies that have examined the Big Five personality traits. The N under each trait indicates the number of twin studies that have examined that trait. The chart plots the average correlations obtained for identical and fraternal twins in these studies. As you can see, identical twins have shown greater resemblance in personality than fraternal twins have, suggesting that personality is partly inherited. (Based on data from Loehlin, 1992)

are more easily understood through a graphic rather than word format. In the graph in Figure 14.14, you will see the results of some notable twin studies. To interpret this graph it is important to analyze what is represented by carefully looking at all the labels both on the left side of the graph and at the bottom of the graph.

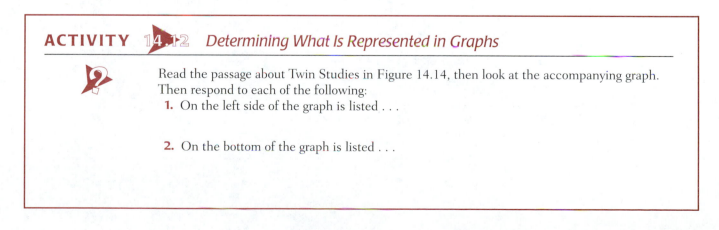

ACTIVITY 14.12   *Determining What Is Represented in Graphs*

Read the passage about Twin Studies in Figure 14.14, then look at the accompanying graph. Then respond to each of the following:

1. On the left side of the graph is listed . . .

2. On the bottom of the graph is listed . . .

DETERMINING WHAT IS COMPARED

For the graph in Figure 14.14 did you note that on the left side of the graph there are five personality traits? At the bottom of the graph is the title "Correlation of Scores" and the range of correlations from 0 to .80. Now the question is "What is being compared?" Essential to interpreting the graph is using the key, which identifies "identical twins" and "fraternal twins." The graph shows the results of twin studies that compared the personality traits of identical twins and fraternal twins. When you look at each of the comparisons, you can see that identical twins are more similar in their personalities than fraternal twins are. This data gives support to genetic factors in the "nature versus nurture" debate that questions whether or not personality is inherited or develops through interaction with one's environment.

Comparisons of data can be represented in graphic form in a variety of ways. In addition to the use of charts (as shown above) two other popular forms are the line graph and the table. In both of these forms, the strategy of analyzing the graph is the same: First look at the headings to see what is represented, then look at what is compared. In each of the following two activities analyze the accompanying graphic.

FIGURE 14.15
Status Dropouts

Source: From J. Wirt, S. Choy, S. Provasnik, P. Rooney, A. Sen, and R. Tobin, *The Condition of Education 2003* (Washington, DC: National Center for Education Statistics, 2003), p. 42.

Elementary/Secondary Persistence and Progress

Status Dropout Rates, by Race/Ethnicity

Since 1972, status dropout rates for Whites and Blacks ages 16–24 have declined; rates for Hispanics have not decreased and remain higher than those for other racial/ethnic groups.

Dropouts from high school are more likely to be unemployed and earn less when they are employed than those who complete high school (NCES 2002–114). In addition, high school dropouts are more likely to receive public assistance than high school graduates who do not go to college (NCES 98–013, *indicator 34*).

The status dropout rate represents the percentage of an age group that is not enrolled in school and has not earned a high school credential (i.e., diploma or equivalent, such as a GED). According to this measure, 11 percent of

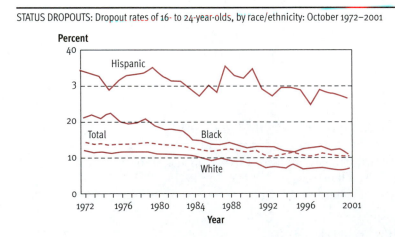

STATUS DROPOUTS: Dropout rates of 16- to 24-year-olds, by race/ethnicity: October 1972–2001

NOTE: Due to relatively small sample sizes, American Indians or Alaska Natives and Asians or Pacific Islanders are included in the total but are not shown separately. The erratic nature of the Hispanic status rates reflects, in part, the historically small sample size of Hispanics. Black includes African American, and Hispanic includes Latino. Race categories exclude Hispanic origin unless specified.

SOURCE: U.S. Department of Commerce, Bureau of the Census, Current Population Survey (CPS), October 1972–2001.

Continued

FIGURE 14.15, *Continued*
Status Dropouts

16- to 24-year-olds were out of school without a high school credential in 2001. Although the status dropout rate declined for young adults as a group between the early 1970s and 2001, it remained fairly stable from 1992 to 2001.

Racial/ethnic differences exist in the status dropout rates and in the changes in the rates over time. Each year between 1972 and 2001, the status dropout rate was lowest for Whites and highest for Hispanics. Between 1972 and 2001, the status dropout rates for White and Black young adults declined, while the rate for Hispanics remained relatively constant. The gap between Blacks and Whites narrowed during the 1970s and 1980s, but not in the period since then.

Greater dropout rates among Hispanic immigrants partly account for the persistently high dropout rates for all Hispanic young adults. Among Hispanic 16- to 24-year-olds who were born outside the 50 states and the District of Columbia, the status dropout rate of 43 percent in 2001 was more than double the rates for first- or later-generation Hispanic young adults born in the United States (15 percent and 14 percent, respectively). Nevertheless, Hispanic young adults born in the United States are more likely to be high school dropouts than their peers of other race/ethnicities.

ACTIVITY 14.13 *Determining What Is Compared in a Line Graph*

Read the passage about dropout rates in Figure 14.15, then look at the accompanying graph. Then respond to each of the following:

1. The heading of this graph is . . .

2. On the left side of the graph is listed . . .

3. On the bottom of the graph is listed . . .

4. The four lines in the graph represent . . .

5. This graph shows that in relation to the total population, the group with the highest high school dropout rate is . . .

6. This graph shows that in relation to the total population, the group with the lowest high school dropout rate is . . .

7. Describe the trend in high school dropouts among black young adults during the last thirty years.

FIGURE 14.16
Services and Accommodations for Students with Disabilities

Source: From J. Wirt, S. Choy, S. Provasnik, P. Rooney, A. Sen, and R. Tobin, *The Condition of Education 2003* (Washington, DC: National Center for Education Statistics, 2003), p. 160.

Services and Accommodations for Students With Disabilities

Table 34-1. Percentage distribution of students reporting disabilities according to type of disability, and among students reporting disabilities, their service receipt status, by type of disability: 1999–2000

Type of disability reported	Percentage distribution of students reporting disabilities	Percentage of students reporting disabilities who reported receiving disability-related services	Percentage of students reporting disabilities who reported needing disability-related services, but did not receive them
All disabilities	100.0	26.0	22.0
Orthopedic or mobility impairment	29.4	19.0	20.5
Mental illness or depression	17.1	30.3	24.1
Health impairment or problem	15.1	19.5	19.6
Visual or hearing impairment	11.9	22.0	13.7
Learning disability or ADD	11.4	51.1	31.7
Other disability	15.1	25.4	23.6

NOTE: Disabilities are defined as those that created difficulties for the undergraduate as a student. Detail may not sum to totals because of rounding.
SOURCE: U.S. Department of Education, NCES, 1999–2000 National Postsecondary Student Aid Study (NPSAS:2000).

ACTIVITY 14.14 *Determining What Is Compared in a Table*

Look at the table entitled "Services and Accommodations for Students with Disabilities" in Figure 14.16. Then, respond to each of the following:

1. What type of disabilities are listed in this table?

2. What are the three types of percentages in the table?

3. Students with what type of disability received the most services? What data did you use for this conclusion?

4. Which students reported a disability but had the lowest percentage of services provided to them?

5. What conclusions can you make about the services provided to students with disabilities?

ANALYZING VISUAL TEXT

Compared to fifty years ago, our contemporary world explodes with visual images because of the abundance of pictures and graphics on television, the Internet, and emerging technologies. No longer is it sufficient for you to read and respond just to printed words. You are expected to be able to interpret, evaluate, and use visual images in many different media, whether they are in books, on television, in films, on the computer, on signs, in your mail, in magazines, in newspapers, in brochures, on posters, or in art. As a critical reader and as a critical consumer, it is important for you to look at the message, its impact, and the overall composition, style, graphic features, and use of symbols in communicating a message. In today's world, to be literate means that you have acquired critical literacy processes in reading and responding to media in all of its visual forms.

In the previous discussions of interpreting and analyzing text, we focused primarily on printed text in word form. In this section we focus on text in pictorial form. As you look at the examples, recall our discussion of understanding the social, historical, and other cultural contexts of text; this will be particularly applicable for understanding other visuals. Therefore, as a critical reader, consider not just what is in the picture but also the larger context of when, where, for whom, and why the visual was created. A primary goal of critical literacy is to use inquiry processes to interpret and analyze the symbols in the picture, the message, and the overall impact on you and other viewers.

LEARNING FROM PICTURES, PHOTOGRAPHS, AND DRAWINGS

Most textbooks (apart from literary novels) include visual text for two reasons: first, visuals inform you about many of the concepts in the text passage. Visuals often provide concrete examples of abstract concepts. Visuals bring ideas to life, clarify complex relationships, communicate important details, and provide a rich context for the ideas in the text passage. For instance, if you see a close-up photograph of soldiers at war, the photograph shows with stark realism the human dimension of war. If you see an illustration of medieval life, you see how people lived, what they wore, what they did, where they lived, and other details that describe how life was different from life today. The saying "A picture tells a thousand words" underscores the power of pictures in bringing words to life. Secondly, visual images add interest to the text and provide a visual appeal. Most people enjoy looking at pictures; the attention to visual effects, including color, layout, and design, add an aesthetic quality. Most textbook publishers use first-rate graphic designers and artists to create textbooks that not only are well-written but are beautifully composed with graphics and visual images.

Each discipline area uses visuals for displaying information unique to that discipline. For instance, in textbooks in the areas of history and political science, you will find pictures of people, historical events, and geographical places. A photograph can capture how people live, their attitudes about an event, and what they look like; if the text passage describes a famous person, an accompanying photograph will show what he or she looked like. The social sciences, such as anthropology, psychology, and sociology, use visuals to illustrate specialized concepts and show people in different societies throughout the world. Science textbooks amply use photographs, pictures, and line drawings to illustrate relationships, particularly ones that need clarification and elaboration. For instance, biol-

FIGURE 14.17

Sound Waves: Music Versus an Explosion

Source: From R. J. Sternberg, *Psychology: In Search of the Human Mind,* 3d ed. (Fort Worth, TX: Harcourt, 2001), p. 140.

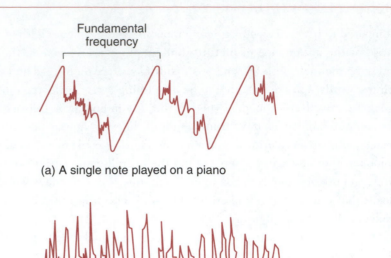

(a) A single note played on a piano

(b) Explosion (noise)

SOUND WAVES: MUSIC VERSUS AN EXPLOSION. As you look at these two sets of sound waves, how would you explain the differences in our sensation of a single note played on a piano versus an explosion?

ogy textbooks illustrate different organisms, biological processes, and different structures. A geology textbook shows different earth formations, rocks, landscapes, coastlines, geologic times, and organisms. Let us look at some examples.

When there are similarities and differences among two or more items, a good illustration can show those distinctions. For instance, note how the illustration about sound waves shows the differences between a musical note and an explosion. (See Figure 14.17.) This picture is helpful for seeing the graphs of the sound waves of these two sounds.

You will find many illustrations in science textbooks, particularly to demonstrate biological concepts, processes, structures, and organisms. In Figure 14.18 there is a set of illustrations that show the human lung. Note how the illustration not only shows you the structure but also labels the components of the respiratory system; this illustration will help you become familiar with the terminology used in biology. The illustration shows you where the different components of the human respiratory system are located, along with two cross-sections that show you how the trachea (windpipe) is composed and the alveoli.

Illustrations and pictures help you visualize relationships of space and design. If you are following a set of directions, you will find it easier to match the correct materials and

FIGURE 14.18

The Human Lung

Source: From G. T. Miller, *Living in the Environment: Principles, Connections, and Solutions,* 11th ed. (Pacific Grove, CA: Brooks/Cole, 2000), p. 487.

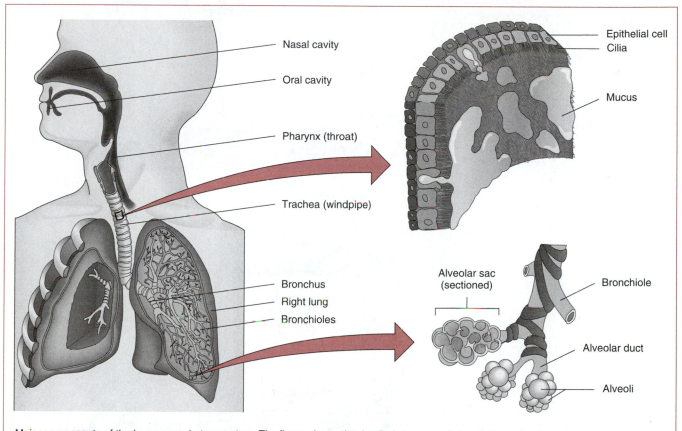

Major components of the human respiratory system. The figure shows the detailed structure of alveoli, the main sites where oxygen diffuses into the blood and carbon dioxide diffuses out into the lungs.

the sequence of steps if you have a good illustration that you can use as a guide. A line drawing can illustrate important principles for building. For instance, in the set of drawings about designs for houses with passive solar energy, note the placement and type of windows, the flow of air, and the construction of the walls. (See Figure 14.19.)

When you read about cause-effect relationships, an illustration can show those relationships. For instance, in the area of environmental science, it is important to understand the delicate balance in ecosystems and the effects of environmental problems, such as pollution, on living organisms and the earth. Figure 14.20 shows you sources and types of air pollutants.

FIGURE 14.19

Passive Solar Design

Source: From G. T. Miller, *Living in the Environment: Principles, Connections, and Solutions,* 11th ed. (Pacific Grove, CA: Brooks/Cole, 2000), p. 410.

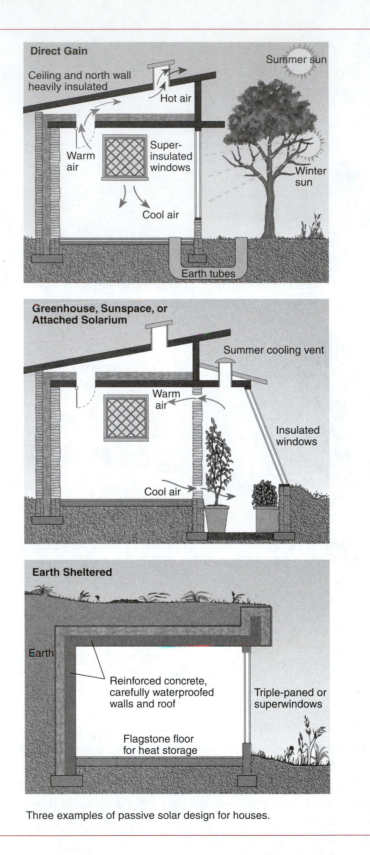

Three examples of passive solar design for houses.

FIGURE 14.20

Sources and Types of Air Pollutants

Source: **From G. T. Miller,** *Living in the Environment: Principles, Connections, and Solutions,* **11th ed. (Pacific Grove, CA: Brooks/Cole, 2000), p. 474.**

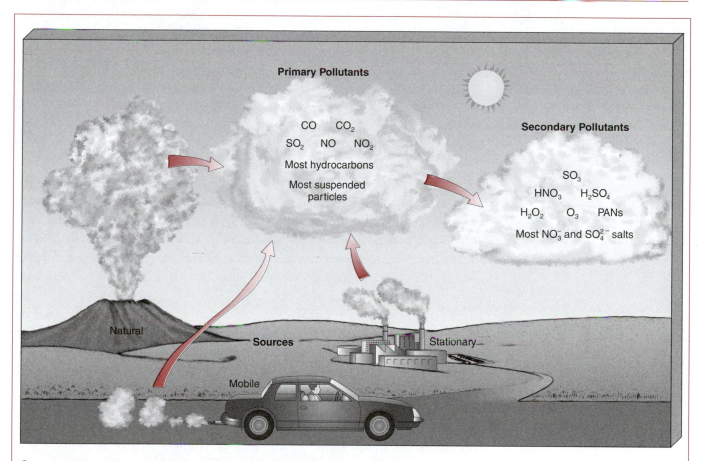

Sources and types of air pollutants. Human inputs of air pollutants may come from mobile sources (cars) and stationary sources (industrial and power plants). Some primary air pollutants may react with one another or with other chemicals in the air to form secondary air pollutants.

ACTIVITY   14.15   *Learning from Illustrations and Pictures*

Study the illustrations in Figures 14.17, 14.18, 14.19, and 4.20. Choose one. Then, respond to the following prompts:

1. Summarize the ideas in this illustration or picture.

2. Describe what you learned from this illustration or picture.

ACTIVITY 14.16 *Where Are You Now?*

Now that you have completed this chapter, take a few minutes to return to the beginning of this chapter and repeat Activity 14.1, Where Are You Now? What have you learned about reading for critical comprehension? What are you going to do differently now? How are you going to change your analytical reading strategies?

Summary

As a college student, you use critical reading strategies to interpret, analyze, question, and reflect on the texts you read; these processes are also essential for understanding the ideas in the discipline you are learning. This chapter focused on analytical reading strategies that asked you to determine the author's purpose, point of view, and tone; detect bias; and determine facts from opinions. Reading for critical literacy also involves understanding underlying historical, scientific, religious, philosophical, and social beliefs and perspectives; determining existing social contexts and power relationships; and reflecting on your own perspectives, biases, and beliefs in relation to the text. In this chapter you also extended your analytical skills to graphics, specifically charts, tables, graphs, and visuals. For these you read to determine what was represented, then to determine what was compared.

Review Questions

Terms You Should Know: Make a flash card for each term.

Analytical comprehension	Facts	Philosophical context
Author's purpose	Graphs	Point of view
Bias	Historical context	Religious context
Critical comprehension	Opinions	Social context
Evidence	Perspective	Tone

Completion: Fill in the blank to complete each of the following statements. You may use the terms and concepts listed above.

1. When you read for _____ _____, you read to analyze the ideas in the text and question the logic of those ideas.

2. When you determine the author's _____, which is also described as point of view, then you are able to determine the author's opinion.

3. When you analyze when a text was written, how people thought, and how they lived, you consider the _____ context.

4. Another word for _____ is inclination.

5. When you read _____, it is important to analyze what the headings represent and what data is being compared.

Multiple Choice: Circle the letter of the best answer for each of the following questions. Be sure to underline key words and eliminate wrong answers.

6. Which of the following is an example of a factual statement?
   A. The weather report said that today's temperature will be 68 degrees.
   B. Today's temperature will be delightful.
   C. I don't care for rainy weather.
   D. If the weather is good today, then I'd like to go outside for a walk.

7. An author who writes to be persuasive:
   A. uses a detached, impersonal tone.
   B. combines facts with strong opinions.
   C. omits his or her own perspectives.
   D. writes to entertain.

Short Answer–Essay: On a separate sheet answer each of the following questions.

8. Describe the goals of critical comprehension.

9. Describe how to determine an author's point of view.

10. Provide at least two questions each for determining the historical, scientific, and social contexts of a text passage.

15 Summarizing and Synthesizing Texts

In this chapter you will learn how to:

➤ Read to summarize and synthesize ideas in a text

➤ Write a summary of the main points in a text

➤ Write a synthesis of the main points in multiple texts

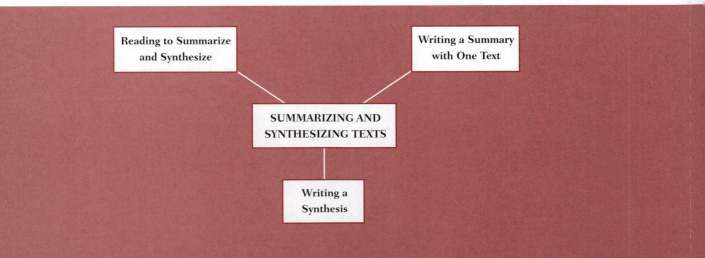

ACTIVITY 15.1   *Where Are You Now?*

Take a few minutes to answer *yes* or *no* to the following questions; choose *yes* if you do this most of the time; choose *no* if you do not consistently do it or if you are not sure.

	YES	NO
1. Are you familiar with problem-solving strategies for reading?	_____	_____
2. Are you a critical reader?	_____	_____
3. After reading a college textbook assignment, do you summarize the main points?	_____	_____
4. When you read two different articles about the same topic, do you look for common ideas and opinions about them?	_____	_____
5. Do you know how to write a summary of an article?	_____	_____
6. Do you know how to write a synthesis of two articles?	_____	_____
7. Do you know how to use evidence in writing research papers?	_____	_____
8. When using other sources to write your own papers, do you copy the text without full bibliographic citations?	_____	_____
9. When writing your own college-level papers, do you write clearly and cohesively?	_____	_____
10. Do you write well in your college classes?	_____	_____
Total Points	_____	

Score yourself 1 point for each *yes* answer to questions 1–7 and 9–10 and *no* to question 8. Total up your points. A low score indicates that you will need to develop strategies for responding to text with good summaries and syntheses. A high score indicates that you are familiar with strategies for critical reading at the synthesis level.

READING TO SUMMARIZE AND SYNTHESIZE

In this chapter you build on the ideas and skills that you've learned in the previous chapters. As an analytical reader, you've learned how to look closely at the text, determine key ideas and supporting points, look for an author's point of view, look for any bias, and determine the broader contexts of the text in relation to historical, social, scientific, religious, and philosophical perspectives. As a critical reader, you've practiced asking the "why" questions, digging deeper into the text's ideas. In this chapter you will build on these analytical strategies and learn to respond to the text as a critical reader. In this chapter you will work on a sophisticated level of critical reading: reading to synthesize. As noted in Figure 15.1, when you synthesize information, you use a combination of

FIGURE 15.1
Reader Purposes

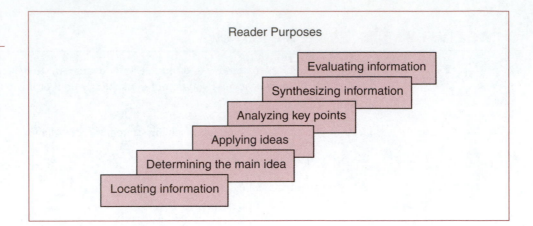

processes: application, analysis, and synthesis. Your approach to text is multifaceted, complex, and sophisticated.

As a critical reader and a critical thinker, your process of comprehending a text involves much more than determining the main points and details; your goal is to use your creativity in making thoughtful, unique responses that show a deep understanding of the text. We have previously discussed in Chapter 14 the importance of applying the ideas in the text to new situations and to make connections of those ideas with your own life and the world we live in. We've discussed the importance of taking a step back and asking the "why" questions: Why is this important? Why is it important for me and for the world we live in? Let us continue this discussion of critical reading in this chapter.

CRITICAL AND CREATIVE READING

Your goal as a critical reader is to interpret, analyze, and evaluate the texts you read; your goal as a creative reader is to explore the ideas of the text, go beyond the ideas of the text, and come up with fresh perspectives, new ideas, and conclusions (Harris & Sipay, 1990).[1] It is important to read for both of these goals when you are reading college level texts. For instance, if you are reading literature, you could think of a different ending or think of a different way some of the characters would act. On the other hand, if you are reading expository text (such as that found in a science textbook), you could design your own experiment to test a hypothesis.

As a critical reader, you stay focused on the text and look for significant ideas, details, and the conclusions of the author. As a creative reader, you have the opportunity to write unique responses to the text and add your own perspectives. As a creative reader, you have the opportunity to create something new, be innovative, use your imagination, or design something after you have read about the ideas in the text. A key distinction is that when you are reading and thinking at the synthesis level (see Figure 15.1), you have the opportunity to think divergently, in contrast to convergent thinking. Divergent thinking occurs when you think of alternative answers; you stretch your thinking to arrive at possible solutions to a problem. On the other hand, when you use convergent thinking, you are looking for a specific correct answer. Both of these types of thinking are important for problem solving.

---

[1] A. J. Harris and E. R. Sipay, *How to Increase Reading Ability,* 9th ed. (New York: Longman, 1990).

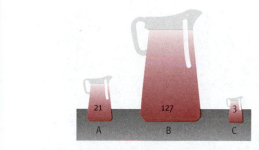

Water jar problem
Suppose that you have a 21-cup jar, a
127-cup jar, and a 3-cup jar. Drawing
and discarding as much water as you
like, you need to measure out exactly
100 cups of water. How can this be
done?

FIGURE 15.2

The Water Jug Problem

Source: From W. Weiten,
*Psychology: Themes and
Variations,* 6th ed. (Belmont, CA:
Wadsworth/Thomson Learning,
2004), p. 315.

READING, INQUIRY, AND PROBLEM SOLVING

When you are reading and responding to text at the synthesis level, you are asking questions and using your own unique, creative perspectives. Integral to critical reading is reading to be a problem solver. When you read to be a problem solver, you need to search for plausible solutions. You need to stretch your thinking and try strategies for figuring out possible ideas. In this section of the chapter you will have the opportunity to try a few activities designed to challenge your problem-solving skills and encourage you to think creatively. To start, look at the problem in Figure 15.2 and try the accompanying activity. This is a classic problem that psychologists use to encourage divergent thinking.

ACTIVITY   15.2   *Creative Problem Solving*

Look at the figure and read "The Water Jar Problem" in Figure 15.2. Then, using the Journal Entry Form located on the *College Reading and Study Strategies* Web site, copy the figure and the problem in your journal.

Then, try to solve the problem. Be prepared to share your responses in class.
Think of the strategies you use to solve this problem; write down those strategies in your journal. What approach(es) did you use?

How did you solve this problem? Check your work in comparison with the solution that Weiten (2004) provides[2]:

---

[2]W. Weiten, *Psychology: Themes and Variations,* 6th ed. (Belmont, CA: Wadsworth/Thomson Learning, 2004), pp. 316 and 317.

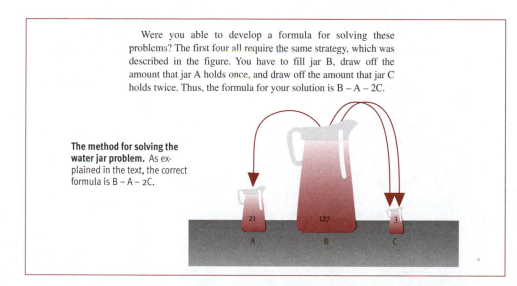

Were you able to develop a formula for solving these problems? The first four all require the same strategy, which was described in the figure. You have to fill jar B, draw off the amount that jar A holds once, and draw off the amount that jar C holds twice. Thus, the formula for your solution is B – A – 2C.

The method for solving the water jar problem. As explained in the text, the correct formula is B – A – 2C.

FIGURE 15.3

*Solution to the Water Jug
Problem*

Source: From W. Weiten,
*Psychology: Themes and
Variations,* 6th ed. (Belmont, CA:
Wadsworth/Thomson Learning,
2004), pp. 316 and 317.

FIGURE 15.4

The Tower of Hanoi Problem

Source: From W. Weiten, *Psychology: Themes and Variations*, 6th ed. (Belmont, CA: Wadsworth/Thomson Learning, 2004), p. 318.

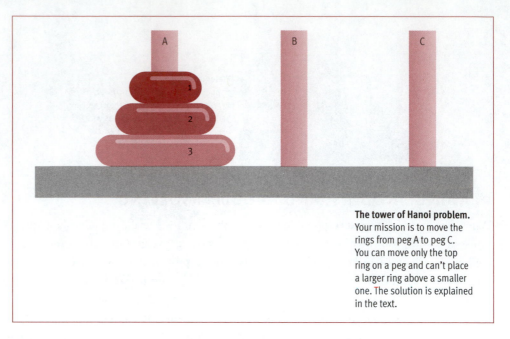

The tower of Hanoi problem. Your mission is to move the rings from peg A to peg C. You can move only the top ring on a peg and can't place a larger ring above a smaller one. The solution is explained in the text.

Did you use a formula to solve this problem, too? When you are reading and responding to text as a problem solver, you can use a strategy proposed by Bransford and Stein (1984), called the IDEAL model of problem solving. According to Bransford and Stein, when solving a problem, use these steps of the IDEAL model in sequence:

1. Identify the problem.

2. Define the problem.

3. Explore strategies for solving the problem.

4. Act on those strategies.

5. Look back and evaluate the results of those strategies.[3]

What this model proposes is that you closely read the text to determine the problem, and based on the available information, you generate possible solutions. However, a critical step is to evaluate these solutions for their feasibility. (We will find in Chapter 16 that judging the feasibility of a solution is an integral component of critical reading.) Try the problem in Figure 15.4 using the IDEAL steps as your guide. As you work on this problem, think of the steps and strategies you use to solve this problem.

---

[3] J. D. Bransford and B. Stein, *The IDEAL Problem Solver* (New York: W. H. Freeman, 1984).

ACTIVITY 15.3   *Using the Ideal Problem Solver*

Look at the problem in Figure 15.4. Then, respond to the prompts listed below, using the IDEAL model. After you identify and define the problem, write down your solution. Try out your solution and evaluate its effectiveness. Be prepared to share your responses in class.

1. Identify the problem; describe the overall goal:

2. Define the problem; be specific what you need to do:

3. Explore strategies for solving the problem; write down your solution:

4. Act on those strategies; try out your solution:

5. Look back and evaluate the results of those strategies; evaluate your solution:

One solution to this problem was proposed by Weiten (2004), as noted in Figure 15.5.[4] How did you do? You can apply the IDEAL problem-solving strategy to texts that you read. When an author poses a problem, you can create solutions that are plausible. The author may provide solutions to the problem; however, you do not have to accept the author's solutions as the only ones. You can look back at the solutions the author suggests and evaluate their effectiveness. According to the IDEAL problem-solving model, a critical step is to look back and evaluate the effectiveness of all of the proposed solutions.

---

[4]W. Weiten, *Psychology: Themes and Variations,* 6th ed. (Belmont, CA: Wadsworth/Thomson Learning, 2004), p. 318.

FIGURE 15.5

Solution to The Tower of Hanoi Problem

Source: From W. Weiten, *Psychology: Themes and Variations,* 6th ed. (Belmont, CA: Wadsworth/Thomson Learning, 2004), p. 318.

Solution to the Tower of Hanoi Problem

The wisdom of formulating subgoals can be seen in the *tower of Hanoi problem.* The terminal goal for this problem is to move all three rings on peg A to peg C, while abiding by two restrictions: only the top ring on a peg can be moved, and a ring must never be placed above a smaller ring. See whether you can solve the problem before continuing.

Dividing this problem into subgoals facilitates a solution (Kotovsky, Hayes, & Simon, 1985). If you think in terms of subgoals, your first task is to get ring 3 to the bottom of peg C. Breaking this task into sub-subgoals, subjects can figure out that they should move ring 1 to peg C, ring 2 to peg B, and ring 1 from peg C to peg B. These maneuvers allow you to place ring 3 at the bottom of peg C, thus meeting your first subgoal. Your next subgoal—getting ring 2 over to peg C—can be accomplished in just two steps: move ring 1 to peg A and ring 2 to peg C. It should then be obvious how to achieve your final subgoal—getting ring 1 over to peg C.

For the following activity, read the author's suggestions for "Learning to Relax" in Figure 15.6. Use the IDEAL problem-solving model to generate solutions of your own. When you have finished exploring alternative solutions, take a look at your list and evaluate the effectiveness of your suggestions as well as those of the author.

FIGURE 15.6

Learning to Relax

Source: From W. Weiten, *Psychology: Themes and Variations,* 6th ed. (Belmont, CA: Wadsworth/Thomson Learning, 2004), p. 554.

Learning to Relax

Relaxation is a valuable stress management technique that can soothe emotional turmoil and reduce problematic physiological arousal (Lehrer & Woolfolk, 1984, 1993; Smyth et al., 2001). The value of relaxation became apparent to Herbert Benson (1975; Benson & Klipper, 1988) as a result of his research on meditation. Benson, a Harvard Medical School cardiologist, believes that relaxation is the key to the beneficial effects of meditation. According to Benson, the elaborate religious rituals and beliefs associated with meditation are irrelevant to its effects. After "demystifying" meditation, Benson set out to devise a simple, nonreligious procedure that could provide similar benefits. He calls his procedure the *relaxation response.* Although there are several other worthwhile approaches to relaxation training, we'll examine Benson's procedure, as its simplicity makes it especially useful. From his study of a variety of relaxation techniques, Benson concluded that four factors promote effective relaxation:

1. *A quiet environment.* It's easiest to induce the relaxation response in a distraction-free environment. After you become experienced with the relaxation response, you may be able to practice it in a crowded subway. Initially, however, you should practice it in a quiet, calm place.

Continued

2. *A mental device.* To shift attention inward and keep it there, you need to focus your attention on a constant stimulus, such as a sound or word recited repetitively.

3. *A passive attitude.* It's important not to get upset when your attention strays to distracting thoughts. You must realize that such distractions are inevitable. Whenever your mind wanders from your attentional focus, calmly redirect attention to your mental device.

4. *A comfortable position.* Reasonable body comfort is essential to avoid a major source of potential distraction. Simply sitting up straight generally works well. Lying down is too conducive to sleep.

ACTIVITY 15.4 *Generating Solutions*

As a problem solver, you can extend the author's solutions. Read the passage in Figure 15.6 entitled "Learning to Relax." Then, using the Journal Entry Form located on the *College Reading and Study Strategies* Web site, respond to these prompts:

1. Identify the problem:

2. Describe the problem:

3. Describe the author's recommendations for relaxing:

4. Add to this list your own recommendations:

5. Try out those recommendations:

6. Look back at your lists and describe the effectiveness of the author's suggestions and your own:

FIGURE 15.7

The Image

Source: From W. Weiten, *Psychology: Themes and Variations,* 6th ed. (Belmont, CA: Wadsworth/ Thomson Learning, 2004), p. 145.

As an analytical, critical, creative reader, you can question what you read and look for alternative explanations other than those proposed by the author. When you were trying to solve the previous problems, did you try out different solutions? Perhaps you found an acceptable solution other than those Weiten proposed.

On the other hand, do you find that for some problems you are just stuck when you are trying to find an answer? In some cases what we see the first time may need a different perspective. Problem solving sometimes requires stepping away from the problem, looking at it from a different perspective, then using your creativity for coming up with a solution. Let's try looking at a figure from different perspectives. What do you see when you look at the image in Figure 15.7?

ACTIVITY 15.5 *Using a Different Perspective*

Look at the image in Figure 15.7. In the space below describe what you see.

1. When I look at the image in Figure 15. 7, I see:

Look at Figure 15.7 again. Try a different perspective. Do you see a different image? Be prepared to share your responses in class.

2. When I look at the image in Figure 15.7 again, I see:

Using the process of inquiry enables you to ask questions that go beyond the text, to use different perspectives, and to look for connections of the text ideas in different ways. Later in this chapter we will look at different perspectives about an issue; perhaps you have a perspective that differs from theirs as well. It is important to remember that different readers bring different perspectives to the text. Therefore, when you read, look for the perspective of the author and think about the perspective you hold.

READING AND RESPONDING TO SINGLE AND MULTIPLE TEXTS

As a college student, your professors will expect that you are able to read for critical comprehension, to understand different perspectives, and to ask probing questions. To demonstrate that you have read your text assignments and that you are able to interpret, analyze, and evaluate the texts you have read, you will be expected to write about them. Most college writing includes a combination of summary and synthesis. Therefore, to be a successful college student, you will need to know not only how to read critically but also to write good summaries and syntheses. For this reason we turn our attention to the topic of responding to text through writing.

As you work with different texts in this chapter, you will see that the twin processes of summarization and synthesis can be used for single texts and for multiple texts. Depending on the assignment you have, you may need to summarize the ideas in a single text. In this case your focus is to work with that text, look for the main ideas and supporting points, and generate your summary. On the other hand, your assignment may be to read two different texts, then to look for common or contrasting opinions and ideas between the two; in this case your task would be to write a synthesis.

In some cases your text may be visual text, such as a picture, photograph, or graph. Your summary of the visual text can include a description of the main theme and the specific characteristics or details. Some professors expect that you know how to compare the visual text with a written text. Whether the text is in word form or in visual form, the tasks of summarization and synthesis are similar in that you are looking to boil down the ideas in the text(s) to the main points. In the next sections of this chapter we will look at how to create a summary and how to create a synthesis.

WRITING A SUMMARY WITH ONE TEXT

What is a summary? According to *The Literacy Dictionary*, a summary is "a brief statement that contains the essential ideas of a longer passage or selection."[5] Note the key point of this definition: a summary contains the *essential* ideas. In your college classes the length of your summaries will depend on the length and complexity of your reading assignments. A summary may be written or oral; most of your summaries will most likely be written. Most likely, your professors will expect that your summary papers be at least a one-page, well-written paper that has good support for the main points you make. Let us turn now to the process of writing a summary.

---

[5] T. L. Harris and R. E. Hodges, *The Literacy Dictionary: The Vocabulary of Reading and Writing* (Newark, DE: International Reading Association, 1995), p. 247.

SUMMARIZING MAIN IDEAS

The goal of writing a summary is to condense the original text passages so that the main ideas remain. When you write a summary, you should aim to write a brief version of the original text. To write a good summary you want to construct a well-written paragraph (or several paragraphs, if the original text is quite long) that provides a condensed version of what the author states. In a summary you do not add your own opinions but stay close to the original text.

For example, if you read a story and a friend asked you to summarize it, you would give a brief version of the story. You would give the relevant details, such as the name of the characters, the location of the story, and important details. However, you would skip many of the details because you would want to give the main point of the story.

When you write a summary, you need an introduction, a series of "one-sentence summaries," and a conclusion. The "one-sentence summaries" describe the main points of your texts. Many students use the strategy of returning to the original text, annotating it for the key points, then writing one-sentence summaries based on the annotations in each paragraph. If there is a stated main idea in the paragraph, then the stated main idea can be used in the summary. If there is an implied main idea, then the reader needs to generate a one-sentence summary that paraphrases what the text means. For additional suggestions for writing a summary read the Tip Block on writing a summary.

TIP

TIPS FOR WRITING A SUMMARY

WRITE A SHORT INTRODUCTORY SENTENCE. Your introduction should provide the context for your paper. In your introduction state the topic and text passages that you are summarizing. This introduction begins your summary.

LOOK FOR A TOPIC SENTENCE OR STATED MAIN IDEA IN EACH PARAGRAPH IN THE TEXT YOU ARE READING. Return to your text reading and look for a topic sentence or stated main idea; it may be located in the first sentence of the paragraph or in the last sentence. Annotate your text and underline the stated main ideas.

WRITE A ONE-SENTENCE SUMMARY FOR EACH PARAGRAPH. For each of the paragraphs with a stated main idea or topic sentence, paraphrase the main idea in your own words; keep your one-sentence summary sentences to the point, and do not add extra information that is not in the original text. For each paragraph where there is not a stated main idea, look for an implied main idea; look for a "super-ordinate" idea, that is, a general idea that ties together the specific points. Write the implied main idea as a

one-sentence summary. Include in your summary each of your one-sentence summary sentences.

LOOK FOR INFORMATION THAT IS TRIVIAL OR REDUNDANT IN YOUR ORIGINAL TEXT. Do **not** include this information in your summary. Your summary should not include information that is trivial.

WRITE SPECIFIC, SUPPORTING IDEAS FOR EACH OF YOUR SUMMARY SENTENCES. For each general idea stated in your one-sentence summaries, include specific, supporting evidence to clarify your point.

WRITE A CONCLUDING SENTENCE IN YOUR SUMMARY. Your conclusion completes your paper.

READ YOUR SUMMARY FOR CLARITY. Read your summary to see that it is well-written, clear, and generally follows the sequence of ideas in the original text.

ACKNOWLEDGE YOUR SOURCES. Check to be sure that you acknowledge all your sources with full bibliographic citations.

For practice writing one-sentence summaries, read the passage entitled "A Society Grows Old" in Figure 15.8, then write "sentence summaries," that is, a sentence for each paragraph that summarizes the main point of the paragraph. As you are reading, keep focused on the major ideas of the text; if there is a sentence directly stated in the paragraph that summarizes the main ideas, you can paraphrase it as your sentence summary.

Figure 15.8
A Society Grows Old

Source: **From M. L. Andersen and H. F. Taylor,** *Sociology: Understanding a Diverse Society,* **3d ed. (Stamford, CT: Wadsworth/Thomson Learning, 2004), pp. 388–389.**

A Society Grows Old

Never before have so many people in the United States lived so long. This fact, in itself, has a number of implications for how society is organized and the issues to be faced in years to come. Current generations—whether young, middle aged, or old—will be profoundly influenced by the *graying of America.* The proportion of old people in the population is increasing dramatically. In addition to this fact, consider the following:

- A growing proportion of the population of Black and Native Americans will be those over age 55 (U.S. Census Bureau 2002).
- Women will continue to outnumber men in old age, especially among the oldest old.

Currently structured into society are certain assumptions that guide the expectations and obligations that exist between generations of people. Sociologists speak of these assumptions as the *contract between generations.* Imagine this contract exists between your generation, your parents' generation, and your grandparents' generation. Not a formal contract, but a set of social norms and traditions, the contract between generations is the expectation that the first generation (say, your grandparents' generation) will grow up and raise the second generation (your parents' generation) who, in turn, produce a third generation (your generation). The expectation has been that each generation cares for the next, and the second or third generation will care for the first when they become old. The expectation has been that parents care for children who in turn care for their children; the children and grandchildren then care for their parents or grandparents once they are too old to care for themselves.

Currently, however, the shrinking size of families means that the proportion of elderly people is growing faster than the number of younger potential caretakers. Moreover, as life expectancy increases and people live longer, the traditional contract is upset. Women, who shoulder the work of elder care, can expect to spend more years as the care giver of an elderly parent than as the mother of children under eighteen (Watkins 1987). As a result, family members can now expect to spend more time in intergenerational family roles than ever before. This in-between grouping has come to be called the *sandwich generation,* because of the time and resources its members spend with both their parents and their own offspring. In many ways this sandwich generation corresponds roughly to the Baby Boom generation—although on average the boomers are a bit older—now mostly in their forties and fifties, a "bulge" moving over the years through the population pyramid and who are probably of the age of the parents of many who are reading this book.

Changes in family structure further alter the traditional patterns of intergenerational care. Childless couples may not have a younger generation family member to care for them in their older years. Those in single-parent families, particularly women, have the extra burden of caring not only for their own children, but perhaps also for an elderly parent—a heavy burden. Men and women in their middle ages may have to find ways, often with few institutional supports, to care for older, and perhaps ill, parents. Given the geographic mobility that has characterized modern life,

Continued

Figure 15.8, *Continued*
A Society Grows Old

they may have to do so over long distances. What we may be experiencing is a classic case of *culture lag,* in which the norms of care and support have not changed as rapidly as the composition of the population.

Currently, Social Security is one of the older and most successful national social policies. Established in 1935 under the Social Security Act, the Old Age, Survivors' and Disability Insurance commission created the Social Security system. Together with Medicare (established in 1966 as a national health care system for those over age sixty-five), Social Security expenditures are more than one-third of the federal budget for human resources (U.S. Census Bureau 2002). Can these expenses continue? This is presently a hot political issue. The statistics are striking: In 1945, the Social Security system had thirty-five working people paying into the fund for every recipient drawing upon it; this is a ratio of 35 to 1. By the late 1970s, the ratio of wage earners to recipients was down to 3.2 to 1. With this dramatic drop in the ratio of earners to recipients, recent estimates note that sufficient funds are available to pay those turning sixty-five in the late 1990s and soon after the year 2000, but without significant changes in Social Security policy, most agree that there will not be enough workers to support the number of retirees by about the year 2020 (Kingson and Quadagno 1995). This prediction has led politicians to search for new ideas for funding the Social Security system, such as investing the system's funds in the stock market.

For the most part, this looming social issue has been posed as a matter of fairness between generations. Social Security is frequently an issue in political campaigns, pitting young against old. Most people assume that more support for other groups could come only at the expense of the elderly. This debate is referred to as the question of **generational equity**—whether one age group or generation is unfairly taxed to support the needs and interests of another generation. There are those who argue that, as the proportion increases of individuals over age sixty-five, a disproportionate share of the burden of supporting them will fall upon the younger generations. Consequently, so this argument goes, the younger generations are not treated equally and are not treated fairly. This debate has its origins in the aging of the population, budgetary crises in the federal government, growing health care costs, increased poverty among children, and, as some sociologists note, a declining faith in social institutions on the part of the public (Kingson and Williamson 1993, Atchley 2000).

Sociologists who have assessed the generational equity debate have argued that this need not be a divisive issue. Studies of other nations find there is no necessary connection between high spending for older adults and

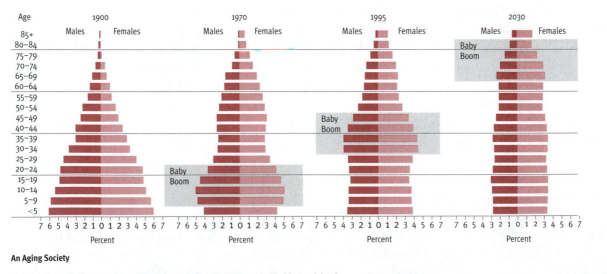

An Aging Society

SOURCE: U.S. Census Bureau. 2002. *Statistical Abstract of the United States.* 2001. Washington, DC: U.S. Government Printing Office.

Continued

Figure 15.8, *Continued*
A Society Grows Old

lower spending for children and the poor (Pampel 1994, Pampel and Adams 1992). Other industrialized nations where governments sponsor programs for strong family allowance systems do not target one group at the expense of another (Adams and Dominick 1995). Instead, sociologists suggest that the problems associated with the graying of America could be addressed by having a changed public agenda—one that provides universal access to the basic needs of income, housing, and health care, a change that would require tax increases and some reduction in benefits such as health insurance (Kingson and Quadagno 1995, Kingson and Williamson 1991, 1993).

To date, such a solution has not gained political appeal. The nation's response may be to exacerbate stereotypes of the aged as "greedy geezers" and to blame the victim, rather than try to solve the problem. This debate about generational equity also has the risk of potentially increasing age prejudice in society, while failing to address the problems of the elderly, children, or the poor.

ACTIVITY 15.6   *Writing One-Sentence Summaries*

Read the passage in Figure 15.9 entitled "A Society Grows Old." Then, annotate the text and underline the main ideas. Next, write an introduction, a one-sentence summary for each paragraph, and a conclusion. Your one-sentence summaries should summarize the main point of each paragraph. Then reread the passage and your sentence summaries to check your summary for clarity. Hint: You will find that this activity works best if you compose your sentence summaries with a computer word processing program.

Introductory Sentence:

Sentence Summary 1: (Include the two bulleted items in your summary.)

Sentence Summary 2:

Sentence Summary 3:

Sentence Summary 4:

Sentence Summary 5:

Sentence Summary 6:

Sentence Summary 7:

Sentence Summary 8:

Concluding Sentence:

ACTIVITY **15.7** *Writing Sentence Summaries from Your Own Textbooks*

Choose a four- to five-paragraph passage from one of your own textbooks. Then, using the Journal Entry Form located on the *College Reading and Study Strategies* Web site, write a sentence summary for each paragraph. Write an introductory sentence, then your sentence summaries, followed by a concluding

sentence. (Hint: You will find that this activity works best if you compose your sentence summaries with a computer word processing program.) Did you have difficulty writing the sentence summaries? What questions do you have about using this strategy?

WRITING WITH SUFFICIENT EVIDENCE

Most of the time when you write an academic summary, you are expected not only to write the main points but also to give enough evidence to support them. Let us return to the passage in Figure 15.8 entitled "A Society Grows Old." In the first paragraph the authors introduce the idea mentioned in the title, that is, that in our current world the proportion of old people is increasing. The authors state the problem in the first paragraph when they say, "Never before have so many people in the United States lived so long."

Let's consider the sixth paragraph in Figure 15.8, beginning with the sentence "Currently, Social Security is one of the older and most successful national social policies." The authors present the problem that the Social Security program, as it is presently organized, will be in jeopardy in the years ahead unless significant changes occur. What evidence do the authors provide? The authors note that today's Social Security expenditures, together with Medicare, are more than one-third of the federal budget for human resources. The expectation is that by the year 2020 there will not be enough workers to support the retirees. These facts are important evidence for the premise that the Social Security program will be in jeopardy in the years ahead unless some drastic changes take place.

Therefore, when you write your summary, include key data that provide support for your paper. A well-written summary captures both the main points and the significant details. Without good evidence, a summary tends to be too general, lacking enough information to provide a meaningful discussion of a topic. As a writer, you can include key details to make your paper interesting, substantive, and lively. The point of including such data is that you need to be sure that your summary includes sufficient evidence for the main thesis.

ACTIVITY **15.8** *Writing with Sufficient Evidence*

Return to your Journal responses for Activity 15.6. Reread the passage entitled "A Society Grows

Old." Now, add to your sentence summaries at least one supporting point.

ACTIVITY **15.9** *Writing with Sufficient Evidence from a Textbook Passage*

Return to your Journal responses for Activity 15.7. Reread the textbook passage you selected for this

activity. Now, add to your sentence summaries at least one supporting point.

When you write your summary, choose evidence that proves a point. When you are reading a textbook passage and looking for evidence, look for facts, statistics, definitions, and descriptions. If your textbook passage includes graphs or tables, look for statistics, trends, or comparisons. For instance, return to Figure 15.8 and view the accompanying graph entitled "An Aging Society." Do you see the changing trends since 1900? Note the predictions for the year 2030. Reread the text in Figure 15.8 and see how the graph supports the text's point that "The proportion of old people in the population is increasing dramatically." In particular, note how the band representing the Baby Boom changes from 1970 to 1995 to 2030. The critical reader looks for this evidence and makes a note about these changes. The implications of this trend are many, particularly on the services that will need to be available to the elderly, such as health care.

The following activity will give you additional practice in summarizing. As you read the text passage in Figure 15.9, also look at the accompanying graphs that provide support for the authors' main points. As you read this passage, look for the main point in each paragraph so that you will be able to write your one-sentence summaries. Then, complete the outline in Activity 15.10, noting evidence from the text passage.

As you read this passage, look for the approach that the authors use to address their question "Prisons: Deterrence or Rehabilitation?" As we noted in Chapter 14, as a critical reader it is important to look for the author's perspective and determine the larger point in the context of social and historical issues. As you read this passage, consider the authors' opinions, as well as your own. As you read, consider which main points and which data you would like to include in your summary. However, note that a summary does not include your opinion; a summary objectively reports the authors' main points and key evidence. When you write persuasive papers (as noted in Chapter 16), you can add your own perspectives to the information you summarize.

FIGURE 15.9
Prisons: Deterrence or Rehabilitation?

Source: From M. L. Andersen and H. F. Taylor, *Sociology: Understanding a Diverse Society*, 3d ed. (Stamford, CT: Wadsworth/Thomson Learning, 2004), pp. 242–244.

Prisons: Deterrence or Rehabilitation?

More than half of the federal and state male prisoners in the United States are racial minorities. Blacks have the highest rates of imprisonment, followed by Hispanics, then Native Americans and Asians who together are less than 1 percent of the total prison population. Among prisoners, Black and White men are the vast majority, Blacks being a large percentage relative to their representation in the general population and Hispanics being the fastest growing minority group in prison (U.S. Bureau of Justice Statistics 2002). Native Americans, though a small proportion of the prison population, are still overrepresented in prisons. In theory, the criminal justice system is supposed to be unbiased, able to objectively weigh guilt and innocence. In reality, the criminal justice system reflects the racial and class stratification and bias in society.

Continued

FIGURE 15.9, *Continued*
Prisons: Deterrence or Rehabilitation?

The United States and Russia have the highest rate of incarceration in the world (The Sentencing Project 2001, Mauer 1999, see Figure 9.4). In the United States, the rate of imprisonment has been rapidly growing (see Figure 9.5). By all signs, the population of state and federal prisons continues to grow, with the population in prisons exceeding the capacity of the facilities. The total cost to the nation of keeping people behind bars is approximately $130 billion (U.S. Bureau of Justice Statistics 2002).

The rate of prison growth in the United States has been so high in recent years that a new trend has emerged—the operation of prisons by private companies. Running corrections systems is now big business, and the "prison market" is expected to more than double in years ahead. For those looking for a business investment, running a prison is a good proposition because, as one business publication has argued, it is like running a hotel with 100 percent occupancy, booked for years in the future!

The privatization of prisons raises new questions for social policy. In the interest in running a profit center, prison managers may overcrowd prisons, reduce staffing, and cut back on food, medical care, or staff training. What

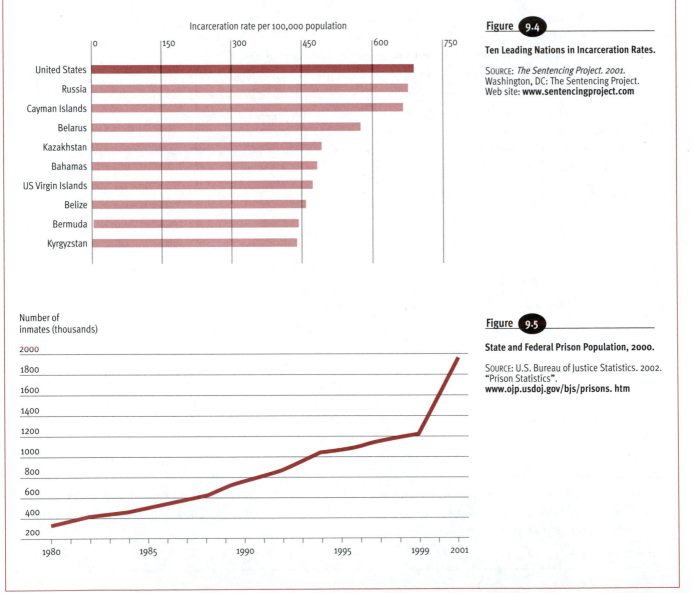

Figure 9.4

Ten Leading Nations in Incarceration Rates.

SOURCE: *The Sentencing Project. 2001.* Washington, DC: The Sentencing Project. Web site: **www.sentencingproject.com**

Figure 9.5

State and Federal Prison Population, 2000.

SOURCE: U.S. Bureau of Justice Statistics. 2002. "Prison Statistics". **www.ojp.usdoj.gov/bjs/prisons. htm**

Continued

FIGURE 15.9, *Continued*
Prisons: Deterrence or Rehabilitation?

may be sound business practice can result in less humane treatment of prisoners, which is locked away from the eyes of the public. Investigators are beginning to see that there are other costs to privatization. The rate of violence in private prisons is higher than in state facilities, and because the private prisons receive money from the state to house prisoners, there is financial incentive to keep people in prison longer—at the taxpayers' expense (Bates 1998).

Why is there such growth in the prison population when the crime rate has recently been declining? A major reason for the increasing number of individuals behind bars is the increased enforcement of drug offenses and the mandatory sentencing that has been introduced. Nearly one-quarter of state prisoners are serving a drug sentence. Sixty percent of federal prisoners are serving drug sentences, more than double since 1980. Although the number of drug offenders has grown dramatically, so has the number of violent offenders (U.S. Bureau of Justice Statistics 2002, Mumola and Beck 1997).

The number of women behind bars has also increased at a faster rate than for men, although the numbers of women in prison are small by comparison. Women comprise only 8 percent of all state and federal prisoners (U.S. Bureau of Justice Statistics 2002). Like men, three-fourths of the women in federal prisons are there because of drug-related offenses, which include theft, prostitution, and robbery (Chesney-Lind 1992). Often, they have participated in these crimes by going along with the behavior of their boyfriends (Miller 1986). The typical woman in prison is a poor, young minority who dropped out of high school, is unmarried, and is the mother of two or more children. Fifty-seven percent of women in prison are African American. Of all women prisoners, about two-thirds have been victims of sexual abuse. Women prisoners are also more likely than men to be positive for HIV-infection (Greenfield and Snell 1999).

Women in prison face unique problems, in part because they are in a system designed for men and run mostly by men, which tends to ignore the special needs of women. For example, 25 percent of women entering prison are pregnant or have just given birth, but they often get no prenatal or obstetric care. Male prisoners are trained for such jobs as auto mechanics, whereas women are more likely to be trained in relatively lower status jobs such as beauticians or launderers. The result is that few women offenders are rehabilitated by their experience in prison.

The United States is putting offenders in prison at a record pace. Is crime being deterred? Are prisoners being rehabilitated? If the deterrence argument were correct, we would expect that increasing the risk of imprisonment would lower the rate of crime. For example, we would expect drug use to decline as enforcement of drug laws increased. In the past few years, there has been a marked increase in drug law enforcement, but not the expected decrease in drug use. Although the use of drugs did decline slightly, overall there has been an increase in use among Black Americans and inner-city youth—those most likely to feel the crackdown of increased enforcement (Mauer 1999). If drug use is an example, it appears that the threat of imprisonment does not deter crime.

There is also little evidence that the criminal justice system rehabilitates offenders. With drugs use the example again, only 20 percent who are imprisoned for drug offenses ever receive drug treatment. Although law enforcement is getting "tough on crime," it is doing little to see that offenders do not continue to commit drug crimes once they are released from prison.

In general, prisons seem to rarely deter or rehabilitate offenders. Prisons certainly do nothing to address the societal problems known to promote criminal activity. They concentrate on individual wrongdoers, not on the social structural causes of crime. Although there has been an enormous increase in the number of prisons built and the number of people in prison, it appears that imprisonment is doing little to solve the problem of crime.

If the criminal justice system fails to reduce crime, what does it do? Some sociologists contend that the criminal justice system is not meant to reduce crime but has other functions, namely, to reinforce the stereotype of crime as a threat from the poor and from racial groups. The prison experience is demeaning and poorly suited to training prisoners in marketable skills or allowing them to repay their debt to society. In the end, prisons seem, at least in some cases, to refine criminals, not rehabilitate them.

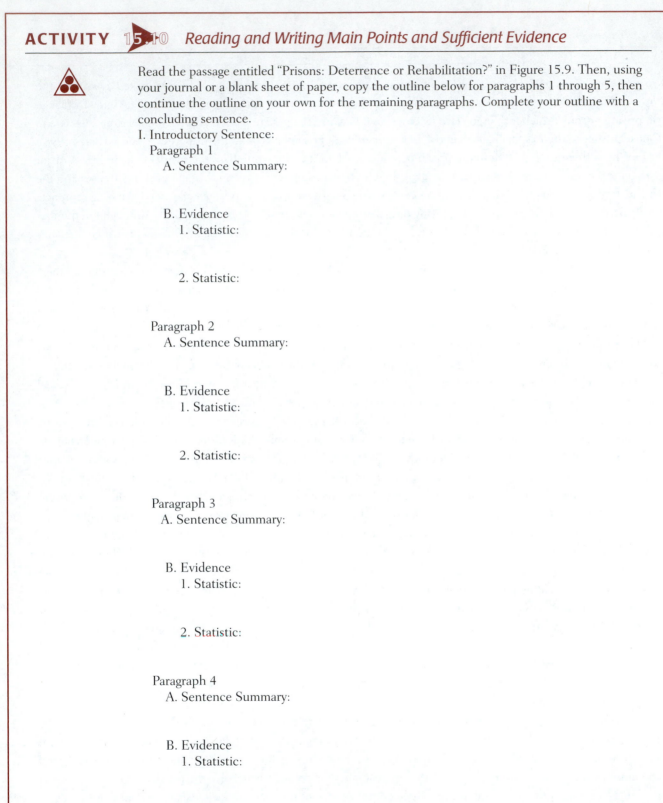

ACTIVITY 15.10   *Reading and Writing Main Points and Sufficient Evidence*

Read the passage entitled "Prisons: Deterrence or Rehabilitation?" in Figure 15.9. Then, using your journal or a blank sheet of paper, copy the outline below for paragraphs 1 through 5, then continue the outline on your own for the remaining paragraphs. Complete your outline with a concluding sentence.

I. Introductory Sentence:

Paragraph 1
   A. Sentence Summary:

   B. Evidence
     1. Statistic:

     2. Statistic:

Paragraph 2
   A. Sentence Summary:

   B. Evidence
     1. Statistic:

     2. Statistic:

Paragraph 3
   A. Sentence Summary:

   B. Evidence
     1. Statistic:

     2. Statistic:

Paragraph 4
   A. Sentence Summary:

   B. Evidence
     1. Statistic:

     2. Statistic:

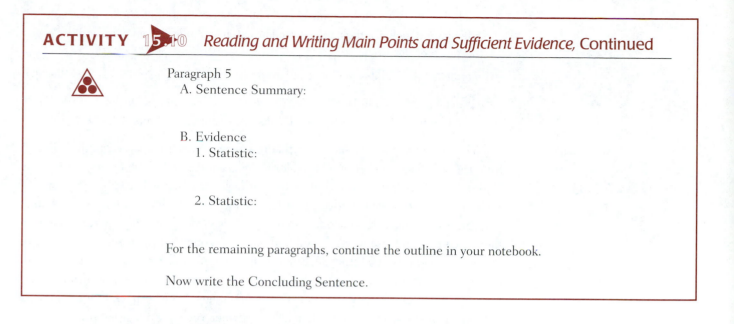

ACTIVITY 15.10 *Reading and Writing Main Points and Sufficient Evidence,* Continued

Paragraph 5
A. Sentence Summary:

B. Evidence
1. Statistic:

2. Statistic:

For the remaining paragraphs, continue the outline in your notebook.

Now write the Concluding Sentence.

ACTIVITY 15.11 *Summary Writing*

When you complete Activity 15.10, you have an outline of the main ideas and supporting evidence for the passage entitled "Prison: Deterrence or Rehabilitation?" in Figure 15.9. To write a summary, follow your outline in sequence. Write a complete sentence for your sentence summary, and then write complete sentences for your supporting evidence. Be sure that your summary has a clear introduction and conclusion.

ACKNOWLEDGING RESEARCH SOURCES

When you write an academic paper, whether it is a short summary paper or a longer research paper, it is paramount that you acknowledge your sources. This means that if you directly quote text written by someone else, you must do the following:

➤ Acknowledge that you are directly quoting someone else by using quotation marks (" ") around the words you quote. If you are quoting longer passages, the generally accepted format is to indent the sentences in your text.

➤ In your own text, note the name of the author, year of publication, and page number of the source from where you chose the quote.

➤ If you do not directly quote an author but you do paraphrase that author's work, acknowledge the name of the author and year of publication of the text you quoted.

➤ At the end of your paper include a reference page that includes a full bibliographic citation. This means that you note all the information that will help a reader find the original source. There are several formats for writing bibliographic citations (APA, MLA, Chicago). However, even though the order of the information may vary from one format to another, they all have the following information: author's name, year of publication of the text, the name of the text. For a book, the citation also includes the name of the publisher and place of publication; for a journal article, the citation includes the name of the journal, its volume and number, and the page numbers of the article.

For instance, the bibliographic citation for the passage in Figure 15.9 is the following:

Andersen, M. L., and H. F. Taylor. *Sociology: Understanding a Diverse Society,* 3d ed. Stamford, CT: Wadsworth Thomson Learning, 2004, pp. 242–245.

This bibliographic citation means that the passage was from pages 242 through 245 from the sociology book entitled *Sociology: Understanding a Diverse Society,* which was written by authors Andersen and Taylor; the textbook was published in 2004 by Wadsworth Thomson Learning in Stamford, Connecticut. Since there are different formats for writing bibliographic citations, it is important to see which one your professor requires you to use, then to consistently use it. When you find out which one your professor requires you to use, it is important to pay strict attention to the punctuation, capitalization, indentation, and overall format required by that bibliographic style; available to you are manuals and Web sites that describe how to create different citations. Each of these different formats has style manuals that you can use as a reference when you are writing your papers.

Most importantly, for all text that is quoted or paraphrased, you must acknowledge your source. In other words, you cannot copy and fail to give the full bibliographic citation in your paper. If you do copy without acknowledging your source, you are guilty of plagiarism. This is a very serious offense in college, one that is so serious you could be dismissed and not allowed to continue your studies. Under no circumstance should you copy another person's work without acknowledging your source.

If you paraphrase someone else's work, refer to someone's research, or use specific terminology created by someone else, then you also need to include a bibliographic citation for that work in your paper's reference section. If you are not sure whether or not you need to acknowledge the source, it is better to err on the side of "yes, include it" rather than failing to acknowledge it.

WRITING WITH COHESIVE TIES

When you have completed writing a first draft of your summary paper, it is a good idea to reread your text for clarity and for cohesiveness. When you read your paper for clarity, check to be sure that your writing is clear and that it makes sense. When you read your paper for cohesiveness, you check your transitions to see if your sentences flow smoothly from one idea to the next.

Here are some questions for checking for clarity and cohesiveness: If you introduce a new idea, do you use a transition phrase to mark it as a new idea? If you are comparing ideas, do you use words that indicate comparison (such as "compared to," "similar to," or "like")? If you are contrasting ideas, do you use words that indicate differences (such as "in contrast to," "unlike," or "different from")? When you begin new paragraphs, do you include transition words? Such transitions help the reader keep track of the ideas you are presenting. In Chapter 13 you used transition words as a strategy for determining which details provide support for a main idea. You can use these same transition words in your own writing to establish cohesiveness in your text. In other words, by using these transition words your writing will flow smoothly from one idea to the next; the ideas will be connected to each other with clear ties that show the relationships of one idea with another. Figure 15.10 contains a listing of these transition words for creating clear, cohesive text.

Transition Words

FIGURE 15.10
Transition Words

Text Pattern	Transitions
Listing, sequence, chronology	A, B, C First, Second, Third In addition Next Last Finally
Description	For example To illustrate For instance Such as
Classification	Similar to Like
Comparison and contrast	Similar . . . different In contrast to Like . . . unlike However Although But on the other hand
Cause and effect	As a result Consequently Why Because
Conclusion	Thus In conclusion Therefore In summary

ACTIVITY 15.12 *Writing with Cohesive Ties*

Return to the summary you wrote for Activity 15.11. Check your summary for clarity and cohesiveness. Add transitions between paragraphs and main points, where needed. Reread your summary to see if the ideas flow smoothly from one idea to the next. With a partner in class try out your summary; ask your partner to read your summary for clarity and cohesiveness.

ACTIVITY 15.13 *Summary Writing with Cohesive Ties*

Choose a contemporary issue in our society. Using Infotrac, search for a short article that speaks to that issue. Then, using the Journal Entry Form located on the *College Reading and Study Strategies* Web site, write a summary of the article, incorporating an introductory paragraph, sentence summary for each paragraph, key supporting details, and a conclusion. Then, reread your summary; where needed, include transitions for clarity and cohesiveness.

WRITING A SYNTHESIS

In the previous examples and throughout most of the exercises in this textbook, you have worked with single passages to practice your literal, interpretive, inferential, and analytical skills. Many college professors, however, expect that you work with multiple texts, not just a single text. Many of your text assignments will be in print, some will be in graphic form, and others will be in electronic form, which most likely will include a combination of print and visual images. In these cases both the printed text passage and the accompanying visual information complement each other; they both talk about the same information and share the same perspective about the subject matter.

If you are asked to summarize the ideas from two very different text passages, however, you will find that different authors hold different beliefs and perspectives, even though the topic in both texts may be the same. Your task, then, as a critical reader is to synthesize the ideas from the two different passages. Different authors may not necessarily present the same facts as evidence; in addition, they may not come to the same conclusions. In this next section we will introduce you to the process of creating a response that interprets different perspectives, synthesizes key points shared by different texts, and uses clear evidence to do so.

INTERPRETING MULTIPLE PERSPECTIVES

Writing well-composed syntheses in college is perhaps one of the most highly prized skills for success throughout your academic years. The first essential step in writing a good synthesis as a response to reading multiple text passages is to interpret the perspectives and main points in each text passage. The assumption here is that the text passages talk about similar content. In other words, when you write a synthesis based on two or more reading assignments, the two passages should be about the same topic. For instance, you might read two different articles about the reasons for a budget deficit, or two different articles about Shakespeare as a playwright, or two different articles about stress management. Therefore, for each passage you should identify the topic to check that the two different articles share a common topic. Remember that when visual information is also presented along with a printed text, look for the information in each that discusses the same topic.

Next, for each text you read, you should identify the author's perspective about it. In other words, what is the author's point of view about it? Is the author favorable? Unfavorable? Supportive? Not supportive? When you read multiple texts, you will find that different authors may have different points of view toward the subject matter. For instance, when you read about current events, consider the background of the author and possible reasons for the author's perspective. When authors of different political, social, or cultural backgrounds write about an event, you will see differences in their interpretations.

For instance, in the text in Figure 15.9 previously discussed, consider the author's point of view about the plight of prisoners currently in prison. What was the author's perspective? Was the author favorable? Unfavorable? If you read other articles about the current status of prisoners in the United States, you will hear the perspectives of others as well. The question "Deterrence or Rehabilitation?" points to the controversy.

ACTIVITY 15.14 *Writing About Multiple Perspectives*

Search for an article about the controversy of the current prison system in the United States. Summarize the author's perspective. As you read the article, note who the author is, the author's point of view, and the type of evidence the author uses to support his/her perspective. Then, compare and contrast the author's perspective with the authors of the text passage in Figure 15.9.

SYNTHESIZING KEY POINTS

When you read multiple texts, it is often helpful to create your own set of visual notes in order to keep track of the ideas that are presented in the different texts. One useful tool is a Venn diagram, particularly if there are two topics or people being compared. (See Figure 15.11.) You can use a Venn diagram to record the ideas and details that are common or unique. You can use this tool for recording ideas within an article as well as ideas and details compared across two different articles.

The details you select for your Venn diagram should support the main concepts, themes, and perspectives in each text. In other words, as you read each text, you can annotate the text to pull out the most significant details. Then, after you have read each text, you can look back and see which ideas, details, opinions, and points of view are common to each text.

Let us now read two different text passages written about the same topic but written at different time periods and written with very different perspectives. The first text passage is about the Lewis and Clark expedition, told from the perspective of historians two hundred years after this famous expedition. (See Figure 15.12.) As you read this first text, entitled "Leading Men," note the perspective of the writer about this historical expedition. Also, as you read, look for specific descriptions that compare and contrast the different explorers, look for the description of President Jefferson, and look for descriptions of Native Americans who both helped and challenged the explorers.

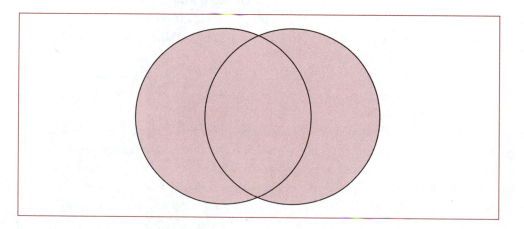

FIGURE 15.11
Venn Diagram

FIGURE 15.12
Leading Men

Source: From L. Y. Jones, "Leading Men," *Time,* July 8, 2002, pp. 56–60. Reprinted by permission of Time, Inc.

Leading Men

They spent roughly a thousand days and nights together, from the rainy October morning they left the falls of the Ohio until they finally pulled their canoes out of the Mississippi three years later in St. Louis. They slept in impossibly close quarters, often sharing the same buffalo-skin teepee with an Indian woman, a French-Canadian interpreter and their baby. They, and several enlisted men, kept journals whose published throw weight equals 13 volumes, 30 lbs., 18 in. of bookshelf and approximately 1 million words. All that evidence notwithstanding, the more we learn about the two captains who gave their names to the Lewis and Clark Expedition, the more powerful becomes their pull on our imagination.

Historians traditionally distinguish them by contrasting their personalities—the brooding Meriwether Lewis played off against the genial William Clark—Jeremy Irons hitting the road with John Goodman. Gary Moulton, editor of the explorers' journals, says, "The differences existed, but they may have been exaggerated." In reality, the two men had far more in common. They were both Virginians. They were both Army officers, six-footers and experienced outdoorsmen, who first met eight years before the expedition when they were serving in Indian campaigns in the Ohio Valley. They shared with their friend Thomas Jefferson a passion for such Enlightenment sciences as ethnology, paleontology, zoology and botany.

They were both fearless spellers. Clark took "Looner" observations, ate slices of "Water millions," tracked "bearfooted Indians" and was proud to serve the "Untied States." Clark's spelling is more famously imaginative—he found 27 different ways to spell the word *Sioux.* (In fairness, even the best-educated Americans displayed erratic spelling until Noah Webster's dictionary standardized spelling two decades later.)

Older than Lewis by four years—they were 33 and 29 when the expedition began—Clark was the more experienced soldier and frontiersman. His five older brothers had fought in the American Revolution. One, General George Rogers Clark, had led raids that kept the lower Great Lakes region out of British hands. As an Army officer, William had trekked the Ohio Valley, leading troops at least once in a skirmish with Indians. "He is a youth of solid and promising parts, and as brave as Caesar," reported a family member.

But by 1803 George was sinking into alcoholism, and William had resigned his commission in part to help settle his brother's debts. The two were living together on a point of land overlooking the Ohio River just below Louisville when William received an astonishing letter from his old Army buddy.

FOR THE PREVIOUS TWO YEARS, Lewis had been working in the White House as Jefferson's private secretary. Like Jefferson, Lewis had lost his father at an early age; now he was in daily contact with the President, who was practically a surrogate father to him. Lewis told Clark that Jefferson had placed him in charge of a mission to explore "the interior of the continent of North America, or that part of it bordering on the Missourie & Columbia Rivers." Moreover, Lewis wanted Clark to be his co-commander.

Jefferson had once discussed a similar mission with George Rogers Clark. But now, leaving George in his family's care, William accepted "cheerfully," and "with much pleasure"—just in time to prevent Lewis from signing up his backup choice, an Army lieutenant named Moses Hooke.

Lewis and Clark got along well from the start. When Clark's anticipated commission as a captain instead came through as second lieutenant—a misstep that still rankled years later—they never told their men and treated each other as equals—placing them among the few effective co-CEOS in organizational history.

They apportioned their operating responsibilities: Clark was the better boatman and navigator, Lewis the planner and natural historian, often walking ashore far ahead of the vessels being laboriously hauled against the Mis-

Continued

FIGURE 15.12, *Continued*
Leading Men

souri's current. Clark clearly had the cooler head. He brokered the crucial early compromise that ended a stare-down with the Teton Sioux. The more mercurial Lewis hurled a puppy into the face of an Indian who angered him, and killed a Blackfeet in the corps's only violent incident.

During their long winter at Fort Mandan, near today's Bismarck, N.D., Lewis and Clark encountered Charles McKenzie, a British trader who later wrote, "[Captain Lewis] could not make himself agreeable to us. He could speak fluently and learnedly on all subjects, but his inveterate disposition against the British stained, at least in our eyes, all his eloquence. [Clark] was equally well informed, but his conversation was always pleasant, for he seemed to dislike giving offense unnecessarily."

Nothing reveals the captains more than their treatment of Sacagawea. Lewis could be aloof, dismissing their interpreter's wife as "the Indian woman," observing that "if she has enough to eat and a few trinkets to wear I beleive she would be perfectly content anywhere." But the less formal Clark nicknamed her "Janey" and treated her warmly. She repaid him with gifts, including "two Dozen white weazils tails" on Christmas Day 1805. At the expedition's end, Clark offered to educate her son Pomp, "a butifull promising Child."

Either captain could assume sole leadership in a pinch—and often did. When Clark was waylaid with a boil on his ankle and abrasions on his feet from dragging the boats up the shallow Beaverhead River, Lewis forged ahead to find the Shoshone and the horses they desperately needed to cross the mountains. But just a few weeks later, when the entire party was near starvation on the Lolo Trail, it was Clark's turn to strike out ahead to hunt for food. If there ever was tension between them along the way, it was not recorded. Each captain consistently referred to the other as "my friend Capt. C." or "my worthy friend Capt. Lewis" and seemed to mean it. After he was accidentally shot in the backside by Pierre Cruzatte on a hunting trip, Lewis spent the next three weeks lying on his stomach in a canoe while Clark cleaned and dressed his wounds every day. The party trusted both leaders completely. Perplexed at the junction of the Missouri and Marias rivers, the men unanimously "pronounced the [north] fork to be the Missouri," Lewis noted. But when the captains overruled them (correctly), "They said very cheerfully that they were ready to follow us any wher we thought proper to direct."

We know these details because Lewis and Clark kept perhaps the most complete journals in the history of human exploration. We can look over their shoulders as they and their party of 31 contend with hunger, disease, blizzards, broiling sun, boiling rapids, furious grizzly bears and unrelenting plagues of tormenting "musquetors." We know about the Indians who helped them, and we know that they had to eat dogs and horses to survive. We are in the canoe with Clark when he writes, "Ocian in view! O! the joy," straining to hear the waves breaking on the shore he had sought for so long.

Jefferson had given Lewis an unambiguous mission: to find "the most direct & practicable water communication across this continent." Judged by that yardstick, the captains had utterly failed. What Jefferson hoped would be a "practicable" water route had turned out to be a brutal portage across parts of Montana and Idaho that included some of the most rugged wilderness in North America. If nothing else, later traders and settlers, appalled by the expedition's experience, learned where not to go and found a friendlier route along the Platte River across Nebraska and over South Pass in Wyoming.

Rather than admit failure, Jefferson devised a solution any spinning politician would recognize: he changed objectives. The expedition, he advised Congress, "has had all the success which could have been expected." Its goal, he said, was actually the understanding "of numerous tribes of Indians hitherto unknown," not to mention examining the trunkloads of specimens of plants and animals that Lewis and Clark had collected along the way.

The last task of the voyage—publishing their account—fell to Lewis. He had kept the raw notes and journals he and Clark had painstakingly carried to the Pacific and back with the goal of editing them into final form. But

Continued

FIGURE 15.12, *Continued*

Leading Men

beset by administrative battles in his new job as Governor of Louisiana Territory, frustrated in his romantic aspirations and sinking into a depression fueled by alcohol and possibly disease, Lewis developed one of history's monumental cases of writer's block. He never turned in a single line.

On Oct. 28, 1809, Clark read the shocking report in a Kentucky newspaper that Lewis had killed himself on the Natchez Trace, near Nashville, Tenn. "I fear O! I fear the waight of his mind has over come him," he wrote to his brother Jonathan. (The cause of Lewis' death is still hotly debated, though most historians believe it was suicide.) A month after Lewis' death, in a remarkable letter published in May in James Holmberg's *Dear Brother: Letters of William Clark to Jonathan Clark,* William wrote that, in his final delirium, Lewis would apparently conceive "that he herd me Comeing on, and Said that he was certain [I would] over take him, that I had herd of his Situation and would Come to his releaf."

In one sense, Clark did exactly that in taking over the project. After further delays, including the bankruptcy of the original publisher, the journals finally came out in a two-volume edition in 1814 that left out most of the expedition's significant scientific discoveries.

WHAT IT DID INCLUDE WAS A cartographic masterpiece: Clark's map of the West. For the first time the blank spaces on the continent had been filled in with generally accurate representations of mountain ranges and rivers. Prominently marked on Clark's map were the names of dozens of tribes that lived there, in bold type that continues to undermine the notion that the West was ever an unpopulated wilderness.

The press run was a paltry 1,417 copies. It sold poorly. Two years later, Clark still had not received his own copy. By that time the nation was beginning to forget about Lewis and Clark. Well-publicized explorations led by John Charles Fremont through the Rockies to California and John Wesley Powell down the Colorado River eventually eclipsed the Voyage of Discovery in the public's imaginings of the West. Yet publishing would revive their reputations. New editions of the journals were published in 1893 and 1904-05, bringing the saga to life a century after it happened.

When the men of the Corps of Discovery had arrived back in St. Louis in 1806, the residents "Huzzared three cheers." But they otherwise did not seem to know what to make of this crew or its achievement. Two nights later, they feted the captains at William Christy's inn. There they raised toasts to, among others, President Jefferson ("the polar star of discovery") . . . Christopher Columbus ("his hardihood, perseverence and merit") . . . and Agriculture and Industry ("The farmer is the best support of government"). But when the revelers got to the captains in the 18th and final toast, they seemed to be at a loss for words. Finally they settled for saluting "their perilous services [that] endear them to every American heart."

It has been that way ever since.

ACTIVITY 15.15 *Using a Venn Diagram*

Read the article entitled "Leading Men" in Figure 15.12. As you read, compare and contrast Lewis with Clark, using a Venn diagram to record your notes. Also look for descriptions of other prominent people, including the Native Americans who assisted these explorers. Note the author's perspective about this famous expedition.

WRITING TO INTEGRATE EVIDENCE

Your final task in writing a synthesis is to write a clear, cohesive comparison and contrast essay that integrates evidence from the two texts. When you write a synthesis, you want to highlight in your paper the themes that are present in both of the texts, then show support for these with evidence from both texts. When you are working with multiple texts, first read one text and annotate it for the main ideas and key details, including those that describe the author's perspective. Then read the second text similarly.

When you are reading multiple texts, read all accompanying visuals that inform you about the key details. When you are reading to integrate evidence, you are looking not only for common themes but also for details in the text that support these themes. You most likely will not find an exact match of descriptions and details. Therefore, you will need to piece together the information you have to form a coherent statement. As a writer, when you are writing a synthesis paper, you compare and contrast the significant points in the paper. You can also zero in on specific sections that discuss certain topics.

For instance, let us work with a second text that describes the Lewis and Clark expedition. This article was published in the *New York Times* almost a year after the first article (which appeared in *Time* magazine). As you read the article in Figure 15.13, consider the Native American perspective about the Lewis and Clark expedition. Look for descriptions about this expedition. (See Figure 15.13.)

FIGURE 15.13

Two Centuries Later

Source: From T. Egan, "Two Centuries Later, a Moment for Indians to Retell the Past," *New York Times,* June 15, 2003, pp. 1, 16. Reprinted by permission of the New York Times Co.

Two Centuries Later, a Moment For Indians to Retell the Past

NEW TOWN, N.D.—Indian Country is a place where people gather in late June to celebrate the day Custer was whipped at Little Big Horn, where cars sometimes run only in reverse and casinos run all night, and where a Nez Percé guide who led Lewis and Clark over the Bitterroot Mountains is remembered by his native name, which means "Furnishes White Men With Brains."

But on the map—be it the road atlas handed out by the state or the statistical one issued by the Census Bureau—the homelands of the first Americans seem to possess little life or magic. Across vast stretches of the northern plains, Indian lands are blank patches, nations within a nation, landlocked islands foreign to most other Americans.

Certainly, the scars of memory are layered as thick as the dam water that buries so many old Indian villages and sacred sites here. Generations after the scourges of smallpox, war and forced resettlement, much of what a traveler finds in Indian Country is emptiness.

Still, those looking to find some link across 200 years, to the people whose nations Lewis and Clark passed through, need only peek into daily life on the reservations along the trail from St. Louis to the Pacific.

Here in New Town, home of the Mandan, Hidatsa and Arikara, Amy Mossett has just planted her garden, using seed corn that is the antithesis of genetically engineered agriculture; it is the same sweet corn given members of the American expedition to help them through the winter of 1804-05, at their fort just down river. At that time, the Indian urban complex 1,600 miles from the mouth of the Missouri River had more people (about 4,000) than St. Louis or Washington.

Continued

FIGURE 15.13, *Continued*
Two Centuries Later

"Indians have the strongest sense of place of anyone in the world," said Ms. Mossett, a Mandan-Hidatsa who is a scholar on Sacagawea, the young Lemhi Shoshone woman who saved Lewis and Clark from disaster at two points when the expedition was at low ebb. "Look at me: why would I choose to live in little New Town, North Dakota, when I could live anywhere? It's because we've been a part of the Missouri River for a thousand years."

New Town, by its name, raises the question of what happened to Old Town. And this is where the Mandans, who did perhaps more than any other tribe to help Lewis and Clark, turn bitter.

It was one thing for the tribe to lose 90 percent of its members to smallpox, a disease that did more than the United States Cavalry to wipe out American Indians. But in the mid-20th century, just as the population was rebounding, the federal government built the Garrison Dam. It choked off the Missouri River here and buried 155,000 acres of prime Indian farmland under a reservoir, dividing a tight-knit reservation into five districts. Many tribal members wound up in this community, on higher ground.

"Some gratitude, huh?" said Frederick Baker, the Mandan-Hidatsa archivist at the tribal museum here. "One guy I know had his house moved as he was eating dinner. But, hey, we want people to understand our people are alive. Everywhere else in North Dakota, schools are closing and towns are dying. We're growing. We're alive!"

The Corps of Volunteers for North Western Discovery, as Lewis called the expedition, passed through roughly 50 Indian nations in their journey of nearly 8,000 miles. Some of those tribes were forcibly removed to Oklahoma. Others—including the Chinook, who lived at the mouth of the Columbia River on the Pacific Coast—are today without a homeland, even a tiny reservation.

The indignities are piled like bleached buffalo bones. Some of the friendliest tribes were later treated the worst. The Nez Percé, who saved the corps from starvation in Idaho, were chased from their treaty-promised homeland and rounded up near the Canadian border in 1877. The Lemhi Shoshone were erased from the land they had lived on for hundreds of years, and lumped with other tribes in the desert of southern Idaho.

But now as then, big pieces of the trail, particularly in the Dakotas, run through solid Indian Country. These lands hold the bones of Sitting Bull, the great Sioux chief, and of Sacagawea. They contain towns full of heartbreak, where suicide is the No. 1 killer. They also hold prairie grass untouched by the plow, and bison herds roaming free, giving the tribes something to connect pop-culture-jaded teens on the reservation of 2003 to the warriors whose spirit so impressed travelers in 1803.

This year, even the Blackfeet of Montana, the only nation to lose people in mortal conflict with Lewis and Clark, and the aggressive Teton Sioux of the Plains, have the bicentennial.

It is time, the Indians say, to tell their own story of Lewis and Clark, an epic about Indians bailing out whites, showing them where to go, what to eat, whom to avoid along the way, and how to get back home in one piece.

"One reason we're opening our doors to people is because there are so many dumb images of what Indians are like," said Denelle High Elk of the Cheyenne River Sioux Reservation in South Dakota, "I was in Monticello in January, for the kickoff of the bicentennial, and the cab driver said to me, 'Oh, you're Indian. You people still live in tepees, don't you?'"

Forgotten by History

President Thomas Jefferson knew he was sending an expedition through lands populated by people who did not care a whit for lines drawn on maps in Paris or Virginia. But Jefferson, an Enlightenment-age man, had conflicted views of the native people. He thought some Indians could be "civilized" back East, while others had to be removed to the far Western plains, the continental equivalent of Mars.

Continued

FIGURE 15.13, *Continued*
Two Centuries Later

"Jefferson appears both as the scholarly admirer of Indian character, archaeology and language, and the planner of cultural genocide, the architect of the removal policy, the surveyor of the Trail of Tears," wrote the historian Anthony F. C. Wallace, in his book, "Jefferson and the Indians: the Tragic Fate of the First Americans."

Lewis and Clark had trouble finding Indians at first. The swift plague of smallpox had come before them, and in some places it left a deathly resonance.

On Aug. 12, 1804, the corps passed the empty village of Tonwantonga, where the once powerful Omahas had lived. Today Nebraska's largest city is named for this tribe, which has a tiny toehold in the state.

Further north lived the Otoe, who joined the Missouri Tribe about 200 years ago. They were the first Indians to have a council with Lewis and Clark.

Today the Otoe and the Missouri have vanished from the trail. They can found in distant Oklahoma, where about 1,300 members live near Red Rock. They feel forgotten by history, some members said, left out of the bicentennial.

But in rummaging through the belongings of a well-traveled tribe, the Otoe found something recently that has electrified historians—two documents written by Meriwether Lewis, which are not in his journal, describing Indians on the middle Missouri.

"My grandmother kept these in her trunk," said Rhoda Dent, treasurer of the tribe. "After she died, my cousin found them. It was just phenomenal for us to read them, even though Lewis refers to native people as children."

The documents are now in the Oklahoma Museum of History, and curators there say they believe they are authentic.

The Otoe would like to reconnect to their old homeland. "We were the first to greet Lewis and Clark, and look what happened to us," Ms. Dent said.

Upriver, the expedition met different reactions among the large nations that roamed the Dakota prairie. Among the Yankton Sioux, the men dined at a tidy village on a meal of stewed dog meat—"good & well-flavored," as one expedition member described it.

William Clark described the Yankton Sioux this way: "Stout bold looking people (the young men hand Sum) and well made. The Warriors are Very much deckerated with porcupin quils & feathers, large legins & mockersons, all with Buffalow roabes of Different colours."

The late historian Stephen Ambrose called such descriptions "pathbreaking ethnology." But the next encounter, with the Teton Sioux, appears to have been a textbook case of diplomatic blundering.

The corps showed off its air gun and a magnifying glass, while offering medals and tobacco. The Teton Sioux, unimpressed, wanted something in return for letting these people pass through their lands. At one point guns were drawn, arrows aimed, and the small cannon mounted to the corps' keelboat ready to fire. The standoff ended peacefully after three days, but with both sides steamed.

Clark never forgot nor forgave. "They are the vilest miscreants of the savage race and must ever remain the pirates of the Missouri," he wrote of the Teton Sioux.

Living Between 2 Worlds

The Sioux fought for their lands to the end, helping to defeat Custer, only to be slaughtered at Wounded Knee in 1890. Today the bands of the Great Sioux Nation, as they call themselves, are spread throughout South Dakota, while Jefferson's granite visage is carved near an Indian sacred site in the Badlands.

They have shown the same fierce spirit in taking hold of the Lewis and Clark bicentennial in their state, despite opposition from some Sioux elders, and some initial snubs from other tribes. The Sioux have organized an in-

Continued

FIGURE 15.13, *Continued*
Two Centuries Later

tertribal tourism council, and set up a Native American Scenic Byway—"a journey through the lands of the least known and most misunderstood nations in America," as the Indians say in a brochure for the road and its highlights.

"We were entrepreneurs back then," said Daphne Richards Cook, who lives on the Lower Brule Sioux Reservation in South Dakota. "And we're entrepreneurs now."

The reservations are breathtaking, the prairie grass high and green, the towns bursting with one quirky story after another. They are the biggest population centers for hundreds of miles, with 12,000 Indians living on the Cheyenne River Reservation, 11,000 on the Standing Rock, and 4,300 total on the smaller Crow Creek and Lower Brule reservations. One out of every 12 people in South Dakota, population 756,600, is Indian.

"I call Indian Country the last of the real frontier," said Wanda Wells Crowe of the Crow Creek Sioux. "Take a look—it's not your typical America."

The Sioux say they walk a fine line between two worlds. "A lot of Indians don't want people here," Ms. Crowe said, "And in truth, I sometimes wonder myself why I'm doing this, trying to promote Lewis and Clark as a way to tell our story." Perhaps the greatest cross-cultural mingling on the expedition happened in what is now North Dakota, where the corps wintered just across the river from Mandan and Hidatsa villages. Lewis and Clark spent more time in the area than anywhere else.

What the natives who descended from those tribes want people to know is that they already had an advanced society when Lewis and Clark arrived. It was a sophisticated agricultural society, with clans and large earth lodges run by women. The Indians shared food, building tips and wives with the newcomers.

"Jefferson wanted to make Indians into farmer and traders," Ms. Mossett said between bites of a fajita salad at a restaurant here in New Town. "But we were already doing all of that. The difference is, we were doing it without slave labor."

Of course, the Mandan and Hidatsa captured other Indians in raids, and later adopted them into their culture. That is how Sacagawea came to live with the Mandan and Hidatsa. She joined the corps in the winter, just after giving birth to a boy she would carry across the West and back.

"In some ways, the Hidatsa thought these guys were a joke," said Mr. Baker, the museum archivist. "We saw them as a trading opportunity, but also felt sorry for them. And we joked about their crummy trade items."

Farther along the trail, the Nez Percé also pitied the corps. At one point, the explorers might have been killed just after crossing the Continental Divide, but a Nez Percé woman intervened.

"The expedition owed more to Indian women than either captain ever acknowledged," Mr. Ambrose wrote in "Undaunted Courage," his best-selling account of the voyage. Mr. Ambrose also noted the bitter irony that when the Nez Percé were driven out of their homeland in 1877, among the stragglers were a handful of old men who had been children when Lewis and Clark visited.

The Nez Percé, alone among American Indian tribes, selectively bred horses, and say they produced the appaloosa. On this bicentennial, the tribe is reviving its horsebreeding registry and language as part of a Lewis and Clark Rediscovery Project.

A sign on the Weippe Prairie, in Idaho, reads: "Lewis and Clark Route, First Contact Between Two Cultures."

Like the Sioux, the Nez Percé, with 3,296 tribal members today, suffered the indignity of not even being called by their real name. Sioux is a Chippewa word, shortened by the French, which means little snake, or enemy. Nez Percé is also a French misnomer. Tribal members say they did not pierce their noses.

Continued

FIGURE 15.13, *Continued*
Two Centuries Later

> At the very least, the Nez Percé, like other Indians along the route from the flatlands to the ocean, hope the Lewis and Clark bicentennial will dispel certain myths.
>
> With the kind of humor found often in Indian Country, the tribe is taking to the revisionist task. After discussing efforts to restore salmon in rivers stapled with government dams, the Nez Percé report on their Web site that "we also frequent restaurants and eat modern foods."

ACTIVITY 15.16   *Looking for Evidence*

Read the article entitled "Two Centuries Later, A Moment for Indians to Retell the Past" in Figure 15.13. As you read this text, annotate the text for evidence that describes the Lewis and Clark expedition, Sacagawea, and the perspective of those interviewed in the article. Using the Journal Entry Form located on the *College Reading and Study Strategies* Web site, make three columns: the "Lewis and Clark Expedition," "Sacagawea," and "Native American Perspectives." Write evidence from the text under each of these columns.

Now, return to the article entitled "Leading Men" in Figure 15.12. Reread the text looking for evidence about the Lewis and Clark expedition, Sacagawea, and the author's perspectives. Using the Journal Entry Form located on the *College Reading & Study Strategies* Web site, make three columns: for the "Lewis and Clark Expedition," "Sacagawea," and "Author's Perspectives." Write evidence from the text under each of these columns.

Now that you have selected evidence from your two texts, you are ready to write a synthesis. The most important step in this process is that as a writer you need to decide what your main purpose is going to be. What do you want to accomplish in your paper? When you write your paper, you will use the notes you have generated (in Activity 15.16) to make a statement about the major ideas in the two papers you have read to prove a point. Therefore, the first step is to decide your purpose. For instance, in the two papers you have read, you could compare and contrast perspectives about Sacagawea. Or, you could compare and contrast perspectives held by contemporary Native Americans and by non–Native Americans.

Then, based on your selection of a controlling thesis, revisit your notes and select the notes that most clearly support your point. It is a good idea to develop an outline for your paper so that you will be able to organize your notes. Then, as in any good paper, write a clear introduction, followed by your supporting paragraphs. Use evidence from the text; it is important to cite where you get that evidence. Therefore, pay strict attention to the punctuation and format for quoting your sources and acknowledging where they were published. Then, wrap up your paper with a clear conclusion. As you should for any academic paper, reread your paper and revise it for clarity, coherence, spelling, grammar, and mechanics.

ACTIVITY 15.17 *Writing a Synthesis*

Revisit your notes from Activity 15.16. Decide on a main thesis for your paper. Using the Journal Entry Form located on the *College Reading and Study Strategies* Web site, write an outline for your paper, noting where you will include evidence from the text. Then, write an introduction and supporting paragraphs; include evidence from the text, citing your sources. Finally, write a conclusion for your paper. Reread your paper to edit it for clarity, coherence, spelling, grammar, and mechanics.

ACTIVITY 15.18 *Where Are You Now?*

Now that you have completed this chapter, take a few minutes to return to the beginning of this chapter and repeat Activity 15.1, Where Are You Now? What have you learned about reading for critical comprehension? What have you learned about summarizing and synthesizing text? What are you going to do differently now? How are you going to change your reading strategies?

Summary

As a critical and creative reader you interpreted and analyzed multiple texts in this chapter for the purpose of generating your own response. Some of these texts were printed passages, while others were visual texts, such as graphs. After you analyzed the texts, you generated your own response to them using evidence from the texts to support your theses.

Since summary writing and synthesis writing are essential tasks in college classes, this chapter emphasized several points for writing academic papers. First, when you are writing summaries and syntheses, it is important to search for the main ideas in the text. These main ideas can be summarized as sentence summaries, which hold the essential ideas in a paragraph. If you are reading graphs or tables, it is important to look for the data summarized in the graphs. If you are working with multiple texts, it is important to search for the themes that cross these texts and to discern the different perspectives that different authors hold. Likewise, it is important to consider the historical, social, political, and cultural contexts in order to understand deeper meanings of the text, as well as to reflect on your own perspectives about it.

Second, when writing summary and syntheses papers, it is important to look for and write about the supporting evidence in the text, such as essential details and statistics that provide data as support for the main ideas. Third, whenever you directly use or indirectly describe another person's work, it is required that you give a full bibliographic citation for that work. Failure to do so is plagiarism, which is considered a serious offense in college. Finally, after you write the first draft of your paper, it is important to revise your paper with cohesive ties, then check for mechanics, spelling, and grammar, as well as the overall clarity of your response.

Review Questions

Terms You Should Know: Make a flash card for each term.

Analysis	Divergent thinking	Summary
Bibliographic citation	Evidence	Synthesis
Cohesive ties	IDEAL problem solver	Theme
Convergent thinking	Inquiry	Visual text
Creative reader	Plagiarism	
Critical reader	Sentence summary	

Completion: Fill in the blank to complete each of the following statements.

1. As a _____ _____, you read in order to generate a response to text.

2. When you condense the main points of a paragraph into one sentence, you are
   writing _____ _____.

3. When you write a summary of a single text, it is important to look for the author's
   main points and _____ that supports those points.

4. If you do not appropriately acknowledge the sources you quote in your paper, then
   you are guilty of _____, a serious offense.

5. The purpose of using _____ _____ in your writing is
   to provide transitions between ideas and provide clarity to your ideas.

Multiple Choice: Circle the letter of the best answer for each of the following questions.
Be sure to underline key words and eliminate wrong answers.

6. A bibliographic citation for a quote must include all of the following:
   A. Author(s), publication year of the text, name of the text, place of
      publication, name of publisher, page number of the quote.
   B. Author(s), name of the text, page number of the quote.
   C. Author(s), publication year of the text, name of the text, place of
      publication, name of publisher, page number of the quote, summary of the
      quote.
   D. Author(s), page number of the quote.

7. A summary paper, in contrast to a synthesis paper,
   A. describes the main ideas and supporting evidence of a single text.
   B. provides your opinion of an issue in order to persuade the reader.
   C. tells a story about an event in history.
   D. presents solutions to contemporary problems.

Short Answer–Essay: On a separate sheet answer each of the following questions.

8. Describe the steps in problem solving.

9. Describe how to write a summary.

10. Describe how to write a synthesis paper.

16 Evaluating Information

In this chapter you will learn how to:

➤ Critically read to evaluate information

➤ Recognize propaganda and fallacies in reasoning

➤ Evaluate arguments

➤ Write a paper with solid arguments

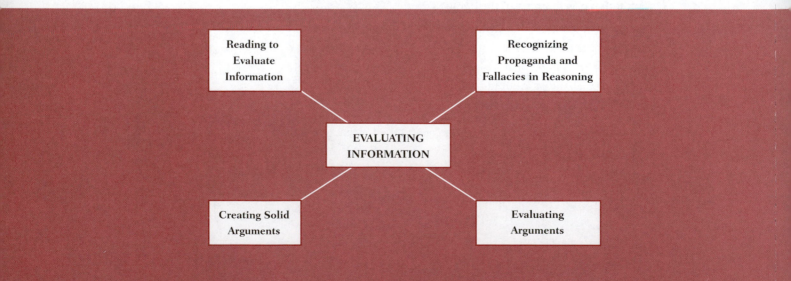

ACTIVITY 16.1   *Where Are You Now?*

Take a few minutes to answer *yes* or *no* to the following questions; choose *yes* if you do this most of the time; choose *no* if you do not consistently do it or if you are not sure.

	YES	NO
1. When reading a passage that was written to convince you about someone or something, do you critically evaluate the main argument and supporting evidence?	_____	_____
2. When you read passages about a controversy, do you let yourself disagree with the writer?	_____	_____
3. When you read informational text, do you check to see who wrote the passage?	_____	_____
4. When you watch or read advertisements, can you identify common propaganda techniques?	_____	_____
5. When you read a passage that was written to convince you about someone or something, can you find fallacies in the reasoning?	_____	_____
6. When you read a persuasive text passage, do you evaluate the evidence that is presented?	_____	_____
7. When you write a paper intended to convince someone, do you use your opinion as evidence?	_____	_____
8. When you read your college textbooks, can you identify the writer's opinion?	_____	_____
9. Do you write academic papers with one-sided arguments?	_____	_____
10. Do you write academic papers with solid arguments and evidence?	_____	_____

Total Points   _____

Score yourself 1 point for each *yes* answer to questions 1–6, 8, and 10 and *no* to questions 7 and 9. Total up your points. A low score indicates that you will need to learn how to evaluate textual information and write persuasive text with solid arguments, good evidence, and reputable sources. A high score indicates that you have already developed many good strategies for reading and responding to text at the evaluative level.

READING TO EVALUATE INFORMATION

When you read texts about controversial topics, do you find yourself getting involved in the topic? Do you sometimes disagree with the writer? Do you find yourself talking about the topic with your friends and/or family members? If you answer "yes" to these questions, then you are reading at a critical level and using some of the strategies for reading as an evaluative, critical reader. As a critical reader, particularly about hot

FIGURE 16.1
Reader Purposes

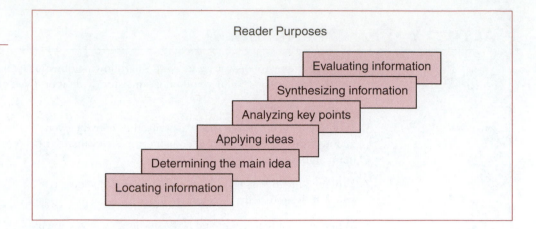

Reader Purposes

Evaluating information

Synthesizing information

Analyzing key points

Applying ideas

Determining the main idea

Locating information

topics, you will find yourself involved in the text. Most likely, if you already know much about the topic, you will be able to extend the discussion with other information. Most likely, you will have your own opinions, too.

In previous chapters you have learned to read on the first levels of this framework: to locate essential details, determine the main idea of a text passage, analyze those ideas, and synthesize information. In this chapter you will use reading strategies to evaluate the ideas in a text. This last step is the true test of a critical reader.

Although the goal of this chapter is to help you become a critical reader and successful student in your college classes, you will be able to apply many of the ideas in this chapter to your everyday life. You will find that many of the texts that you view, such as commercials and advertisements, are excellent practice materials for the ideas in this chapter. In addition to critiquing nonprint materials, you will be able to critique essays, letters, and many of the print materials you meet both in and out of college.

In this chapter you will read to analyze and critique information. Much of the material that you read in a college-level textbook is informational text, which is text that informs and teaches you about something. However, there is also another type of text that you read in college: persuasive text, which tries to convince you about something. When you read persuasive text, the writer wants you to have an opinion about the topic; most likely, the writer wants you to agree with the position that is presented.

As you read the text passages in this chapter, consider the writer's goal and look for passages that not only inform you about something but also try to convince you about something. Some persuasive text passages are easy to identify because the writer clearly informs you about the purpose of the passage. Some persuasive text passages are harder to identify; sometimes the writer presents information and very subtly includes an opinion. As you read the text passages in this chapter, look for both informational and persuasive texts and practice using the strategies of a critical reader.

DETERMINING ARGUMENTS AND SUPPORT

Your first task when reading persuasive text is to determine the central argument the writer presents, then check to see how those arguments are supported. The first key questions are to ask "What is the main point?" and "What does the writer want you to believe?" Then, it is important to ask "What related details does the writer use to prove the point?"

FIGURE 16.2
Stereotypical Portrayals of Men and Women

Source: From J. T. Wood, *Gendered Lives: Communication, Gender, and Culture* (Belmont, CA: Wadsworth/Thomson Learning, 2001), pp. 283–284.

Stereotypical Portrayals of Men and Women

In general, media continue to present both men and women in stereotyped ways that limit our perceptions of human possibilities. Typically, men are portrayed as active, adventurous, powerful, sexually aggressive, and largely uninvolved in human relationships. Just as consistent with cultural views of gender are depictions of women as sex objects who are usually young, thin, beautiful, passive, dependent, and often incompetent and dumb.

Stereotypical portrayals of men. According to James Doyle (1989), whose research focuses on masculinity, children's television typically shows males as "aggressive, dominant, and engaged in exciting activities from which they receive rewards from others for their 'masculine' accomplishments" (p. 111). Relatedly, other studies reveal that the majority of men on prime-time television are independent, aggressive, and in charge (McCauley, Thangavelu, & Rozin, 1988). Television programming for all ages disproportionately depicts men as serious, confident, competent, powerful, and in high-status positions. Gentleness in men, which was briefly evident in the 1970s, has receded as established male characters are redrawn to be more tough and distanced from others (Boyer, 1986). Highly popular films such as *Lethal Weapon, Pulp Fiction,* the James Bond series, *Die Hard with a Vengeance, Scent of a Woman, In the Company of Men,* and *Cliffhanger* star men who embody the stereotype of extreme masculinity. Media, then, reinforce longstanding cultural ideals of masculinity: Men are presented as hard, tough, independent, sexually aggressive, unafraid, violent, totally in control of all emotions, and—above all—in no way feminine.

Equally interesting is how males are *not* presented. Specifically, they are seldom portrayed as nurturers. Men are seldom shown doing housework (Brown & Campbell, 1986). Boys and men are rarely presented caring for others, and they are typically represented as uninterested in and incompetent at homemaking, cooking, and child care (Horovitz, 1989). Each season's new ads for cooking and cleaning supplies include several that caricature men as incompetent buffoons who are klutzes in the kitchen and no better at taking care of children. Although children's books have made a limited attempt to depict women engaged in activities outside of the home, there has been little parallel effort to show men involved in family and home life. When someone is shown taking care of a child, it is usually the mother, not the father. This perpetuates a negative stereotype of men as uncaring and uninvolved in family life.

Some rap stars have led the way in offering enlarged portrayals of men and their roles. A 1997 video by LL Cool J opens with a gospel choir and portraits of young children. In his video, "Retrospect for Life," 25-year old Common shows a young pregnant Black woman who is facing single motherhood until the father returns to stay with her. What accounts for the change? In an interview with *Newsweek's* Veronica Chambers, Common says, "A lot of my friends were getting turned off to hip-hop music because we were growing up" (Chambers, 1998, p. 66). LL Cool J, who has children with a woman to whom he wasn't married, offers a different answer: "I went to see my kids and my son asked me, 'Daddy, are you going to marry Mommy?' That was deep to listen to. That told me he was yearning for a family" (Chambers, 1998, p. 67). Since LL Cool J marched to the altar, he's been followed by Snoop Doggy Dogg and Coolio. Family values and men's roles as husbands and fathers are a new theme in the hip-hop community.

Let's take a look at the passage entitled "Stereotypical Portrayals of Men and Women" in Figure 16.2. When you read this passage, look for the central argument and then identify support for that argument. As you are reading, look for the examples, facts, and information the writer uses to prove the main point. At this point in your reading, stay close to the text, even though you may want to insert your own opinion as you read.

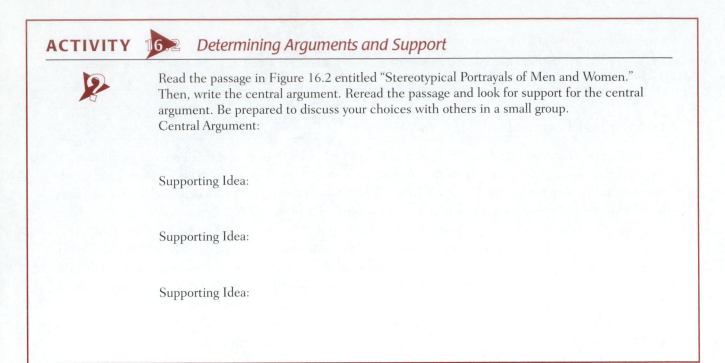

ACTIVITY 16.2 *Determining Arguments and Support*

Read the passage in Figure 16.2 entitled "Stereotypical Portrayals of Men and Women." Then, write the central argument. Reread the passage and look for support for the central argument. Be prepared to discuss your choices with others in a small group.

Central Argument:

Supporting Idea:

Supporting Idea:

Supporting Idea:

The central argument for this passage is stated in the first paragraph and in the headings. Did you find the central argument in the first sentence? When you are reading, you can underline the central argument, then notate the supporting points that follow. Notice that the second sentence in the first paragraph provides the explanation of the argument: media continue to present men in stereotypical ways, as "active, adventurous, powerful, sexually aggressive, and largely uninvolved in human relationships." Do you see the writer's point of view in this statement? One characteristic of an argument is that the writer has a belief about a topic that clearly reveals a point of view.

What did you find as support for this argument? Note that each paragraph following the introductory one gives support for the central argument. In Figure 16.2 the writer describes male stereotypes on prime-time television, then describes how men are not presented on prime-time television, then describes a counterimage portrayed by rap stars.

After you located the central argument and the writer's support, could you think of other supporting ideas for the writer's argument? Or, did you think that the writer did not really have a good argument? What is your opinion on this topic? After first determining the central argument and support, you can extend these ideas with your own opinion. Before you add your own opinion, however, it is important to be objective and identify the author's point of view before presenting your own. When you are reading to evaluate the writer's argument, first be sure you locate and describe the writer's perspective. Then, when you write your own persuasive text, you can state your own point of view.

ACTIVITY 16.3 *Responding to Arguments and Support*

Reread the passage in Figure 16.2 entitled "Stereotypical Portrayals of Men and Women." Then, in your journal write your own response to this passage. Do you agree with the writer?

Include support for your point of view about stereotypical portrayals of men and women in media. Be prepared to discuss your response in class.

The final step in analyzing the argument and the support is to determine whether the writer's conclusions make sense. When we learned about the Bransford and Stein (1984) IDEAL Problem Solving Approach in Chapter 15, we learned to identify the problem, define the problem, explore solutions, act on the solutions, then look back and evaluate the effectiveness of the solutions. This last step is critical. When we evaluate the final conclusions, we want to see whether they make sense. We want to consider the implications and consequences of the writer's conclusions to see whether there would be difficulties or unreasonable consequences. As you test the appropriateness of the writer's conclusions, don't be afraid to trust your own common sense and your ability to ask hard questions. In the process of testing the appropriateness of the writer's conclusions, it is also a good idea to review the evidence presented. Let us now turn to that topic.

DETERMINING EVIDENCE

When you read persuasive text, it is important not only to identify the central argument and the supporting ideas but also to determine what type of evidence the writer uses to prove the main point. It is important to see whether what the writer is using as proof is good evidence. What counts as evidence? Writers typically use these types of evidence as support for their arguments:

> **Facts and Figures** When you read to locate the evidence in support of an argument, you look for statistics, facts, and other figures that will prove the writer's claims as truthful. For instance, if the writer said, "Last winter was the snowiest winter on record," what would you expect to see in support of this statement? Yes, you would expect to see statistics about snowfall amounts during the past one hundred or so years. When you are a critical reader, not only do you look for the statistics but you also ask yourself, "Are the facts and figures appropriate as evidence?" As a critical reader, check to see whether what is presented to you as factual evidence is indeed solidly factual and not flimsy evidence. As a critical reader, check to see whether what is presented as evidence is good support, is substantive, and is well documented.

> **Research Studies** Particularly in the sciences and social science, you will see references to research studies as proof in support of an argument. For instance, in the passage entitled "Stereotypical Portrayals of Men and Women" in Figure 16.2, did you notice the first sentence in the second paragraph? The writer cites the research of James Doyle (1989). The writer also cites numerous other research studies about the way males are portrayed on television.

If you want to check whether or not the cited research studies are really any good as evidence, you would need to do your homework and go find the original sources and read them to check the caliber of research. What type of research was conducted? Was it good research? What were the conclusions of the research? Were the original research studies good ones? In some cases research studies may be quoted inaccurately; so, does the writer accurately summarize the original research? Most likely, as you study the research in a specific field, you begin to know the names of the leading researchers in your area.

➤ **Examples**   If the writer uses examples as evidence, the writer wants to illustrate and bring to life the main point. For instance, in the text passage cited above, did you notice the names of films used to support the argument? As a critical reader you can ask, "Did the examples provide good evidence?" On the other hand, as a critical reader you may want to ask, "Did the examples show only a narrow perspective? How truthful were the examples?" For instance, the writer in the sample text passage cites popular films such as *Lethal Weapon, Pulp Fiction,* and *Die Hard with a Vengeance.* However, there are other popular films that show a very different portrayal of men: Robin Williams's *Mrs. Doubtfire,* Tom Hanks's *Sleepless in Seattle,* or the father in the full-length animated film *Finding Nemo.* These three popular films would not provide evidence as support for the writer's argument about the stereotypical male.

Let's take a look at another text passage. In Figure 16.3, look for evidence in support of the writer's discussion about the impact of television.

FIGURE 16.3
Impact of Television

Source: **From K. H. Jamieson and K. K. Campbell, *The Interplay of Influence: News, Advertising, Politics, and the Mass Media,* 5th ed. (Belmont, CA: Wadsworth/Thomson Learning, 2001), p. 181.**

Impact of Television

Although some disconfirming studies exist, in general scholars have found that those who rely on newspapers for political information are better informed than those who rely on television. The two audiences start with different dispositions. The better educated are more likely to rely on newspapers for information.[81]

Currently, paid daily newspaper circulation is 57 million, rising to 60.8 million on Sundays. Dailies reach 59.3 percent of households; Sundays, 62.9 percent.[82] More people still read a newspaper on a daily basis than do not. In general, those who do not read newspapers fall at "the lower end of the socio-economic ladder; [they] lack resources and cognitive skills due to low education, and lack of social contacts and lack of leisure time."[83] People who are more involved in their communities tend to be regular newspaper readers.

Television has replaced newspapers as the prime source of information for the U.S. public. Researchers account for this decline by noting the increased mobility of the population, a mobility that works against the community involvement and familiarity with coverage and layout that characterize newspaper subscribers.

Local retail advertising, the largest slice of newspaper ad revenues, comes primarily from food and drugs, entertainment and hobbies, housing and decoration, and clothing and general merchandise. Clothing and general

Continued

FIGURE 16.3, *Continued*

Impact of Television

Source: **From K. H. Jamieson and K. K. Campbell,** *The Interplay of Influence: News, Advertising, Politics, and the Mass Media,* **5th ed. (Belmont, CA: Wadsworth/Thomson Learning, 2001), p. 181.**

merchandise represent nearly half of all retail advertising in newspapers, a fact that makes newspapers vulnerable to any new medium able to provide a large audience for advertising from department and clothing stores.[84]

Cable television may pose such a threat because it can carry advertising to selected audiences, and when it is interactive, consumers can order products without leaving their living rooms.

[81] Jack M. McLeod and Daniel G. McDonald, "Beyond Simple Exposure: Media Orientations and Their Impact on Political Processes." *Communication Research* 12 (1985): 3–33.
[82] "Daily Newspapers," *Marketer's Guide to the Media* (New York: BPI Communications, 1998), p. 190.
[83] Steven H. Chaffee and Sun Yuel Choe, "Newspaper Reading in Longitudinal Perspective: Beyond Structural Constraints," *Journalism Quarterly* 58 (Summer 1981): 201.
[84] Anthony Smith, *Goodbye Gutenberg: The Newspaper Revolution of the 1980's* (New York: Oxford, 1980), pp. 65–66.

ACTIVITY 16.4 *Determining Evidence*

Read the passage in Figure 16.3 entitled "Impact of Television" and find evidence in the text that describes the impact of television. Then, record in the space below or in your notebook the details used as evidence. Be prepared to discuss your response in class.
Evidence used in the text:

EVALUATING THE CREDIBILITY OF SOURCES

Besides checking the credibility of the research studies, it is also the mark of a critical reader to evaluate the expertise of the writer. Does the writer have extensive experience? What are the credentials of the writer, that is, what type of training does the writer have? Do the writer's credentials match the discipline under discussion? For many of the textbooks that you read in college, there is typically a biographical page describing the author's background and experience. You can check the authors' credentials by reading the bibliographical notes.

If the writer quotes someone as evidence in support of the main argument, it is a good idea to check the credentials of the person who is quoted. Is the person an expert?

Why was this person selected? Is special training needed in this area? The purpose of checking the credibility of sources is to see whether the opinions stated are from an expert who has much experience about the topic or from someone who does not have much experience. Clearly, if the sources are not reputable and credible, then the evidence cited is questionable.

ACTIVITY 16.5   *Determining the Credibility of Sources*

Locate a textbook you are using for one of your classes. Then, respond to the following prompts:

1. The name of the textbook is . . .

2. The name of the author is . . .

3. The author's professional background is . . .

4. The author's background matches (or does not match) the topics in the textbook in the following ways . . .

RECOGNIZING PROPAGANDA AND FALLACIES IN REASONING

As a critical reader, when you are reading or viewing text, you should be able to spot fallacies in the presentation of evidence and the conclusions that the writer makes about a topic. In this section of the chapter you will meet some of the most widely used propaganda techniques in both print and visual text; you will also meet some of the most common fallacies that writers use (perhaps unknowingly) in faulty arguments. The purpose of learning about the different propaganda techniques and fallacies in reasoning is to be able to critically evaluate the worth of the information a writer uses in attempting to convince you about something.

PROPAGANDA APPROACHES

Commonly used in advertising to persuade people to buy a product, propaganda techniques slant the way information is presented. In other words, when the advertiser uses propaganda approaches, you as a consumer see positive connections with the product. The typical commercial on television is fifteen seconds; in that short time span the advertiser wants to make a strong impression on you so that you will buy the product. While you are reading about different types of propaganda approaches, think of some advertisements you see both in print and in the visual media. Writers use these popular propaganda approaches in persuasive texts to convince you about the worth of the product.

> **Bandwagon** Have you ever bought something because you saw that other people had one and you didn't want to be left out because you didn't have one? Commercials using the bandwagon technique create the impression that everyone is using the product and, therefore, you should, too. (Interestingly, the truth may be that many people may not be using the product.) The reason that this is a propaganda technique is that the commercial does not inform you about the advantages and disadvantages of the product. In fact, the commercial avoids showing the merits or any problems associated with the product. Rather, you are pressured to conform to be like the group and to use the product; if you want to "be cool," you must buy it.

> **Testimonial** Have you bought something because you saw a famous person on television endorse it? For instance, in the world of sports you see football players, basketball players, and Olympic champions promote a product, such as sports clothing. The impression is that if you want to be a champion, too, then you should buy the product. This is a propaganda technique because the basis for buying the product is for you to identify with the champion, not particularly to consider the worth of the product. Can you think of any commercials that feature famous movie stars, sports figures, or even politicians? Hint: Think sports!

> **Plain Folks** Similar to the testimonial is the propaganda technique of "Plain Folks" in which the advertisement shows everyday people—just like you and me—using the product. The implication is that "if the guy next door uses this product, then it must be okay for me to use it, too." Some of my favorite commercials that use this approach are food commercials. For instance, you see the alarm set for 7:00 A.M.; a woman is waking up. She goes into the kitchen. She pours herself a fresh cup of Coffee X. It's a bright new day, full of promise. . . . The implication is that when you drink Coffee X, then you, too, will start the day off well, just like the woman in the commercial. Can you think of some other examples that use plain folks as a propaganda technique?

> **Transfer** In the previous examples the propaganda approach is that advertisers want you to identify with a person or group who uses the product, and then because of that association with the product, you will be motivated to go out and buy it. In the propaganda technique of "transfer," the advertisers evoke strong emotions through images that are compelling and motivating; when the product is associated with those images, then you will want to buy it. For instance, consider this commercial: You see the wide, open, free expanse of a deserted western valley. Then, climbing over rocks, sagebrush, and more rocks, a 4 x 4 truck straddles a mountain ridge. The truck stops. The view is breathtaking. After seeing such a fantastic place and the superior performance of the truck, wouldn't you, too, want to buy that truck?

➤ **Stacking the Deck**   In this propaganda technique the advertisers inform you about the merits of the product. However, they tell you *only* about the merits of their product, and they contrast their product with the negative attributes of a rival product. The conclusion that is shown in the commercial is "Why would anyone want to buy the competitor's product when there are so many problems with it? Instead, buy our product because of the superior quality." The truth is that the competitor's product may not be as bad as what is shown in the commercial.

➤ **Glittering Generalities**   Advertisers want to show their product in the best light possible. However, sometimes what they claim to be true may be just empty words. Advertisers may use descriptions of their product that do not have any real data as proof for their claim. Yet the words sound good and evoke a strong, positive emotion. For instance, a magazine advertisement for a bank had the subheading "Embracing ingenuity." In the same magazine an advertisement for a television said, "See, hear, and feel things like never before. The world's first and largest . . ." Another advertisement for a car had the heading "Pure comfort for the driver . . ." Perhaps you can find some additional examples in both printed text and in the visual media. The following three activities will give you practice in identifying and describing propaganda approaches.

ACTIVITY 16.6   *Propaganda Approaches in Magazine Advertisements*

Select a popular magazine, such as *Newsweek* or *Time*. Then, find examples for each of the following propaganda approaches. Describe why you selected the advertisement. Be prepared to discuss your response in class.

• Bandwagon

• Testimonial

• Plain Folks

• Transfer

• Stacking the Deck

• Glittering Generalities

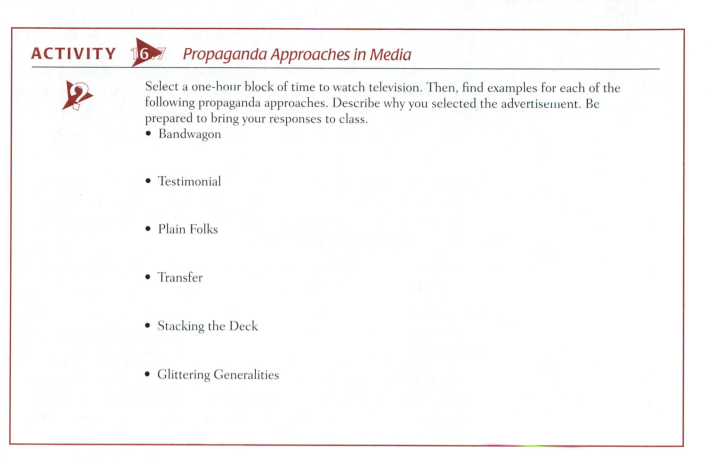

ACTIVITY   16.7   *Propaganda Approaches in Media*

Select a one-hour block of time to watch television. Then, find examples for each of the following propaganda approaches. Describe why you selected the advertisement. Be prepared to bring your responses to class.

- Bandwagon

- Testimonial

- Plain Folks

- Transfer

- Stacking the Deck

- Glittering Generalities

ACTIVITY   16.8   *Propaganda Techniques*

We have explored six of the most commonly used propaganda techniques in advertising. Other propaganda techniques are used in advertising as well. Using InfoTrac College Edition, search for an article about propaganda techniques. Then, using the Journal Entry Form located on the *College Reading and Study Strategies* Web site, write a short description of the propaganda techniques you found. Be prepared to discuss your findings in class.

TYPES OF FALLACIES

In our discussion of propaganda, we noted that advertisers commonly and intentionally use different types of propaganda to persuade the viewer to buy a product. In this section we will explore different types of fallacies that thwart an argument. Fallacies are "false statements," and, as such, are errors in reasoning. It is important for critical readers to see the type of evidence the writer uses and how the writer draws conclusions from the argument. If there are errors in reasoning, then the argument itself is suspect. In some cases a writer may make such fallacies deliberately; in other cases a writer may simply not be aware that he or she is making a fallacy. Critical readers, therefore, look carefully at the conclusions the writer makes.

The underlying reason for examining a text for a fallacy is to check the worth of the argument. According to Aristotelian logic, persuasive text may appeal to reason (logos), character (ethos), or emotions (pathos).[1] There can be errors in each of these three ways of constructing an argument. Hammond (1989) lists some of the more common fallacies writers may use either knowingly or unknowingly:

1. Hasty generalization (weak induction: not enough facts considered). Example: "I can't write. I got D's on my first two papers."

2. The citing of illegitimate authorities (devious deduction: use of an authority's opinion as a fact to reinforce an inference you want to make, when that authority's qualifications for offering the opinion are suspect). Example: "Dick Butkus and Bubba Smith think that the beer tastes great."

3. Unstated assumptions (devious deduction: not stating the principles of your arguments). Example: "He'll never graduate. He's an athlete."

4. Undefined key terms (weak or devious deduction: carelessness about whether the audience really knows what you mean). Example: "He's more qualified than she is. We'll hire him."

5. Inappropriate comparisons or analogies (weak or devious deduction: unstated general principle is that the two items compared are essentially alike). Example: "Since Napolean made France strong again by attacking Austria and Italy, we should make the United States strong again by attacking Canada."

6. Unsubstantiated cause-effect claims (weak or devious deduction: unstated general principle is that your cause caused your effect.) Example: "The English are a morose people because their weather is so cloudy."

7. A claim that there are only two choices (weak or devious deduction: unstated general principle is that are only two possibilities). Example: "Either fight communism wherever it rears its head, or live in a world in which we have no friends."

8. Ignoring the point at issue (absence of logos: not constructing arguments that are to the point). Example from a paper on nuclear power plant safety: "A hydrogen bomb could destroy half of Connecticut."

9. The hurling of insults (misuse of pathos: trying to get readers emotional about irrelevant matters). Example: "You're not going to trust the word of a bureaucrat!"

10. Appeal to irrelevant emotions (misuse of pathos: this one is often very difficult to decide). Example: "No one who loves children can fail to put $25 in an envelope and send it to P. O. Box 47, New York, New York."

11. Exaggeration (abuse of ethos: readers won't trust a writer who overreacts). Example: "'You can't judge a book by its cover' is a very familiar saying, and probably the best one yet."[2]

---

[1] E. P. J. Corbett, *Classical Rhetoric for the Modern Student* (New York, NY: Oxford University Press, 1965), p. 39.
[2] E. R. Hammond, *Critical Thinking, Thoughtful Writing* (New York: McGraw-Hill, 1989), pp. 98–99.

When you are reading persuasive text, look for these fallacies. One place where you most likely will find clear examples of these fallacies is in the Letters to the Editor section in your local paper. Likewise, when you read the editorial page in your local paper, read the essays carefully for any of these fallacies. You will also need to be aware of these fallacies when you are writing your own papers.

ACTIVITY 16.9   *Finding Fallacies*

Read the "Letters to the Editor" section in a newspaper of your choice. Then, using the Journal Entry Form located on the *College*

Reading and Study Strategies Web site, list the fallacies that you find. Label them, using the list from Hammond (1989).

EVALUATING ARGUMENTS

To this point in the chapter we have located arguments and the evidence used as support. We have also looked at propaganda approaches that can influence the reader, sometimes unwittingly. We have also looked at fallacies in reasoning that can block the effectiveness of an argument. Now let us focus on how the text passage presents the argument in a persuasive passage. We will focus on three questions to evaluate an argument:

➤ Does the writer present just one side of the issue or give other viewpoints?

➤ Does the writer provide good, clear, relevant, substantive, sufficient evidence in support of the claim?

➤ Does the writer give opinions or facts?

ONE-SIDED ARGUMENTS

A good persuasive paper presents both sides of an issue. In a well-written persuasive paper, the writer will present the argument, then explore one side of the issue, presenting good evidence in favor of the writer's claim. Next, the writer will explore the opposing side. The writer will speak to the issue, showing how the opposing perspective is limited. In this phase the writer needs good evidence showing why the opposing perspective is limited. Therefore, if the writer presents only one side of an argument, then the reader does not have the full story. When the writer acknowledges and explores the opposing perspective, then the reader knows that the writer is fully aware of the issues, has thoughtfully analyzed them, and can discuss the strengths and weaknesses of both sides of the issue. In a persuasive writing piece, however, the writer wants to convince you, the reader, about the benefit of believing the writer's perspective. So, keep in mind that the purpose of discussing the opposing perspective is to convince you of the merit of the writer's conclusions.

Let's look at an example. The article "What Makes Us Do It?" in Figure 16.4 explores the classic nature versus nurture theory. As you read this article, look for the opposing beliefs and their supporting points. This article also gives a historical perspective; how has this debate changed over the past one hundred years? What was the reason for the change? On the whole does this article present a one-sided argument? Or, does it fairly and accurately voice the perspectives on both sides of the issue?

FIGURE 16.4
What Makes Us Do It?

Source: From M. D. Lemonick, "What Makes Us Do It?" *Time,* October 26, 2002, p. 54. Reprinted by permission of Time, Inc.

What Makes Us Do It?

In one important sense, the argument over nature and nurture has been resolved. For centuries, the nature camp said that personalities are born, not made, that our character is pretty much formed by the time we pop out of the womb. The nurture people countered with the metaphor of the tabula rasa: our mind starts out as a blank slate, and it's how we are reared that determines what gets written on it. Modern science, though—especially our fast-growing understanding of the human genome—makes it clear that both sides are partly right. Nature endows us with inborn abilities and personality traits; nurture takes these raw materials and molds them as we learn and mature.

But if you think this compromise has stopped the arguments, think again. Scientists and philosophers are still getting steamed up over the issue, but now they're fighting over percentages, over how much of human character is shaped by genes and how much by environment. And according to Steven Pinker, a professor of psychology at the Massachusetts Institute of Technology, we continue to give far too much credit to the latter. In a series of articles, a lecture tour and especially in a new book, *The Blank Slate: The Modern Denial of Human Nature* (Viking), Pinker argues that ignorance, prejudice and political correctness have kept scientists and the public from appreciating the power of our genes.

Anyone who has read Pinker's earlier books—including *How the Mind Works* and *The Language Instinct*—will rightly guess that his latest effort is similarly sweeping, erudite, sharply argued, richly footnoted and fun to read. It's also highly persuasive. The view that environment is paramount began, he says, with the philosophers of the Enlightenment: John Locke, Jean-Jacques Rousseau, René Descartes and John Stuart Mill. And it was reinforced in the 1950s by Harvard psychologist B.F. Skinner, who said that all human behavior was simply a set of conditioned responses.

That jibed nicely with 20th century liberal social theory: violence, crime and poverty were not the fault of the violent, the lawless and the poor but of society. Improve living conditions and you will cure the problems. Even mental illness and homosexuality were the result of family dynamics, went this line of reasoning. These notions, of course, flew in the face of everything conservatives held dear—the idea that the lower classes were inherently stupid and lazy, for example, and that rehabilitating lawbreakers was an exercise in futility—which may have been part of their appeal.

Then, in the 1970s, science began to show that the nurture-only view was indeed too simplistic—which triggered a backlash from the left. When researchers like Richard Herrnstein and E.O. Wilson demonstrated that genes do play a significant role in human intelligence and behavior, for example, they were vilified by many of their colleagues. And just a few years ago, a conference designed to explore the genetic roots of violence had to be canceled in the face of widespread condemnation.

The backlash was understandable, says Pinker. Once you suggest that human nature is in any way hardwired, it's easier for the unscrupulous to write off entire groups as genetically inferior—as the Nazis did with Jews, Poles, Gypsies and gays. If have-nots are genetically lacking in drive or intelligence or ambition, what's the point of fighting poverty?

Continued

FIGURE 16.4, *Continued*
What Makes Us Do It?

Plenty, says Pinker. Compassion and altruism (which he thinks also are at least partly hardwired) are good reasons to make life better for those who start out at a disadvantage. And while he's cranky about society's unwillingness to accept scientific discoveries about the roots of human behavior, Pinker also admits, albeit in a less strident voice, that environment plays a significant part in how we turn out. It's just not the whole story.

But those nuances are generally lost in Pinker's all-out assault on those who insist that nurture explains everything—as if anybody still believes that anymore. And his evidence for the power of our genes is, at best, a work in progress. Are liberal and conservative political attitudes really, as Pinker confidently asserts, "largely, though far from completely, heritable"? Are art and literature "in trouble" because they've drifted away from what our genes would prefer to see and hear? Maybe. Yet as with any polemic, this one is delivered with more certainty than it merits. The book is hugely entertaining and highly informative. But readers would be wise to apply some skepticism, whether it's native or nurtured.

ACTIVITY 16.10   *Reading for Two Sides of an Argument*

Read the article entitled "What Makes Us Do It?" in Figure 16.4. Then, respond to the following prompts. Be prepared to discuss your responses in class.

1. The author's main points about the importance of "nature" as the influence on our behavior are . . .

2. The author's main points about the importance of "nurture" as the influence on our behavior are . . .

3. The author's point of view about this issue is . . .

4. In my opinion the author did/did not fairly present both sides of the issue. Why?

INSUFFICIENT EVIDENCE

To be effective, persuasive text must have good, clear, solid, sufficient evidence. If the evidence is not substantial, then it is difficult for the reader to be convinced, particularly if the reader holds an opinion or perspective quite different from that of the writer. If the writer is presenting a hypothesis, then the evidence needs to be complete, grounded in factual material, and well researched. As we noted previously, the evidence must be from reputable, credible sources. Otherwise, it will be difficult to believe the writer's claims because the support will be lacking.

Reread the article in Figure 16.4. As you read, check to see whether the evidence is clear, grounded in factual material, and sufficient for proving the classic theory for nature or for nurture. As you are reading, you may also have some questions that you would like to have answered; write these in your journal as well.

ACTIVITY 16.11 *Reading for Evidence*

Reread the article entitled "What Makes Us Do It?" in Figure 16.4. Then, respond to the following prompts. Be prepared to discuss your responses in class.

1. The writer uses the following evidence in favor of the theory that nature is responsible for human behavior:

2. The writer uses the following evidence in favor of the theory that the environment shapes our human behavior:

3. I am persuaded to believe this theory:

4. My questions for the writer are:

OPINION INSTEAD OF FACTS

For a persuasive paper to be credible, the support needs to be documented with factual evidence and not with the writer's opinion. The factual evidence needs to be from credible sources. Particularly for the sciences and social sciences, the factual material should be drawn from reputable research studies. When a research study is cited, the writer needs to document where the research study was published; most textbooks and peer-reviewed journals use a standard format for this, such as the one recommended by the American Psychological Association. In the article in Figure 16.5, read to check to see what type of evidence is used. Is it factual? Is it primarily the writer's opinion? Does the writer use research-based sources?

FIGURE 16.5

Gender Differences in Relationship Jealousy

Source: From W. Weiten, *Psychology: Themes and Variations,* 5th ed. (Belmont, CA: Wadsworth/Thomson Learning, 2001), p. 402.

Gender Differences in Relationship Jealousy

In their analyses of human sexual behavior, evolutionary psychologists have also come up with some interesting hypotheses about gender differences in the events that most readily activate jealousy (Bailey et al., 1994; Buss, 1996). Males of many species have to worry about *paternity uncertainty*—that is, whether their children are really theirs. The males of some species solve this adaptive problem by literally guarding their mate around the clock to prevent other males from obtaining sexual access to the partner. Although some possessive men seem to mimic this approach, mate guarding is not a particularly realistic strategy among humans. In any event, the issue of paternity uncertainty means that *sexual infidelity* by one's partner ought to be particularly threatening to the reproductive success of men. In contrast, females are always certain that their offspring are theirs, but they supposedly have to worry more about losing a male partner's material resources, which depend on his emotional commitment. Hence, males' *emotional infidelity* ought to be particularly threatening to the reproductive success of females (see Figure 10.13). In a test of these hypotheses, Buss and his colleagues (1992) found that sexual infidelity elicited the greatest jealousy in men, whereas emotional infidelity triggered the greatest jealousy in women (see Figure 10.14). Another study replicated these results in the United States, Germany, and the Netherlands (Buunk et al., 1996).

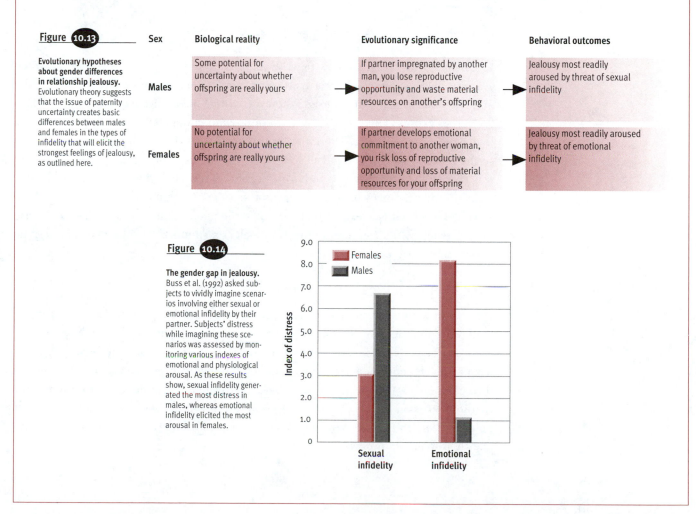

Figure 10.13

Evolutionary hypotheses about gender differences in relationship jealousy. Evolutionary theory suggests that the issue of paternity uncertainty creates basic differences between males and females in the types of infidelity that will elicit the strongest feelings of jealousy, as outlined here.

Sex	Biological reality	Evolutionary significance	Behavioral outcomes
Males	Some potential for uncertainty about whether offspring are really yours	If partner impregnated by another man, you lose reproductive opportunity and waste material resources on another's offspring	Jealousy most readily aroused by threat of sexual infidelity
Females	No potential for uncertainty about whether offspring are really yours	If partner develops emotional commitment to another woman, you risk loss of reproductive opportunity and loss of material resources for your offspring	Jealousy most readily aroused by threat of emotional infidelity

Figure 10.14

The gender gap in jealousy. Buss et al. (1992) asked subjects to vividly imagine scenarios involving either sexual or emotional infidelity by their partner. Subjects' distress while imagining these scenarios was assessed by monitoring various indexes of emotional and physiological arousal. As these results show, sexual infidelity generated the most distress in males, whereas emotional infidelity elicited the most arousal in females.

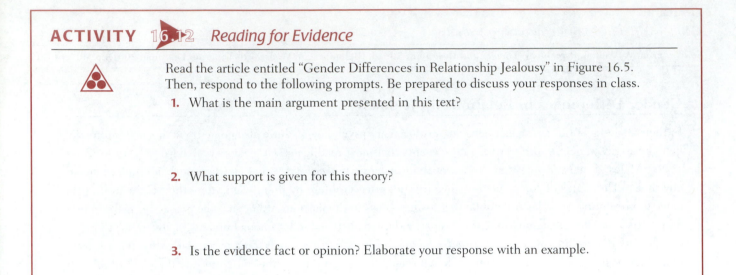

ACTIVITY 16.12 *Reading for Evidence*

Read the article entitled "Gender Differences in Relationship Jealousy" in Figure 16.5. Then, respond to the following prompts. Be prepared to discuss your responses in class.

1. What is the main argument presented in this text?

2. What support is given for this theory?

3. Is the evidence fact or opinion? Elaborate your response with an example.

CREATING SOLID ARGUMENTS

In Chapter 15 you learned how to write summaries and syntheses. If you recall, when you write either a summary or a synthesis paper, you need to objectively describe the main points and supporting ideas. When you write a persuasive paper, a central goal is for you to express your perspective and to provide enough evidence to persuade the reader to agree with you. Therefore, in this section of the chapter, the goal is to describe how to write a good persuasive paper. The purpose of including this section in this chapter is to provide you with a strategy for responding to text on a critical level. You will find that many of your college professors expect that you will not only read on a critical level but also expect that you will write good academic papers as a response to your reading. You can refer to the Tip Block as a summary of suggestions for writing a good persuasive paper.

PRESENTING KEY POINTS

When you write a persuasive paper, you first need to focus your paper on your main argument; in other words, what is the main point of your paper? Typically, your main point states your perspective about the topic. As a writer, you can decide how you wish to reach your audience. As we had noted previously, persuasive text may appeal to reason (logos), appeal to one's character (ethos), or appeal to one's emotions (pathos). Or, you may decide to combine all three approaches. Some students find it helpful to organize their papers with an outline, particularly to designate the issues and their main point of view.

TIP WRITING PERSUASIVE PAPERS

WRITE TO CONVINCE YOUR AUDIENCE. A good persuasive paper speaks to a clear audience. As you write your paper, think of your audience so that your reader will agree with you.

DESCRIBE THE ISSUE OR PROBLEM. Before you articulate your perspective, give a full explanation of the controversy or problem. In this way your reader will have a context for understanding your point of view and the perspectives of others. It is important to describe why the issue is important, particularly the significance of any action taken to solve the problem.

CLEARLY ARTICULATE YOUR PERSPECTIVE. When you write a persuasive paper, the reader should be able to clearly identify your point of view

about a topic. Your paper should have a style that reveals how you feel and think. To do that, choose your words carefully.

SPEAK TO THE ISSUE WITH EVIDENCE. A convincing paper provides good evidence, such as facts, research results, and related data. When you cite other sources, include full bibliographic documentation.

DESCRIBE THE OPPOSING PERSPECTIVE. Good persuasive papers describe opposing perspectives and describe the limitations of those perspectives. Some of your readers may hold perspectives opposing your own; therefore, the power to convince your reader is to acknowledge those perspectives and to show why the opposing arguments fall short.

ACTIVITY 16.13 *Presenting Key Points*

Choose a topic that is controversial and one that is familiar to you. Then, respond to the following prompts. Be prepared to discuss your responses in class.

My main topic for this paper is . . .

I am choosing this topic because . . .

The issues related to this topic are . . .

My perspective about this topic is . . .

PROVIDING EVIDENCE

As we had noted in our discussion about sufficient evidence, when you write your own persuasive paper, you need to have clear, substantive, well-documented evidence. In other words, you need to do your own homework so that you will have well-documented support for both sides of the issue. As you read about this topic, check your sources carefully, and include full documentation about them in your bibliography. Your evidence can include facts, figures, research conclusions, and expert opinion. It is important that you clearly note which information is factual and which information is your own perspective.

ACTIVITY 16.14 *Providing Evidence*

Continue your journal notes from Activity 16.13. Search for evidence for your topic on the Internet. As you choose your evidence, pay attention to the source of your evidence so that you have credible support for your argument. Also, search the Web for information related to the opposing perspective. Create an outline with the following included:

My perspective:

Evidence for this (include documented sources):

1.

2.

3.

4.

5.

The opposing perspective:

Evidence for this (include documented sources):

1.

2.

3.

4.

5.

REFUTATIONAL TEXT

When you write a good persuasive essay, you use the strategy of writing refutational text. Similar to the process of a debate, your paper should first articulate the issue and describe why it is controversial. When you are writing your introduction to your paper, you can state your point of view. However, so that your paper does not contain fallacies in reasoning, you need to position your perspective with evidence that is factual. Therefore, as you would in a debate, you should clearly spell out your perspective in the next section of your paper, providing good evidence as support. Next, it is important to discuss the opposing perspective, clarifying as objectively as possible the distinctions in perspective. After you describe the beliefs from the opposing perspective, it is important to refute these beliefs; this means that you need to clearly point out why the opposing perspective lacks the benefits of your perspective. Finally, you can return to your perspective and provide additional evidence that supports your beliefs and would persuade the reader to side with your position.

ACTIVITY   16.15   *Writing Refutational Text*

Continue your work from Activity 16.14. Create a draft of persuasive text in which you state your position, refute the opposing perspective, and show why someone should believe your position. After you finish your draft, reread it. Is your position clear? Have you provided good evidence as support?

Writing academic papers with solid arguments is one of the most sophisticated forms of college writing. Yet if you carefully locate appropriate evidence for your paper, logically present your points, and summarize your paper with well-substantiated conclusions, then you will be able to perform well as a college student. The tasks of critically reading both print and nonprint texts, then responding through inquiry, analysis, summarization, synthesis, and evaluation clearly are the trademarks of the successful student.

ACTIVITY   16.16   *Where Are You Now?*

Now that you have completed this chapter, take a few minutes to return to the beginning of this chapter and repeat Activity 16.1, Where Are You Now? What have you learned about evaluating information as a critical reader? What are you going to do differently now?

Summary

The key to reading and writing persuasive and informational texts is to apply critical, evaluative strategies for analyzing the arguments and perspectives in them. As a critical reader, it is important to analyze and judge the credibility of the evidence and the source of the evidence, distinguish facts from opinions, and note any fallacies in reasoning. When you make an evaluation, you make an informed opinion about the worth of something. To do so, you carefully check the examples, facts, and other information the writer provides as proof for an argument. It is important to see whether the evidence is sufficient, both sides of an argument are presented, and opinions are clearly noted as such and not presented as factual.

Evidence that a writer uses in support of an argument should be good evidence, grounded in research studies, good data, and relevant examples. When looking at the evidence a writer uses, it is important to check the credibility of the sources. It is important to see whether the background training and experiences of the writer is appropriate.

This chapter also presented a variety of commonly used propaganda techniques in advertising: Bandwagon, Testimonial, Plain Folks, Transfer, Stacking the Deck, and Glittering Generalities. When viewing television and reading advertisements, it is important to recognize these common techniques in order to evaluate the worth of the evidence presented. This chapter also presented a variety of fallacies in reasoning; these "false statements" show faulty logic and diminish the writer's argument.

Finally, this chapter showed how to write a good persuasive paper. The key to writing good persuasive papers is to write refutational text. This involves presenting both sides of an issue, along with an analysis of the opposing perspective's claims, showing how your perspective is superior. In sum, as a critical reader and writer, you use strategies of analysis, synthesis, and evaluation to make solid judgments about the texts you meet in your college experiences.

Review Questions

Terms You Should Know: Make a flash card for each term.

Argument	Glittering generalities	Propaganda techniques
Bandwagon	Hasty generalizations	Refutational text
Credibility of sources	Informational text	Stacking the deck
Ethos	Logos	Support
Evaluative reading	Opinions	Testimonial
Evidence	Pathos	Transfer
Facts	Persuasive text	
Fallacies in reasoning	Plain folks	

Completion: Fill in the blank to complete each of the following statements.

1. Central to understanding persuasive text is the analysis of the _____, which states what the writer believes about the topic.

2. Aristotelian logic states that persuasive text may appeal to _____, _____, and _____.

3. When you write persuasive text, it is important to use _____ _____ in order to show both sides of an issue and to show why the reader should not believe the opposing perspective.

4. When checking the _____ _____ _____ it is important to check the background expertise of the person who wrote the evidence.

5. When reading to check _____ and figures as evidence, you check to see whether they are accurate and sufficient.

Multiple Choice: Circle the letter of the best answer for each of the following questions. Be sure to underline key words and eliminate wrong answers.

6. A soft drink company shows a TV commercial that shows its Cola X is much better than Cola Y, which is made by its rival company. The propaganda technique used in this commercial is
    A. Bandwagon.
    B. Glittering generalities.
    C. Testimonial.
    D. Stacking the deck.

7. An advertisement shows a famous actress using a new shampoo; she encourages you to buy it, too. The propaganda technique used in this commercial is
    A. Bandwagon.
    B. Glittering generalities.
    C. Testimonial.
    D. Stacking the deck.

Short Answer–Essay: On a separate sheet answer each of the following questions.

8. Describe and give two examples of a propaganda technique.

9. Describe two types of fallacies in reasoning.

10. Describe how to create refutational text.

Index